A TREASURY OF
LAUGHTER

Consisting of Humorous Stories, Poems, Essays, Tall Tales, Jokes,
Boners, Epigrams, Memorable Quips, and Devastating Crushers

SELECTED AND EDITED, WITH AN INTRODUCTION BY

LOUIS UNTERMEYER

ILLUSTRATED BY **LUCILLE CORCOS**

SIMON AND SCHUSTER, NEW YORK

Acknowledgments

Much of the material in this volume is copyright by other publishers, and may not be reprinted or reproduced without the permission of the owners. A complete list of the holders of the copyright, or their agents, follows. Any errors are accidental and will be corrected in future printings upon advice to the editor or publisher.

D. APPLETON-CENTURY COMPANY—for "David Harum's Horse Trade" from *David Harum* by Edward Noyes Westcott, copyright, 1898, by D. Appleton-Century Company; 1926, by Philip N. Westcott.

ALBERT AND CHARLES BONI, INC.—for the selection from Donald Ogden Stewart's *The Crazy Fool*, copyright, 1925, by Albert and Charles Boni, Inc.

ROARK BRADFORD—for "Green Pastures" from *Ol' Man Adam an' His Chillun*, copyright, 1928, by Harper & Brothers.

BRANDT & BRANDT—for "The Quiet Afternoon" from *Penrod*, copyright, 1914, 1942, by Booth Tarkington, published by Doubleday, Doran and Company, Inc.

CURTIS BROWN, LTD.—for "All Yankees Are Liars" from *Sam Small Flies Again* by Eric Knight, copyright, 1938, by the Curtis Publishing Company and reprinted by permission of Mrs. Eric Knight.

MRS. LAURA S. COBB—for "Speaking of Operations" by Irvin S. Cobb, copyright, 1915, by Doubleday & Co., 1943, by Irvin S. Cobb.

A. E. COPPARD and JONATHAN CAPE, London—for "Alas, Poor Bollington" from *The Black Dog* by A. E. Coppard, published in America by Alfred A. Knopf, Inc., and reprinted here by special permission of the author.

DODD, MEAD & COMPANY, INC.—for "Confessions of a Gallomaniac" from *The Margin of Hesitation* by Frank Moore Colby, copyright, 1921, by Dodd, Mead & Company, Inc.; "Ring Out Wild Bells" from *A Bed of Neuroses* by Wolcott Gibbs; "My Financial Career" from *Literary Lapses* by Stephen Leacock and "Gertrude, the Governess" from *Nonsense Novels* by Stephen Leacock. The foregoing are reprinted by permission of Dodd, Mead & Company, Inc.

DOUBLEDAY & COMPANY, INC.—for "A Pair of Sexes" from *The Column Book of F. P. A.*, copyright, 1911, by Doubleday & Co.; "The Rich Man" from *Tobogganing on Parnassus* by Franklin P. Adams, copyright, 1911, by Doubleday & Co.; "The Fable of the Spotlighters and the Spotter" and "The Ninny Who Swam Away from the Life Preserver" from *Hand-Made Fables* by George Ade, copyright, 1920, by Doubleday & Co.; "Pigs Is Pigs" from the book of the same name by Ellis Parker Butler, copyright, 1906, by Doubleday & Co.; "the coming of archy," "mehitabel was once cleopatra," and "the song of mehitabel" from *"archy and mehitabel"* by Don Marquis, copyright, 1927, 1930, by Doubleday & Co.; "The Ransom of Red Chief" from *Whirligigs* by O. Henry, copyright, 1931, by Doubleday & Co.; "Uncle Fred Flits By" from *Young Man in Spats* by P. G. Wodehouse, copyright, 1916, by Doubleday & Co.

MESSRS. GERALD DUCKWORTH & COMPANY, LTD., London—for permission to reprint the selections from Hilaire Belloc's *Cautionary Verses and Other Poems* in Canada as well as the U. S. A.

ESQUIRE, INC. and ROBERT O. FOOTE—for "Who Was Joe Miller?" by Robert O. Foote, copyright, 1942, by Esquire, Inc., Chicago, Ill.

SAMUEL FRENCH—for "If Men Played Cards as Women Do," copyright, 1923, by George S. Kaufman; copyright, 1926, by Samuel French. All rights reserved. *Caution*: professionals and amateurs are hereby warned that "If Men Played Cards as Women Do," being fully protected under the copyright laws of the United States of America, the British Empire, including the Dominion of Canada, and other countries of the Copyright Union, is subject to a royalty. All rights, including professional, amateur, motion pictures, recitation, public reading, radio broadcasting and the rights of translation into foreign languages are strictly reserved. Amateurs may produce this play upon payment of a royalty of Five Dollars for each performance, payable one week before the play is to be given, to Samuel French, at 25 West 45th Street, New York, N. Y. or 811 West 7th Street, Los Angeles, Calif., or, if in Canada, to Samuel French (Canada) Ltd., at 480 University Ave., Toronto, Canada.

GOOD HOUSEKEEPING—for "A Bachelor Keeps House" by Louis Untermeyer, copyright, 1945, by *Good Housekeeping*.

HARCOURT, BRACE AND COMPANY, INC.—for "My Father Goes to Court" from *The Laughter of My Father* by Carlos Bulosan, copyright, 1944, by Harcourt, Brace and Company, Inc.; "The Sock Hunt" from *My Sister Eileen*, copyright, 1938, by Ruth McKenney; "The Education of Hyman Kaplan" from *The Education of Hyman Kaplan* by Leonard Q. Ross, copyright, 1937, by Harcourt, Brace and Company, Inc.; Two Parodies from *Selected Poems and Parodies of Louis Untermeyer*, copyright, 1935, by Harcourt, Brace and Company, Inc.; "Lincoln, the Laughing President" from *Abraham Lincoln: The Prairie Years* by Carl Sandburg, copyright, 1926, by Harcourt, Brace and Company, Inc.; "The Fifty Yard Dash" and "The Circus" from *My Name Is Aram*, copyright, 1940, by William Saroyan. By permission of Harcourt, Brace and Company, Inc.

HARPER & BROTHERS—for "The Treasurer's Report" from *The Treasurer's Report and Other Aspects of Community Singing*, copyright, 1930, by Robert Benchley; "Kiddie-Kar Travel" from *Pluck and Luck* by Robert Benchley, copyright, 1925, by Harper & Brothers; "The Sycophantic Fox" and "The Vainglorious Oak" from *Fables for the Frivolous* by Guy Wetmore Carryl, copyright, 1898, 1926, by Harper & Brothers; "Alcohol as Food" from *Mr. Dooley's Philosophy* by Finley Peter Dunne, copyright, 1900, by Robert Howard Russell; 1928, by Finley Peter Dunne; "How Tom Whitewashed the Fence" from *The Adventures of Tom Sawyer* by Mark Twain; "The Celebrated Jumping Frog" from *Sketches New and Old* by Mark Twain; and "The Camel's Appetite" from *Roughing It* by Mark Twain.

LUCIEN HARRIS—for "The Wonderful Tar Baby Story" from *Uncle Remus; His Songs and Sayings* by Joel Chandler Harris.

HENRY HOLT AND COMPANY, INC.—for "The Indomitable Duck" from *Past the End of the Pavement* by Charles G. Finney, copyright, 1939, by Henry Holt and Company, Inc.; "Brown's Descent" from *Collected Poems of Robert Frost*, copyright, 1930, 1939, by Henry Holt and Company, Inc.; 1936, by Robert Frost; "When I Was One and Twenty" and "See How Thick the Goldcup Flowers" from *A Shropshire Lad* by A. E. Housman, 1924, Authorized Edition.

HERBERT JENKINS and P. G. WODEHOUSE—for permission to reprint P. G. Wodehouse's "Uncle Fred Flits By" in Canada as well as the U. S. A.

ALFRED A. KNOPF, INC.—for the selections from *Cautionary Verses* and other poems by Hilaire Belloc; "The Egg" from *Thoughts Without Words*, copyright, 1923, 1928, by Clarence Day; "The Noblest Instrument" from *Life With Father*, copyright, 1920, 1922, 1923, 1924, 1933, 1935, by Clarence Day; "Rain" and "The Belle of the Balkans" from *Theatre Guyed*, copyright, 1931, 1932, 1933, by Newman Levy; "Downfall of a Revolutionary" from *Heathen Days* by H. L. Mencken, copyright, 1941, 1942, 1943, by Alfred A. Knopf, Inc.

JOHN LANE THE BODLEY HEAD LTD., London—for permission to reprint the selections from *The Short Stories of Saki* in Canada as well as the U. S. A.

J. B. LIPPINCOTT COMPANY—for "Butch Minds the Baby" from *Guys and Dolls*, copyright, 1931, by Damon Runyon, published by J. B. Lippincott Company.

LITTLE, BROWN & COMPANY—for "The Evening Out," "The Common Cold," "To a Small Boy Standing on My Shoes," "Seven Spiritual Ages of Mrs. Marmaduke Moore," from *The Face Is Familiar* by Odgen Nash; "A Trip to Hollywood" from *A Pearl in Every Oyster* by Frank Sullivan.

THE MACMILLAN COMPANY—for "The Unselfish Hostess" from *As Others Hear Us* by E. M. Delafield.

HOWARD MAIER—for "What Price Heaven": A Play for Radio, copyright by Howard Maier.

HAROLD MATSON—for "Mary," copyright, 1939, by John Collier; "Another American Tragedy," copyright, 1940, John Collier; "Ever Fall in Love with a Midget?" copyright, 1938, by William Saroyan.

THE NEW YORKER—for the following selections which first appeared in the pages of that magazine: "Between Madison and Park" by Sally Benson, copyright, 1941, by Sally Benson; "We Have Been Here

Lardner, copyright, 1924, by Charles Scribner's Sons; "Mr. and Mrs. Fix-It" from *The Love Nest and Other Stories* by Ring Lardner, copyright, 1926, by Charles Scribner's Sons; "Cora, or Fun at a Spa," "Clemo Uti," and "I Gaspiri," from *First and Last* by Ring Lardner, copyright, 1926, by Charles Scribner's Sons; "The Axolotl" and "Epitaph to a Waiter," from *Bay Window Ballads* by David McCord, copyright, 1935, by Charles Scribner's Sons.

SIMON AND SCHUSTER, INC.—for "From Pillar to Post" and "Come One, Come *One,*" from *How To Do Practically Anything,* copyright, 1942, by Jack Goodman and Alan Green.

THE SOCIETY OF AUTHORS, as the literary representative of the Trustees of the Estate of the late A. E. Housman, and JONATHAN CAPE, LTD., publishers of A. E. Housman's Collected Poems, for permission to print "When I Was One and Twenty" and "See How Thick the Goldcup Flowers" in Canada as well as in the U. S. A.

JAMES THURBER—for "What Do You Mean It *Was* Brillig?" and "The Secret Life Of Walter Mitty," from *My World and Welcome To It* by James Thurber, published by Harcourt, Brace and Company, Inc. and "The Greatest Man In the World."

LOUIS UNTERMEYER—for "A Bachelor Keeps House," which originally appeared in *Good Housekeeping.*

VIKING PRESS, INC.—for "The Elephant Cutlet" from *My War with the United States,* copyright, 1937, by Ludwig Bemelmans; the selections from *Boners* and *More Boners,* copyright, 1931, by The Viking Press, Inc.; "The Mouse" and "The Story-Teller" from *The Short Stories of Saki* (H. H. Munro), copyright, 1930, by The Viking Press, Inc.; "You Were Perfectly Fine" and "Little Words," copyright 1930, 1931, 1944, by Dorothy Parker, from *The Portable Dorothy Parker;* "Entrance Fee" from *While Rome Burns,* copyright, 1934, by Alexander Woollcott. All of the foregoing are reprinted by permission of The Viking Press, Inc., New York.

VOGUE—for "A Wit with a Whim of Iron" by Frank Crowninshield, copyright, 1942, by the Condé Nast Publications, Inc., New York.

It is with real gratitude that the editor thanks the many people who have given permission to reprint their works or quote parts of them. Besides the obligation to friends for countless stimulating suggestions, he is especially indebted to the foregoing authors, publishers, and agents.

The work itself was first suggested to me by M. Lincoln Schuster and Richard L. Simon, to whom I am indebted not only for data and documents, but for unflagging and enthusiastic encouragement.

For suggestive comments, research, and gentle but persistent prodding I am especially obliged to my friends Jack Goodman, Albert Leventhal, Wallace Brockway, Quincy Howe, Maria Leiper, Vida Ginsberg, Philip Van Doren Stern, Fred Schwed, and Mary Jane Gaffney. Lastly, I am indebted to Kay Margolis, who guided the book through proof and goaded me into deleting some of the worst jokes I had long cherished.

L. U.

THIS BOOK IS FOR MARY
FOR MORE THAN LAUGHS

Contents

Introduction

It is an unwritten but carefully observed law that books of humor must begin with the observation that man, differing from other beasts, is the laughing animal. But few of the books point out that man's way of laughing, as well as his reasons for laughter, change from generation to generation. The very word "humor" has meant different things to different centuries. In the sixteenth century, for example, the prime meaning of humor was "a disorder of the blood"; the Greeks, according to Hippocrates, believed the human body contained four "humors": namely, blood, phlegm, yellow bile, and black bile.

There are people who, confused by satire or stung by wit, still look on humor as a kind of intellectual biliousness. They have forgotten the distinctions, if they ever learned them. Wit is sudden and startling and usually scornful; it leaps audaciously and wickedly. Humor is slower; it is rarely malicious; it does not fly to assault the mind but laughs its way into the heart. Satire is probing and critical; it cuts through pretension with quick corrosive acid; its purpose is coldly destructive. But humor seldom analyzes; it is warmly sympathetic, playful, sometimes high-hearted, sometimes hilarious. Unlike the poisoned barb of satire and the killing point of wit, humor is healing. It is not only wholesome, but recreative and rejuvenating.

This, then, is a book of humor. If wit and satire manage to work their way in, it is without my consent. The aim of this book is the communication of the comic; its object is to make the reader laugh. If the reader should pause to ponder or philosophize, that is his right, but it is not my business. This editor's chief concern is with such pieces in prose, and occasionally in verse, which have made readers grin, smile, chortle, chirrup, giggle, titter, crow, cackle, shout—where's that thesaurus? Ah yes—leap, roar, burst and die with laughter. Obviously not every page in this collection will cause all these pleasant reactions, nor are they meant to. But each selection has its devotees and has won from them the genial chuckle or the side-splitting guffaw.

Since I believe that humor suffers violently, almost fatally, in translation, my selections are confined to the two languages in which they were written: English and American. Dialect is here, but kept to a minimum. There is nothing essentially comic in mispronunciation and misspelling —who today can laugh at the printing of tu for "to" or reddy for "ready" or invenshun for "invention"?—and the reader of this book will find examples of only the few dialect writers and artificially rustic illiterates who created character or who achieved humorous situations in spite of, rather than because of, odd typographical devices. Research students and historically minded tabulators who look for the names of Petroleum V. Nasby, Eli Perkins, Orpheus C. Kerr, John Phoenix, Jr., and the Danbury News Man will have to look elsewhere. If our taste in fun changes with every generation, dialect is the most inflexibly dated form of humor; it is rigidly tied to its time.

It might be objected that I have been ungenerous to dialect and too tolerant of jokes. A joke is supposed to be even lower than a pun, proverbially the lowest form of wit; it is, according to Clifton Fadiman, international in a bad sense, "not laughter's true tongue but its lingua franca." Nevertheless a joke might be defined as something everyone decries and everyone tries to tell; even so solemn an analyst as Dr. Sigmund Freud insists that "a new joke acts like an event of universal interest. It passes from person to person like news of the latest conquest." Without claiming too much for it, I would say that the reason for the popularity of a joke is its extraordinary condensation: a character is presented and disposed of, a problem is stated and solved, all in one breath. A joke is a compressed short story—a story stripped to its point. Contrariwise, many short stories, such as O. Henry's and Guy de Maupassant's, are extended jokes. Jokes, therefore, are a legitimate part of this collection. But, since a long assembly of jokes, anecdotes, and funny say-

ings are bound to pall, the editor has divided them not only in character but in space. In this volume the jokes serve as the dressing, the accompaniment to the meal, not the meal itself.

As to the omissions which every reader will inevitably hold against the editor, there is this to say: Nothing is more personal than an anthology. Every anthologist says in effect: Here are some (though not all) of the things I've collected for years, and I hope you, the reader, will like them, too. If you ask me why I have left out some of your own favorites, I would offer one or more of these excuses: (a) Times change and taste changes with them. Some of the pieces I roared at in my youth still seem the best of their kind; some of the things that doubled me up last year seem pretty dull stuff to me today. (b) I admire the broad humor of Fielding, the delicate innuendoes of Sterne, the lively satirical novels of Thackeray, the breakfast-table repartee of Oliver Wendell Holmes; but much though I relish their works, I found nothing in them which seemed easily detachable or self-sufficient or actually funny by itself. (c) In spite of a lifetime spent in reading and an acquired air of omniscience, it is just possible that I've never encountered your particular favorite.

Finally, I must warn the reader that this is neither a textbook nor a treatise. It does not presume to explain the motives or analyze the effects of humor. E. B. White, that sapient essayist, once compared the analyst and professional producer of humor with a man who had become the champion soap-bubble blower of America. "He had," wrote White in A Subtreasury of American Humor, "perfected the business of blowing bubbles, refined it, doubled it, squared it, and had even worked himself up into a convenient lather. The effect was not pretty. It was, if anything, a rather repulsive sight. Humor is a little like that: it won't stand much blowing up, and it won't stand much poking. It has a certain fragility, an evasiveness, which one had best respect. Essentially, it is a complete mystery."

It is on this note of mystery that the editor ushers in his book and bows himself out. And, combining a couple of Latin quotations, his last words are: "Laugh, if you are wise—for the man who laughs is the man who knows the truth."

L. U.

A TREASURY OF
LAUGHTER

F. P. A.

He was born Franklin Pierce Adams, but people who would never recognize that resounding combination of presidential names know him simply as F. P. A. A Chicago journalist at twenty-two, he followed the example of his illustrious hometown predecessors, Eugene Field and Bert Leston Taylor: he started a "column." His first New York venture in that field was in 1904; it was headed "Always in Good Humor," a misleading caption soon discarded for "The Conning Tower," and F. P. A. kept on conducting columns for various newspapers until he became one of the board of experts on the radio program "Information Please." He insists that he prefers almost anything —poker, tennis, his family—to writing; but he has, somehow, managed to put together more than a dozen volumes, from his own sprightly Tobogganing on Parnassus to Innocent Merriment, an anthology of light verse. Moreover, in between his various activities, F. P. A. collaborated with O. Henry on a comic opera that never reached Broadway, translated Horace into nimble American idioms, and compiled The Diary of Our Own Samuel Pepys, in which he told salient facts about everyone except himself.

A Pair of Sexes

I. A MAN TELEPHONES

"Ed? . . . Lunch at one. Whyte's. Right."

II. A WOMAN TELEPHONES

"Hello, operator. Operator? I want Caledonia five eight six seven, please. Oh, this *is* Caledonia five eight six seven? Oh, I beg your pardon, I'm terribly sorry. I thought it was the operator. I've had so much trouble with the telephone lately. May I speak to Miss Lucille Webster, please? Oh, *speaking?* Oh, I'm terribly sorry. Is this Miss Webster? Is this you, Lucille? I didn't recognize your voice at first. First I thought it was the operator, and then I thought it was somebody answering for you, Lucille. I didn't recognize your voice at first. Got a cold or something? Oh, you sound as though you had. There's so much of it around this wretched weather. I never saw anything like it in my whole life. Well, I'm glad you haven't got a cold, though at first you certainly sounded like it. . . . I was just talking to Ethel for a second, and she had such a cold she could hardly talk. That's the reason I asked you. There's an *awful* lot of it around this wretched weather. . . . Oh, nothing particular. . . . Oh, yes, there is too. How silly of me! I was so interested in what you were saying, I almost forgot. Lucille, what are you doing tomorrow? . . . No, about lunch time. Or a little earlier. Or a little later. It doesn't matter. Because I expect to be in your part of town about that time, around lunch time, oh, maybe one or one-thirty or so, I have an appointment at twelve-thirty, and it oughtn't to take me more than half an hour, or at the most three quarters, surely not over an hour, I'm almost certain, and probably I'll be through in half an hour, but, anyway, I ought to be all through by one-thirty, and I could meet you anywhere you say. . . . Oh, I know, but Maillard's is pretty crowded about that time, and isn't there some place nearer? My appointment is on Forty-seventh Street near Madison—no, it's near Fifth, I guess. But that doesn't matter. I'll take a cab. If I can get one. Did you ever see anything like how hard it is to get a cab nowadays? My dear, last night I was twenty-five minutes trying to get one, and it got me late for dinner, and I *know* they didn't believe me. But if I can't get one I'll walk. It's only a block. And I guess a little exercise wouldn't do me any harm . . . Maillard's. . . . How about the Ritz? No, there's such a jam there. And it's hard to meet. Well, any place *you*

2

say. . . . Oh, Lucille, that's a dreadful place. The food's so—oh, I don't know. You know. So—bad; if you know what I mean. Well, let's take a chance on Maillard's. Only it's so crowded. . . . Oh, no, I never heard that. . . . No, I haven't. I haven't read a thing in months, absolutely months. Where the time goes to I don't know. *I* simply do not know where the time goes to. Lucille, you're sure you've got tomorrow at lunch free? Because if you haven't, or there's something you'd rather do, just say so and we'll try again. Well, suppose we say at Maillard's at—oh, do you know that little tea shop on Forty-seventh? I think it's between Park and Madison on the—let's see—on the downtown, that's the south side of the street. I'll be there by one, or anyway one-thirty, and if I'm there first I'll get a table, and you do the same if you are. But I ought to be there by one. My appointment is for half-past twelve, and it may take me only a few minutes. I might be there before one. But surely by quarter past, and certainly by one-thirty. . . . All right, then. Suppose we say about one, at Maillard's. . . . Oh, no, what am I thinking of? We decided that would be too crowded, didn't we? Unless you'd rather go there. That little tea shop is very nice. . . . Well, yes, I'd just as soon go to Maillard's. It doesn't matter much. It's seeing you I care about. There's a *lot* I want to talk to you about. These little snatches at the telephone are so, well, so sort of unsatisfactory, if you know what I mean. . . . All right, suppose we say Maillard's, then. And then if we don't like the looks of things we can go somewhere else. . . . All right, then, at . . . oh, let's go to the tea room. It's quieter. . . . All right then. I'm longing to see you, Lucille. . . . Tomorrow, then. At the tea shop, that's on Forty-seventh between Park and Madison, on the downtown, that's the south side of the street. Tomorrow, then, about one. That's Wednesday. . . . What? Is it Tuesday? . . . Well, I'm *all* turned around. I thought it was Wednesday. I'm terribly sorry, Lucille. I can't *possibly* meet you tomorrow if it's Tuesday. I've got a luncheon appointment I've had for ages, simply for weeks, and I've postponed it so often I don't dare do it again. . . . You can't Wednesday? I'm terribly sorry. . . . Well, I'll try again. Ring me up. I'll be in all afternoon until five twenty-five, and then I have to go uptown. . . . Yes. . . . Well, I'm glad we had a nice little talk, anyway. . . . And I'll see you soon. . . . What? No, *soon*—S for Sam. . . . Yes, soon. . . . Good-bye, Lucille. . . . Good-bye. Good-bye. Good-bye."

The Rich Man

The rich man has his motor-car,
   His country and his town estate.
He smokes a fifty-cent cigar
   And jeers at Fate.

He frivols through the livelong day,
   He knows not Poverty, her pinch.
His lot seems light, his heart seems gay;
   He has a cinch.

Yet though my lamp burns low and dim,
   Though I must slave for livelihood—
Think you that I would change with him?
   You bet I would!

George Ade

Out of a small town in Indiana (Kentland, to be exact) a Hoosier, born in 1866, added a new dimension to our speech. George Ade's Fables in Slang not only enlivened but enriched the American language. A few critics referred to Ade's style as the American Slanguage, but it survived puns and patronization. Meanwhile, having carved his monument out of living words, Ade went on to write for the theater, with which he had always been in love. "By a queer set of circumstances," wrote Ade, "I have been known to the general public as a writer of slang. I never wanted to be a comic or tried to be one. Always I wrote for 'the family trade,' and I used no word or phrase which might give offense to mother and the girls—or to a professor of English."

Critical comments have not been obtained from mother and the girls, but professors of English were anything but offended. On the contrary, every appraisal ended in praise. Although the style of Fables in Slang is somewhat dated, the spirit is still fresh. Ade, who died in 1944, was one of our best vernacular philosophers, "a continuer," said Carl Van Doren, "of the old wisdom and the inventor of a new idiom."

The Fable of the Spotlighters and the Spotter

nce a Traveller arrived at a Cure where the Water of the Healing Springs smelled so awful that the Management felt justified in asking $10 a Day.

This Traveller was a City Yap, which is worse than being a Begosher, because the R.F.D. Boob usually knows that he is below Par.

The City Yap is a Vertebrate with Shiny Hair, living under the dominion of the Traffic Cops.

He will stand in front of a Window, with others of his Kind, for an Hour at a time, watching a powerful Blonde demonstrate a Fireless Cooker.

When $100,000,000 gets married to a Title, it is the City Yap who has to be clubbed back by the Police so that the Bride can get her Purchase into the Sanctuary.

When Jack Dempsey or Prince Blozotski arrives by Special Train, the City Yap is the poor Google-Eye that you see standing in the Rain.

He believes that Greatness means having one's Name on the Front Page; consequently it is better to jump off the Williamsburg Bridge than to be an Emeritus Professor at Johns Hopkins.

Perhaps the Reader will ask: "Could a City Yap afford to put up at one of these Ten-a-Day Resorts?"

Listen!

Some of the City Yaps have been to Harvard. They have tailor-made Underwear, Gold Service for Company, De Luxe Editions, Divorce Papers—Everything.

This particular Species of Metropolitan Mokus used to Boast that he could walk into any Hotel and the Clerks would hoist the Flag.

Such a Claim might not seem Portentous to one residing in Grand Island or Waupaca, but there are Favoured Spots within the Republic at which being known by the Boys behind the Desk is the very Essence of Fame.

Sure enough, the Lad who gives out the Keys recognized the Traveller and called him by Name and let on as though the Tavern had just opened and here was the first Customer.

After the newly arrived Delegate from the Asphalt Jungles had read a Telegram saying that Frazzingham Preferred had advanced from

¾ to ⅞ on a Report that the King of Rumania had received a Letter from the King of Greece, he brushed up a little and then sauntered back to the Bureau of Information and asked the Room Clerk if any one was stopping in the House.

Of course he knew that some 500 Transients of fair Business Standing and the usual Family connections were scattered about the Premises.

When he said "Any One," he meant did they have any one who would get Attention from the Head Waiter Himself.

A true Worshipper of the Exalted Few regards the common Run of Humanity as mere Whitebait. If you wish to hand him a Thrill, you must show him a Tarpon.

"We have so many Stars here that even the Manager is trembling," replied Cuthbert, the refined Room Clerk. "Do you see that Bunch out on the Piazza, taking the Sun? Leave me call them off to you. First, there is Jimmy Hooper, supposed to be the nerviest Plunger on the Exchange. He can lose or win a Million without disturbing the Ash on his Cigarette. He makes all the other High Rollers in the world look like Marble Players. He is King of the Gilt-Edge Gams."

"I have read all about him in the Papers," said the Roof-Garden Rufus.

"Then there is Mr. Hiram Cherrib, who has closed out all his big Interests and puts in his Time endowing Hospitals and slipping Coin to Presbyterian Colleges. He allows that he will shoot every Bean in the old Tin Box and die Poor if he can do good to those that he formerly Did so successfully."

"For years I have yearned to get a peek at Mr. Cherrib," said the Café Habitué.

"And lookie! There is Mrs. Beverly Margrave, often called the uncrowned Empress of the American Hote Mond. You've heard of her!"

"HAVE I?" exclaimed the Bumpkin from the Boulevards.

His Nostrils were quivering.

"She was a Terwhilligus from Baltimore, you may recall. I know People who would give their Eye-Teeth just to have her Insult them. Then they could say they had Met her. Right next to her Nobs is the famous preacher, Rev. Ormsby Toncell. They say he pulls down the biggest Salary and has the swellest lot of Box-Holders of any Parson in this whole Country. Even the English think he's English. He must be a talented Guy, all right!"

"Hardly a week passes but I see an Interview with him," said the Subway Simp.

"As I live and breathe, she's out there, too!" ejaculated the highly intelligent Room Clerk.

"Who?" asked the eager Cosmopolite.

"Lottie Limmet, the big Hit in that new Piece called 'Oh, Lizzie!'
You remember—the Police made them change it. She had a Song that
caused a Strike in the Orchestra. Some of the Musicians said they had
Families."

"I tried to buy Seats"—in a Choking Whisper—"but they were sold
out Eight Weeks in advance, and the Speculators asked Ten for Two
on the Aisle."

"She is Some Gal. It is reported that they are going to put up a Statue
of her at Yale. The Female Party right near her is supposed to be the
Richest Woman in the Western Hemisphere."

"You don't mean Jane Plummer, the Widow that gets a Full Page
in the Sunday Issue every two or three weeks?" asked the City Chap,
his Cup of Joy just about ready to slop over.

"None other. I remember reading how much her Income would
weigh if she changed it into Nickels. By the way, there's another Big
Gun out there. I didn't notice him at first. Probably you've read the
Editorial Attacks on Steve Gurney, the Political Boss."

"You don't mean the head of the Venal State Machine, who sits in
a Back Room and gives orders to the Legislature and dictates Appoint-
ments and pulls all that Coarse Stuff, do you?"

"That's the Bird! I can see that you're well read. They've been trying
for Years to get something on him and take his Measure, but he is still
riding the Tractor."

"Me to put myself next," said Mr. H. Polloi. "I don't often get a
Close-Up of these Immortals, and I'm sure going to Periscope."

So he edged out into the Sunlight and stalked his Prey.

There was one empty Chair right in the thick of the Who's Who, and
he nailed it.

Oh, Joy! Oh, Bliss! And a couple of Raptures!

He found himself within smelling-distance of Lottie Limmet, the
Forty-Second Street Parisienne.

There was no mistaking the much talked-of Cutie.

If Colours could be converted into Sounds her Costume would have
been a Siren Whistle.

She had her Limbs crossed in such a way as to prove that she spared
no Expense, but, nevertheless, her Knee-Caps were modestly concealed.

He knew it was She or Her because alongside of the Gay Creature
and very Chummy was the famous Wall Street Blokie, Jimmy Hooper,
dressed up like a Horse.

Yes, indeed! Shepherd's Plaid, Stripes on the Shirt, and a Bow Tie that looked like a Clot of Blood.

He had "Gambler" placarded all over him.

Our Hero knew that every Soubrette has a Gentleman Broker Friend who gives her Tips on the Market, so that ofttimes she will clean up as much as $300,000 at a Crack and then send her Mother a Watch.

He knew, because that was the part of the Paper he devoured.

It is easy to get acquainted with an Actress, so in a few minutes George W. Fresh was carrying on with the Footlight Favourite and exchanging Hot Ones with Jimmy the Sport.

Presently the one who had been identified as Steve Gurney, Malefactor and Enemy of the People, edged over with his Rocking Chair and joined in the gay chatter of the Bohemians.

After giving Steve the Up-and-Down, it was easy to believe all that had been printed about him in the Righteous Press.

He was undershot and had Fuzz on the Back of his Hands.

He looked like a Vessel Unloader who had put on a Mail Order Suit in order to attend a Clam Bake.

The sort of Person you wouldn't care to meet in a Lonesome Street on a Rainy Night.

While the Investigator was letting himself go, in the company of these Abandoned Characters, and wondering what the Boys at the Lunch Club would say when he pulled it on them, he sized the other Notables close at hand.

Mrs. Beverly Margrave was perceptibly annoyed by the immediate presence of the *Canaille,* meaning Ordinary Skates.

Her prim but high-priced Suit of Quaker Gray, the chiselled suggestion of Patrician Reserve on her cold features, the wince of Pain and the lifted Eyebrow when Steve Gurney guffawed loudly, and the fact that she was reading George Moore—all these Items meant much to the Observant Traveller.

Why deny Class Distinction when even a Stranger can single out a True Genevieve with Pink Corpuscles?

Near the Queen of the Swagger Set, a pale Gentleman in somber Attire seemed quite lost in contemplation of the hazy Landscape.

He gave no heed to the gabby Groundlings only a few feet away.

He held daintily between the Forefinger and Thumb a White Rose with slender Stem.

At intervals he would lift the gorgeous Bloom to the Olfactory Orifices and inhale in a conservative manner, closing his Eyes and seeming to pass into a pleasant Trance.

It was a Cinch to place this Party as the Rev. Ormsby Toncell.

The absence of Jewellery, the Ascetic Pallor, the simple adoration of Purity's Emblem—all these bespoke a Nature more Spiritual than Broadway.

Out by the Veranda Rail, seemingly lost in Meditation as he propped his Chin with a Newspaper made into a Roll, sat Horace Cherrib, the foremost Benefactor of his Time.

The City Fellow knew him by the Side Whiskers.

In every Good Show, the Elderly Person with Money who is trying to save some one else from Ruin and bring Happiness to the Deserving carries quite a mess of Ivy in front of each Listener.

Even if there had been no Trade-Marks, it would have been a Pipe to make the eminent Philanthropist.

The Light of Goodness twinkled in his Baby Blue Eyes and a Smile of infinite Kindliness illumined his Handsome Diagram.

He seemed oblivious, detached, quite unaware that others were watching him.

He was planning, dreaming—what? Possibly new Hospitals for the Crippled Children, more Colleges for the Farm Hands.

It was worth a Day's Journey just to sit and look at the great Cherrib.

You may be sure that the Lynx also improved this Golden Opportunity to get a line on Jane Plummer, the good old Standby of the Sunday Editor.

He knew her by the Ear-Bobs, which were Pearls about the size of Ripe Olives.

He had put in a lot of time studying Price Tags and he judged the Pearls would fetch close to $50,000 apiece, or $100,000 for the Two.

But, of course, she could afford it, so it was none of his Business.

Mrs. Plummer, whose Vast Fortune if converted into $1 Bills and placed End to End would reach from Boston to Omaha, was engaged in some sort of Fancy Work on a Tambourine Frame.

She chatted in a care-free way as her jewelled Fingers plied the busy Needle.

Her remarks were addressed to a timid little Woman in rusty Black, who seemed more or less Cowed, which proved that she must be the hired Companion.

The Boy from the City had learned by a careful course of Reading, while lying in Bed, that every Woman of tremendous Wealth is trailed by a Female Friday who is addressed by her last Name.

He tried to pick out a Label for this Worm and decided that it might be Wiggins or Tubbs.

While he was wallowing in blissful Juxtaposition to the Prominent, some one touched him on the Shoulder.

It was the Room Clerk.

"I am off Watch," said the Employee, "and will take you on for Nine Holes."

Excusing himself from the Musical Comedy Star and the bold Speculator and the unprincipled Corrupter, he started for the Locker Room with Cuthbert, who had put him next to the King Pins.

"You are unquestionably the Child of Fortune," said the Room Clerk. "I take it that Mixer is your Middle Name. You work fast."

"One is always safe in flagging a theatrical Fairy," was the modest Reply. "I had no hesitancy about busting in as soon as I heard my friend Jimmy Hooper kidding her along."

"Why, you poor Fish! You have been getting gay for a Half Hour with Mrs. Beverly Margrave, acknowledged Leader of the Young Married Set."

"You must be mistaken. Mrs. Margrave was dressed in Gray and reading one of them High-Brow Books, and she got peeved because we made so much Racket."

"The Lady in Gray who won't speak to any one is Lottie Limmet. She won't even sign Autograph Albums."

"Back up! Do you mean to tell me that Mrs. Beverly Margrave, who comes of the most Aristocratic Family in Maryland, would stand for all that Joshing from a Rounder like Hooper?"

"Are you talking about that Buddie with the Loud Checks and the Crimson Cravat?"

"Sure."

"That was the Rev. Ormsby Toncell, and, take it from me, he's a regular Human Being."

"I think you're Twisted."

"No chance. Room Clerks know everything."

"I'm almost positive that the Reverend Toncell sat over to my right. He was dressed something like an Undertaker and kept smelling a Rose."

"You just got them reversed, that's all. The one with the Rose was Jimmy Hooper. He's Nuts about Flowers and keeps a fresh Bouquet on his Desk all the time."

"Have you got the unblushing Face to tell me that the Jolly Party with the Make-Up was the exclusive Matron and that a celebrated Preacher wore any such Stripes on his Shirt?"

"That's what I'm trying to Convey."

"Well, I'll prove that you're off. Do you think Mrs. Beverly Margrave and the Rev. Ormsby Toncell would hobnob with Steve Gurney after what all the newspapers have printed about him?"

"They didn't hobnob with Steve. They couldn't. He never goes near a Silk Stocking unless he wants to use him, and then he sends for him."

"Didn't I see it with my own Eyes?"

"Oh, you mean the big, square-jawed Burly that never buttons his Vest! That was Horace Cherrib, whom I told you about—the one that's going to save the World by feeding it $10 Bills."

"I don't think you took a good Look."

"Cert'nly I did. Steve wasn't near you Folks. He sat over there by himself and never chirped. 'Silent Steve,' his Friends call him."

"I refuse to believe that a kind-faced and gentle Soul like that is really the Boss of a disreputable Machine."

"No other kind could be. He wins out by making Friends."

"Well, anyway, I made no miscue on the Rich Widow. I marked her by the Expensive Pearls."

"Where do you get that Noise? Her Bill for Jewellery last year was 85 cents. She bought a jet Hat-Pin."

"Oh, come off! You don't mean to say——"

"Yes; the scared little Dame in the Black Gown, purchased direct from one of our largest Department Stores, has more Currency than you and I could shovel with two Shovels in two Weeks."

"How about the one with the enormous Pearls and the seven Rings?"
"Oh, that's her French Maid—from Wisconsin."

Moral: *The recognized Types never run true to Form during the Vacation Period.*

The Ninny Who Swam Away from the Life Preserver

Once there was a Citizen who put in most of his Time acting as Custodian of a Thirst.

He could inhale through a Straw, bury his Nose in it or leave it flow from the Original Package.

After he had bombarded the Innards with Aqua Fortis for a matter of 20 years, he awoke one Morning suffering from a combination of Pin-wheels, Moving-Pictures and a General Alarm of Fire.

Doc came in answer to a Hurry-Up and found that he was on the Job about 8 years too late.

The Patient had something like 15 Things the matter with him, ranging from Cirrhosis of the Liver to Water on the Brain, although the latter did not sound Reasonable.

He had six Weeks in which to settle up his Affairs before receiving the Wreaths and Pillows.

During that time he chopped on the Fire-Water because he somewhat blamed the Old Stuff for sending him away at 42 when he might have stuck around to be 87.

His Pals came to see him just before he winked out.

They found him very white and drawn and sort of Aghast at the Record he had established.

After the funeral the Pall-Bearers took off many Dark Gloves and flew at the High Balls.

One of them expressed the Opinion that what killed Jim was cutting out the Stimulants. The Shock was too much for him.

All the other Diagnosticians nodded their heads gravely.

And the Host went to the Cellar for another Load.

Moral: *It is absolutely Harmless unless Discontinued.*

Max Adeler

Charles Heber Clark (1841–1915) is a name unknown to all but a few zealous researchers in obscure Americana. Even "Max Adeler," the pseudonym under which Clark wrote, is forgotten. Yet Out of the Hurly-Burly sold more than a quarter of a million copies, and its author was known as the Maryland Marvel. Incidentally, there are those who maintain that Adeler, and not Graham (see page 300), was the originator of the "Little Willie" rhymes which are still going the rounds and are still being credited to that prolific author "Anonymous."

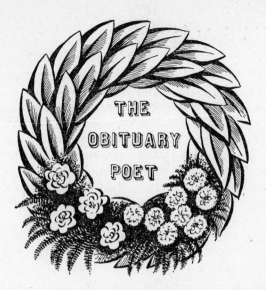

THE OBITUARY POET

A rather unusual sensation has been excited in the village by the *Morning Argus* within a day or two; and while most of the readers of that wonderful sheet have thus been supplied with amusement, the soul of the editor has been filled with gloom and wrath and despair. Colonel Bangs recently determined to engage an assistant to take the place made vacant by the retirement of the eminent art-critic, Mr. Murphy, and he found in one of the lower counties of the State a person who appeared to him to be suitable. The name of the new man is Slimmer. He has often contributed to the *Argus* verses of a distressing character, and I suppose Bangs must have become acquainted with him through the medium of the correspondence thus begun. No one in the world but Bangs would ever have selected such a poet for an editorial position. But Bangs is singular—he is exceptional. He never operates in accordance with any known laws, and he is more than likely to do any given thing in such a fashion as no other person could possibly have adopted for the purpose. As the *Argus* is also *sui generis*, perhaps Bangs does right to conduct it in a peculiar manner. But he made a mistake when he employed Mr. Slimmer.

The colonel, in his own small way, is tolerably shrewd. He had observed the disposition of persons who have been bereaved of their relatives to give expression to their feelings in verse, and it occurred to him that it might be profitable to use Slimmer's poetical talent in such a way as to make the *Argus* a very popular vehicle for the conveyance to the public of notices of deaths. That kind of intelligence, he well

15

knew, is especially interesting to a very large class of readers, and he believed that if he could offer to each advertiser a gratuitous verse to accompany the obituary paragraph, the *Argus* would not only attract advertisements of that description from the country round about the village, but it would secure a much larger circulation.

When Mr. Slimmer arrived, therefore, and entered upon the performance of his duties, Colonel Bangs explained his theory to the poet, and suggested that whenever a death-notice reached the office, he should immediately write a rhyme or two which should express the sentiments most suitable to the occasion.

"You understand, Mr. Slimmer," said the colonel, "that when the death of an individual is announced I want you, as it were, to cheer the members of the afflicted family with the resources of your noble art. I wish you to throw yourself, you may say, into their situation, and to give them, f'r instance, a few lines about the deceased which will seem to be the expression of the emotion which agitates the breasts of the bereaved."

"To lighten the gloom in a certain sense," said Mr. Slimmer, "and to—"

"Precisely," exclaimed Colonel Bangs. "Lighten the gloom. Do not mourn over the departed, but rather take a joyous view of death, which, after all, Mr. Slimmer, is, as it were, but the entrance to a better life. Therefore, I wish you to touch the heart-strings of the afflicted with a tender hand, and to endeavor, f'r instance, to divert their minds from a contemplation of the horrors of the tomb."

"Refrain from despondency, I suppose, and lift their thoughts to—"

"Just so! And at the same time combine elevating sentiment with such practical information as you can obtain from the advertisement. Throw a glamour of poesy, f'r instance, over the commonplace details of the every-day life of the deceased. People are fond of minute descriptions. Some facts useful for this purpose may be obtained from the man who brings the notice to the office; others you may perhaps be able to supply from your imagination."

"I think I can do it first rate," said Mr. Slimmer.

Mr. Slimmer had charge of the editorial department the next day during the absence of Colonel Bangs in Wilmington. Throughout the afternoon and evening death-notices arrived; and when one would reach Mr. Slimmer's desk, he would lock the door, place the fingers of his left hand among his hair and agonize until he succeeded in completing a verse that seemed to him to accord with instructions.

The next morning Mr. Slimmer proceeded calmly to the office for the purpose of embalming in sympathetic verse the memories of other departed ones. As he came near to the establishment he observed a crowd of people in front of it, struggling to get into the door. Ascending some steps upon the other side of the street, he overlooked the crowd, and could see within the office the clerks selling papers as fast as they could handle them, while the mob pushed and yelled in frantic efforts to obtain copies, the presses in the cellar meanwhile clanging furiously. Standing upon the curbstone in front of the office there was a long row of men, each of whom was engaged in reading *The Morning Argus* with an earnestness that Mr. Slimmer had never before seen displayed by the patrons of that sheet. The bard concluded that either his poetry had touched a sympathetic chord in the popular heart, or that an appalling disaster had occurred in some quarter of the globe.

He went around to the back of the office and ascended to the editorial rooms. As he approached the sanctum, loud voices were heard within. Mr. Slimmer determined to ascertain the cause before entering. He obtained a chair, and placing it by the side door, he mounted and peeped over the door through the transom. There sat Colonel Bangs, holding *The Morning Argus* in both hands, while the fringe which grew in a semicircle around the edge of his bald head stood straight out, until he seemed to resemble a gigantic gun-swab. Two or three persons stood in front of him in threatening attitudes. Slimmer heard one of them say:

"My name is McGlue, sir!—William McGlue! I am a brother of the late Alexander McGlue. I picked up your paper this morning, and perceived in it an outrageous insult to my deceased relative, and I have come around to demand, sir, WHAT YOU MEAN by the following infamous language:

" 'The death-angel smote Alexander McGlue,
    And gave him protracted repose;
He wore a checked shirt and a Number Nine shoe,
    And he had a pink wart on his nose.
No doubt he is happier dwelling in space
    Over there on the evergreen shore.
His friends are informed that his funeral takes place
    Precisely at quarter-past four.'

"This is simply diabolical! My late brother had no wart on his nose, sir. He had upon his nose neither a pink wart nor a green wart, nor a cream-colored wart, nor a wart of any other color. It is a slander! It is a gratuitous insult to my family, and I distinctly want you to say *what do you mean* by such conduct?"

"Really, sir," said Bangs, "it is a mistake. This is the horrible work of a miscreant in whom I reposed perfect confidence. He shall be punished by my own hand for this outrage."

"How could I know," murmured Mr. Slimmer to the foreman, who with him was listening, "that the corpse hadn't a pink wart? I used to know a man named McGlue, and *he* had one, and I thought *all* the McGlues had. This comes of irregularities in families."

"And who," said another man, addressing the editor, "authorized you to print this hideous stuff about my deceased son? Do you mean to say, Bangs, that it was not with your authority that your low comedian inserted with my advertisement the following scandalous burlesque? Listen to this:

" 'Willie had a purple monkey climbing on a yellow stick,
And when he sucked the paint all off it made him deathly sick;
And in his latest hours he clasped that monkey in his hand,
And bade good-bye to earth and went into a better land.

" 'Oh! no more he'll shoot his sister with his little wooden gun;
And no more he'll twist the pussy's tail and make her yowl, for fun.
The pussy's tail now stands out straight; the gun is laid aside;
The monkey doesn't jump around since little Willie died.'

"The atrocious character of this libel will appear when I say that my son was twenty years old, and that he died of liver complaint."

"Infamous!—utterly infamous!" groaned the editor as he cast his eyes over the lines.

"And yet," whispered Slimmer to the foreman, "he told me to lighten the gloom and to cheer the afflicted family with the resources of my art; and I certainly thought that idea about the monkey would have that effect, somehow. Bangs is ungrateful!"

Just then there was a knock at the door, and a woman entered, crying.

"Are you the editor?" she inquired of Colonel Bangs.

Bangs said he was.

"W-w-well!" she said, in a voice broken by sobs, "wh-what d'you mean by publishing this kind of poetry about m-my child? M-my name is Sm-Smith; and wh-when I looked this m-morning for the notice of Johnny's d-death in your paper, I saw this scandalous verse:

" 'Four doctors tackled Johnny Smith—
They blistered and they bled him;
With squills and anti-bilious pills
And ipecac, they fed him.

They stirred him up with calomel,
And tried to move his liver;
But all in vain—his little soul
Was wafted o'er The River.' "

"Madam, I shall go crazy!" exclaimed Bangs. "This is not my work.
It is the work of a villain whom I will slay with my own hand as soon
as he comes in."

"Strange! strange!" said Slimmer. "And this man told me to combine
elevating sentiment with practical information. If the information concerning the squills and ipecac is not practical, I have misunderstood the
use of that word. And if young Smith didn't have four doctors, it was
an outrage. He ought to have had them, and they ought to have excited
his liver. Thus it is that human life is sacrificed to carelessness."

At this juncture the sheriff entered, his brow clothed with thunder.
He had a copy of *The Morning Argus* in his hand. He approached the
editor, and pointing to a death-notice, said, "Read that outrageous burlesque, and tell me the name of the writer!"

The editor read as follows:

"We have lost our little Hanner in a very painful manner,
And we often asked, How can her harsh sufferings be borne?
When her death was first reported, her aunt got up and snorted
With the grief that she supported, for it made her feel forlorn.

"She was such a little seraph that her father, who is sheriff,
Really doesn't seem to care if he ne'er smiles in life again.
She has gone, we hope, to heaven, at the early age of seven
(Funeral starts off at eleven), where she'll nevermore have pain."

"As a consequence of this, I withdraw all the county advertising from
your paper. A man who could trifle in this manner with the feelings of
a parent is a savage and a scoundrel!"

As the sheriff went out, Colonel Bangs placed his head upon the table
and groaned.

"Really," Mr. Slimmer said, "that person must be deranged. I tried,
in his case, to put myself in his place, and to write as if I was one of the
family, according to instructions. That allusion to the grief of the aunt,
particularly, seemed to me to be very happy. It expresses violent emotion with a felicitous combination of sweetness and force. These people
have no soul—no appreciation of the beautiful in art."

While the poet mused, hurried steps were heard upon the stairs, and
in a moment a middle-aged man dashed in abruptly, and seizing the

colonel's scattered hair, bumped his prostrate head against the table three or four times with considerable force. Having expended the violence of his emotion in this manner, he held the editor's head down with one hand, shaking it occasionally by way of emphasis, and with the other hand seized the paper and said,

"You disgraceful old reprobate! You disgusting vampire! You hoary-headed old ghoul! What d'you mean by putting such stuff as this in your paper about my deceased son?

" 'Oh! bury Bartholomew out in the woods,
    In a beautiful hole in the ground,
Where the bumble-bees buzz and the woodpeckers sing,
    And the straddle-bugs tumble around;
So that, in winter, when the snow and the slush
    Have covered his last little bed,
His brother Artemas can go out with Jane
    And visit the place with his sled.'

"I'll teach you to talk about straddle-bugs! I'll instruct you about slush! I'll enlighten your insane old intellect on the subject of singing woodpeckers!"

At the end of every phrase the visitor gave the editor's head a fresh knock against the table. When the exercise was ended, Colonel Bangs explained and apologized in the humblest manner, promising at the same time to give his assailant a chance to flog Mr. Slimmer, who was expected to arrive in a few moments.

"The treachery of this man," murmured the poet to the foreman, "is dreadful. Didn't he desire me to throw a glamour of poesy over commonplace details? But for that I should never have thought of alluding to woodpeckers and bugs, and other children of Nature. The man objects to the remarks about the sled. Can the idiot know that it was necessary to have a rhyme for 'bed'? Can he suppose that I could write poetry without rhymes? The man is a lunatic!"

The poet determined to leave before any more criticisms were made upon his performances. He jumped down from his chair and crept softly toward the back staircase.

The story told by the foreman relates that Colonel Bangs at the same instant resolved to escape any further persecution, and he moved off in the direction taken by the poet. The two met upon the landing, and the colonel was about to begin his quarrel with Slimmer, when an enraged old woman who had been groping her way up stairs suddenly plunged her umbrella at Bangs, and held him in the corner while she handed a copy of the *Argus* to Slimmer, and pointing to a certain stanza, asked him to read it aloud. He did so in a somewhat tremulous voice and with frightened glances at the enraged colonel. The verse was as follows:

"Little Alexander's dead;
　Jam him in a coffin;
Don't have as good a chance
　For a fun'ral often.
Rush his body right around
　To the cemetery;
Drop him in the sepulchre
　With his Uncle Jerry."

When Mr. Slimmer had concluded his portion of the entertainment, he left the colonel in the hands of the enemy and fled. He has not been seen in New Castle since that day, and it is supposed that he has returned to Sussex county for the purpose of continuing in private his dalliance with the Muses. Colonel Bangs appears to have abandoned the idea of establishing a department of obituary poetry, and the *Argus* has resumed its accustomed aspect of dreariness.

It may fairly boast, however, that once during its career it produced a profound impression upon the community.

TEN  TALES

It's a tall country, mister, said the Old Settler. And the stories have got to grow to match those tall buildings and that tall timber. Why, out in the Paul Bunyan country—that's the country that runs from Michigan through Minnesota clear out to Oregon and the Pacific—they say the trees grow so high it takes a man a whole week to see the top of them.

And, speaking of Paul Bunyan, that giant lumberjack, did you ever hear of the house he built in the north woods? It was so high that he had to put the last five stories on hinges to let the moon go by.

Yes, sir—and the time Paul Bunyan went hunting. He was the surest shot and the fastest runner that ever waded across the Mississippi. They still talk of it out in the Northwest. It seems Paul sighted a big buck a mile away; it was standing on the edge of a cliff—and Paul knew if he shot him, the buck would fall off the edge and down the cliff. So Paul pulled the trigger—and as soon as the bullet left the gun, Paul ran to where the buck was standing. He ran so fast he got there ahead of the shot—he had to duck his head to let the bullet go by. Yes, sir.

And the buck? Oh, the buck was killed all right. But not by the bullet. When it saw Paul standing there, that buck was plumb scared to death. It died without waiting for the shot to reach it.

That's how things happened in the Paul Bunyan country.

And out in Iowa, where the black loam is twenty feet deep, the corn grows so high they have to climb ladders to get down the ears. Why, once out near Ames there was a boy who saw a shoot of corn coming out of the earth and when it got as high as his shoulder he started climbing it just for fun. Before he could yell "Whoa!" the cornstalk was higher than the silo, and it was still going strong. They had to shoot biscuits up to the boy to keep him from starving. Pretty soon the cornstalk got beyond rifle range and they had to drop food to the boy by airplane. Then they put an axe to the stalk, but Paul Bunyan and all his loggers couldn't have chopped it down.

23

It grew all through the winter, and it lasted until the big blizzard the following year. The boy, poor kid, was never seen again. And if you don't believe the story, they'll show you the very place where the cornstalk grew.

In Ohio they still talk about Mike Fink, who was half horse and half alligator and the rest of him snapping turtle. He was the toughest fighter ever was; his fists went round like a windmill, and he never was licked in his life.

Never? Well, just once, maybe. And that was by Davy Crockett's wife—Mary Jane Whirlwind Thunder and Lightning Crockett. Just to scare her, Mike dressed himself in an old alligator skin and came crawling into Mary Jane's cabin.

But Mary Jane didn't scare easy. She'd been brought up on buffalo's milk and she'd cut her teeth on a rusty saw. She put her arm down the alligator's throat and turned him inside out. And there was Mike Fink. She was just about to put her arm down *his* throat when Mike gave a great whoop, dashed off and plunged into the river. He's still there.

And whenever the Ohio goes on a rampage, rising and roaring over its banks, that's Mike Fink thinking of Mary Jane Crockett and lashing his tail. Leastways, that's what they say.

Wyoming—that's great sheep-herding country. And if you want to hold on to your sheep, you got to know how to count 'em too.

They tell about a famous sheep-counter who in a second could size up a herd, no matter how big it was. He never missed. Well, one day a wealthy rancher took him up a mountain and showed him a huge flock of sheep grazing in the valley. "About how many would you say there was?" asked the rancher.

"I wouldn't say *about* how many," said the sheep-counter. "I'd say there was exactly eight hundred and three sheep."

"That's right," said the rancher. "Now come on over to the other side of the mountain, and see if you can guess how many there is in my other herd."

"I don't guess," said the counter, and walked over to the other side of the mountain. "That's a bigger bunch—there are two thousand, five hundred and sixty-six—no, sixty-seven—sheep there."

"Gosh!" said the rancher. "That's wonderful! How do you do it?"

"It's easy," said the counter. "I just count their feet and divide by four."

Florida's the place for snakes—rattlers, copperheads, moccasins, pretty little coral snakes that are the worst of the lot. One day I was starting to fish near the Okefenokee when I noticed I had forgotten to bring any bait. I looked around—and there, behind a log, was a great big venomous copperhead with a fat worm in his mouth.

I needed that worm, so just before the snake swallowed it, I reached into my back-pocket, took out my flask of whiskey, and quickly poured a few drops down the snake's throat. The whiskey was strong, and it must have burned, for the snake dropped the worm and slid off in a hurry.

I caught my fish all right, a big fellow, too. But I was still short of bait.

Then I heard a little slithering sound. It was the snake. He was back —with another worm in his mouth.

You talk about worms and things like that—Georgia, that's the state for vermin. Especially cockroaches. You never saw such roaches. Big as a man's arm. And smart! Even the small ones—the two-foot cockroaches—would eat you instead of trying to drag you off. They knew if they waited, a larger cockroach would take you away from them.

During the war the Georgia cockroaches won one battle after another. They had organization, they had! Soldiers coming back to the barracks would hear a shuffling noise in the darkness. When the light was switched on, there were the cockroaches—drilling. And they were using the company's rifles!

The hottest place in the country? Southern Texas. But you get used to it—you get so that nothing nowhere else can ever be warm enough.

They tell about a man from Texas who came up to Michigan for work. It was early spring but there was still a touch of snow in the air. But the Texan couldn't stand it. He fell to the sidewalk and stiffened out.

They tried to revive him, but he didn't respond. They tried to pour whiskey down his throat, but it was no use.

"He's dead," they said. "There's nothing we can do with him. We'll have to cremate him and send the ashes home."

So they put his rigid body into a crematory oven and stoked up the fire.

Two hours later they opened the door of the furnace, and there was the man from Texas sitting bolt upright.

"For heaven's sake," he shouted. "Close that door! I'll catch my death of cold in a draft like that!"

Texas—that's the place where everything grows Bigger and Better. Even the dust-storms. They say that out in the Panhandle a rancher went to town to borrow money on his ranch. "Before I can let you have anything," said the banker, shouting above the high wind, "I'll have to go out and take a look at your place." " 'Twon't be necessary," said the rancher. "Here comes the place now."

And the Texas Rangers—they grow big, too. Seems there was a riot or something in one of the towns and the mayor wired for a company of Rangers to come and disperse the mob. Pretty soon a lone Ranger showed up. "Hey," said the mayor, "it's a tough mob—I wired for a company of Rangers, not just one Ranger!"

"Well," drawled the Ranger, "you ain't got but one mob, ain't you?"

Illinois—that's where they get things done, and get them done fast! Especially in Chicago.

It seems a fellow from Chicago was visiting a friend in New York and they were walking down Fifth Avenue together.

"That building there," said the man from Chicago, pointing to one of the big hotels, "how long did it take to put that up?"

"Oh, about two years," said his New York friend.

"Not bad. But in Chicago we could have built it in half the time. And that structure—how long did *that* take?"

"That? The Public Library?" said the New Yorker, trying to out-boast the Chicagoan. "Less than four months."

"Four months? We could have done it in two. And this one?" said the visitor, pointing to the hundred stories of the Empire State sky-scraper.

"I can't say," replied the New Yorker cautiously. "It wasn't here last night."

Talk about fogs! In California the fogs are so thick that ships often sail right across country till they hit the Sierra Nevada mountains. Sure thing—they even tell how they shingle houses ten feet beyond the roof and nail the shingles to the fog. And it gets so cold at night your shadow freezes on the wall and they have to use blowtorches to thaw it out.

But that ain't nothing compared to Kansas, the home of the torna-does that will pick up telephone poles and set them down—in the same order—two states away. And the telephone girls with them. Why, one morning at milking time, a Kansas tornado came along and picked up a whole town, and dropped it in Nebraska—including the wheel-tracks.

Yes, sir, it's a tall country. And growing taller all the time.

Hilaire Belloc

Born in Paris (1870) of a French father and an English mother, educated at Oxford and trained in a regiment of French artillery, the versatile Hilaire Belloc learned to write easily on anything and everything. He even wrote authoritatively (according to the title of one of his books of essays) On Nothing. His fertility was a legend which happened to be a fact. Before he was seventy he had become the author of about one hundred volumes of prose and poetry—histories, biographies, travel sketches, religious philosophy, satirical fiction, parables and polemics. Most of these books reveal Belloc's delight in controversy, a light-hearted truculence which might be characterized as simple Bellocosity.

Belloc's most quoted works are his least ambitious: The Bad Child's Book of Beasts, More Beasts for Worse Children, and Cautionary Tales, three booklets of verse which combine the oversimplification of a child's Primer and the heavy moralizing of Sunday school verse, and then turn the morals upside down.

Jim

There was a Boy whose name was Jim;
His Friends were very good to him.
They gave him Tea, and Cakes, and Jam,
And slices of delicious Ham,
And Chocolate with pink inside
And little Tricycles to ride,
And read him Stories through and through,
And even took him to the Zoo—
But there it was the Dreadful Fate
Befell him, which I now relate.

You know—at least you ought to know,
For I have often told you so—
That Children never are allowed
To leave their Nurses in a Crowd;
Now this was Jim's especial Foible,
He ran away when he was able,
And on this inauspicious day
He slipped his hand and ran away!

He hadn't gone a yard when—Bang!
With open Jaws, a Lion sprang,
And hungrily began to eat
The Boy: beginning at his feet.
Now, just imagine how it feels
With first your toes and then your heels,
And then by gradual degrees,
Your shins and ankles, calves and knees,
Are slowly eaten, bit by bit.
No wonder Jim detested it!

No wonder that he shouted "Hi!"
The Honest Keeper heard his cry,
Though very fat he almost ran
To help the Little Gentleman.
"Ponto!" he ordered as he came
(For Ponto was the Lion's name),
"Ponto!" he cried, with angry Frown,

"Let go, Sir! Down, Sir! Put It down!"
The Lion made a sudden stop,
He let the Dainty Morsel drop,
And slunk reluctant to his Cage,
Snarling with Disappointed Rage.
But when he bent him over Jim,
The Honest Keeper's Eyes were dim.
The Lion having reached his Head,
The Miserable Boy was dead!

When Nurse informed his Parents, they
Were more Concerned than I can say:—
His Mother, as She dried her eyes,
Said, "Well—it gives me no surprise,
He would not do as he was told!"
His Father, who was self-controlled,
Bade all the Children round attend
To James's miserable end,
And always keep a-hold of Nurse
For fear of finding Something Worse.

Henry King

The Chief Defect of Henry King
Was chewing little bits of String.
At last he swallowed some which tied
Itself in ugly Knots inside.

Physicians of the Utmost Fame
Were called at once; but when they came
They answered, as they took their Fees,
"There is no Cure for this Disease.

"Henry will very soon be dead."
His Parents stood about his Bed
Lamenting his Untimely Death,
When Henry, with his Latest Breath,

Cried, "Oh, my Friends, be warned by me,
That Breakfast, Dinner, Lunch, and Tea
Are all the Human Frame requires. . . ."
With that, the Wretched Child expires.

Algernon

Young Algernon, the Doctor's Son,
Was playing with a Loaded Gun.
He pointed it towards his Sister,
Aimed very carefully, but missed her.

His Father, who was standing near,
The Loud Explosion chanced to hear,
And reprimanded Algernon
For playing with a Loaded Gun.

The Yak

As a friend to the children commend me the Yak.
  You will find it exactly the thing:
It will carry and fetch, you can ride on its back,
  Or lead it about with a string.

The Tartar who dwells on the plains of Thibet
  (A desolate region of snow)
Has for centuries made it a nursery pet,
  And surely the Tartar should know!

Then tell your papa where the Yak can be got,
  And if he is awfully rich
He will buy you the creature—or else he will not.
  (I cannot be positive which.)

The Lion

The Lion, the Lion, he dwells in the waste,
He has a big head and a very small waist;
But his shoulders are stark, and his jaws they are grim,
And a good little child will not play with him.

Four Epigrams

ON HIS BOOKS

When I am dead, I hope it may be said:
"His sins were scarlet—but his books were read."

ON THE POLITICIAN

Here, richly, with ridiculous display,
The Politician's corpse was laid away.
While all of his acquaintance sneered and slanged,
I wept: for I had longed to see him hanged.

ON LADY POLTAGRUE, A PUBLIC PERIL

The Devil, having nothing else to do,
Went off to tempt my Lady Poltagrue.
My Lady, tempted by a private whim,
To his extreme annoyance, tempted him.

FATIGUED

I'm tired of Love; I'm still more tired of Rhyme;
But Money gives me pleasure all the time.

Ludwig Bemelmans

If not a whole atlas in himself, Ludwig Bemelmans is at least a small continent of varied cultures and backgrounds. His father was Belgian, a happy-go-lucky painter. His mother was Bavarian, daughter of a prosperous brewer. Born in the Tyrol, in a district that was alternately Austrian and Italian, Bemelmans was educated in Germany, apprenticed to his uncle who owned a string of hotels in the Alps, and, after a succession of misadventures, was given (so he insists) the choice of a Reform School or immigration to America. He chose the latter. That was in 1914.

When he arrived in New York he was sixteen and was put to work in the dining-room of a hotel which he only slightly disguised in one of the best of his books, Hotel Splendide. Here he gradually rose to the proud eminence of waiter and a confidante of the maître d'hôtel. During the first World War, Bemelmans was naturalized and served with the U. S. Army—an episode he has recorded in My War with the United States. He had always "played" with drawing; now he turned to it in earnest. The war over, he decorated studios, designed settings for the stage, and illustrated his books with the same ease and amiable nonchalance which is his way of writing. An affable recluse, he claims that he does most of his thinking, like Diogenes, in the tub. His books, he says, are the result of insomnia; if he could sleep soundly, he would never write again.

The Elephant Cutlet

Once upon a time there were two men in Vienna who wanted to open a restaurant. One was a Dentist who was tired of fixing teeth and always wanted to own a restaurant, and the other a famous cook by the name of Souphans.

The Dentist was, however, a little afraid. "There are," he says, "already too many restaurants in Vienna, restaurants of every kind, Viennese, French, Italian, Chinese, American, American-Chinese, Portuguese, Armenian, Dietary, Vegetarian, Jewish, Wine and Beer Restaurants, in short all sorts of restaurants."

But the Chef had an Idea. "There is one kind of restaurant that Vienna has not," he said.

"What kind?" said the Dentist.

"A restaurant such as has never existed before, a restaurant for cutlets from every animal in the world."

The Dentist was afraid, but finally he agreed, and the famous Chef went out to buy a house, tables, and chairs, and engaged help, pots and pans and had a sign painted with big red letters ten feet high saying:

"Cutlets from Every Animal in the World."

The first customer that entered the door was a distinguished lady, a Countess. She sat down and asked for an Elephant Cutlet.

"How would Madame like this Elephant Cutlet cooked?" said the waiter.

"Oh, Milanaise, sauté in butter, with a little spaghetti over it, on that a filet of anchovy, and an olive on top," she said.

"That is very nice," said the waiter and went out to order it.

"Jessas Maria und Joseph!" said the Dentist when he heard the order and he turned to the Chef and cried: "What did I tell you? Now what are we going to do?"

The Chef said nothing, he put on a clean apron and walked into the dining room to the table of the Lady. There he bowed, bent down to her and said: "Madame has ordered an Elephant Cutlet?"

"Yes," said the Countess.

"With spaghetti and a filet of anchovy and an olive?"

"Yes."

"Madame is all alone?"

"Yes, yes."

"Madame expects no one else?"

"No."

"And Madame wants only one cutlet?"

"Yes," said the Lady, "but why all these questions?"

"Because," said the Chef, "because, Madame, I am very sorry, but for one Cutlet we cannot cut up our Elephant."

Robert Benchley

"America's leading writer of nonsense for nonsense's sake." "Misfortune's fool, he makes capital of a handicap." "A character where anomaly is the norm and inconsistency the standard." These are a few of the tributes paid to Robert Benchley (born in Worcester, 1889; B. A. Harvard, 1912) by his fellow humorists. Benchley himself was not flattered by such praise. His chief desire in life was to be a social service worker, his literary ambition to write a life of Queen Anne. He gratified at least part of his aims, for he fought for social justice, even for the awkward and ridiculous people he burlesqued. A born Master of Ceremonies, Benchley also acted in Hollywood productions, as well as in his own motion picture and radio shows. In 1936 he won the award of the Academy of Motion Picture Arts and Sciences with a memorable piece of mock-research, "How to Sleep." He died suddenly November 21, 1945.

Benchley's ready gift for bewilderment is best illustrated by "The Treasurer's Report," which started as a parlor trick and has become the anthologist's standby, and by the books gravely entitled 20,000 Leagues Under the Sea or, David Copperfield and My Ten Years in a Quandary and How They Grew.

The Treasurer's Report

The report is delivered by an Assistant Treasurer who has been called in to pinch-hit for the regular Treasurer who is ill. He is not a very good public-speaker, this assistant, but after a few minutes of confusion is caught up by the spell of his own oratory and is hard to stop.

I shall take but a very few moments of your time this evening, for I realize that you would much rather be listening to this interesting entertainment than to a dry financial statement . . . but I *am* reminded of a story—which you have probably all of you heard.

It seems that there were these two Irishmen walking down the street when they came to a—oh, I should have said in the first place that the parrot which was hanging out in *front* of the store—or rather belonging to one of these two fellows—the *first* Irishman, that is—was—well, *anyway,* this parrot——

(After a slight cogitation, he realizes that, for all practical purposes, the story is as good as lost; so he abandons it entirely and, stepping forward, drops his facile, story-telling manner and assumes a quite spurious businesslike air.)

Now, in connection with reading this report, there are one or two points which Dr. Murnie wanted brought up in connection with it, and he has asked me to bring them up in connec—to bring them up.

In the first place, there is the question of the work which we are trying to do up there at our little place at Silver Lake, a work which we feel not only fills a very definite need in the community but also fills a very definite need—er—in the community. I don't think that many members of the Society realize just how big the work is that we are trying to do up there. For instance, I don't think that it is generally known that most of our boys are between the age of fourteen. We feel that, by taking the boy at this age, we can get closer to his real nature—for a boy *has* a very real nature, you may be sure—and bring him into closer touch not only with the school, the parents, and with each other, but also with the town in which they live, the country to whose flag they pay allegiance, and to the—ah—*(trailing off)* town in which they live.

Now the fourth point which Dr. Murnie wanted brought up was that in connection with the installation of the new furnace last Fall. There seems to have been considerable talk going around about this not having been done quite as economically as it might—have—been—done, when, as a matter of fact, the whole thing *was* done just as economically as possible—in fact, even *more* so. I have here a report of the Furnace Committee, showing just how the whole thing was handled from start to finish.

(*Reads from report, with considerable initial difficulty with the stiff covers.*)

Bids were submitted by the following firms of furnace contractors, with a clause stating that if we did not engage a firm to do the work for us we should pay them nothing for submitting the bids. This clause alone saved us a great deal of money.

The following firms, then, submitted bids:

Merkle, Wybigant Co., the Eureka Dust Bin and Shaker Co., The Elite Furnace Shop, and Harris, Birnbauer and Harris. The bid of Merkle, Wybigant being the lowest, Harris Birnbauer were selected to do the job.

(*Here a page is evidently missing from the report, and a hurried search is carried on through all the pages, without result.*)

Well, that pretty well clears up that end of the work.

Those of you who contributed so generously last year to the floating hospital have probably wondered what became of the money. I was speaking on this subject only last week at our up-town branch, and, after the meeting, a dear little old lady, dressed all in lavender, came up on the platform, and, laying her hand on my arm, said: 'Mr. So-and-so (calling me by name), Mr. So-and-so, what the hell did you do with all the money we gave you last year?' Well, I just laughed and pushed her off the platform, but it has occurred to the committee that perhaps some of you, like that little old lady, would be interested in knowing the disposition of the funds.

Now, Mr. Rossiter, unfortunately our treasurer—or rather Mr. Rossiter our *treasurer, unfortunately* is confined at his home tonight with a bad head-cold and I have been asked (*he hears someone whispering at him from the wings, but decides to ignore it*) and I have been asked if I would (*the whisperer will not be denied, so he goes over to the entrance and receives a brief message, returning beaming and laughing to himself*). Well, the joke seems to be on *me!* Mr. Rossiter has *pneumonia!*

Following, then, is a summary of the Treasurer's Report:

(Reads, in a very businesslike manner.)

During the year 1929—and by that is meant 1928—the Choral Society received the following in donations:

B. L. G.	$500
G. K. M.	500
Lottie and Nellie W.	500
In memory of a happy summer at Rye Beach	10
Proceeds of a sale of coats and hats left in the boat-house	14.55
And then the Junior League gave a performance of 'Pinafore' for the benefit of the Fund which, unfortunately, resulted in a deficit of	300
Then, from dues and charges	2,354.75
And, following the installation of the new furnace, a saving in coal amounting to $374.75—which made Dr. Murnie very happy, you may be sure.	
Making a total of receipts amounting to	$3,645.75

This is all, of course, reckoned as of June.

In the matter of expenditures, the Club has not been so fortunate. There was the unsettled condition of business, and the late Spring, to contend with, resulting in the following—er—rather discouraging figures, I am afraid.

Expenditures	$23,574.85
Then there was a loss, owing to—several things—of	3,326.70
Car-fare	4,452.25
And then, Mrs. Rawlins' expense account, when she went down to see the work they are doing in Baltimore, came to $256.50, but I am sure that you will all agree that it was worth it to find out—er—what they are doing in Baltimore.	
And then, under the general head of Odds and Ends	2,537.50
Making a total disbursement of	
(hurriedly)	$416,546.75

or a net deficit of—ah—several thousand dollars.

Now, these figures bring us down only to October. In October my sister was married, and the house was all torn up, and in the general confusion we lost track of the figures of May and August. All those wishing the *approximate* figures for May and August, however, may obtain them from me in the vestry after the dinner, where I will be with pledge cards for those of you who wish to subscribe over and above your annual dues, and I hope that each and every one of you here tonight will look deep into his heart and (*archly*) into his pocketbook, and see if he cannot find it there to help us to put this thing over with a bang (*accompanied by a wholly ineffectual gesture representing a bang*) and to help and make this just the biggest and best year the Armenians have ever had. . . . I thank you.

(*Exits, bumping into proscenium.*)

Kiddie-Kar Travel

In America there are two classes of travel—first class, and with children. Traveling with children corresponds roughly to traveling third-class in Bulgaria. They tell me there is nothing lower in the world than third-class Bulgarian travel.

The actual physical discomfort of traveling with the Kiddies is not so great, although you do emerge from it looking as if you had just moved the piano upstairs single-handed. It is the mental wear-and-tear that tells and for a sensitive man there is only one thing worse, and that is a church wedding in which he is playing the leading comedy rôle.

There are several branches of the ordeal of Going on Choo-Choo, and it is difficult to tell which is the roughest. Those who have taken a very small baby on a train maintain that this ranks as pleasure along with having a nerve killed. On the other hand, those whose wee companions are in the romping stage, simply laugh at the claims of the first group. Sometimes you will find a man who has both an infant *and* a romper with him. Such a citizen should receive a salute of twenty-one guns every time he enters the city and should be allowed to wear the insignia of the Pater Dolorosa, giving him the right to solicit alms on the cathedral steps.

There is much to be said for those who maintain that rather should the race be allowed to die out than that babies should be taken from place to place along our national arteries of traffic. On the other hand, there *are* moments when babies are asleep. (Oh, yes, there are. There *must* be.) But it is practically a straight run of ten or a dozen hours for your child of four. You may have a little trouble in getting the infant to doze off, especially as the train newsboy waits crouching in the vestibule until he sees signs of slumber on the child's face and then rushes in to yell, "Copy of *Life*, out today!" right by its pink, shell-like ear. But after it *is* asleep, your troubles are over except for wondering how you can shift your ossifying arm to a new position without disturbing its precious burden.

If the child is of an age which denies the existence of sleep, however, preferring to run up and down the aisle of the car rather than sit in its chair (at least a baby can't get out of its chair unless it falls out and even then it can't go far), then every minute of the trip is full of fun. On the whole, having traveled with children of all the popular ages, I would be inclined to award the Hair-Shirt to the man who successfully completes the ride with a boy of, let us say, three.

In the first place, you start with the pronounced ill-will of two-thirds of the rest of the occupants of the car. You see them as they come in, before the train starts, glancing at you and yours with little or no attempt to conceal the fact that they wish they had waited for the four o'clock. Across from you is perhaps a large man who, in his home town, has a reputation for eating little children. He wears a heavy gold watch chain and wants to read through a lot of reports on the trip. He is just about as glad to be opposite a small boy as he would be if it were a hurdy-gurdy.

In back of you is a lady in a black silk dress who doesn't like the porter. Ladies in black silk dresses always seem to board the train with an aversion to the porter. The fact that the porter has to be in the same car with her makes her fussy to start with, and when she discovers that in front of her is a child of three who is already eating (you simply have to give him a lemon-drop to keep him quiet at least until the train starts) she decides that the best thing to do is simply to ignore him and not give him the slightest encouragement to become friendly. The child therefore picks her out immediately to be his buddy.

For a time after things get to going all you have to do is answer questions about the scenery. This is only what you must expect when you have children, and it happens no matter where you are. You can always say that you don't know who lives in that house or what that cow is doing. Sometimes you don't even have to look up when you say that you don't know. This part is comparatively easy.

It is when the migratory fit comes on that you will be put to the test. Suddenly you look and find the boy staggering down the aisle, peering into the faces of people as he passes them. "Here! Come back here, Roger!" you cry, lurching after him and landing across the knees of the young lady two seats down. Roger takes this as a signal for a game and starts to run, screaming with laughter. After four steps he falls and starts to cry.

On being carried kicking back to his seat, he is told that he mustn't run down the aisle again. This strikes even Roger as funny, because it is such a flat thing to say. Of course he is going to run down the aisle again and he knows it as well as you do. In the meantime, however, he is perfectly willing to spend a little time with the lady in the black silk dress.

"Here, Roger," you say, "don't bother the lady."

"Hello, little boy," the lady says, nervously, and tries to go back to her book. The interview is over as far as she is concerned. Roger, however, thinks that it would be just dandy to get up in her lap. This has to be stopped, and Roger has to be whispered to.

He then announces that it is about time that he went to the wash-room. You march down the car, steering him by the shoulders and both lurching together as the train takes the curves and attracting wide attention to your very obvious excursion. Several kindly people smile knowingly at you as you pass and try to pat the boy on the head, but their advances are repelled, it being a rule of all children to look with disfavor on any attentions from strangers. The only people they want to play with are those who hate children.

On reaching the wash-room you discover that the porter has just locked it and taken the key with him, simply to be nasty. This raises quite a problem. You explain the situation as well as possible, which turns out to be not well enough. There is every indication of loud crying and perhaps worse. You call attention to the Burrows Rustless Screen sign which you are just passing and stand in the passage way

by the drinking-cups, feverishly trying to find things in the landscape
as it whirls by which will serve to take the mind off the tragedy of the
moment. You become so engrossed in this important task that it is
some time before you discover that you are completely blocking the
passage way and the progress of some fifteen people who want to get
off at Utica. There is nothing for you to do but head the procession
and get off first.

Once out in the open, the pride and prop of your old age decides that
the thing to do is pay the engineer a visit, and starts off up the platform at a terrific rate. This amuses the onlookers and gives you a little
exercise after being cramped up in that old car all the morning. The
imminent danger of the train's starting without you only adds to the
fun. At that, there might be worse things than being left in Utica. One
of them is getting back on the train again to face the old gentleman
with the large watch chain.

The final phase of the ordeal, however, is still in store for you when
you make your way (and Roger's way) into the diner. Here the plung-
ing march down the aisle of the car is multiplied by six (the diner is
never any nearer than six cars and usually is part of another train).
On the way, Roger sees a box of animal crackers belonging to a little
girl and commandeers it. The little girl, putting up a fight, is promptly
pushed over, starting what promises to be a free-for-all fight between
the two families. Lurching along after the apologies have been made,
it is just a series of unwarranted attacks by Roger on sleeping travelers
and equally unwarranted evasions by Roger of the kindly advances of
very nice people who love children.

In the diner, it turns out that the nearest thing they have suited to
Roger's customary diet is veal cutlets, and you hardly think that his
mother would approve of those. Everything else has peppers or sardines
in it. A curry of lamb across the way strikes the boy's fancy and he
demands some of that. On being told that he has not the slightest
chance in the world of getting it but how would he like a little crackers-
and-milk, he becomes quite upset and threatens to throw a fork at the
Episcopal clergyman sitting opposite. Pieces of toast are waved allur-
ingly in front of him and he is asked to consider the advantages of
preserved figs and cream, but it is curry of lamb or he gets off the train.
He doesn't act like this at home. In fact, he is noted for his tractability.
There seems to be something about the train that brings out all the
worst that is in him, all the hidden traits that he has inherited from his
mother's side of the family. There is nothing else to do but say firmly:
"Very well, then, Roger. We'll go back *without* any nice dinner," and

carry him protesting from the diner, apologizing to the head steward for the scene and considering dropping him overboard as you pass through each vestibule.

In fact, I had a cousin once who had to take three of his little ones on an all-day trip from Philadelphia to Boston. It was the hottest day of the year and my cousin had on a woolen suit. By the time he reached Hartford, people in the car noticed that he had only two children with him. At Worcester he had only one. No one knew what had become of the others and no one asked. It seemed better not to ask. He reached Boston alone and never explained what had become of the tiny tots. Anyone who has ever traveled with tiny tots of his own, however, can guess.

Sally Benson

Sally Benson must be tired of the words "witty" and "penetrating." They have been endlessly applied not only to her work but to her personality. Born in St. Louis in 1900, mother of a grown daughter, she still looks as though she might have stepped off the stage of one of Broadway's better musical comedies. As a matter of record, her acquaintance with the theater is more than casual; a dramatization of her vignettes of adolescence, Junior Miss, ran for almost two years on Broadway, after which it was adapted as a motion picture. Junior Miss was preceded by People Are Fascinating and Emily; it was followed by Meet Me in St. Louis, a graphic and nostalgic reminiscence of things past, and Women and Children First, a collection which is perhaps Miss Benson's most—er—witty and penetrating.

In these volumes, especially in the last, there is an almost scientific study of fate's little twists and life's little miseries. It is all done by suggestion and understatement; the perceptivity is sharpened because the shrewdness is tempered with sympathy. Much has been written about the revealing character drawing of the Russians, but not enough has been said about Miss Benson's ability to examine individuals of every sort with wry humor, with a keenness that is sometimes cruel and yet compassionate.

Between Madison and Park

One morning, when Mrs. Gibson awoke, she realized that she didn't feel very well. She had a choking sensation in her throat and couldn't seem to catch her breath. She took a warm bath and a cold shower and went into the dining room, where she sat down at the table and stared at her grapefruit. Mr. Gibson had almost finished his bacon and eggs before she spoke to him. "Ted," she said, "I feel funny."

He looked up from his paper. "How do you mean, funny?" he asked.

"I can't explain it," she said. "I have a choking sensation. You know, as though I were being strangled."

"You're probably coming down with something," he said. "Better take an aspirin."

She pushed her chair back from the table and stood up. "I believe I will," she said. "I certainly don't want any breakfast."

She took two aspirins and began to get dressed. Before she put on her dress she felt so bad that she decided to lie down for a few minutes. She was still lying down when Mr. Gibson came into the bedroom to say good-bye before he left for his office. "Better?" he asked.

"No," she said. "I really think I feel worse with my head down."

"Does your back ache?" he asked.

"No," she said. "It doesn't ache at all. My head doesn't ache, either, and I'm pretty sure I'm not running a temperature. I just feel funny."

"Well, if you don't ache anywhere, you can't have the flu," he said. He stooped to kiss her. "I'll call you up this afternoon. Take care of yourself."

When her husband had gone, Mrs. Gibson reached for the telephone, which stood on the table between the twin beds, and dialled Marion Tyler's number. "Hello, Marion," she said. "How are you?"

"I'm exhausted," Mrs. Tyler said. "I'm thinking about putting up the living-room curtains. You know what a job that is! All those little rings, and getting the cord just right so that they'll pull without getting snarled. Besides, I think that man shrank them. The lining shows below the chintz. I'm worn out thinking about struggling with them. Why don't you come over for lunch?"

"I don't think I'd better," Mrs. Gibson said. "I feel awfully funny. I have sort of a choking sensation and can't get my breath. I think maybe I'll call up Dr. Hammond."

Mrs. Tyler's voice sounded cheerful. "A choking sensation?" she repeated.

47

"As though I were being strangled," Mrs. Gibson said.

"Well, I wouldn't bother going to see Dr. Hammond about that. I don't think he'll know a thing about it. It certainly sounds to me as though it were just plain nerves, and Hammond doesn't know anything about nerves. If you'll take my advice, you'll go to see Mitchell."

Mrs. Gibson turned on her side and propped her head up with another pillow. "Mitchell?" she asked. "What does he do?"

"What does he *do?*" Marion Tyler said. "What *doesn't* he do? I'm surprised you've never heard of him. He's a neurologist, and he knows all about psychiatry, too. He's the one who did so much for Peggy Crandall. Remember how jittery she used to be, and remember the day we were playing at my house and she simply threw her hand down on the table and said she couldn't play another minute?"

"I remember, all right," Mrs. Gibson said. "She was minus seventy-six. And over five dollars of it was mine."

"I'd forgotten about that," Marion Tyler said. "The main point is that Mitchell's the man who got her back on her feet. I really think you'd better call him. His office is in the Eighties, between Madison and Park. Anyway, you can find it in the telephone book. John Lorimer Mitchell."

At that moment, Mrs. Gibson's choking sensation became so bad that she drew in her breath sharply. It frightened her, and her voice grew nervous and strained. "I'll have to hang up," she said. "But I'll call him right away. I'll tell him Peggy Crandall recommended him. That'll be best, don't you think?"

"Yes, I do," Mrs. Tyler said. "He's terribly busy, but if he knows Peggy sent you and that it's really urgent, he'll probably see you today. Let me know what happens."

When they had said their good-byes, Mrs. Gibson reached for the telephone book and then dialled Dr. Mitchell's office. The nurse who answered made an appointment for her to see Dr. Mitchell at eleven-thirty that morning.

Mrs. Gibson took a taxi to the Doctor's office, which was on the main floor of an apartment building on East Eighty-third Street, between Madison and Park. The building was red brick with white trim, which gave it a rather homey appearance until one looked up and saw that it was at least twelve stories high. Dr. Mitchell's office was to the right of the entrance. She rang the bell and stood tapping her foot as she waited. The young woman who answered the door was not in uniform. She wore a neat navy-blue dress with white collar and cuffs, and she had the pleasant, tolerant smile of a kindergarten teacher.

"Mrs. Gibson?" she asked. "This way. Dr. Mitchell will be ready for you in a few moments." She waved her hand toward a room at her right and disappeared into her own small office.

Mrs. Gibson went into the waiting room and sat down in an easy chair which was covered with chartreuse-colored leather. The room was sunny. There was a white iron wall bracket between the windows that held three pots of healthy-looking ivy, and pots of sensevieria stood on either end of the mantelshelf. There was a large table covered with magazines: *Harper's Bazaar, Time, Fortune, Reader's Digest, Vogue,* and the *Saturday Evening Post.* The walls of the room were painted a soft green. Mrs. Gibson looked with interest at the pictures. In a spot where the light was just right for it hung a painting that she thought might be a Matisse. There were also several nice etchings and a woodcut. The floor was covered with a fine Oriental rug. As she looked about her, Mrs. Gibson's choking sensation seemed less unpleasant. She felt that help was at hand and, judging by the appearance of the room, intelligent help. She thought of Dr. Hammond's office, with its worn black leather chairs, the ancient magazines, and the small sign that requested his patients to refrain from smoking.

After a while the door across the small foyer opened and a woman came out. "Next Tuesday then!" she called back cheerfully.

When the nurse appeared at the doorway of her office and nodded pleasantly, Mrs. Gibson understood that it was her turn. Her knees shook a little as she entered Dr. Mitchell's office. The office was not as sunny as the waiting room, but it looked out into a courtyard planted with flowering shrubs and small evergreen trees. Dr. Mitchell was seated behind a kneehole desk that had a top covered with red leather. He reminded Mrs. Gibson of someone she had seen before. His forehead was high and broad, with a receding hairline which accentuated it. His eyes were blue and sharp, with thick lids that moved slowly when he blinked. He wore a beautifully tailored tweed suit, a soft-blue hand-woven tie, and a blue cornflower in the buttonhole of his coat. He sat with his back to the window, so when Mrs. Gibson sat down facing him, the light shone full on her face.

He got up from his chair as she approached and shook hands with her warmly. Then he sat down again, leaned back in his chair, and clasped his hands together. His hands were brown and his nails were healthy and well polished. "So you're a friend of Mrs. Crandall," he said. He frowned at some memory and then his face cleared again. It was as though, in that brief moment, some disaster had loomed before his eyes and had somehow magically been averted.

"Oh, yes," Mrs. Gibson said. "I've known her for years."

"Charming person," he said. "And doing beautifully now, I hear."

"Yes," Mrs. Gibson said. She began to open and shut the zipper on her handbag. "Well, Dr. Mitchell, first I want you to understand that I am not a woman who thinks she has something the matter with her when she hasn't and keeps running to doctors all the time."

He laughed pleasantly. "You don't have to tell me that," he said. "I can see that you're not."

"You'll just have to take my word for it that I'm not," Mrs. Gibson said. "It's just that—well, when I woke up this morning I felt funny. I felt as though I were choking. I mean I don't feel *sick* at all. I just have this choking sensation."

Dr. Mitchell closed his eyes.

Mrs. Gibson saw that there was a bust of Shakespeare in the center of the bookshelves that ran across the side of the room to the right of the Doctor's desk. "Oh!" she cried. "Isn't that the funniest thing! You know, when I came in I was almost sure I'd seen you before, and I guess I was simply thinking of Shakespeare. I mean you would look almost exactly like Shakespeare if you wore a beard."

He opened his eyes. "Now, that's very odd," he said. "So many of my patients have told me the same thing. Personally, I don't see the resemblance. But I suppose one never does see one's own self." He leaned forward and looked at her steadily. "About this choking sensation which you have . . ."

Mrs. Gibson laughed nervously. "I suppose I *imagine* it, really."

"But aren't the things we imagine real to us?" Dr. Mitchell asked softly.

"I daresay they are," Mrs. Gibson said. "At least, I see what you mean. If I thought I were Napoleon, I would really think I *was* Napoleon."

"Let's hope it won't be as bad as that, dear lady," Dr. Mitchell said. He closed his eyes again. "Now, tell me, has anything been worrying you lately?"

Mrs. Gibson thought a minute. "I can't say that it has," she said. "Of course, there's the war, and lately I've noticed that I can't stand riding on the Madison Avenue buses. I didn't used to mind them at all, but really, I've been going out of my way to avoid riding on them."

"I see," he said. "And Mr. Gibson? Now, I don't expect you to tell me your private affairs. You are obviously an adult person and conduct your affairs in an adult manner, but you and Mr. Gibson—"

"Oh, Ted," Mrs. Gibson said. "He's fine."

"Money?" Dr. Mitchell asked.

"Not any more than usual."

"Have you any children?"

"No," Mrs. Gibson said. "I haven't." She added sociably, "Have you?"

"Yes, two," Dr. Mitchell said. "One twelve and the other sixteen. The younger boy is fine. Just a fine, healthy, happy-go-lucky youngster. A real boy. But Lorimer . . ."

"Yes?"

"I can't explain it," Dr. Mitchell said. "Lorimer seems to set the wrong values on the wrong things. We had to change his school again this year, and the other day we got word that he won't graduate with his class."

"Oh," Mrs. Gibson said. "That's a shame. He's probably too mischievous and doesn't like to study. I have a nephew who is like that. Simply won't study."

"Lorimer likes to study," Dr. Mitchell said. "But he only studies what he wants to study. He wants to be a writer. Now, if anyone can understand that feeling, I certainly am that one. I wanted to be a writer myself when I was a boy. But that didn't mean that I neglected my other studies. I feel that Lorimer can be a writer and still follow that pattern of life, the pattern we must follow if we are to live in peace with our fellow-men. I explained it to him when he went away last fall, but he doesn't seem to have understood me."

"Of course, he's only sixteen," Mrs. Gibson said.

"Old enough, though," Dr. Mitchell said sternly, "to realize that he is a human being in a world of human beings. Frankly, Mrs. Mitchell and I don't know what to do with him."

"Does he get into trouble?" Mrs. Gibson asked. "I mean serious trouble."

"Oh, no. Nothing of that sort. He just doesn't like people. He wants to be away by himself. He's either up in the clouds or down in the dumps."

"Maybe if you didn't send him to school and let him go to work for a while," Mrs. Gibson suggested.

Dr. Mitchell breathed in deeply. "I hadn't thought of that," he said. "I'll talk it over with Mrs. Mitchell." He closed his eyes and nodded. "That might be the solution," he said. He opened his eyes and smiled at Mrs. Gibson and she smiled back. "Now, that choking sensation," he said. He took out a prescription blank from the drawer of his desk, wrote hurriedly on it, and handed it to her. The prescription was written in Latin, but at the bottom of the blank were two words in English. "For tension," they read.

"Thank you," Mrs. Gibson said. She arose to go and they shook hands. "I hope your boy will be all right. I'm *sure* he will. After all, you must realize he's only sixteen."

"I'd like to see you again in about a week," Dr. Mitchell said. "And we'll see if that choking sensation hasn't cleared up. It may be a form of claustrophobia, or it may be that you are overtired and your nerves are playing tricks. Will you stop and make an appointment with Miss Devers, my nurse?"

"Yes, I will," Mrs. Gibson said. "Good-bye."

In the small office next to the waiting room she found Miss Devers. Mrs. Gibson left her name and address and made an appointment to see Dr. Mitchell again a week from Wednesday. "Would you mind telling me what Dr. Mitchell charges?" Mrs. Gibson asked. "My husband will want to know. You know how men are."

"Of course," Miss Devers answered brightly. "Twenty-five dollars for the first visit and fifteen dollars for all other visits, unless you wish him to come to your home. That would be slightly more."

"I see," Mrs. Gibson said. She tucked the prescription in her bag and nodded good-bye to Miss Devers.

The weather was clear and the sky was very blue. Mrs. Gibson remembered that she had had no breakfast and realized that she was hungry. She frowned, thinking of Dr. Mitchell's boy Lorimer. She was fond of children, and as she started toward Madison Avenue she wondered if Dr. Mitchell was handling the boy in the right manner.

She thought that maybe if she could have a little talk with Lorimer sometime, she might understand him better than his parents did. She decided to ride down to Marion Tyler's and have lunch with her after all. She could leave her prescription at the drugstore and pick up her medicine on her way home. She ran across Madison Avenue, hailed a bus, and got on it without thinking about it at all.

"Josh Billings"

He never thought of being an author until he was in his late forties. Born in 1818 in Massachusetts, Henry Wheeler Shaw became a farmer and quickly tired of the soil. At various times he was an explorer in the West, a river boatman, a real estate salesman. He employed his talents vocally, even vociferously; he excelled as the town auctioneer in Poughkeepsie.

At forty-five he began writing odd pieces for small newspapers. Passing himself off as a cracker-box philosopher, he wrote over the pseudonym "Josh Billings." His style was a mass of incongruities—absurd logic, purposeful errors, violent puns —all embedded in a peculiar spelling of his own. It was both phonetic and funny, and its author was hailed not only as a comic but a deflater of humbugs. His almanacs (spelled Allminax) were published annually for a dozen years, and in the 1870's everybody seemed to be reading Josh Billings, His Sayings and Josh Billings' Trump Kards. He was still popular when he died in 1885.

The Mule

The mule is haf hoss, and haf Jackass, and then kums tu a full stop, natur diskovering her mistake. Tha weigh more, akordin tu their heft, than enny other kreetur, except a crowbar. Tha kant hear enny quicker, nor further than the hoss, yet their ears are big enuff for snow shoes. You kan trust them with enny one whose life aint worth enny more than the mules. The only wa tu keep them into a paster, is tu turn them into a medder jineing, and let them jump out. Tha are reddy for use, just as soon as they will du tu abuse. Tha haint got enny friends, and will live on huckel berry brush, with an ockasional chanse at Kanada thissels. Tha are a modern invenshun, i dont think the Bible deludes tu them at tall. Tha sel for more money than enny other domestik animile. Yu kant tell their age by looking into their mouth, enny more than you kould a Mexican cannons. Tha never hav no dissease that a good club wont heal. If tha ever die tha must kum rite tu life agin, for i never herd nobody sa "ded mule." Tha are like sum men, very korrupt at harte; ive known them tu be good mules for 6 months, just tu git a good chanse to kick sumbody. I never owned one, nor never mean to, unless there is a United Staits law passed, requiring it. The only reason why tha are pashunt, is bekause tha are ashamed ov themselfs. I have seen eddikated mules in a sirkus. Tha kould kick, and bite, tremenjis. I would not sa what I am forced tu sa again the mule, if his birth want an outrage, and man want tu blame for it. Enny man who is willing tu drive a mule ought to be exempt by law from running for the legislatur. Tha are the strongest creeturs on earth, and heaviest, ackording tu their sise; I herd tell ov one who fell oph from the tow path, on the Eri kanawl, and sunk as soon as he touched bottom, but he kept rite on towing the boat tu the nex stashun, breathing thru his ears, which stuck out ov the water about 2 feet 6 inches; i didn't see this did, but an auctioneer told me ov it, and i never knew an auctioneer tu lie unless it was absolutely convenient.

Pioneers

God bless the pironeers—the whole ov them—inkluding the man who fust rode a mule. Hiz name was Stickfasst, he will be remembered az long az black wax will be, hiz posterity have aul bin good stickers, sum

ov the best clothes-pins the world ever saw, cum from this familee. . . .
I remember olde Buffaloo. He waz a sunsett pironeer; he started tew
discover, "out west," 40 years ago, hiz property was a wife, with the side
ake, 2 galls, just busting thru their clothes into womanhood, 2 boys, who
kould kill a skunk at 3 paces, and dodge the smell, a one-hoss wagging,
a rifle, and a brasskittle; he squat at Rock River, in the Illinoise, for 6
months, and then moved on more westly, the last that ware seen ov him,
was the hind-board ov hiz wagging, just doubling the top ov the rocky
mountains. . . . And thare waz Beltrigging, who fust diskovered the
tempranse question, he had bin a suckcessful rumdrinker, and seller for
36 years, and had retired with a pile, he diskovered kold water one day,
on the back side ov hiz farm, digging out foxes; he lektured nex day, in
a 7-day babtiss church, and told his xperiense; he made 13 hundred dollars lekturing, and died 9 years afterwards, in grate agony, having drank
4 drops ov french brandee, on a lump ov brown sugar bi mistake. He
begot Springwater, and Springwater begot Rainwater, and Rainwater
begot Dewdrop, and Dewdrop begot Morning-Mist, awl ov them sele-
brated tempranse lekturers. . . . And there waz Solomon Saw-dust, the
author ov bran-bred, and nailrod-soup; he waz a champion ov lite
weights; he fit the dispepshee in aul its forms; he lived for 18 months,
at one heat, on the smell ov a red herring, and gained 9 pounds in wind.
He had menny admirers and immitaturs the moste grate ov which was
Wet Pack and Water Kure. . . . And there waz Mehitable Saffron, the
virgin-hero ov wimmins' rights; i herd her fust orashun, in the town
hall; she spoke without notes, at arms' length. She ced, "woman had a
destiny that man kouldn't fill for her, and az for her, she could go it
alone, she did n't want no he-creeter around her, she had on a pair of
kowhide pegged boots, and closed up bi holding hi in the air, a pair ov
corduroy breeches, which she swore bi the good olde Mozes, waz awl
enny man had to brag ov. . . . She waz the first pironeer in the corduroy
britches business, she died celibate, and haz had menny followers amung
her sexes, but none that had the jism she had. . . . And then thare waz
Old Perpetual; he got crazee at last, but not till he had invented a pitch-
pine dog, with a bass-wood tail, that would bark and chase every wagging that cum along, clean down to the bridge over bean kreek. He got
out a patent for a sorrel horse, and a nu milch cow, and lived till he was
90 years olde, and then died from a kold he had caught, down seller,
trieing tew make soft sope, out ov bull's liver. On hiz grave stun waz
these affekting paragraph: "State, and county rights for sale, enquire ov
—the widder."

Morris Bishop

"The everlasting effort to write is like trying to fight a feather-bed," said the English traveler, soldier, and scholar, T. E. Lawrence. The American critic, Richard P. Blackmur, enlarged on the theme. "You meet a writer today," said Blackmur, "and you ask him where he teaches. If he doesn't teach, the chances are he does something else such as working for Mr. Luce [arbiter of Time and Life] which appears to be a kind of fur-lined purgatory."

Morris Bishop, born in Willard, New York, in 1893, has lived in more than one "fur-lined purgatory." He was professor of Romance Languages at Cornell for a score of years and left Ithaca to supervise the Italian desk at the Office of War Information. Incomparably versatile, he wrote a murder mystery (The Widening Stain) under a pseudonym and a series of limericks (Limericks Long After Lear) which were—oddly enough—funny without being indecent. As a writer of light verse, Mr. Bishop is not an originator like Ogden Nash, but he knows how to surprise the reader with a combination of round humor and barbed nonsense. "We Have Been Here Before" is a fine burlesque of a hundred stereotyped nostalgias.

We Have Been Here Before

I think I remember this moreland,
  The tower on the tip of the tor;
I feel in the distance another existence;
  I think I have been here before.

And I think you were sitting beside me
  In a fold in the face of the fell;
For Time at its work'll go around in a circle,
  And what is befalling, befell.

"I have been here before!" I asserted,
  In a nook on a neck of the Nile.
I once in a crisis was punished by Isis,
  And you smiled. I remember your smile.

I had the same sense of persistence
  On the site of the seat of the Sioux;
I heard in the teepee the sound of a sleepy
  Pleistocene grunt. It was you.

The past made a promise, before it
  Began to begin to begone.
This limited gamut brings you again. Damn it,
  How long has this got to go on?

Sonnet and Limerick

The sonnet with her Mona Lisa smile
  Broods on the world with other-worldly stare.
  Priestess of melancholy, darkly fair,
Serene above our fury, guilt, and guile,
She, in her deeps, has learned to reconcile
  Life's contradictions. Really, I declare,
  I'd gladly trust a sonnet anywhere,

That pure, seraphic sedentary. While
The limerick's furtive and mean;
You must keep her in close quarantine,
   Or she sneaks to the slums,
   And promptly becomes
Disorderly, drunk, and obscene.

Limericks Long After Lear

I

There's a tiresome young man in Bay Shore;
When his fiancée cried, "I adore
   The beautiful sea!"
   He replied, "I agree
It's pretty; but what is it *for?*"

II

Said a fervent young lady of Hammels,
"I object to humanity's trammels!
   I want to be free!
   Like a bird! Like a bee!
Oh, why am I classed with the mammals?"

III

A ghoulish old fellow in Kent
Encrusted his wife in cement;
   He said, with a sneer:
   "I was careful, my dear,
To follow your natural bent."

IV

A contemptuous lady in Shoreham
Behaved with extreme indecorum;
   She snapped a sarcastic
   And secret elastic
Throughout the Community Forum.

V

There's a dowager near Sneden Landing
Whose manners are bluff and commanding;
   It is one of her jests
   To trip up her guests,
For she hates to keep gentlemen standing.

Roark Bradford

Although he is a descendant of Governor William Bradford of Massachusetts, Roark Bradford's family has lived in the South since colonial days. All during his youth, Bradford listened to the songs and stories of the black man, and his books are full of their gusty echoes. His first volume, Ol' Man Adam an' His Chillun, paraphrased stories from the Bible as they might have been rendered by illiterate but highly imaginative colored preachers. Marc Connelly (see page 165) used the title of one of the stories and made the book into a play, Green Pastures, which won the Pulitzer Prize in 1930, and subsequently became an unusual motion picture. A sort of sequel, King David an' the Philistine Boys, sustained the notes of broad humor and innocent irreverence.

Green Pastures

After ole King Solomon died de kings got to comin' and goin' so fast dat hit made de Lawd dizzy tryin' to keep up wid who was de king and who wa'n't de king. So he say, "Dis ain't gittin' nowheres. Ef my people can't keep a king long enough for me to get acquainted wid him, well, I'm gonter see what gonter happen."

So hit was a king over in de next town name Nebuchadnezzar which yared de news, so he say, "Well, when de Lawd was sidin' wid de Hebrew boys they was doin' some mighty struttin'. But now wid de Lawd layin' back and watchin', I'll jest drap over and raise me some sand." And so he did.

So ole King Nebuchadnezzar lined up his army and lit out.

"Halt, who comin' yar?" say de Hebrew sentry.

"Sad news is comin' yar," say King Nebuchadnezzar.

"Ain't yo' name King Nebuchadnezzar?" say de sentry.

"Dat's what dey calls me," he say. "What's yo' name?"

"Daniel," say de sentry.

"Well, Daniel," say Nebuchadnezzar, "I'm bringin' you some sad news. I'm bringin' you de news which say I'm gonter raise me some sand in dis town."

"You better let dis town alone," say Daniel. "When you raise a ruckus in dis town you's raisin' a ruckus in de Lawd's town."

"I kotched de Lawd away f'm home, dis time," say Nebuchadnezzar.

"You didn't kotch me away f'm home," say Daniel.

"Naw," say Nebuchadnezzar, "and I'm gonter use you. I'm gonter feed my pet' lines on you."

So de soldiers captured Daniel and de army marched into town and raised a ruckus. They got drunk and they shot up de place. Den when de sheriff tried to arrest 'em, dey locked de sheriff up in his own jail and den burned de jail down wid him in hit. So they busted out de window lights and they tore down de gyarden fences. So they driv off de men and women and scared all de chillun.

"King Nebuchadnezzar," say Queen Nebuchadnezzar when he got back home, "did you spile dat town?"

"Did I spile hit?" say de king. "Queen Nebuchadnezzar, I didn't spile hit, I jest natchally ruint hit."

"Well, did you bring me somethin' back?" say de queen.

"I brang back some solid-gold drinkin' cups, and I brang back a few Hebrew boys to feed my lines on," King Nebuchadnezzar say.

"You's always bringin' back somethin' to drink out of, and somethin' to feed yo' lines on," say de queen, "but you ain't brang back nothin' to build me no fire wid, And yar poor me, settin' round de house queenin' all day long and 'bout to freeze to death."

"Well, queen," say de king, "I'm good-hearted. You kin have a few of my Hebrew boys to pitch on de fire."

So dey brought out a few of de Hebrew boys and pitch 'em on de fire. But when dey got to doin' de Hebrew boys like dat, de Lawd tuck a hand. "Jest go on and git pitched in de fire," say de Lawd, " 'cause I ain't gonter let you git burnt." So when dey put de Hebrews in de fire hit jest sputtered a couple er times and went out.

"No wonder they won't burn," say King Nebuchadnezzar; "you ain't got no kindlin' in yar." So dey brang a armful of pine knots and toch off. And de pine knots burned and blazed, and de Hebrew chillun jest sot round on de coals. "Bring my overcoat, King Nebuchadnezzar," say one of de Hebrew boys. "Hit's a draft in yar and I'm cold, and I don't want to git tuck down wid de phthisic."

"Well, dat whups me," say King Nebuchadnezzar. "I b'lieve I'll go on out and feed my lines. Bring dat boy Daniel out yar so I kin feed him to my lines."

So dey brang Daniel out, but Daniel wa'n't skeered. He been tawkin' wid de Lawd 'bout dem lines.

"Dem lines ain't hongry," say Daniel.

"Well, you kin stay among 'em to dey gits hongry," say de king.

"Well," say Daniel, "I wish you'd fix me up a bed and bring me some vittles, 'cause I'm gonter git mighty tired sleepin' on de ground wid nothin' but a line for my pillow till dem scound'els gits hongry enough to eat me."

"Dat's jest you and de lines about dat," say Nebuchadnezzar. "I'm goin' and put on my robes and wash my face and hands and git ready for de big doin's tonight."

So dat night ole King Nebuchadnezzar had a mighty feast. All de big folks and de quality folks in de town came, and hit kept de hand-maidens busy dancin' and singin' and makin' music, and hit kept de handmen busy rollin' out de licker and knockin' out de bungs.

"When I invites y'all to come to a mighty feast," say Nebuchadnez-zar, "do y'all have a mighty feast or don't you?"

"Yo' Majesty," say all de people, "we does."

"Well, den, is ev'ybody happy?" say Nebuchadnezzar.

"Don't we look happy?" say de people.

"Well, jest make yo' own fun," say Nebuchadnezzar. So some er de menfolks got to drinkin' de licker outer de bungholes, and some er de women got to passin' out and fallin' to sleep under de tables, and ev'ybody got to carryin' on scandalous.

"Whar all dem solid-gold cups which I tuck f'm de Hebrew boys?" say ole King Nebuchadnezzar.

"Put away," say de haid waiter.

"Well, bring 'em out so My Majesty kin drink some licker outer dem solid-gold drinkin'-cups," say ole King Nebuchadnezzar. And right dar was whar he made a big mistake, 'cause dem cups wa'n't de Hebrew boys' cups. Dem was de Lawd's cups. So 'bout de time ole King Nebuchadnezzar drunk out of a solid-gold cup, de Lawd stepped right through de wall and wrote somethin' on hit, and den stepped right back again.

"I seen a ha'nt," say King Nebuchadnezzar.

"Hit's de licker," say de gal which is settin' in his lap. "Hit'll make you see mighty nigh anything."

"Naw, hit ain't de licker," say Nebuchadnezzar. "Licker makes me see snakes. You can't fool me 'bout licker. I know when I sees snakes. I tell you I seen a ha'nt."

"Well," say de gal, "le's call him over and give him a drink."

"Ain't no time to git funny wid me now, gal," say Nebuchadnezzar. "I sees some writin' on de wall. Dat's what I sees."

"What do hit say?" say de gal.

"I didn't brought my glasses," say Nebuchadnezzar.

"I'm too drunk to read hit, too," say de gal. "Whyn't you call dat boy Daniel which is sleepin' wid de lines? He ain't drunk."

So dey sont for Daniel out in de lines' den.

"Read hit to me, Daniel," say Nebuchadnezzar, "and I'll give you de best job in my kingdom."

So Daniel look at de writin' and den he look at de king. "Ole King Nebuchadnezzar," he say, "you can't give me no job in yo' kingdom, 'cause f'm what I reads yonder on de wall, you ain't got no kingdom no more."

"Is dat a fack?" say Nebuchadnezzar. "What do hit say?"

"It's de Lawd's own handwritin'," say Daniel.

"Lawd writin' me a letter, is he?" say Nebuchadnezzar. "What he writin' to me, Daniel?"

" 'Dear King Nebuchadnezzar,' hit say," say Daniel, " 'Heavy, heavy hangs over yo' haid. Yours truly, Lawd.' "

"Sounds like he's writin' me a riddle instid of a letter," say de king.

"Well, riddle or letter," say Daniel, "dat's what hit say. And hit

means dat de Lawd is done got tired er yo' foolishness and is done quit playin' wid you. Hit means dat befo' sunup you ain't gonter be no king no more. Dat is what hit means."

"So de Lawd don't like my style er bein' king?" say Nebuchadnezzar. "Well, I be doggone!"

"De Lawd don't like yo' style and he ain't gonter try to change hit," say Daniel.

"What he gonter do?" say Nebuchadnezzar.

"He gonter change kings," say Daniel.

"Well," say Nebuchadnezzar, "bein' king ain't much fun, anyway. Y'all boys and gals go right on wid de party as long as de licker holds out. I b'lieve I'm gonter go out and eat me a little grass."

Carlos Bulosan

In the winter of 1939 Carlos Bulosan, a twenty-five-year-old poet, was broke and out of work. Standing in the rain outside a California fish cannery with a crowd of other job seekers, he thought of his childhood in the Philippine village of Binalonan, where he had been born. Before he reached the head of the line he had composed the title story of his gay and guileless reminiscences, The Laughter of My Father. It was bought by The New Yorker, and Bulosan proceeded to re-create the casual but astonishing events of his strange past.

When the stories were published in a volume, Bulosan was compared to Hans Christian Andersen for his artlessness, to Clarence Day (see page 202) for his active memory, and to Boccaccio for his raciness. It is to Bulosan's credit that his work survived the comparisons.

My Father Goes to Court

When I was four, I lived with my mother and brothers and sisters in a small town on the island of Luzon. Father's farm had been destroyed in 1918 by one of our sudden Philippine floods, so for several years afterward we all lived in the town, though he preferred living in the country. We had as a next door neighbor a very rich man, whose sons and daughters seldom came out of the house. While we boys and girls played and sang in the sun, his children stayed inside and kept the windows closed. His house was so tall that his children could look in the windows of our house and watch us as we played, or slept, or ate, when there was any food in the house *to* eat.

Now, this rich man's servants were always frying and cooking something good, and the aroma of the food was wafted down to us from the windows of the big house. We hung about and took all the wonderful smell of the food into our beings. Sometimes, in the morning, our whole family stood outside the windows of the rich man's house and listened to the musical sizzling of thick strips of bacon or ham. I can remember one afternoon when our neighbor's servants roasted three chickens. The chickens were young and tender and the fat that dripped into the burning coals gave off an enchanting odor. We watched the servants turn the beautiful birds and inhaled the heavenly spirit that drifted out to us.

Some days the rich man appeared at a window and glowered down at us. He looked at us one by one, as though he were condemning us. We were all healthy because we went out in the sun every day and bathed in the cool water of the river that flowed from the mountains into the sea. Sometimes we wrestled with one another in the house before we went out to play. We were always in the best of spirits and our laughter was contagious. Other neighbors who passed by our house often stopped in our yard and joined us in laughter.

Laughter was our only wealth. Father was a laughing man. He would go into the living room and stand in front of the tall mirror, stretching his mouth into grotesque shapes with his fingers and making faces at himself; then he would rush into the kitchen, roaring with laughter.

There was always plenty to make us laugh. There was, for instance, the day one of my brothers came home with a small bundle under his arm, pretending that he brought something good to eat, maybe a leg of lamb or something as extravagant as that, to make our mouths water. He rushed to Mother and threw the bundle into her lap. We all stood

67

around, watching Mother undo the complicated strings. Suddenly a black cat leaped out of the bundle and ran wildly around the house. Mother chased my brother and beat him with her little fists, while the rest of us bent double, choking with laughter.

We made so much noise that all our neighbors except the rich family came into the yard and joined us in loud, genuine laughter.

It was like that for years.

As time went on, the rich man's children became thin and anemic, while we grew even more robust and full of life. Our faces were bright and rosy, but theirs were pale and sad. The rich man started to cough at night; then he coughed day and night. His wife began coughing too. Then the children started to cough, one after the other. At night their coughing sounded like the barking of a herd of seals. We hung outside their windows and listened to them. We wondered what had happened. We knew that they were not sick from lack of nourishing food, because they were still always frying something delicious to eat.

One day the rich man appeared at a window and stood there a long time. He looked at my sisters, who had grown fat with laughing, then at my brothers, whose arms and legs were like the *molave*, which is the sturdiest tree in the Philippines. He banged down the window and ran through his house, shutting all the windows.

From that day on, the windows of our neighbor's house were always closed. The children did not come outdoors any more. We could still hear the servants cooking in the kitchen, and no matter how tight the windows were shut, the aroma of the food came to us in the wind and drifted gratuitously into our house.

One morning a policeman from the *presidencia* came to our house with a sealed paper. The rich man had filed a complaint against us. Father took me with him when he went to the town clerk and asked him what it was about. He told Father the man claimed that for years we had been stealing the spirit of his wealth and food.

When the day came for us to appear in court, Father brushed his old Army uniform and borrowed a pair of shoes from one of my brothers. We were the first to arrive. Father sat on a chair in the center of the courtroom. Mother occupied a chair by the door. We children sat on a long bench by the wall. Father kept jumping up from his chair and stabbing the air with his arms, as though he were defending himself before an imaginary jury.

The rich man arrived. He had grown old and feeble; his face was scarred with deep lines. With him was his young lawyer. Spectators came in and almost filled the chairs. The judge entered the room and sat on a high chair. We stood up in a hurry and than sat down again.

After the courtroom preliminaries, the judge looked at Father. "Do you have a lawyer?" he asked.

"I don't need any lawyer, Judge," he said.

"Proceed," said the judge.

The rich man's lawyer jumped up and pointed his finger at Father. "Do you or do you not agree that you have been stealing the spirit of the complainant's wealth and food?"

"I do not!" Father said.

"Do you or do you not agree that while the complainant's servants cooked and fried fat legs of lamb or young chicken breasts you and your family hung outside his windows and inhaled the heavenly spirit of the food?"

"I agree," Father said.

"Do you or do you not agree that while the complainant and his children grew sickly and tubercular you and your family became strong of limb and fair of complexion?"

"I agree," Father said.

"How do you account for that?"

Father got up and paced around, scratching his head thoughtfully. Then he said, "I would like to see the children of the complainant, Judge."

"Bring in the children of the complainant."

They came in shyly. The spectators covered their mouths with their hands, they were so amazed to see the children so thin and pale. The children walked silently to a bench and sat down without looking up. They stared at the floor and moved their hands uneasily.

Father could not say anything at first. He just stood by his chair and looked at them. Finally he said, "I should like to cross-examine the complainant."

"Proceed."

"Do you claim that we *stole* the spirit of your wealth and became a laughing family while yours became morose and sad?" Father asked.

"Yes."

"Do you claim that we *stole* the spirit of your food by hanging outside your windows when your servants cooked it?" Father asked.

"Yes."

"Then we are going to *pay* you right now," Father said. He walked over to where we children were sitting on the bench and took my straw hat off my lap and began filling it up with *centavo* pieces that he took out of his pockets. He went to Mother, who added a fistful of silver coins. My brothers threw in their small change.

"May I walk to the room across the hall and stay there for a few minutes, Judge?" Father asked.

"As you wish."

"Thank you," Father said. He strode into the other room with the hat in his hands. It was almost full of coins. The doors of both rooms were wide open.

"Are you ready?" Father called.

"Proceed," the judge said.

The sweet tinkle of the coins carried beautifully into the courtroom. The spectators turned their faces toward the sound with wonder. Father came back and stood before the complainant.

"Did you hear it?" he asked.

"Hear what?" the man asked.

"The spirit of the money when I shook this hat?" he asked.

"Yes."

"Then you are paid," Father said.

The rich man opened his mouth to speak and fell to the floor without a sound. The lawyer rushed to his aid. The judge pounded his gavel.

"Case dismissed," he said.

Father strutted around the courtroom. The judge even came down from his high chair to shake hands with him. "By the way," he whispered, "I had an uncle who died laughing."

"You like to hear my family laugh, Judge?" Father asked.

"Why not?"

"Did you hear that, children?" Father said.

My sisters started it. The rest of us followed them and soon the spectators were laughing with us, holding their bellies and bending over the chairs. And the laughter of the judge was the loudest of all.

Ellis Parker Butler

One of the foremost names on every list of American humorists, author of more than thirty books, Ellis Parker Butler is known to most readers because of one short but hilarious story: Pigs Is Pigs. Born in 1869 in Muscatine, Iowa, where Mark Twain lived for a while, Butler had to stop his education at the first year of high school. He earned his living as a clerk and occasional contributor to trade papers until The American Magazine published Pigs Is Pigs. That was in 1905. The story was republished as a book and has been in demand ever since. A shrewd appraiser of character, Butler attempted to write novels, but with no success. His stories are at their best when they approach caricature.

Butler died in 1937, in his sixty-eighth year.

Pigs Is Pigs

Mike Flannery, the Westcote agent of the Interurban Express Company, leaned over the counter of the express office and shook his fist. Mr. Morehouse, angry and red, stood on the other side of the counter, trembling with rage. The argument had been long and heated, and at last Mr. Morehouse had talked himself speechless. The cause of the trouble stood on the counter between the two men. It was a soap box across the top of which were nailed a number of strips, forming a rough but serviceable cage. In it two spotted guinea-pigs were greedily eating lettuce leaves.

"Do as you loike, then!" shouted Flannery, "pay for thim an' take thim, or don't pay for thim and leave thim be. Rules is rules, Misther Morehouse, an' Mike Flannery's not goin' to be called down fer breakin' of thim."

"But, you everlastingly stupid idiot!" shouted Mr. Morehouse, madly shaking a flimsy printed book beneath the agent's nose, "can't you read it here—in your own plain printed rates? 'Pets, domestic, Franklin to Westcote, if properly boxed, twenty-five cents each.' " He threw the book on the counter in disgust. "What more do you want? Aren't they pets? Aren't they domestic? Aren't they properly boxed? What?"

He turned and walked back and forth rapidly, frowning ferociously.

Suddenly he turned to Flannery, and forcing his voice to an artificial calmness spoke slowly but with intense sarcasm.

"Pets," he said. "P-e-t-s! Twenty-five cents each. There are two of them. One! Two! Two times twenty-five are fifty! Can you understand that? I offer you fifty cents."

Flannery reached for the book. He ran his hand through the pages and stopped at page sixty-four.

"An' I don't take fifty cints," he whispered in mockery. "Here's the rule for ut. 'Whin the agint be in anny doubt regardin' which of two rates applies to a shipment, he shall charge the larger. The consign-ey may file a claim for the overcharge.' In this case, Misther Morehouse, I be in doubt. Pets thim animals may be, an' domestic they be, but pigs I'm blame sure they do be, an' me rules says plain as the nose on yer face, 'Pigs Franklin to Westcote, thirty cints each.' An', Misther Morehouse, by me arithmetical knowledge two times thirty comes to sixty cints."

Mr. Morehouse shook his head savagely. "Nonsense!" he shouted, "confounded nonsense, I tell you! Why, you poor ignorant foreigner, that rule means common pigs, domestic pigs, not guinea-pigs!"

Flannery was stubborn.

"Pigs is pigs," he declared firmly. "Guinea-pigs or dago pigs or Irish pigs is all the same to the Interurban Express Company an' to Mike Flannery. Th' nationality of the pig creates no differentiality in the rate, Misther Morehouse! 'Twould be the same was they Dutch pigs or Rooshun pigs. Mike Flannery," he added, "is here to tind to the expriss business and not to hould conversation wid dago pigs in sivinteen languages fer to discover be they Chinese or Tipperary by birth an' nativity."

Mr. Morehouse hesitated. He bit his lip and then flung out his arms wildly.

"Very well!" he shouted, "you shall hear of this! Your president shall hear of this! It is an outrage! I have offered you fifty cents. You refuse it! Keep the pigs until you are ready to take the fifty cents, but, by George, sir, if one hair of those pigs' heads is harmed I will have the law on you!"

He turned and stalked out, slamming the door. Flannery carefully lifted the soap box from the counter and placed it in a corner. He was not worried. He felt the peace that comes to a faithful servant who has done his duty and done it well.

Mr. Morehouse went home raging. His boy, who had been awaiting the guinea-pigs, knew better than to ask him for them. He was a normal boy and therefore always had a guilty conscience when his father was angry. So the boy slipped quietly around the house. There is nothing so soothing to a guilty conscience as to be out of the path of the avenger.

Mr. Morehouse stormed into the house. "Where's the ink?" he shouted at his wife as soon as his foot was across the doorsill.

Mrs. Morehouse jumped guiltily. She never used ink. She had not seen the ink, nor moved the ink, nor thought of the ink, but her husband's tone convicted her of the guilt of having borne and reared a boy, and she knew that whenever her husband wanted anything in a loud voice the boy had been at it.

"I'll find Sammy," she said meekly.

When the ink was found Mr. Morehouse wrote rapidly, and he read the completed letter and smiled a triumphant smile.

"That will settle that crazy Irishman!" he exclaimed. "When they get that letter he will hunt another job, all right!"

A week later Mr. Morehouse received a long official envelope with the card of the Interurban Express Company in the upper left corner. He tore it open eagerly and drew out a sheet of paper. At the top it bore the number A6754. The letter was short. "Subject—Rate on guinea-pigs," it said. "Dear Sir,—We are in receipt of your letter regarding rate on guinea-pigs between Franklin and Westcote, addressed to the president of this company. All claims for overcharge should be addressed to the Claims Department."

Mr. Morehouse wrote to the Claims Department. He wrote six pages of choice sarcasm, vituperation and argument, and sent them to the Claims Department.

A few weeks later he received a reply from the Claims Department. Attached to it was his last letter.

"Dear Sir," said the reply. "Your letter of the 16th inst., addressed to this Department, subject rate on guinea-pigs from Franklin to Westcote, rec'd. We have taken up the matter with our agent at Westcote, and his reply is attached herewith. He informs us that you refused to receive the consignment or to pay the charges. You have therefore no claim against this company, and your letter regarding the proper rate on the consignment should be addressed to our Tariff Department."

Mr. Morehouse wrote to the Tariff Department. He stated his case clearly, and gave his arguments in full, quoting a page or two from the encyclopedia to prove that guinea-pigs were not common pigs.

With the care that characterizes corporations when they are systematically conducted, Mr. Morehouse's letter was numbered, O.K.'d, and started through the regular channels. Duplicate copies of the bill of lading, manifest, Flannery's receipt for the package and several other pertinent papers were pinned to the letter, and they were passed to the head of the Tariff Department.

The head of the Tariff Department put his feet on his desk and yawned. He looked through the papers carelessly.

"Miss Kane," he said to his stenographer, "take this letter. 'Agent, Westcote, N. J. Please advise why consignment referred to in attached papers was refused domestic pet rates.'"

Miss Kane made a series of curves and angles on her notebook and waited with pencil poised. The head of the department looked at the papers again.

"Huh! guinea-pigs!" he said. "Probably starved to death by this time! Add this to that letter: 'Give condition of consignment at present.'"

He tossed the papers on to the stenographer's desk, took his feet from his own desk and went out to lunch.

When Mike Flannery received the letter he scratched his head.

"Give prisint condition," he repeated thoughtfully. "Now what do thim clerks be wantin' to know, I wonder! 'Prisint condition,' is ut? Thim pigs, praise St. Patrick, do be in good health, so far as I know, but I niver was no veternairy surgeon to dago pigs. Mebby thim clerks wants me to call in the pig docther an' have their pulses took. Wan thing I do know, howiver, which is, they've glorious appytites for pigs of their soize. Ate? They'd ate the brass padlocks off of a barn door! If the paddy pig, by the same token, ate as hearty as these dago pigs do, there'd be a famine in Ireland."

To assure himself that his report would be up to date, Flannery went to the rear of the office and looked into the cage. The pigs had been transferred to a larger box—a dry goods box.

"Wan,—two,—t'ree,—four,—foive,—six,—sivin,—eight!" he counted. "Sivin spotted an' wan all black. All well an' hearty an' all eatin' loike ragin' hippypottymusses." He went back to his desk and wrote.

"Mr. Morgan, Head of Tariff Department," he wrote, "why do I say dago pigs is pigs because they is pigs and will be til you say they ain't which is what the rule book says stop your jollying me you know it as well as I do. As to health they are all well and hoping you are the same. P. S. There are eight now the family increased all good eaters. P. S. I paid out so far two dollars for cabbage which they like shall I put in bill for same what?"

Morgan, head of the Tariff Department, when he received this letter, laughed. He read it again and became serious.

"By George!" he said, "Flannery is right, 'pigs is pigs.' I'll have to get authority on this thing. Meanwhile, Miss Kane, take this letter: 'Agent, Westcote, N. J. Regarding shipment guinea-pigs, File No. A6754. Rule 83, General Instructions to Agents, clearly states that agents shall collect from consignee all costs of provender, etc., etc., required for live stock while in transit or storage. You will proceed to collect same from consignee.'"

Flannery received this letter next morning, and when he read it he grinned.

"Proceed to collect," he said softly. "How thim clerks do loike to be talkin'! *Me* proceed to collect two dollars and twinty-foive cints off Misther Morehouse! I wonder do thim clerks *know* Misther Morehouse? I'll git it! Oh, yes! 'Misther Morehouse, two an' a quarter, plaze.' 'Cert'nly, me dear frind Flannery. Delighted!' *Not !*"

Flannery drove the express wagon to Mr. Morehouse's door. Mr. Morehouse answered the bell.

"Ah, ha!" he cried as soon as he saw it was Flannery. "So you've come to your senses at last, have you? I thought you would! Bring the box in."

"I hev no box," said Flannery coldly. "I hev a bill agin Misther John C. Morehouse for two dollars and twinty-foive cints for kebbages aten by his dago pigs. Wud you wish to pay ut?"

"Pay—Cabbages—!" gasped Mr. Morehouse. "Do you mean to say that two little guinea-pigs——"

"Eight!" said Flannery. "Papa an' mamma an' the six childer. Eight!"

For answer Mr. Morehouse slammed the door in Flannery's face. Flannery looked at the door reproachfully.

"I take ut the con-*sign*-y don't want to pay for thim kebbages," he said. "If I know signs of refusal, the con-*sign*-y refuses to pay for wan dang kebbage leaf an' be hanged to me!"

Mr. Morgan, the head of the Tariff Department, consulted the president of the Interurban Express Company regarding guinea-pigs, as to whether they were pigs or not pigs. The president was inclined to treat the matter lightly.

"What is the rate on pigs and on pets?" he asked.

"Pigs thirty cents, pets twenty-five," said Morgan.

"Then of course guinea-pigs are pigs," said the president.

"Yes," agreed Morgan, "I look at it that way, too. A thing that can come under two rates is naturally due to be classed as the higher. But are guinea-pigs, pigs? Aren't they rabbits?"

"Come to think of it," said the president, "I believe they are more like rabbits. Sort of half-way station between pig and rabbit. I think the question is this—are guinea-pigs of the domestic pig family? I'll ask Professor Gordon. He is authority on such things. Leave the papers with me."

The president put the papers on his desk and wrote a letter to Professor Gordon. Unfortunately the Professor was in South America collecting zoological specimens, and the letter was forwarded to him by his wife. As the Professor was in the highest Andes, where no white man had ever penetrated, the letter was many months in reaching him. The president forgot the guinea-pigs, Morgan forgot them, Mr. Morehouse forgot them. But Flannery did not. One half of his time he gave to the duties of his agency; the other half was devoted to the guinea-pigs. Long before Professor Gordon received the president's letter Morgan received one from Flannery.

"About them dago pigs," it said, "what shall I do they are great in family life, no race suicide for them, there are thirty-two now shall I sell them do you take this express office for a menagerie, answer quick."

Morgan reached for a telegraph blank and wrote:

"Agent, Westcote. Don't sell pigs."

He then wrote Flannery a letter calling his attention to the fact that the pigs were not the property of the company but were merely being held during a settlement of a dispute regarding rates. He advised Flannery to take the best possible care of them.

Flannery, letter in hand, looked at the pigs and sighed. The dry goods box cage had become too small. He boarded up twenty feet of the rear of the express office to make a large and airy home for them, and went about his business. He worked with feverish intensity when out on his rounds, for the pigs required attention and took most of his time. Some months later, in desperation, he seized a sheet of paper and wrote "160" across it and mailed it to Morgan. Morgan returned it asking for explanation. Flannery replied:

"There be now one hundred sixty of them dago pigs, for heaven's sake let me sell off some, do you want me to go crazy, what?"

"Sell no pigs," Morgan wired.

Not long after this the president of the express company received a letter from Professor Gordon. It was a long and scholarly letter, but the point was that the guinea-pig was the *Cavia aparoea*, while the common pig was the genus *Sus* of the family *Suidae*. He remarked that they were prolific and multiplied rapidly.

"They are not pigs," said the president, decidedly, to Morgan. "The twenty-five cent rate applies."

Morgan made the proper notation on the papers that had accumulated in File A6754, and turned them over to the Audit Department. The Audit Department took some time to look the matter up, and after the usual delay wrote Flannery that as he had on hand one hundred and sixty guinea-pigs, the property of consignee, he should deliver them and collect charges at the rate of twenty-five cents each.

Flannery spent a day herding his charges through a narrow opening in their cage so that he might count them.

"Audit Dept.," he wrote, when he had finished the count, "you are way off there may be was one hundred and sixty dago pigs once, but wake up don't be a back number. I've got even eight hundred, now shall I collect for eight hundred or what, how about sixty-four dollars I paid out for cabbages."

It required a great many letters back and forth before the Audit Department was able to understand why the error had been made of billing one hundred and sixty instead of eight hundred, and still more time for it to get the meaning of the "cabbages."

Flannery was crowded into a few feet at the extreme front of the office. The pigs had all the rest of the room and two boys were employed constantly attending to them. The day after Flannery had counted the guinea-pigs there were eight more added to his drove, and by the time the Audit Department gave him authority to collect for eight hundred Flannery had given up all attempts to attend to the receipt or the delivery of goods. He was hastily building galleries around the express office, tier above tier. He had four thousand and sixty-four guinea-pigs to care for. More were arriving daily.

Immediately following its authorization the Audit Department sent another letter, but Flannery was too busy to open it. They wrote another and then they telegraphed:

"Error in guinea-pig bill. Collect for two guinea-pigs, fifty cents. Deliver all to consignee."

Flannery read the telegram and cheered up. He wrote out a bill as rapidly as his pencil could travel over paper and ran all the way to the Morehouse home. At the gate he stopped suddenly. The house stared at him with vacant eyes. The windows were bare of curtains and he could see into the empty rooms. A sign on the porch said, "To Let." Mr. Morehouse had moved! Flannery ran all the way back to the express office. Sixty-nine guinea-pigs had been born during his absence. He ran out again and made feverish inquiries in the village. Mr. Morehouse had not only moved, but he had left Westcote. Flannery returned to the express office and found that two hundred and six guinea-pigs had entered the world since he left it. He wrote a telegram to the Audit Department.

"Can't collect fifty cents for two dago pigs consignee has left town address unknown what shall I do? Flannery."

The telegram was handed to one of the clerks in the Audit Department, and as he read it he laughed.

"Flannery must be crazy. He ought to know that the thing to do is to return the consignment here," said the clerk. He telegraphed Flannery to send the pigs to the main office of the company at Franklin.

When Flannery received the telegram he set to work. The six boys he had engaged to help him also set to work. They worked with the haste of desperate men, making cages out of soap boxes, cracker boxes, and all kinds of boxes, and as fast as the cages were completed they filled them with guinea-pigs and expressed them to Franklin. Day after day the cages of guinea-pigs flowed in a steady stream from Westcote to Franklin, and still Flannery and his six helpers ripped and nailed and packed—relentlessly and feverishly. At the end of the week they had shipped two hundred and eighty cases of guinea-pigs, and there were in the express office seven hundred and four more pigs than when they began packing them.

"Stop sending pigs. Warehouse full," came a telegram to Flannery. He stopped packing only long enough to wire back, "Can't stop," and kept on sending them. On the next train up from Franklin came one of the company's inspectors. He had instructions to stop the stream of guinea-pigs at all hazards. As his train drew up at Westcote station he saw a cattle-car standing on the express company's siding. When he reached the express office he saw the express wagon backed up to the

door. Six boys were carrying bushel baskets full of guinea-pigs **from** the office and dumping them into the wagon. Inside the room Flannery, with his coat and vest off, was shoveling guinea-pigs into bushel baskets with a coal scoop. He was winding up the guinea-pig episode.

He looked up at the inspector with a snort of anger.

"Wan wagonload more an' I'll be quit of thim, an' niver will ye catch Flannery wid no more foreign pigs on his hands. No, sur! They near was the death o' me. Nixt toime I'll know that pigs of whativer nationality is domestic pets—an' go at the lowest rate."

He began shoveling again rapidly, speaking quickly between breaths.

"Rules may be rules, but you can't fool Mike Flannery twice wid the same thrick—whin ut comes to live stock, dang the rules. So long as Flannery runs this expriss office—pigs is pets—an' cows is pets—an' horses is pets—an' lions an' tigers an' Rocky Mountain goats is pets—an' the rate on thim is twinty-foive cints."

He paused long enough to let one of the boys put an empty basket in the place of the one he had just filled. There were only a few guinea-pigs left. As he noted their limited number his natural habit of looking on the bright side returned.

"Well, annyhow," he said cheerfully, " 'tis not so bad as ut might be. What if thim dago pigs had been elephants!"

Anecdotes of the Great and the Near Great

It has never been ascertained whether more anecdotes have been credited to the great than have been uttered by them. Some of the most incisive remarks credited to Whistler in his time or to Woollcott in our own day were never spoken by either of those waspish wits. But a good jest, unlike a good wine, needs a bush, a signboard, a name to give it authority. Thus we find that the best witticisms of one season will be attributed to Dorothy Parker, and next year the very same bon mots will be laid at the door of Groucho Marx. Speaking of two contending script writers, Goodman Ace, the radio writer, said, "If you locked both of them in a room with a typewriter, the typewriter would fight its way out." But the same remark was made about Goodman Ace and *his* collaborator! Lincoln amused his Cabinet with jests from Artemus Ward who stole them from Joe Miller who . . .

But let us examine some of these anecdotes without further introduction, for, as Eddie Cantor (undoubtedly quoting someone else) said, "You don't introduce people to old friends." And that is no less true of anecdotes. Alphabetically then. . . .

BARRYMORE, JOHN

Coming of a long lineage of aristocrats of the theater, the three Barrymores, Lionel, Ethel, and John were dubbed "The Royal Family" and Edna Ferber collaborated in a play with George S. Kaufman about them, using that title. Nevertheless, there were times when the youngest and most famous of the trio was not recognized. Once, at the height of his fame, he went into a Hollywood shop and, after selecting some articles, said, "Charge it as usual."

"And the name?" asked the clerk.

"Barrymore," coldly replied the actor.

"And the first name?" pursued the clerk.

Barrymore's glare froze the atmosphere. "Ethel," he said.

Perhaps the most quoted of all the Barrymore snubs occurred when he was summoned to the telephone by the secretary of one of the largest motion picture producers in Hollywood.

"I am speaking for Mr. Laskwyn, who wants you to attend an important party he is giving tomorrow," said the voice.

"And I," said Barrymore, "am speaking for John Barrymore, who has a previous engagement which he will make as soon as you have hung up."

BEECHER, HENRY WARD

Henry Ward Beecher and Park Benjamin, the writer and humorist, were great friends. "But why," asked Beecher, "don't you ever come to hear me preach?"

"I'd like to," replied Benjamin, "but I make it a rule never to go to places of amusement on Sunday."

Trying to sell the reverend Henry Ward Beecher a horse, the owner of the stable said, "Now here's one that is gentle and well-behaved. Stands anywhere without hitching; does anything you ask him. He hasn't a bad trait, won't kick, and listens carefully to everything you say."

"Ah," said Beecher wistfully, "if that horse were only a member of my congregation!"

Equally memorable is the following limerick:

> To the hen said the eminent preacher,
> "My dear, you're an elegant creature."
> The hen, just for that,
> Laid an egg in his hat.
> And thus did the hen reward Beecher.

CARUSO, ENRICO

The greatest of tenors was so well known that he could afford to poke fun at himself. He was fond of telling how, when his car broke down, a farmer helped him and gave him lunch while the automobile was being repaired. As a gesture of thanks Caruso sang, and when the farmer asked his name, replied with a slight swagger, "Caruso."

"Think of that!" exclaimed the farmer. "I've read about you for years!"

"Yes?" said the eminent star of opera, with a self-satisfied smirk.

"Yes," echoed the farmer. "And to think I've had you sing for me, here in my own kitchen! Caruso, the great, the famous traveler, Robinson Caruso!"

Caruso also acquired fame as an enormous eater. Yet here he yielded first place to the oversize contralto, Ernestine Schumann-Heink. Seeing her in a restaurant with a huge steak in front of her, Caruso exclaimed: "Steena, you're not going to eat that steak alone, are you?"

"Certainly not," replied Schumann-Heink. "With potatoes."

CHOATE, JOSEPH

The famous lawyer and statesman, Joseph Choate, was more than usually busy. But the young man insisted on pushing his way into the advocate's office.

"Take a chair," said Choate gently.

"I," blustered the intruder, without apologizing for the interruption, "I am the son of Bishop Maxwell."

"Oh," said Choate, "please take *two* chairs."

Always suave, Choate was so brilliant in the courtroom that he capti- vated the jury. Once, in Westchester County, his opponent tried to offset Choate's strength and his own weak case, by saying, "I hope the gentlemen of the jury will not be influenced by my opponent's Chester- fieldian urbanity."

"And *I* hope," replied Choate, "that the gentlemen will not be misled by my opponent's Westchesterfieldian suburbanity."

COOLIDGE, CALVIN

President Coolidge, who, said Alice Longworth, "looked as though he had been weaned on a pickle," was so laconic that his brevity of speech became proverbial. Even his wife could get little but the barest re- sponses from him. One Sunday after returning from church to the White House, where his wife was confined with a cold, he was asked whether he enjoyed the sermon.

"Yes," said the President.

"And what was it about?" asked Mrs. Coolidge, trying to engage him in conversation.

"Sin," said Coolidge.

"But what did he *say?*" she persisted.

"He was against it."

It became a sort of standing challenge to force President Coolidge to talk. One Washington matron frankly told him so at a White House dinner.

"I've made a wager, Mr. President," she said, with a disarming smile. "I've bet that I can make you say at least three words."

"You lose," said Coolidge.

The motto "Keep cool with Coolidge" was so persuasive that even Coolidge believed in it. He evaded all controversial issues. At the height of his campaign he maintained silence on practically everything.

"Have you anything to say on Prohibition?" asked the interviewers at one of the conferences.

"No," replied Coolidge.

"Will you say something about unemployment?"

"No," he repeated.

"Will you tell us your views about the world situation?"

"No."

"About your message to Congress?"

"No."

Then, as the meeting broke up, he added, "And don't quote me."

When he was Vice-President, Coolidge was invited to attend many dinners, but his hostesses were always in despair because he refused to make conversation. One lady tried to solve the difficulty by seating him next to the brilliant daughter of Theodore Roosevelt, Alice Roosevelt Longworth. Even she, with all her sparkle, failed to rouse any response and, finally, toward the end of the meal, Mrs. Longworth said icily, "You go to so many dinners. You must get terribly bored."

"Well," said Coolidge, "a man must eat."

DISRAELI, BENJAMIN

The rivalry between Disraeli, first earl of Beaconsfield, prime minister and author, and Gladstone, the scholar-statesman, was intense. Disraeli was Queen Victoria's favorite and, when people wondered how the sharp-witted and malicious writer had ingratiated himself with the prim monarch, Disraeli said, "It is simple. Gladstone speaks to the Queen as though she were a public institution. I treat her with the knowledge that she is a woman."

Called upon to tell the difference between a misfortune and a calamity, Disraeli hesitated and then answered: "There is a similarity, but there is also a profound difference. If, let us say, Mr. Gladstone were to fall into the Thames, that would be a misfortune. But if anyone were to pull him out, that would be a calamity."

EDISON, THOMAS A.

Electric storms had caused considerable damage in the neighborhood of Edison's New Jersey home. One of his friends called to ask the inventor's opinion about preventing further damage to a large structure.

"Lightning rods might help, don't you think?" he asked.

"What kind of a building is it?" inquired Edison.

"A church," said his friend.

"By all means put on lightning rods," said Edison. "Providence is sometimes mighty absent-minded."

Edison was a heavy smoker, and he was annoyed to find that his friends helped themselves liberally to his expensive Havana cigars. He decided to play a trick on them. He had a tobacconist construct a lot of cigars made entirely of cabbage leaves and brown paper wrapping. He left these on his desk and, a day later, departed for a short trip. When he returned, his Havanas started disappearing again.

"But what did you do with those—er—new cigars I ordered?" Edison asked his secretary.

"Oh, those," said his secretary. "I took it for granted that those were something special. So I put that box in your suitcase."

"My God!" exclaimed Edison. "You mean to say that I smoked every one of those damned things myself!"

FIELD, EUGENE

Before Eugene Field became celebrated throughout America as a poet and columnist, he was the drama critic for the *Denver Post*. Two lines of his review of a performance of *King Lear* have become immortal. "Last night," wrote Field, "a visiting actor, who shall be nameless, played *King Lear*. He played the king as though he expected someone to play the ace."

Another of Field's reviews was even terser. "Mr. X played Hamlet," wrote Field. "He played it until one o'clock."

GOLDWYN, SAMUEL

There is no limit to the stories about Samuel Goldwyn, the Hollywood mogul. Many of the tales are shrewd, many are flatly incredible —or as Goldwyn is supposed to have said about a bad actor, "in two words: im-possible!" Some Goldwynisms follow:

Goldwyn had heard of Dorothy Parker's quick wit and he determined to have her come to Hollywood and write for him.

"But," objected one of his assistants, "don't you think she's rather caustic?"

"What do I care how much she costs?" shouted Goldwyn. "Get her!"

~/~

"Gentlemen," Goldwyn is reported to have said at a conference about a scenario, "I'm willing to admit that I may not always be right—but I'm never wrong."

~/~

"La Prisonnière" had been a great success in France, and Goldwyn was anxious to purchase the film rights.

"But you can't film that play," said one of his directors. "It's about a group of Lesbians."

"So what!" exclaimed Goldwyn. "We'll make them Americans!"

~/~

Goldwyn stories are endless, but one is an unforgettable classic. The place was England, and Goldwyn was dickering with George Bernard Shaw. The Irish playwright was not at all eager to have his plays made into films and made his terms almost impossibly stiff. Finally Goldwyn attempted to appeal to the creator rather than to the businessman. "Think, Mr. Shaw," said Goldwyn, "think of the millions who have never had a chance to see your plays on the stage, think of the millions who will now have the opportunity to get acquainted with your art."

"Ah, Mr. Goldwyn," said the mischievous Shaw, "you think of nothing but Art, while I think of nothing but money."

GRANT, U. S.

It has always been a question whether Ulysses S. Grant actively disliked music or was just apathetic to it. Once, while he was President, he was compelled to attend a concert of classical pieces.

"Did you enjoy the music, Mr. President?" he was asked.

"How could I?" said Grant. "I know only two tunes. One of them is 'Yankee Doodle' and the other isn't."

~/~

One of Grant's advisers was arguing against Sumner, saying that Sumner was an agnostic. "Why," continued the speaker, "he doesn't even believe in the Bible."

"Why should he?" replied Grant. "He didn't write it."

HULL, CORDELL

As Secretary of State, Cordell Hull never passed judgment without examining all the evidence. On one of his western trips he and a friend were looking out of the window when they observed a large flock of sheep.

"Those sheep have just been shorn," said his friend.

"Well," said the cautious statesman, "at least on this side."

JERROLD, DOUGLAS

One of the greatest of nineteenth century wits, Douglas Jerrold dreaded nothing so much as bores. One of them, accosting Jerrold, said breezily, "Well, Jerrold, what's going on?"

"I am," said Jerrold, suiting the action to the word.

∿

Jerrold was a playwright who was always nervous on the first night of his plays. One of his colleagues, who had a reputation for plagiarism, reproached him.

"Look at me," said he, "I'm never nervous at my first nights."

"Why should you be?" replied Jerrold. "Your new pieces have *always* been successful."

KREISLER, FRITZ

Although Kreisler preferred playing in public to appearing at private houses, he was persuaded, to perform for the famed but obnoxious Mrs. Astorbilt. His fee was a thousand dollars.

"A thousand dollars?" said the rich hostess. "Isn't that rather high?"

"That is my fee," said Kreisler.

"Well, I suppose I'll have to pay it," said she. "But remember, you are an entertainer, and as such you must not mingle with my guests."

"In that case," said the violinist, "my fee will be five hundred dollars."

MASSEY, RAYMOND

Everyone who saw Robert Sherwood's immensely successful play about Abraham Lincoln remarked on Raymond Massey's extraordinary interpretation of the character. He looked the part even without his makeup; he began to make offstage pithy utterances; it was maliciously said that he was trying to grow a wart to look still more like Lincoln.

"Uncanny, isn't it?" someone said to the playwright, George S. Kaufman.

"Uncanny indeed," said Kaufman. "Massey won't be satisfied until he's assassinated!"

MORGAN, J. P.

The eminent financier, J. P. Morgan, was coming to tea at the home of Mrs. Dwight Morrow, and Mrs. Morrow was worried. She had two charming but outspoken daughters; Mr. Morgan had an unusually brilliant and conspicuous nose. Mrs. Morrow was particularly afraid that the observant Anne (later Anne Lindbergh) would make a comment that would ruin the afternoon. Therefore she took pains to explain that children should be prepared for odd things without speaking of them and, particularly, to say nothing about any of Mr. Morgan's features which might seem strange.

The hour came, and so did Mr. Morgan. The children were brought in and were fascinated. After being introduced Anne gazed wonderingly at the famous Morgan nose, but did not utter an undiplomatic syllable. Finally the girls curtsied and left the room. Mrs. Morrow breathed a great sigh of relief.

"And now, Mr. Morgan," she said to her guest, "will you have one or two lumps of sugar in your nose?"

PHELPS, WILLIAM LYON

Most of the late William Lyon Phelps's classes felt that they were attending "snap courses." But, as if to admonish his students, the professor set a rather stiff examination just before Christmas. One of the more light-hearted classmen wrote nonchalantly across his paper: "God knows the answer to these questions. Merry Christmas."

Phelps returned the paper with this notation: "God gets an A. You get an F. Happy New Year."

PINCHOT, MRS. AMOS

In a strange dream Mrs. Amos Pinchot felt that the secrets of the universe had been unveiled. In tune with the infinite, she began to write the world's most profound poem.

Waking in a half-trance, she scribbled down what was still vibrating in her mind. In the morning she had forgotten all except the vaguest outlines of the dream. But the scrawled piece of paper was on the table beside her. She picked it up and read the masterpiece which had come out of her subconsciousness. It was this:

> Hoggamus, higgamus,
> Men are polygamous.
> Higgamus, hoggamus,
> Women monogamous.

ROOSEVELT, THEODORE

Theodore Roosevelt, sometimes known as Roosevelt the First, was a President who knew his value; he did not cheapen himself by under-estimating it. "Father always had to be the center of attention," said one of his children. "When he went to a wedding, he wanted to be the bride. When he went to a funeral, he was sorry that he couldn't be the corpse."

During one of his campaign speeches, Theodore Roosevelt was continually interrupted by a heckler who kept shouting, "I am a Democrat."

Finally Roosevelt had to do something. With disarming gentleness he inquired, "May I ask the gentleman why he is a Democrat?"

"My grandfather was a Democrat," replied the heckler. "My father was a Democrat. And I am a Democrat."

"And suppose," continued Roosevelt, "that your grandfather had been a jackass, and your father had been a jackass, what would you be?"

The heckler shouted back, "A Republican!"

SHAW, GEORGE BERNARD

Perhaps the best-known anecdote concerning the Irish playwright and master of repartee is the one involving Sam Goldwyn, which ap-

pears on page 88. But there are several others almost equally well
authenticated and gleefully retold. A popular legend has it that the
famous dancer and free spirit, Isadora Duncan, wrote Shaw a fervent
letter which ended with the proposal that it would be a good thing for
eugenics, as well as posterity, if they should become the parents of a
child.

"Think," urged Miss Duncan, "what a fortunate child it would be
with your brains and my body."

Shaw replied that he was flattered, but he declined the invitation.

"The child," he wrote in reply, "might not be so lucky. It might
have my body and your brains."

It was the first performance of *Arms and the Man,* one of Shaw's
most illustrious opening nights. But as he answered the curtain call,
one man in the gallery shouted, "Rotten!"

With that roguish smile for which the Irish are famous, the playwright bowed. "My friend, I completely agree with you. But," he
added, shrugging his shoulders and pointing to the applauding audience,
"what are we two against so many?"

Shaw's vegetarianism led to many brusque retorts. Lady Randolph
was startled to receive a curt refusal to her bid inviting Shaw to
luncheon. "Certainly not," wired Shaw. "What makes you think I
would alter my well-known habits!"

To which Lady Randolph replied: "Know nothing about your habits. Hope they are not as bad as your manners."

Shaw saw no reason why he should suffer fools gladly; in fact he refused to suffer them at all. Once, at dinner, he had to listen to a so-called child-expert explain progressive education. Shaw remained silent until the enthusiast exclaimed, "Youth! Youth is the most wonderful thing in the world."

"Yes," murmured Shaw. "Isn't it a pity it's wasted on the young?"

TWAIN, MARK

The right place to find Mark Twain's best stories is, obviously, in Twain's own books. But there are many anecdotes of his personal life which never found their way into his volumes. One such anecdote concerns Twain's attendance as a guest of honor at the Metropolitan Opera House. It took place in a box and his wealthy hostess had been unusually talkative all through the performance. At the end of the opera, she thanked Twain for coming and added, "I do hope you'll be my guest again. What about next Wednesday? The opera will be *Carmen*."

"I'd love to," said the author. "I've never heard you in *Carmen*."

Mark Twain was a born borrower, especially of books. One of his neighbors undertook to cure him. When Twain asked for the loan of a book, his neighbor said, "Certainly. But I've made a rule that any volume taken from my library must be read on the premises."

A week later, the neighbor came to borrow Twain's lawn-mower. "Of course you may have it," said Twain. "But I've made a rule that any lawn-mower of mine must be used only on my own lawn."

When he was lecturing in Utah, a Mormon acquaintance argued with Twain on the question of polygamy. After a long and rather heated discussion, the Mormon said, "Can you find a single passage of Scripture which *forbids* polygamy?"

"Certainly," said Twain. " 'No man can serve two masters.' "

Twain was visiting the studio of Whistler, and started to touch part of a painting. "Look out!" cried Whistler, testily. "Can't you see it isn't dry yet?"

"Oh, I don't mind," said Twain. "I've got gloves on."

WEBSTER, NOAH

Webster's severe choice of words, the discrimination which led him to compile the dictionary, also led to his most quoted distinction.

One day his wife came suddenly into the pantry and found Webster kissing the pretty chambermaid. "Mr. Webster!" exclaimed his wife. "I am surprised!"

"No, my dear," said Webster, with a reproving smile. "You are astounded. It is I who am surprised."

WHISTLER, JAMES MCNEILL AND WILDE, OSCAR

Friends and rivals in malicious wit, the painter James McNeill Whistler and the poet-playwright Oscar Wilde were continually trying to outwit each other. Once, when Whistler had said something particularly brilliant, Wilde sighed enviously, "Jimmie, I wish I had said that!"

"Don't worry, Oscar," said Whistler. "You will."

The gossip column of an English newspaper printed this paragraph: "James McNeill Whistler and Oscar Wilde were seen yesterday at Brigton talking, as usual, about themselves."

Whistler sent the clipping to Wilde with this line: "I wish reporters would be more accurate. You may remember, Oscar, we were talking about me."

Wilde answered: "True Jimmie, we were talking about you—but I was thinking about myself."

Whistler's conceit was superb. No one enjoyed his boundless immodesty more than Whistler himself. On one occasion a duchess, wishing to be polite, remarked, "I believe you know King Edward, Mr. Whistler."

"No, madame," said Whistler curtly.

"That's odd," she murmured. "I met the king at a dinner party a few weeks ago, and he said he knew you."

"Oh," said Whistler, "he was just boasting."

Whistler's egotism was surpassed only by Wilde's. Arriving at the club after the first performance of one of his least successful plays, he was asked how the drama was received.

"Oh," said Wilde airily, "the play was a great success. But the audience was a failure."

Once the audience retaliated. The place was Boston and Wilde had been haranguing his hearers on their insensitivity to art. "You are Philistines," he said superciliously. "Philistines who have invaded the sacred sanctum."

"And you," cried a voice in the audience, "are driving us forth with the jawbone of an ass."

WOOLLCOTT, ALEXANDER

Alexander Woollcott, often called "the smartest of Alecs," was telling a story at his class reunion. A fellow alumnus interrupted, "Hello, Alex! You remember me, don't you?"

"I can't remember your name," said Woollcott, "but don't tell me."

Always in love with the stage, Woollcott was both a playwright and a critic; there was a time when he was an actor. His estimate of his own acting may be guessed by the telegram he sent Sinclair Lewis on the opening of "Angela is Twenty-Two," a play which Lewis wrote and in which he appeared "in person." "Greetings," wrote Woollcott, "from one elderly exhibitionist who knows he can't act to another who still thinks he can."

Lewis Carroll

He was the reverend Charles Lutwidge Dodgson, a university lecturer, a noted mathematician, and a deacon in holy orders. Under another name, Lewis Carroll, he wrote a series of books for children—Alice's Adventures in Wonderland, Through the Looking Glass, Sylvie and Bruno—nonsense as logical as it was lovable.

But Dodgson kept himself apart from Carroll; to the last he refused to identify himself with his pseudonym. It is said that Queen Victoria was one of the few who discovered that Dodgson was the creator of the Alice books; she let it be known that she would be willing to sponsor his work. Whereupon Dodgson sent her the manuscript of a new volume of which he was proud; its title was An Elementary Treatise on Determinants.

Part of Carroll's charm is inspired nonsense, part is calculated parody. The seemingly irresponsible rhymes of "Father William" are actually a satire on Robert Southey's "The Old Man's Comforts, and How He Gained Them," a moral poem which begins:

"You are old, Father William," the young man
    cried,
    "The few locks which are left you are gray;

> You are hale, Father William, a hearty old
>   man,
>   Now tell me the reason, I pray."
>
> "In the days of my youth," Father William
>   replied,
>   "I remembered that youth would fly fast,
> And abused not my health and my vigor at
>   first,
>   That I never might need them at last."

With a flick of the pen, Carroll turned Southey's sanctimonious old babbler into an agile-bodied and alert-minded gentleman who makes his youthful questioner seem ridiculous.

Father William

FROM "ALICE'S ADVENTURES IN WONDERLAND"

> "You are old, Father William," the young man said,
>   "And your hair has become very white;
> And yet you incessantly stand on your head—
>   Do you think, at your age, it is right?"
>
> "In my youth," Father William replied to his son,
>   "I feared it might injure the brain;
> But, now that I'm perfectly sure I have none,
>   Why, I do it again and again."
>
> "You are old," said the youth, "as I mentioned before,
>   And have grown most uncommonly fat;
> Yet you turned a back-somersault in at the door—
>   Pray, what is the reason of that?"
>
> "In my youth," said the sage, as he shook his grey locks,
>   "I kept all my limbs very supple.

By the use of this ointment—one shilling the box—
   Allow me to sell you a couple?"

"You are old," said the youth, "and your jaws are too weak
   For anything tougher than suet;
Yet you finished the goose, with the bones and the beak—
   Pray, how did you manage to do it?"

"In my youth," said his father, "I took to the law,
   And argued each case with my wife;
And the muscular strength, which it gave to my jaw,
   Has lasted the rest of my life."

"You are old," said the youth, "one would hardly suppose
   That your eye was as steady as ever;
Yet you balanced an eel on the end of your nose—
   What made you so awfully clever?"

"I have answered three questions, and that is enough,"
   Said his father. "Don't give yourself airs!
Do you think I can listen all day to such stuff!
   Be off, or I'll kick you down stairs!"

"Jabberwocky" is often considered the greatest nonsense poem in the English language, a piece of riotous surrealism, a composition of meaningless but unforgettable music. It defies explanation. Nevertheless, Carroll himself teasingly "explained" a part of it. Most of the words, wrote Carroll, are "portmanteau" words—in which two or more ideas are telescoped into one word. If the reader were to think of "fretful" and "furious" and "fuming" simultaneously and tried to say all three words at the same time, the result would be an explosive portmanteau word exactly like "frumious." After the hero has slain the Jabberwock, he comes back "galloping" in "triumph"—therefore he comes back "galumphing."

Later in Through the Looking Glass, Humpty Dumpty attempts to explain some of the other difficult words to Alice. "Brillig," he said, "means four o'clock in the afternoon—the time when you begin broiling things for dinner."

"That'll do very well," said Alice: "and 'slithy'?"

"Well, 'slithy' means 'lithe and slimy.' 'Lithe' is the same as 'active.' You see it's like a portmanteau—there are two meanings packed up into one word."

"I see it now," Alice remarked thoughtfully: "and what are 'toves'?"

"Well, 'toves' are something like badgers—they're something like lizards—and they're something like corkscrews." *

"They must be very curious-looking creatures."

"They are that," said Humpty Dumpty: "also they make their nests under sun-dials—also they live on cheese."

"And what's to 'gyre' and to 'gimble'?"

"To 'gyre' is to go round and round like a gyroscope. To 'gimble' is to make holes like a gimlet."

"And 'the wabe' is the grass-plot around a sun-dial, I suppose?" said Alice, surprised at her own ingenuity.

"Of course it is. It's called 'wabe,' because it goes a long way before it, and a long way behind it—"

"And a long way beyond it on each side," Alice added.

"Exactly so. Well, then, 'mimsy' is 'flimsy' and 'miserable' (there's another portmanteau for you). And a 'borogove' is a thin shabby-looking bird with its feathers sticking out all round—something like a live mop."

"And then 'mome raths'?" said Alice. "I'm afraid I'm giving you a great deal of trouble."

"Well, a 'rath' is a sort of green pig: but 'mome' I'm not certain about. I think it's short for 'from home'—meaning that they'd lost their way, you know."

Jabberwocky

FROM "THROUGH THE LOOKING GLASS"

'Twas brillig, and the slithy toves
   Did gyre and gimble in the wabe ;
All mimsy were the borogoves,
   And the mome raths outgrabe.

---

* It is suspected that *"toves"* are really a cross between "toads" and "doves." (Editor.)

"Beware the Jabberwock, my son!
   The jaws that bite, the claws that catch!
Beware the Jubjub bird, and shun
   The frumious Bandersnatch!"

He took his vorpal sword in hand:
   Long time the manxome foe he sought—
So rested he by the Tumtum tree,
   And stood awhile in thought.

And as in uffish thought he stood,
   The Jabberwock, with eyes of flame,
Came whiffling through the tulgey wood,
   And burbled as it came!

One, two! One, two! And through and through
   The vorpal blade went snicker-snack!
He left it dead, and with its head
   He went galumphing back.

"And hast thou slain the Jabberwock?
   Come to my arms, my beamish boy!
O frabjous day! Callooh! Callay!"
   He chortled in his joy.

'Twas brillig, and the slithy toves
   Did gyre and gimble in the wabe;
All mimsy were the borogoves,
   And the mome raths outgrabe.

Humpty Dumpty's Recitation

FROM "THROUGH THE LOOKING GLASS"

In winter, when the fields are white,
I sing this song for your delight——

In spring, when woods are getting green,
I'll try and tell you what I mean.

In summer, when the days are long,
Perhaps you'll understand the song:

In autumn, when the leaves are brown,
Take pen and ink, and write it down.

I sent a message to the fish:
I told them "This is what I wish."

The little fishes of the sea,
They sent an answer back to me.

The little fishes' answer was
"We cannot do it, Sir, because——"

I sent to them again to say
"It will be better to obey."

The fishes answered with a grin,
"Why, what a temper you are in!"

I told them once, I told them twice:
They would not listen to advice.

I took a kettle large and new,
Fit for the deed I had to do.

My heart went hop, my heart went thump;
I filled the kettle at the pump.

Then someone came to me and said,
"The little fishes are in bed."

I said to him, I said it plain,
"Then you must wake them up again."

I said it very loud and clear;
I went and shouted in his ear.

But he was very stiff and proud;
He said, "You needn't shout so loud!"

And he was very proud and stiff;
He said, "I'd go and wake them, if——"

I took a corkscrew from the shelf:
I went to wake them up myself.

And when I found the door was locked,
I pulled and pushed and kicked and knocked.

And when I found the door was shut,
I tried to turn the handle, but——

The Mad Gardener's Song

FROM "SYLVIE AND BRUNO"

He thought he saw an Elephant
    That practised on a fife:
He looked again, and found it was
    A letter from his wife.
"At length I realise," he said,
    "The bitterness of Life!"

He thought he saw a Buffalo
    Upon the chimney-piece:
He looked again, and found it was
    His Sister's Husband's Niece.
"Unless you leave this house," he said,
    "I'll send for the Police!"

He thought he saw a Rattlesnake
    That questioned him in Greek:
He looked again, and found it was
    The Middle of Next Week.

"The one thing I regret," he said,
  "Is that it cannot speak!"

He thought he saw a Banker's Clerk
  Descending from the bus:
He looked again and found it was
  A Hippopotamus.
"If this should stay to dine," he said,
  "There won't be much for us!"

He thought he saw a Kangaroo
  That worked a coffee-mill:
He looked again, and found it was
  A Vegetable-Pill.
"Were I to swallow this," he said,
  "I should be very ill!"

He thought he saw a Coach-and-Four
  That stood beside his bed:
He looked again, and found it was
  A bear without a Head.
"Poor thing," he said, "poor silly thing!
  It's waiting to be fed!"

Guy Wetmore Carryl

An extraordinary versifier—with the exception of Ogden Nash, perhaps the most brilliant American writer of light verse—the precocious Guy Wetmore Carryl was born in New York City, March 4, 1873. He had published five volumes of surprising prose and verse when he died at thirty-one.

A juggler of intricate rhymes, Carryl was able to keep a battery of bristling rhymes, astounding puns, and topsy-turvy morals in the air at one time and in one poem. His titles indicate the manner: Mother Goose for Grownups, Fables for the Frivolous, Grimm Tales Made Gay. Never have antique tales and modern parables been more dexterously balanced.

The Sycophantic Fox and the Gullible Raven

A raven sat upon a tree,
  And not a word he spoke, for
His beak contained a piece of Brie
  Or, maybe, it was Roquefort.
    We'll make it any kind you please—
    At all events it was a cheese.

Beneath the tree's umbrageous limb
  A hungry fox sat smiling;
He saw the raven watching him,
  And spoke in words beguiling:
    "*J'admire*," said he, "*ton beau plumage*,"
    (The which was simply persiflage).

Two things there are, no doubt you know,
  To which a fox is used:
A rooster that is bound to crow,
  A crow that's bound to roost;
    And whichsoever he espies
    He tells the most unblushing lies.

"Sweet fowl," he said, "I understand
  You're more than merely natty,
I hear you sing to beat the band
  And Adelina Patti.
    Pray render with your liquid tongue
    A bit from 'Götterdämmerung.' "

This subtle speech was aimed to please
  The crow, and it succeeded;
He thought no bird in all the trees
  Could sing as well as he did.
    In flattery completely doused,
    He gave the "Jewel Song" from "Faust."

But gravitation's law, of course,
   As Isaac Newton showed it,
Exerted on the cheese its force,
   And elsewhere soon bestowed it.
      In fact, there is no need to tell
      What happened when to earth it fell.

I blush to add that when the bird
   Took in the situation
He said one brief, emphatic word,
   Unfit for publication.
      The fox was greatly startled, but
      He only sighed and answered "'Tut."

The Moral is: A fox is bound
   To be a shameless sinner.
And also: When the cheese comes round
   You know it's after dinner.
      But (what is only known to few)
      The fox is after dinner, too.

The Vainglorious Oak and the Modest Bulrush

A bulrush stood on a river's rim,
   And an oak that grew near by
Looked down with cold *hauteur* on him,
   And addressed him this way: "Hi!"
The rush was a proud patrician, and
   He retorted, "Don't you know,
What the veriest boor should understand,
      That 'Hi' is low?"

This cutting rebuke the oak ignored.
   He returned, "My slender friend,
I will frankly state that I'm somewhat bored

With the way you bow and bend."
"But you quite forget," the rush replied,
    "It's an art these bows to do,
An art I wouldn't attempt if I'd
        Such boughs as you."

"Of course," said the oak, "in my sapling days
    My habit it was to bow,
But the wildest storm that the winds could raise
    Would never disturb me now.
I challenge the breeze to make me bend,
    And the blast to make me sway."
The shrewd little bulrush answered, "Friend,
        Don't get so gay."

And the words had barely left his mouth
    When he saw the oak turn pale,
For, racing along south-east-by-south,
    Came ripping a raging gale.
And the rush bent low as the storm went past,
    But stiffly stood the oak,
Though not for long, for he found the blast
        No idle joke.

    *   *   *   *   *   *   *   *

Imagine the lightning's gleaming bars,
    Imagine the thunder's roar,
For that is exactly what eight stars
    Are set in a row here for!
The oak lay prone when the storm was done,
    While the rush, still quite erect,
Remarked aside, "What under the sun
        Could one expect?"

And *The Moral,* I'd have you understand,
    Would have made La Fontaine blush,
For it's this: Some storms come early, and
        Avoid the rush!

Irvin S. Cobb

LADIES & GENTLEMEN

A toastmaster once introduced Cobb by saying, "And now let me present a man who is a ready wit. All you have to do is put a dinner in his mouth, and out comes his speech." In reply Cobb said, "Your toastmaster is far more remarkable. All you have to do is put a speech in his mouth, and out comes your dinner."

Cobb's fame as a story-teller was undoubtedly enhanced by his dinner-table reputation. But it was Speaking of Operations which ranked him as one of the leading humorists of his time. Born in Paducah, Kentucky, in 1876, Cobb had been a reporter at sixteen; he was an undistinguished journalist until Speaking of Operations sold more than three hundred thousand copies.

In 1941 Cobb published a friendly, rambling account of his life, Exit Laughing. The title was prophetically justified. Three years later, on March 10, 1944, Cobb died, leaving a 1500-word letter describing the kind of funeral and burial he wanted. "Keep it cheerful," he said. "If anybody tries to insert me into one of those dismal numbers run up by the undertaker's dressmaking department, I'll come back and ha'nt 'em! Nor do I crave to make my mortal exit in a tail-coat with white tie and artificial pearl studs. I'll be done with after-dinner speaking forever, so why dispatch me hence in the regalia of the craft? When a man dies with his sins, let the sins die with the man. That's what I say and it sums up such speculations as I might ever have had touching on the future state, if any. For me a suitable epitaph would be: 'Anyhow, he left here.'"

"Speaking of Operations"

Now that the last belated bill for services professionally rendered has been properly paid and properly receipted; now that the memory of the event, like the mark of the stitches, has faded out from a vivid red to a becoming pink shade; now that I pass a display of adhesive tape in a drug-store window without flinching—I sit me down to write a little piece about a certain matter—a small thing, but mine own—to wit, That Operation.

For years I have noticed that persons who underwent pruning or remodeling at the hands of a duly qualified surgeon, and survived, like to talk about it afterward. In the event of their not surviving I have no doubt they still liked to talk about it, but in a different locality. Of all the readily available topics for use, whether among friends or among strangers, an operation seems to be the handiest and most dependable.

For mixed companies a whale is one of the best and the easiest things to talk about that I know of. In regard to whales and their peculiarities you can make almost any assertion without fear of successful contradiction. Nobody ever knows any more about them than you do. You are not hampered by facts. If someone mentions the blubber of the whale and you chime in and say it may be noticed for miles on a still day when the large but emotional creature has been moved to tears by some great sorrow coming into its life, everybody is bound to accept the statement. For after all how few among us really know whether a distressed whale sobs aloud or does so under its breath? Who, with any certainty, can tell whether a mother whale hatches her own egg her own self or leaves it on the sheltered bosom of a fjord to be incubated by the gentle warmth of the midnight sun? The possibilities of the proposition for purposes of informal debate, pro and con, are apparent at a glance.

The weather, of course, helps out amazingly when you are meeting people for the first time, because there is nearly always more or less weather going on somewhere and practically everybody has ideas about it. The human breakfast is also a wonderfully good topic to start up during one of those lulls. Try it yourself the next time the conversation seems to drag. Just speak up in an offhand kind of way and say that you never care much about breakfast—a slice of toast and a cup of weak tea start you off properly for doing a hard day's work. You will be surprised to note how things liven up and how eagerly all present join in. The lady on your left feels that you should know she always takes two lumps of sugar and nearly half cream, because she simply cannot abide hot milk, no matter what the doctors say. The gentleman on your right will be moved to confess he likes his eggs boiled for exactly three minutes, no more and no less. Buckwheat cakes and sausage find a champion and oatmeal rarely lacks a warm defender.

But after all, when all is said and done, the king of all topics is operations. Sooner or later, wherever two or more are gathered together, it is reasonably certain that somebody will bring up an operation.

Until I passed through the experience of being operated on myself, I never really realized what a precious conversational boon the subject is, and how great a part it plays in our intercourse with our fellow beings on this planet. To the teller it is enormously interesting, for he is not only the hero of the tale but the rest of the cast and the stage setting as well—the whole show, as they say; and if the listener has had a similar experience—and who is there among us in these days that has not taken a nap 'neath the shade of the old ether cone?—it acquires a doubled value.

"Speaking of operations——," you say, just like that, even though nobody present has spoken of them; and then you are off, with your new acquaintance sitting on the edge of his chair, or hers as the case may be and so frequently is, with hands clutched in polite but painful restraint, gills working up and down with impatience, eyes brightened with desire, tongue hung in the middle, waiting for you to pause to catch your breath, so that he or she may break in with a few personal recollections along the same line. From a mere conversation it resolves itself into a symptom symposium, and a perfectly splendid time is had by all.

If an operation is such a good thing to talk about, why isn't it a good thing to write about, too? That is what I wish to know. Besides, I need the money. Verily, one always needs the money when one has but recently escaped from the ministering clutches of the modern hospital. Therefore I write.

It all dates back to the fair, bright morning when I went to call on a prominent practitioner here in New York, whom I shall denominate as Doctor X. I had a pain. I had had it for days. It was not a dependable, locatable pain, such as a tummyache or a toothache is, which you can put your hand on; but an indefinite, unsettled, undecided kind of pain, which went wandering about from place to place inside of me like a strange ghost lost in Cudjo's Cave. I never knew until then what the personal sensations of a haunted house are. If only the measly thing could have made up its mind to settle down somewhere and start light housekeeping I think I should have been better satisfied. I never had such an uneasy tenant. Alongside of it a woman with the moving fever would be comparatively a fixed and stationary object.

Having always, therefore, enjoyed perfectly riotous and absolutely unbridled health, never feeling weak and distressed unless dinner happened to be ten or fifteen minutes late, I was green regarding physicians and the ways of physicians. But I knew Doctor X slightly, having met him last summer in one of his hours of ease in the grand stand at a ball game, when he was expressing a desire to cut the umpire's throat from ear to ear, free of charge; and I remembered his name, and remembered, too, that he had impressed me at the time as being a person of character and decision and scholarly attainments.

He wore whiskers. Somehow in my mind whiskers are ever associated with medical skill. I presume this is a heritage of my youth, though I believe others labor under the same impression. As I look back it seems to me that in childhood's days all the doctors in our town wore whiskers.

I recall one old doctor down there in Kentucky who was practically lurking in ambush all the time. All he needed was a few decoys out in front of him and a pump gun to be a duck blind. He carried his calomel about with him in a fruit jar, and when there was a cutting job he stropped his scalpel on his bootleg.

You see, in those primitive times germs had not been invented yet and so he did not have to take any steps to avoid them. Now we know that loose, luxuriant whiskers are unsanitary, because they make such fine winter quarters for germs; so, though the doctors still wear whiskers, they do not wear them wild and waving. In the profession bosky whiskers are taboo; they must be landscaped. And since it is a recognized fact that germs abhor orderliness and straight lines they now go elsewhere to reside, and the doctor may still retain his traditional aspect and yet be practically germproof. Doctor X was trimmed in accordance with the ethics of the newer school. He had trellis whiskers. So I went to see him at his offices in a fashionable district, on an expensive side street.

Before reaching him I passed through the hands of a maid and a nurse each of whom spoke to me in a low, sorrowful tone of voice, which seemed to indicate that there was very little hope.

I reached an inner room where Doctor X was. He looked me over, while I described for him as best I could what seemed to be the matter

with me, and asked me a number of intimate questions touching on
the lives, works, characters and peculiarities of my ancestors; after
which he made me stand up in front of him and take my coat off, and
he punched me hither and yon with his forefinger. He also knocked
repeatedly on my breastbone with his knuckles, and each time, on doing
this, would apply his ear to my chest and listen intently for a spell,
afterward shaking his head in a disappointed way. Apparently there was
nobody at home. For quite a time he kept on knocking, but without
getting any response.

He then took my temperature and fifteen dollars, and said it was
an interesting case—not unusual exactly, but interesting—and that it
called for an operation.

From the way my heart and other organs jumped inside of me at
that statement I knew at once that, no matter what he may have
thought, the premises were not unoccupied. Naturally I inquired how
soon he meant to operate. Personally I trusted there was no hurry about
it. I was perfectly willing to wait for several years, if necessary. He
smiled at my ignorance.

"I never operate," he said; "operating is entirely out of my line. I
am a diagnostician."

He was, too—I give him full credit for that. He was a good, keen,
close diagnostician. How did he know I had only fifteen dollars on me?
You did not have to tell this man what you had, or how much. He
knew without being told.

I asked whether he was acquainted with Doctor Y—, Y being a
person whom I had met casually at a club to which I belong. Oh, yes, he
said he knew Doctor Y. Y was a clever man, X said—very, very
clever; but Y specialized in the eyes, the ears, the nose and the throat.
I gathered from what Doctor X said that any time Doctor Y ventured
below the thorax he was out of bounds and liable to be penalized; and
that if by any chance he strayed down as far as the lungs he would
call for help and back out as rapidly as possible.

This was news to me. It would appear that these up-to-date practi-
tioners just go ahead and divide you up and partition you out among
themselves without saying anything to you about it. Your torso belongs to one man and your legs are the exclusive property of his brother
practitioner down on the next block, and so on. You may belong to as
many as half a dozen specialists, most of whom, very possibly, are
total strangers to you, and yet never know a thing about it yourself.

It has rather the air of trespass—nay, more than that, it bears some
of the aspects of unlawful entry—but I suppose it is legal. Certainly

judging by what I am able to learn, the system is being carried on generally. So it must be ethical.

Anything doctors do in a mass is ethical. Almost anything they do singly and on individual responsibility is unethical. Being ethical among doctors is practically the same thing as being a Democrat in Texas or a Presbyterian in Scotland.

"Y will never do for you," said Doctor X when I had rallied somewhat from the shock of these disclosures. "I would suggest that you go to Doctor Z, at such-and-such an address. You are exactly in Z's line. I'll let him know that you are coming and when, and I'll send him down my diagnosis."

So that same afternoon, the appointment having been made by telephone, I went, full of quavery emotions, to Doctor Z's place. As soon as I was inside his outer hallway I realized that I was nearing the presence of one highly distinguished in his profession.

A pussy-footed male attendant, in a livery that made him look like a cross between a headwaiter and an undertaker's assistant, escorted me through an anteroom into a reception-room, where a considerable number of well-dressed men and women were sitting about in strained attitudes, pretending to read magazines while they waited their turns, but in reality furtively watching one another.

I sat down in a convenient chair, adhering fast to my hat and my

umbrella. They were the only friends I had there and I was determined not to lose them without a struggle. On the wall were many colored charts showing various portions of the human anatomy and what ailed them. Directly in front of me was a very thrilling illustration, evidently copied from an oil painting, of a liver in a bad state of repair. I said to myself that if I had a liver like that one I should keep it hidden from the public eye—I would never permit it to sit for its portrait. Still, there is no accounting for tastes. I know a man who got his spleen back from the doctors and now keeps it in a bottle of alcohol on the what-not in the parlor, as one of his most treasured possessions, and sometimes shows it to visitors. He, however, is of a saving disposition.

Presently a lady secretary, who sat behind a roll-top desk in a corner of the room, lifted a forefinger and silently beckoned me to her side. I moved over and sat down by her; she took down my name and my age and my weight and my height, and a number of other interesting facts that will come in very handy should anyone ever be moved to write a complete history of my early life. In common with Doctor X she shared one attribute—she manifested a deep curiosity regarding my forefathers—wanted to know all about them. I felt that this was carrying the thing too far. I felt like saying to her:

"Miss or madam, so far as I know there is nothing the matter with my ancestors of the second and third generations back, except that they are dead. I am not here to seek medical assistance for a grandparent who succumbed to disappointment that time when Samuel J. Tilden got counted out, or for a great-grandparent who entered into Eternal Rest very unexpectedly and in a manner entirely uncalled for as a result of being an innocent bystander in one of those feuds that were so popular in my native state immediately following the Mexican War. Leave my ancestors alone. There is no need of your shaking my family tree in the belief that a few overripe patients will fall out. I alone—I, me, myself—am the present candidate!"

However, I refrained from making this protest audibly. I judged she was only going according to the ritual; and as she had a printed card, with blanks in it ready to be filled out with details regarding the remote members of the family connection, I humored her along.

When I could not remember something she wished to know concerning an ancestor I supplied her with thrilling details culled from the field of fancy. When the card was entirely filled up she sent me back to my old place to wait. I waited and waited, breeding fresh ailments all the time. I had started out with one symptom; now if I had one I had a million and a half. I could feel goose flesh sprouting out all over me.

If I had been taller I might have had more, but not otherwise. Such is the power of the human imagination when the surroundings are favorable to its development.

Time passed; to me it appeared that nearly all the time there was passed and that we were getting along toward the shank-end of the Christian era mighty fast. I was afraid my turn would come next and afraid it would not. Perhaps you know this sensation. You get it at the dentist's, and when you are on the list of after-dinner speakers at a large banquet, and when you are waiting for the father of the Only Girl in the World to make up his mind whether he is willing to try to endure you as a son-in-law.

Then some more time passed.

One by one my companions, obeying a command, passed out through the door at the back, vanishing out of my life forever. None of them returned. I was vaguely wondering whether Doctor Z buried his dead on the premises or had them removed by a secret passageway in the rear, when a young woman in a nurse's costume tapped me on the shoulder from behind.

I jumped. She hid a compassionate smile with her hand and told me that the doctor would see me now.

As I rose to follow her—still clinging with the drowning man's grip of desperation to my hat and my umbrella—I was astonished to note by a glance at the calendar on the wall that this was still the present date. I thought it would be Thursday of next week at the very least.

Doctor Z also wore whiskers, carefully pointed up by an expert hedge trimmer. He sat at his desk, surrounded by freewill offerings from grateful patients and by glass cases containing other things he had taken away from them when they were not in a condition to object. I had expected, after all the preliminary ceremonies and delays, that we should have a long séance together. Not so; not at all. The modern expert in surgery charges as much for remembering your name between visits as the family doctor used to expect for staying up all night with you, but he does not waste any time when you are in his presence.

I was about to find that out. And a little later on I was to find out a lot of other things; in fact, that whole week was of immense educational value to me.

I presume it was because he stood so high in his profession, and was almost constantly engaged in going into the best society, that Doctor Z did not appear to be the least bit excited over my having picked him out to look into me. In the most perfunctory manner he shook the hand that has shaken the hands of Jess Willard, George M. Cohan and Henry

Ford, and bade me be seated in a chair which was drawn up in a strong light, where he might gaze directly at me as we conversed and so get the full values of the composition. But if I was a treat for him to look at he concealed his feelings very effectually.

He certainly had his emotions under splendid control. But then, of course, you must remember that he probably had traveled about extensively and was used to sight-seeing.

From this point on everything passed off in a most businesslike manner. He reached into a filing cabinet and took out an exhibit, which I recognized as the same one his secretary had filled out in the early part of the century. So I was already in the card-index class. Then briefly he looked over the manifest that Doctor X had sent him. It may not have been a manifest—it may have been an invoice or a bill of lading. Anyhow, I was in the assignee's hands. I could only hope it would not eventually become necessary to call in a receiver. Then he spoke:

"Yes, yes-yes," he said; "yes-yes-yes! Operation required. Small matter—hum, hum! Let's see—this is Tuesday? Quite so. Do it Friday! Friday at"—he glanced toward a scribbled pad of engagement dates at his elbow—"Friday at seven A.M. No; make it seven-fifteen. Have important· tumor case at seven. St. Germicide's Hospital. You know the place?—up on Umpty-umph Street. Go' day! Miss Whoziz, call next visitor."

Thursday at noon I received from Doctor Z's secretary a note stating that arrangements had been made for my admission into St. Germicide that same evening and that I was to spend the night there. This hardly seemed necessary. Still, the tone of the note appeared to indicate that the hospital authorities particularly wished to have me for an overnight guest; and as I reflected that probably the poor things had few enough bright spots in their busy lives, I decided I would humor them along and· gladden the occasion with my presence from dinner-time on.

About eight o'clock I strolled in very jauntily. In my mind I had the whole program mapped out. I would stay at the hospital for, say, two days following the operation—or, at most, three. Then I must be up and away. I had a good deal of work to do and a number of people to see on important business, and I could not really afford to waste more than a week-end on the staff of St. Germicide's. After Monday they must look to their own devices for social entertainment. That was my idea. Now when I look back on it I laugh, but it is a hollow laugh and there is no real merriment in it.

Indeed, almost from the moment of my entrance little things begun to come up that were calculated to have a depressing effect on one's spirits. Downstairs a serious-looking lady met me and entered in a book a number of salient facts regarding my personality which the previous investigators had somehow overlooked. There is a lot of book-keeping about an operation. This detail attended to, a young man, dressed in white garments and wearing an expression that stamped him as one who had suffered a recent deep bereavement, came and relieved me of my hand bag and escorted me upstairs.

As we passed through the upper corridors I had my first introduction to the hospital smell, which is a smell compounded of iodoform, ether, gruel, and something boiling. All hospitals have it, I understand. In time you get used to it, but you never really care for it.

The young man led me into a small room tastefully decorated with four walls, a floor, a ceiling, a window sill and a window, a door and a doorsill, and a bed and a chair. He told me to go to bed. I did not want to go to bed—it was not my regular bedtime—but he made a point of it, and I judged it was according to regulations; so I undressed and put on my night clothes and crawled in. He left me, taking my other clothes and my shoes with him, but I was not allowed to get lonely.

A little later a ward surgeon appeared, to put a few inquiries of a pointed and personal nature. He particularly desired to know what my trouble was. I explained to him that I couldn't tell him—he would have to see Doctor X or Doctor Z; they probably knew, but were keeping it a secret between themselves.

The answer apparently satisfied him, because immediately after that he made me sign a paper in which I assumed all responsibility for what was to take place the next morning.

This did not seem exactly fair. As I pointed out to him, it was the surgeon's affair, not mine; and if the surgeon made a mistake the joke would be on him and not on me, because in that case I would not be here anyhow. But I signed, as requested, on the dotted line, and he departed.

After that, at intervals, the chief house surgeon dropped in, without knocking, and the head nurse came, and an interne or so, and a ward nurse, and the special nurse who was to have direct charge of me. It dawned on me that I was not having any more privacy in that hospital than a gold-fish.

About eleven o'clock an orderly came, and, without consulting my wishes in the matter, he undressed me until I could have passed almost anywhere for September Morn's father, and gave me a clean shave, twice over, on one of my most prominent plane surfaces. I must confess I enjoyed that part of it. So far as I am able to recall, it was the only shave I have ever had where the operator did not spray me with cheap perfumery afterward and then try to sell me a bottle of hair tonic.

Having shaved me, the young man did me up amidships in a neat cloth parcel, took his kit under his arm and went away.

It occurred to me that, considering the trivial nature of the case, a good deal of fuss was being made over me by persons who could have no personal concern in the matter whatsoever. This thought recurred to me frequently as I lay there, all tied in a bundle like a week's washing. I did not feel quite so uppish as I had felt. Why was everybody picking on me?

Anon I slept, but dreamed fitfully. I dreamed that a whole flock of surgeons came to my bedside and charted me out in sections, like one of those diagram pictures you see of a beef in the Handy Compendium of Universal Knowledge showing the various cuts and the butcher's pet name for each cut. Each man took his favorite joint and carried it away and when they were all gone I was merely a recent site, full of reverberating echoes and nothing else.

I have had happier dreams in my time; this was not the kind of dream I should have selected had the choice been left to me.

When I woke the young sun was shining in at the window, and an orderly—not the orderly who had shaved me, but another one—was there in my room and my nurse was waiting outside the door. The orderly dressed me in a quaint suit of pyjamas cut on the half shell and buttoning stylishly in the back, *princess mode*. Then he rolled in a flat litter on wheels and stretched me on it, and covered me up with a white tablecloth, just as though I had been cold Sunday-night supper, and we started for the operating-room at the top of the building; but before we started I lit a large black cigar, as Gen. U. S. Grant used to do when he went into battle. I wished by this to show how indifferent I was. Maybe he fooled somebody, but I do not believe I possess the same powers of simulation that Grant had. He must have been a very remarkable man—Grant must.

The orderly and the nurse trundled me out into the hall and loaded me into an elevator which was to carry us up to the top of the hospital. Several other nurses were already in the elevator. As we came aboard one of them remarked that it was a fine day. A fine day for what? She did not finish the sentence.

Everybody wore a serious look. Inside of myself I felt pretty serious too—serious enough for ten or twelve. I had meant to fling off several very bright, spontaneous quips on the way to the table. I thought them out in advance, but now, somehow, none of them seemed appropriate. Instinctively, as it were, I felt that humor was out of place here.

I never knew an elevator to progress from the third floor of a building to the ninth with such celerity as this one on which we were traveling progressed. Personally I was in no mood for haste. If there was anyone else in all that great hospital who was in a particular hurry to be operated on I was perfectly willing to wait. But alas, no! The mechanism of the elevator was in perfect order—entirely too perfect. No accident of any character whatsoever befell us en route, no dropping back into the basement with a low, grateful thud; no hitch; no delay of any kind. We were certainly out of luck that trip. The demon of a joy-rider who operated the accursed device jerked a lever and up we soared at a distressingly high rate of speed. If I could have had my way about that youth he would have been arrested for speeding.

Now we were there! They rolled me into a large room, all white, with a rounded ceiling like the inside of an egg. Right away I knew what the feelings of a poor, lonely little yolk are when the spoon begins to chip the shell. If I had not been so busy feeling sorry for myself I think I might have developed quite an active sympathy for yolks.

My impression had been that this was to be in the nature of a private affair, without invitations. I was astonished to note that quite a crowd had assembled for the opening exercises. From his attire and general deportment I judged that Doctor Z was going to be the master of the revels, he being attired appropriately in a white domino, with rubber gloves and a fancy cap of crash toweling. There were present, also, my diagnostic friend, Doctor X, likewise in fancy-dress costume, and a surgeon I had never met. From what I could gather he was going over the course behind Doctor Z to replace the divots.

And there was an interne in the background, playing caddy, as it were, and a head nurse, who was going to keep the score, and two other nurses, who were going to help her keep it. I only hoped that they would show no partiality, but be as fair to me as they were to Doctor Z, and that he would go round in par.

So they placed me right where my eyes might rest on a large wall cabinet full of very shiny-looking tools; and they took my cigar away from me and folded my hands on the wide bowknot of my sash. Then they put a cloth dingus over my face and a voice of authority told me to breathe. That advice, however, was superfluous and might just as well have been omitted, for such was my purpose anyhow. Ever since I can recall anything at all, breathing has been a regular habit with me. So I breathed. And, at that, a bottle of highly charged sarsaparilla exploded somewhere in the immediate vicinity and most of its contents went up my nose.

I started to tell them that somebody had been fooling with their ether and adulterating it, and that if they thought they could send me off to sleep with soda pop they were making the mistake of their lives, because it just naturally could not be done; but for some reason or other I decided to put off speaking about the matter for a few minutes. I breathed again—again—agai——

I was going away from there. I was in a large gas balloon, soaring up into the clouds. How pleasant! . . . No, by Jove! I was not in a balloon —I myself was the balloon, which was not quite so pleasant. Besides Doctor Z was going along as a passenger; and as we traveled up and up he kept jabbing me in the midriff with the ferrule of a large umbrella which he had brought along with him in case of rain. He jabbed me harder and harder. I remonstrated with him. I told him I was a bit tender in that locality and the ferrule of his umbrella was sharp. He would not listen. He kept on jabbing me. . . .

Something broke! We started back down to earth. We fell faster and

faster. We fell nine miles, and after that I began to get used to it. Then I saw the earth beneath and it was rising up to meet us.

A town was below—a town that grew larger and larger as we neared it. I could make out the bonded indebtedness, and the Carnegie Library and the moving-picture palaces, and the new dancing parlor, and other principal points of interest.

At the rate we were falling we were certainly going to make an awful splatter in that town when we hit. I was sorry for the street-cleaning department.

We fell another half mile or so. A spire was sticking up into the sky directly beneath us, like a spear, to impale us. By a supreme effort I twisted out of the way of that spire, only to strike squarely on top of the roof of a greenhouse back of the parsonage, next door. We crashed through it with a perfectly terrific clatter of breaking glass and landed in a bed of white flowers, all soft and downy, like feathers.

And then Doctor Z stood up and combed the débris out of his whiskers and remarked that taking it by and large, it had been one of the pleasantest little outings he had enjoyed in the entire course of his practice. He said that as a patient I was fair, but as a balloon I was immense. He asked me whether I had seen anything of his umbrella and began looking round for it. I tried to help him look, but I was too tired to exert myself much. I told him I believed I would take a little nap.

I opened a dizzy eye part way. So this was heaven—this white expanse that swung and swam before my languid gaze? No, it could not be—it did not smell like heaven. It smelled like a hospital. It was a hospital. It was my hospital. My nurse was bending over me and I caught a faint whiff of the starch in the front of her crisp blue blouse. She was two-headed for the moment, but that was a mere detail. She settled a pillow under my head and told me to lie quiet.

I meant to lie quiet; I did not have to be told. I wanted to lie quiet and hurt. I was hurty from head to toe and back again, and crosswise and cater-cornered. I hurt diagonally and lengthwise and on the bias. I had a taste in my mouth like a bird-and-animal store. And empty! It seemed to me those doctors had not left anything inside of me except the acoustics. Well, there was a mite of consolation there. If the over-hauling had been as thorough as I had reason to believe it was from my present sensations, I need never fear catching anything again so long as I lived, except possibly dandruff.

I waved the nurse away. I craved solitude. I desired only to lie there in that bed and hurt—which I did.

I had said beforehand I meant to stay in St. Germicide's for two or three days only. It is when I look back on that resolution I emit the hollow laugh elsewhere referred to. For exactly four weeks I was flat on my back. I know now how excessively wearied a man can get of his own back, how tired of it, how bored with it! And after that another two weeks elapsed before my legs became the same dependable pair of legs I had known in the past.

I did not want to eat at first, and when I did begin to want to they would not let me. If I felt sort of peckish they let me suck a little glass thermometer, but there is not much nourishment really in thermometers. And for entertainment, to wile the dragging hours away, I could count the cracks in the ceiling and read my temperature chart, which was a good deal like Red Ames' batting average for the past season—ranging from ninety-nine to one hundred and four.

Also, through daily conversations with my nurse and with the surgeons who dropped in from time to time to have a look at me, I learned, as I lay there, a great deal about the medical profession—that is, a great deal for a layman—and what I learned filled me with an abiding admiration for it, both as a science and as a business. This surely is one profession which ever keeps its face to the front. Burying its past mistakes and forgetting them as speedily as possible, it pushes straight forward into fresh fields and fresh patients, always hopeful of what the future may bring in the way of newly discovered and highly expensive ailments. As we look backward upon the centuries we are astonished by its advancement. I did a good deal of looking backwards upon the centuries during my sojourn at St. Germicide's.

Take the Middle Ages now—the period when a barber and a surgeon were one and the same. If a man made a failure as a barber he turned his talents to surgery. Surgeons in those times were a husky breed. I judge they worked by the day instead of by piecework; anyhow the records show they were very fond of experiments, where somebody else furnished the raw material.

When there came a resounding knock at the tradesman's entrance of the moated grange, the lord of the manor, looking over the portcullis and seeing a lusty wight standing down below, in a leather apron, with his sleeves rolled up and a kit of soldering tools under his arm, didn't know until he made inquiry whether the gentle stranger had come to mend the drain or remove the cook's leg.

A little later along, when gunpowder had come into general use as a humanizing factor of civilization, surgeons treated a gunshot wound by pouring boiling lard into it, which I would say was calculated to take the victim's mind off his wound and give him something else to think about—for the time being, anyhow. I assume the notion of applying a mustard plaster outside one's stomach when one has a pain inside one's stomach is based on the same principle.

However, one doesn't have to go clear back to medieval times to note the radical differences in the plan of treating human ailments. A great many persons who are still living can remember when the doctors were not nearly so numerous as they are now. I, for one, would be the last to reverse the sentence and say that because the doctors were not nearly so numerous then as they are now, those persons are still living so numerously.

In the spring of the year, when the sap flowed and the birds mated, the sturdy farmer felt that he was due to have something the matter with him, too. So he would ride into the county-seat and get an almanac. Doubtless the reader, if country raised, has seen copies of this popular work. On the outside cover, which was dark blue in color, there was a picture of a person whose stomach was sliced four ways, like a twenty-cent pie, and then folded back neatly, thus exposing his entire interior arrangements to the gaze of the casual observer. However, this party, judging by his picture, did not appear to be suffering. He did not even seem to fear that he might catch cold from standing there in his own draught. He was gazing off into space in an absent-minded kind of way, apparently not aware that anything was wrong with him; and on all sides he was surrounded by interesting exhibits, such as a crab, and a scorpion, and a goat, and a chap with a bow and arrow—and one thing and another.

Such was the main design of the cover, while the contents were made up of recognized and standard varieties in the line of jokes and the line of diseases which alternated, with first a favorite joke and then a favorite disease. The author who wrote the descriptions of the diseases was one of the most convincing writers that ever lived anywhere. As a realist he had no superiors among those using our language as a vehicle for the expression of thought. He was a wonder. If a person wasn't particular about what ailed him he could read any page at random and have one specific disease. Or he could read the whole book through and have them all, in their most advanced stages. Then the only thing that could save him was a large dollar bottle.

Again, in attacks of the breakbone ague or malaria it was customary to call in a local practitioner, generally an elderly lady of the neighborhood, who had none of these latter-day prejudices regarding the use of

tobacco by the gentler sex. One whom I distantly recall, among childhood's happy memories, carried this liberal-mindedness to a point where
she not only dipped snuff and smoked a cob pipe, but sometimes chewed
a little natural leaf. This lady, on being called in, would brew up a large
caldron of medicinal roots and barks and sprouts and things; and then
she would deluge the interior of the sufferer with a large gourdful of
this pleasing mixture at regular intervals. It was efficacious, too. The
inundated person either got well or else he drowned from the inside.
Rocking the patient was almost as dangerous a pastime as rocking the
boat. This also helps to explain, I think, why so many of our forebears
had floating kidneys. There was nothing else for a kidney to do.

By the time I attained to long trousers, people in our town mainly
had outgrown the unlicensed expert and were depending more and more
upon the old-fashioned family doctor—the one with the whisker-jungle
—who drove about in a gig, accompanied by a haunting aroma of iodoform and carrying his calomel with him in bulk.

He probably owned a secret calomel mine of his own. He must have;
otherwise he could never have afforded to be so generous with it. He
also had other medicines with him, all of them being selected on the
principle that unless a drug tasted like the very dickens it couldn't possibly do you any good. At all hours of the day and night he was to be
seen going to and fro, distributing nuggets from his private lode. He
went to bed with his trousers and his hat on, I think, and there was a
general belief that his old mare slept between the shafts of the gig, with
the bridle shoved up on her forehead.

It has been only a few years since the old-time general practitioner
was everywhere. Just look round and see now how the system has
changed! If your liver begins to misconduct itself the first thought of
the modern operator is to cut it out and hide it someplace where you
can't find it. The old-timer would have bombarded it with a large
brunette pill about the size and color of a damson plum. Or he might
put you on a diet of molasses seasoned to taste with blue mass and
quinine and other attractive condiments. Likewise, in the spring of the
year he frequently anointed the young of the species with a mixture
of mutton suet and asafetida. This treatment had an effect that was
distinctly depressing upon the growing boy. It militated against his
popularity. It forced him to seek his pleasures outdoors, and a good
distance outdoors at that.

It was very hard for a boy, however naturally attractive he might be,
to retain his popularity at the fireside circle when coated with mutton
suet and asafetida and then taken into a warm room. He attracted attention which he did not court and which was distasteful to him. Keeping

quiet did not seem to help him any. Even if they had been blindfolded, others would still have felt his presence. A civet-cat suffers from the same drawbacks in a social way, but the advantage to the civet-cat is that as a general thing it associates only with other civet-cats.

Except in the country the old-time, catch-as-catch-can general practitioner appears to be dying out. In the city one finds him occasionally playing a limit game in an office on a back street—two dollars to come in, five to call; but the tendency of the day is toward specialists. Hence the expert who treats you for just one particular thing. With a pain in your chest, say, you go to a chest specialist. So long as he can keep the trouble confined to your chest, all well and good. If it slips down or slides up he tries to coax it back to the reservation. If it refuses to do so, he bids it an affectionate adieu, makes a dotted mark on you to show where he left off, collects his bill and regretfully turns you over to a stomach specialist or a throat specialist, depending on the direction in which the trouble was headed when last seen.

Or, perhaps the specialist to whom you take your custom is an advocate of an immediate operation for such cases as yours and all others. I may be unduly sensitive on account of having recently emerged from the surgeon's hands, but it strikes me now that there are an awful lot of doctors who take one brief glance at a person who is complaining, and say to themselves that here is something that ought to be looked into right away—and immediately open a bag and start picking out the proper utensils. You go into a doctor's office and tell him you do not feel the best in the world—and he gives you a look and excuses himself, and steps into the next room and begins greasing a saw.

Mind you, in these casual observations as compiled by me while bedfast and here given utterance, I am not seeking to disparage possibly the noblest of professions. Lately I have owed much to it. I am strictly on the doctor's side. He is with us when we come into the world and with us when we go out of it, oftentimes lending a helping hand on both occasions. Anyway, our sympathies should especially go out to the medical profession at this particular time when the anti-vivisectionists are railing so loudly against the doctors. The anti-vivisection crusade has enlisted widely different classes in the community, including many lovers of our dumb-animal pets—and aren't some of them the dumbest things you ever saw!—especially chow dogs and love birds.

I will admit there is something to be said on both sides of the argument. This dissecting of live subjects may have been carried to extremes on occasions. When I read in the medical journals that the eminent Doctor Somebody succeeded in transferring the interior department of a pelican to a pointer pup, and vice versa, with such success that the pup drowned while diving for minnows, and the pelican went out in the back yard and barked himself to death baying at the moon, I am interested naturally; but, possibly because of my ignorance, I fail to see wherein the treatment of infantile paralysis has been materially advanced. On the other hand, I would rather the kind and gentle Belgian hare should be offered up as a sacrifice upon the operating table and leave behind him a large family of little Belgian heirs and heiresses—dependent upon the charity of a cruel world—than that I should have something painful which can be avoided through making him a martyr. I would rather any white rabbit on earth should have the Asiatic cholera twice than that I should have it just once. These are my sincere convictions, and I will not attempt to disguise them.

Thanks, too, to medical science we know about germs and serums and diets and all that. Our less fortunate ancestors didn't know about them. They were befogged in ignorance. As recently as the generation immediately preceding ours people were unacquainted with the simplest rules of hygiene. They didn't care whether the housefly wiped his feet before he came into the house or not. The gentleman with the drooping cream-separator mustache was at perfect liberty to use the common drinking cup on the railroad train. The appendix lurked in its snug retreat, undisturbed by the prying fingers of curiosity. The fever-bearing skeeter buzzed and flitted, stinging where he pleased. The germ theory was unfathomed. Suitable food for an invalid was anything the invalid could afford to buy. Fresh air, and more especially fresh night air, was regarded as dangerous, and people hermetically sealed themselves in before retiring. Not daily as at present was the world gladdened by the tidings that science had unearthed some new and particularly unpleasant disease. It never occurred to a mother that she should sterilize the slipper before spanking her offspring. Babies were not reared antiseptically, but just so. Nobody was aware of microbes.

In short, our sires and our grandsires abode in the midst of perils. They were surrounded on all sides by things that are immediately fatal to the human system. Not a single one of them had a right to pass his second birthday. In the light of what we know, we realize that by now this world should be but a barren waste, dotted at frequent intervals with large graveyards and populated only by a few dispossessed and hungry bacteria, hanging over the cemetery fence singing: Driven From Home!

In the conditions generally prevalent up to twenty-five years ago, most of us never had any license, really, to be born at all. Yet look how many of us are now here. In this age of research I hesitate to attempt to account for it, except on the entirely unscientific theory that what you don't know doesn't hurt you. Doubtless a physician could give you a better explanation, but his would cost you more than mine has.

But we digress. Let us get back to our main subject, which is myself. I shall never forget my first real meal in that hospital. There was quite a good deal of talk about it beforehand. My nurse kept telling me that on the next day the doctor had promised I might have something to eat. I could hardly wait. I had visions of a tenderloin steak smothered in fried onions, and some French-fried potatoes, and a tall table-limit stack of wheat cakes, and a few other incidental comfits and kickshaws. I could hardly wait for that meal.

The next day came and she brought it to me, and I partook thereof. It was the white of an egg. For dessert I licked a stamp; but this I did clandestinely and by stealth, without saying anything about it to her. I was not supposed to have any sweets.

On the occasion of the next feast the diet was varied. I had a sip of one of those fermented milk products. You probably know the sort of thing I mean. Even before you've swallowed it, it tastes as though it had already disagreed with you. The nurse said this food was predigested but did not tell me by whom. Nor did I ask her. I started to, but thought better of it. Sometimes one is all the happier for not knowing too much.

A little later on, seeing that I had not suffered an attack of indigestion from this debauch, they gave me junket. In the dictionary I have looked up the definitions of junket. I quote:

JUNKET, v. I. t. To entertain by feasting; regale. II. i. To give or take part in an entertainment or excursion; feast in company; picnic, revel. JUNKET, n. A merry feast or excursion; picnic.

When the author of a dictionary tries to be frivolous he only succeeds in making himself appear foolish.

I know not how it may be in the world at large, but in a hospital, junket is a custard that by some subtle process has been denuded of those ingredients which make a custard fascinating and exciting. It tastes as though the eggs, which form its underlying basis, had been laid in a fit of pique by a hen that was severely upset at the time.

Hereafter when the junket is passed round somebody else may have my share. I'll stick to the mince pie à la mode.

And the first cigar of my convalescence—ah, that, too, abides as a vivid memory! Dropping in one morning to replace the wrappings Doctor Z said I might smoke in moderation. So the nurse brought me a cigar, and I lit it and took one deep puff; but only one. I laid it aside. I said to the nurse:

"A mistake has been made here. I do not want a cooking cigar, you understand. I desire a cigar for personal use. This one is full of herbs and simples, I think. It suggests a New England boiled dinner, and not a very good New England boiled dinner at that. Let us try again."

She brought another cigar. It was not satisfactory either. Then she showed me the box—an orthodox box containing cigars of a recognized and previously dependable brand. I could only conclude that a root-and-herb doctor had bought an interest in the business and was introducing his own pet notions into the formula.

But came a day—as the fancy writers say when they wish to convey the impression that day has come, but hate to do it in a commonplace manner—came a day when my cigar tasted as a cigar should taste and food had the proper relish to it; and my appetite came back again and found the old home place not so greatly changed after all.

And then shortly thereafter came another day, when I, all replete with expensive stitches, might drape the customary habiliments of civilization about my attenuated frame and go forth to mingle with my fellow beings. I have been mingling pretty steadily ever since, for now I have something to talk about—a topic good for any company; congenial, an absorbing topic.

I can spot a brother member a block away. I hasten up to him and give him the grand hailing sign of the order. He opens his mouth to speak, but I beat him to it.

"Speaking of operations——" I say. And then I'm off.

Believe me, it's the life!

Waifs and Strays

Scraps of sourceless verse continually crop up in conversation, slip into newspaper columns, and even find themselves between the more or less imperishable covers of a book. Their origins have been lost; they all seem to be the work of that industrious and often-quoted author "Anonymous." Obviously, they were once written by someone, someone with a name. But the name has disappeared, and these miniature comedies, bits of parodies, and burlesque aphorisms are all that remain of some writer's affair with the fickle and forgetful Muse. They are the waifs and strays of poetry. Here are a few of them.

> King David and King Solomon
>   Lived merry, merry lives
> With many, many lady friends
>   And many, many wives;
> But when old age crept onward,
>   With all its many qualms,
> King Solomon wrote the Proverbs
>   And King David wrote the Psalms.

> I often pause and wonder
>   At fate's peculiar ways,
> For nearly all our famous men
>   Were born on holidays.

> A centipede was happy quite,
>   Until a frog, in fun,
> Said, "Pray, which leg comes after which?"
> This raised her mind to such a pitch
> She lay distracted in a ditch,
>   Considering how to run.

> Tobacco is a filthy weed—
>   I like it.
> It satisfies no normal need—
>   I like it.

It makes you thin, it makes you lean,
It takes the hair right off your bean;
It's the worst darned stuff I've ever seen.
　　I like it.

'Twixt optimist and pessimist,
　The difference is droll:
The optimist sees the doughnut,
　The pessimist sees the hole.

If you your lips would save from slips,
　Five things observe with care:
Of whom you speak, to whom you speak,
　And how, and when, and where.

Little Miss Muffet decided to rough it
　In a cabin quite old and medieval.
A rounder espied her and plied her with cider
　And now she's the forest's prime evil.

The saddest words of tongue or pen
Perhaps may be "It might have been."
The sweetest words we know, by heck,
Are simply these: "Enclosed find check."

A doctor fell in a deep well,
　And broke his collarbone.
The Moral: Doctor, mind the sick
　And leave the well alone!

She wore her stockings inside out
   All through the summer heat.
She said it cooled her off to turn
   The hose upon her feet.

Girls, to this advice give heed—
In your affairs with men
If at first you don't succeed,
Cry, cry again.

Knows he that never took a pinch,
   Nosey! the pleasure thence which flows?
Knows he the titillating joy
   Which my nose knows?

Oh, nose! I am as fond of thee
   As any mountain of its snows!
I gaze on thee, and feel that pride
   A Roman knows!

Whene'er a hen lays eggs, with each
She is impelled to make a speech.
The selfsame urge stirs human bones
Whenever men lay cornerstones.

I never see my rector's eyes;
   He hides their light divine—
For when he prays he shuts his own;
   And, when he preaches, mine.

Women's faults are many,
   Men have only two:
Everything they say,
   And everything they do.

Frank Moore Colby

In his early thirties when he published Outlines of General History, it was assumed that Frank Moore Colby, born in Washington in 1865, would become a heavily serious historian and a plodding political scientist. When he became an editor and encyclopedist it seemed that his career as a creator was over.

Then the essays began appearing, quiet, unobtrusive essays, but so spiked with wit that readers fortunate enough to find them could not forget them. At that time the critic Hamilton Wright Mabie was the fashionable idol of women's clubs, but he ceased to be literary arbiter the day that Colby wrote, "Hamilton Wright Mabie conducted women into the suburbs of literature and left them there." Colby delighted to twist the neck of many a respectable platitude. He observed that "from the advertisements one would never guess that encyclopedias are made by human beings"; he thought "self-esteem is the most voluble of the emotions"; he spoke of Horace Walpole "with his even flow of animal spites."

In 1926, a year after Colby's death, his unique sense of humor was comprehensively revealed in The Colby Essays, edited in two volumes by Clarence Day (see page 202). Anthologists were slow to discover the books, but Colby's pages are now being carefully, if belatedly, rifled; several of the best have been preserved in Clifton Fadiman's richly personal Reading I've Liked and in E. B. White and Katharine White's excellent A Subtreasury of American Humor. Of "Confessions of a Gallomaniac" Philip Littell wrote, "As a whole it is to Mark Twain on the German Language what comedy is to farce."

Confessions of a Gallomaniac

Down to the outbreak of the war I had no more desire to converse with a Frenchman in his own language than with a modern Greek. I thought I understood French well enough for my own purposes, because I had read it off and on for twenty years, but when the war aroused sympathies and sharpened curiosities that I had not felt before, I realized the width of the chasm that cut me off from what I wished to feel. Nor could it be bridged by any of the academic, natural, or commercial methods that I knew of. They were either too slow or they led in directions that I did not wish to go. I tried a phonograph, and after many bouts with it I acquired part of a sermon by Bossuet and real fluency in discussing a quinsy sore throat with a Paris physician, in case I ever went there and had one. I then took fourteen conversation lessons from a Mme. Carnet, and being rather well on in years at the start, I should, if I had kept on diligently, have been able at the age of eighty-five to inquire faultlessly my way to the post office. I could already ask for butter and sing a song written by Henry IV—when my teacher went to France to take care of her half-brother's children. I will say this for Mme. Carnet. I came to understand perfectly the French for all her personal and family affairs. No human being has ever confided in me so abundantly as she did. No human being has ever so sternly repressed any answering confidences of my own. Her method of instruction, if it was one, was that of jealous, relentless, unbridled soliloquy.

Thrown on the world with no power of sustaining a conversation on any other subject than the members of the Carnet family, I nevertheless resolved to take no more lessons but to hunt down French people and make them talk. What I really needed was a governess to take me to and from my office and into the park at noon, but at my age that was out of the question. Then began a career of hypocritical benevolence. I scraped acquaintance with every Frenchman whom I heard talking English very badly, and I became immensely interested in his welfare. I formed the habit of introducing visiting Frenchmen to French-speaking Americans, and sitting, with open mouth, in the flow of their conversation. Then I fell in with M. Bernou, the commissioner who was over here buying guns, and whose English and my French were so much alike that we agreed to interchange them. We met daily for two weeks and walked for an hour in the park, each tearing at the other's language. Our conversations, as I look back on them, must have run about like this:

"It calls to walk," said he, smiling brilliantly.

133

"It is good morning," said I, "better than I had extended."

"I was at you yestairday ze morning, but I deed not find."

"I was obliged to leap early," said I, "and I was busy standing up straight all around the forenoon."

"The book I prayed you send, he came, and I thank, but positively are you not deranged?"

"Don't talk," said I. "Never talk again. It was really nothing anywhere. I had been very happy, I reassure."

"Pardon, I glide, I glode. There was the hide of a banane. Did I crash you?"

"I noticed no insults," I replied. "You merely gnawed my arm."

Gestures and smiles of perfect understanding.

I do not know whether Bernou, who like myself was middle-aged, felt as I did on these occasions, but by the suppression of every thought that I could not express in my childish vocabulary, I came to feel exactly like a child. They said I ought to think in French and I tried to do so, but thinking in French when there is so little French to think with, divests the mind of its acquisitions of forty years. Experience slips away for there are not words enough to lay hold of it. Knowledge of good and evil does not exist; the sins have no names; and the mind under its linguistic limitations is like a rather defective toy Noah's ark. From the point of view of Bernou's and my vocabulary, Central Park was as the Garden of Eden after six months—new and unnamed things everywhere. A dog, a tree, a statue taxed all our powers of description, and on a complex matter like a policeman our minds could not meet at all. We could only totter together a few steps in any mental direction. Yet there was a real pleasure in this earnest interchange of insipidities and they were highly valued on each side. For my part I shall always like Bernou, and feel toward him as my childhood's friend. I wonder if he noticed that I was an old, battered man, bothered with a tiresome profession. I certainly never suspected that he was. His language utterly failed to give me that impression.

After I lost Bernou I fastened upon an unfrocked priest who had come over here and gone into the shoe trade—a small, foxy man, who regarded me, I think, in the light of an aggressor. He wanted to become completely American and forget France, and as I was trying to reverse the process, I rather got in his way. He could talk of mediæval liturgies and his present occupation, but nothing in between, and as he spoke English very well, his practical mind revolted at the use of a medium of communication in which one of us almost strangled when there was another available in which we were both at ease. I could not pump much French out of him. He would burst into English rather resentfully. Then I took to the streets at lunch-time and tried newsdealers, book-shops, restaurants, invented imaginary errands, bought things that I did not want, and exchanged them for objects even less desirable. That kept a little conversation going day by day, but on the whole it was a dry season. It is a strange thing. There are more than thirty thousand of them in the city of New York, and I had always heard that the French are a clannish folk and hate to learn another language, but most of my overtures in French brought only English upon me. The more pains I took the more desirable it seemed to them that I should be spared the trouble of continuing. I was always diving into French and they were always pulling me out again. They thought they were humane.

French people hate broken French worse than most of us hate broken English. But when dragged out into the light of English I tried to talk just as foolishly in order that they might think it was not really my French that was the matter with me. Sometimes that worked quite well. Finding me just as idiotic in my own language they went back to theirs. It certainly worked well with my friend M. Bartet, a paralytic tobacconist in the West Thirties near the river, to whom my relation was for several months that of a grandchild, though, I believe, we were of the same age. He tried to form my character by bringing me up on such praiseworthy episodes of his early life as he thought I was able to grasp.

Now at the end of a long year of these persistent puerilities I am able to report two definite results: In the first place a sense of my incapacity and ignorance infinitely vaster than when I began, and in the second a profound distrust, possibly vindictive in its origin, of all Americans in the city of New York who profess an acquaintance with French culture, including teachers, critics, theater audiences, lecture audiences, and patronesses of visiting Frenchmen.

It was perhaps true, as people said at the time, that a certain French theatrical experiment in New York could not continue for the simple reason that it was too good a thing for the theater-going public to support. It may be that the precise equivalent of the enterprise, even if not hampered by a foreign language, could not have permanently endured. Yet from what I saw of its audiences, critics, enthusiasts, and from what I know of the American Gallophile generally, including myself, I believe the linguistic obstacle to have been more serious than they would have us suppose—serious enough to account for the situation without dragging in our æsthetic incapacity. It was certainly an obstacle that less than one-half of any audience ever succeeded in surmounting.

I do not mean that the rest of the audience got nothing out of it, for so expressive were the players by other means than words, that they often sketched the play out in pantomime. The physical activities of the troupe did not arise, as some of the critics declared, from the vivacity of the Gallic temperament; nor were they assumed, as others believed, because in the seventeenth century French actors had been acrobats. These somewhat exaggerated gestures were occasioned by the perception that the majority of the spectators were beginners in French. They were supplied by these ever-tactful people as a running translation for a large body of self-improving Americans.

I do not blame other Americans for dabbling in French, since I myself am the worst of dabblers, but I see no reason why any of us should pretend that it is anything more than dabbling. The usual way of reading French does not lead even to an acquaintance with French literature. Everybody knows that words in a living language in order to be understood have to be lived with. They are not felt as a part of living literature when you see them pressed out and labeled in a glossary, but only when you hear them fly about. A word is not a definite thing susceptible of dictionary explanation. It is a cluster of associations, reminiscent of the sort of men that used it, suggestive of social class, occupation, mood, dignity or the lack of it, primness, violences, pedantries, or platitudes. It hardly seems necessary to say that words in a living literature ought to ring in the ear with the sounds that really belong to them, or that poetry without an echo cannot be felt.

It may be that there is no way out of it. Perhaps it is inevitable that the colleges which had so long taught the dead languages as if they were buried should now teach the living ones as if they were dead. But there is no need of pretending that this formal acquaintance with books results in an appreciation of literature. No sense of the intimate quality of a writer can be founded on a verbal vacuum. His plots, his place in literature, his central motives, and the opinion of his critics could all be just as adequately conveyed, if his books were studied in the language of the deaf and dumb. Of course, one may be drawn to an author by that process but it would hardly be the artistic attraction of literature; it is as if one felt drawn to a woman by an interest exclusively in her bones.

Elementary as these remarks may seem I offer them to Gallophiles without apology. On the contrary I rather fear that I am writing over their heads.

From the Cynic's Dictionary

Psychologists say we protect ourselves by pretending to take lightly those things which affect us most seriously. It may be, as Socrates said, that "the genius of Comedy and Tragedy are essentially the same." It may be that we make fun of the things we cherish because we are afraid to feel them too deeply.

In any case there is something of the cynic in all of us. We delight to make or laugh at jokes about man's oldest institutions and deepest emotions, especially love and marriage. "Love," says the skeptical Henry L. Mencken, "is the delusion that one woman differs from another"—and every one, at least every married man, smiles broadly. "A bachelor," says a much-married man—and every one waits for the cynical remark which is to complete the humorous definition.

Here, then, are a few definitions from the cynic's dictionary.

A Bachelor (to complete the definition begun above) has been variously defined as "a man who never makes the same mistake once," "a man who knows when to stop," or "a man who thinks before he acts—and then doesn't act," or "a man who knows more about women than married men do—which is one reason why he's a bachelor," or "a cowardly, cruel, and wholly selfish man who is cheating some nice woman out of a profitable divorce," or "a man who has no children to speak of," or "a man who believes that other men marry in haste and repent at leisure," or "a man who has been lucky in love." Obviously these definitions have been made by envious husbands.

A Husband on the other hand is (by the same token) merely "a bachelor who has weakened," or "a man who never knows when he is well off—because he never is," or "a man who has been married for batter—or worse," or "a man who is not merely against marriage, but up against it."

Marriage, that institution for those who are not yet ready to be sent to an institution, has been defined as "a word which is not a word but a sentence," or "a word which was originally spelled 'm-i-r-a-g-e,'" or "the

137

only life sentence which is suspended because of bad behavior," or "an arrangement which takes two people to complete: a girl and her mother," or "a business in which the husband is the silent partner," or "the association of two persons for the benefit of one," or "a lottery in which the wife sometimes loses—she does not always become a widow," or "a condition to which most women aspire and to which most men submit."

As for the Wife (usually referred to as "the bitter half") she is the one who "generally speaking, is generally speaking"; who remembers her birthday but forgets which one it is; who no longer demands that her husband satisfy her slightest wish as long as he takes care of the larger ones; who first picks her husband's clothes and then his pockets; who would be less dangerous if a man could fall into her arms without falling into her hands; who is attractive at twenty, attentive at thirty, and adhesive at forty.

Love, that perpetual emotion, sometimes classified as the greatest indoor sport, is treated even more caustically by the cynics. It is "the feeling that makes a woman make a man make a fool of himself"; it is a heart attack or, to point it with a pun, "a softening of the hearteries"; a farcical tragedy, "a comedy of Eros"; the most universal thing in the world because it is all-embracing; the form of insanity which prompts a woman to marry her employer so she can work for him for nothing.

Life, according to the cynics, is a protracted disease contracted at birth; an everlasting struggle to keep money coming in and teeth and hair from falling out; a continually failing attempt to foresee the unforeseen. Differing from Love, Life is just one fool thing after another, while Love is just two fool things after each other.

Ambrose Bierce, the most severe and spectacular cynic of his day (1842–1913), wrote a book of witticisms which is still extensively quoted. It was called *The Devil's Dictionary* and it was so widely imitated that many of the epigrams became current in popular speech. Here are a few of Bierce's bitter mockeries:

ABORIGINES. Persons of little worth found cumbering the soil of a newly discovered country. They soon cease to cumber; they fertilize.

ABSURDITY. A belief manifestly inconsistent with one's own opinion.

ADMIRATION. Our polite recognition of another's resemblance to ourselves.

ALLIANCE. In politics, the union of two thieves who have their hands so deeply inserted in each other's pocket that they cannot separately plunder a third.

BELLADONNA. In Italian a beautiful lady; in English a deadly poison. A striking example of the essential identity of the two languages.

COMFORT. A state of mind produced by contemplation of a neighbor's uneasiness.

DIPLOMACY. The patriotic art of lying for one's country.

EGOTIST. A person of low taste, more interested in himself than in me.

OCCIDENT. The part of the world lying west (or east) of the Orient. It is largely inhabited by Christians, a powerful subtribe of the Hypocrites, whose principal industries are murder and cheating, which they are pleased to call "war" and "commerce." These, also, are the principal industries of the Orient.

PEACE. In international affairs, a period of cheating between two wars.

POSITIVE. Mistaken at the top of one's voice.

SUCCESS. The one unpardonable sin against one's fellows.

Say "Adult" to the cynic, and he will say: "A person who has stopped growing—except in the middle." Say "Criminal" and he will define him as "The fellow who got caught." To the cynic a "Jury" is "a group of twelve men selected to decide who has the better lawyer"; and "Executive Conference" is a meeting to talk about what shouldn't be done, "where minutes are kept and hours are wasted"; a "Pessimist" is "an optimist who tried to practice what he preached"; a "Self-made man" is "a horrible example of unskilled labor," and the "Average man" is "one who is sure he isn't."

Bierce defended the cynic by declaring that he is a "blackguard whose faulty vision sees things as they are, not as they ought to be." Nevertheless, the cynic doesn't escape his own cynicism. After all, he is a man who as Oscar Wilde said, knows the price of everything and the value of nothing. Suffering from what might be called skeptic poisoning, the cynic has no faith in anything and tries to make others share his belief. Let us forget him.

John Collier

Three contemporary John Colliers succeeded each other in the public prints. There was the late John Collier, English portrait painter and author of A Primer of Art. There was the American John Collier, champion of and spokesman for the Indians of the Southwest. And (no relation to either) there is the John Collier who was born in London a little more than forty years ago, and who came to the United States in 1941.

The character of Collier's work is faintly indicated by the titles of his books: His Monkey Wife, Presenting Moonshine, Defy the Foul Fiend, and The Touch of Nutmeg. This author blends humor and horror with so ingenious a style that he has been compared to an insouciant Poe and an overripe O. Henry. "Bizarre," "aromatic," "fiendish," "orchidaceous," "acetic" (not "ascetic"!), "dandiacal" and "demonic" are a few of the adjectives used most frequently to describe Collier's tales. Clifton Fadiman writes that Collier's mind is subtle, "working only with the unexpected, the wild, and the lightly diabolic." Perhaps it is most remarkable when it is blandly deceptive, when, as in "Another American Tragedy," the diabolic turns into the hilarious and concocts a tale that is frightful and, at the same time, frightfully funny.

Another American Tragedy

A young man entered the office of a prominent dentist, and seated himself in the chair. He scornfully waved aside the little probe and mirror with which the dentist smilingly approached him. "Rip 'em all out," he said.

"But," said the dentist, "your teeth seem perfectly good."

"So," said the young man, "is my money."

The dentist hesitated a little. "It would hardly be ethical," said he, "to take out teeth which are sound—unless there is a very good reason for it."

The young man, who had begun to smile at the word "ethical," here extended his smile into a cavernous gape, which laid bare the hindermost of his ivories. At the same time he twitched out a small roll of bills from his vest pocket, and held them noticeably in his hand.

The dentist utterly ignored these bills. "If you want those excellent teeth out," said he, "you must certainly be mad. Now I have a little theory: *mental* derangement is caused by *dental* derangement. It is a sign of something wrong way up behind the roots of the teeth, especially those of the upper row. Viewed from that angle——"

"Cut it, and pull them out," said the young man, impatient of these professional niceties.

The dentist shrugged and obeyed. As if in fear that the young man might become altogether too sane at the end of the operation, he humorously tweaked away the roll of bills with a thirty-third frisk of his forceps.

The young man made no comment, but only called for a mirror, in which he surveyed his numb and fallen chops with every appearance of satisfaction. He asked when his temporary denture would be ready, made the appointment, and went his way.

"Dear me!" thought the dentist. "Perhaps the trouble was not in his teeth after all. Certainly he is still as crazy as a coot."

Here the dentist made a big mistake. The young man was perfectly sane, and knew very well what he was about. It happened that he had spent all his money, in some years of the vilest dissipation, but he had a very far-reaching and water-tight plan for getting some more.

He accordingly returned to the dentist on the appointed day, and was equipped with his temporary grinders, which he sucked at and gnashed in the most ordinary fashion. He paid for them with almost his last dollar, went out, and got into his racy-looking roadster, and drove out of town as if pursued by the finance company, as he certainly would have been had they caught sight of him.

He drove till nightfall, and resumed his journey next day. Late in the afternoon he arrived in that part of the country where old and miserly uncles live in remote, dilapidated farm houses. Our young man was more or less fortunate in possessing one of the oldest and richest of these uncles, whose house was the remotest and most dilapidated of all.

Arriving at this secluded dwelling, our hero drew up before a porch upon which no money had been squandered for years. "So much the more in the old sock," reflected the nephew, as he knocked upon the door.

He was a little disconcerted to hear the tap of high heels within, instead of the shuffle of a deaf and surly retainer, and his jaw dropped when the door was opened by a plump and squarish blonde, a baby of some thirty years and about a hundred and fifty pounds. Her mouth was as wide and as red as a slice of watermelon, she had well-darkened lashes and brows, and an abundance of phony gold hair flowing girlishly down over her shoulders. Our friend was to some extent reassured when he realized that she was dressed in what might be called a nurse's uniform, but the fact that her garters were bright scarlet, and adorned with enormous bows, caused him to wonder if his dear uncle was getting the very best of professional care.

Nevertheless it is important to get on the right side of the nurse, especially when she stands solidly in the doorway. Our hero removed his hat, and put on so soapy a smile that his false teeth nearly dropped out of his head. "I have driven all the way from the big city," said he, "to see my poor, dear, bed-ridden old uncle—God bless him! I did not expect to see so charming a nurse."

The nurse, not budging an inch, responded with a surly and suspicious stare.

"I fear he must be sinking," continued the nephew. "In fact, I had an intuition, a sort of telepathic S.O.S., telling me to hasten out here before it was too late. Let me rush to his bedside."

The nurse still hesitated, but at that moment a peculiar sound, resembling the croaking of giant bull frogs, arose in the dim depths of the house. This was the good old uncle himself, vociferating toothlessly for an immediate sight of his nephew, whose expressions of affection and concern had been audible in every corner of the dwelling. The old boy knew very well that his relative was after money, and he was eager for the pleasure of turning him down.

The nurse somewhat grudgingly stepped aside. Our hero, with a well-rehearsed whinny of delight, scuttled into the bedroom.

Nothing is more affecting than the greetings of near relatives after a long separation, especially when they are as fond of each other as these two. "My dear Uncle!" cried the nephew. "What a pleasure it is to see you again! But why does your hand tremble so? Why are your eyes so sunken? Why are you so thin and pale?"

"If it comes to that," said his uncle, "you are not too stout and rosy yourself. Yes, you are very worn and emaciated, my boy. Your hair is thin and grey; you have lines, bags, and creases all over your face. If it were not for your handsome white teeth, I believe you would look every bit as old as I do."

"That," said the nephew, "is the effect of ceaseless toil and moil. It is a hard struggle, Uncle, to make good in these days, especially without any capital."

"So you are making good?" said the old man. "Do you not drink any more?"

"No, Uncle, I never drink now," replied the nephew.

"Well, that's tough," said his uncle, producing a giant flask from under his pillow. "In that case I can't ask you to join me." With that, he took a mighty swig, and, wiping his lips, he continued, "I have, thank heaven, a good doctor. A typical tough, bluff, hard-hitting, straight-shooting country doc of the old school. We call him the horse 'n' buggy doc. He recommends me this as medicine."

"Perhaps that is why your hand trembles so," said his nephew.

"Your own is none too steady," rejoined his uncle. "Evidently you work too hard. Tell me, Nephew, do you ever take a little flutter with the cards?"

"Good heavens, no!" cried the nephew. "I cured myself of that folly long ago."

"I am sorry to hear it," replied his uncle. "We might have played a little cut-throat. The old horse 'n' buggy doc says the excitement keeps me lively. We often play together till after midnight."

"That is why your eyes are sunken so deep," said the nephew.

"I think yours are equally hollow," replied the old man. "You should take a little rest now and then. I suppose, my dear Nephew, you still have an occasional frolic with the girls."

"Girls!" cried the nephew, lifting up his hands. "What an odious suggestion! It is years since I have even looked at a girl."

"Well, that's too bad," said his uncle. "The old horse 'n' buggy doc has up-to-date views. It was he who sent me Birdie." And, turning to the nurse, who happened to be arranging his pillows, he gave her a certain sort of caress such as is far better imagined than described.

"No wonder!" cried his nephew, when the nurse had gone bridling and smirking from the room. "No wonder, my poor Uncle, that you are so extremely thin and pale!"

"You are equally so," replied his uncle, "and you are only half my age."

"Well," said the nephew, trying a new tack, "perhaps your doctor is right. Perhaps I had better take your treatment."

"I heartily advise it," said the old man.

"The only thing," said the nephew, "is that I can hardly work at the same time. I suppose you would not care to give me a little money, so that I can enjoy the benefits of the system."

"Well, no," said his uncle. "I would not. Definitely not."

"I thought as much," said his nephew. "I fear I shall have to keep on toiling. How upset your good old horse 'n' buggy doc would be! Tell me one thing, however; indulge my curiosity in one trifling respect. Is there any hope I shall come into your money? Have you arranged it in your will?"

"Oh, come!" said his uncle. "Why bother your head with matters of that sort?"

"Do tell me," pressed the nephew. "You have no idea how interested I am."

"Well, if you really want to know," said his uncle, "I have left it all to the old horse 'n' buggy doc, a true downright, straight-living, hard-faced, crusty, soft-hearted country saw-bones of the old school, and you cannot imagine how agreeable his treatment is to me."

"Is that really so?" said the nephew. "I must say I expected something of the sort. Fortunately I have made my plans against just such a contingency. Allow me, my dear Uncle."

With that he twitched a pillow from under the old man's head, and pressed it over his face. The old uncle gave a petulant kick or two, but what with one thing and another there was very little life left in him, and soon that little was gone.

The nephew, with a wary glance at the door, quickly divested himself of his clothing, which he stowed under the bed. Next, possibly feeling a little chilly, he took the liberty of borrowing his uncle's night-shirt. Then stowing his uncle's shrunken body under the bed also, he climbed into his place between the sheets. Finally he expectorated his false teeth into a clean pocket handkerchief, which he had brought

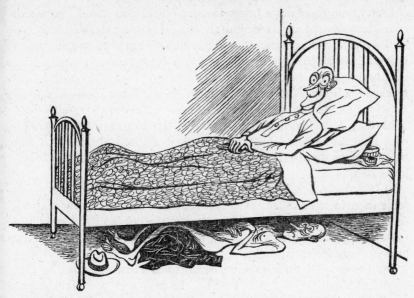

especially for the purpose, and leaned back upon the pillows, the very spit and image of the old man.

Soon he set up a pipe: "Birdie! Birdie!"

At his call the nurse came hurrying in. "Why, honey-boy," said she, "where's your worthless nephew gone?"

"He has just slipped out for a stroll around the old place," croaked our hero. "Moreover, I don't think you should call him worthless. No, I have misjudged that young man, and I want you to send for the lawyer, so that I can do him justice in my will."

"Why, Daddy?" cried the nurse. "What's made this change in you?"

"Change?" said the nephew hastily. "There's no change in me, my dear, except perhaps I feel my latter end approaching. Otherwise I am just the same." And to reassure her on this point, he gave her a friendly little caress, exactly as his uncle had done. She emitted an hilarious squeal and went giggling on her errand.

The nephew lay at his ease, waiting only for the arrival of the lawyer. "I shall dictate a new will," thought he, "and sign it before the very eyes of the lawyer, in a shaky imitation of the old man's crabbed hand. I shall then express a desire to be left alone for a short nap, replace my poor uncle in the bed, put on my clothes, put back my teeth, and step out of the window, to march in at the front door as if newly returned from my walk. What bucketfuls of tears I shall shed, when we discover that the poor old boy has passed peacefully away!"

Pretty soon there was a heavy footstep on the porch, and a large and rough-hewn individual strode into the room, bearing a sizable black bag.

"I am glad you have come," said our hero. "I am eager to make out a new will. I wish to leave everything to my nephew."

"My dear old friend," replied the newcomer, "I fear your malady has reached the brain. Who would have thought my old pal could have mistaken me for the lawyer? You must let me make a brief examination." With that, he pulled down the sheet, and began to probe the nephew with a hard and horny finger. The nephew realized too late that this was no lawyer, but the horse 'n' buggy doc himself, and he uttered a hollow groan.

"I feared as much," said the doctor. "There is something very wrong somewhere in here. I must act at once if you are to recover your reason." As he spoke, he turned the nephew over in the bed, and whisked out a monster hypodermic from his black bag. "Fortunately," said he, "I am always ready for emergencies."

Our hero tried to protest, but he hardly knew what to say, fearing that his uncle would be discovered under the bed, and the circumstance would tend to his prejudice. The doctor, all in a moment, injected a pint of icy fluid into the small of his back, which numbed his whole middle, and paralysed all his faculties, except that of rolling the eyes, which he indulged to the point of excess.

"I am only an old, rough, goldarn horse 'n' buggy doc," observed the doctor, "but I keep abreast of the times. Mental derangement is often caused by abdominal derangement. If you will get out my instruments, nurse, I think we shall soon find the source of the trouble."

In a moment the unfortunate nephew was laid open under his own eyes, which he never ceased to roll. The doctor, unpacking him like a Gladstone bag, kept up a running commentary. "Take this," said he to the nurse, "and put it on the wash-stand. Put these on the chair. Don't get them mixed up, or I shall have the devil of a job getting them back again. It is a pity that nephew is not back: it is more ethical to have the consent of a relative before operating. I see nothing wrong with this pancreas, considering the age of the patient. Put it on the chest of drawers. Hang these over the bed-rail.

"Hold the candle a little closer," he continued. "I still have not found the cause of his madness. Don't let the candle drip; that is hardly hygienic. Anyway, he is certainly mad, or he would not think of leaving his money to that scallawag of a nephew. It is well you let me know, my dear, instead of bothering the lawyer. When this is all over, we must take a little trip together."

Saying this, he gave the nurse a caress, similar to that which both uncle and nephew had bestowed on her. The sight of this caress not only shocked our hero, but depressed him abominably, and lowered his powers of resistance. "It is most unprofessional," thought he, "and, what's even worse, it smacks hatefully of conspiracy." This thought caused him to roll his eyes for the last time, and next moment he was a goner.

"Dear me," said the doctor, "I fear I have lost my patient. Sometimes I quite envy the city doctor, with his well-appointed operating theater. However, their biographies usually sell very poorly, and, after all, I did my best for the old boy, and he has remembered me in his will. Had he lived, he might have altered it. What an extraordinary trick of fate! Pass me over the various organs, my dear, and I will put them roughly into position, for I expect the nephew will be back very shortly, and he would hate to see them lying around."

Mary

There was in those days—I hope it is there still—a village called Ufferleigh, lying all among the hills and downs of North Hampshire. In every cottage garden there was a giant apple tree, and when these trees were hung red with fruit, and the newly lifted potatoes lay gleaming between bean-row and cabbage-patch, a young man walked into the village who had never been there before.

He stopped in the lane just under Mrs. Hedges's gate, and looked up into her garden. Rosie, who was picking the beans, heard his tentative cough, and turned and leaned over the hedge to hear what he wanted. "I was wondering," said he, "if there was anybody in the village who had a lodging to let."

He looked at Rosie, whose cheeks were redder than the apples, and whose hair was the softest yellow imaginable. "I was wondering," said he in amendment, "if *you* had."

Rosie looked back at him. He wore a blue jersey such as seafaring men wear, but he seemed hardly like a seafaring man. His face was brown and plain and pleasant, and his hair was black. He was shabby and he was shy, but there was something about him that made it very certain he was not just a tramp. "I'll ask," said Rosie.

With that she ran for her mother, and Mrs. Hedges came out to interview the young man. "I've got to be near Andover for a week," said he, "but somehow I didn't fancy staying right in the town."

"There's a bed," said Mrs. Hedges. "If you don't mind having your meals with us——"

"Why, surely, ma'am," said he. "There's nothing I'd like better."

Everything was speedily arranged; Rosie picked another handful of beans, and in an hour he was seated with them at supper. He told them his name was Fred Baker, but, apart from that, he was so polite that he could hardly speak, and in the end Mrs. Hedges had to ask him outright what his business was. "Why, ma'am," said he, looking her straight in the face, "I've done one thing and another ever since I was so high, but I heard an old proverb once, how to get on in the world. 'Feed 'em or amuse 'em,' it said. So that's what I do, ma'am. I travel with a pig."

Mrs. Hedges said she had never heard of such a thing.

"You surprise me," said he. "Why, there are some in London, they tell me, making fortunes on the halls. Spell, count, add up, answer questions, anything. But let them wait," said he, smiling, "till they see Mary."

"Is that the name of your pig?" asked Rosie.

"Well," said Fred, shyly, "it's what I call her just between ourselves like. To her public, she's Zola. Sort of Frenchified, I thought. Spicy, if you'll excuse the mention of it. But in the caravan I call her Mary."

"You live in a caravan?" cried Rosie, delighted by the doll's-house idea.

"We do," said he. "She has her bunk, and I have mine."

"I don't think I should like that," said Mrs. Hedges. "Not a pig. No."

"She's as clean," said he, "as a new-born babe. And as for company, well, you'd say she's human. All the same, it's a bit of a wandering life for her—up hill and down dale, as the saying goes. Between you and me I shan't be satisfied till I get into one of these big London theatres. You can see us in the West End!"

"I should like the caravan best," said Rosie, who seemed to have a great deal to say for herself, all of a sudden.

"It's pretty," said Fred. "Curtains, you know. Pot of flowers. Little stove. Somehow I'm used to it. Can't hardly think of myself staying at one of them big hotels. Still, Mary's got her career to think of. I can't stand in the way of her talent, so that's that."

"Is she big?" asked Rosie.

"It's not her size," said he. "No more than Shirley Temple. It's her brains and personality. Clever as a wagonload of monkeys! You'd like her. She'd like you, I reckon. Yes, I reckon she would. Sometimes I'm

afraid I'm a bit slow by way of company for her, never having had
much to do with the ladies."

"Don't tell me," said Mrs. Hedges archly, as convention required.

" 'Tis so, ma'am," said he. "Always on the move, you see, ever since
I was a nipper. Baskets and brooms, pots and pans, then some acrobat
stuff, then Mary. Never two days in the same place. It don't give you
the time to get acquainted."

"You're going to be here a whole week, though," said Rosie artlessly,
but at once her red cheeks blushed a hundred times redder than before,
for Mrs. Hedges gave her a sharp look, which made her see that her
words might have been taken the wrong way.

Fred, however, had noticed nothing. "Yes," said he, "I shall be here a
week. And why? Mary ran a nail in her foot in the market-place,
Andover. Finished her act—and collapsed. Now she's at the vet's, poor
creature."

"Oh, poor thing!" cried Rosie.

"I was half afraid," said he, "it was going wrong on her. But it seems
she'll pull round all right, and I took opportunity to have the van repaired a bit, and soon we'll be on the road again. I shall go in and see
her tomorrow. Maybe I can find some blackberries, to take her by way
of a relish, so to speak."

"Colley Bottom," said Rosie. "That's the place where they grow big
and juicy."

"Ah! If I knew where it was—" said Fred tentatively.

"Perhaps, in the morning, if she's got time, she'll show you," said
Mrs. Hedges, who began to feel very kindly disposed towards the
young man.

In the morning, surely enough, Rosie did have time, and she showed
Fred the place, and helped him pick the berries. Returning from
Andover, later in the day, Fred reported that Mary had tucked into
them a fair treat, and he had little doubt that, if she could have spoken,
she would have sent her special thanks. Nothing is more affecting than
the gratitude of a dumb animal, and Rosie was impelled to go every
morning with Fred to pick a few more berries for the invalid pig.

On these excursions Fred told her a great deal more about Mary, a bit
about the caravan, and a little about himself. She saw that he was very
bold and knowing in some ways, but incredibly simple and shy in others.
This, she felt, showed he had a good heart.

The end of the week seemed to come very soon, and all at once they
were coming back from Colley Bottom for the last time. Fred said he
would never forget Ufferleigh, nor the nice time he had there.

"You ought to send us a postcard when you're on your travels," said Rosie.

"Yes," he said. "That's an idea. I will."

"Yes, do," said Rosie.

"Yes," said he again. "I will. Do you know, I was altogether down-hearted at going away, but now I'm half wishing I was on the road again already. So I could be sending that card right away," said he.

"At that rate," said Rosie, looking the other way, "you might as well make it a letter."

"Ah!" said he. "And do you know what I should feel like putting at the bottom of that letter? If you was my young lady, that is. Which, of course, you're not. Me never having had one."

"What?" said Rosie.

"A young lady," said he.

"But what would you put?" said she.

"Ah!" said he. "What I'd put. Do you know what I'd put? If—*if*, mind you—if you was my young lady?"

"No," said she, "what?"

"I don't hardly like to tell you," said he.

"Go on," she said. "You don't want to be afraid."

"All right," said he. "Only mind you, it's *if*." And with his stick he traced three crosses in the dust.

"If I was anybody's young lady," said Rosie. "I shouldn't see anything wrong in that. After all, you've got to move with the times."

Neither of them said another word, for two of the best reasons in the world. First, they were unable to; second, it was not necessary. They walked on with their faces as red as fire, in an agony of happiness.

Fred had a word with Mrs. Hedges, who had taken a fancy to him from the start. Not that she had not always looked down upon caravan people, and could have been knocked over with a feather, had anyone suggested, at any earlier date, that she would allow a daughter of hers to marry into such a company. But right was right: this Fred Baker was different, as anyone with half an eye could see. He had kept himself to himself, almost to a fault, for his conversation showed that he was as innocent as a new-born babe. Moreover, several knowledgeable people in the village had agreed that his ambitions for Mary, his pig, were in no way unjustified. Everyone had heard of such talented creatures, re-clining on snow-white sheets in the best hotels of the metropolis, drink-ing champagne like milk, and earning for their fortunate owners ten pounds, or even twenty pounds, a week.

So Mrs. Hedges smilingly gave her consent, and Rosie became Fred's real, genuine, proper young lady. He was to save all he could during the winter, and she to stitch and sing. In the spring, he would come back and they were to get married.

"At Easter," said he.

"No," said Mrs. Hedges, counting on her fingers. "In May. Then tongues can't wag, caravan or no caravan."

Fred had not the faintest idea what she was driving at, for he had lived so much alone that no one had told him certain things that every young man should know. However, he well realized that this was an unusually short engagement for Ufferleigh, and represented a great concession to the speed and dash of the entertainment industry, so he respectfully agreed, and set off on his travels.

MY DARLING ROSIE,

Well here we are in Painswick having had a good night Saturday at Evesham. Mary cleverer than ever that goes without saying now spells four new words thirty-six in all and when I say now Mary how do you like Painswick or Evesham or wherever it is she picks FINE it goes down very well. She is in the best of health and I hope you are the same. Seems to understand every word I say more like a human being every day. Well I suppose I must be getting our bit of supper ready she always sets up her cry for that specially when I am writing to you.

With true love
FRED XXX

In May the apple trees were all in bloom, so it was an apple-blossom wedding, which in those parts is held to be an assurance of flowery days. Afterwards they took the bus to the market town, to pick up the caravan, which stood in a stable yard. On the way Fred asked Rosie to wait a moment, and dived into a confectioner's shop. He came out with a huge box of chocolates. Rosie smiled all over her face with joy. "For me?" she said.

"Yes," said he. "To give to her as soon as she claps eyes on you. They're her weakness. I want you two to be real pals."

"All right," said Rosie, who was the best-hearted girl in the world.

The next moment they turned into the yard: there was the caravan. "Oh, it's lovely!" cried Rosie.

"Now you'll see her," said Fred.

At the sound of his voice a falsetto squeal rose from within.

"Here we are, old lady," said Fred, opening the door. "Here's a friend of mine come to help look after you. Look, she's brought you something you'll fancy."

Rosie saw a middle-sized pig, flesh-colored, neat, and with a smart collar. It had a small and rather calculating eye. Rosie offered the chocolates: they were accepted without any very effusive acknowledgment.

Fred put the old horse in, and soon they were off, jogging up the long hills to the west. Rosie sat beside Fred on the driving seat; Mary took her afternoon nap. Soon the sky began to redden where the road divided the woods on the far hill-top. Fred turned into a green lane, and they made their camp.

He lit the stove, and Rosie put on the potatoes. They took a lot of peeling, for it seemed that Mary ate with gusto. Rosie put a gigantic rice pudding into the oven, and soon had the rest of the meal prepared.

Fred set the table. He laid three places.

"I say," said Rosie.

"What?" said Fred.

"Does she eat along with us?" said Rosie. "A pig?"

Fred turned quite pale. He beckoned her outside the caravan. "Don't say a thing like that," said he. "She won't never take to you if you say a thing like that. Didn't you see her give you a look?"

"Yes, I did," said Rosie. "All the same— Well, never mind, Fred. I don't care, really. I just thought I did."

"You wait," said Fred. "You're thinking of ordinary pigs. Mary's different."

Certainly Mary seemed a comparatively tidy eater. All the same, she gave Rosie one or two very odd glances from under her silky straw-colored lashes. She seemed to hock her rice pudding about a bit with the end of her nose.

"What's up, old girl?" said Fred. "Didn't she put enough sugar in the pudden? Never mind—can't get everything right first time."

Mary, with a rather cross hiccup, settled herself on her bunk. "Let's go out," said Rosie, "and have a look at the moon."

"I suppose we might," said Fred. "Shan't be long, Mary. Just going about as far as that gate down the lane." Mary grunted morosely and turned her face to the wall.

Rosie and Fred went out and leaned over the gate. The moon, at least, was all that it should be.

"Seems funny, being married and all," said Rosie softly.

"Seems all right to me," said Fred.

"Remember them crosses you drew in the dirt in the road that day?" said Rosie.

"That I do," said Fred.

"And all them you put in the letters?" said Rosie.

"All of 'em," said Fred.

"Kisses, that's what they're supposed to stand for," said Rosie.

"So they say," said Fred.

"You haven't given me one, not since we was married," said Rosie. "Don't you like it?"

"That I do," said Fred. "Only, I don't know——"

"What?" said Rosie.

"It makes me feel all queer," said Fred, "when I kiss you. As if I wanted——"

"What?" said Rosie.

"I dunno," said Fred. "I don't know if it's I want to eat you all up, or what."

"Try and find out, they say," said Rosie.

A delicious moment followed. In the very middle of it a piercing squeal rose from the caravan. Fred jumped as if he were shot.

"Oh dear," he cried. "She's wondering what's up. Here I come, old girl! Here I come! It's her bed-time, you see. Here I come to tuck you in!"

Mary, with an air of some petulance, permitted this process. Rosie stood by. "I suppose we'd better make it lights out," said Fred. "She likes a lot of sleep, you see, being a brain worker."

"Where do *we* sleep?" said Rosie.

"I made the bunk all nice for you this morning," said Fred. "Me, I'm going to doss below. A sack full of straw, I've got."

"But—" said Rosie. "But——"

"But what?" said he.

"Nothing," said she. "Nothing."

They turned in. Rosie lay for an hour or two, thinking what thoughts I don't know. Perhaps she thought how charming it was that Fred should have lived so simple and shy and secluded all these years, and yet be so knowing about so many things, and yet be so innocent, and never have been mixed up in bad company— It is impossible to say what she thought.

In the end she dozed off, only to be wakened by a sound like the bag-pipes of the devil himself. She sat up, terrified. It was Mary.

"What's up? What's up?" Fred's voice came like the ghost's in *Hamlet* from under the floor. "Give her some milk," he said.

Rosie poured out a bowl of milk. Mary ceased her fiendish racket while she drank, but the moment Rosie had blown out the light, and got into bed again, she began a hundred times worse than before.

There were rumblings under the caravan. Fred appeared in the door-

way, half dressed and with a straw in his hair.

"She *will* have me," he said, in great distress.

"Can't you— Can't you lie down here?" said Rosie.

"What? And you sleep below?" said Fred, astounded.

"Yes," said Rosie, after a rather long pause. "And me sleep below."

Fred was overwhelmed with gratitude and remorse. Rosie couldn't help feeling sorry for him. She even managed to give him a smile before she went down to get what rest she could on the sack of straw.

In the morning, she woke feeling rather dejected. There was a mighty breakfast to be prepared for Mary; afterwards Fred drew her aside.

"Look here," he said. "This won't do. I can't have you sleeping on the ground, worse than a gippo. I'll tell you what I'm going to do. I'm going to get up my acrobat stuff again. I used to make a lot that way, and I like it fine. Hand springs, double somersaults, bit of conjuring: it went down well. Only I didn't have time to keep in practice with Mary to look after. But if you'd do the looking after her, we'd make it a double turn, and soon we'd have a good bit of cash. And then——"

"Yes?" said Rosie.

"Then," said Fred, "I could buy you a trailer."

"All right," said Rosie, and turned away. Suddenly she turned back with her face flaming. "You may know a lot about pigs," she said bitterly. "And about somersaults, and conjuring and baskets and brooms and I don't know what-all. But there's *one* thing you *don't* know." And with that she went off and cried behind a hedge.

After a while she got the upper hand of it, and came back to the caravan. Fred showed her how to give Mary her morning bath, then the depilatory—that was very hard on the hands—then the rubbing with Cleopatra Face Cream—and not on her face merely—then the powdering, then the manicuring and polishing of her trotters.

Rosie, resolved to make the best of it, conquered her repugnance, and soon mastered these handmaidenly duties. She was relieved at first that the spoiled pig accepted her ministrations without protest. Then she noticed the gloating look in its eye.

However, there was no time to brood about that. No sooner was the toilet finished than it was time to prepare the enormous lunch. After lunch Mary had her little walk, except on Saturdays when there was an afternoon show, then she took her rest. Fred explained that during this period she liked to be talked to, and have her back scratched a bit. Mary had quite clearly decided that in future she was going to have it scratched a lot. Then she had her massage. Then tea, then another little walk, or the evening show, according to where they were, and then it was time to prepare dinner. At the end of the day Rosie was thankful to curl up on her poor sack of straw.

When she thought of the bunk above, and Fred, and his simplicity, her heart was fit to break. The only thing was, she loved him dearly, and she felt that if they could soon snatch an hour alone together, they might kiss a little more, and a ray of light might dispel the darkness of excessive innocence.

Each new day she watched for that hour, but it didn't come. Mary saw to that. Once or twice Rosie suggested a little stroll, but at once the hateful pig grumbled some demand or other that kept her hard at work till it too late. Fred, on his side, was busy enough with his practising. He meant it so well, and worked so hard—but what did it lead to? A trailer!

As the days went by, she found herself more and more the slave of this arrogant grunter. Her back ached, her hands got chapped and red, she never had a moment to make herself look nice, and never a moment alone with her beloved. Her dress was spotted and spoiled, her smile was gone, her temper was going. Her pretty hair fell in elf locks and tangles, and she had neither time nor heart to comb it.

She tried to come to an explanation with Fred, but it was nothing but cross purposes and then cross words. He tried in a score of little ways to show that he loved her: these seemed to her a mere mockery, and she gave him short answers. Then he stopped, and she thought he loved her no longer. Even worse, she felt she no longer loved him.

So the whole summer went by, and things got worse and worse, and you would have taken her for a gipsy indeed.

The blackberries were ripe again; she found a whole brake of them. When she tasted one, all sorts of memories flooded into her heart: she went and found Fred. "Fred," she said, "the blackberries are ripe again. I've brought you one or two." She held out some in her grubby hand. Fred took them and tasted them; she watched to see what the result would be.

"Yes," said he, "they're ripe. They won't gripe her. Take her and pick her some this afternoon."

Rosie turned away without a word, and in the afternoon she took Mary across the stubbles to where the ripe berries grew. Mary, when she saw them, dispensed for once with dainty service, and began to help herself very liberally. Rosie, finding she had nothing more urgent to attend to, sat down on a bank and sobbed bitterly.

In the middle of it all she heard a voice asking what was the matter. She looked up and there was a fat, shrewd, jolly-looking farmer. "What is it, my girl?" said he. "Are you hungry?"

"No," said she. "I'm fed up."

"What with?" said he.

"A pig!" said she, with a gulp.

"You've got no call to bawl and cry," said he. "There's nothing like a bit of pork. I'd have the indigestion for that, any day."

"It's not pork," she said. "It's a pig. A live pig."

"Have you lost it?" said he.

"I wish I had," said she. "I'm that miserable I don't know what to do."

"Tell me your troubles," said he. "There's no harm in a bit of sympathy."

So Rosie told him about Fred, and about Mary, and what hopes she'd had and what they'd all come to, and how she was the slave of this insolent, spoiled, jealous pig, and in fact she told him everything except one little matter which she could hardly bring herself to repeat, even to the most sympathetic of fat farmers.

The farmer, pushing his hat over his eyes, scratched his head very thoughtfully. "Really," said he. "I can't hardly believe it."

"It's true," said Rosie, "every word."

"I mean," said the farmer. "A young man—a young gal—the young gal sleeping down on a sack of straw—a pretty young gal like you. Properly married and all. Not to put too fine a point on it, young missus, aren't the bunks wide enough, or what?"

"He doesn't know," sobbed Rosie. "He just doesn't know no more'n a baby. And she won't let us ever be alone a minute. So he'd find out."

The farmer scratched his head more furiously than ever. Looking at her tear-stained face, he found it hard to doubt her. On the other hand it seemed impossible that a pig should know so much and a young man should know so little. But at that moment Mary came trotting through the bushes, with an egotistical look on her face, which was well besmeared with the juice of the ripe berries.

"Is this your pig?" said the farmer.

"Well," said Rosie, "I'm just taking her for a walk."

The shrewd farmer was quick to notice the look that Rosie got from the haughty grunter when it heard the expression "your pig." This, and Rosie's hurried, nervous disclaimer, convinced the worthy man that the story he had heard was well founded.

"You're taking her for a walk?" said he musingly. "Well! Well! Well! I'll tell you what. If you'd ha' been here this time tomorrow you'd have met *me* taking a walk, with a number of very dear young friends of mine, all very much like her. You might have come along. Two young sows, beautiful creatures, though maybe not so beautiful as that one. Three young boars, in the prime of their health and handsomeness. Though I say it as shouldn't, him that's unattached—he's a prince. Oh, what a beautiful young boar that young boar really is!"

"You don't say?" said Rosie.

"For looks and pedigree both," said the farmer, "he's a prince. The fact is, it's their birthday, and I'm taking 'em over to the village for a little bit of a celebration. I suppose this young lady has some other engagement tomorrow."

"She has to have her sleep just about this time," said Rosie, ignoring Mary's angry grunt.

"Pity!" said the farmer. "She'd have just made up the party. Such fun they'll have! Such refreshments! Sweet apples, cakes, biscuits, a bushel of chocolate creams. Everything most refined, of course, but plenty. You know what I mean—plenty. And that young boar—you know what I mean. If she *should* be walking by——"

"I'm afraid not," said Rosie.

"Pity!" said the farmer. "Ah, well. I must be moving along."

With that, he bade them good afternoon, raising his hat very politely to Mary, who looked after him for a long time, and then walked sulkily home, gobbling to herself all the way.

The next afternoon Mary seemed eager to stretch out on her bunk, and, for once, instead of requiring the usual number of little attentions from Rosie, she closed her eyes in sleep. Rosie took the opportunity to pick up a pail and go off to buy the evening ration of fresh milk. When she got back Fred was still at his practice by the wayside, and Rosie went round to the back of the caravan, and the door was swinging open, and the bunk was empty.

She called Fred. They sought high and low. They went along the roads, fearing she might have been knocked over by a motor car. They went calling through the woods, hoping she had fallen asleep under a tree. They looked in ponds and ditches, behind haystacks, under bridges, everywhere. Rosie thought of the farmer's joking talk, but she hardly liked to say anything about it to Fred.

They called and called all night, scarcely stopping to rest. They sought all the next day. It grew dark, and Fred gave up hope. They plodded silently back to the caravan.

He sat on a bunk, with his head in his hand.

"I shall never see her again," he said. "Been pinched, that's what she's been.

"When I think," he said, "of all the hopes I had for that pig——

"When I think," he said, "of all you've done for her! And what it's meant to you——

"I know she had some faults in her nature," he said. "But that was artistic. Temperament, it was. When you got a talent like that——

"And now she's gone!" he said. With that he burst into tears.

"Oh, Fred!" cried Rosie. "Don't!"

Suddenly she found she loved him just as much as ever, more than ever. She sat down beside him and put her arms round his neck. "Darling Fred, don't cry!" she said again.

"It's been rough on you, I know," said Fred. "I didn't ever mean it to be."

"There! There," said Rosie. She gave him a kiss, and then she gave him another. It was a long time since they had been as close as this. There was nothing but the two of them and the caravan; the tiny lamp, and darkness all round; their kisses, and grief all round. "Don't let go," said Fred. "It makes it better."

"I'm not letting go," she said.

"Rosie," said Fred. "I feel— Do you know how I feel?"

"I know," she said. "Don't talk."

"Rosie," said Fred, but this was some time later. "Who'd have thought it?"

"Ah! Who would, indeed?" said Rosie.

"Why didn't you tell me?" said Fred.

"How could I tell you?" said she.

"You know," said he. "We might never have found out—never!—if she hadn't been pinched."

"Don't talk about her," said Rosie.

"I can't help it," said Fred. "Wicked or not, I can't help it—I'm glad she's gone. It's worth it. I'll make enough on the acrobat stuff. I'll make brooms as well. Pots and pans, too."

"Yes," said Rosie. "But look! It's morning. I reckon you're tired, Fred—running up hill and down dale all day yesterday. You lie abed now, and I'll go down to the village and get you something good for breakfast."

"All right," said Fred. "And tomorrow I'll get yours."

So Rosie went down to the village, and bought the milk and the bread and so forth. As she passed the butcher's shop she saw some new-made pork sausages of a singularly fresh, plump, and appetizing appearance. So she bought some, and very good they smelled while they were cooking.

"That's another thing we couldn't have while she was here," said

Fred, as he finished his plateful. "Never no pork sausages, on account of her feelings. I never thought to see the day I'd be glad she was pinched. I only hope she's gone to someone who appreciates her."

"I'm sure she has," said Rosie. "Have some more."

"I will," said he. "I don't know if it's the novelty, or the way you cooked 'em, or what. I never ate a better sausage in my life. If we'd gone up to London with her, best hotels and all, I doubt if ever we'd have had as sweet a sausage as these here."

School Days

Education has always been fair game for the funsters. Classroom jokes are relished equally by the graduate and by the badly educated—which includes most of us. There are two main variations: the traditional Teacher and Johnny pattern, and the more recent and more unpredictable twist inspired by the modern progressive school.

In the second category, there is the tale of the mother who wished to enter her child in an up-to-the-minute kindergarten. But the child was only five, and the age requirement was six. "I think," said the mother, "she can pass the six-year-old test."

"We shall see," said the examiner. Then, to the child, "Dear, just say a few words that come into your mind."

"Mother," said the five-year-old candidate, "does the lady want logically connected sentences or purely irrelevant words?"

It was the end of the term at the progressive nursery school, and a mother was waiting downstairs to see the principal about registering her child for the next term. The clock struck three, and a horde of children rushed out, practically throwing the visitor over. The last child, instead of running off with the others, stopped and apologized. At that moment the head of the school appeared.

"Please excuse that youngster," said the principal. "He's a new pupil, and he isn't quite adjusted to us yet."

Perhaps the most incisive story about the progressive method is the one about the school psychologist who is putting a young girl through a series of tests to determine her intellectual fitness.

"Now first," said the psychologist, "are you a boy or a girl?"

"A boy," said the girl promptly.

"Well," said the psychologist, taken aback, "that's interesting. And

161

what are you going to be when you grow up?"

"A father," said the child.

"But, darling," interrupted her mother, "you know better than that. Why do you *say* such things to the doctor?"

"Because," said the child in all seriousness, "if he's going to ask silly questions I'm going to give silly answers."

So much for jests about progressive education. Most humorists rely on the old formula—the formula which represents Teacher and Johnny matching wits in the classroom. It is a foregone conclusion that Johnny must win. For example, Teacher inquires: "Where was the Declaration of Independence signed?" And Johnny is bound to reply: "At the bottom."

Here are a few more examples of the age-long struggle between the wish to instruct and the will to resist.

TEACHER: "We've been talking about recent inventions. Now, Johnny, name something which did not exist twenty-five years ago."

JOHNNY: "Me."

TEACHER: "Why is Lapland so thinly populated?"

JOHNNY: "Because there are so few Lapps to the mile."

TEACHER: "When I say 'I have went' what is wrong with that sentence?"

JOHNNY: "It's wrong because you ain't went yet."

Johnny was having a wonderful time with crayons and a sheet of paper when his mother came in and asked what he was drawing. He answered:

"I'm making a picture of God."

Surprised but interested, the fond parent queried: "How can you do that? No one in the world knows what God looks like."

"Well," replied Johnny with assurance, "they will when I get through!"

Freddy took a long time to show his report card. "Perhaps I'd better explain it first," he said. "*A* stands for excellent. *B* means good. *C* is fair. And *D* is what I got."

Coming home from Sunday School two girls were discussing the morning's lesson. "Do you believe there's a devil?" asked one.

"Of course not," said the other. "It's just like Santa Claus. It's only your father."

TEACHER: "If you had seven apples and I asked you for two, how many would you have left?"
JOHNNY: "Seven."

TEACHER: "How would you define 'unaware'?"
JOHNNY: "It's the last thing I take off at night."

TEACHER: "When Archimedes leaped from his bath shouting 'Eureka! I have found it!' What did he mean?"
JOHNNY: "The soap."

TEACHER: "Give the plural of 'man.'"
JOHNNY: "Men."
TEACHER: "And the plural of 'child'?"
JOHNNY: "Twins."

As a final triumph for Johnny, there is the story of the mental drill which, this time, centered about the calendar. Said the teacher: "Which month has twenty-eight days in it?" Johnny thought a moment and replied: "They all have."

It is not so much of an educational leap from school to college. The struggle goes on, but this time the antagonists are the professor (proverbially absent-minded but, nevertheless, sarcastic in the classroom) and the not-too-innocent victim who is, in name at least, a student. The pattern remains practically the same. For example:

PROFESSOR: "And now, Mr. Johns, what do you know about French syntax?"
STUDENT: "I didn't know they had to pay for it."

PROFESSOR: "Give the most important fact about nitrates."
STUDENT: "They're cheaper than the day rates."

STUDENT: "Sir, I don't think I deserve an absolute zero."
PROFESSOR: "I don't either. But it's the lowest mark I can possibly give."

PROFESSOR: "Think carefully, and state the number of tons of copper exported from the United States in any given year."
STUDENT (*thinking carefully*): "The year 1492—none."

STUDENT: "Sir, what was the figure you gave when you predicted the end of the world?"
PROFESSOR: "I said approximately fifty million years."
STUDENT: "Thank God. I thought you said only *fifteen* million!"

Marc Connelly

At twenty Marc (Marcus Cook) Connelly, born in McKeesport, Pennsylvania, in 1890, was a reporter for the Pittsburgh Sun. Five years later he went to New York to see a musical comedy which included some of his lyrics. The show was an emphatic failure, but Connelly stayed on and became a pronounced success. Within a few years he had a reputation as a man-of-all-work in the theater: as sketch-writer, adapter, collaborator, and director. His first published play, Dulcy, was one of several comedies written with George S. Kaufman, followed by The Wisdom Tooth and The Green Pastures (adapted from Roark Bradford's Ol' Man Adam and His Chillun), which received the Pulitzer Prize in 1930 and which is one of the classics of the contemporary stage.

Besides his activities as playwright, Connelly has worked energetically for the establishment of an international copyright for plays. Recounting the difficulties, Connelly once testified before the Patent Office that, after Dulcy was successfully performed in Holland, all he got was a copy of the program—on which his name had been misspelled.

The Guest

The scene is Room 1257 in the North American Hotel. Mr. Kenneth Mercer is sitting on the edge of his bed, in his nightshirt, using the telephone.

MR. MERCER—Hello, Aussel, Aussel, Coyne, and Mehoff? . . . Mr. Watson, please. . . . No, ma'am, I haven't an appointment. I *did* have one at nine-thirty but they didn't waken me at the hotel. . . . Yes, ma'am, I know it's ten o'clock. . . . But I've been traveling three days just to see him before he left for Europe. Will you connect me with him? (*While he waits for Mr. Watson, Mr. Mercer reads the card under the glass top of his bed-table. It tells all about the Service Plus which one receives in North American Hotels. It seems the North American Chain has gone the limit in making every patron feel he is 'not merely a guest but a friend.' Mr. Mercer finally gets tired reading, and jiggles the hook of the telephone.*) Hello. . . . Is this Aussel, Aussel, Coyne, and Mehoff? . . . Oh, the hotel operator. . . . No, ma'am, I wasn't through. . . . Will you please get them back for me? . . . Barker 2348. . . . And in the meantime I'd like to have a little breakfast. . . . Which button? . . . All right. Get that number, please.

(*Mr. Mercer goes to an idiotic instrument near the door. It has a mouthpiece and several buttons. Beside it is a neat card reading:*

MEALDICATOR

Just another example of North American Hotels, Inc., Service Plus. Merely press the button and state what you wish from our kitchens. 'Waiting for the waiter' never bothers a North American Hotel guest.

Mr. Mercer faces the mouthpiece and pushes the button. Nothing happens.)

MR. MERCER—A cup of coffee, please. (*Nobody seems to care.*) A cup of coffee, please. (*Mr. Mercer waits a moment, hopes somebody heard him, and looks around the room for the suit of clothes which he'd ordered to be pressed and delivered at eight-thirty sharp this morning. He goes to the telephone again.*) Hello, operator. . . . What? . . . (*Excitedly*) Aussel, Aussel, Coyne, and Mehoff? . . . Operator, did you have them back on there? . . . Yes, I *did* want them. . . . Please get them back and . . . Look, operator, last night I gave a bellboy a gray suit I wanted pressed and . . . Which button?

166

(He goes to a panel near the door with a few more buttons about it and a small sign reading:

THE QUIET VALET

Just another example of North American Service Plus. Merely press the top button and the clothing you wished cleaned or pressed will be returned to you moth-free and fresh in this Byer-Schlaffing All-Cedar Suit Protector.

Mr. Mercer presses the button, the panel swings open and there is somebody's full-dress suit. Mr. Mercer goes to the telephone again.)

MR. MERCER—Look, operator, that isn't my suit. . . . I say, that isn't my suit. . . . Well, it's just somebody else's suit. . . . What number? . . . Certainly, I want that number. . . . All right, keep working on that number. . . . Never mind the suit. *(Mr. Mercer goes into the bathroom to shave. Just as his face is nicely lathered he hears a voice in his bedroom.)*

THE VOICE—Good morning! Good morning! You wished to be called at eight-thirty. Well, eight-thirty it is. Eight-thirty of a beautiful morning. *(Mr. Mercer has now run back into the bedroom and is looking frantically for the speaker.)*

MR. MERCER—You lie! It's after ten o'clock. Don't tell me it's any eight-thirty, because I happen to have a watch that . . . *(Mr. Mercer observes that the voice is coming from the Time Announcer, just another example of North American Service Plus, over his bed.)*

THE VOICE—And now for a tip-top breakfast, eh? Merely instruct the Mealdicator what you wish and it will be served piping hot in jig time. *(The Time Announcer stops announcing and Mr. Mercer, a little self consciously, goes to the Mealdicator again. He presses a button.)*

MR. MERCER—Don't forget the coffee.

(Mr. Mercer sees several other buttons about the Mealdicator and presses them all, one at a time. The last one turns on a beautiful waltz from the room radio, which he hadn't noticed before. Mr. Mercer does not want to hear the radio, so he presses the button again to make it stop. It doesn't. About a foot away is a loud speaker and under it is another inviting button which Mr. Mercer presses. This makes the waltz become louder. Mr. Mercer decides he might as well go back to the bathroom and finish shaving. As he picks up his razor there is a knock on the door.)

MR. MERCER—Come in. *(A bellboy enters with a plate of dog meat.)* Well?

BELLBOY—For the dog, sir.

MR. MERCER—For the dog?

BELLBOY—Yes, sir.

MR. MERCER—Do they give you a dog here too? (*The bellboy laughs pleasantly.*)

BELLBOY—It's just the way you ordered it, sir.

MR. MERCER—I ordered a cup of coffee.

BELLBOY—One should never give coffee to a dog.

MR. MERCER—The coffee is for me.

BELLBOY—Well, this is for the dog. (*The bellboy puts the plate on the floor and looks around for the dog. Mr. Mercer wishes he had an old-fashioned instead of a safety razor.*)

MR. MERCER—Would you mind fixing that radio? (*He goes back into the bathroom. The bellboy does something to the radio which makes it louder.*)

BELLBOY—Better, sir?

MR. MERCER—Ideal. (*Mr. Mercer freshens the lather on his face and the telephone rings.*)

BELLBOY—I'll answer it, sir. (*The bellboy hears something over the phone which makes him laugh.*) What? (*He laughs again.*) No, this isn't Ausser, Ausser, Coyle, and Mehaugh . . . (*Mr. Mercer has run out of the bathroom and has seized the telephone.*)

MR. MERCER—Hello. . . . Operator. . . . Did you have them back on there? . . . Yes, I do want them. . . . Well, that was a mistake. . . . I'll hold the line. (*The door from the hall opens. An assistant manager and two electricians enter.*)

ASSISTANT MANAGER—I beg your pardon, sir, we thought this room was vacant. I'm afraid the Time Announcer over your bed is out of order.

MR. MERCER (*at the phone*)—Look, operator, I'm in a sort of a hurry . . .

ASSISTANT MANAGER—So with your permission we will fix it. All right, boys. (*The two electricians climb over Mr. Mercer and begin hammering at the Time Announcer. There is another knock at the door.*) Come in. (*A head waiter and two other waiters enter with a table set for four. Two busboys follow them bearing a large nickel food-warmer. Mr. Mercer, who has been trying to talk over the telephone from under a pillow, comes up for air and sees them.*)

MR. MERCER—Is that the coffee?

HEAD WAITER—Did you want the coffee now, sir? (*This disturbs Mr. Mercer's patience and he speaks sternly into the telephone.*)

MR. MERCER—Operator, I wish to make a complaint! (*The others are aghast.*)

HEAD WAITER—They distinctly said they wanted the coffee afterwards.

MR. MERCER (*to the assemblage*)—Excuse my being in this nightshirt with soap on my face, gentlemen, but I am a little upset. I can't get called in time, I can't get a suit of clothes I ordered, I can't get a cup of coffee, I can't get a telephone call through, and that young man over there brings me dog meat. I've been in hotels all over this country, but . . . (*The air is suddenly charged with electricity. All the others begin to murmur 'Mr. Pitcairn!' because T. Francis Pitcairn, general Eastern manager of the North American Hotels Chain, has entered the room too.*)

MR. PITCAIRN—What is this about a complaint? (*His manner is very benign.*)

MR. MERCER (*witheringly*)—Oh, nothing, nothing.

MR. PITCAIRN—We are not used to complaints in the North American Chain. We of the Chain pride ourselves and rightly so on the fact that there is no comfort, no luxury which we do not provide in more than full measure to our guests. However, we do not like having our guests take advantage of our good nature. In fact we are resolute in insisting that our hotels be not turned into bedlams. Turn off that radio. (*One of the electricians turns it off.*) That's better. Now what is our guest's name?

ASSISTANT MANAGER—Kenneth Mercer, Columbus, Ohio.

MR. PITCAIRN—Ah, I have many friends in Columbus.

MR. MERCER—I've only been trying to get a little service.

MR. PITCAIRN—You have been getting plenty of service. Probably more than you have ever enjoyed in your own home. Fortunately, the hotel man of today knows how to protect himself from persons of your stripe, Mr. Mercer, and has taken legal measures to do so. (*There is now a deathlike hush.*)

MR. MERCER—You mean you're going to sue?

MR. PITCAIRN—If our attorneys so advise us. Just pack up his things. He will now leave the hotel. (*Everybody but Mr. Mercer begins to pack his things. The assistant manager offers Mr. Mercer his hat and overcoat.*)

MR. MERCER—But I have a nightgown on.

MR. PITCAIRN—You will notice, gentlemen, he is refusing to go.

MR. MERCER—No, I'm not.

BELLBOY—May I carry your bag, sir?

MR. MERCER—Thank you. I have no change; I'll have to break a bill downstairs.

BELLBOY—That's quite all right, sir. (*Mr. Mercer starts to leave the room.*)

MR. PITCAIRN—By the bye, who are your attorneys?

MR. MERCER—Aussel, Aussel, Coyne, and Mehoff. (*Mr. Mercer stops at the Mealdicator, just as he goes out. He presses a button and steps to the mouthpiece.*) Never mind the coffee.

A. E. Coppard

Before he became famous as a short story writer of peculiar charm and sensitivity, Alfred Edgar Coppard had been an office boy, a salesman, an accountant to an engineering firm, an all-round amateur athlete, and a professional sprinter. His father was a tailor, his mother a housemaid; "Except for these," he wrote, "I have no notable ancestors."

Coppard did not emerge as an author until he was in his forties; his first volume, the fanciful Adam and Eve and Pinch Me appeared in 1921. Since that time some hundreds of Coppard's unconventional stories and tartly flavored poems have been collected in twenty books, most of them with such imaginative titles as Clorinda Walks in Heaven, Nixey's Harlequin, Fishmonger's Fiddle, and Ninepenny Flute.

Alas, Poor Bollington!

"I walked out of the hotel, just as I was, and left her there. I never went back again. I don't think I intended anything quite so final, so dastardly; I had not intended it, I had not thought of doing so, but that is how it happened. I lost her, lost my wife purposely. It was heartless, it was shabby, for she was a nice woman, a charming woman, a good deal younger than I was, a splendid woman, in fact she was very beautiful, and yet I ran away from her. How can you explain that, Turner?"

Poor Bollington looked at Turner, who looked at his glass of whiskey, and that looked irresistible—he drank some. Bollington sipped a little from his glass of milk.

I often found myself regarding Bollington as a little old man. Most of the club members did so too, but he was not that at all, he was still on the sunny side of fifty, but *so* unassertive, no presence to speak of, no height, not enough hair to mention—if he had had it would surely have been yellow. So mild and modest he cut no figure at all, just a man in glasses that seemed rather big for him. Turner was different, though he was just as bald; he had stature and bulk, his very pince-nez seemed twice the size of Bollington's spectacles. They had not met each other for ten years.

"Well, yes," Turner said, "but that was a serious thing to do."

"Wasn't it!" said the other, "and I had no idea of the enormity of the offense—not at the time. She might have been dead, poor girl, and her executors advertising for me. She had money, you know, her people had been licensed victuallers, quite wealthy. Scandalous!"

Bollington brooded upon his sin until Turner sighed: "Ah well, my dear chap."

"But you have no idea," protested Bollington, "how entirely she engrossed me. She was twenty-five and I was forty when we married. She was entrancing. She had always lived in a stinking hole in Balham, and it is amazing how strictly some of those people keep their children; licensed victuallers, did I tell you? Well, I was forty, and she was twenty-five; we lived for a year dodging about from one hotel to another all over the British Isles, she was a perfect little nomad. Are you married, Turner?"

No, Turner was not married, he never had been.

"Oh, but you should be," cried little Bollington. "It's an extraordinary experience, the real business of the world is marriage, marriage. I was deliriously happy and she was learning French and Swedish—that's

172

where we were going later. She was an enchanting little thing, fair, with blue eyes; Phoebe her name was."

Turner thoughtfully brushed his hand across his generous baldness, then folded his arms.

"You really should," repeated Bollington, "you ought to, really. But I remember we went from Killarney to Belfast, and there something dreadful happened. I don't know, it had been growing on her, I suppose, but she took a dislike to me there, had strange fancies, thought I was unfaithful to her. You see, she was popular wherever we went, a lively little woman, in fact she wasn't merely a woman, she was a little magnet, men congregated and clung to her like so many tacks and nails and pins. I didn't object at all—on the contrary, 'Enjoy yourself, Phoebe,' I said, 'I don't expect you always to hang around an old fogey like me.' Fogey was the very word I used; I didn't mean it, of course, but that was the line I took, for she was so charming until she began to get so bad-tempered. And believe me, that made her angry, furious. No, not the fogey, but the idea that I did not object to her philandering. It was fatal, it gave colour to her suspicions of me—Turner, I was as innocent as any lamb—tremendous colour. And she had such a sharp tongue! If you ventured to differ from her—and you couldn't help differing sometimes —she'd positively bludgeon you, and you couldn't help being bludgeoned. And she had a passion for putting me right, and I always seemed to be so very wrong, always. She would not be satisfied until she had proved it, and it was so monstrous to be made to feel that because you were rather different from other people you were an impertinent fool. Yes, I seemed at last to gain only the pangs and none of the prizes of marriage. Now there was a lady we met in Belfast to whom I paid some attention . . ."

"Oh, good Lord!" groaned Turner.

"No, but listen," pleaded Bollington, "it was a very innocent friend-ship—nothing was further from my mind—and she was very much like my wife, very much, it was noticeable, everybody spoke of it—I mean the resemblance. A Mrs. Macarthy, a delightful woman, and Phoebe simply loathed her. I confess that my wife's innuendoes were so mean and persistent that at last I hadn't the strength to deny them, in fact at times I wished they were true. Love is idolatry if you like, but it cannot be complete immolation—there's no such bird as the phoenix, is there, Turner?"

"What, what?"

"No such bird as the phoenix."

"No, there is no such bird, I believe."

"And sometimes I had to ask myself quite seriously if I really hadn't been up to some infidelity! Nonsense, of course, but I assure you that was the effect it was having upon me. I had doubts of myself, frenzied doubts! And it came to a head between Phoebe and me in our room one day. We quarrelled. Oh, dear, how we quarrelled! She said I was sly, two-faced, unfaithful, I was a scoundrel, and so on. Awfully untrue, all of it. She accused me of dreadful things with Mrs. Macarthy and she screamed out: 'I hope you will treat her better than you have treated me.' Now what did she mean by that, Turner?"

Bollington eyed his friend as if he expected an oracular answer, but just as Turner was about to respond, Bollington continued: "Well, I never found out, I never knew, for what followed was too terrible. 'I shall go out,' I said, 'it will be better, I think.' Just that, nothing more. I put on my hat and I put my hand on the knob of the door when she said most violently: 'Go with your Macarthys, I never want to see your filthy face again!' Extraordinary you know, Turner. Well, I went out, and I will not deny I was in a rage, terrific. It was raining but I didn't care, and I walked about in it. Then I took shelter in a bookseller's doorway opposite a shop that sold tennis rackets and tobacco, and another one that displayed carnations and peaches on wads of coloured wool. The rain came so fast that the streets seemed to empty, and the passersby were horribly silent under their umbrellas, and their footsteps splashed so dully, and I tell you I was very sad, Turner, there. I debated whether to rush across the road and buy a lot of carnations and peaches and take them to Phoebe. But I did not do so, Turner, I never went back, never."

"Why, Bollington, you, you were a positive ruffian, Bollington."

"Oh, scandalous," rejoined the ruffian.

"Well, out with it, what about this Mrs. Macarthy?"

"Mrs. Macarthy? But, Turner, I never saw her again, never, I . . . I forgot her. Yes, I went prowling on until I found myself at the docks and there it suddenly became dark; I don't know, there was no evening, no twilight, the day stopped for a moment—and it did not recover. There were hundreds of bullocks slithering and panting and steaming in the road, thousands; lamps were hung up in the harbour, cabs and trollies rattled round the bullocks, the rain fell dismally and everybody hurried. I went into the dock and saw them loading the steamer, it was called S. S. *Frolic,* and really, Turner, the things they put into the belly of that steamer were rather funny: tons and tons of monstrous big chain, the links as big as soup plates, and two or three pantechnicon vans. Yes, but I was anything but frolicsome, I assure you, I was full of misery and trepidation and the deuce knows what. I did not know what I wanted to do, or what I was going to do, but I found myself buying a ticket to go to Liverpool on that steamer, and, in short, I embarked. How wretched I was, but how determined. Everything on board was depressing and dirty, and when at last we moved off the foam slewed away in filthy bubbles as if that dirty steamer had been sick and was running away from it. I got to Liverpool in the early morn, but I did not stay there, it is such a clamouring place, all trams and trollies and teashops. I sat in the station for an hour, the most miserable man alive, the most miserable ever born. I wanted some rest, some peace, some repose, but they never ceased shunting an endless train of goods trucks, banging and screeching until I almost screamed at the very porters. Criff was the name on some of the trucks, I remember, Criff, and everything seemed to be going criff, criff, criff. I haven't discovered to this day what Criff signifies, whether it's a station or a company, or a manufacture, but it was Criff, I remember. Well, I rushed to London and put my affairs in order. A day or two later I went to Southampton and boarded another steamer and put to sea, or rather we were ignominiously lugged out of the dock by a little rat of a tug that seemed all funnel and hooter. I was off to America, and there I stopped for over three years."

Turner sighed. A waiter brought him another glass of spirit.

"I can't help thinking, Bollington, that it was all very fiery and touchy. Of course, I don't know, but really it was a bit steep, very squeamish of you. What did your wife say?"

"I never communicated with her, I never heard from her, I just dropped out. My filthy face, you know, she did not want to see it again."

"Oh, come, Bollington! And what did Mrs. Macarthy say?"

"Mrs. Macarthy! I never saw or heard of her again. I told you that."

"Ah, yes, you told me. So you slung off to America."

"I was intensely miserable there for a long while. Of course I loved Phoebe enormously, I felt the separation, I . . . Oh, it is impossible to describe. But what was worst of all was the meanness of my behavior, there was nothing heroic about it, I soon saw clearly that it was a shabby trick, disgusting, I had bolted and left her to the mercy of . . . well, of whatever there was. It made such an awful barrier—you've no idea of my compunction—I couldn't make overtures—'Let us forgive and forget.' I was a mean rascal, I *was* filthy. That was the barrier—myself; I was too bad. I thought I should recover and enjoy life again; I began to think of Phoebe as a cat, a little cat. I went everywhere and did everything. But America is a big country, I couldn't get into contact, I was lonely, very lonely, and although two years went by I longed for Phoebe.

Everything I did I wanted to do with Phoebe by my side. And then my cousin, my only relative in the world—he lived in England—he died. I scarcely ever saw him, but still he was my kin. And he died. You've no comprehension, Turner, of the truly awful sensation such a bereavement brings. Not a soul now would have the remotest interest in my welfare. Oh, I tell you, Turner, it was tragic, tragic, when my cousin died. It made my isolation complete. I was alone, a man who had made a dreadful mess of life. What with sorrow and remorse I felt that I should soon die, not of disease, but disgust."

"You were a great ninny," ejaculated his friend. "Why the devil didn't you hurry back, claim your wife, let bygones be bygones; why, bless my conscience, what a ninny, what a great ninny!"

"Yes, Turner, it is as you say. But though conscience is a good servant it is a very bad master, it overruled me, it shamed me, and I hung on to America for still another year. I tell you my situation was unbearable, I was tied to my misery, I was a tethered dog, a duck without water— even dirty water. And I hadn't any faith in myself or in my case; I knew I was wrong, had always been wrong, Phoebe had taught me that. I hadn't any faith, I wish I had had. Faith can move mountains, so they say, though I've never heard of it actually being done."

"No, not in historical times," declared Turner.

"What do you mean by that?"

"Oh, well, time is nothing, it's nothing, it comes and off it goes. Has it ever occurred to you, Bollington, that in 5,000 years or so there will be nobody in the world speaking the English language, our very existence even will be speculated upon, as if we were the Anthropophagi? Oh, good lord, yes."

And another whiskey.

"You know, Bollington, you were a perfect fool. You behaved like one of those half-baked civil service hounds who lunch in a dairy on a cup of tea and a cream horn. You wanted some beef, some ginger. You came back, you must have come back because there you are now."

"Yes, Turner, I came back after nearly four years. Everything was different, ah, how strange! I could not find Phoebe, it is weird how people can disappear. I made enquiries, but it was like looking for a lost umbrella, fruitless after so long."

"Well, but what about Mrs. Macarthy?"

Mr. Bollington said, slowly and with the utmost precision: "I did not see Mrs. Macarthy again."

"Oh, of course, you did not see her again, not ever."

"Not ever. I feared Phoebe had gone abroad too, but at last I found her in London . . ."

"No," roared Turner, "why the devil couldn't you say so and done with it? I've been sweating with sympathy for you. Oh, I say, Bollington!"

"My dear Turner, listen. Do you know, she was delighted to see me, she even kissed me, straight off, and we went out to dine and had the very deuce of a spread and we were having the very deuce of a good time. She was lovelier than ever, and I could see all her old affection for me was returning, she was so . . . well, I can't tell you, Turner, but she had no animosity whatever, no grievance, she would certainly have taken me back that very night. Oh, dear, dear . . . and then! I was anxious to throw myself at her feet, but you couldn't do that in a public café, I could only touch her hands, beautiful, as they lay on the white linen cloth. I kept asking: 'Do you forgive me?' and she would reply: 'I have nothing to forgive, dear, nothing.' How wonderful that sounded to my truly penitent soul—I wanted to die.

" 'But you don't ask me where I've been!' she cried gaily, 'or what I've been doing, you careless old Peter. I've been to France, and Sweden too!'

"I was delighted to hear that, it was so very plucky.

" 'When did you go?' I asked.

" 'When I left you,' she said.

" 'You mean when I went away?'

" 'Did you go away? Oh, of course, you must have. Poor Peter, what a sad time he has had.'

"I was a little bewildered, but I was delighted; in fact, Turner, I was hopelessly infatuated again, I wanted to wring out all the dregs of my detestable villainy and be absolved. All I could begin with was: 'Were you not very glad to be rid of me?'

" 'Well,' she said, 'my great fear at first was that you would find me again and make it up. I didn't want that then, at least, I thought I didn't.'

" 'That's exactly what I felt,' I exclaimed, 'but how could I find you?'

" 'Well,' Phoebe said, 'you might have found out and followed me. But I promise never to run away again, Peter dear, never.'

"Turner, my reeling intelligence swerved like a shot bird.

" 'Do you mean, Phoebe, that you ran away from *me?*'

" 'Yes, didn't I?' she answered.

" 'But I ran away from *you*,' I said. 'I walked out of the hotel on that dreadful afternoon we quarrelled so, and I never went back. I went to America. I was in America nearly four years.'

" 'Do you mean you ran away from me?' she cried.

" 'Yes,' I said, 'didn't I?'

" 'But that is exactly what I did—I mean, I ran away from you. *I* walked out of the hotel directly you had gone—*I* never went back, and I've been abroad thinking how tremendously I had served you out, and wondering what you thought of it all and where you were.'

"I could only say, 'Good God, Phoebe, I've had the most awful four years of remorse and sorrow, all vain, mistaken, useless, thrown away.' And she said: 'And I've had four years—living in a fool's paradise after all. How dared you run away, it's disgusting!'

"And, Turner, in a moment she was at me again in her old dreadful way, and the last words I had from her were: 'Now I *never* want to see your face again, never, this *is* the end!'

"And that's how things are now, Turner. It's rather sad, isn't it?"

"Sad! Why you chump, when was it you saw her?"

"Oh, a long time ago, it must be nearly three years now."

"Three years! But you'll see her again!"

"Tfoo! No, no, no, Turner. God bless me, no, no, no!" said the little old man.

Frederic Swartout Cozzens

Frederic Swartout Cozzens (1818–1869) was a
genial American wine merchant who was, nevertheless, so temperate that he groaned whenever he
was joked about his "high spirits." It is said that
Cozzens became a humorist in self-defense. At any
rate, his was a defensive humor, best illustrated by
The Sparrowgrass Papers, which portrays the joys
and maladjustments of the city-dweller who deter-
mines to become a countryman.

Living in the Country

It is a good thing to live in the country. To escape from the prison-walls of the metropolis—the great brickery we call "the city"—and to live amid blossoms and leaves, in shadow and sunshine, in moonlight and starlight, in rain, mist, dew, hoarfrost, and drought, out in the open campaign and under the blue dome that is bounded by the horizon only. It is a good thing to have a well with dripping buckets, a porch with honey-buds and sweet-bells, a hive embroidered with nimble bees, a sundial mossed over, ivy up to the eaves, curtains of dimity, a tumbler of fresh flowers in your bedroom, a rooster on the roof, and a dog under the piazza.

When Mrs. Sparrowgrass and I moved into the country, with our heads full of fresh butter, and cool, crisp radishes for tea; with ideas entirely lucid respecting milk, and a looseness of calculation as to the number in family it would take a good laying hen to supply with fresh eggs every morning; when Mrs. Sparrowgrass and I moved into the country, we found some preconceived notions had to be abandoned, and some departures made from the plans we had laid down in the little back parlor of Avenue G.

One of the first achievements in the country is early rising! with the lark—with the sun—while the dew is on the grass, "under the opening eyelids of the morn," and so forth. Early rising! What can be done with five or six o'clock in town? What may not be done at those hours in the country? With the hoe, the rake, the dibble, the spade, the watering-pot? To plant, prune, drill, transplant, graft, train, and sprinkle! Mrs. S. and I agreed to rise *early* in the country. Early rising in the country is not an instinct; it is a sentiment, and must be cultivated.

A friend recommended me to send to the south side of Long Island for some very prolific potatoes—the real hippopotamus breed. Down went my man, and what, with expenses of horse-hire, tavern bills, toll-gates, and breaking a wagon, the hippopotami cost as much apiece as pine-apples. They were fine potatoes, though, with comely features, and large languishing eyes, that promised increase of family without delay. As I worked my own garden (for which I hired a landscape gardener at two dollars per day to give me instructions), I concluded that the object of my first experiment in early rising should be the planting of the hippo-potamuses. I accordingly arose next morning at five, and it rained! I rose next day at five, and it rained! The next, and it rained! It rained for two weeks! We had splendid potatoes every day for dinner. "My

180

dear," said I to Mrs. Sparrowgrass, "where did you get these fine potatoes?" "Why," said she, innocently, "out of that basket from Long
Island!" The last of the hippopotamuses were before me, peeled, and
boiled, and mashed, and baked, with a nice thin brown crust on the top.

I was more successful afterward. I did get some fine seed-potatoes in
the ground. But something was the matter; at the end of the season I did
not get as many out as I had put in.

Mrs. Sparrowgrass, who is a notable housewife, said to me one day,
"Now, my dear, we shall soon have plenty of eggs, for I have been
buying a lot of young chickens." There they were, each one with as
many feathers as a grasshopper, and a chirp not louder. Of course, we
looked forward with pleasant hopes to the period when the first cackle
should announce the milk-white egg, warmly deposited in the hay which
we had provided bountifully. They grew finely, and one day I ventured
to remark that our hens had remarkably large combs, to which Mrs. S.
replied, "Yes indeed, she had observed that; but if I wanted to have a
real treat I ought to get up early in the morning and hear them crow."
"Crow!" said I, faintly, "our hens crowing! Then, by 'the cock that
crowed in the morn, to wake the priest all shaven and shorn,' we might
as well give up all hopes of having any eggs," said I; "for as sure as you
live, Mrs. S., our hens are all roosters!" And so they were roosters!
They grew up and fought with the neighbors' chickens, until there was
not a whole pair of eyes on either side of the fence.

A *dog* is a good thing to have in the country. I have one which I raised
from a pup. He is a good, stout fellow, and a hearty barker and feeder.
The man of whom I bought him said he was thoroughbred, but he begins
to have a mongrel look about him. He is a good watchdog, though; for
the moment he sees any suspicious-looking person about the premises he
comes right into the kitchen and gets behind the stove. First, we kept
him in the house, and he scratched all night to get out. Then we turned
him out, and he scratched all night to get in. Then we tied him up at the
back of the garden, and he howled so that our neighbor shot at him
twice before daybreak. Finally we gave him away, and he came back;
and now he is just recovering from a fit, in which he has torn up the
patch that has been sown for our spring radishes.

A good, strong gate is a necessary article for your garden. A good,
strong, heavy gate, with a dislocated hinge, so that it will neither open
nor shut. Such a one have I. The grounds before my fence are in common, and all the neighbors' cows pasture there. I remarked to Mrs. S.,
as we stood at the window in a June sunset, how placid and picturesque
the cattle looked, as they strolled about, cropping the green herbage.

Next morning I found the innocent creatures in my garden. They had not left a green thing in it. The corn in the milk, the beans on the poles, the young cabbages, the tender lettuce, even the thriving shoots on my young fruit trees had vanished. And there they were, looking quietly on the ruin they had made. Our watchdog, too, was foregathering with them. It was too much; so I got a large stick and drove them all out, except a young heifer, whom I chased all over the flower-beds, breaking down my trellises, my woodbines and sweet-briers, my roses and petunias, until I cornered her in the hotbed. I had to call for assistance to extricate her from the sashes, and her owner has sued me for damages.

We are worried about our cucumbers. Mrs. S. is fond of cucumbers, so I planted enough for ten families. The more they are picked, the faster they grow; and if you do not pick them, they turn yellow and look ugly. Our neighbor has plenty, too. He sent us some one morning, by way of a present. What to do with them we did not know, with so many of our own. To give them away was not polite; to throw them away was sinful; to eat them was impossible. Mrs. S. said, "Save them for seed." So we did. Next day, our neighbor sent us a dozen more. We thanked the messenger grimly and took them in. Next morning another dozen came. It was getting to be a serious matter; so I rose betimes the following morning, and when my neighbor's cucumbers came I filled his man's basket with some of my own, by way of exchange. This bit of pleasantry was resented by my neighbor, who told his man to throw them to the hogs. His man told our girl, and our girl told Mrs. S., and in consequence, all intimacy between the two families has ceased; the ladies do not speak, even at church.

We have another neighbor, whose name is Bates; he keeps cows. This year our gate has been fixed; but my young peach trees near the fences are accessible from the road; and Bates's cows walk along that road morning and evening. The sound of a cow-bell is pleasant in the twilight. Sometimes, after dark, we hear the mysterious curfew tolling along the road, and then with a louder peal it stops before our fence and again tolls itself off in the distance. The result is, my peach trees are as bare as bean-poles. One day I saw Mr. Bates walking along, and I hailed him: "Bates, those are your cows there, I believe?" "Yes, sir; nice ones, ain't they?" "Yes," I replied, "they are *nice* ones. Do you see that tree there?" —and I pointed to a thrifty peach, with as many leaves as an exploded skyrocket. "Yes, sir." "Well, Bates, that red-and-white cow of yours yonder ate the top off that tree; I saw her do it." Then I thought I had made Bates ashamed of himself, and had wounded his feelings, perhaps, too much. I was afraid he would offer me money for the tree, which I made up my mind to decline at once. "Sparrowgrass," said he, "it don't hurt a tree a single mossel to chaw it if it's a young tree. For my part, I'd rather have my young trees chawed than not. I think it makes them grow a leetle better. I can't do it with mine, but you can, because you can wait to have good trees, and the only way to have good trees is to have 'em chawed."

We have put a dumb-waiter in our house. A dumb-waiter is a good thing to have in the country, on account of its convenience. If you have company, everything can be sent up from the kitchen without any trouble; and if the baby gets to be unbearable, on account of his teeth, you can dismiss the complainant by stuffing him in one of the shelves and letting him down upon the help. To provide for contingencies, we had all our floors deafened. In consequence, you cannot hear anything that is going on in the story below; and when you are in the upper room of the house there might be a democratic ratification meeting in the cellar and you would not know it. Therefore, if any one should break into the basement it would not disturb us; but to please Mrs. Sparrowgrass, I put stout iron bars in all the lower windows. Besides, Mrs. Sparrowgrass had bought a rattle when she was in Philadelphia; such a rattle as watchmen carry there. This is to alarm our neighbor, who, upon the signal, is to come to the rescue with his revolver. He is a rash man, prone to pull trigger first and make inquiries afterward.

One evening Mrs. S. had retired and I was busy writing, when it struck me a glass of icewater would be palatable. So I took the candle and a pitcher and went down to the pump. Our pump is in the kitchen. A country pump in the kitchen is more convenient; but a well with buckets is certainly more picturesque. Unfortunately, our well water has not been sweet since it was cleaned out. First I had to open a bolted door that lets you into the basement hall, and then I went to the kitchen door, which proved to be locked. Then I remembered that our girl always carried the key to bed with her and slept with it under her pillow. Then I retraced my steps, bolted the basement door, and went up into the dining-room. As is always the case, I found, when I could not get any water, I was thirstier than I supposed I was. Then I thought I would wake our girl up. Then I concluded not to do it. Then I thought of the well, but I gave that up on account of its flavor. Then I opened the closet doors: there was no water there; and then I thought of the dumb-waiter! The novelty of the idea made me smile. I took out two of the movable shelves, stood the pitcher on the bottom of the dumb-waiter, got in myself with the lamp; let myself down, until I supposed I was within a foot of the floor below, and then let go!

We came down so suddenly that I was shot out of the apparatus as if it had been a catapult; it broke the pitcher, extinguished the lamp, and landed me in the middle of the kitchen at midnight, with no fire and the air not much above the zero point. The truth is, I had miscalculated the distance of the descent—instead of falling one foot, I had fallen five. My first impulse was to ascend by the way I came down, but I found that impracticable. Then I tried the kitchen door; it was locked. I tried to force it open; it was made of two-inch stuff, and held its own. Then I hoisted a window, and there were the rigid iron bars. If ever I felt angry at anybody it was at myself for putting up those bars to please Mrs. Sparrowgrass. I put them up, not to keep people in, but to keep people out.

I laid my cheek against the ice-cold barriers and looked out at the sky; not a star was visible; it was as black as ink overhead. Then I made a noise. I shouted until I was hoarse, and ruined our preserving kettle with the poker. That brought our dogs out in full bark, and between us we made night hideous. Then I thought I heard a voice and listened—it was Mrs. Sparrowgrass calling to me from the top of the staircase. I tried to make her hear me, but the infernal dogs united with howl, and growl, and bark, so as to drown my voice, which is naturally plaintive and tender. Besides, there were two bolted doors and double-deafened floors between us; how could she recognize my voice, even if she did hear it? Mrs. Sparrowgrass called once or twice and then got frightened; the next thing I heard was a sound as if the roof had fallen in, by which I understood that Mrs. Sparrowgrass was springing the rattle! That called out our neighbor, already wide awake; he came to the rescue with a bull-terrier, a Newfoundland pup, a lantern, and a revolver. The moment he saw me at the window he shot at me, but fortunately just missed me. I threw myself under the kitchen table and ventured to expostulate with him, but he would not listen to reason. In the excitement I had forgotten his name, and that made matters worse. It was not until he had roused up everybody around, broken in the basement door with an ax, gotten into the kitchen with his cursed savage dogs and shooting-iron, and seized me by the collar, that he recognized me—and then he wanted me to explain it! But what kind of an explanation could I make to him? I told him he would have to wait until my mind was composed, and then I would let him understand the whole matter fully. But he never would have had the particulars from me, for I do not approve of neighbors that shoot at you, break in your door, and treat you, in your own house, as if you were a jailbird. He knows all about it, however—somebody has told him—*somebody* tells everybody everything in our village!

Down on the Farm

All collections of rural stories seem to begin with one of the oldest of farm jokes.

"Doesn't your son help you with the farm work?" asked the stranger.

"No," replied the farmer. "He can't. He's a bootblack in the city."

"I see," said the stranger. "You make hay while the son shines."

It was late dusk; the moon was just showing on the horizon. The farm boy and the girl from town were leaning on the pasture bars watching the calf and its mother rubbing noses.

"Gee!" said the farm boy. "I'd like to be doing that."

"Go ahead," smiled the girl. "It's your cow."

The rooster, crossing the barnyard, came across the football that the schoolboy had been kicking around.

"Ladies," he crowed, "come here and observe carefully. I don't want to complain, but I'd like you to see what's being done in other yards."

"You mustn't take it too hard, Silas," consoled the minister, driving back from the funeral. "You and Martha were married forty years. That's a long time for man and wife to live together."

"That's right, parson," said Silas. "Martha made me a good wife. But, do you know something, deacon, somehow I never got to like her."

"That peculiar odor," said the lady from the city, "it seems to be coming from the plowed field. What can it be?"

"That's fertilizer," answered the farmer.

"For the land's sake!" exclaimed the lady.

"Yes," said the farmer.

186

"How's your uncle doing on that farm of his?" asked Brown.

"Not so good," said Green. "There's no money in eggs, and he loses money on the milk he sells. But he's awful busy."

"What does he do?" asked Brown.

"He sits up nights," said Green, "thinking of something else for the cows and hens to work at."

"Yep, my uncle was the dumbest farmer in the whole county. He had two windmills to begin with, but he took down one because he said there wasn't wind enough for two of them. He'd order certain kinds of seeds from last year's catalogue because he read it took two years for them to bloom. He'd raise a mixture of cucumbers, celery, tomatoes and lettuce all in one patch because the summer boarders asked for combination salad. He liked to tell stories about the year when the rain fell for weeks without stopping until the roads ran faster than the streams. Once, he said, he saw a hat lying in the middle of one of those muddy roads, but when he went to pick it up he saw there was a man's head under it. "Can I help you, stranger?" asked my uncle. "No, thanks," said the stranger. "I got a good horse under me."

It was in Kentucky; the night was dark. Two men banged on the old cabin door. "Joe and me, we just found a body down in the holler, and we were afraid it might be you. It was too dark to tell."

"What did the body look like?"

"About your height; sort of scraggy——"

"Did he have on a shirt?"

"Yep."

"Flannel?"

"Yep."

"Was he shaved?"

"I think so."

"Well, then, it warn't me."

"Giddap," called the Vermont farmer to his tired horse. The horse stumbled and fell to his knees.

"Giddap there, I'm telling you!" But the horse went down, and lay on its side, looking up dejectedly.

This was more than the farmer could stand. "Giddap for the last time! If you don't git up, I'll drive right over you!"

"Is this the Woman's Exchange?" asked Reuben.
"Of course. What did you want to see?"
"Well, if you're the woman, I guess I'll keep Sarah."

It was Farmer Brown's first visit to the big town. In the window of the department store he read a sign: "Ladies Ready to Wear Clothes."
"Gosh," he said, "it's about time."

Frank Crowninshield

Frank (originally Francis Welch) Crowninshield, born in 1872, has not only known—as far as any one man can know—every interesting person in all fields of contemporary culture, but he has practically total recall about all of them. Modest about most accomplishments, including his editing of various magazines, he likes to boast that he took Edith Wharton on her first trip on the subway and introduced her to her first five-and-ten. A great raconteur, he prefers to tell stories rather than write them. His articles are mosaics: a reminiscence here, an incident there, a dash of data, a whiff of nostalgia—and the pieces fall into place.

Such a mosaic is "A Wit with a Whim of Iron," a eulogy which is also a blithe elegy of one of Crowninshield's best friends.

A Wit with a Whim of Iron

Macabre as it may seem, one of the jolliest luncheons ever held at The Players Club, in New York, was composed of men who, but an hour before, had been the pallbearers at the funeral of a man they had all loved. Of that jollity, the dead man would have been the first to approve, for it was as a mark of deep affection and respect that Oliver Herford's friends were sitting there together, mourning him in their hearts, but, recalling, reciting, and laughing over some of his inimitable epigrams, ripostes, and *jeux d'esprit*.

They must all have recalled his appearance, which, in itself, suggested fantasy: short, slight, and predominantly grey—an ill-fitting grey suit, and fluffy, profuse, and disordered grey hair. ("For Heaven's sake," his wife used to say, "stop looking like a penwiper!") Along with that grey suit, there were always black shoes, a black tie, a monocle attached to a black ribbon, spats, and, sometimes, a black silk hat of an archaic design. A cigar burned eternally between his fingers, the ashes, in time, burying him—in the manner of the old Pompeians—from view. His reticence was marked, his voice low and musical, his eyes a childish blue. Think of an embarrassed field-mouse, and Oliver Herford will rise from the shadowy mists, and stand before you.

His position as a writer and illustrator—1895–1935—was, probably, a minor one. Though known in New York, and Boston, he attained little general renown. His works—forty of them in all—were too slight to achieve a wide sale, though he regularly published his poems, squibs, and drawings in *Life, Harper's Weekly, The Century,* and *Vanity Fair*.

Fortunately, his needs were simple, as his income was meagre and irregular. Indeed, there never was a time when he would not have welcomed a few extra dollars.

His tailor once wrote him a letter expressing pained surprise that he had, for so long a time, paid no attention to his bill. "How, possibly," Oliver had written back, "can you say anything so monstrous? As a matter of record, I have shown it *every* attention; I took it on a delightful week-end to the Berkshires; also to a luncheon at Mrs. Charles Dana Gibson's (Lady Astor's sister); to a tea given by William Dean Howells (Mark Twain was a fellow guest) at his charming flat overlooking Central Park; and was, in fact, on the verge of taking it to Newport, for the yacht races, when your letter arrived."

On another occasion, he bought a female bear cub, which he nursed and tended as a mother might. But, after many tragedies—the destruc-
190

tion of property, and the loss of friends—he turned the animal over to the Zoo. Asked as to his original motive in acquiring the beast, he said: "Well, a few months ago, I came into a small inheritance, and was so afraid I'd spend the money foolishly—that I bought Brunhild."

For thirty-five years much of his time was spent at The Players, and many of the anecdotes concerning him had their happy origins in that delightful Club.

One morning Herford arrived at the Club wearing an exaggerated, not to say impossible, hat. Derided for it, he explained that the choice had not been his. "It was a whim of my wife's," he said. "Disregard all that, and throw the hat away," his friends said. "You don't know her," he said, "she has a whim of iron."

Two anecdotes concerned Edward Simmons, the painter, who had long fatigued his fellow members by prolix and, often, pointless monologues. Finally, Herford, believing that the time for action had arrived, hand-lettered a sign, which he fastened over the door of the sitting-room. The sign read, laconically: "EXIT, IN CASE OF SIMMONS."

On another occasion, the same unfortunate Simmons had been insulted by a tipsy fellow member who had offered him fifty dollars if he would resign from the Club. Simmons immediately imparted his grievance to Herford and repeated the insult, *con brio*. "Don't take it," said Oliver, "you're bound to get better offers."

Robert Reid, the painter (six-feet-three and a little mellow with wine), seeing Herford at a writing-desk in the Club, slapped him, with exaggerated gusto, on the back. Oliver, trembling, fixed him with his sad blue eyes and said: "Your face and your name have escaped me, but your manners are most familiar."

Once, coming into The Players, and seeing the name of George Barr McCutcheon posted on the Club's "death board," Oliver adjusted his monocle, read the name reverently, and murmured: "Always the wrong man."

At a Ladies' Day, at the Club, Otis Skinner was showing a group of visitors a collection of death masks made by Laurence Hutton. A lady, pointing to a mask of Richard Brinsley Sheridan, observed: "I had no idea he was so frail a man." "Well," explained Oliver, "when *that* was taken, Sheridan was really not himself."

For one English writer—Arnold Bennett—he nourished a strong dislike. "Tell me, Oliver, on your honour," Francis Wilson—an inveterate reader and book collector, and an actor of great renown—once asked him, point-blank, "have you ever read a single book by Arnold Bennett?"

"I'll be very frank with you," he said. "When Bennett published his first novel—*Buried Alive*—I reviewed it for *The New York Times;* and that review so prejudiced me against the man that I never read another word he wrote."

In 1910, having published several little books with the Century Company, on a ten per cent. royalty basis, he asked me (since I was an Editor there) to plead with Frank H. Scott, the President of the Company, for a more generous arrangement of royalties. We went into the den, to beard the lion.

"No," said Mr. Scott, tapping out a tune on his teeth with a thin, blue pencil. "No, I can't very well do that, Mr. Herford, for there really isn't the money in book publishing that people commonly suppose. To begin with, there is the forty per cent. discount to the wholesalers; then there is the ten per cent. to the author; the twenty-eight per cent. for paper, printing, and binding; ten per cent. for advertising and selling; ten per cent. for overhead and depreciation; five per cent. for . . ."

"Stop, stop," said Oliver. "I can only felicitate myself that I never invested my hard-earned savings in your unfortunate enterprise."

On visiting Dr. Coakley—the nose and throat specialist—he observed a dozen or so sinus patients sitting in an anteroom recovering from their treatments. Pointing to them, he said: "They came to cough, but remained to spray."

He was the least punctual of men, his tardiness—on occasions—being exasperating. (He said he was not made for clocks, clothes, conventions, or cold weather.) Arthur Bartlett Maurice, annoyed with him for having arrived twenty minutes late for dinner, wrote two lines on a dinner-card and passed them along, down the table: "The man who's twenty minutes late, to dinner, is a reprobate." Oliver turned the card and wrote on the back, without hesistancy: "A man who comes ahead of time is capable of any crime."

Once, when breakfasting with friends in the country and seeing a comb of honey on their breakfast table, he remarked: "How wonderful, to keep a bee!"

During a somewhat heated Biblical discussion, he said: "Jehovah has always seemed to me the most fascinating character in all fiction." . . . Of house guests: "Many are called, but few get up." . . . A little maxim in morality: "Only the young die good."

To a lady who had thanked him for picking up her handkerchief: "Nothing too small for personal attention—remember the flea." . . . A random thought about the ladies: "Women's minds are cleaner than men's; they change them more often." . . . When discussing the Ver-

sailles Treaty, he spoke of it as: "The peace that passeth all understanding."

Mrs. James Brown Potter (Cora Urquhart—the mother of Mrs. James
Stillman) had left her husband—the nephew of Bishop Henry C. Potter—in order to go on the stage with Kyrle Bellew. Oliver comforted the
Bishop by remarking that "Actresses *will* happen in the best-regulated
families."

E. V. Lucas, the English writer, had said, in a literary essay, that Herford was a veritable elf. "From that day to this," Oliver used to say,
"I've felt painfully elf-conscious."

In 1894—a year after the Hotel Waldorf had been built and opened,
by William Waldorf Astor—Herford described the hotel as "An institution designed to supply exclusiveness to the masses."

A landlady of his was once bemoaning the death of her greatly loved
cat. "It must," she said, sobbingly, "have eaten the paste on my new
wallpaper."

Herford, looking with considerable disapproval at the paper: "Probably not the paste, but the pattern," he explained.

Maxfield Parrish had created a poster for *St. Nicholas,* in which a
plump boy was blowing soap-bubbles, in a magical garden—against an
azure sky. Oliver, as he was gazing at the slightly epicene figure, remarked, with feeling, "How beautiful! A youth blossoming into womanhood."

There was, in Herford's humour, no trace of vulgarity, no evidence of
the *common* man. (His limericks, however stupefying, were miracles of
style and literary taste.) Indeed, in looking back, I recall but a single
remark of his that seemed a little out of character: a remark about his
grey suits.

Charles Hanson Towne once asked him why he invariably wore a
grey suit. "It saves me a world of trouble," he answered. "When spring
and autumn come around, I merely write to my tailor, send him a small
sample of dandruff, and tell him to match it exactly."

There was also the story of The Farragut Club, which, he contended,
was the most exclusive club in America. He proposed me for membership in it, and I was promptly blackballed. However, I later took solace
in the fact that other of my friends—Reginald Birch, Francis Wilson,
John Drew, even the Rt. Rev. Henry C. Potter, Bishop of New York,
had been similarly humiliated. The final "pay off," in the anecdote, was
that Herford, in his own person, composed the entire membership of the
Club, and was its President, Secretary, House Committee, and office boy
as well. I still treasure a set of formal resolutions (printed up by The

Farragut Club), bewailing my departure for Europe. It was signed by the Club's six officers, the signatures all variants of Oliver's name, finished with: "Ollie, Office Boy."

A few years later, I learned the reason for the Club's name. Herford, during the summer months, often dined at Delmonico's on Twenty-Sixth Street. After his dinner, he would saunter across Fifth Avenue to Madison Square and leisurely smoke a cigar on the little ledge beneath Saint Gaudens' statue of Admiral Farragut.

An unwelcome caller once interrupted a supper party which he was giving at his apartment on Eighteenth Street. "So this is your coterie," the interloper remarked, with interest. "Yes," said Oliver, "and over there is my vestry, and, just under it, are my pantries."

Many of his little books he both wrote and illustrated. In one of them, the dedication ran as follows: "To the Illustrator, in grateful acknowledgment of his admirable condescension in rendering his exquisitely distinguished art to the embellishment of these poor verses.—The Author."

I went with him, once, to a clothing store where an impressive floor-walker approached us, smiling benignly. "Coatings, suitings, or trouserings?" we were asked with the proper, and invariable, unction. "No," said Oliver, apologetically. "Only some paltry collarings and cuffings."

In animals of every kind he was inordinately interested—kittens in particular. He had also a high respect for crabs. "The crab," he said, "more than any of God's creatures, has formulated the perfect philosophy of life. Whenever he is confronted by a great moral crisis in life, he first makes up his mind what is right, and then goes sideways as fast as he can."

I remember that, once, forty years ago, I was dining at old Martin's on University Place, when a Western Union messenger boy arrived with a letter for me. The writer of it had expressed keen regret at not having seen me for two weeks; inquired about my health and that of my mother (the writer said that he liked her greatly), and ended by demanding an introduction to the lady with whom I was dining.

As the letter was unsigned, I scanned, fruitlessly, all the faces in the room. Finally—with his back two feet from mine—I discovered Herford —grey, retiring, modest—the field-mouse, par excellence.

With the exception of Edward Lear, Herford was, perhaps, the best of all limerick writers. Many of his are quotable; some indelicate; a few Rabelaisian. But, whatever their type, they were never mulled over, but emerged, spontaneously, from the mazes of his fecund brain. Booth Tarkington recently reminded me that, once, while sitting at The Players (everybody engaged in quoting limericks), Oliver entered the room unexpectedly. John Drew immediately made a challenging gesture toward Tarkington. "Here, Oliver," he said, "what could you do with *him,* in a limerick ?" Herford paused not at all :

> "There was a young feller called Booth,
> Whose habits, at times, were uncouth;
> Once, he sat a whole day
> Drinking absinthes frappées,
> Then tossed off six quarts of vermouth."

His limericks, however bold, were saved from vulgarity by their literary skill, the aptitude of their metaphors, and the avoidance of scarifying words. I am sorry that the sharp eye of the Editor will prevent my quoting a hundred or two such classics, and that I must, therefore, leave readers in doubt as to the final fate of the young lady of Exeter, so fair that all men craned their necks at her ; or that I may not, since the proof-reading censors are everywhere, explain why it is that "the sexual desires of a camel are odder than anyone thinks, and include, in their fanciful orbit, illicit *amours* with the Sphinx. . . ."

But most of Herford's limericks fell a good deal short of indelicacy. They were, as a rule, on a par with the following threnody:

> "A lady, athletic and handsome,
> Got wedged in her sleeping room transom;
> When she offered much gold,
> For release, she was told
> That the view was worth more than the ransom."

At another time, on learning that *meles mephitica* was the scientific name for skunk, he wrote this tragic verse :

> "Said a man to a meles mephitica,
> 'I'd give all I own for your pretty fur,'
> Now, he'd barter a throne
> For some eau de Cologne,
> And all he can say is 'Gee, Whittaker.' "

At one time, Herford, as a bachelor, was living at the Hotel Grenoble, on Seventh Avenue—where Kipling so long hovered between life and death. Pressed for his bill, he said to the manager : "Really, if your bill is going to get any larger, I shall have to ask you for a larger room."

A friend, who ran a kennel of setters near the Meadow Brook Club, asked him to design a coat-of-arms for his letter-heads. The task was executed without delay; but several years passed before the kennel owner noticed that, across the shield, over a setter, rampant, Oliver had drawn a bend sinister.

As a young illustrator, he once sold a picture of a two-horned rhinoceros (with an appropriate verse) to William F. Clarke, the Editor of *St. Nicholas*. Herford had asked $35 for his double feature. When a check arrived for only $25, he borrowed the drawing from a clerk at the magazine and removed one of the horns from the rhinoceros. "I could not," he said, "in justice to an animal doubly favoured by God, permit him to be thus humiliated."

The details of his marriage are wholly in character. Here they are, as Cissie Loftus gave them to me.

One morning, in May, 1905, Miss Loftus' telephone rang. "How quickly can a man get married?" the voice said. "I mean, married, *right away?* Peggy has said 'yes,' but you know Peggy."

Miss Loftus, commanding him to call back in twenty minutes, rang up her lawyer, who, luckily, knew a Justice of the Peace. When Oliver again telephoned, she told him to bring his bride in an hour and a half.

"Oh, my God! I can't hold her *that* long!"

Peggy was so wobbly during the ceremony that it surprised Miss Loftus not a little that the marriage proved a remarkably happy one until the two died—only five months apart.

His wife was always tolerant of his foibles. She seemed, indeed, not only to condone, but sympathize with them: with his custom, for example, of never opening his Christmas cards until July. "It's so much nicer," he used to say, "when everybody else is complaining of the heat, I am having a bracing time looking at pictures of snow and reindeer and Donner and Blitzen and Santa Claus himself."

There is still another story; the last and most typical of them all.

The Herfords lived, for thirty years, at 142 East Eighteenth Street, which was then, and still is, the oldest apartment-house in New York, having been known as early as the 'Seventies, as "The French Flats," for the reason that the apartments in it had been arranged in the French manner; that is to say, all the rooms on one floor.

On July 5, 1935, as Oliver lay dying, his wife, his sister—Beatrice—Ethel Watts Mumford (Mrs. Grant), and another feminine admirer had assembled in the room, hearing that the end might be near.

Herford opened his eyes, and, looking long at the ladies, beckoned to the doctor—a faint flicker in his eye. The doctor stooped low and put his ear to Oliver's lips.

"To think that I should die—the President of a Woman's Club. . . ."

The effort proved too much for him; he sank back on his pillow, never to speak again.

Will Cuppy

William Jacob Cuppy, born in 1884 in Auburn, Indiana, is a researcher in reverse. He knows more irrelevant facts about unrelated (and mostly uninteresting) objects than any man alive. His thoughts are not only devastating but highly uneducational; assembled from an ever-accumulating pile of 3 x 5 cards on which Cuppy jots them down, they represent the last extremity of How to— books. Cuppy's How to Be a Hermit was followed by How to Tell Your Friends from the Apes. Another book, How to Become Extinct, is succeeded logically by a volume on which Cuppy has been working for years; it is called The Decline and Fall of Everybody, and will probably prove its case.

As a naturalist Cuppy is somewhat unorthodox. He maintains, for example, that the Dodo became extinct because that was all it was good for. Furthermore, he insists, we can learn nothing from the fate of this peculiar bird. It is an idée fixe with Cuppy that nobody ever learns anything from anybody. But, he adds—or his publishers add for him —his volumes have a practical side for everybody. "If the reader wishes to become extinct and is willing to take the trouble, he has merely to read about the Dinosaur and the Pterodactyl, and act accordingly." The reader should be warned, however, that paying close attention will not benefit him in the slightest.

The Goldfish

Goldfish come of a very old family, but it seems to do them no good. They have no place to go.[1] Goldfish were invented by the Early Chinese, who had little to do.[2] They have been cultivated so long that they are now useless. Goldfish have most uninteresting habits. Several times each year the males drive the females around the aquarium to teach them a lesson.[3] Queen Victoria had a Goldfish.[4] The Common or Ten Cent Goldfish has xanthochromism and cares less. He is the only kind known to some people. These people are just as well off. The Fantail is more expensive because his tail is bifid or trifid. The male Fringetail is a matter of taste. He has long floating draperies and is often petulant.[5] When enraged, he flounces about, but nobody cares.[6] He is also subject to twitters.[7] He cannot help it, because he was always like that. The Japanese Lionhead or Buffalohead or Shishigashira looks very strange and probably is. Do not worry about your Goldfish. The chances are eighty-two to eighty-one that whatever you do for them will be wrong.[8]

---

[1] The Olivaceous Goldfish of the Potomac River has succeeded in escaping from ornamental fountains in Washington. The Bar-tailed Flathead, the Large-mouthed Bass and the Common Perch do not try to escape.

[2] Much the same thing may be said of printing, which broke out in the province of Kansu in 868 A.D. The Early Chinese simply could not let well enough alone.

[3] These races provide the only clue to the sex of your Goldfish, the females invariably being the ones in front. In a small bowl, however, it is difficult to tell which one is in front.

[4] This statement is offered without documentation. It is based upon the self-evident truth that if Queen Victoria did *not* have a Goldfish, then history has no meaning and might as well stop.

[5] Goldfish quickly take on the attributes of their owners. Show me a peevish, ill-natured Goldfish and I'll show you the usual family.

[6] He particularly hates being bumped into by Tadpoles. If looks could kill there would be some dead Tadpoles in most aquaria.

[7] Cutting down on his flake food sometimes brings him to reason. If not, better trade him for something else—almost anything else.

[8] Goldfish are fond of nibbling at a bit of Anacharis, also called Waterweed or Ditchmoss or Babington's Curse. Mr. Babington had a really frightful time with it. There are nine kinds of Ludwigia in the United States. You don't need all of them.

The Pterodactyl

Life was very difficult for the average reptile in the Mesozoic Era, what
with the Dinosaurs and the humidity, so some of them took to the air
to get away from it all. The Pterodactyls grew leathery wings attached
to their outer digits and hind legs, which enabled them to fly in a clumsy
sort of way.[1] They tumbled through the air more or less as Bats do today,
and they were never quite sure where they were going to light.[2] They
were even worse off on land, as they were constantly tripping over their
wings, involved as these were with the wrong parts of their body. The

Rhamphorhynchus, an early Pterodactyl, had pointed jaws full of teeth,
a long tail with a membranous tip, and a somewhat half-witted expression. The Rhamphorhynchus could never have become popular, if only
because of his name. Lots of people wouldn't get it. The Pteranodon, a

---

[1] In those days animals thought nothing of growing a new limb or organ to
adapt themselves to conditions. We seem to have lost the knack.

[2] Some scientists say the Pterodactyls merely glided and never attained true
flight. As a matter of fact, they flew.

much larger Pterodactyl, lived in Kansas in the Cretaceous Period. He had no teeth and no tail and may be regarded as an improvement.[1] He also had a birdlike beak and a bony crest almost two feet long on the back of his skull which gave him a rather topheavy look. We do not know exactly what this thing was for, but the Pteranodon probably knew. It was clever of the Pterodactyls to think of flying, but that's all you can say for them. They were doomed from the start because they had no feathers and no wishbone, or furcula, as flying vertebrates should have. Pretty soon the Archaeopteryx, a genuine bird, came along, and the Pterodactyls faded away. They didn't belong in the picture and public opinion was against them.[2] The Archaeopteryx was not much of a bird, but at least it had feathers. As for the Pterodactyls, the best thing to do is just to forget them.[3]

The Plesiosaur

There were no real Sea Serpents in the Mesozoic Era, but the Plesiosaurs were the next thing to it. The Plesiosaurs were reptiles who had gone back to the water because it seemed like a good idea at the time. As they knew little or nothing about swimming, they rowed themselves around in the water with their four paddles, instead of using their tails for propulsion like the brighter marine animals.[4] This made them too slow to catch fish, so they kept adding vertebrae to their necks until their necks were longer than all the rest of their body. Then they would dart their heads at the fish from a distance of twenty-five or thirty feet.[5] Thus the Plesiosaurs resembled the modern Sea Serpent above the water-line, though they were almost a total loss farther down. They might have had a useful career as Sea Serpents, but they were before their time. There was nobody to scare except fish, and that was hardly worth while. Their heart was not in the work. As they were made so poorly, Plesiosaurs had

---

[1] If you call the lack of one's teeth and tail an improvement.

[2] If you're booked for extinction, there's nothing much you can do about it.

[3] Bats are going to flop, too, and everybody knows it except the Bats themselves. Well, that's always the way.

[4] Such as the Ichthyosaurs, who used their paddles for balancing and steering. The Plesiosaurs did everything wrong.

[5] They got the fish, but it would have been much simpler to learn the Australian crawl.

ery little fun. They had to go ashore to lay their eggs and that sort of
hing.[1] They also tried to get along with gizzards instead of stomachs,
wallowing pebbles after each meal to grind their food. At least, pebbles
have been found near fossil Plesiosaurs, and to a scientist that means the
Plesiosaur had a gizzard.[2] During the Cretaceous Period many of the
nland seas dried up, leaving the Plesiosaurs stranded without any fish.[3]
Just about that time Mother Nature scrapped the whole Age of Reptiles
and called for a new deal. And you see what she got.

---

[1] The Ichthyosaurs stayed right in the water and gave birth to living young. It
can be done if you know how.

[2] This is Gimmick's Law.

[3] Here we see the working of another Law of Nature: No water, no fish.

Clarence Day

Clarence (Shepard) Day immortalized a family that was fairly well established when he inherited it. His grandfather, Benjamin H. Day, was the founder of the New York Sun; his uncle, Ben Day, invented a process for engraving which still bears his name; his father was a governor of the Stock Exchange. Born in New York in 1874, young Day became the partner of his colorful and choleric father, but, at the outbreak of the Spanish-American War, left to join the Navy.

It was at this time that Day contracted the arthritis that made him an invalid the rest of his life. Crippled so badly that he was rarely able to leave his bed, he nevertheless conducted a glove business, attended to his affairs as a stock broker, and wrote and illustrated a series of remarkable books—This Simian World, God and My Father, Life with Father—unique in their combination of satire and sympathy, shrewdness and tenderness. As Day grew older his infirmity increased; after middle age he was scarcely able to move more than a finger. Yet his writing continued serene; there was never a trace of bitterness or self-pity.

The paradox of his career continued to the end: when he died at sixty-one it was not the arthritis that killed him but an attack of pneumonia. His posthumous life began with the dramatized version of Life with Father, a play that has become a fixture in the American theater.

FROM *"Life with Father"*
THE NOBLEST INSTRUMENT

Father had been away, reorganizing some old upstate rail-road. He returned in an executive mood and proceeded to shake up our home. In spite of my failure as a singer, he was still bound to have us taught music. We boys were summoned before him and informed that we must at once learn to play on something. We might not appreciate it now, he said, but we should later on. "You, Clarence, will learn the violin. George, you the piano. Julian—well, Julian is too young yet. But you older boys must have lessons."

I was appalled at this order. At the age of ten it seemed a disaster to lose any more of my freedom. The days were already too short for our games after school; and now here was a chunk to come out of playtime three days every week. A chunk every day, we found afterward, because we had to practice.

George sat at the piano in the parlor, and faithfully learned to pound out his exercises. He had all the luck. He was not an inspired player, but at least he had some ear for music. He also had the advantage of playing on a good robust instrument, which he didn't have to be careful not to drop, and was in no danger of breaking. Furthermore, he did not have to tune it. A piano had some good points.

But I had to go through a blacker and more gruesome experience. It was bad enough to have to come in from the street and the sunlight and go down into our dark little basement where I took my lessons. But that was only the opening chill of the struggle that followed.

The whole thing was uncanny. The violin itself was a queer, fragile, cigar-boxy thing, that had to be handled most gingerly. Nothing sturdy about it. Why, a fellow was liable to crack it putting it into its case. And then my teacher, he was queer too. He had a queer pickled smell.

I dare say he wasn't queer at all really, but he seemed so to me, be-cause he was different from the people I generally met. He was probably worth a dozen of some of them, but I didn't know it. He was one of the violinists in the Philharmonic, and an excellent player; a grave, middle-aged little man—who was obliged to give lessons.

He wore a black, wrinkled frock coat, and a discolored gold watch-chain. He had small, black-rimmed glasses; not tortoise-shell, but thin rims of metal. His violin was dark, rich, and polished, and would do anything for him.

Mine was balky and awkward, brand new, and of a light, common color.

The violin is intended for persons with a passion for music. I wasn't that kind of person. I liked to hear a band play a tune that we could march up and down to, but try as I would, I could seldom whistle such a tune afterward. My teacher didn't know this. He greeted me as a possible genius.

He taught me how to hold the contraption, tucked under my chin. I learned how to move my fingers here and there on its handle or stem. I learned how to draw the bow across the strings, and thus produce sounds. . . .

Does a mother recall the first cry of her baby, I wonder? I still remember the strange cry at birth of that new violin.

My teacher, Herr M., looked as though he had suddenly taken a large glass of vinegar. He sucked in his breath. His lips were drawn back from his teeth, and his eyes tightly shut. Of course, he hadn't expected my notes to be sweet at the start; but still, there was something unearthly about that first cry. He snatched the violin from me, examined it, readjusted its pegs, and comforted it gently, by drawing his own bow across it. It was only a new and not especially fine violin, but the sounds it made for him were more natural—they were classifiable sounds. They were not richly musical, but at least they had been heard before on this earth.

He handed the instrument back to me with careful directions. I tucked it up under my chin again and grasped the end tight. I held my bow exactly as ordered. I looked up at him, waiting.

"Now," he said, nervously.

I slowly raised the bow, drew it downward. . . .

This time there were *two* dreadful cries in our little front basement. One came from my new violin and one from the heart of Herr M.

Herr M. presently came to, and smiled bravely at me, and said if I wanted to rest a moment he would permit it. He seemed to think I might wish to lie down awhile and recover. I didn't feel any need of lying down. All I wanted was to get through the lesson. But Herr M. was shaken. He was by no means ready to let me proceed. He looked around desperately, saw the music book, and said he would now show me that. We sat down side by side on the window-seat, with the book in his lap, while he pointed out the notes to me with his finger, and told me their names.

After 'a bit, when he felt better, he took up his own violin, and instructed me to watch him and note how he handled the strings. And then at last, he nerved himself to let me take my violin up again. "Softly, my child, softly," he begged me, and stood facing the wall. . . .

We got through the afternoon somehow, but it was a ghastly experience. Part of the time he was maddened by the mistakes I kept making, and part of the time he was plain wretched. He covered his eyes. He seemed ill. He looked often at his watch, even shook it as though it had stopped; but he stayed the full hour.

That was Wednesday. What struggles he had with himself before Friday, when my second lesson was due, I can only dimly imagine, and of course I never even gave them a thought at the time. He came back to recommence teaching me, but he had changed—he had hardened. Instead of being cross, he was stern; and instead of sad, bitter. He wasn't unkind to me, but we were no longer companions. He talked to himself, under his breath; and sometimes he took bits of paper, and did little sums on them, gloomily, and then tore them up.

During my third lesson I saw the tears come to his eyes. He went up to Father and said he was sorry but he honestly felt sure I'd never be able to play.

Father didn't like this at all. He said he felt sure I would. He dismissed Herr M. briefly—the poor man came stumbling back down in two minutes. In that short space of time he had gallantly gone upstairs in a glow, resolved upon sacrificing his earnings for the sake of telling the truth. He returned with his earnings still running, but with the look of a lost soul about him, as though he felt that his nerves and his sanity were doomed to destruction. He was low in his mind, and he talked to himself more than ever. Sometimes he spoke harshly of America, sometimes of fate.

But he no longer struggled. He accepted this thing as his destiny. He regarded me as an unfortunate something, outside the human species, whom he must simply try to labor with as well as he could. It was a grotesque, indeed a hellish experience, but he felt he must bear it.

He wasn't the only one—he was at least not alone in his sufferings. Mother, though expecting the worst, had tried to be hopeful about it, but at the end of a week or two I heard her and Margaret talking it over. I was slaughtering a scale in the front basement, when Mother came down and stood outside the door in the kitchen hall and whispered, "Oh, Margaret!"

I watched them. Margaret was baking a cake. She screwed up her face, raised her arms, and brought them down with hands clenched.

"I don't know what we shall do, Margaret."

"The poor little feller," Margaret whispered. "He can't make the thing go."

This made me indignant. They were making me look like a lubber. I wished to feel always that I could make anything go. . . .

I now began to feel a determination to master this thing. History shows us many examples of the misplaced determinations of men—they are one of the darkest aspects of human life, they spread so much needless pain: but I knew little history. And I viewed what little I did know romantically—I should have seen in such episodes their heroism, not their futility. Any role that seemed heroic attracted me, no matter how senseless.

Not that I saw any chance for heroism in our front basement, of course. You had to have a battlefield or something. I saw only that I was appearing ridiculous. But that stung my pride. I hadn't wanted to learn anything whatever about fiddles or music, but since I was in for it, I'd do it, and show them I could. A boy will often put in enormous amounts of his time trying to prove he isn't as ridiculous as he thinks people think him.

Meanwhile Herr M. and I had discovered that I was nearsighted. On account of the violin's being an instrument that sticks out in front of one, I couldn't stand close enough to the music book to see the notes clearly. He didn't at first realize that I often made mistakes from that cause. When he and I finally comprehended that I had this defect, he had a sudden new hope that this might have been the whole trouble, and that when it was corrected I might play like a human being at last.

Neither of us ventured to take up this matter with Father. We knew that it would have been hard to convince him that my eyes were not perfect, I being a son of his and presumably made in his image; and we knew that he immediately would have felt we were trying to make trouble for him, and would have shown an amount of resentment which it was best to avoid. So Herr M. instead lent me his glasses. These did fairly well. They turned the dim grayness of the notes into a queer bright distortion, but the main thing was they did make them brighter, so that I now saw more of them. How well I remember those little glasses. Poor, dingy old things. Herr M. was nervous about lending them to me; he feared that I'd drop them. It would have been safer if they had been spectacles: but no, they were pince-nez; and I had to learn to balance them across my nose as well as I could. I couldn't wear them up near my eyes because my nose was too thin there; I had to put them about halfway down where there was enough flesh to hold them. I also had to tilt my head back, for the music-stand was a little too tall for me. Herr M. sometimes mounted me on a stool, warning me not to step off. Then when I was all set, and when he without his glasses was blind, I would smash my way into the scales again.

All during the long winter months I worked away at this job. I gave no thought, of course, to the family. But they did to me. Our house was heated by a furnace, which had big warm air pipes; these ran up through the walls with wide outlets into each room, and sound traveled easily and ringingly through their roomy, tin passages. My violin could be heard in every part of the house. No one could settle down to anything while I was practicing. If visitors came they soon left. Mother couldn't even sing to the baby. She would wait, watching the clock, until my long hour of scale-work was over, and then come downstairs and shriek at me that my time was up. She would find me sawing away with my forehead wet, and my hair wet and stringy, and even my clothes slowly getting damp from my exertions. She would feel my collar, which was done for, and say I must change it. "Oh, Mother! Please!"—for I was in a hurry now to run out and play. But she wasn't being fussy about my collar, I can see, looking back; she was using it merely as a barometer or gauge of my pores. She thought I had better dry myself before going out in the snow.

It was a hard winter for Mother. I believe she also had fears for the baby. She sometimes pleaded with Father; but no one could ever tell Father anything. He continued to stand like a rock against stopping my lessons.

Schopenhauer, in his rules for debating, shows how to win a weak case by insidiously transferring an argument from its right field, and discussing it instead from some irrelevant but impregnable angle. Father knew nothing of Schopenhauer, and was never insidious, but, nevertheless, he had certain natural gifts for debate. In the first place his voice was powerful and stormy, and he let it out at full strength, and kept on letting it out with a vigor that stunned his opponents. As a second gift, he was convinced at all times that his opponents were wrong. Hence, even if they did win a point or two, it did them no good, for he dragged the issue to some other ground then, where he and Truth could prevail. When Mother said it surely was plain enough that I had no ear, what was his reply? Why, he said that the violin was the noblest instrument invented by man. Having silenced her with this solid premise he declared that it followed that any boy was lucky to be given the privilege of learning to play it. No boy should expect to learn it immediately. It required persistence. Everything, he had found, required persistence. The motto was, Never give up.

All his life, he declared, he had persevered in spite of discouragement, and he meant to keep on persevering, and he meant me to, too. He said that none of us realized what he had had to go through. If he had been the kind that gave up at the very first obstacle, where would he have been now—where would any of the family have been? The answer was, apparently, that we'd either have been in a very bad way, poking round for crusts in the gutter, or else nonexistent. We might have never even been born if Father had not persevered.

Placed beside this record of Father's vast trials overcome, the little difficulty of my learning to play the violin seemed a trifle. I faithfully spurred myself on again, to work at the puzzle. Even my teacher seemed impressed with these views on persistence. Though older than Father, he had certainly not made as much money, and he bowed to the experience of a practical man who was a success. If he, Herr M., had been a success he would not have had to teach boys; and sitting in this black pit in which his need of money had placed him, he saw more than ever that he must learn the ways of this world. He listened with all his heart, as to a god, when Father shook his forefinger, and told him how to climb to the heights where financial rewards were achieved. The idea he got was that perseverance was sure to lead to great wealth.

Consequently our front basement continued to be the home of lost causes.

Of course, I kept begging Herr M. to let me learn just one tune. Even though I seldom could whistle them, still I liked tunes; and I knew that, in my hours of practicing, a tune would be a comfort. That is, for myself. Here again I never gave a thought to the effect upon others.

Herr M., after many misgivings, to which I respectfully listened—though they were not spoken to me, they were muttered to himself, pessimistically—hunted through a worn old book of selections, and after much doubtful fumbling chose as simple a thing as he could find for me—for me and the neighbors.

It was spring now, and windows were open. That tune became famous.

What would the musician who had tenderly composed this air, years before, have felt if he had foreseen what an end it would have, on Madison Avenue; and how, before death, it would be execrated by that once peaceful neighborhood. I engraved it on their hearts; not in its true form but in my own eerie versions. It was the only tune I knew. Consequently I played and replayed it.

Even horrors when repeated grow old and lose part of their sting. But those I produced were, unluckily, never the same. To be sure, this tune kept its general structure the same, even in my sweating hands. There was always the place where I climbed unsteadily up to its peak, and that difficult spot where it wavered, or staggered, and stuck ; and then a sudden jerk of resumption—I came out strong on that. Every afternoon when I got to that difficult spot, the neighbors dropped whatever they were doing to wait for that jerk, shrinking from the moment, and yet feverishly impatient for it to come.

But what made the tune and their anguish so different each day? I'll explain. The strings of a violin are wound at the end around pegs, and each peg must be screwed in and tightened till the string sounds just right. Herr M. left my violin properly tuned when he went. But suppose a string broke, or that somehow I jarred a peg loose. Its string then became slack and soundless. I had to re-tighten it. Not having an ear, I was highly uncertain about this.

Our neighbors never knew at what degree of tautness I'd put such a string. I didn't myself. I just screwed her up tight enough to make a strong reliable sound. Neither they nor I could tell which string would thus appear in a new role each day, nor foresee the profound transformations this would produce in that tune.

All that spring this unhappy and ill-destined melody floated out through my window, and writhed in the air for one hour daily, in sunshine or storm. All that spring our neighbors and I daily toiled to its peak, and staggered over its hump, so to speak, and fell wailing through space.

Things now began to be said to Mother which drove her to act. She explained to Father that the end had come at last. Absolutely. "This awful nightmare cannot go on," she said.

Father pooh-poohed her.

She cried. She told him what it was doing to her. He said that she was excited, and that her descriptions of the sounds I made were exaggerated and hysterical—must be. She was always too vehement, he shouted. She must learn to be calm.

"But you're downtown, *you* don't have to hear it!"

Father remained wholly skeptical.

She endeavored to shame him. She told him what awful things the neighbors were saying about him, because of the noise I was making, for which he was responsible.

He couldn't be made to look at it that way. If there really were any unpleasantness then I was responsible. He had provided me with a good teacher and a good violin—so he reasoned. In short, he had done his best, and no father could have done more. If I made hideous sounds after all that, the fault must be mine. He said that Mother should be stricter with me, if necessary, and make me try harder.

This was the last straw. I couldn't try harder. When Mother told me his verdict I said nothing, but my body rebelled. Self-discipline had its limits—and I wanted to be out: it was spring. I skimped my hours of practice when I heard the fellows playing outside. I came home late for lessons—even forgot them. Little by little they stopped.

Father was outraged. His final argument, I remember, was that my violin had cost twenty-five dollars; if I didn't learn it the money would be wasted, and he couldn't afford it. But it was put to him that my younger brother, Julian, could learn it instead, later on. Then summer came, anyhow, and we went for three months to the seashore; and in the confusion of this Father was defeated and I was set free.

In the autumn little Julian was led away one afternoon, and imprisoned in the front basement in my place. I don't remember how long they kept him down there, but it was several years. He had an ear, however, and I believe he learned to play fairly well. This would have made a happy ending for Herr M. after all; but it was some other teacher, a younger man, who was engaged to teach Julian. Father said Herr M. was a failure.

The Egg

Oh who that ever lived and loved
Can look upon an egg unmoved?
The egg it is the source of all.
'Tis everyone's ancestral hall.
The bravest chief that ever fought,
The lowest thief that e'er was caught,
The harlot's lip, the maiden's leg,
They each and all came from an egg.

The rocks that once by ocean's surge
Beheld the first of eggs emerge—
Obscure, defenseless, small and cold—
They little knew what eggs could hold.
The gifts the reverent Magi gave,
Pandora's box, Aladdin's cave,
Wars, loves, and kingdoms, heaven and hell
All lay within that tiny shell.
Oh, join me, gentlemen, I beg,
In honoring our friend, the egg.

E. M. Delafield

She was christened Edmée Elizabeth Monica De
la Pasture; her father was Count Henry De la
Pasture of Llandogo, Monmouthshire, the De la
Pastures having come to England after the French
Revolution. As an author she wrote more than
thirty books and, using her initials and an English
translation of her French name, signed them
"E. M. Delafield."

A witty traveler and a wise observer, she has
traveled extensively, lectured in America, and recorded her accurate impressions of significant details in a series of diaries, of which The Diary of a
Provincial Lady is the most famous. Among her
recreations she lists "reading other people's books
and criminology." There is probably no connection
between the latter and her duties as Justice of the
Peace in Devon.

The Unselfish Hostess

"Do take that chair, dear—it's the only really comfortable one in the room."

"But what about you?"

"Oh, I'm quite all right—really I am. You see, I'm *used* to it. I'm just going to get you a cushion."

"Please don't bother."

"It's no bother at all. Wait a minute—there's a nicer one in the next room—I'll just get it—"

"No, no—please—"

"Yes, really—I like it. I *love* running about and waiting on people—I'm quite funny, like that. There! That's better."

"Thank you so much. Now, do tell me all your news."

"No, no, I want to hear yours. But you'd like a fire-screen—"

"No, thanks."

"Sure? It's no trouble. I can move that big one in from the dining-room in a minute. It isn't nearly as heavy as it looks."

"Honestly, I don't want a screen."

"Just exactly as you like, dear. It's so nice to have you here at last. Tell me, do you still like peppermints? I remember you always used to like my home-made peppermint creams."

"Of course I do! How kind of you to—"

"I said, 'Never mind whether I've got time or not, I *must* make some of my peppermint creams for Elizabeth.' I'm afraid I didn't get to bed till long after twelve last night."

"Oh dear—what a shame."

"No, no. I was up at seven just the same—or a little bit earlier, really, because I was *determined* to have plenty of spare time while you were here. It just meant a little reorganising, that was all."

"I know how busy you must be."

"I suppose I am, really. There always seems to be *something* to do for *somebody*. But then, as I always say, 'What are we here for, except to help one another?'"

"I'm sure you do a great deal."

"Ah well, I'm afraid I'm one of those silly people who *like* working for others. Now look here, I'm just going to pop into the next room and bring you that screen. Yes, really . . ."

"Please . . ."

"It's all right, it's quite all right. . . ."

212

"Let me . . ."

"I can manage. Yes, really, I can do it better by myself, I know just how to . . . was that your foot, dear? I'm so dreadfully sorry. . . . I hope it didn't hurt you. There! Isn't that better, keeping the fire off your face?"

"Well, thank you—"

"Now, tell me all about yourself. Or wait one second—I'm just going to give you that footstool. It's one I always use myself, it makes all the difference."

"Please, please keep it."

"No, no—I'd rather you had it. I know how miserably uncomfortable one can be without it. Now, I want you to tell me just what you'd like to do tomorrow. I've kept the day entirely free."

"How very kind of you. But what about your own plans?"

"No, dear, don't give them a thought. I said only this morning: 'Now whatever happens, I'm going to sacrifice *everything* while Elizabeth's here, I can make up for lost time *somehow,* afterwards.' "

"I'd so much rather you didn't bother about me. I can be quite happy with a book."

"My dear, what an idea! I shouldn't dream of it. Now do, do be perfectly honest. Isn't there somewhere you'd like to go, or someone you'd like to see, while you're in the neighbourhood?"

"I should very much like to have a look at Stonehenge, if that's at all possible. It isn't very far away, is it?"

"*Quite* near. Of course you shall. Now, let me see how we can possibly manage it. I could put off seeing the District Nurse in the morning, and try and get through my letters by eleven, and if we had lunch half an hour later than—no, no, that won't do. It's Cook's afternoon out. Still, I daresay I could—"

"No, no, please don't think of it. Really, I don't care—it isn't at all important."

"But, dear, of *course* it is! I know it can be done somehow, if I think it out. It's only just that the car— But perhaps I could hire the village car."

"No, no, no!"

"Or I daresay we could manage it in the afternoon. I'm not really supposed to be out late at this time of year, because of my wretched throat —but I daresay it wouldn't hurt me for once. I could risk it."

"I shouldn't dream of letting you, I don't really want to see Stonehenge at all—I can't think what made me say I did—I should *hate* it."

"That screen isn't really shielding you—I'll just move it. It doesn't matter about me— I never mind getting my face scorched. So long as *you're* all right. Now, we simply *must* find out how to get you to Stonehenge, if that's what you've set your heart on."

"I haven't—really and truly."

"Yes, dear, you have—and I'm determined to get you there, by hook or by crook, even if it means sacrificing an entire day. I'd half thought we might go and—but it doesn't matter."

"Oh, what?"

"Nothing, dear, nothing at all. Just a little scheme of my own. Don't give it a thought."

"But I'd so much rather you told me."

"No, no—it doesn't matter. I can probably manage it some other way —and if I can't, what does it matter? I want *you* to enjoy yourself. That's what you're here for."

Finley Peter Dunne

His name was Finley Peter Dunne, but most people called him "Mr. Dooley." He disliked it, for it was a proof that the fictional character had grown larger—and livelier—than its creator.

Dunne was in his late twenties when, in 1893, he invented the skeptical Mr. Dooley, who, in a series of Socratic dialogues, argued with his friend, the gullible Hennessy, about industry and art, politics and sports. When Dunne died in 1936 at the peak of his power, critics of every persuasion mourned the loss of a man who, without raising his fists or his voice, delivered so many blows against selfishness and stupidity. T. A. Daly called Dunne "a kind of leprechaun" and Henry Seidel Canby praised the perfection of the "marvelous little satires, with a twist at the end as incomparable as the last line of a sonnet."

Dunne's dialect is tricky and many of his topics are dated. But among such masculine pairs as Robinson Crusoe and his man Friday, Huckleberry Finn and Tom Sawyer, Sherlock Holmes and his faithful if blundering Dr. Watson, readers will remember the shrewd Mr. Dooley and the wide-eyed Hennessy.

Alcohol as Food

"If a man come into this saloon—" Mr. Hennessy was saying.

"This ain't no saloon," Mr. Dooley interrupted. "This is a resthrant."

"A what?" Mr. Hennessy exclaimed.

"A resthrant," said Mr. Dooley. "Ye don't know, Hinnissy, that liquor is food. It is though. Food—an' dhrink. That's what a doctor says in the pa-apers, an' another doctor wants th' gover'mint to sind tubs iv th' stuff down to th' Ph'lipeens. He says 'tis almost issintial that people shud dhrink in thim hot climates. Th' perspiration don't dhry on thim afther a hard pursoot iv Aggynaldoo an' th' capture iv Gin'ral Pantaloons de Garshy; they begin to think iv home an' mother sindin' down th' lawn-sprinkler to be filled with bock, an' they go off somewhere, an' not bein' able to dhry thimsilves with dhrink, they want to die. Th' disease is called nostalgia or home-sickness, or thirst.

" 'What we want to do f'r our sojer boys in th' Ph'lipeens besides killin' thim,' says th' ar-rmy surgeon, 'is make th' place more homelike,' he says. 'Manny iv our heroes hasn't had th' deleeryum thremens since we first planted th' stars an' sthripes,' he says, 'an' th' bay'nits among th' people,' he says. 'I wud be in favor iv havin' th' rigimints get their feet round wanst a week, at laste,' he says. 'Lave us,' he says, 'reform th' reg'lations,' he says, 'an' insthruct our sojers to keep their powdher dhry an' their whistles wet,' he says.

"Th' idee ought to take, Hinnissy, f'r th' other doctor la-ad has discovered that liquor is food. 'A man,' says he, 'can live f'r months on a little booze taken fr'm time to time,' he says. 'They'se a gre-reat dale iv nourishment in it,' he says. An' I believe him, f'r manny's th' man I know that don't think iv eatin' whin he can get a dhrink. I wondher if the time will iver come whin 'ye'll see a man sneakin' out iv th' fam'ly enthrance iv a lunch-room hurridly bitin' a clove! People may get so they'll carry a light dinner iv a pint iv rye down to their wurruk, an' a man'll tell ye he niver takes more thin a bottle iv beer f'r breakfast. Th' cook'll give way to th' bartinder and th' doctor'll ordher people f'r to ate on'y at meals. Ye'll r-read in th' pa-apers that 'Anton Boozinski, while crazed with ham an' eggs, thried to kill his wife an' childher.' On Pathrick's day ye'll see th' Dr. Tanner Anti-Food Fife an' Drum corpse out at th' head iv th' procession instead iv th' Father Macchews, an' they'll be places where a man can be took whin he gets th' monkeys fr'm immodhrate eatin'. Th' sojers'll complain that th' liquor was unfit to dhrink an' they'll be inquiries to find out who sold embammin' flood
216

to th' ar-rmy. Poor people'll have simple meals—p'raps a bucket iv beer an' a little crame de mint, an' ye'll r-read in th' pa-apers about a family found starvin' on th' North side, with nawthin' to sustain life but wan small bottle iv gin, while th' head iv th' family, a man well known to the polis, spinds his wages in a low doggery or bakeshop fuddlin' his brains with custard pie. Th' r-rich'll inthrajoose novelties. P'raps they'll top off a fine dinner with a little hasheesh or proosic acid. Th' time'll come whin ye'll see me in a white cap fryin' a cocktail over a cooksthove, while a nigger hollers to me: 'Dhraw a stack iv Scotch,' an' I holler back: 'On th' fire.' Ye will not."

"That's what I thought," said Mr. Hennessy.

"No," said Mr. Dooley. "Whisky wudden't be so much iv a luxury if 'twas more iv a necessity. I don't believe 'tis a food, though whin me frind Schwartzmeister makes a cocktail all it needs is a few noodles to look like a biled dinner. No, whisky ain't food. I think better iv it thin that. I wudden't insult it be placin' it on th' same low plane as a lobster salad. Father Kelly puts it r-right, and years go by without him lookin' on it even at Hallowe'en. 'Whisky,' says he, 'is called th' divvle, because,' he says, ' 'tis wan iv th' fallen angels,' he says. 'It has its place,' he says, 'but its place is not in a man's head,' says he. 'It ought to be th' reward iv action, not th' cause iv it,' he says. 'It's f'r th' end iv th' day, not th' beginnin',' he says. 'Hot whisky is good f'r a cold heart, an' no whisky's good f'r a hot head,' he says. 'Th' minyit a man relies on it f'r a crutch he loses th' use iv his legs. 'Tis a bad thing to stand on, a good thing to sleep on, a good thing to talk on, a bad thing to think on. If it's in th' head in th' mornin' it ought not to be in th' mouth at night. If it

laughs in ye, dhrink; if it weeps, swear off. It makes some men talk like good women, an' some women talk like bad men. It is a livin' f'r orators an' th' death iv bookkeepers. It doesn't sustain life, but, whin taken hot with wather, a lump iv sugar, a piece iv lemon peel, and just th' dustin' iv a nutmeg-grater, it makes life sustainable.' "

"D'ye think ye-ersilf it sustains life?" asked Mr. Hennessy.

"It has sustained mine f'r many years," said Mr. Dooley.

Mr. Dooley on Expert Testimony

"Anything new?" said Mr. Hennessy, who had been waiting patiently for Mr. Dooley to put down his newspaper.

"I've been r-readin' th' tistimony iv th' Lootgert case," said Mr. Dooley.

"What d'ye think iv it?"

"I think so," said Mr. Dooley.

"Think what?"

"How do I know?" said Mr. Dooley. "How do I know what I think? I'm no combi-nation iv chemist, doctor, osteologist, polisman, an' sausage-maker, that I can give ye an opinion right off th' bat. A man needs to be all iv thim things to detarmine annything about a murdher trile in these days. This shows how intilligent our methods is, as Hogan says. A large German man is charged with puttin' his wife away into a breakfas'-dish, an' he says he didn't do it. Th' on'y question, thin, is, Did or did not Alphonse Lootgert stick Mrs. L. into a vat, an' rayjooce her to a quick lunch? Am I right?"

"Ye ar-re," said Mr. Hennessy.

"That's simple enough. What th' coort ought to've done was to call him up, an' say: 'Lootgert, where's ye'er good woman?' If Lootgert cudden't tell, he ought to be hanged on gin'ral principles; f'r a man must keep his wife around th' house, an' whin she isn't there, it shows he's a poor provider. But, if Lootgert says, 'I don't know where me wife is,' the coort shud say: 'Go out, an' find her. If ye can't projooce her in a week, I'll fix ye.' An' let that be th' end iv it.

"But what do they do? They get Lootgert into coort an' stand him up befure a gang iv young rayporthers an' th' likes iv thim to make pitchers iv him. Thin they summon a jury composed iv poor tired, sleepy expressmen an' tailors an' clerks. Thin they call in a profissor from a colledge. 'Profissor,' says th' lawyer f'r the State, 'I put it to ye if a wooden vat three hundherd an' sixty feet long, twenty-eight feet deep, an' sivinty-five feet wide, an' if three hundherd pounds iv caustic soda boiled, an' if the leg iv a guinea pig, an' ye said yestherdah about bi-carbonate iv soda, an' if it washes up an' washes over, an' th' slimy, slippery stuff, an' if a false tooth or a lock iv hair or a jawbone or a goluf ball across th' cellar eleven feet nine inches—that is, two inches this way an' five gallons that?' 'I agree with ye intirely,' says th' profissor. 'I made lab'ratory experiment in an ir'n basin, with bichloride iv gool, which I will call soup-stock, an' coal tar, which I will call ir'n filings. I mixed th' two over a hot fire, an' left in a cool place to harden. I thin packed it in ice, which I will call glue, an' rock-salt, which I will call fried eggs, an' obtained a dark, queer solution that is a cure f'r freckles, which I will call antimony or doughnuts or annything I blamed please.'

" 'But,' says th' lawyer f'r th' State, 'measurin' th' vat with gas,—an' I lave it to ye whether this is not th' on'y fair test,—an' supposin' that two feet acrost is akel to tin feet sideways, an' supposin' that a thick green an' hard substance, an' I daresay it wud; an' supposin' you may, takin' into account th' measuremints,—twelve be eight,—th' vat bein' wound with twine six inches fr'm th' handle an' a rub iv th' green, thin ar-re not human teeth often found in counthry sausage?' 'In th' winter,' says th' profissor. 'But th' sisymoid bone is sometimes seen in th' fut, sometimes worn as a watch-charm. I took two sisymoid bones, which I will call poker dice, an' shook thim together in a cylinder, which I will call Fido, poored in a can iv milk, which I will call gum arabic, took two pounds iv rough-on-rats, which I rayfuse to call; but th' raysult is th' same.' Question be th' coort: 'Different?' Answer: 'Yis.' Th' coort: 'Th' same.' Be Misther McEwen: 'Whose bones?' Answer: 'Yis.' Be Misther Vincent: 'Will ye go to th' divvle?' Answer: 'It dissolves th' hair.'

"Now what I want to know is where th' jury gets off. What has that collection iv pure-minded pathrites to larn fr'm this here polite discussion, where no wan is so crool as to ask what anny wan else means? Thank th' Lord, whin th' case is all over, the jury'll pitch th' tistimony out iv th' window, an' consider three questions: 'Did Lootgert look as though he'd kill his wife? Did his wife look as though she ought to be kilt? Isn't it time we wint to supper?' An', howiver they answer, they'll be right, an' it'll make little diff'rence wan way or th' other."

THOSE IRISH ULLS

Someone once attempted to define an Irish bull by saying that it was a horse of another color. But that is an example of an Irish bull, rather than a definition. An Irish bull (to make one more futile attempt) is a statement that twists itself into an absurdity, a contradiction in its own terms, an idea which starts out reasonably and ends ridiculously.

"Whenever he speaks he commits an error," would be the commonplace way of referring to a man with a talent for embarrassing himself and his friends; but an Irish bull puts it more neatly: "Every time he opens his mouth he puts his foot in it!"

Here are a few other examples of the sudden turn of speech which transforms a quietly dull statement into a roaring Irish bull:

"You're a nuisance," said the exasperated father to his unruly child. "The next time I take you out I'll leave you home."

Why do Irishmen seem to enjoy a brawl? According to his own countrymen, "an Irishman is never at peace except when he's fighting."

"Mary," wrote McCaffrey, "this is the third time I've written to you asking you to be my wife. If you won't do it, then return this letter unopened."

"Your money or your life!" cried the holdup man, producing a pistol. "Take my life then," said Brannigan, "for I'm saving my money for my old age."

"Brady," said Flynn to his friend who had fallen into a pit, "Brady, are you killed? Answer me. If you're killed, say so!"

"No, Flynn," replied Brady. "I'm not killed. But I can't answer you. I've been knocked speechless."

"No Irishman will ever let himself be buried in any but an Irish cemetery. He'd rather die first."

"Tell me, Denny," said Barney as he put down the last glass and rose uncertainly to his feet, "do you know where I left my coat?"

"Sure, Barney," said his friend, "you've got it on."

"Thanks for telling me. And it's a good thing you noticed it, or I'd have gone home without it."

"That was a terrible thunder and lightning storm last night," said Mrs. Magee to her husband.

"It was, was it?" replied Magee. "Then why didn't you wake me up? You know I can't sleep when it thunders!"

"Abstinence," said Dennis, "is a good thing. But it should always be practiced in moderation."

For final authority we turn to Webster's Unabridged. Webster calls an Irish bull "a grotesque blunder in language," and gives us this almost perfect example: "He remarked in all seriousness that it was hereditary in his family to have no children."

Eugene Field

He was a reporter in St. Louis, where he was born in 1850, a drama critic in Denver, a columnist in Chicago. He was also a wit (see page 87), a practical joker and a Latin scholar who transported Horace from his Sabine farm to the Windy City of the Midwest. But to most readers he was (and is) childhood's laureate. Like his English counterpart, Robert Louis Stevenson, Field was unashamedly simple and tender, but the humorist was usually on hand to stop the sentiment from running away into sentimentality.

Field was beginning to express a deeper strain when he died prematurely at forty-five.

Seein' Things

I ain't afraid uv snakes or toads, or bugs or worms or mice,
An' things 'at girls are skeered uv I think are awful nice!
I'm pretty brave I guess; an' yet I hate to go to bed,
For, when I'm tucked up warm an' snug an' when my prayers are said,
Mother tells me "Happy Dreams" an' takes away the light,
An' leaves me lyin' all alone an' seein' things at night!

Sometimes they're in the corner, sometimes they're by the door,
Sometimes they're all a-standin' in the middle uv the floor;
Sometimes they are a-sittin' down, sometimes they're walkin' round
So softly and so creepy-like they never make a sound!
Sometimes they are as black as ink, an' other times they're white—
But color ain't no difference when you see things at night!

Once, when I licked a feller 'at had just moved on our street,
An' father sent me up to bed without a bite to eat,
I woke up in the dark an' saw things standin' in a row,
A-lookin at me cross-eyed an' p'intin' at me—so!
Oh, my! I wuz so skeered 'at time I never slep' a mite—
It's almost alluz when I'm bad I see things at night!

Lucky thing I ain't a girl or I'd be skeered to death!
Bein' I'm a boy, I duck my head an' hold my breath.
An' I am, oh so sorry I'm a naughty boy, an' then
I promise to be better an' I say my prayers again!
Gran'ma tells me that's the only way to make it right
When a feller has been wicked an' sees things at night!

An' so when other naughty boys would coax me into sin,
I try to skwush the Tempter's voice 'at urges me within;
An' when they's pie for supper, or cakes 'at's big an' nice,
I want to—but I do not pass my plate f'r them things twice!
No, ruther let Starvation wipe me slowly out o' sight
Than I should keep a-livin' on an' seein' things at night!

Charles G. Finney

Charles Grandison Finney, born in Sedalia, Missouri, December 1, 1905, is distinguished for his brilliant, unpredictable prose and for three personal idiosyncrasies: snake-catching, pistol-shooting, and a refusal to live in New York. After graduating from the University of Missouri, he enlisted in the army, and served three years as a sharpshooter in China.

At twenty-five, Finney returned to America, found himself (and a job) in Tucson, Arizona, became a journalist, and began The Circus of Dr. Lao, which won the American Booksellers' prize for the most original novel of the year. The Circus of Dr. Lao is a phantasmagoria of delicate nuances and nightmare, of irony and ribaldry. It was followed by the partly autobiographical Past the End of the Pavement, a homespun contrast to its predecessor, a nostalgic work which combines sensitive imagination and the broadest possible humor. The chapter which follows is not only a sympathetic study of boyhood, but an outrageous piece of zoology.

The Indomitable Duck

Mrs. Farrier had been by turns amused, amazed, and exasperated by the interests which successively held her sons' attention, but the discoveries at Frogpond gave a new direction to her thoughts. The more she reflected on them the more she decided she was greatly distressed by their frank enthusiasm for the high mysteries of amphibian sex life and reproduction. She felt it was not right for two such small boys to have witnessed so much and to be able to recount it with such accuracy and delight. She doubted if she was bringing them up properly.

So, not knowing quite what else to do, she took the matter up with the Reverend Mr. Jackson, pastor of Grace Episcopal Church. She wound up by saying, "And that's all they talk about any more, Mister Jackson. It's just awful. I don't know what to think. Isn't there something I can do about it?"

Mr. Jackson pulled at his lip. "There is," he said, "nothing essentially wrong in their knowing such things. Of course, it is a pity they are not somewhat older. I believe the best thing to do is to distract their attention from the frogs and center it on something else. Boys never concentrate on things very long. Find something else to interest them, Misses Farrier."

"But bugs and frogs and things for pets are all that does interest them!" wailed Mrs. Farrier.

"Very well! Get them some other pet! Some less . . . uh . . . exotic pet, if that's the word I want. Get them a chicken, Misses Farrier!"

"A chicken?"

"Yes. Certainly. They evidence interest in pets, you say. Very well! Get them a pet that is domesticated—something which will be profitable for them to study and care for. In that way, you mold and shape your sons' natural inclinations. They have this zest for observing animal life. Very well! Put it to use, Misses Farrier."

"Well, I don't know," she said doubtfully. "I just can't picture them somehow, getting very excited about a chicken . . . but I'll try."

She called her boys to her next morning. "If," she said, "you will both promise me faithfully to take good care of them, I will get you some chickens, and you may have them for pets. They're far more interesting than frogs, and, if they lay any eggs, we can have them for breakfast."

No immediate enthusiasm was discernible on her sons' countenances.

In fact, Willie said, "Aw, heck, mamma, chickens are so *dumb*. Ever'-body, pretty near, has got chickens."

"They're not dumb at all," said Mrs. Farrier firmly. She knew if the boys ever started arguing it would mean the end of the chicken project. "You've never had any chickens, so you don't know a single thing about them. As a matter of fact, chickens are very interesting. You can even train them to do little tricks. When I was a girl I had a bantam rooster that would ride around on my shoulder. I know you'll both love chickens after you have them a while."

"Yeh, but, look, mamma, we like wild stuff that we got to catch. Don't we, Tom? Like those frogs at Frogpond."

"Uh huh," said Tom. "Chickens ain't no fun at all. They're dumb. Ever'body's got 'em."

"Nevertheless," said Mrs. Farrier in desperation, "I think it would be good for you to have some chickens. If, after a month or so, you de-cide you don't like them, you can get rid of them. But I'm going to in-sist that you give them a fair trial."

She called the community market where the local farmers sold their wares through a sort of brokerage system. The clerk there, who knew her, told her she could get young live pullets for fifty cents apiece.

"Now, Willie," she said, "here's a dollar and a half. You and Tom go to the market and buy three pullets. The clerk knows you're coming, and he'll see that you get nice ones. He'll put them in a box for you, and you bring them home. You can keep them in the woodshed till you build them a regular coop."

The boys went to market, but went reluctantly. "Doggone," they kept wondering to each other, "whur did mamma ever get the idear we wanted any old fool chickens?"

The market, a hollow square with pens all around, aroused their in-terest slightly. Its acrid poultry smell piqued their nostrils, and the cries of the fowls piqued their ears. They wandered round and round, talking and looking.

Just at the end of their tour of inspection, they saw the muscovy drake. After seeing him that once, they looked at nothing else.

He was a huge snow-white brute of a duck with wattles that were blood red and a thin, cruelly hooked yellow beak. His short tail feathers curled into tight knots; his gnarled webbed feet were broader than the boys' outspread hands. He was arrogant and rude and in a vile temper, and he flew at them whenever they came too close to his bars. They looked at him and fell in love with him, for he was no ordinary barnyard fowl. He was something heraldic, as strange as a wild bird from a wild, far-off island. They looked at him and decided they must have him.

They went straightway to the clerk.

"We're Misses Farrier's kids," Willie told him, "and we come to get that big white duck down there . . . if he ain't too expensive."

"Now, wait a minute," said the clerk. "I thought yer mother said you was to git some chickens. I know cockeyed well she did."

"Naw," said Willie. "Mamma said we could get chickens if we didn't find nothing else that suited us better. But we think now we'll take that duck."

"Well, I think now I'd better phone yer old lady and make sure," said the clerk.

"It won't do no good," said Willie. "She went downtown and won't be back for a long time."

"Well . . . look here: are you kids lying to me?"

"No, sir. If mamma'd seen the duck 'fore she called yuh, she'd a'said for you to sell it to us 'stead of any old fool chickens."

"Well . . . all right. It's not my funeral. Come on and git it. It's two bucks."

Both boys said simultaneously, "Good gosh!"

"Now what's the matter?" demanded the clerk.

"We ain't got that much money."

"How much have you got?"

"Dollar and a half."

"Well, that's just too tough, boys. The duck's two bucks. Old man Renfro brought it in from the farm and put the price on it himself."

The boys were very near to tears. "Wouldn't Mister Renfro sell it just a little cheaper?" Tom finally asked.

"I dunno. Whyn't yuh ask him? There he is over there—the big guy in the straw hat. It's his duck."

They went dubiously to Mr. Renfro.

"Mister Renfro . . ."

"That's me, gentlemen."

"Uh . . . we wanta buy yer duck."

"My duck? Here, now, you ought to break these things to a fellah more gentle-like. Which duck? I've got better'n three hundred."

"We mean the big white one in the coop over there," said Willie timidly.

"Oh! Well, now, that can be arranged real simple-like. Two bucks, an' the bird's yers forever."

"But we ain't got but a dollar and a half," explained Tom.

"No sale," said Mr. Renfro.

"Aw, gosh, couldn't you please just sell him to us a little bit cheaper?"

Mr. Renfro looked at the boys carefully for the first time. They were twitching with nervousness, and their eyes were full of tears.

"Hey, wait a minute!" he protested. "Don't make yerselves sick over it, fer gosh sakes. What do you kids want with a fool duck, anyhow?"

"We want him for a pet," sobbed Tom. "But we ain't got but a dollar and a half."

"Here, here!" said Mr. Renfro. "Take it easy, boy. Take it easy. Who are you kids? What's yer names?"

"We're Misses Farrier's boys," said Willie.

"Do you know 'em?" Mr. Renfro asked the clerk.

"I know their mother," said the clerk. "They're all right, I guess."

"Well, leave 'em have the damn duck, then," said Mr. Renfro. "I never did see kids act such a way before. Lord!"

"You mean we can have it for a dollar and a half?" asked Willie.

"Yep. Take it and get out of here."

"Oh, gee! Thanks! Gosh, that's nice of yuh! C'mon, Tom!"

"Wait! Wait!" said the clerk. "How you going to get him home?"

"Aw, we can carry him," said Willie. "Under our arms."

"Aw, no, you can't," said Mr. Renfro. "That drake's a regular man-killer. Get a gunny sack and pack him home in that. If he starts to act rambunctious, slap him up agin a telephone pole, and that'll tone him down."

The clerk found a burlap bag and attempted to sack up the fowl.

At once a magnificent battle took place. The drake used wings and claws and beak; the clerk fished about feebly with one hand. When the battle was over the drake still huffed and snorted in the coop, the clerk was blown and perspiring, and his hand and forearm were lacerated and scratched.

"That thing sure 'nough is a man-killer," he acknowledged to Mr. Renfro.

Mr. Renfro had watched the battle with a great deal of interest. "I'll git the so-and-so out of there for you," he said determinedly. "You mustn't fool around the way you do. After all, that ain't no weak-kneed chicken in there. That's a real bird. Hold the sack wide open, boys; I aim to git some action."

Mr. Renfro shoved his big brawny arm into the pen, and, after long preliminary maneuvers, got the drake by the neck and choked it down.

"Look out! Yer gonna kill it!" screamed Willie.

"Shut up!" grunted Mr. Renfro. "Who's catching this duck? Git ready with that bag like I tole yuh."

He yanked the drake out in a rumpled mass and thrust it deep into the burlap sack. He twisted a length of baling wire about the sack's mouth, sealing it tight.

"There! That's the way to handle 'em! Now, take the fool thing and git out of here."

Willie picked up the sack at one end and Tom picked up the other. They left the market in jubilation. The drake squawked and thrashed about and made rousing trouble in the sack, but the boys never released their grips till they got him home.

Tom said, "We better get him in the woodshed 'fore we let him out."

Willie said, "Yeh, and we better close the door good, too."

Their mother was on the back porch as they came into the yard. She called to them brightly, "Did you get nice chickens, boys?"

They looked at each other in alarm; they had forgotten her completely.

Willie said in a low voice, "Better go ahead and tell her and get it over with." And in a loud and studiedly casual voice he said, "Mamma, the chickens they had there weren't no good, so we got us a duck instead."

"A duck? Willie, I told you plainly to get chickens!"

"But, mamma, the chickens wasn't any good."

"Now, Willie, why can't you ever do as you're told?"

"Aw, mamma, they ain't really much difference between chickens and ducks, 'cept that ducks are lots better. Gee, we got a swell duck, mamma!"

"Let me see it," said Mrs. Farrier.

"Well, you'll hafta look at him in the woodshed, mamma, for he's kinda wild. It'll be a couple of days 'fore we get him tamed good."

"For heaven's sake, what kind of duck is it?"

"It's a big white one," said Tom.

Mrs. Farrier went with her sons to the woodshed. There, they entered, closed the door carefully, and let their prize out of the sack. The prize appraised his new surroundings and masters with loud, exasperated hisses. He took immediate command of the interior of the woodshed. First, he stalked about haughtily, flapping his wings and nibbling at his back feathers. Then he made a quick rush at Tom and drove him into a corner. He made a similar rush at Mrs. Farrier and drove her to the door. He hissed warningly at Willie, plainly indicating to him to keep his distance.

"Now, what in the world," said Mrs. Farrier in distress, "will you ever be able to do with the horrible thing? He won't ever get tame or gentle. I never saw such ferocity in all my life."

"Aw, mamma," Willie assured her, "if we just let him alone for a while till he sorta gets used to the place, he'll be all right. I think he'll get real tame, mamma."

"Well, you watch him while I get out of here. I might have known something like this would happen. I send you down to get three nice little chickens, and you come back with this atrocious goose, or whatever it is. Really, Willie, I don't know what to think of you sometimes. I'm awfully provoked."

"Yeh, but, heck, mamma, he can't hurt nothing in the shed."

"Well, mind you keep him here, then. You remember that, too, Tom; don't ever let him out of here."

"Aw, we'll take good care of him, mamma. Gee, I guess we ought to feed him. What does he eat, mamma?"

"Raw meat, from the looks of him," said Mrs. Farrier. "But, come on in, and I'll give you some bread crusts. He might like them. He ought to have a pan of water, too."

They fed their great drake and watered him, and, after subsequent experimental feedings, they found he would eat anything and everything in the way of fish, flesh, fowl, fruit, root, or leafy vegetable or insect. He had an overwhelming, outrageous appetite, and his table manners were terrible. He would rush upon the boys when they came bearing him foodstuffs, knock the pan from their hands, batter them away with his thrashing wings, and gobble up ravenously every speck of what they brought him. Then he would strut about and hiss at them, dash his head into his pan of water, throwing drops and rivulets over his back and tail, and, done with that rite, he would march up and face them and make loud, guttural noises in demand of more food.

On the whole, however, the drake's career in the woodshed was harmless and fairly peaceable. It was when the boys prevailed upon their mother to let them take him out for an airing that travail began in the neighborhood.

They said one day, "Heck, mamma, he's getting so tame now that he'll eat out of his pan real gentle-like without first trying to knock it outta your hand like he used to all the time. Why can't we just tie a cord to his leg and take him out so's he can walk around a little? He's probably awful tired of being cooped up in the woodshed all the time."

"No," said Mrs. Farrier. "I still don't trust him."

"But, mamma, there can't possibly nothing happen. We'll tie a good, strong cord to his leg, and we'll watch him real close."

"No."

"Aw, mamma, please!"

"Well . . . but just for a little while."

So they secured a long piece of jute wrapping twine and went to give their drake an airing.

A wild ten-minute free-for-all took place before they overpowered him and hobbled him with the string. Shaken and definitely uncertain, they were nevertheless determined to go through with the project; they opened the door and ushered him out.

The drake strode out scolding and gabbling, turning now and then to hiss violently at them without the faintest trace of conciliation or gratitude in his tone. He proved exceptionally intractable on his leash, and they discovered almost at once that the sole way to make any progress was to follow along behind him wherever he wanted to go and not attempt to guide him themselves.

He toured the back yard haphazardly, muttering discontentedly to himself, and snarling at them whenever the cord impeded his newest whim. He pulled up flowers abandonedly, shaking them about in his beak and spitting them out without eating them. He came upon the washtub half full of water, jumped in with a great delighted splash, and gave himself such a hectic bath that when he was through the boys were as wet as he was from his splashings.

"Maybe we better put him back now," said Tom, who was becoming weary of the strain.

"Yeh, I guess we better," agreed Willie. "He's had a good bath and a lotta exercise."

But there was no agreement at all on the part of the drake. At the first tug on the cord, he went into a frenzy. He tried to snatch himself free of them but succeeded only in ignominiously tripping himself when the cord jerked his foot from under him. That brought his rage to the explosion point. He swooped at Willie and buffeted him with his wing knobs. He gave a lunge at Tom, while Willie yanked desperately at the cord.

Then the cord snapped off at the drake's ankle, and the big white bird was free.

"Golly, he's got loose!" gasped Willie. He jumped for him and made a futile flying tackle.

It was futile because the drake uncovered a brand new accomplishment; at least, it was brand new to the harassed Farriers. He ran a short distance along the ground, spread his wings, flapped mightily, and soared ponderously into the air to light on the roof of the woodshed. There, contemptuously, he looked down at them. Beneath him, all around, were the other back yards of the neighborhood. He surveyed them in triumph. He gave vent to a bugling scream of victory.

"Gosh, how we ever gonna get him back?" despaired Tom.

"I dunno," said Willie. "Maybe we can't."

He was right; they couldn't. The drake looked down at them once more, then catapulted himself from the woodshed roof and went flapping off. They didn't see him again for some time, but they heard plenty about him.

Mrs. Farrier, when her sons tearfully told her of their prize's escape, was sincerely and deeply relieved; she even counseled them not to search for him too hard. "He'll get run over, or a dog will kill him, or something. It really isn't much use looking for him," she said.

Tom and Willie did not, at first, look very much, for they didn't know just where to look. They thought that perhaps the drake had flown off to the wilds somewhere and was living as drakes normally should live—amid ponds and mud banks and water-waving greenery. Only a few days were necessary, however, to demonstrate that actually the fowl had remained in the immediate neighborhood and therein had uncovered new deviltries unsuspected even by his former masters.

The first news they heard about him after his escape was brought by Joseph L. (Tar) Beach, who lived a block down the street from the Farriers'. Tar Beach was a carpenter who sold and installed tarpaper roofs. He was a thin, constantly embittered person; the only pleasure of his life was his chickens: he had a back yard full of fine plymouth rocks which were the feathered apples of his acrimonious eye.

Tar's news about the drake was bad.

He came to the Farrier house the fourth day after the drake had left, and he pounded loudly on the Farrier back door.

"Why, hello, Mister Beach," said Mrs. Farrier. "How are you this morning?"

"Well, I'm a-doing all right, thank ye, but, now, lissen here, Miz Farrier, ain't them kids of your'n got 'em a big ole white duck?"

"Well . . . uh . . . they did have, but it got away a few days ago and we haven't seen it since."

"Uh huh? Yeh. That's what I figgered. That's jest zackly what I figgered. Now, lissen here, Miz Farrier, that there doggone duck got in among my plymouth rocks right early this morning an' he jest raised ole tunket. Yer a lady, Miz Farrier, an' I cain't tell yuh jest what it was he did, but I am a-tellin yuh this: you better keep that critter away from my plymouth rocks er there'll be hell tuh pay."

"Oh, dear!" said Mrs. Farrier. "Did he hurt your chickens?"

"Well, he like tuh kilt three uh the roosters, m'am, but that ain't nothing at all compared with what he done to my hens. Why, I never seen sech a thing in all my life! A doggone duck actin' thataway with hens! That there duck ain't nacheral, Miz Farrier. Why . . . why, it's a devil—that's what it is, a doggone devil."

"I wish," said Mrs. Farrier, "you would have killed it. I wouldn't have objected in the least."

"Kilt it? Why, doggonit, Miz Farrier, what d'yuh figger I tried tuh do? I went after it with a club the first time, but the doggone thing flew up on the barn and scritched at me. So then I went an' got my ole double-bar'l. But I didn't have nothin' but quail loads, an' they didn't faze him a bit. Anyhow, that duck ain't nacheral, an' you better do something about him. He's your'n, ain't he?"

"But what can I do, Mister Beach?"

"I dunno," said Tar Beach. "But you gotta do something. I cain't have that thing a-botherin' my hens no more like he done. I still dunno what's gonna come of it."

"Well . . . I'll try, Mister Beach. And I'm really awfully sorry that it happened."

"Yer sorry? Well, so'm I sorry. I kin sure tell yuh that!" And Tar Beach went broodingly home, unhappy, uncertain, and indignant over what had befallen his flock.

The drake, in addition to his other unpleasant characteristics, was a fearful and perverted lecher. Tar Beach's placid plymouth rocks had

caught the drake's wicked eye that morning, doubtless as he was winging down the alley back of Tar's chicken yard.

He swooped around short and lighted right among them with a loud, lewd gabble. Tar's roosters rushed to the protection of their harem, but there was nothing on earth the mighty muscovy welcomed more than a rough-and-tumble brawl with a choice pullet as the guerdon for the victor. The roosters were already handicapped, for Tar had clipped their spurs to neutralize any fights they might have among themselves; they were virtually helpless against the rage of the drake. He attacked them almost before they showed indication of attacking him; he weighed as much as all three of them together; and his beak and wing knobs did fearful damage.

Once they lay gasping in corners, he turned his attention to the hens. It was while he was vigorously disporting himself among them that Tar came out to see what the excitement was about.

Ordinarily no more profane than the average man, Tar, at the sight of the drake and what he was doing, strained his vocabulary to the point where it was reduced to mere gibberish. He seized a mop handle and made for the white demon. The muscovy saw Tar coming, read his intent, whirled about, and launched himself at Tar's head. Tar's experience with poultry had never encompassed fighting with a horn-mad duck; he retreated without honor. When he reappeared on his back-porch stoop, armed with his fowling piece and yelling imprecations, he could not loose a volley, for the drake had shielded himself with hens. And, when the drake did eventually fly to the barn peak, Tar's ill-aimed broadside was ineffective; the light birdshot bounced off the duck as if they were raindrops.

Mrs. Farrier told her boys a censored version of what Tar had told her and sent them out to look for the muscovy. "The moment I set eyes on that duck I knew he was going to make trouble," she said. "Oh, if you'd only gotten chickens as I told you!"

"Yeh, but the doggone thing musta gone crazy," said Willie. "Shoot, I don't see why a duck should wanta fight chickens. I thought they got along swell."

Tom said, "Maybe he's like a eagle or something. They all-a time attack chickens, don't they, mamma?"

"Yes," said Mrs. Farrier, "but not the way your duck does."

Willie and Tom took broom handles and went off on what was the first of many duck hunts. But they failed to locate the big drake; and the score stood one up for the muscovy and one down for the neighborhood.

Mrs. George Multin, Sr., lived several houses farther down the street from Tar Beach. She was pretty much against pets in general and on principle. ("They are such fearful nuisances, my dear!"), and she restricted her son George, Jr., to one rabbit. It was a big fluffy white rabbit named Lulu; it had pink ears and the gentlest of mien. Mrs. Multin had personally selected the rabbit for her son, and she felt toward it a certain tolerance. In fact, whenever Mrs. Multin thought of Lulu it was with definite amiability. For Lulu didn't bark, as would a dog; Lulu didn't have kittens all the time, as would a cat; Lulu didn't require a lot of care, as would a canary; and Lulu wasn't delicate, as is a goldfish. "Furthermore," Mrs. Multin would say, "Lulu isn't outlandish like those horrible things the Farrier boys are always catching and bringing home. I really enjoy George Junior's having Lulu. It's educational for boys to have pets."

Mrs. Multin, too, was pretty much against the Farrier boys in general and on principle. "I don't see how a nice woman like Helen Farrier could have had such brats, and if I've told George Junior once I've told him a million times that I'll tan the hide off him if I ever catch him playing with them!"

Lulu had a little hutch where she stayed most of the time but sometimes in the cool of the morning George, Jr., would put Lulu in the side yard, which was fenced in, and let her hop around and nibble at grass.

And, so, one day when Lulu had been put in the side yard and was hopping about nibbling at grass, Mrs. Multin went to the window and looked out to see if Lulu were all right before she, Mrs. Multin, went to the grocery store.

She looked out the window, and the pleasant smile on her face switched to an expression of frigid horror. For a great white bird with blood-red wattles clustered about its eyes and beak was chasing Lulu round and round the fenced side yard. It hissed as undoubtedly hisses a demon; its wings were half-spread like a demon's; its predatory beak was open, avid to seize Lulu.

Lulu doubled and redoubled with astonishing agility, but the great white bird was as relentless as death is supposed to be. It never ceased pursuit for a second; finally, it made a quick turn on its awkward webbed feet, got hold of Lulu by one large pink ear and, at the same time, folded her under its immense wing.

Lulu gave a shrill squeak; there followed a scene which gave Mrs. Multin nightmares for a long while afterward. It was atrocious and outrageous and unbelievable. It was fantastic and downright insane. It was incredible that such a thing could happen on a sunny summer morning

in the Multins' fenced side yard. And the most hideous thing about it all was that Lulu seemed to enjoy it. It was as if Lulu were, indeed, another Leda. . . .

"Lulu! Lulu!" screamed Mrs. Multin. "Stop that! Get away from that awful thing! Oh, Lulu . . . how could you . . . oh, dear!"

She felt that she ought to interfere, but she didn't quite know how to go about it. She remained inside and had a case of nerves until George, Jr., came home.

"Go out right away and look at Lulu," she ordered. "It was the most ghastly thing! I'm afraid to step foot out of the house."

"What was it happened, mother?" asked her bewildered son.

"A big white bird attacked Lulu. It was awful, I tell you. Go see if she's all right."

Lulu seemed to be, as far as George, Jr.'s, cursory examination could indicate. "What was it happened to her, mother?" he pressed. "I cain't see nothing wrong."

"Well, I still can't believe it, George Junior. But I looked out the window, and there was a horrible goose or something chasing her about. I thought surely it would . . . uh . . . kill her."

"Was it a big ole white duck?" asked George, Jr

"Oh, heavens, it was far too large for a duck!"

"I betcha," said George, Jr., inspiredly, "it was that doggone duck that Tom and Willie Farrier got at the market last month. They tole me it got away and that ole Tar Beach was raising cain 'cause it liked to killed some of his chickens."

"Lord, I might have known it came from the Farriers!" cried Mrs.

Multin. "I'm going to call that woman up and tell her a few things! The idea of letting something dangerous like that loose in the neighborhood! And you see here, George Junior, if I ever catch you playing with those Farrier boys, I'll . . . I'll tan the hide right offen you!"

She phoned Mrs. Farrier.

"But, Misses Multin," pleaded Mrs. Farrier, "what can I do? The duck escaped last week, and we never have been able to catch him again. I'm terribly sorry, naturally, about Lulu, but this whole duck business has gotten completely out of my control."

"You should never have let your boys get the thing in the first place," was all the comfort Mrs. Multin would give her. "I've a good mind to complain to the police."

That evening Mrs. Farrier went to call on her best friend, rich, old Mrs. Barsdel who lived one block over and two blocks down. She poured out all her woes to Mrs. Barsdel.

Mrs. Barsdel, to Mrs. Farrier's surprise, cackled with unbridled glee. "Why, that's the funniest thing I ever heard tell of!" she exclaimed. "A duck scaring folks so! Haw, haw, haw! Too bad we don't have more of them ducks around here. Might wake people up."

Her unsuppressed enthusiasm for the drake's doings aroused a similar, if not quite as hearty, enthusiasm in Helen Farrier; and Mrs. Farrier went away from her visit to Mrs. Barsdel thinking that perhaps the drake might not be the unadulterated villain she had long considered him.

Mrs. Barsdel herself went to bed that night still cackling intermittently over the muscovy. And, when she arose in the morning, she remembered him again and cackled all over. She ate a large and leisurely breakfast; then, as was her wont, went to her garden to feed her goldfish.

She had the largest and most beautiful goldfish pool in town. It was as big as a wading pool and almost deep enough to swim in. At one end of it there stood a mirrored gazing globe, larger than a man's head. It rested on a slender bronze pillar, and it mirrored the goldfish pool and the entire garden. It was very lovely.

Mrs. Barsdel would have nothing in her pool but Japanese fantails, the pearly colored beauties with huge cloudlike tails, lacy, delicate fins, and scales so minute and transparent that even the intestines within the fish are clearly visible. Her fish were so tame that they would eat from Mrs. Barsdel's fingers, and they always swarmed to the pool top at the first sign of her approach. She loved them very much; she had named each one, and she spent much time talking to them.

So, after a large and leisurely breakfast, Mrs. Barsdel went out in her garden to feed her goldfish. But even as Tar Beach had discovered in his chicken yard and as Mrs. Multin had discovered in her side yard, so also did Mrs. Barsdel discover in her fish pool an intruder.

The muscovy drake rode high on the water with all the aplomb in the world; as methodical as a Chinese fisherman's trained cormorant, he hunted down the goldfish. They could not escape him by seeking refuge in deep water, for he could dive like an otter and his great beak never missed. Mrs. Barsdel was privileged to watch him make his last splendid dive and catch poor Pitty Sing, her final fantail. His craw already bulged with Pitty Sing's fourteen former companions.

The drake rose to the surface with a swirl, Pitty Sing flopping feebly in his beak. He eyed Mrs. Barsdel angrily, threw up his head to swallow Pitty Sing with a gurgling gulp, and hissed at Mrs. Barsdel, treading water and plainly on his guard.

Mrs. Barsdel was a strong-minded woman, not one to be cowed by a duck. She snatched up a convenient garden rake and made for him, intent on slaughter or worse. For some reason, the drake decided against fighting back; instead of returning the attack, he took to the air. He rose from the goldfish pond with the speedy ponderosity of a large amphibian plane, and, as he left it with a grand noisy rush, knocked over the gazing globe with his left wingtip and smashed it to smithereens on the concrete.

Mrs. Barsdel followed in the footsteps of Tar Beach and Mrs.

Multin; she called up Helen Farrier, read the riot act, and emptied out vials of wrath.

"An'," yelled Mrs. Barsdel over the telephone in peroration, "when I seen that damn duck swaller poor Pitty Sing an' then bust my mirror ball, why, I could of jest set down an' bawled!"

Mrs. Farrier did weep. The thing was getting to be too much for her, and she gave way to despair. When her sons came in for lunch, though, she had herself more or less under control and decided to go through the whole matter with them again.

"Willie, this just can't go on any further. You and Tom simply have to catch that awful duck and chop off his head or something. I won't have the neighbors call me up every day and scream at me. I just won't have it!"

"But, mamma, we cain't catch him!" Willie wailed. "We been trying our durndest, too. We seen him the other day over to Thompson's grocery trying to get at some chickens Mister Thompson had in a coop there, but, gosh, he flew off 'fore we could get within fifty feet of him. Gosh, mamma, you really oughtta see him now. He can fly just like a eagle or something!"

"I never want to see the beastly thing again!" snorted Mrs. Farrier. "But if you can't catch your own pet duck, I'm going to get somebody that can."

Said Willie scornfully, "I'd like tuh see anybody catch him if we cain't. Who you gonna get?"

"I'm going to get the police," said Mrs. Farrier determinedly. And she went straight to the telephone. Tom and Willie sat very silent; it was the first time their mother had ever had to have recourse to the police. It must be very serious.

After the chief of police talked to Mrs. Farrier, he hung up the receiver and said to a patrolman, "Well, kin you tie that up?"

"What?"

"It's Miz Farrier. She claims her kids had 'em a pet duck. It got loose a while back, and now it's raising hell all over the neighborhood, and ever'body's scared of the thing. She wants us to go get it."

"Shouldn't be no trick to that," said the patrolman.

"Yeh, but kin you imagine anybody so dumb that they got to call the p'lice department to help 'em catch a damn duck?"

"Well, it takes lots uh people to make the world," philosophized the patrolman.

"Horsecollar," said the chief. But he also said, "I guess you better go on over to her place and catch it fer 'em, anyhow."

"Do I git to keep it if I catch it?" asked the patrolman.

"That's up to Miz Farrier," said the chief.

There was a knocking at the Farrier front door. Willie opened it and found a burly, bluecoated policeman.

"Hello, laddie," said the officer. "You the folks with the duck?"

"We hadda duck," admitted Willie timidly, "but it got away."

"Yer the folks I'm looking for, then," said the policeman. "Whur's yer mother?"

"Gosh, you ain't gonna arrest us, are yuh?"

"Haw, haw, haw! Nope. I just come down to catch yer duck fer yuh. I got a reputation on the force fer being the finest duck-catcher west of the Mississippi River, and I got to keep in practice."

So Willie summoned his mother. She told the policeman to be very careful; the drake was accounted to be uncommonly vicious.

"Oh, I'll handle him, m'am," he assured her. "Don't worry 'bout me a-tall. Whatcha want done with him when I git him?"

"Oh, dear, take him away and do anything you like—except return him here!"

"Kin I have him?"

"You certainly can—with my blessing!"

"Well, thanks, Miz Farrier," said the delighted officer. "We ain't et no duck over to our place fer so long that I'm halfway scared the old lady's fergot how to cook 'em. But mebbe she kin git her hand in again."

And he said to the Farrier sons, "How 'bout you two gennelmen showing me the stomping ground of this here renegade, if yer mamma kin spare yuh fer a few minutes?"

"They'll be glad to help any way they can," said Mrs. Farrier. And the boys said, "Gosh, yes!"

Proud to be guides for a uniformed officer with a big revolver, they led him out through the back yard and down the alley.

"It was over there," said Willie, pointing, "that he like to killed George Junior Multin's rabbit."

"Over on that next block," said Tom, also pointing, "is where he ate all Miz Barsdel's goldfish."

"Down here a little ways," said Willie, "is where he killed a lot of old Tar Beach's chickens."

"That duck certainly gets around," said the policeman.

"I never could figger," mused Willie, "what made him get so mean that way all of a sudden. Why, he was just as gentle when we first got him, wasn't he, Tom?"

"Kinda," said Tom.

They were in the alley at the rear of Tar Beach's place, and, just as they arrived there, a roaring noise and a cloud of smoke came from Tar's chicken yard. It was followed by a fancy assortment of profanity.

"I betcha," said Willie, "that's old Tar shooting at the duck again."

"Well, he better watch hisself firing off firearms within the city limits," said the policeman. "It's strickly agin the law. Come on, boys, I wanta talk to that guy."

He pulled open Tar's wooden gate and strode in, followed by the Farriers. Sure enough, there was Tar with a smoking shotgun in his hands. Two tattered, dead plymouth rocks lay at his feet; other bewildered chickens ran all about. And up on the highest peak of Tar's two-story house, the great white muscovy sat and preened his feathers.

"Look a-here," said the policeman sternly, "it's agin the law to shoot guns in town. You oughtta know that."

"'I God," said Tar Beach, "it ain't agin the law to perteck yer own proputty, is it?"

"What d'yuh mean?" asked the policeman.

Tar pointed at the miscreant on his rooftop. "That's what I mean! That's the third time this week that doggoned duck has got at my fryin' hens. I'm gonna kill that son of a bastard if it's the last mortal thing I ever do. Look at him a-settin' there on my house laughin' at me! 'I God, wait'll I reload! I went an' kilt two uh my own fryers on account of I missed him jest now while he was amongst 'em on the ground, but I aim tuh give him both bar'ls this time an' shoot the guts clean outta him."

"Now, wait a minute," said the policeman. "I jest got through tellin' yuh it was agin the law tuh shoot in town, didn't I?"

"Is it agin the law fer *you* to shoot?" demanded Tar.

"Course not. I'm an officer."

"Aw right!" said Tar. "Here." He handed the policeman his shotgun. "Now you shoot him and ever'thing'll be law-abiding an' jim-dandy."

"Well, I dunno," said the policeman, scratching his head. "I ain't never done nothin' like this before. . . . Still an' all, however, I was sent here with orders to git the duck. I guess mebbe it'll be all right. Gimme a couple uh loads, an' I'll knock him offen there fer yuh. I used tuh be a pretty fair hand at duck-shootin'."

Tar fished around in his pockets; then looked sheepish and irritated. "I ain't got no more loads," he said disgustedly. "That musta been the last I had what I touched off jest now."

"Well, how come yuh missed when he was settin' on the ground?"

"I never missed them there hens," said Tar sadly.

Willie had an idea. "Why don'tcha shoot him with your pistol?" he asked the policeman.

"Well," said the officer doubtfully, "it's sorta long range fer hand-gun shootin'."

"Gimme the gun!" cried Tar. "I don't keer how long the range is."

"Nope," said the patrolman. "If there's any more shootin' done, I'm gonna do it."

He took his revolver from its holster, looked at it speculatively, and then at the drake still preening himself on the roof.

"I ain't had much practice lately on account uh pistol loads costin' so doggoned much," he explained, "but mebbe I kin do it. Stand back, you kids; the muzzle blast is bad."

He sighted long and closely, and fired. The drake still preened.

He took the revolver in both hands, sighted still more closely, and fired. The drake still preened.

He rested the revolver against a tree trunk, and fired. The drake still preened.

He lost his temper and fired the three remaining cartridges as fast as he could pull the trigger. The drake still preened.

The policeman sighed and put away his weapon. "Well," he said, "that's that, I reckon."

"What d'yuh mean 'that's that'?" demanded Tar Beach.

"I ain't got no more loads either," explained the cop.

"Well, what d'yuh aim tuh do?"

"I dunno—'less I go back to the station an' git me a rifle."

"Lordy-Lord! You mean go all the way back on foot?"

"Sure. Whatcha think I came here on—the passenger train?"

" 'I God," said Tar despairingly, "I dunno what it is, but that there duck has got a jinx on me. The thing ain't nacheral. I shoot at him a-settin' in my own chicken yard an' miss him a mile an' kill two uh my own fryin' hens. You shoot at him on the roof an' miss him six times. Now, there ain't neither of us got ary loads left fer more shootin', an' the gol-danged thing sets up there an' laughs at us. No, sir, that duck ain't nacheral."

"Tell yuh what," said the cop. "I hate tuh be beat by a doggone ornery duck, an' I don't aim tuh be. You all stay here an' watch him. I'll hike back to the station quick as I kin an' git me a rifle. I'm a shore cinch tuh hit him with a rifle, even if I cain't with a doggone six-shooter."

"Yeh, but you got ary reason tuh believe he's a-gonna set there an' wait fer yuh to fetch a rifle all the way back here?"

"Well, that's why I want you all tuh watch him. You can sorta foller him if he takes a notion to go somewhere er other. Honest, it's the only thing I kin think of."

"Well, it hain't much of an idear," said Tar scornfully.

Willie broke in, saying excitedly, "Hey, look at the duck now, wouldja?"

They all looked. The drake was standing up on his big flat feet, apparently through for the day with his preening. He looked insolently down at his foes and shook himself. He thrust out first one wing, then the other, stretching them leisurely. Then he flapped both wings violently, as if to make sure they were in good working order.

"Looks like," said Tar, "he's already got his notion to go somewhere er other."

"Well, I cain't think of no way off hand to stop him," said the cop.

The muscovy walked slowly along the roof till he reached its very edge. There, majestically, he launched himself into the air, falling nearly twenty feet before his thrashing pinions took hold. Then he climbed with massive wing-beats above the level of the neighborhood roofs. He circled Tar Beach's back yard twice, rising higher and higher, then headed west and went lumbering out of sight with the grace of a threshing machine.

"Mebbe he's gone fer good," said the cop optimistically.

"Mebbe," said Tar.

"I done the best I could, anyhow," said the cop.

"Well, I sure thank yuh fer yer help," said Tar.

"I 'spect I better be gettin' on back, though," said the cop. "So long, you kids. Tell yer mother I done the best I could."

"Yeh, we will," said the Farriers. They left, too. "Good-by, Mister Beach."

" 'By, boys," said Tar absently. He went over and picked up his two dead frying hens.

Back at the station, the chief asked the patrolman about reports coming in of much shooting in the neighborhood where the patrolman had been sent to catch the duck.

"That must of been me," said the cop. "I fired a time er two."

"Didja git him?" asked the chief.

"Nope, but I sure scared hell out of him."

Three days after the policeman's efforts, Mrs. Farrier was sitting on her front porch, sewing and rocking. A big green farm wagon stopped in the street in front. From it, after he twisted the reins around the brake handle, alighted a large, genial-looking man in overalls. He came to the porch step and took off his hat. "Are you Miz Farrier?" he asked politely.

"Yes."

"Well, I'm Mister Renfro; I live out towards Muddy Creek a ways."

"Yes?"

"Well, some time back, I think it was your two boys who bought a duck offen me at the market."

"Oh, dear! Now what's happened?"

"Why, nothing much. 'Cept this morning I thought I seen that duck I sold your kids back in with my others, and I was wondering if he could of got away from yuh or something. If he did, I'll be more'n glad to return him."

"No! No!" cried Mrs. Farrier. "It's not our duck. There's been a mistake. We don't want any ducks. We don't like ducks."

"Well, but, ma'am, if he's yourn, looks like you'd want him back."

"No!" said Mrs. Farrier. "We don't want him. Please don't bring any ducks around here. Please!"

"Well . . . okay," said Mr. Renfro. "I jest thought I'd ask, on account of being in town today. Mebbe I'm a duck to the good."

He left somewhat bewildered.

Mrs. Farrier fiddled around uncertainly for a while and then decided that the occasion demanded some unusual manifestation in the way of celebrating. She made a hurried trip to town and then busied herself in the kitchen. When Tom and Willie came trooping in, asking about supper, they were startled to the soles of their shoes to see ice cream and cake on the table.

Robert O. Foote

Robert O. Foote confessed that, having progressed from reporter to managing editor before he was thirty, he settled on that traditional journalistic sinecure: sports-writing. But even the best-laid plans of sports-writers go awry, and one day Foote was caught reading a book—apparently so amazing a cultural activity in a sports-writer that he was made literary editor of the Pasadena Star-News.

Foote has had other activities more or less nefarious. He was a political correspondent for newspapers on the Atlantic seaboard, and he once made a decent—or, at least, a soft—living as a pulp-writer. His favorite hobby is browsing among the musty volumes in the Huntington Library, one of California's noblest literary monuments, and it was there he obtained the scholarly background for his examination of "Joe Miller" and his sources.

Who Was Joe Miller?

Humor, say philosophers, is the index of an era's sophistication. Because the present day laughs at broad jokes, it is inclined to fancy itself as tolerant; "modern" is the popular word. The stories we tell in mixed company would only have been whispered by grandfather to his bar-room cronies. Ipso facto, we're pretty darn sophisticated. But are we?

Examine a case example: You see a cartoon—or will shortly when the gag men realize what they have been overlooking—which shows a young man getting out of bed in which still reposes a lovely dame. The caption says "I think I'll get up and rest."

Now, except for the manner of its telling through the aid of a drawing reproduction process unknown to our ancestors, instead of completely by words as was necessary with them, that is the identical joke at which our forbears of two hundred years ago were snickering. Here is its exact wording, No. 164 in the now priceless first edition of *Joe Miller's Jests*:

"A Young Lady who had been Married but a Short Time, seeing her Husband going to Rise pretty early in the Morning, said, 'What, my Dear, are you getting up already? Pray lie a little longer and rest yourself.' 'No, my Dear,' replied the husband, 'I'll get up and rest myself.'"

Even then it was an old joke, like all of Joe Miller's, of whom more anon, as he would say. It is cited here merely as a single demonstration, among hundreds of possible ones, that the love of what the Puritan calls "dirty jokes" is firmly implanted in the Anglo-Saxon. The Jest Books which are treasured possessions of the great libraries were the *Esquires* and *New Yorkers* of the 15th, 16th, 17th centuries, until nasty niceness forced them onto the back shelves for more than one hundred years.

Those ancient tomes afford rewarding research to a man who, like the late Justice Oliver W. Holmes, finds the facts of life and the expression thereof rather amusing. Their study and the tracing of their relationship with the now happily emancipated laughter of the present has been the favorite relaxation of this writer for years.

While there is no record of any joke book having been compiled in English prior to the invention of printing, that innovation was applied to the service of laughter even before it came to the aid of piety. The first complete Bible in our language was that issued by Miles Coverdale in 1535; almost ten years before that, in 1526, there was issued the first jest book, called *C Mery Tayls*.

This *Hundred Merry Tales* (to translate its title into our spelling) is one of the rarest of all books, there are only two known copies. Great

246

Britain possesses one, badly mutilated. The other is a perfect copy that reposes, or at least did before Hitler cut loose, in the Library of the University of Guttingen, which bears this legend on its title page:

"Emprynted at London at the Sign of the Merymayd at Powlys Gate next to Chepesyde. The Year of our Lorde MDXXVI: the XXII day of November."

One fourth of its jokes would be unprintable, even by our relaxed standards. That is a fair approximation of the proportion of overly risqué that persisted in the humorous literature of the following two hundred years. Yet examination of copies of that earliest jest book, which have reached this country, reveals that its conviction that marriage is an essentially comic matter to all but the victims, would easily pass current as keen wit in this day. Here is a specimen:

"A man asked his neighbor which was but late married to a widow how he agreed with his wife, for he said that her first husband and she could never agree. 'By God, quoth the other, we agree marvelous well.' 'I pray thee how so?' 'I shall tell you, quoth the other, when I am merry she is merry and when I am sad she is sad, for when I go out of my doors I am merry to go from her and so is she and when I come in again I am sad and so is she.' "

A fascinating perusal of many old jest books reveals that the early years of each succeeding century seem to have been especially fruitful in laughter. In 1526 came *C Mery Tayls*. In 1633 or thereabouts came John Taylor, the Water Poet, and Archie Armstrong, King Charles I's jester, to lend a terser and slightly cleaner tinge to the humor of the people. In 1739 came Joe Miller, to act as stepfather to all the earlier smiles. By about the middle of the 1800's appear Mark Lemon in England and Artemus Ward in this country, signifying a sad falling off in the soul of wit. In the 1920's there was a speeding up of sophistication in the humor of America and a return to the frankness of four hundred years previously.

Most of these old books are extremely rare and there is a constant search for them. Among the finest collection in America, though not segregated even there, are the handsome specimens of original John Taylors, Archie Armstrongs, Joe Millers and many others among the treasures of the Henry E. Huntington Library in California.

Archie was the most urbane of the early jesters. His stories told in 1633 and 1639 are not only an improvement in expression and point over those of earlier date, they also excel those which were perpetrated a hundred years later in the notorious name of Joe Miller.

There is a modern twist to much of Archie's humor. The popular gag of one favorite cartoonist of today, that of having a husband, or wife, thinking of something else all the time the other is engaged in telling a long-winded yarn, harks back directly to Archie's tale of:

"One making a long and tedious speech to a grave counselor on the conclusion thereof made an apologie to excuse himself for being so troublesome; who gave him answer, I'll assure you, sir, you have not been troublesome to me at all, for all the time you were speaking my mind was of another matter."

There were Farmer's Daughters in humor nearly four hundred years ago. Indeed, it is possible to trace with almost exactitude the time that she stepped into folklore. In that first jest book of 1526 is a story of a bridegroom who was forced to allow his bride to wait at the church, while at the instigation of the irate father of another sweetheart he made a pecuniary settlement upon the previous object of his affections. The point of the tale is that the bride, upon later wheedling the facts out of her new husband, proved herself above small reproaches. She was content to comment that the girl had been foolish to betray the affair to her father. She, the bride, had been carrying on, she said, in like fashion with a man-servant for a year but her husband was now the first person to whom she had ever made it known.

When the tale reappears a century later in *Archie's Jests* of 1639 (and much better told) the deceived sweetheart has become not simply the "mayd" she was in the earlier version, but a "Farmer's Daughter"—her first appearance as a stock character of ribald wit.

It took intense, but extremely captivating research, much burrowing into the treasures of ancient libraries for this inquirer to fix, even within a hundred years, that important date in the history of humor. Many men have gone honored to their graves for lesser achievements.

Once embarked, however, upon such a research project, no true student could let the matter drop. It went on and on, eventually bringing the conviction that the Elizabethans recognized the essentials of lasting humor exactly as we do. To every age its own language; to all the ages the same fundamental risibility.

Their primary conviction was that the fact of there being two sexes was quite a joke upon humanity; exactly the same imperishable joke to be found in the last issue of any smart magazine. Many of the jests of those gusty early Englishmen were sadly naïve. Their practical jokes, their execrable puns, their witty retorts, their puncturing of ostentation, take a decided sharpening up for modern taste, though it is being done daily, in print and on the air. But when they wanted a belly laugh they went to the relationship of the sexes, just as we do.

Whether or not we do it any better is a matter of opinion, taking into consideration the fact that our ancestors could not illustrate their jests. Here is one from which you may draw your own conclusions, Archie first committed it to print:

"A Scholar having married a young wife and being still at his book, preferring his serious study before dalliance with her; as she was one day sitting lonely, whilst he was reading, 'Sir,' saith she, 'I would with myself I had been a book, for then you would be still pouring over me and I would never, night or day, be without your attention.' 'So would I, sweetheart,' answered he, 'so I might choose the book.' To whom she again answered, 'And what book would you wish me to be?' 'Sweetheart,' saith he, 'an almanack for so I might have a new one every year.' "

To trace the development of such tales, which now appear again as the "very latest—stop me if you've heard it before," is a rare delight. Most such yarns, particularly the bawdy ones, have been printed over and over, down the centuries. Occasionally a squawk is raised over joke-stealing. It is not actual theft, the joke always belongs to the last person who tells it, if he can improve upon it, so much the better. That, at least, was the admirable attitude of John Taylor in his *Wit and Mirth* published 313 years ago, when he said in his preface:

"Because I have had many of these tales by relation and hearsay, I am in doubt that some of them may be in print in some other authors, which I do assure you is more than I do know; which if it be so, I pray you to tolerate and let the authors make twice as bold with me at any time."

Since it is not the happy lot of all to be able to pursue from original source such an entrancing research as this, it would seem to be doing a distinct service at this point to offer some of the early versions from which matrimonial favorites have been drawn. So, slightly purified as to language, with the spelling modernized for ease in reading, here is, as the old title pages used to say, "A Choice Banquet of Jests":

The Emperor Augustus, being shown a young Grecian who very much resembled him, asked the Young Man if his Mother had not been at Rome. "No, sir," answered the Grecian, "but my Father has."—*Joe Miller, 1739*.

A young Gentleman playing at Questions and Commands with some very pretty young Ladies, was commanded to take off the Garter from one of them; but she, as soon as he had laid hold of her Petticoats, ran away into the next Room, "Now, Madam," said he, tripping up her heels, "I bar squealing." "Bar the door, you fool," cry'd she.—*Joe Miller, 1739*.

A handsome Wench, for some suspicious business, being brought before a Justice somewhat late in the evening and he taking compassion of her because she was fair and seeming modest, wished the man that brought her before him, to take her home and lodge her that night and he would hear the case more at length in the morning: "With all my heart," saith the man, "Master Justice, so you will commit my wife, which is now at home, to the jail till the morning."—*Archie's Jests, 1639.*

Upon a time Tarlton and His wife, as passengers, came sailing towards London a mighty storm arose and endangered the ship, whereupon the captain charged every man to throw into the seas the heaviest thing he could best spare, to the end to lighten somewhat the ship. Tarlton, that had his wife there, offered to throw her overboard; but the company rescued her and being asked wherefore he meant so to do, he answered "She is the heaviest thing I have and I can best spare her." —*Tarlton's Jests, 1570.*

A Waiting Gentlewoman being summoned into a Court to take an oath, the Examiner asked her how he should write her down: a Maid, a Wife or a Widow? She told him he should write her down a Maid, for she never had any husband. He finding her a pretty handsome smug Wench, asked her how old she was; she told him about the age of six and twenty: saith he (willing to sport with her), "Then take heed what you swear, for you are now upon your oath and therefore may I securely set you down Maid, being of those years?" The Wench made a pause and considered a while with herself: "I pray you, sir," saith she, "stay your hand a little and write me down a Young Woman."—*Archie, 1639.*

A Company of Rustics, having taken a Wolf, consulted on some exquisite torment, which one of them presently thought of: "Let him," saith he, "be married to two wifes as I am and hell itself can add no greater torment."—*Archie, 1633.*

A woman in Scotland lay dying, to whom her husband said, "Wife, now thou art about to leave me alone, I pray thee tell me with whom I shall marry?" She replied, "Art thou in haste to marry before the breath be out of my body, then marry the devil's dam." "Not so, Wife," saith he, "I have his daughter already an I should mate with his mother too, then I should be guilty of incest."—*John Taylor, 1629.*

This sort of stuff demonstrates that humor has changed less in the last four hundred years than in a thousand previous years. Joe Miller, despite the popular assumption of the contrary opinion, was not the first man to collect ancient wheezes. The very first of whom there is record was one Hierocles of the Fifth Century, about whose exact identity scholars still quarrel but about whose list of twenty-one alleged jokes there can be little dispute—they are the foundation of the most ghastly wit in all creation. Suffer through a few of the least intolerable; you probably have heard their revision within the last month on the air:

A scholar wishing to teach his horse to eat little, gave him no food at all; and the horse dying, "How unlucky," said he, "as soon as I had taught him to live without food, he died."

Another meaning to sell a house, carried about a stone of it as a specimen.

A pedant sealed a wine vessel he had, but his man bored the bottom and stole the liquor. He was astonished at the liquor's diminishing, though the seal was entire; and another saying, "Perhaps it is taken out at the bottom," the pedant answered, "Most foolish of men, it is not the under part but the upper part that is deficient."

A man hearing that crows lived two hundred years, bought one, saying, "I wish to make the experiment."

A scholar meeting a person, said to him, "I heard you were dead." To which the other answered, "You see I am alive." The scholar replied, "Perhaps so, but he who told me was a man of much more credit than you."

Hearing that one of two twins was dead, when he met the other, a scholar asked, "Which of you was it that died? You or your brother."

A scholar in Greece receiving a letter from a friend desired him to buy some books there, neglected the business. But the friend arriving some time after, the scholar said, "I am sorry I did not receive your letter about the books."

This latter is one of the standard jokes of the world, in every age and every language. Joe Miller's version of it is hung upon an Irish lawyer who left this note for his servant: "I am gone to the Elephant and Castle where you shall find me and if you can't read this Note, carry it down to the Stationer's and he will read it for you."

Which brings us back to the most famous of all humorists and the least deserving of the title. Almost exactly two hundred years ago an enterprising publisher gave to the English reading world its most universally accepted designation for an old joke—a "Joe Miller."

Too dead to resist, Joe Miller had immortality thrust upon him. He was a fairly popular actor who had died the previous year. Following the custom of the times, his name was hung upon the next London collection of supposedly funny stories, most of which he probably never had heard. The book, *Joe Miller's Jests* became upon its publication in 1739 the first best seller on record and it has had the longest run in history. It is still being reissued, in modern guise. Joe Miller's chestnuts are never so stale but a re-roasting will revive their flavor.

Joe Miller's Grandchildren

It is impossible to decide which are *the* most famous jokes of all time. Every comedian has his own private (or public) stock, a collection which experience has assured him will always rouse the responsive laugh. But Eddie Cantor's edition of the *World's Best Jokes* differs considerably from Powers Moulton's *2,500 Jokes for All Occasions* and Bennett Cerf's not-too-strictly-contemporaneous *Try and Stop Me.* Josh Billings wrote ungrammatically but accurately, "There is very few good judges of humor, and they don't agree."

The antiquity of a joke is nothing against it, as Joe Miller's imitators have proved; nor, on the other hand, is age a guarantee of the power to make people laugh. The oldest joke is said to have originated in the Garden of Eden when Eve asked Adam, "What's wrong about eating this apple?" and Adam answered, "I'll bite."

Edward ("Senator") Ford confesses that he cannot understand why people continue to laugh at mothers-in-law—nobody ever makes jokes about a father-in-law—and suspects that the custom dates back to antediluvian days. Ford imagines that when the caveman started writing with flint and chisel—undoubtedly the first chiseler—someone shouted to him, "Hey! Hurry! A saber-tooth tiger is fighting with your mother-in-law!" "All right, let 'em fight," said the caveman, calmly proceeding with his chiseling. "What do I care what happens to a saber-tooth tiger."

Surprise is the prime feature of the best jokes—the surprise of the unexpected ending, the incongruous retort, the impossible treated as though it were inevitable. Here is an example:

The scene is a livery stable. Enter a man. "Sixteen of us want to rent a cart and horse for the day," he says.

"Sixteen of you! With one horse!" replies the livery stable keeper. "That's impossible!"

"Don't worry," says the customer with a leer, "we've got whips."

Some of the editor's friends think that is one of the funniest stories they've ever heard—absurd, incongruous, but screamingly funny. Others consider it, if they consider it at all, completely without humor. Josh Billings was right; there is little chance of agreement among experts on humor. Or, rather, there are no experts; the only real test is personal taste.

The following, then, may not be the best jokes you have ever heard. But they are favorite "classics" of the editor and, according to an informal poll, his friends. Many of them are, as a classic must be, old as

Joe Miller, possibly older. But, to those who love a familiar face, they are no worse for being happily remembered. Freshness has charm, but there is also an undeniable appeal in familiarity.

"I've contracted this terrible habit," said the patient to the psychiatrist. "Wherever I am, I start talking to myself. In the subway, at my office, even in the bath. Can you do anything for me?"

"I suppose so," replied the psychiatrist. "But I should warn you it will take a long time. The treatment is slow. It's painful. What's more, it's extremely expensive. And, after all, suppose you do talk to yourself. Is that so terrible?"

"No, I suppose not," said the man. "But I'm *such* a bore."

It was in the hills of Kentucky that a traveler saw a farmer holding a pig in his arms so that the creature could eat the apples right off the tree.

"Won't it take a long time to fatten your hog that way?" asked the traveler.

"I suppose so," replied the farmer. "But what's time to a durned old hog?"

Innumerable stories have been told about Samuel Goldwyn, the Hollywood mogul, sometimes called "Czar of all the Rushes." Most of his maladjustments in language (known as "malapropisms" or just "Goldwynisms") may be legend rather than fact, but they often have come near being truth. What's more they have become famous. Two remarks are now part of current speech.

It took place at a long conference of directors, producers, and bigwigs. They were all trying to induce Goldwyn to join them in a project which he disliked. Finally he turned to them and said, "Gentlemen, the best I can give you is a definite maybe." Then, a few minutes later, he said, "I've reconsidered my decision. Gentlemen, you may include me out."

A more recent story has been credited both to Goldwyn and to a Washington bureaucrat. A secretary came to Goldwyn (or the Washington bureaucrat) saying, "Our files are so crowded that I suggest destroying all correspondence more than six years old."

"By all means," said Mr. G. (or the W. b.), "by all means. But be sure to make copies."

"Did you hear about the woman who married four times? Her first husband was a millionaire. Her second was a famous actor. Her third was a well-known minister. And her last was an undertaker."

"I see. One for the money; two for the show; three to get ready; and four to go."

Ginsberg made it plain to the purser he wanted to have a table by himself. But the first night out he found himself sharing a table with a Frenchman who rose, bowed, and said, "Bon appetit."

Annoyed but not to be outdone, Ginsberg bowed and said, "Ginsberg."

This performance lasted all of the voyage. On the last night out, Ginsberg went to the purser. "I'm glad the trip is about over. Every meal this same introduction business goes on—I'm sick of this Mr. Bon Appetit."

"But you don't understand," said the purser. "That's not his name; it's a French expression meaning, 'I wish you a pleasant meal.'"

"Is that so?" said Ginsberg, and went to the table and waited.

This time it was Ginsberg who got up first, made a deep bow, and said, "Bon appetit."

The Frenchman smiled and murmured, "Ginsberg."

The American language has graduated to a dictionary of its own; it is used with equal freedom by truckdrivers and debutantes. One of the latter was visiting her grandmother, who still insisted on pure and formal English for her family.

"My dear," said the old lady, "I hate to reprimand you, but you *must* do something to improve your vocabulary. There are just two words you use over and over again. One is 'swell' and the other is 'lousy'."

"Yes, grandma," agreed the deb. "And what *are* the two words?"

"Some people object to divorce," said the Reno lawyer. "But a large number of divorces proves that America is the land of the free."

"Perhaps," said the lawyer from New York. "But the steady persistence of marriage shows that it's also the home of the brave."

Fred's hours became more and more irregular. One night his wife, becoming alarmed, wired to five of his best friends: "Fred not home. Is he spending the night with you?"

Fred's friends were loyal, a little too loyal. When Fred arrived home his wife had received five telegrams all reading: "Yes."

This story might be classified as an Irish bull (see page 220), but it is an established classic on its own feet.

"Pat, you must have had a lot of trouble with your five sons," said his friend.

"Trouble?" answered Pat. "Me? Never. I've never laid violent hands on any one of those boys except in self-defense."

"Mother sent me to get a package of diapers for the new baby."

"Here's the package," said the storekeeper. "That'll be fifty cents for the diapers and two cents for the tax."

"Never mind the tacks," said the boy. "Mother uses safety pins."

"Father," said his only son, "what is electricity?"

"Well," temporized his father, "I don't know much about electricity."

"Father," said the boy a few minutes later, "how does the gas make the engine go?"

"Son," answered his father, "I'm afraid I don't know much about motors."

"Father," said the boy, "what is radio-therapy?"

"Radio-therapy?" frowned his father. "I really don't know."

"Gee, dad, I guess I'm making a nuisance of myself."

"Not at all, son. If you don't ask questions you'll never learn anything."

"A man," said she bitterly, "wants everything he can get."

"A woman," he rejoined, "wants anything she can't get."

There was a terrific tumult aboard ship. "Man overboard!" shouted a sailor. The lifeboats were about to be lowered when the sailor, in great embarrassment, stepped up to the captain.

"Beg pardon, sir," he said, saluting. "I made an error when I shouted 'Man overboard.'"

"Thank God," breathed the captain with relief.

"Yes," said the sailor, "it was a woman."

"Is she a natural blonde or a platinum blonde?"

"Neither. She's a suicide blonde."

"A suicide blonde? What's that?"

"Dyed by her own hand."

Noah had packed the last pair of animals in the Ark. There wasn't room for another insect. In the commotion a field-mouse crowded against the elephant's toe.

"Look out!" trumpeted the elephant. "Who do you think you're pushing!"

Two travelers had been making a night of it in London. After riding a considerable distance on the bus, the first traveler said, "Is this Wembley?"

"No," said the second. "This isn't Wembley. This is Thursday."

"Good," said the first. "I'm thirsty too. Let's get off and have another drink."

"Here comes the parade, Johnny. Call your mother. Where is she?"

"Upstairs, dad, waving her hair."

"Goodness! Can't we afford a flag?"

"How can I woo you?" asked the fond lover, "and win you?"

"With three little words," said the Hollywood starlet, softly.

"And what are they?" said he.

"One million dollars."

"Tell the truth, Mabel," asked her unmarried friend. "Did you ever catch your husband flirting?"

"I certainly did. That's exactly *how* I caught him."

"Yes," said the proud mother, "my daughter is an accomplished linguist."

"How is her French?" asked a friend.

"Perfect," replied the mother. "She has a pure Parisian accent."

"And her Italian?"

"You would swear she was born in Rome."

"Spanish?"

"Everyone takes her for a Spaniard."

"Can she talk Esperanto, too?"

"Esperanto? Like a native!"

"Who is that horribly ugly looking woman sitting by herself over there?" said the stranger to his host.

"That, sir," said the host, "happens to be my sister."

"Of course," said the embarrassed guest. "I didn't notice the resemblance."

"Frank, would you rather be in a collision or an explosion?"

"A collision, of course."

"Why 'of course'?"

"Well, in a collision there you are. But in an explosion, where are you?"

A judge and a bishop were arguing about their relative authority. "I'm afraid there isn't much room for debate," said the bishop. "After all, *you* can only say, 'You be hanged,' whereas *I* have the power to say, 'You be damned!' "

"Very true," said the jurist. "But when a judge says to a man, 'You be hanged,' he *is* hanged."

The same bishop, worried about his health, was playing chess one evening with a charming young lady. Suddenly he sank back in his chair.

"It's come," he said, turning white. "My left side is paralyzed."

"Heavens!" exclaimed the young lady. "Are you sure?"

"Positive," groaned the bishop. "I've been pinching my left leg, and I feel absolutely no sensation."

"Your Grace," said the young lady, blushing, "that was my leg you were pinching."

Eccentricity has been the subject of a hundred incredible tales. Perhaps the prize eccentric was the one who went to a bakery shop and ordered an expensive chocolate cake. "But," he insisted, "I'm a fussy man, and I must have the cake in the shape of a 'B'. Can you do it?"

"I think so," said the baker. "But I'll have to do it entirely by hand. And it will take three days."

"Good," said the man. "I'll be back."

Three days later the baker showed him the finished creation, a triumph of difficult workmanship. But the man looked dissatisfied. "It isn't your fault. But I can't use it. This is a script 'B' and I should have specified more exactly. What I want is a capital roman letter 'B'. I'll pay the difference if you can still make it."

"I'll make it," said the baker grimly. "Nobody can complain about my work."

Three days later the customer was back. "Ah!" he exclaimed, when the baker exhibited the newly made confection. "Perfect! A masterpiece! Just what I hoped for!"

"I'm glad," said the gratified baker. "Shall I wrap it up now?"

"Oh, no," replied the eccentric customer. "I'll eat it here."

A woman visitor to the Zoo had been unable to get any intelligent replies from the new keeper. Finally she ventured one more question.

"Is that hippopotamus a male?" she asked. "Or a female?"

"That, madam," replied the keeper, "is a question which should interest only another hippopotamus."

Stories of absent-mindedness are usually credited to college professors. The college professor proverbially combs his cigar and lights his hair, winds up his key and opens the door with his watch, fondles mice and sets traps for the baby, says his prayers when he enters a theater and leaves the church for a smoke between the acts. But no professor was ever more absent-minded than the German poet Gotthold Lessing.

Coming home one dark night, Lessing discovered he had forgotten to take his housekey with him. He knocked at the door, whereupon a servant opened an upper window and called out, "The professor isn't home."

"Very well," said Lessing. "Tell him I'll call some other time."

"Really?" whispered the gushing girl to the ardent actor. "Really, if I refuse to marry you, will you really commit suicide?"

"That," said the actor with great dignity, "has been my customary procedure."

Two friends were discussing why they had remained single all these years.

"Why, only a few days ago," said the first, "I met a girl and fell in love with her at first sight."

"Well, then," said the second, "why didn't you marry her?"

"I took a second look."

Perhaps the oldest "He and She" joke in any language is the following:

He: "Darling, am I good enough for you?"

She: "N-no. But you're too good for any other girl."

"My wife is driving me mad," complained the harassed man. "She has the worst memory!"

"You mean," said his friend sympathetically, "she can't remember anything?"

"On the contrary. She remembers everything."

It was their first quarrel, and the sordid subject was money.

"Before we were married," she cried bitterly, "you told me you were well off."

"I was," he snarled. "But I didn't know it."

He was a little henpecked man. He didn't flirt, he didn't drink, and he never argued with his wife. Once, however, after being tongue-lashed all evening, he went out and proceeded to fortify himself with strong liquor. On his way home, he suddenly got sleepy just as he was passing the Zoo, opened a small door, crawled into the lion's cage, and went to sleep with his head on the largest lion.

Next morning his wife began to search for him and finally saw him, still sleeping in the lion's cage. Whereupon she shook her fist at him and shouted: "Come out of there, you coward!"

"Yes, sir," said Harrison, "I'll simply have to put my foot down. I'll just have to tell her we must economize, that we're going on a budget, and that she'll have to cut out most of her fool luxuries."

"Well," said his friend a few days later, "what was the result of your lecture? Was it effective?"

"Yes indeed," said Harrison. "I'm going to give up cigarettes."

"Why do you act so unhappy? Anything wrong?"

"I had to shoot my dog."

"Was he mad?"

"He wasn't exactly pleased about it."

It was a very convivial evening—very. One of the guests, who fancied herself, began whirling about the room in the manner of a ballerina.

"I'm just about the most graceful dancer in this state," she said confidently.

"You may be in this state," purred her best friend. "But not when you're sober."

"No," said the man at the wheel, "I can't say I've ever had to complain of back-seat driving. In fifteen years I've never had a word from behind."

"What kind of a car do you drive?"

"A hearse."

"When the judge decreed that you would have to pay back alimony, how did you feel?" asked Black of a friend.

"Chagrined."

"And how did your ex-wife feel?"

"She grinned."

Applying for a job, the boaster failed to realize he was making anything but a good impression. "Yes, *sir*," he concluded, "I throw my personality, my whole self into everything I undertake. Is there anything—*anything*—you'd like me to do to prove it?"

"Yes," replied the bored employer. "Go and dig a deep well."

Two specialists in tall tales were trying to see who could tell the biggest lie.

"You talk about hens," said the first. "Why, I had a hen that would hatch out anything you put under her—golf balls, tennis balls, lemons, even grapefruit. Once I put a small box under her, and she laid the most beautiful square eggs—eggs that could never roll and break."

"That's nothing," said the second. "I had a hen that was sort of club-footed, so she didn't mind feeding on wood instead of chicken-feed. She actually preferred sawdust to corn. And she hatched out the most wonderful lot of eggs you ever saw—eleven of the chicks raised themselves on stilts and the twelfth was a woodpecker."

"And, O my brethren," quavered the preacher at the end of his sermon, "for the wicked there will be wailing in the next world, weeping and wailing and gnashing of teeth."

"But, reverend," said a member of the congregation, "how about those who have no teeth?"

"Brother," said the preacher sternly, "teeth will be provided."

It was Christmas in the country and two of Brown's friends were approaching his gaily lit house.

"Look," said the first. "Brown has not forgotten a single Yuletide touch. See—the holly-covered windows, the sprig of mistletoe, the old-fashioned candle-lighted tree, even a group of children to sing Christmas hymns. And—look—they're even carrying in the Yule log."

"That's no Yule log," said the second. "That's Brown."

It was during the days of coffee rationing.

"It looks like rain," said the amiable waiter, serving the demi-tasse.

"Tastes like it, too," said the customer. "Bring me a cup of tea."

It was little Jane's first visit to the country. The night was warm, the window was open, the insect noises were strange.

"Mummy," whimpered Jane, "it's dark here. And everything buzzes. And I'm afraid."

"Don't be afraid, Janie," comforted her mother. "Remember the angels are watching over you. They are right there with you."

There was a pause, and then the whimper changed to a loud wail.

"Mummy!" cried Jane. "One of the angels just bit me!"

The story has been credited to various philosophers, but the expression of Harvard belligerence ("To hell with Yale") has never been more humorously twisted than by two Harvard magnificoes. Dean Briggs, accompanied by Edward Everett Hale, was on his way to the stadium when he was stopped by a friend.

"Tell me, Dean," he was asked, "where are you going?"

"Oh," replied Briggs, "to yell with Hale."

"Darling," sighed the enraptured young man, "when I think that tomorrow is your birthday, and when I think that I didn't know you a year ago—"

"Sweetheart," murmured his darling, "don't let's talk about our past. Let's talk about my present."

"Now, James," said the English teacher, "give me a sentence using the word 'archaic.' "

"Archaic," repeated James. "We can't have archaic and eat it, too."

As a fine example of hospitality there is the tired host who insisted on accompanying his guest downstairs.

"Please don't bother," said his guest. "Don't trouble to see me to the door."

"It's no trouble," said his host. "It's a pleasure."

The king was tired of his clown, an inveterate punster. "Unless you make a pun at once—and a good one—you shall be hanged."

"Very well," said the punster. "Name a subject."

"Myself," said the monarch. "The king."

"The king," punned the clown, "is not a subject."

"Well, then," said the king, concealing his irritation, "why do you make fun of my figure?"

"Sire," said the clown, "everyone likes to make fun at someone else's expanse."

"As to royalty," pursued the king, "why do you say that Queen Elizabeth was greater than Joan of Arc?"

"Joan of Arc was a wonder," replied the clown. "But Queen Elizabeth was a Tudor."

"Enough!" cried the king. "Hang him!"

But as the noose was around the punster's neck, the king said, "I'll grant you your life on one condition: that, as soon as the noose is removed, you'll promise never to make another pun."

"I promise, your Majesty," said the jester. "No noose is good news."

So they hanged him.

Corey Ford

Corey Ford is divided into at least two parts. The eastern half writes under the pseudonym of John Riddell; the western half is Corey Ford. Some say it is vice versa; and some say it is impossible, or at least unpleasant, to draw a hard and fast line of demarcation. Under either name, he is the author of such brilliant travesties as The John Riddell Case, in which that erudite detective Philo Vance is rudely handled, and such free fantasias as "Is the Telephone a Success?" "How to Keep a Bee," and "Here We Go Round Revolving Doors," from a volume inappropriately entitled The Gazelle's Ears.

"Wanted, Dead or Alive"

One of my ancestors must have robbed a bank. There must be *something* in my family history to account for the guilty way in which I stammer and blush and glance shiftily out of the corner of my eye whenever I try to cash a cheque, or give references for an apartment, or open a charge account in a department store. The very thought of opening a charge account makes me a little queasy; and only the fact that I needed a pair of garters very badly, and I hadn't a cent of change, prompted me yesterday to embark upon such a course of action at all. For a time I stood miserably outside the store and argued with myself.

"Come, come," I insisted, "this is no way to act. Be a man. You have every right in the world to open a charge account. In fact, they ought to be very glad to get you. Where is your pride? Buck up, man. Throw out your chin. Square your shoulders. So!"

(Of course, I didn't really say all those things to myself. I might have *thought* them to myself; but I didn't stand there on the sidewalk and mutter out loud that way. I don't go making a fool of myself, even for this article.)

I was probably the most suspicious-looking person that ever entered that store, as I slunk through the door and made my way cautiously across the floor. Slowly I edged toward the hosiery counter, glancing uneasily behind me. At the sound of the clerk's voice in my ear I started violently, and dropped my umbrella.

"Garters," I explained huskily.

The clerk appeared mildly interested.

"Don't want to buy 'em," I added in short gasps. "Don't want to pay for 'em, that is. Want to," loosening my collar, "charge 'em."

"In whose name?" asked the clerk.

"In the name of the great Jehovah and . . . Ford," I checked myself. "My own name. I want to open an account."

"*I* see," said the clerk quietly, with the sort of look that seemed to add: "And maybe *this* will clear up the mystery of those solid-silver belt-buckles that have been disappearing lately." And he exclaimed in a loud voice: "Mr. Messersmith."

There was a slight odor of sulphur, and Mr. Messersmith appeared, rubbing his hands. "Ah?"

"This is Mr. Ford," said the clerk significantly.

"Ah. Of course," said Mr. Messersmith, casting a grateful look at the clerk.

"Mr. Ford," added the clerk, with an ill-concealed smile, "says he would like to open an account!"

I could see a look almost of respect creep into Mr. Messersmith's eyes, as he contemplated this bit of sheer bravado on my part. At least, he reflected, this crook had his nerve with him. "Won't you come with me?" he urged, leading me gently by the arm toward the elevator.

As I emerged at the sixth floor, I detected a stir of interest that swept the entire Business Department. Evidently news of my capture had spread before me. Several girls left off typing, and one or two whispered together, as I marched down the aisle behind Mr. Messersmith, head erect and fists clenched, and followed him dutifully into a small compartment. I heard the door click behind me, and sighed. Well, there was no escape now.

"Mr. Alvord," announced Mr. Messersmith gleefully, "will take care of *you!*"

Mr. Alvord glanced at me briefly over the top of a pair of pince-nez glasses, took out his fountain pen, and sat down at a small table. "Name?" he barked. I thought rapidly.

"What's your name?" he repeated.

"My name?" parrying for time.

He paused, pen in hand, and looked up at me.

"What," he pronounced slowly, "is your name?"

"Now, listen, Mr. Alvord, as one gentleman to another," I began hurriedly in a low, tense undertone, "I wonder if this thing can't be fixed up somehow, just between us two? It's all a big misunderstanding . . . don't you see what it means to me? . . . Think of my family! Think of my name. . . ."

Mr. Alvord screwed the cap back on his fountain pen deliberately. "When you do think of your name," he said, "let me know."

"Perhaps it's on your driver's license in your wallet," insinuated Mr. Messersmith.

Mechanically I took out my wallet and looked inside. There was my driver's license; and there, just as he said, was my name. Evidently they had the goods on me. I handed the yellow slip to Mr. Alvord, and shuddered.

"And now," said Mr. Alvord presently, handing me back my license and blotting his questionnaire grimly, "have you ever had a charge account before?" "No," I lied bravely. "Are you *sure?*" frowned Mr. Alvord. "Think," Mr. Messersmith added darkly in my ear. I sagged. "Once," I admitted weakly, "I opened a charge account with Brooks." I leaned forward impulsively. "But that was years ago, Mr. Alvord . . .

I was a mere boy then. Surely you can't hold against me the follies of my . . ." "Any other account?" patiently. "No," I insisted, watching him like a cat.

With a gleam of triumph I watched him turn the page. At least, he had not found out that I had an account with Abercrombie & Fitch.

Slowly Mr. Alvord raised his eyes to meet mine. "Do you propose," he inquired, fixing me sternly, "to include anyone else beside yourself in this account?"

I drew myself up proudly.

"Mr. Alvord," I said, my voice breaking slightly, "I may have a number of faults, but I do not betray my friends. There will be no one else dragged into this charge account through any admission of mine. I . . . I'll face the music alone!"

Perhaps I had touched a sympathetic chord in their hearts. They glanced significantly at one another, and Mr. Alvord shut his fountain pen. Mr. Messersmith grasped me warmly by the hand.

"Thank you," he smiled. "That is all."

"You mean? . . ." I gasped, unable to believe my ears.

Mr. Messersmith nodded.

"Mr. Messersmith . . . Mr. Alvord . . ." I made an effort to control myself. "Sirs . . . you can't know what this means to me. To be free . . . free to buy what I please . . . to be able to look any clerk in the face and say: 'Charge it' . . ." The tears were streaming down my cheeks . . . "Fellows, I want to . . . to thank you. . . ."

Mr. Messersmith led me, still overcome with emotion, to the elevator.

"I believe," he reminded me gently, "you wished to purchase something."

And at this point it suddenly occurred to me that I could hardly go down now and ask for a pair of garters. The whole thing would sound so flat, after opening a charge account and everything. I had a sneaking feeling that Mr. Messersmith would not take it quite the right way. As I followed him out of the elevator, I thought quickly.

"Hmmm . . . nice-looking neckties . . ." I fingered them carelessly, and yawned to the clerk: "Might let me have a half dozen . . . and handkerchiefs to match, of course. Shirts? Ah, there they are . . . I might take a dozen . . . did I mention socks?"

I glanced at Mr. Messersmith. He was still not impressed.

"And I wanted a pair of sport shoes," I continued swiftly, "something serviceable . . . golf shoes, you know." I took a deep breath. "Oh, and you might toss in a golf suit, while you're at it . . . and . . . let me see . . . a light overcoat" (I already have three overcoats) "and . . .

ah, yes . . . a set of golf clubs" (I don't play golf) "and a dozen balls . . ."

The clerk was writing rapidly. I looked around desperately.

"A polo helmet . . . let me see, a fishing rod . . . tackle . . . archery outfit . . . have you a croquet set? . . . tennis . . . canoe with an out-board motor . . . I guess that will be all . . . and . . ."

I turned weakly, backed into Mr. Messersmith, bowed apologetically, upset the tie-rack, and steadied myself.

". . . and you may charge it, please," I called over my shoulder; and lurched through the door.

At least, I have until the end of the month to pay for it all. And, in the meantime, I can keep up my socks with elastic bands.

Robert Frost

American literature is full of geographical contradictions. "My Old Kentucky Home" and "Old
Black Joe" are traditionally southern ballads; but
these nostalgic compositions were written by
Stephen Collins Foster, son of a Pennsylvania
merchant. "Dixie," the rebel song of the South,
was made up by a minstrel man, Dan Emmett of
Mt. Vernon, Ohio. Robert Frost, laureate of New
England, was born in San Francisco.

In 1884, when Frost was ten years old, he was
brought back to the towns and hills where his
ancestors had lived for eight generations, and
where he became New England's most pungent
interpreter. Subtly blending exact observation and
alert imagination, he wrote about universal things
in a colloquial tone of voice. His outer seriousness
and inner humor have enriched American literature with a spirit that is both playful and profound.

Brown's Descent

OR, THE WILLY-NILLY SLIDE

Brown lived at such a lofty farm
 That everyone for miles could see
His lantern when he did his chores
 In winter after half-past three.

And many must have seen him make
 His wild descent from there one night,
'Cross lots, 'cross walls, 'cross everything,
 Describing rings of lantern light.

Between the house and barn the gale
 Got him by something he had on
And blew him out on the icy crust
 That cased the world, and he was gone!

Walls were all buried, trees were few:
 He saw no stay unless he stove
A hole in somewhere with his heel.
 But though repeatedly he strove

And stamped and said things to himself,
 And sometimes something seemed to yield,
He gained no foothold, but pursued
 His journey down from field to field.

Sometimes he came with arms outspread
 Like wings revolving in the scene
Upon his longer axis, and
 With no small dignity of mien.

Faster or slower as he chanced,
 Sitting or standing as he chose,
According as he feared to risk
 His neck, or thought to spare his clothes,

He never let the lantern drop.
   And some exclaimed who saw afar
The figure he described with it,
   "I wonder what those signals are

"Brown makes at such an hour of night!
   He's celebrating something strange.
I wonder if he's sold his farm,
   Or been made Master of the Grange."

He reeled, he lurched, he bobbed, he checked;
   He fell and made the lantern rattle
(But saved the light from going out).
   So half-way down he fought the battle

Incredulous of his own bad luck.
   And then becoming reconciled
To everything, he gave it up
   And came down like a coasting child.

"Well—I—be—" that was all he said,
   As standing in the river road,
He looked back up the slippery slope
   (Two miles it was) to his abode.

Sometimes as an authority
   On motor-cars, I'm asked if I
Should say our stock was petered out,
   And this is my sincere reply:

Yankees are what they always were.
   Don't think Brown ever gave up hope
Of getting home again because
   He couldn't climb that slippery slope;

Or even thought of standing there
   Until the January thaw
Should take the polish off the crust.
   He bowed with grace to natural law,

And then went round it on his feet.
    He jogged the lantern, saying, "Ile's
'Bout out!" and took the long way home
    By road, a matter of several miles.

Wolcott Gibbs

Who's Who in America lists Wolcott Gibbs (born
in New York, March 15, 1902) as a "writer, critic."
But that designation defines neither Gibbs's activities nor his abilities. Originally engaged as a copy-
reader for The New Yorker, he became one of that
metropolitan weekly's most valuable contributors,
author of remarkable feature stories, and, later, its
trenchant dramatic critic. It was largely due to
Gibbs that The New Yorker has been studied as a
repository of some of the best prose written in
America during the last two decades. Gibbs's own
style is less fantastic than indicated by the punning
title of his collected pieces: A Bed of Neuroses.

Ring Out, Wild Bells

When I finally got around to see Max Reinhardt's cinema version of "A Midsummer-Night's Dream," and saw a child called Mickey Rooney playing Puck, I remembered suddenly that long ago I had taken the same part.

Our production was given on the open-air stage at the Riverdale Country School, shortly before the war. The scenery was only the natural scenery of that suburban dell, and the cast was exclusively male, ranging in age from eleven to perhaps seventeen. While we had thus preserved the pure, Elizabethan note of the original, it must be admitted that our version had its drawbacks. The costumes were probably the worst things we had to bear, and even Penrod, tragically arrayed as Launcelot in his sister's stockings and his father's drawers, might have been embarrassed for us. Like Penrod, we were costumed by our parents, and like the Schofields, they seemed on the whole a little weak historically. Half of the ladies were inclined to favor the Elizabethan, and they had constructed rather bunchy ruffs and farthingales for their offspring; others, who had read as far as the stage directions and learned that the action took place in an Athenian wood, had produced something vaguely Athenian, usually beginning with a sheet. Only the fairies had a certain uniformity. For some reason their parents had all decided on cheesecloth, with here and there a little ill-advised trimming with tinsel.

My own costume was mysterious, but spectacular. As nearly as I have ever been able to figure things out, my mother found her inspiration for it in a Maxfield Parrish picture of a court jester. Beginning at the top, there was a cap with three stuffed horns; then, for the main part, a pair of tights that covered me to my wrists and ankles; and finally slippers with stuffed toes that curled up at the ends. The whole thing was made out of silk in alternate green and red stripes, and (unquestionably my poor mother's most demented stroke) it was covered from head to foot with a thousand tiny bells. Because all our costumes were obviously perishable, we never wore them in rehearsal, and naturally nobody knew that I was invested with these peculiar sound effects until I made my entrance at the beginning of the second act.

Our director was a man who had strong opinions about how Shakespeare should be played, and Puck was one of his favorite characters. It was his theory that Puck, being "the incarnation of mischief," never ought to be still a minute, so I had been coached to bound onto the stage,

274

and once there to dance up and down, cocking my head and waving my arms.

"I want you to be a little whirlwind," this man said.

Even as I prepared to bound onto the stage, I had my own misgivings about those dangerously abundant gestures, and their probable effect on my bells. It was too late, however, to invent another technique for playing Puck, even if there had been room for anything but horror in my mind. I bounded onto the stage.

The effect, in its way, must have been superb. With every leap I rang like a thousand children's sleighs, my melodies foretelling God knows

what worlds of merriment to the enchanted spectators. It was even worse when I came to the middle of the stage and went into my gestures. The other ringing had been loud but sporadic. This was persistent, varying only slightly in volume and pitch with the vehemence of my gestures. To a blind man, it must have sounded as though I had recklessly decided to accompany myself on a xylophone. A maturer actor would probably have made up his mind that an emergency existed, and abandoned his gestures as impracticable under the circumstances. I was thirteen, and incapable of innovations. I had been told by responsible authorities that gestures went with this part, and I continued to make them. I also continued to ring—a silvery music, festive and horrible.

If the bells were hard on my nerves, they were even worse for the rest of the cast, who were totally unprepared for my new interpretation. Puck's first remark is addressed to one of the fairies, and it is mercifully brief.

I said, "How now, spirit! Whither wander you?"

This unhappy child, already embarrassed by a public appearance in cheesecloth and tinsel, was also burdened with an opening speech of sixteen lines in verse. He began bravely:

> "Over hill, over dale,
>   Thorough bush, thorough brier,
> Over park, over pale,
>   Thorough flood, thorough fire . . ."

At the word "fire," my instructions were to bring my hands up from the ground in a long, wavery sweep, intended to represent fire. The bells pealed. To my startled ears, it sounded more as if they exploded. The fairy stopped in his lines and looked at me sharply. The jingling, however, had diminished; it was no more than as if a faint wind stirred my bells, and he went on:

> "I do wander every where,
>   Swifter than the moone's sphere . . ."

Here again I had another cue, for a sort of swoop and dip indicating the swiftness of the moone's sphere. Again the bells rang out, and again the performance stopped in its tracks. The fairy was clearly troubled by these interruptions. He had, however, a child's strange acceptance of the inscrutable, and was even able to regard my bells as a last-minute adult addition to the program, nerve-racking but not to be questioned. I'm sure it was only this that got him through that first speech.

My turn, when it came, was even worse. By this time the audience had succumbed to a helpless gaiety. Every time my bells rang, laughter swept the spectators, and this mounted and mingled with the bells until everything else was practically inaudible. I began my speech, another long one, and full of incomprehensible references to Titania's change-ling.

"Louder!" said somebody in the wings. "You'll have to talk louder."

It was the director, and he seemed to be in a dangerous state.

"And for heaven's sake, stop that jingling!" he said.

I talked louder, and I tried to stop the jingling, but it was no use. By the time I got to the end of my speech, I was shouting and so was the audience. It appeared that I had very little control over the bells, which continued to jingle in spite of my passionate efforts to keep them quiet.

All this had a very bad effect on the fairy, who by this time had many symptoms of a complete nervous collapse. However, he began his next speech:

> "Either I mistake your shape and making quite,
> Or else you are that shrewd and knavish sprite
> Call'd Robin Goodfellow: are you not he
> That . . ."

At this point I forgot that the rules had been changed and I was supposed to leave out the gestures. There was a furious jingling, and the fairy gulped.

"Are you not he that, that . . ."

He looked miserably at the wings, and the director supplied the next line, but the tumult was too much for him. The unhappy child simply shook his head.

"Say anything!" shouted the director desperately. "Anything at all!"

The fairy only shut his eyes and shuddered.

"All right!" shouted the director. "All right, Puck. *You* begin *your* next speech."

By some miracle, I actually did remember my next lines, and had opened my mouth to begin on them when suddenly the fairy spoke. His voice was a high, thin monotone, and there seemed to be madness in it, but it was perfectly clear.

"Fourscore and seven years ago," he began, "our fathers brought forth on this continent a new nation, conceived . . ."

He said it right through to the end, and it was certainly the most successful speech ever made on that stage, and probably one of the most successful speeches ever made on any stage. I don't remember, if I ever knew, how the rest of us ever picked up the dull, normal thread of the play after that extraordinary performance, but we must have, because I know it went on. I only remember that in the next intermission the director cut off my bells with his penknife, and after that things quieted down and got dull.

W. S. Gilbert

Long before he became half of Gilbert and Sullivan, William Schwenck Gilbert (1836–1911) had written melodramas, pantomimes, burlesques, and a series of hilarious rhymes collected under the title The Bab Ballads. The verses were both logical and nonsensical, and Gilbert borrowed their grave absurdities for many of the plots of the librettos he fashioned so skillfully for Sullivan's music. "The Rival Curates," for example, was enlarged, twisted about, pointed at the Wilde-Pre-Raphaelite cult of estheticism, and became the enchanting and ever-popular Patience.

The Rival Curates

List while the poet trolls
    Of MR. CLAYTON HOOPER,
Who had a cure of souls
    At Spiffton-extra-Sooper.

He lived on curds and whey,
    And daily sang their praises,
And then he'd go and play
    With buttercups and daisies.

Wild croquet HOOPER banned,
    And all the sports of Mammon,
He warred with cribbage, and
    He exorcised backgammon.

His helmet was a glance
    That spoke of holy gladness;
A saintly smile his lance,
    His shield a tear of sadness.

His Vicar smiled to see
    This armour on him buckled;
With pardonable glee
    He blessed himself and chuckled:

"In mildness to abound
    My curate's sole design is,
In all the country round
    There's none so mild as mine is!"

And HOOPER, disinclined
    His trumpet to be blowing,
Yet didn't think you'd find
    A milder curate going.

A friend arrived one day
    At Spiffton-extra-Sooper,
And in this shameful way
    He spoke to MR. HOOPER:

"You think your famous name
    For mildness can't be shaken,
That none can blot your fame—
    But, HOOPER, you're mistaken!

"Your mind is not as blank
    As that of HOPLEY PORTER,
Who holds a curate's rank
    At Assesmilk-cum-Worter.

"*He* plays the airy flute,
    And looks depressed and blighted,
Doves round about him 'toot,'
    And lambkins dance delighted.

"*He* labours more than you
    At worsted work, and frames it;
In old maids' albums, too,
    Sticks seaweed—yes, and names it!"

The tempter said his say,
    Which pierced him like a needle—
He summoned straight away
    His sexton and his beadle.

These men were men who could
    Hold liberal opinions:
On Sundays they were good—
    On week-days they were minions.

"To HOPLEY PORTER go,
    Your fare I will afford you—
Deal him a deadly blow,
    And blessings shall reward you.

"But stay—I do not like
    Undue assassination,
And so, before you strike,
    Make this communication:

"I'll give him this one chance—
    If he'll more gaily bear him,
Play croquet, smoke and dance,
    I willingly will spare him."

They went, those minions true,
    To Assesmilk-cum-Worter,
And told their errand to
    THE REVEREND HOPLEY PORTER.

"What?" said that reverend gent,
    "Dance through my hours of leisure?
Smoke?—bathe myself with scent?—
    Play croquet? Oh, with pleasure!

"Wear all my hair in curl?
    Stand at my door, and wink—so—
At every passing girl?
    My brothers, I should think so!

"For years I've longed for some
    Excuse for this revulsion:
Now that excuse has come—
    I do it on compulsion!!!"

He smoked and winked away—
    This REVEREND HOPLEY PORTER—
The deuce there was to pay
    At Assesmilk-cum-Worter.

And HOOPER holds his ground,
    In mildness daily growing—
They think him, all around,
    The mildest curate going.

*Ridiculing the popular fads of the day, Gilbert poked fun at the preten-
sions of the Victorian era. Iolanthe mocks the Peerage in general and the
House of Lords in particular. Ruddigore and The Pirates of Penzance
satirize the pomp of titles. Pinafore laughs at the importance of office-
holders and the means of attaining power.*

The Ruler of the Queen's Navee

FROM "PINAFORE"

When I was a lad I served a term
As office boy to an attorney's firm.
I cleaned the windows and I swept the floor,
And I polished up the handle of the big front door.
   I polished up that handle so carefullee
   That now I am the Ruler of the Queen's Navee!

As office boy I made such a mark
That they gave me the post of a junior clerk.
I served the writs with a smile so bland,
And I copied all the letters in a big round hand—
   I copied all the letters in a hand so free,
   That now I am the Ruler of the Queen's Navee!

In serving writs I made such a name
That an articled clerk I soon became;
I wore clean collars and a brand-new suit
For the pass-examination at the Institute.
   And that pass-examination did so well for me,
   That now I am the Ruler of the Queen's Navee!

Of legal knowledge I acquired such a grip
That they took me into the partnership
And that junior partnership, I ween,
Was the only ship I ever had seen.
   But that kind of ship so suited me,
   That now I am the Ruler of the Queen's Navee!

I grew so rich that I was sent
By a pocket borough into Parliament.
I always voted at my party's call,
And I never thought of thinking for myself at all.
   I thought so little, they rewarded me
   By making me the Ruler of the Queen's Navee!

Now, landsmen all, whoever you may be,
If you want to rise to the top of the tree,
If your soul isn't fettered to an office stool,
Be careful to be guided by this golden rule—
　　Stick close to your desk and never go to sea,
　　And you *all* may be Rulers of the Queen's Navee!

The Bab Ballads have been compared to the madcap rhymes of Edward
Lear and Lewis Carroll. But Gilbert created a new world of fantasy, a
world populated by an unreal but plausible race of people, caricatures
more convincing, and often more endearing, than reality.

Etiquette

The *Ballyshannon* foundered off the coast of Cariboo,
And down in fathoms many went the captain and the crew;
Down went the owners—greedy men whom hope of gain allured:
Oh, dry the starting tear, for they were heavily insured.

Besides the captain and the mate, the owners and the crew,
The passengers were also drowned excepting only two:
Young PETER GRAY, who tasted teas for BAKER, CROOP AND CO.,
And SOMERS, who from Eastern shores imported indigo.

These passengers, by reason of their clinging to a mast,
Upon a desert island were eventually cast.
They hunted for their meals, as ALEXANDER SELKIRK used,
But they couldn't chat together—they had not been introduced.

For PETER GRAY, and SOMERS, too, though certainly in trade,
Were properly particular about the friends they made;
And somehow thus they settled it without a word of mouth—
That GRAY should take the northern half, while SOMERS took the south.

On PETER's portion oysters grew—a delicacy rare,
But oysters were a delicacy PETER couldn't bear.
On SOMERS' side was turtle, on the shingle lying thick,
Which SOMERS couldn't eat, because it always made him sick.

GRAY gnashed his teeth with envy as he saw a mighty store
Of turtle unmolested on his fellow-creature's shore:
The oysters at his feet aside impatiently he shoved,
For turtle and his mother were the only things he loved.

And SOMERS sighed in sorrow as he settled in the south,
For the thought of PETER's oysters brought the water to his mouth.
He longed to lay him down upon the shelly bed, and stuff:
He had often eaten oysters, but had never had enough.

How they wished an introduction to each other they had had
When on board the *Ballyshannon!* And it drove them nearly mad
To think how very friendly with each other they might get,
If it wasn't for the arbitrary rule of etiquette!

One day, when out a-hunting for the *mus ridiculus*,
GRAY overheard his fellow-man soliloquising thus:
"I wonder how the playmates of my youth are getting on,
M'CONNELL, S. B. WALTERS, PADDY BYLES, and ROBINSON?"

These simple words made PETER as delighted as could be,
Old chummies at the Charterhouse were ROBINSON and he!
He walked straight up to SOMERS, then he turned extremely red,
Hesitated, hummed and hawed a bit, then cleared his throat, and said:

"I beg your pardon—pray forgive me if I seem too bold,
But you have breathed a name I knew familiarly of old.
You spoke aloud of ROBINSON—I happened to be by—
You know him?" "Yes, extremely well." "Allow me—so do I!"

It was enough: they felt they could more sociably get on,
For (ah, the magic of the fact!) they each knew ROBINSON!
And MR. SOMERS' turtle was at PETER's service quite,
And MR. SOMERS punished PETER's oyster-beds all night.

They soon became like brothers from community of wrongs;
They wrote each other little odes and sang each other songs;
They told each other anecdotes disparaging their wives;
On several occasions, too, they saved each other's lives.

They felt quite melancholy when they parted for the night,
And got up in the morning soon as ever it was light;
Each other's pleasant company they reckoned so upon,
And all because it happened that they both knew ROBINSON!

They lived for many years on that inhospitable shore,
And day by day they learned to love each other more and more.
At last, to their astonishment, on getting up one day,
They saw a vessel anchored in the offing of the bay!

To PETER an idea occurred. "Suppose we cross the main?
So good an opportunity may not occur again."
And SOMERS thought a minute, then ejaculated, "Done!
I wonder how my business in the City's getting on?"

"But stay," said MR. PETER: "when in England, as you know,
I earned a living tasting teas for BAKER, CROOP, AND CO.,
I may be superseded—my employers think me dead!"
"Then come with me," said SOMERS, "and taste indigo instead."

But all their plans were scattered in a moment when they found
The vessel was a convict ship from Portland, outward bound!
When a boat came off to fetch them, though they felt it very kind,
To go on board they firmly but respectfully declined.

As both the happy settlers roared with laughter at the joke,
They recognised an unattractive fellow pulling stroke:
'Twas ROBINSON—a convict, in an unbecoming frock!
Condemned to seven years for misappropriating stock!!!

They laughed no more, for SOMERS thought he had been rather rash
In knowing one whose friend had misappropriated cash;
And PETER thought a foolish tack he must have gone upon
In making the acquaintance of a friend of ROBINSON.

At first they didn't quarrel very openly, I've heard;
They nodded when they met, and now and then exchanged a word:
The word grew rare, and rarer still the nodding of the head,
And when they meet each other now, they cut each other dead.

To allocate the island they agreed by word of mouth,
And PETER takes the north again, and SOMERS takes the south;
And PETER has the oyster, which he loathes with horror grim,
And SOMERS has the turtle—turtle disagrees with him.

Jack Alan

(GOODMAN) (GREEN)

Jack Alan is a split personality; one half is Jack Goodman and the other half is Alan Green. Both Goodman (born in 1909) and Green (born in 1907) are expert advertising men, the former with Simon and Schuster, Inc., publishers, the latter with Green-Brodie, Inc., a New York agency. Besides the stories and articles written as separate individuals, the two men have collaborated on a hilarious travesty of the "How to—" books which entices the reader with unfounded faith and false sense of power. With the advertiser's understanding of humanity's ill-matched awkwardness and ambition, the book was entitled How to Do Practically Anything and its subtitle was not merely significant but definitive: "An Easy Guide to Complete Chaos." The book was assured of success; it made incompetence more popular than ever.

From Pillar to Post

OR, HOW TO RAISE A DOG

Dog owners, arise! Too long has the actual head of your family not even paid an income tax. Too long have you tried to conceal from your dog the fact that he really owns you. Too long have you searched in vain for the counsel you so sorely need when, panting and tongue hanging out, you fall back into the nearest chair and finally admit to yourself that the lively little fellow isn't going to sit up and beg, hasn't the slightest intention of leaving that frayed end of the tapestry alone, and is unshakeably convinced that the mathematical center of the living-room rug is the Comfort Station Supreme.

You can expect no help from dog books or dog doctors. In this all-important emergency, all they do is back away, muttering incoherent statements about Training and Psychology. And you are left holding the bag, one end of which has already been chewed away, like everything else you own.

I am no expert. I might as well tell you right now that I generally go to sleep with a large, greasy bone under my pillow because I have failed to sway my dog in his opinion that there isn't a better spot in town for bone hiding. My house is thoroughly dog-broken. But I do not intend to leave my fellow man with his dog having the upper paw in the household.

I believe my predicament to be an average one, a valuable case history. I will show you how I deal with my dog. Maybe you will be able to discover where along the line something went terribly, terribly wrong.

Things started badly when I bought him. I didn't select him, he selected me. When I went to the kennel, I had decided definitely against buying four or five puppies, as I wanted to do. Phyllis claims that this is too many for a small apartment. Cunningly, however, I planned to get around this by getting as much dog as possible for my money—a great Dane.

I looked critically at the batch of puppies, which, while only three months old, were the size of Airedales. Then one detached himself from the mob. He had a lot of filling out to do. He took, I noticed, several steps before his skin started moving along with him. He galloped over, sat down heavily on my feet, and looked me over carefully. I couldn't move, so I had to look at him, too. He was obviously admiring me. His

288

next step was to take my trouser leg in his mouth and shake it, possibly to test the quality of the material. Then he gave several pleased body wiggles, attempted to climb up on me, and washed my hand thoroughly with a salmon-pink tongue. Then he sat down again on my feet and admired me some more.

I had been chosen.

Several months have passed, and we have learned much about each other. Neither of us regrets his choice, although my training methods seem to lack something.

I have found that the very first step must be to Gain His Confidence. To accomplish this, I sit on the floor next to him and say, "*Good* little dog!" This is a flat lie and he knows it, being well aware that he is neither little nor good. He backs away several feet, presses himself close to the floor, and turns up his eyes at me with a wary "You-are-up-to-something-tricky-and-I'm-not-going-to-like-it" expression.

I reach out reassuringly and pat his nearest paw. He withdraws the paw and licks it off fastidiously.

I attempt now to get his attention by cupping both hands and saying coyly: "Guess what I've got here?"

Showing signs of interest, he nuzzles into my hands. I am caught flat-footed with nothing in them. I run to get a dog biscuit to absolve myself. Meanwhile he stalks off bitterly to a corner of the room, tenses his forelegs, digs a hole in the carpet, and lies down in it.

I now change my approach, deciding to try the Great Big Playmate tactic. Crouching on all fours, I advance on him, barking several times with mock ferocity. He decides to humor me by pretending he thinks

I'm a huge, dangerous dog. With a happy yelp, he flashes around a chair and dashes upon me from behind. Since he weighs roughly eighty-two pounds at the moment, I am now flat on the floor with him on top of me. He wants to pretend he is shaking me by the neck. This is too difficult unless he actually does shake me by the back of the neck. So he does.

I get up and brush myself off. I brush him off me, too, several times. I have now succeeded in gaining his confidence and showing him that I am a regular fellow who doesn't mind a good, clean romp, so I am through. But he isn't. He likes it too well to quit. He gets my tie in his teeth and hangs from it. It is some time before I get my breath.

He still refuses to stop. It is therefore time for me to Punish Him. I decide to lock him in the bathroom. This consists of the following steps:

1. He instantly senses my purpose and scrambles into the bedroom under the bed.
2. I rush after him and say, "Come out from under there this minute!"
3. He doesn't.
4. I get down on the floor and look under the bed. We face each other silently for a moment, each trying to outstare the other. I blink, which gives him the round.
5. I mutter several dire threats. So does he.
6. I hold out my handkerchief, hoping he will grab it and pull, thereby enabling me to drag him out.
7. He grabs it and pulls.
8. We are now both under the bed.
9. I seize him firmly and wriggle out.
10. A head bumps severely against the box spring. It is not his.
11. I shove and pull him into the bathroom and back out, closing the door.
12. I stop closing the door to avoid catching his nose in it.
13. I shove him back and close the door, catching my hand in it.
14. We both howl simultaneously.

Returning to the living room, tired but victorious (look up Pyrrhic in any good encyclopedia), I now proceed to describe my dog to you. He is still a puppy, seven months old. He is a good dog to have for a case history because, although a thoroughbred, he has a character which is practically a cross section of that of America's dogs.

Although large and getting larger, it is his opinion that he is a lap dog and as such entitled to climb on my chair whether I am in it or not. When I can catch him to give him a bath, he emerges as a dull gold in color with a mouth fringed with black. This mouth is already large enough to contain my arm and, when I am giving him a bath, does. Like all his breed, he has a short coat, but he sheds it with the success of the collie. He has a way of searching out tidbits in his food which probably reveals that in spite of his pedigree he contains a trace of ant-eater. He has a beery sort of baritone. And he is very democratic in his ideas about love.

When I first got him I called him Gilbert, the name I still introduce him by. The only word he will always answer to, however, is Food, so I generally call him that.

Food, or Gilbert, is still in the bathroom, you will recall. This is my golden opportunity to get something to eat unbeknownst to him. Let me explain.

Since I have known Gilbert, I have had few square meals at home. This is because Gilbert is an adept at a quiet, effective sort of bullying. When I am eating, he is too wily to use strong-arm tactics, realizing that force will be answered with force. He therefore just looks at me tragically. He keeps looking at me. He meditates on man's inhumanity to dog. He sighs. Beginning to feel like a heartless gourmand, I transfer my little morsel of food to my mouth. His glance never wavers. He drools slowly.

As a result, I spend a large part of my time at my dinner table chewing things up a little for Gilbert. Then I give them to him, cursing.

But now that Gilbert is in the bathroom, I turn on the radio full blast and enter the kitchen singing loudly, hoping that both noises will distract him.

It is a losing game. Gilbert, who would sleep soundly through a collision with another planet, easily detects the noiseless opening of the electric icebox. No sooner do I reach a guilty hand to a roast-beef bone than Gilbert utters a series of agonized cries, giving the entire neighborhood the impression that I am murdering him by inches. In self-defense I rush to the bathroom to make him stop.

He is very happy as I open the door, particularly since a well-timed move enables him to snatch the beef bone from my hand and rush back to the bathroom.

I am about to follow him to get back my bone when the doorbell rings.

It is Mrs. Garble, a middle-aged woman I do not like. She is the president of Phyllis' club. She is also a cat lover. She expresses relief at being able to come in for once and not have that great brute of a dog jumping all over her. Looking around nervously, she asks where he is. I tell her.

"What in the world is he doing in the bathroom?" she says.

"Well, really, Mrs. Garble," I reply primly, "he *said* he wanted to wash his hands."

This keeps her quiet for a moment. It then develops that she wants to see Phyllis, who isn't home. She looks at the carpet, which has no more than a normal amount of Gilbert's hair on it.

"Goodness gracious!" she says, clucking, "I don't see *how* you can keep a great Dane in a city apartment! Why, I'd just as soon keep a horse in one!"

I bristle and stifle a desire to say, "Oh, so you don't think I ought to keep my horse, either?"

Gilbert chooses this moment to enter. And not, to my surprise, with his usual attitude, which practically says, "Oh my chin and whiskers! What wonderful things have I been missing!" Instead, he comes in with measured dignity. He casts a sedate glance at Mrs. Garble.

"He seems to be getting much better manners," she says grudgingly. "You certainly are training him to behave like a gentleman!"

I decide that Mrs. Garble, too, seems to be getting better manners. I warm toward her, as I do to all types of characters who have a kind word to say for Gilbert. I even toy with the idea of giving her a drink.

I watch with paternal pride as Gilbert walks slowly over to her. He sniffs at her leg in a genteel way. I beam reassuringly. Mrs. Garble smiles back uncertainly. Gilbert seems about to walk past her. He doesn't. He stops. Trained to observe such matters, I suddenly notice an uncertain attitude, a slight quivering of the muscles of Gilbert's left hind leg.

"GILBERT!" I cry, in the nick of time.

There is no need to go into the next five minutes. It will serve no purpose for me to repeat my weak explanation to the outraged Mrs. Garble that Gilbert, being still in the experimental stage, was merely about to test out a comparatively new idea. And that there was no personal malice or intended criticism involved.

Gilbert and I are alone again—and it is definitely time for me to Take Him Out.

Gilbert *loves* to go out. Five, seven times a day he responds with mad joy to the rattle of his chain, dances with impatience as I attach his collar, and, in a series of chamoislike bounds, precipitates me to our apartment elevator, permitting me to touch the corridor with my feet only intermittently on the way.

If Gilbert is in luck, there will be another passenger in the elevator. This is a stout, very short gentleman with a red face who lives on the floor above us. He is generally on his way to some formal affair. There is something about his frock coats and silk hats which brings out Gilbert's warmest feelings of affection.

It takes Gilbert no time at all to place both his paws on the little man's carefully groomed shoulders. Gilbert's tongue then quickly and deftly leaves a long moist streak from chin to forehead, as Gilbert's body deposits large amounts of hair on the faultless apparel.

The little man's face now becomes even redder, because he does not Understand Dogs. I know he doesn't, because the very first time this occurred, I said to him reassuringly, "It's all right, he is friendly."

To which he replied: "I'm not."

Since then all we say to each other is "Look out!"

Once we have left the elevator and passed through the lobby—a passage too swift for the average vision—Gilbert and I find ourselves outside. It is now that my problems begin and Gilbert's end. This is because we spend a lot of time standing by trees, lampposts, and pillars. It is not the fact that Gilbert is generally standing on one more leg than I am which makes my position more difficult than his. It is rather that I am far more conscious than he of the famous girls' finishing school on our block. Since its dismissal times seem to coincide with our airings, it bothers me to feel that there are hundreds of pretty young girls in the world who believe I spend my entire time standing by upright columns.

It is therefore frequently necessary for me to pretend that I do not know Gilbert. That is difficult, because of the stout chain which connects us. There are various attitudes, however, which I assume:

1. That I happened to be out with a chain and a careless dog got caught in it.
2. That a dog happened to be out with a chain and *I* got caught in it.
3. That a chain happened to be out and the dog and I both got caught in it.

Between lampposts, Gilbert and I walk along with dignity. With as much dignity as possible, that is, considering that we are walking in the gutter.

Sometimes we pause in the gutter and turn around rapidly many times. Then one of us reads a newspaper, while the finishing school, which we are directly in front of, conducts a fire drill.

I could go on interminably. Maybe you think I have already. But anyway, we are agreed that my dog-handling methods are not ideal. Now let me give you some information which is really practical in case you plan to have a dog. Let us examine Gilbert's habits, his point of view, his psychology. I know all about them and it does me no good, but it may forewarn you about your own dog.

I have observed many of Gilbert's moods. They are, I believe, fairly common to his race. Here are a few of them:

1. *The Hooray-Hooray-a-New-Day's-Dawning! Mood.* This manifests itself twice a day. Once at six in the morning, at which time Gilbert lands heavily on my stomach, knocking both breath and sleep out of me. And a second time at a few moments past midnight, just after he has been bedded down, at which time he insists that I throw his rubber bone for him, or take him out with my coat over my pajamas. There must be some way to stop this.

2. *The Aren't-I-Supposed-to-Have-Any-Normal-Instincts-at-All? Mood.* This is caused simply by the fact that Gilbert is devoid of a sense of shame and I am not. It often results in our not speaking to each other and also in other people not speaking to me. There is no way to avoid this.

3. *The I-Was-Asleep-and-Some-Bad-Man-Must-Have-Come-in-and Torn-that-Blue-Bedspread-to-Bits Attitude.* This is accompanied by a brazen, hypocritical simulation of overweening joy at my entrance and is unconvincing because of the large piece of blue cloth which Gilbert is unconsciously carrying on his dewlap. One method of avoiding this is always to leave your bed bare to the springs until retiring.

All right. Now that I have revealed my relationship to my dog in all its squalor, the curious may inquire why I have a dog at all. The curious may, but not the wise.

The answer, of course, is simple. In Gilbert I have found a being to whom I am superior in many ways, in spite of the fact that Phyllis insists that a lot more people stop to admire him than me on the street. Gilbert cannot drive a car. I can. Gilbert cannot wash dishes, pour drinks for people, run errands, or do dozens of other things around the house Phyllis considers necessary. Above all, Gilbert is a living, breathing answer to her contention that I am the most inefficient form of life yet devised.

He is also the finest dog in town, even if he did tear up the very best parts of this piece.

Come One, Come One

OR, HOW TO BE A HOST

Our friends have taken a place in the country this summer—our place. As a result, my wife Phyllis is fit to be tied. And unless I can arrange to have someone do a capable job of tying her before she gets into the car and meets me when I arrive on the 6:37 at Westport, there is going to be some small unpleasantness on the eastbound platform.

Phyllis says that my hospitality is going to result in her hospitalization. But it isn't really my fault. The blame lies in that great American institution, the summer week end. You see, I've just finished phoning to tell her that a couple of guests will be out with me on the train tonight, Friday. When she said, "Do you think Information could give me the number of a reliable concern in the train-wrecking business?" I was offended and decided to hang up. But she beat me to it, muttering something about my not even knowing what tomorrow is.

Of course I know what tomorrow is. It is the day that Bill and Tom and I are getting up at six so that we can play fifty-four holes of golf. I must say that Phyllis has changed. When I married her last year (I've forgotten the exact date, it was somewhere around this time of year, maybe next week, maybe last), she was a gay little thing who liked people, even my friends. She enjoyed our pleasant bantering evenings with them, pitched with enthusiasm into the parlor games we played, and rarely failed to win enough to pay off my small losses.

But these summer week ends have changed her. I'm sure it was no one specific incident. I'm quite convinced it wasn't that business about Sidney and the early American glassware. True, it was our glassware, but it was Sidney's forehead.

Nor could it have been that little matter of Rita and the overstuffed chair. After all, Rita studied chemistry in school, and if she says it was spontaneous combustion, who are we to doubt her word?

Nevertheless, Phyllis always starts biting her nails toward the end of the week. This works out for the best, because by the time our guests leave, she is trying to claw at me with them.

By now I'm an expert on Being a Host. I've devoted a lot of study to both sides of the relieved Monday-morning farewell. I've seen a lot of hands still shaking after they've unclasped. And now I'm in a position to give the world the benefits of my experience. I've been at it all summer and I know that the perfect Host is someone whose heart is in the right place. This place is generally his mouth. A Guest, on the other hand, is someone whose heart is on his sleeve, which is generally in my butter.

In my Guest days, I believed that Hosts lay in wait treacherously for the opportunity to get up in the middle of the night and rearrange all the furniture in the path between a hapless Guest and the bathroom. Now, as a Host, I see the basic truth: Guests are low, skulking, destructive types who like nothing better than to go out of their way to bump into a costly piece of furniture.

There is no problem at all to being a Guest. All you need is a toothbrush and a razor to fit your Host's razor blades in. But being a Host requires not only the toothbrush and razor your Guest has forgotten, but also a cluster of talents in the entertainment and diplomatic fields which could only be found in a character combining the best features of Sally and Talleyrand.

For instance, no Guest need be told the proper etiquette involved in informing his Host that his bathing trunks have just been eaten by the Host's dog. He just tells him, quickly and forcefully. But a whole course could be given on the proper methods of informing the Guest that a large segment of the trunks he has just appeared in at the pool were recently eaten by the Host's dog.

And still another could be given on what to do about the Guest who insists on getting up early. It does no good to lock him in. I tried this a few weeks ago and it was easily parried by my guest's simple gambit of taking a heavy, valuable object and banging it against the wall, unhurriedly and steadily, for the next hour.

People who don't want to face and conquer these and countless other problems involved in being a Host had better spend the sweltering summer week ends in the city, having a good time in some air-cooled movie. Don't for a minute think you can duck your responsibility by airily deciding not to have Guests at all. You will have them. Any Guest who knows his business realizes that the summer is the open season on open houses. He will merely wait for your invitation until the last minute and then drop in uninvited if it doesn't come.

Now let us see How to Be a Host by watching one in actual practice —me. To understand the endless war between Hosts and Guests, to comprehend Phyllis' reaction to my announcement that I was bringing guests out this evening, it will be necessary for us to examine a couple of actual week ends.

These week ends may not be typical. One can speak of a typical week end only in the same sense that one can refer to a typical earthquake.

In both there are great differences of intensity, total damage, and number of human beings trapped. But just as the scientist, picking himself off the floor and painfully working his way back to his seismograph, can discover that what has caused his violent flight through the room has been an "earthquake," so can we glean valuable information from samples of my summer week ends.

Our first week end in July, for instance. I'll give it in brief instead of getting the whole transcript from the court stenographer. Phyllis and I planned this one very carefully, and whatever people say about the best-laid plans of mice and men, I feel that any self-respecting mouse would have given itself up to the nearest cat if its plans had gone that much agley.

We knew it was going to be a long week end, what with the Fourth of July falling on a Tuesday. So we saved it for the people we like best, Graham and Mary Terwilliger.

This, I felt, would be ideal, since Graham could play golf every day with me, while Mary could do whatever it is women do all day with Phyllis. Then in the evenings we could play a few rubbers of bridge and go off to bed early, tired, happy, and at peace with the murmurous country night.

It might have worked out that way if Mary hadn't slammed the train door on Graham's foot on the way out. "You should have been holding it open yourself," she apologized. From that point their conversation had moved rapidly toward a silence which became total by the time their train reached Westport.

Since Phyllis and I are very loyal to our friends, we promptly took sides and soon we weren't talking to each other either. Our conversation at dinner went something like this:

"Phyllis," Mary would say, "would you kindly tell Graham to pass the catsup? Tell him not to bother taking it off his vest—there's still enough in the bottle."

"Of course, dear," Phyllis would answer. "I'm so sorry you have such a little veal chop to put it on. I must tell the maid not to serve Jack first next time."

With a hard laugh I'd say to Graham, "You'd think my salary certainly would be sufficient to get enough veal chops to eat, wouldn't you, Graham?"

"It was," Phyllis explained sweetly to Mary, "until veal went up a cent and a half a pound last week."

"There are certain people," said Graham, drumming his fingers musingly on the table, "that I would like to see trying to run a business office."

"That's a good one, Graham!" I said, slapping my knee apprecia-tively with my right hand, which unfortunately held a piece of well-buttered toast.

"There are certain people," said Mary to Phyllis, "that I would like to see stop *trying* to run a business office and run one for a change. By the way, Graham's still not doing very well with that gold-mine stock he bought last year from the man they arrested in Chicago last week."

"I know," said Phyllis. "Jack isn't doing any better with his, even though he has twice as much of it. It's a shame, too, when you think of how much the boys spent on that airplane trip to buy the stuff."

Somehow or other we didn't get to bridge that night. Instead we all sat around the living room and glared at each other.

At eleven, Mary went upstairs and took a hot bath, using all the water in the tank. When Graham followed later and found no water coming out, he left the faucets turned on.

Sometime in the night the hot water began to flow again, overran the tub, and created a small river along the bathroom floor to the hall. From there it cascaded prettily downstairs into the living room, where it formed a deep and peaceful pool.

In the morning, while Mary was on her hands and knees mopping it up, in Phyllis' best negligee, Graham went out to the garage and drove my car through the wall, not realizing that it is a habit of mine to leave the car in gear with the brake off.

Rushing through the garage door to help him, it did not occur to me that he would be rushing through the same door to tell me what had happened. We came to an abrupt stop, both of us standing on Graham's foot. It was the same one Mary had slammed the train door on, and from that point Graham wouldn't talk to me, either.

Golf now out of the question, I decided to let my guests shift for themselves and busy myself about the house. I took some rubbish out in the back to burn it, little realizing that our stationery store would deliver our Fourth of July fireworks in such old boxes and crumpled newspaper.

For the next two days, Graham sat around with his bandaged foot on a chair while I plied myself with healing oils and preserved a stony silence while Phyllis told Mary that, with my eyebrows off, my fore-head didn't look quite so low.

The next week end we naturally set aside for a little peace and quiet. There were to be just the two of us—and there were—right through until Saturday midnight. It was then that the Wilburs, who were driv-ing down from Maine, stopped off.

They had their garter snakes with them. Mrs. Wilbur did not know this. All she knew was that she didn't want Milton to drive any more because the night air was definitely not sobering him up. Milton had found the garter snakes beside the road when he got out to look at a tire or something and naturally did not want to leave them so far from town. So he helped them into the tonneau among the luggage. And when we sleepily admitted him and his wife, he bedded them down in our kitchen, modestly refraining from mentioning this good deed.

The first inkling we had of the snakes' presence came in the morning when the maid tossed the butter crock through the kitchen window. This crash so startled Milton's process of sleeping it off that he leaped from bed, tore out into the hall, and easily cleared a low railing which stood in his path. This, at the rate of thirty-two feet per second, per second, brought him into our living room downstairs. He had the good fortune to land on our divan. Or, as Phyllis put it, "Why did that divan have to be right there where he would break its valuable springs instead of his own worthless neck?"

Let us pass quickly over the week end with Mr. Megglesworth and his wife. He was my biggest customer, and we simply had to have him out. They arrived Friday evening with six children and departed the following Thursday with seven. After they left, Phyllis murmured something about our week-end house being a family-way-station. She also added musingly that up to this point she thought she had seen every possible method by which an uninvited guest could drop in for the week end. . . .

Altogether, you may now be able to see why Phyllis maintains that if a man's home is his castle, his summer one should have a good, deep moat around it.

You can also see that it is easy to be a Host. All you need is an unlimited income, a capacity for going three days without sleep or the use of your bathroom, and an air of good-fellowship that your guests can cut with a knife and probably will.

If you haven't all these qualities, you might solve the summer problem by taking two places. One could be a tiny affair of one room and a bath for yourself, the other a large, drafty manor some twenty miles away for the misuse of your guests. Phyllis and I toyed with this idea for next summer. We thought of calling the big place Tobacco Roadhouse. The little one would be known as Cold Shoulder Arms.

But we've already abandoned this notion. We are undoubtedly taking this same place again next year. After all, our guests are accustomed to it. And they are *such* creatures of habit.

Harry Graham

Harry Graham was an English soldier in the Coldstream Guards. So, when he wanted a pseudonym for his flippant rhymes, he signed them "Col. D. Streamer." His Ruthless Rhymes for Heartless Homes were quoted and imitated by countless readers who had never heard of Graham except as a cracker. Perhaps the most famous of his calmly savage quatrains were these five:

Aunt Eliza

In the drinking well
   Which the plumber built her,
Aunt Eliza fell.
   We must buy a filter.

Indifference

When Grandmamma fell off the boat
   And couldn't swim, and wouldn't float,
Matilda just stood by and smiled.
   I very nearly slapped the child.

Compensation

Weep not for little Léonie,
Abducted by a French *marquis*.
Though loss of honor was a wrench,
Just think how it improved her French.

Uncle Joe

Alas, alas, for Uncle Joe;
He's gone beyond the stars.
I miss him, oh, I miss him so.
He had *such* good cigars.

Billy

Billy, in one of his nice new sashes,
Fell in the grate and was burnt to ashes.
Now, although the room grows chilly,·
I haven't the heart to poke up Billy.

This was in the early nineteen hundreds. Every paper began to print "ruthless rhymes," and every contributor tried to invent a catastrophe more gory in event and more nonchalant in effect than its predecessor. The favorite "hero" was Willie, and, although other characters sometimes crept into the quatrains, the terse lines became known as "Little Willies." Here are a few of the most popular.

Little Willie

Willie poisoned his father's tea;
Father died in agony.
Mother came, and looked quite vexed:
"Really, Will," she said, "what next?"

Willie fell down the elevator—
Wasn't found till six days later.
Then the neighbors sniffed, "Gee whizz!
What a spoiled child Willie is!"

Little Willie on the track
Heard the engine squeal.
Now the engine's coming back;
They're scraping Willie off the wheel.

Little Willie from the mirror
    Sucked the mercury all off,
Thinking, in his childish error,
    It would cure the whooping cough.
At the funeral his mother,
    Weeping, said to Mrs. Brown:
" 'Twas a chilly day for Willie
    When the mercury went down!"

Willie saw some dynamite,
Couldn't understand it quite;
Curiosity never pays;
It rained Willie seven days.

Little Willie;
Pair of skates;
Hole in the ice;
Golden gates.

Willie scalped his baby brother,
Left him lying hairless;
"Willie," said his worried mother,
"You are getting careless."

Father heard his children scream,
So he threw them in the stream,
Saying, as he drowned the third,
"Children should be seen, not heard!"

Last night I slew my darling wife;
　　Stretched her on the flooring.
I was loath to take her life—
　　But I *had* to stop her snoring.

He shot at Lee Wing,
　　But he winged Willie Wong;
A slight but regrettable
　　Slip of the Tong.

Making toast at the fireside
Nurse fell in the grate and died.
But what makes it ten times worse,
All the toast was burnt with Nurse.

Baby sat on the window-seat;
Mary pushed her into the street.
Baby was spilt all over the area.
And mamma held up her forefinger at Mary.

Little Willie hung his sister;
She was dead before we missed her.
Willie's always up to tricks.
Ain't he cute? He's only six.

The one about little Willie and his sister proved to be the most long-lived. Years later it was used as the basis for a review of the sex-ridden Nineteen Twenties when, as F. P. A. remarked, it was "sex o'clock all over America." This was the terse critical parody:

Little Willie wrote a book.
Woman was the theme he took.
Woman was his only text.
Ain't he cute? He's oversexed.

Joel Chandler Harris

Folk-lore has a way of reversing itself. Sometimes an actual man, such as Davy Crockett, takes on mythical proportions; sometimes a myth, like Paul Bunyan, becomes a man. It is hard to believe that Uncle Remus was not an actual person, but only a character invented by Joel Chandler Harris.

Harris, born at Eatonton, Georgia, in 1848, did not create Uncle Remus as a comic figure but as an American counterpart of Aesop, who, according to legend, was also black and a slave. Uncle Remus' animals were not new; they were playing their roles in fables long before Harris re-animated them. But Brer Fox and Brer Rabbit have become part of American literature; their little villainies and heroisms are identified by a native swagger and an even more native humor. They will be with us a long, long time.

The Wonderful Tar Baby Story

One evening recently, the lady whom Uncle Remus calls "Miss Sally" missed her little seven-year-old boy. Making search for him through the house and through the yard, she heard the sound of voices in the old man's cabin, and, looking through the window, saw the child sitting by Uncle Remus. His head rested against the old man's arm, and he was gazing with an expression of the most intense interest into the rough, weather-beaten face, that beamed so kindly upon him. This is what "Miss Sally" heard:

"Bimeby, one day, arter Brer Fox bin doin' all dat he could fer ter ketch Brer Rabbit, en Brer Rabbit bin doin' all he could fer ter keep 'im fum it, Brer Fox say to hisse'f dat he'd put up a game on Brer Rabbit, en he ain't mo'n got de wuds out'n his mouf twel Brer Rabbit come a lopin' up de big road, lookin' des ez plump, en ez fat, en ez sassy ez a Moggin hoss in a barley-patch.

" 'Hol' on dar, Brer Rabbit,' sez Brer Fox, sezee.

" 'I ain't got time, Brer Fox,' sez Brer Rabbit, sezee, sorter mendin' his licks.

" 'I wanter have some confab wid you, Brer Rabbit,' sez Brer Fox, sezee.

" 'All right, Brer Fox, but you better holler fum whar you stan'. I'm monstus full er fleas dis mawnin',' sez Brer Rabbit, sezee.

" 'I seed Brer B'ar yistiddy,' sez Brer Fox, sezee, 'en he sorter rake me over de coals kaze you en me ain't make frens en live naberly, en I told 'im dat I'd see you.'

"Den Brer Rabbit scratch one year wid his off hinefoot sorter jub'usly, en den he ups en sez, sezee:

" 'All a settin', Brer Fox. Spose'n you drap roun' ter-morrer en take dinner wid me. We ain't got no great doin's at our house, but I speck de old 'oman en de chilluns kin sorter scramble roun' en git up sump'n fer ter stay yo stummuck.'

" 'I'm 'gree'ble, Brer Rabbit,' sez Brer Fox, sezee.

" 'Den I'll 'pen' on you,' sez Brer Rabbit, sezee.

"Nex' day, Mr. Rabbit en Miss Rabbit got up soon, 'fo' day, en raided on a gyarden like Miss Sally's out dar, en got some cabbiges, en some roas'n years, en some sparrer-grass, en dey fix up a smashin' dinner. Bimeby one er de little Rabbits, playin' out in de backyard, come runnin' in hollerin', 'Oh, ma! oh, ma! I seed Mr. Fox a comin'!' En den Brer Rabbit he tuck de chilluns by der years en make um set
306

down, en den him and Miss Rabbit sorter dally roun' waitin' for Brer Fox. En dey keep on waitin', but no Brer Fox ain't come. Atter 'while Brer Rabbit goes to de do', easy like, en peep out, en dar, stickin' fum behime de cornder, wuz de tip-een' er Brer Fox tail. Den Brer Rabbit shot de do' en sot down, en put his paws behime his years en begin fer ter sing:

> " 'De place wharbouts you spill de grease,
> Right dar youer boun' ter slide,
> An' whar you fine a bunch er ha'r,
> You'll sholy fine de hide.'

"Nex' day, Brer Fox sont word by Mr. Mink, en skuze hisse'f kaze he wuz too sick fer ter come, en he ax Brer Rabbit fer ter come en take dinner wid him, en Brer Rabbit say he wuz 'gree'ble.

"Bimeby, w'en de shadders wuz at der shortes', Brer Rabbit he sorter brush up en santer down ter Brer Fox's house, en w'en he got dar, he hear somebody groanin', en he look in de do' en dar he see Brer Fox settin' up in a rockin' cheer all wrop up wid flannil, en he look mighty weak. Brer Rabbit look all 'roun', he did, but he ain't see no dinner. De dish-pan wuz settin' on de table, en close by wuz a kyarvin' knife.

" 'Look like you gwineter have chicken fer dinner, Brer Fox,' sez Brer Rabbit, sezee.

" 'Yes, Brer Rabbit, deyer nice, en fresh, en tender,' sez Brer Fox, sezee.

"Den Brer Rabbit sorter pull his mustarsh, en say: 'You ain't got no calamus root, is you, Brer Fox? I done got so now dat I can't eat no chicken 'ceppin she's seasoned up wid calamus root.' En wid dat Brer Rabbit lipt out er de do' and dodge 'mong de bushes, en sot dar watchin' fer Brer Fox; en he ain't watch long, nudder, kaze Brer Fox flung off de flannil en crope out er de house en got whar he could cloze in on Brer Rabbit, en bimeby Brer Rabbit holler out: 'Oh, Brer Fox! I'll des put yo' calamus root out yer on dish yer stump. Better come git it while hit's fresh,' and wid dat Brer Rabbit gallop off home. En Brer Fox ain't never kotch 'im yet, en w'at's mo', honey, he ain't gwineter."

II

"Didn't the fox *never* catch the rabbit, Uncle Remus?" asked the little boy the next evening.

"He come mighty nigh it, honey, sho's you born—Brer Fox did. One day atter Brer Rabbit fool 'im wid dat calamus root, Brer Fox went ter wuk en got 'im some tar, en mix it wid some turkentime, en fix up a contrapshun wat he call a Tar-Baby, en he tuck dish yer Tar-Baby en he sot 'er in de big road, en den he lay off in de bushes fer to see wat de news wuz gwineter be. En he didn't hatter wait long, nudder, kaze bimeby here come Brer Rabbit pacin' down de road—lippity-clippity, clippity-lippity—dez ez sassy ez a jay-bird. Brer Fox, he lay low. Brer Rabbit come prancin' 'long twel he spy de Tar-Baby, en den he fotch up on his behime legs like he wuz 'stonished. De Tar-Baby, she sot dar, she did, en Brer Fox, he lay low.

"'Mawnin'!' sez Brer Rabbit, sezee—'nice wedder dis mawnin',' sezee.

"Tar-Baby ain't sayin' nothin', en Brer Fox, he lay low.

"'How duz yo' sym'tums seem ter segashuate?' sez Brer Rabbit, sezee.

"Brer Fox, he wink his eye slow, en lay low, en de Tar-Baby, she ain't sayin' nothin'.

"'How you come on, den? Is you deaf?' sez Brer Rabbit, sezee. 'Kaze if you is, I kin holler louder,' sezee.

"Tar-Baby stay still, en Brer Fox, he lay low.

"'Youer stuck up, dat's w'at you is,' says Brer Rabbit, sezee, 'en I'm gwineter kyore you, dat's w'at I'm a gwineter do,' sezee.

"Brer Fox, he sorter chuckle in his stummuck, he did, but Tar-Baby ain't sayin' nothin'.

"'I'm gwineter larn you howter talk ter 'specttubble fokes ef hit's de las' ack,' sez Brer Rabbit, sezee. 'Ef you don't take off dat hat en tell me howdy, I'm gwineter bus' you wide open,' sezee.

"Tar-Baby stay still, en Brer Fox, he lay low.

"Brer Rabbit keep on axin' 'im, en de Tar-Baby, she keep on sayin' nothin', twel present'y Brer Rabbit draw back wid his fis', he did, en blip he tuck 'er side er de head. Right dar's whar he broke his merlasses jug. His fis' stuck, en he can't pull loose. De tar hilt 'im. But Tar-Baby, she stay still, en Brer Fox, he lay low.

"'Ef you don't lemme loose, I'll knock you agin,' sez Brer Rabbit, sezee, en wid dat he fotch 'er a wipe wid de udder han', en dat stuck. Tar-Baby, she ain't sayin' nothin', en Brer Fox, he lay low.

"'Tu'n me loose, fo' I kick de natal stuffin' outen you,' sez Brer Rabbit, sezee, but de Tar-Baby, she ain't sayin' nothin'. She des hilt on, en den Brer Rabbit lose de use er his feet in de same way. Brer Fox, he lay low. Den Brer Rabbit squall out dat ef de Tar-Baby don't tu'n 'im loose he butt'er cranksided. En den he butted, en his head got

stuck. Den Brer Fox, he sa'ntered fort', lookin' des ez innercent ez one er yo' mammy's mockin'-birds.

"'Howdy, Brer Rabbit,' sez Brer Fox, sezee. 'You look sorter stuck up dis mawnin',' sezee, en den he rolled on de groun', en laughed en laughed twel he couldn't laugh no mo'. 'I speck you'll take dinner wid me dis time, Brer Rabbit. I done laid in some calamus root, en I ain't gwineter take no skuse,' sez Brer Fox, sezee."

Here Uncle Remus paused, and drew a two-pound yam out of the ashes.

"Did the fox eat the rabbit?" asked the little boy to whom the story had been told.

"Dat's all de fur de tale goes," replied the old man. "He mout, en den agin he moutent. Some say Jedge B'ar come 'long en loosed 'im— some say he didn't. I hear Miss Sally callin'. You better run 'long."

III

"Uncle Remus," said the little boy one evening, when he had found the old man with little or nothing to do, "did the fox kill and eat the rabbit when he caught him with the Tar-Baby?"

"Law, honey, ain't I tell you 'bout dat?" replied the old darkey, chuckling slyly. "I 'clar ter grashus I ought er tole you dat, but old man Nod wuz ridin' on my eyeleds twel a leetle mo'n I'd a dis'member'd my own name, en den on to dat here come yo' mammy hollerin' atter you.

"W'at I tell you w'en I fus' begin? I tole you Brer Rabbit wuz a monstus soon creetur; leas'ways dat's w'at I laid out fer ter tell you. Well, den, honey, don't you go en make no udder calkalashuns, kaze in dem days Brer Rabbit en his fambly wuz at de head er de gang w'en enny racket wuz on han', en dar de stayed. 'Fo' you begins fer ter wipe yo' eyes 'bout Brer Rabbit, you wait en see whar'bouts Brer Rabbit gwineter fetch up at. But dat's needer yer ner dar.

"W'en Brer Fox fine Brer Rabbit mixt up wid de Tar-Baby, he feel mighty good, en he roll on de ground' en laff. Bimeby he up'n sez, sezee:

" 'Well, I speck I got you dis time, Brer Rabbit,' sezee; 'maybe I ain't, but I speck I is. You been runnin' roun' here sassin' atter me a mighty long time, but I speck you done come ter de een' er de row. You bin cuttin' up yo' capers en bouncin' 'roun' in dis neighborhood ontwel you come ter b'leeve yo'se'f de boss er de whole gang. En den youer allers some'rs whar you got no bizness,' sez Brer Fox, sezee. 'Who ax you fer ter come en strike up a 'quaintance wid dish yer Tar-Baby? En who stuck you up dar whar you iz? Nobody in de roun' worril. You des tuck en jam yo'se'f on dat Tar-Baby widout waitin' fer enny invite,' sez Brer Fox, sezee, 'en dar you is, en dar you'll stay twel I fixes up a bresh-pile and fires her up, kaze I'm gwineter bobby-cue you dis day, sho,' sez Brer Fox, sezee.

"Den Brer Rabbit talk mighty 'umble.

" 'I don't keer w'at you do wid me, Brer Fox,' sezee, 'so you don't fling me in dat brier-patch. Roas' me, Brer Fox,' sezee, 'but don't fling me in dat brier-patch,' sezee.

" 'Hit's so much trouble fer ter kindle a fier,' sez Brer Fox, sezee, 'dat I speck I'll hatter hang you,' sezee.

" 'Hang me des ez high as you please, Brer Fox,' sez Brer Rabbit, sezee, 'but do fer de Lord's sake don't fling me in dat brier-patch,' sezee.

" 'I ain't got no string,' sez Brer Fox, sezee, 'en now I speck I'll hatter drown you,' sezee.

" 'Drown me des ez deep ez you please, Brer Fox,' sez Brer Rabbit, sezee, 'but do don't fling me in dat brier-patch,' sezee.

" 'Der ain't no water nigh,' sez Brer Fox, sezee, 'en now I speck I'll hatter skin you,' sezee.

" 'Skin me, Brer Fox,' sez Brer Rabbit, sezee, 'snatch out my eyeballs, t'ar out my years by de roots, en cut off my legs,' sezee, 'but do please, Brer Fox, don't fling me in dat brier-patch,' sezee.

"Co'se Brer Fox wanter hurt Brer Rabbit bad ez he kin, so he cotch 'im by de behime legs en slung 'im right in de middle er de brier-patch. Dar wuz a considerbul flutter whar Brer Rabbit struck de bushes, en

Brer Fox sorter hang 'roun' fer ter see w'at wuz gwineter happen. Bimeby he hear somebody call 'im, en way up de hill he see Brer Rabbit settin' cross-legged on a chinkapin log koamin' de pitch outen his har wid a chip. Den Brer Fox know dat he bin swop off mighty bad. Brer Rabbit wuz bleedzed fer ter fling back some er his sass, en he holler out:

"'Bred en bawn in a brier-patch, Brer Fox—bred en bawn in a brier-patch!' en wid dat he skip out des ez lively ez a cricket in de embers."

O. Henry

William Sydney Porter was born in Greensboro, North Carolina, but O. Henry became the laureate of Bagdad-on-the-Subway (as he liked to call New York), interpreter of its shopgirls, actors, policemen, tramps, and the city's uncelebrated millions.

The son of an improvident country doctor, Porter worked in a rural drugstore, wandered to Texas and found odd jobs there, as sheepherder, ranch hand, reporter, and bank clerk. The bank was carelessly run, and when a shortage was discovered, Porter foolishly accepted the advice of friends and fled to Honduras. Hearing of his wife's illness, he returned, was arrested, convicted, and served three years. It was in prison that Porter began to write short stories under a pseudonym; the first story which he signed "O. Henry" was published in 1899 when he was thirty-seven.

Success came to him with the first casually told adventures of ordinary people. Editors besieged him with ever-increasing offers; readers never tired of his sympathetic comedies, his flirtations with the sentimental, his quick characterizations, and his fondness for tricky endings. The one-volume omnibus Complete Works of O. Henry includes the contents of fourteen volumes and almost three hundred stories.

The Ransom of Red Chief

It looked like a good thing: but wait till I tell you. We were down South, in Alabama—Bill Driscoll and myself—when this kidnapping idea struck us. It was, as Bill afterward expressed it, "during a moment of temporary mental apparition"; but we didn't find that out till later.

There was a town down there, as flat as a flannel-cake, and called Summit, of course. It contained inhabitants of as undeleterious and self-satisfied a class of peasantry as ever clustered around a Maypole.

Bill and me had a joint capital of about six hundred dollars, and we needed just two thousand dollars more to pull off a fraudulent town-lot scheme in Western Illinois with. We talked it over on the front steps of the hotel. Philoprogenitiveness, says we, is strong in semi-rural communities; therefore, and for other reasons, a kidnapping project ought to do better there than in the radius of newspapers that send reporters out in plain clothes to stir up talk about such things. We knew that Summit couldn't get after us with anything stronger than constables and, maybe, some lackadaisical bloodhounds and a diatribe or two in the *Weekly Farmers' Budget*. So, it looked good.

We selected for our victim the only child of a prominent citizen named Ebenezer Dorset. The father was respectable and tight, a mortgage fancier and a stern, upright collection-plate passer and forecloser. The kid was a boy of ten, with bas-relief freckles, and hair the color of the cover of the magazine you buy at the news-stand when you want to catch a train. Bill and me figured that Ebenezer would melt down for a ransom of two thousand dollars to a cent. But wait till I tell you.

About two miles from Summit was a little mountain, covered with a dense cedar brake. On the rear elevation of this mountain was a cave. There we stored provisions.

One evening after sundown, we drove in a buggy past old Dorset's house. The kid was in the street, throwing rocks at a kitten on the opposite fence.

"Hey, little boy!" says Bill, "would you like to have a bag of candy and a nice ride?"

The boy catches Bill neatly in the eye with a piece of brick.

"That will cost the old man an extra five hundred dollars," says Bill, climbing over the wheel.

That boy put up a fight like a welter-weight cinnamon bear; but, at last, we got him down in the bottom of the buggy and drove away. We took him up to the cave, and I hitched the horse in the cedar brake.

After dark I drove the buggy to the little village, three miles away, where we had hired it, and walked back to the mountain.

Bill was pasting court-plaster over the scratches and bruises on his features. There was a fire burning behind the big rock at the entrance of the cave, and the boy was watching a pot of boiling coffee, with two buzzard tail-feathers stuck in his red hair. He points a stick at me when I come up, and says:

"Ha! cursed paleface, do you dare to enter the camp of Red Chief, the terror of the plains?"

"He's all right now," says Bill, rolling up his trousers and examining some bruises on his shins. "We're playing Indian. We're making Buffalo Bill's show look like magic-lantern views of Palestine in the town hall. I'm Old Hank, the Trapper, Red Chief's captive, and I'm to be scalped at daybreak. By Geronimo! that kid can kick hard."

Yes, sir, that boy seemed to be having the time of his life. The fun of camping out in a cave had made him forget that he was a captive himself. He immediately christened me Snake-eye, the Spy, and announced that, when his braves returned from the warpath, I was to be broiled at the stake at the rising of the sun.

Then we had supper; and he filled his mouth full of bacon and bread and gravy, and began to talk. He made a during-dinner speech something like this:

"I like this fine. I never camped out before; but I had a pet 'possum once, and I was nine last birthday. I hate to go to school. Rats ate up sixteen of Jimmy Talbot's aunt's speckled hen's eggs. Are there any real Indians in these woods? I want some more gravy. Does the trees moving make the wind blow? We had five puppies. What makes your nose so red, Hank? My father has lots of money. Are the stars hot? I whipped Ed Walker twice, Saturday. I don't like girls. You dassent catch toads unless with a string. Do oxen make any noise? Why are oranges round? Have you got beds to sleep on in this cave? Amos Murray has got six toes. A parrot can talk, but a monkey or a fish can't. How many does it take to make twelve?"

Every few minutes he would remember that he was a pesky redskin, and pick up his stick rifle and tiptoe to the mouth of the cave to rubber for the scouts of the hated paleface. Now and then he would let out a war-whoop that made Old Hank the Trapper shiver. That boy had Bill terrorized from the start.

"Red Chief," says I to the kid, "would you like to go home?"

"Aw, what for?" says he. "I don't have any fun at home. I hate to go to school. I like to camp out. You won't take me back home again, Snake-eye, will you?"

"Not right away," says I. "We'll stay here in the cave awhile."

"All right!" says he. "That'll be fine. I never had such fun in all my life."

We went to bed about eleven o'clock. We spread down some wide blankets and quilts and put Red Chief between us. We weren't afraid he'd run away. He kept us awake for three hours, jumping up and reaching for his rifle and screeching: "Hist! pard," in mine and Bill's ears, as the fancied crackle of a twig or the rustle of a leaf revealed to his young imagination the stealthy approach of the outlaw band. At last, I fell into a troubled sleep, and dreamed that I had been kidnapped and chained to a tree by a ferocious pirate with red hair.

Just at daybreak, I was awakened by a series of awful screams from Bill. They weren't yells, or howls, or shouts, or whoops, or yawps, such as you'd expect from a manly set of vocal organs—they were simply indecent, terrifying, humiliating screams, such as women emit when they see ghosts or caterpillars. It's an awful thing to hear a strong, desperate, fat man scream incontinently in a cave at daybreak.

I jumped up to see what the matter was. Red Chief was sitting on Bill's chest, with one hand twined in Bill's hair. In the other he had the sharp case-knife we used for slicing bacon; and he was industriously and realistically trying to take Bill's scalp, according to the sentence that had been pronounced upon him the evening before.

I got the knife away from the kid and made him lie down again. But, from that moment, Bill's spirit was broken. He laid down on his side of the bed, but he never closed an eye again in sleep as long as that boy was with us. I dozed off for a while, but along toward sun-up I remembered that Red Chief had said I was to be burned at the stake at the rising of the sun. I wasn't nervous or afraid; but I sat up and lit my pipe and leaned against a rock.

"What you getting up so soon for, Sam?" asked Bill.

"Me?" says I. "Oh, I got a kind of pain in my shoulder. I thought sitting up would rest it."

"You're a liar!" says Bill. "You're afraid. You was to be burned at sunrise, and you was afraid he'd do it. And he would, too, if he could find a match. Ain't it awful, Sam? Do you think anybody will pay out money to get a little imp like that back home?"

"Sure," said I. "A rowdy kid like that is just the kind that parents dote on. Now, you and the Chief get up and cook breakfast, while I go up on the top of this mountain and reconnoitre."

I went up on the peak of the little mountain and ran my eye over the contiguous vicinity. Over towards Summit I expected to see the sturdy yeomanry of the village armed with scythes and pitchforks beating the countryside for the dastardly kidnappers. But what I saw was a peaceful landscape dotted with one man ploughing with a dun mule. Nobody was dragging the creek; no couriers dashed hither and yon, bringing tidings of no news to the distracted parents. There was a sylvan attitude of somnolent sleepiness pervading that section of the external outward surface of Alabama that lay exposed to my view. "Perhaps," says I to myself, "it has not yet been discovered that the wolves have borne away the tender lambkin from the fold. Heaven help the wolves!" says I, and I went down the mountain to breakfast.

When I got to the cave I found Bill backed up against the side of it, breathing hard, and the boy threatening to smash him with a rock half as big as a cocoanut.

"He put a red-hot boiled potato down my back," explained Bill, "and then mashed it with his foot; and I boxed his ears. Have you got a gun about you, Sam?"

I took the rock away from the boy and kind of patched up the argument. "I'll fix you," says the kid to Bill. "No man ever yet struck the Red Chief but he got paid for it. You better beware!"

After breakfast the kid takes a piece of leather with strings wrapped around it out of his pocket and goes outside the cave unwinding it.

"What's he up to now?" says Bill, anxiously. "You don't think he'll run away, do you, Sam?"

"No fear of it," says I. "He don't seem to be much of a home body. But we've got to fix up some plan about the ransom. There don't seem to be much excitement around Summit on account of his disappearance; but maybe they haven't realized yet that he's gone. His folks may think he's spending the night with Aunt Jane or one of the neighbors. Anyhow, he'll be missed to-day. To-night we must get a message to his father demanding the two thousand dollars for his return."

Just then we heard a kind of war-whoop, such as David might have emitted when he knocked out the champion Goliath. It was a sling that Red Chief had pulled out of his pocket, and he was whirling it around his head.

I dodged, and heard a heavy thud and a kind of a sigh from Bill, like a horse gives out when you take his saddle off. A niggerhead rock the size of an egg had caught Bill just behind his left ear. He loosened himself all over and fell in the fire across the frying pan of hot water for washing the dishes. I dragged him out and poured cold water on his head for half an hour.

By and by, Bill sits up and feels behind his ear and says: "Sam, do you know who my favorite Biblical character is?"

"Take it easy," says I. "You'll come to your senses presently."

"King Herod," says he. "You won't go away and leave me here alone, will you, Sam?"

I went out and caught that boy and shook him until his freckles rattled.

"If you don't behave," says I, "I'll take you straight home. Now, are you going to be good, or not?"

"I was only funning," says he, sullenly. "I didn't mean to hurt Old Hank. But what did he hit me for? I'll behave, Snake-eye, if you won't send me home, and if you'll let me play the Black Scout to-day."

"I don't know the game," says I. "That's for you and Mr. Bill to decide. He's your playmate for the day. I'm going away for a while, on business. Now, you come in and make friends with him and say you are sorry for hurting him, or home you go, at once."

I made him and Bill shake hands, and then I took Bill aside and told him I was going to Poplar Grove, a little village three miles from the cave, and find out what I could about how the kidnapping had been regarded in Summit. Also, I thought it best to send a peremptory letter to old man Dorset that day, demanding the ransom and dictating how it should be paid.

"You know, Sam," says Bill, "I've stood by you without batting an eye in earthquakes, fire and flood—in poker games, dynamite outrages, police raids, train robberies, and cyclones. I never lost my nerve yet till we kidnapped that two-legged skyrocket of a kid. He's got me going. You won't leave me long with him, will you, Sam?"

"I'll be back some time this afternoon," says I. "You must keep the boy amused and quiet till I return. And now we'll write the letter to old Dorset."

Bill and I got paper and pencil and worked on the letter while Red Chief, with a blanket wrapped around him, strutted up and down, guarding the mouth of the cave. Bill begged me tearfully to make the ransom fifteen hundred dollars instead of two thousand. "I ain't attempting," says he, "to decry the celebrated moral aspect of parental affection, but we're dealing with humans, and it ain't human for anybody to give up two thousand dollars for that forty-pound chunk of freckled wildcat. I'm willing to take a chance at fifteen hundred dollars. You can charge the difference up to me."

So, to relieve Bill, I acceded, and we collaborated a letter that ran this way:

EBENEZER DORSET, ESQ. :

We have your boy concealed in a place far from Summit. It is useless for you or the most skillful detectives to attempt to find him. Absolutely, the only terms on which you can have him restored to you are these: We demand fifteen hundred dollars in large bills for his return; the money to be left at midnight to-night at the same spot and in the same box as your reply—as hereinafter described. If you agree to these terms, send your answer in writing by a solitary messenger to-night at half-past eight o'clock. After crossing Owl Creek on the road to Poplar Grove, there are three large trees about a hundred yards apart, close to the fence of the wheat field on the right-hand side. At the bottom of the fence-post, opposite the third tree, will be found a small pasteboard box.

The messenger will place the answer in this box and return immediately to Summit.

If you attempt any treachery or fail to comply with our demand as stated, you will never see your boy again.

If you pay the money as demanded, he will be returned to you safe and well within three hours. These terms are final, and if you do not accede to them no further communication will be attempted.

TWO DESPERATE MEN.

I addressed this letter to Dorset, and put it in my pocket. As I was about to start, the kid comes up to me and says:

"Aw, Snake-eye, you said I could play the Black Scout while you was gone."

"Play it, of course," says I. "Mr. Bill will play with you. What kind of a game is it?"

"I'm the Black Scout," says Red Chief, "and I have to ride to the stockade to warn the settlers that the Indians are coming. I'm tired of playing Indian myself. I want to be the Black Scout."

"All right," says I. "It sounds harmless to me. I guess Mr. Bill will help you foil the pesky savages."

"What am I to do?" asks Bill, looking at the kid suspiciously.

"You are the hoss," says Black Scout. "Get down on your hands and knees. How can I ride to the stockade without a hoss?"

"You'd better keep him interested," said I, "till we get the scheme going. Loosen up."

Bill gets down on his all fours, and a look comes in his eye like a rabbit's when you catch it in a trap.

"How far is it to the stockade, kid?" he asks, in a husky manner of voice.

"Ninety miles," says the Black Scout. "And you have to hump yourself to get there on time. Whoa, now!"

The Black Scout jumps on Bill's back and digs his heels in his side.

"For Heaven's sake," says Bill, "hurry back, Sam, as soon as you can. I wish we hadn't made the ransom more than a thousand. Say, you quit kicking me or I'll get up and warm you good."

I walked over to Poplar Grove and sat around the post-office and store, talking with the chaw-bacons that came in to trade. One whisker-ando says that he hears Summit is all upset on account of Elder Ebenezer Dorset's boy having been lost or stolen. That was all I wanted to know. I bought some smoking tobacco, referred casually to the price of black-eyed peas, posted my letter surreptitiously, and came away. The postmaster said the mail-carrier would come by in an hour to take the mail to Summit.

When I got back to the cave Bill and the boy were not to be found. I explored the vicinity of the cave, and risked a yodel or two, but there was no response.

So I lighted my pipe and sat down on a mossy bank to await developments.

In about half an hour I heard the bushes rustle, and Bill wabbled out into the little glade in front of the cave. Behind him was the kid, stepping softly like a scout, with a broad grin on his face. Bill stopped, took off his hat, and wiped his face with a red handkerchief. The kid stopped about eight feet behind him.

"Sam," says Bill, "I suppose you'll think I'm a renegade, but I couldn't help it. I'm a grown person with masculine proclivities and habits of self-defense, but there is a time when all systems of egotism and predominance fail. The boy is gone. I sent him home. All is off. There was martyrs in old times," goes on Bill, "that suffered death rather than give up the particular graft they enjoyed. None of 'em ever was subjugated to such supernatural tortures as I have been. I tried to be faithful to our articles of depredation; but there came a limit."

"What's the trouble, Bill?" I asks him.

"I was rode," says Bill, "the ninety miles to the stockade, not barring an inch. Then, when the settlers was rescued, I was given oats. Sand ain't a palatable substitute. And then, for an hour I had to try to explain to him why there was nothin' in holes, how a road can run both ways, and what makes the grass green. I tell you, Sam, a human can only stand so much. I takes him by the neck of his clothes and drags him down the mountain. On the way he kicks my legs black and blue from the knees down; and I've got to have two or three bites on my thumb and hand cauterized.

"But he's gone"—continues Bill—"gone home. I showed him the road to Summit and kicked him about eight feet nearer there at one kick. I'm sorry we lose the ransom; but it was either that or Bill Driscoll to the madhouse."

Bill is puffing and blowing, but there is a look of ineffable peace and growing content on his rose-pink features.

"Bill," says I, "there isn't any heart disease in your family, is there?"

"No," says Bill, "nothing chronic except malaria and accidents. Why?"

"Then you might turn around," says I, "and have a look behind you."

Bill turns and sees the boy, and loses his complexion and sits down plump on the ground and begins to pluck aimlessly at grass and little sticks. For an hour I was afraid of his mind. And then I told him that my scheme was to put the whole job through immediately and that we would get the ransom and be off with it by midnight if old Dorset fell in with our proposition. So Bill braced up enough to give the kid a weak sort of a smile and a promise to play the Russian in a Japanese war with him as soon as he felt a little better.

I had a scheme for collecting that ransom without danger of being caught by counterplots that ought to commend itself to professional kidnappers. The tree under which the answer was to be left—and the money later on—was close to the road fence with big, bare fields on all sides. If a gang of constables should be watching for any one to come for the note, they could see him a long way off crossing the fields or in the road. But no, sirree! At half-past eight I was up in that tree as well hidden as a tree toad, waiting for the messenger to arrive.

Exactly on time, a half-grown boy rides up the road on a bicycle, locates the pasteboard box at the foot of the fence-post, slips a folded piece of paper into it, and pedals away again back toward Summit.

I waited an hour and then concluded the thing was square. I slid down the tree, got the note, slipped along the fence till I struck the woods, and was back at the cave in another half an hour. I opened the note, got near the lantern, and read it to Bill. It was written with a pen in a crabbed hand, and the sum and substance of it was this:

Two Desperate Men.

   Gentlemen: I received your letter to-day by post, in regard to the ransom you ask for the return of my son. I think you are a little high in your demands, and I hereby make you a counter-proposition, which I am inclined to believe you will accept. You bring Johnny home and pay me two hundred and fifty dollars in cash, and I agree to take him off your hands. You had better come at night, for the neighbors believe he is lost, and I couldn't be responsible for what they would do to anybody they saw bringing him back. Very respectfully,

EBENEZER DORSET.

"Great pirates of Penzance," says I; "of all the impudent——"

But I glanced at Bill, and hesitated. He had the most appealing look in his eyes I ever saw on the face of a dumb or a talking brute.

"Sam," says he, "what's two hundred and fifty dollars, after all? We've got the money. One more night of this kid will send me to a bed in Bedlam. Besides being a thorough gentleman, I think Mr. Dorset is a spendthrift for making us such a liberal offer. You ain't going to let the chance go, are you?"

"Tell you the truth, Bill," says I, "this little he ewe lamb has somewhat got on my nerves too. We'll take him home, pay the ransom, and make our getaway."

We took him home that night. We got him to go by telling him that his father had bought a silver-mounted rifle and a pair of moccasins for him, and we were to hunt bears the next day.

It was just twelve o'clock when we knocked at Ebenezer's front door. Just at the moment when I should have been abstracting the fifteen hundred dollars from the box under the tree, according to the original proposition, Bill was counting out two hundred and fifty dollars into Dorset's hand.

When the kid found out we were going to leave him at home he started up a howl like a calliope and fastened himself as tight as a leech to Bill's leg. His father peeled him away gradually, like a porous plaster.

"How long can you hold him?" asks Bill.

"I'm not as strong as I used to be," says old Dorset, "but I think I can promise you ten minutes."

"Enough," says Bill. "In ten minutes I shall cross the Central, Southern, and Middle Western States, and be legging it trippingly for the Canadian border."

And, as dark as it was, and as fat as Bill was, and as good a runner as I am, he was a good mile and a half out of Summit before I could catch up with him.

Oliver Wendell Holmes

He was brought up to be a doctor, but Oliver
Wendell Holmes (1809–1894) never built up a
successful practice. He loathed the unctuous "bedside manner" and was too fond of puns; patients
resented being told that "small fevers would be
gratefully received." Holmes learned to restrain his
wit, and the sagacious essays in the Breakfast Table
series are no less keen for being kindly. As a poet,
he was inclined to be sententious; but "The
Deacon's Masterpiece" is a little masterpiece of
New England logic and humor.

The One-Hoss Shay

OR, THE DEACON'S MASTERPIECE

Have you heard of the wonderful one-hoss shay,
That was built in such a logical way
It ran a hundred years to a day,
And then, of a sudden, it—ah, but stay,
I'll tell you what happened without delay,
Scaring the parson into fits,
Frightening people out of their wits,—
Have you ever heard of that, I say?

Seventeen hundred and fifty-five.
Georgius Secundus was then alive,—
Snuffy old drone from the German hive.
That was the year when Lisbon-town
Saw the earth open and gulp her down,
And Braddock's army was done so brown,
Left without a scalp to its crown.
It was on the terrible Earthquake-day
That the Deacon finished the one-hoss shay.

Now in building of chaises, I tell you what,
There is always *somewhere* a weaker spot,—
In hub, tire, felloe, in spring or thill,
In panel, or crossbar, or floor, or sill,
In screw, bolt, thoroughbrace,—lurking still,
Find it somewhere you must and will,—
Above or below, or within or without,—
And that's the reason, beyond a doubt,
A chaise *breaks down,* but doesn't *wear out.*

But the Deacon swore (as Deacons do),
With an "I dew vum," or an "I tell yeou,"
He would build one shay to beat the taown
'N' the keounty 'n' all the kentry raoun';
It should be so built that it *couldn'* break daown:
—"Fur," said the Deacon, " 't's mighty plain

Thut the weakes' place mus' stan' the strain;
'N' the way t' fix it, uz I maintain,
                              Is only jest
T' make that place uz strong uz the rest."

So the Deacon inquired of the village folk
Where he could find the strongest oak,
That couldn't be split nor bent nor broke,—
That was for spokes and floor and sills;
He sent for lancewood to make the thills;
The crossbars were ash, from the straightest trees,
The panels of white-wood, that cuts like cheese,
But lasts like iron for things like these;
The hubs of logs from the "Settler's ellum,"—
Last of its timber,—they couldn't sell 'em,
Never an axe had seen their chips,
And the wedges flew from between their lips,
Their blunt ends frizzled like celery tips;
Step and prop-iron, bolt and screw,
Spring, tire, axle, and linchpin too,
Steel of the finest, bright and blue;
Thoroughbrace bison-skin, thick and wide;
Boot, top, dasher, from tough old hide
Found in the pit when the tanner died.
That was the way he "put her through."—
"There!" said the Deacon, "naow she'll dew!"

Do! I tell you, I rather guess
She was a wonder, and nothing less!
Colts ew horses, beards turned gray,
Deac nd Deaconess dropped away,
Children and grandchildren—where were they?
But there stood the stout old one-hoss shay
As fresh as on Lisbon-earthquake-day!

EIGHTEEN HUNDRED;—it came and found
The Deacon s asterpiece strong and sound.
Eighteen hundred increased by ten;—
"Hahnsum kerridge" they called it then.
Eighteen hundred and twenty came;—
Running as usual; much the same.

Thirty and forty at last arrive,
And then come fifty, and FIFTY-FIVE.

Little of all we value here
Wakes on the morn of its hundredth year
Without both feeling and looking queer.
In fact, there's nothing that keeps its youth,
So far as I know, but a tree and truth.
(This is a moral that runs at large;
Take it.—You're welcome.—No extra charge.)
FIRST OF NOVEMBER—the-Earthquake-day,—
There are traces of age in the one-hoss shay,
A general flavor of mild decay,
But nothing local, as one may say.
There couldn't be,—for the Deacon's art
Had made it so like in every part
That there wasn't a chance for one to start.
For the wheels were just as strong as the thills,
And the floor was just as strong as the sills,
And the panels just as strong as the floor,
And the whipple-tree neither less nor more,
And the back-cross bar as strong as the fore,
And spring and axle and hub *encore*.
And yet, as *a whole,* it is past a doubt
In another hour it will be *worn out!*

First of November, 'Fifty-five!
This morning the parson takes a drive.
Now, small boys, get out of the way!
Here comes the wonderful one-hoss shay,
Drawn by a rat-tailed, ewe-necked bay.
"Huddup!" said the parson. Off went they.
The parson was working his Sunday text,—
Had got to *fifthly,* and stopped perplexed
At what the—Moses—was coming next.
All at once the horse stood still,
Close by the meet'n'-house on the hill.
—First a shiver, and then a thrill,
Then something decidedly like a spill,—
And the parson was sitting up on a rock,
At half-past nine by the meet'n'-house clock,—

Just the hour of the Earthquake shock!
—What do you think the parson found,
When he got up and stared around?
The poor old chaise in a heap or mound,
As if it had been to the mill and ground!
You see, of course, if you're not a dunce,
How it went to pieces all at once,—
All at once, and nothing first,—
Just as bubbles do when they burst.

End of the wonderful one-hoss shay,
Logic is logic. That's all I say.

Contentment

"Man wants but little here below"

Little I ask; my wants are few;
   I only wish a hut of stone
(A *very plain* brownstone will do),
   That I may call my own:—
And close at hand is such a one,
In yonder street that fronts the sun.

Plain food is quite enough for me;
   Three courses are as good as ten;—
If Nature can subsist on three,
   Thank Heaven for three. Amen!
I always thought cold victual nice;—
My *choice* would be vanilla-ice.

I care not much for gold or land;—
   Give me a mortgage here and there,—
Some good bank-stock, some note of hand,
   Or trifling railroad share,—
I only ask that Fortune send
A *little* more than I shall spend.

Honors are silly toys, I know,
   And titles are but empty names;
I would, *perhaps,* be Plenipo,—
   But only near St. James;
I'm very sure I should not care
To fill our Gubernator's chair.

Jewels are baubles; 'tis a sin
   To care for such unfruitful things;—
One good-sized diamond in a pin,—
   Some, *not so large,* in rings.
A ruby, and a pearl, or so,
Will do for me;—I laugh at show.

My dame should dress in cheap attire;
   (Good, heavy silks are never dear;)
I own perhaps I *might* desire
   Some shawls of true Cashmere,—
Some marrowy crapes of China silk,
Like wrinkled skins on scalded milk.

I would not have the horse I drive
   So fast that folks must stop and stare;
An easy gait—two, forty-five—
   Suits me; I do not care;—
Perhaps, for just a *single spurt,*
Some seconds less would do no hurt.

Of pictures, I should like to own
   Titians and Raphaels three or four,—
I love so much their style and tone,—
   One Turner, and no more,
(A landscape,—foreground golden dirt,—
The sunshine painted with a squirt.)

Of books but few,—some fifty score
   For daily use, and bound for wear;
The rest upon an upper floor;—
   Some *little* luxury *there*
Of red morocco's gilded gleam,
And vellum rich as country cream.

Busts, cameos, gems,—such things as these
  Which others often show for pride,
I value for their power to please,
  And selfish churls deride;—
One Stradivarius, I confess,
Two meerschaums, I would fain possess.

Wealth's wasteful tricks I will not learn
  Nor ape the glittering upstart fool;—
Shall not carved tables serve my turn,
  But all must be of buhl.
Give grasping pomp its double share,—
I ask but one recumbent chair.

Thus humble let me live and die,
  Nor long for Midas' golden touch;
If Heaven more generous gifts deny,
  I shall not miss them *much*,—
Too grateful for the blessing lent
Of simple tastes and mind content!

A BIT OF SCOTCH

I had to go all the way to Brussels to hear a new (to me) twist of an old joke. Said my host, "The Scots have a great sense of humor." "So they have," I agreed. "No, no," said my host, "you must ask me why." "Oh," I echoed dutifully, "why?" "Because," said he, "it's a gift."

The Scottish people are, as a people, no more penurious than any other race. According to Robert L. ("Believe It Or Not") Ripley, it was a Scot who originated the custom of tipping—"to insure prompt service," and the first letters of those words make up the word "tips." But humor demands a pattern of fixed types: poets are always asinine, lovers are absurd, mothers-in-law are dreadful, the Irish are comic liars, the French are effeminate, the English are pompous fools—and all Scots are thrifty. When it was discovered that the word "Scotch" meant a "whiskey" as well as "a native of Scotland," the opportunities for jokes were limitless. Samples: "A Scotchman will drink—any given amount." "Recipe for a Scotch toddy: A glass of hot water and someone else's whiskey." "The first day of winter all the natives of Glasgow were going about with their mouths open—because there was a nip in the air."

The Scottish kilt was not invented because it had no pockets; but as long as jokes are made about nationalities, jokesters will define rigid economy as "a dead Scot" and they will tell the story about MacGregor who cried, " 'Tis ma birrrthday, Maggie. Hang the expense—give the canary anither seed." Even Ogden Nash, who does not follow any formula but his own, yielded to the stereotype when he concluded:

> No MacTavish
> Was ever lavish.

Here are a few choice variations on the theme:

A Scotchman, an Irishman, and a Jew had dinner together. When the waiter came with the bill, the Scotchman promptly said he would take it. The next day the newspaper carried a headline: "Death of a Jewish Ventriloquist."

MacDonald, leaving home for a few days, said, "Noo, Maggie, dinna forget to mak' wee Alec tak' off his glasses when he's not lookin' through them."

Angus woke early and found that his wife had passed away during the night. "Maggie! Maggie!" he cried to the servant.

"Aye, sir?" she called back.

"Maggie, ye need boil only one egg the morn!"

A friend was condoling with a Scotchman on the loss of his wife. "Eh, Sandy," he said, " 'tis a sair loss ye hae had!"

"Mon, 'tis that," answered Sandy. "And tae think! 'Twas a week ago that the doctor ordered a box of pills for her, and she hadna time tae take but half of them!"

"Now, McTavish," said the doctor, "it's like this: You've got a hard choice; you must either stop drinking whiskey or lose your eyesight."

"Ay, weel, doctor," said McTavish, "I'm an old man noo, an' I'm thinkin' I ha'e seen about everything worth seein'."

MacPherson bought only one spur. He figured that if one side of the horse went, the other was sure to follow.

A Scotchman came upon an automobile overturned at a railway crossing. Beside it lay a man badly hurt.

"Get a doctor," he moaned.

"Did the train hit you?" asked the Scotchman.

"Yes, yes! Get a doctor!"

"Has the claim agent been here yet?"

"No, no! Please get a doctor!"

"Move over," said the Scot, "till I lie down beside you."

A hunter was returning home from the field with nothing in his bag, when suddenly he spied a flock of ducks swimming in a little pond. An old Scotch farmer was watching them.

"How much do you want to let me take a pot shot at those ducks?" asked the hunter.

"Half a dollar," was the reply. The hunter let fly with both barrels, killing fourteen ducks.

"Well," said the hunter, smiling, as he paid the farmer, "I guess I got the best of that bargain."

"Ah, I dinna ken," replied the Scotchman. "They're not my ducks— and it's not my pond."

In Edinburgh they tell the story of the two burglars who smashed a jeweler's window and were arrested when they came back for the brick.

"Are ye the mon who rescued our little Angus from drowning?" cried the frantic mother. "If ye are, where's his bonnet?"

"Jock!" cried his father, "if you sow your wild oats, sow them in the back yard where they'll do some good."

"Did you hear about Sandy's tragedy? He had to give up golf."
"Poor man. Why?"
"He lost his ball."

"I hear that Anna got married to old MacDonald. How does he treat her?"
"Seldom."

Perhaps the meanest present ever sent was the one Campbell of Glasgow sent to his friend in Edinburgh. It was a homing pigeon.

A. E. Housman

A cloistered Cambridge scholar who composed the most chiselled verse of his day, Alfred Edward Housman (1859–1936) has wittily been called "the finest Latin poet who ever wrote in English." No poems of the period have been more quoted than those in A Shropshire Lad, a seemingly indestructible little volume that has gone into edition after edition since it was first published in 1896. Perhaps this is because Housman's themes are the perennial and indestructible favorites: young love and the countryside, passion and patriotism, beauty and betrayal. Perhaps it is because Housman had the uncanny gift of putting bitter texts to blithe tunes. In any case, his verses sing themselves into the mind and will not be shaken out of it.

When I Was One-and-Twenty

When I was one-and-twenty
   I heard a wise man say,
"Give crowns and pounds and guineas
   But not your heart away;
Give pearls away and rubies
   But keep your fancy free."
But I was one-and-twenty,
   No use to talk to me.

When I was one-and-twenty
   I heard him say again,
"The heart out of the bosom
   Was never given in vain;
'Tis paid with sighs a-plenty
   And sold for endless rue."
And I am two-and-twenty,
   And oh, 'tis true, 'tis true.

Oh, See How Thick the Goldcup Flowers

Oh, see how thick the goldcup flowers
   Are lying in field and lane,
With dandelions to tell the hours
   That never are told again,
Oh, may I squire you round the meads
   And pick you posies gay?
—'Twill do no harm to take my arm.
   "You may, young man, you may."

Ah, spring was sent for lass and lad,
   'Tis now the blood runs gold,
And man and maid had best be glad
   Before the world is old.
What flowers today may flower tomorrow,

But never as good as new.
—Suppose I wound my arm right round.
" 'Tis true, young man, 'tis true."

Some lads there are, 'tis shame to say,
    That only court to thieve,
And once they bear the bloom away
    'Tis little enough they leave.
Then keep your heart for men like me
    And safe from trustless chaps.
My love is true and all for you.
    "Perhaps, young man, perhaps."

Oh, look in my eyes then, can you doubt?
    —Why, 'tis a mile from town.
How green the grass is all about!
    We might as well sit down.
—Ah, life, what is it but a flower?
    Why must true lovers sigh?
Be kind, have pity, my own, my pretty,—
    "Good-by, young man, good-by."

Alva Johnston

Alva Johnston is more laconic than his detailed documents would indicate. He says he has no biography. It has, nevertheless, been learned that he was born in Sacramento, California, in 1888 and served a journalistic apprenticeship in his native state. After his fortieth year he wrote chiefly for The Saturday Evening Post and The New Yorker, and was awarded the Pulitzer Prize for newspaper reporting while on The New York Times for accounts of the meetings of the American Association for the Advancement of Science.

The selection which follows, regarded as one of Johnston's sharpest pieces of portraiture, is a condensation of a "Profile" first published in The New Yorker.

Legend of a Sport

Wilson Mizner, of the Klondike and Times Square, died in Hollywood on April 3, 1933, at the age of fifty-six. His fame has grown steadily since. Although he wrote practically nothing, he is probably quoted more than any other American of this century. His chance remarks have been organized into a literature by his disciples. Like the character in Stendhal who became a noted wit on the strength of six or seven pleasantries inherited from an uncle, scores of men have won recognition as sparkling conversationalists because they have collected small private anthologies of Mizner sayings.

Shortly before he died, a publisher asked him to write the story of his life. "It would be blowing a police whistle," replied Mizner. This was a reasonable excuse. The crime chapters would have occupied a large part of his autobiography. He was fundamentally a confidence man whom circumstances occasionally induced to go straight. But his real reason for refusing to write an autobiography was that he hated to write; he said, "Writing is too damned lonesome." He regarded it as an occupation for starvelings. Jim Tully once badgered him into writing a short story, which appeared in the *Liberty* of May 3, 1930. Mizner received a check for $1,000. He was incensed. "It took me eight hours to write it!" he exclaimed.

The short story is rather poor, although it contains a few typical Mizner lines. After a description of the long, tapering fingers of a cardsharp named Bert, Mizner added that Bert "could do more with fifty-two soda crackers than any other ocean grafter could with a new deck." The last paragraph of the story describes a tombstone erected over the grave of the hero, showing him kneeling, with hands clasped in prayer; the last line is "If you pried his hands open, four dice and a pearl necklace would fall out." Mizner was a little shamefaced over his literary effort. "I wanted to see something of mine in print except my thumbs," he said.

As a wit, Mizner belonged to two distinct schools—the scientific and the O. Henry. His scientific method consisted of bringing a calm spirit of inquiry to bear on boiling emotion. When an excited man rushed up to him exclaiming, "Coolidge is dead," Mizner asked, "How do they know?" The O. Henry school was the school of fantastic exaggeration. During Mizner's formative years, smart conversation consisted mainly of tired hyperboles. A majority of the familiar quotations from Mizner are extravagant figures of speech. He described a thin man as "a trellis

337

for varicose veins." He told a conceited motion-picture producer, "A demitasse cup would fit over your head like a sun-bonnet." Regarding a long-nosed Hollywood magnate, he said, "He's the only man who can take a shower and smoke a cigar at the same time" and "I'd like to take him by the feet and plow a furrow with him." Telling of a Klondike pal who had frozen to death in the act of tying his shoelaces, he said, "We had to bury him in a drum." A strutting little fellow went through bankruptcy and then strutted more than ever. "Failure has gone to his head," said Mizner. Describing his own flight from a madman armed with a revolver, he said, "I got up enough lather to shave Kansas City."

A man with a flourishing head of hair once joined his table at the Brown Derby restaurant in Hollywood, uttered several solemn platitudes, and left. "Now I know," said Mizner, "that hair can grow on anything."

A famous stage beauty, who had risen by five marriages to wealth and a title, attempted to bandy insults with him. "You're nothing but a parlayed chambermaid," he said. "You've compromised so many gentlemen that you think you're a lady," he added.

Talking about Tom Sharkey, the great heavyweight prizefighter, who kept a saloon with the old-fashioned swinging doors, Mizner said, "He was so dumb that he crawled under them for two years before he found out that they swung both ways."

He disapproved of San Francisco at the time when Hiram Johnson was sending grafters to jail in large numbers. "They learn to say 'Guilty' here before they can say 'Papa' and 'Mamma,' " he said.

He was asked by Lew Lipton, stage and screen writer, if a certain actress wasn't a little "mannish." "Mannish!" he said. "Not at all. I understand it took her all winter to color a meerschaum pipe."

Many of Mizner's lines have passed into the language. Some, like "Life's a tough proposition, and the first hundred years are the hardest," are passing out again after long and hard service. His rules "No opium smoking in the elevators" and "Carry out your own dead," which he put into effect as manager of the Hotel Rand in New York in 1907, have become standard hotel practice. Among his philosophical maxims were: "Be nice to people on your way up because you'll meet 'em on your way down," and "If you steal from one author, it's plagiarism; if you steal from many, it's research." H. L. Mencken, in his "New Dictionary of Quotations," attributes to Mizner, "I respect faith, but doubt is what gets you an education" and "A good listener is not only popular everywhere, but after a while he gets to know something." Mizner's comment on Hollywood, "It's a trip through a sewer in a glass-bottomed boat," was converted by Mayor Jimmy Walker into "A reformer is a guy who rides through a sewer in a glass-bottomed boat" and has since become a shopworn jewel of stump oratory. Two of Mizner's thirty-year-old lines have recently had revivals in the movies. A magistrate asked him if he was trying to show contempt of court. "No, I'm trying to conceal it," muttered Mizner. A friend argued that a certain Broadway producer "must have a head" to be so successful. "They put better heads on umbrellas," said Mizner.

Among his miscellaneous lines are "You sparkle with larceny," "He'd steal a hot stove and come back for the smoke," "You're a mouse studying to be a rat," "Another pot of coffee, waiter, and bring it under your arm to keep it warm," "I've had better steaks than this for bad behavior," "You look like a half-portion of cottage cheese," and "If you [a radio chatterer] don't get off the air, I'll stop breathing it."

Mizner usually avoided slang, although he had a few special words of his own, such as "croaker" for "physician," "heart trouble" for "cowardice," and "trap" for a "bank." He disliked puns, although a play on words was worth about $10,000 to him on one occasion. It made a jury laugh and saved him from a verdict for damages. After the Florida real-estate crash a man had sued him to recover the purchase price of a barren plot, asserting that Mizner had falsely informed him that he could grow nuts on it. "Did you tell the plaintiff that he could grow nuts on the land?" Mizner was asked. "Oh, no," he replied. "I told him he could go nuts on it." He perpetrated a sort of physical pun once when playing poker with a man whose credit was not too good. The man threw his wallet on the table and said, "I raise five hundred dollars." Mizner pulled off a shoe and threw it on the table. "If we're betting leather, I call," he said.

The earliest recorded example of Mizner wit belongs to the scientific school. He was in Nome, Alaska, in 1900. One of his pals there was Tex Rickard. Tex had a girl named Goldie, who was famous throughout the northern-lights district. One night Tex ran out of a hotel shooting at a stranger, who escaped in the dark. Men ran up asking what the stranger had done. "He insulted Goldie!" shouted Tex. Others were wild with excitement; Mizner was cold, scientific, scholarly. All he wanted to know was how the thing could be done, how the ingenious and resourceful stranger had accomplished his unparalleled feat. As the others chattered, Tex shrieked again, "He insulted Goldie!" "For God's sake, *how?*" inquired Mizner.

Mizner had a vast first-hand criminal erudition, which he commercialized as a dramatist on Broadway and a screen writer in Hollywood. At various times during his life he had been a miner, confidence man, ballad singer, medical lecturer, man of letters, general utility man in a segregated district, cardsharp, hotel man, songwriter, dealer in imitation masterpieces of art, prizefighter, prizefight manager, Florida promoter, and roulette-wheel fixer. He was an idol of low society and a pet of high. He knew women, as his brother Addison said, from the best homes and houses.

His formal underworld education began in his youth on the Barbary Coast in San Francisco, where he took up opium-smoking as an occasional pastime. After four years in mining camps in Alaska, he continued his school in the New York Tenderloin, and got a final polishing in London, Paris, and the steamship lanes. He acquired the gold-rush psychology in Alaska; his idea of the good life was one bonanza after another. His greatest strike was a $7,500,000 widow whom he married in 1906, but he abandoned this rich claim because he lacked the patience to exploit it. After gaining and dissipating several minor fortunes, he won paper wealth during the Florida boom. He rejected an offer of $1,250,000 for his holdings; a little later the Florida crash left him penniless. After that he became a Hollywood hack, with an interest in the Brown Derby on the side. "Turned traitor to vagrancy at fifty," he said.

Mizner was born in 1876 in Benicia, a town on San Francisco Bay, once the capital of California. He was only the second most distinguished citizen of Benicia, the first being John C. Heenan, the "Benicia Boy," heavyweight champion of America. Heenan's fight with Tom Sayers, at Farnborough, England, in 1860, is described by the Encyclopædia Britannica as "still the most celebrated prizefight of modern times."

Wilson Mizner was born in a house which had been shipped in knockdown condition around Cape Horn in the early gold-rush years. He was practically born to the purple. The Mizners were the great family of Benicia. There is nothing so toplofty as a village noble. Wilson was steeped in feelings of grandeur from childhood and always looked down on others from a towering height. He curried favor with nobody except suckers whom he was planning to fleece. Because he respected nothing and nobody, he was able to give his wit unlimited play. With all his raffishness, he had a superiority and independence of spirit, like that other disreputable aristocrat Sir John Falstaff, who sharpened his wit on princes. A non-commercial comic, Mizner never pandered to public taste. Will Rogers, a good man who liked everybody and humored the entire population, wrote hundreds of thousands of words and is remembered for little except "All I know is what I read in the papers." Mizner, a bad man who despised nearly everybody and wrote almost nothing, put hundreds of lines into circulation. Mizner had other advantages in addition to contempt for the public. Humorous writers comment chiefly on topics and events which go out of date almost immediately; Mizner commented on human behavior, which does not become outmoded. Mizner specialized in exposing himself, so he had an ever-ready and vulnerable butt for his wit. He had one further advantage; using the oral medium, he could freely coin phrases for which rival wits, using the printed medium, would have gone to jail.

A large-headed, spindle-shanked boy during his Benicia days, Wilson was described by his brother as wearing a No. 7 collar and a No. 8 hat. Even at this period he had a genius for getting into trouble with schoolteachers and the village authorities, but he always emerged triumphant because of the glorified status of his family. At the age of twelve, his privileged place in the world was recognized by international law. His father, having supported Benjamin Harrison in 1888, was appointed Minister to Guatemala. The law of nations forbade the arrest of any member of the family for anything except murder. For the rest of his life, Mizner had a sort of subconscious belief that treaties had been entered into by the nations of the world authorizing him to commit anything except capital crimes. His only conviction—for running a gambling house in Mineola in 1919—came as a terrific shock because of his lifelong assumption that he was a man to whom the statutes didn't apply. Although sentence was suspended, he took the conviction to heart. He was so grateful to Al Smith for pardoning him and restoring his rights of citizenship that he named the Brown Derby in his honor.

The family returned to California after two years in Guatemala. Mizner's enjoyment of diplomatic immunity had given him too strong an I-do-as-I-please spirit for school discipline. After being expelled from softer institutions, he was sent to Santa Clara College, famous for changing young hellhounds into saints. Mizner caused a panic at Santa Clara by tying a steak to the rope of a fire gong after curfew, the alarm being sounded when the meat attracted the attention of the large dogs which roamed the campus at night to encourage students to stay in their dormitories. He was expelled for heating a cannon ball for several hours and then bowling it from a fire shovel along a corridor. He cor-

rectly forecast that the severest disciplinarian on the faculty would
rush out and pick it up.

The primary authority on the Klondike chapter of the life of Mizner
is Sid Grauman, proprietor of the famous Egyptian and Chinese Theatres in Hollywood. Going to the Klondike as a boy, Grauman sold
newspapers from the States for a living—a dollar-fifty apiece in Dawson
City and two dollars on the creeks, where deliveries were made by dog
sled. The price was always paid in gold dust poured from a tomato can
into scales, and as the miners made it a point of pride to give good
measure, the newsboy made a little extra on each sale. He once took
in $3,200 in three days.

Grauman lived at McQueston's Hotel, described as an edifice of card-
board and spit. The rate was two dollars a night for a stretch of canvas;
stretches were hung three deep on the walls. The newsboy's attitude
toward Mizner was one of hero worship, inspired partly by the fact that
Mizner had the only private bedroom in McQueston's, that he had an
individual pitcher and basin, and that he owned a private gold-mono-
grammed comb and brush. After becoming friends with his hero, Grauman won the privilege of using Mizner's comb and brush, the only ones
in the Klondike that he would trust. Miners out of luck were employed
as bedmakers. They were a fastidious set. They were ready to face the
animal kingdom in the form of bears or wolves, but man after man
resigned rather than cope with animated nature at McQueston's. Mizner
solved the servant problem by inventing a method of making a bed with
a walking stick, which enabled the bedmaker to remain at a distance.
Mizner, who seldom spoke well of himself, used to be effusive in his
own praise when he described this invention. He also boasted that he
had the finest library in the Klondike, consisting of a table and a powerful kerosene lamp, which made it possible to read the finest seams.

Sometimes weeks passed before Grauman received a shipment of
newspapers. The Spanish-American War was on and the Klondikers
were crazy for news. Once, when a dog-sled shipment arrived, Mizner
offered Grauman $25 for the first paper, provided no others were sold
for forty-five minutes. Grauman accepted, but regretted the bargain.
Mizner filled an empty store with miners at fifty cents a head and read
the news aloud to them. The newsboy stuck to his bargain, although he
believed himself ruined. It turned out to be a good investment, however. Mizner's reading merely whetted the community's appetite for
news and Grauman was soon sold out. Then Mizner gave him $75, half
the proceeds of his show. According to Grauman, Wilson's purpose in

giving the reading was to be the centre of attention, to have hundreds of men hanging on his every word.

Mizner acted the part of big brother to the young newsboy. Once, when his papers were weeks overdue, Grauman was broke and hungry. Mizner invited him to a dinner of bear steaks at seven-fifty each. When they had finished, Grauman ducked out quickly at the suggestion of his host, who, it turned out, was also broke. Mizner casually asked the proprietor to charge it. He escaped with bruises and lacerations.

The Arctic achievement which Mizner was fondest of recalling in later years was his $10,000 coup with a tomato can. He had gone to sleep after having had too much to drink. On awakening, he found that his revolver had been stolen. This was an ill-timed misfortune; a glance at his watch showed that he was already overdue at an engagement to play the part of a damaged husband in a badger game. Cursing his irresponsibility, he picked up a tomato can, stripped off the label, and hurried to the appointment. Crashing the door in with an experienced shoulder, he raged at the culprits and threatened to blow the entire triangle to heaven with the can, which, he gave the home-wrecking stranger to understand, was full of dynamite. The stranger purchased his life with a belt loaded with gold dust. When the heroine asked for her share, Mizner handed her the tomato can. She asked what good that would do her. "It just got me ten thousand dollars," said Mizner.

Mizner returned to San Francisco in 1900. Hearing, on his arrival there, of a new gold strike on the beaches at Nome, he immediately took a boat for the new diggings. At Nome, he operated a hotel, but devoted himself mainly to gambling. Addison Mizner arrived in Nome several months after his brother. He was gratified but a little puzzled at hearing Wilson casually referred to as "the bravest man in Nome." He was told on all sides of Wilson's reckless daring and his crazy disregard for his own safety. This reputation did not quite agree with Addison's mental picture of his brother; he knew that Wilson would fight desperately when the reasons seemed good and sufficient, but he could not conceive of him as a man who went around thoughtlessly wasting heroism.

Everybody told Addison how, as a member of a posse, Wilson, nonchalantly rolling a cigarette with one hand and holding a revolver in the other, had kicked in the door of a cabin to which three desperadoes, one of them wounded, had been traced. The other members of the posse had hung back, regarding it as foolhardy to walk in on trapped bandits.

They all expected to see Mizner filled with bullets. But he walked into the cabin uninjured and came out beckoning to the others with a lighted cigarette. They found the place empty. Fresh bloodstains showed that a wounded man had been there. Addison found Wilson uncommunicative on this subject, but he gradually learned the truth. The three bandits—known as Mit, the Half-Kid, and Two-Tooth Mike —had been caught stealing gold from a sluice box and chased to the cabin after a running fight. They had escaped unseen from the cabin, however, and made their way to Mizner's hotel, where they begged him to conceal them. He hid them in his own room behind a burlap partition. A few minutes later friends rushed in to tell him that a band of desperadoes had been cornered in the cabin; he then joined the posse and gave his memorable exhibition of intrepidity. Three days later, after things had quieted down, he helped smuggle the robbers to safety.

II

Mizner was a star witness on March 14, 1918, at a John Doe inquiry into gambling in the Court of General Sessions. According to the *Sun*, which treated the inquiry with some flippancy, it all started when a German baker, who had lost $35,000 to Mizner at chemin de fer, started to pay off in doughnuts. The *Sun* asserted that tens of thousands of doughnuts were piled up in front of Mizner's apartment on West Forty-third Street, near Sixth Avenue.

Mizner denied on the witness stand in a Magistrates' Court on August 28, 1918, that he lived entirely by gambling. He testified that he had a half-interest in a tannery in Newark and did scenarios on the side. The charge against him was that of assaulting Herman Frank, an actor, in a Times Square restaurant. Frank had accused Mizner of stealing a Ziegfeld beauty from him. According to the testimony, Frank had sent Mizner a challenge to a duel in Van Cortlandt Park and written the challenge in blood. On cross-examination, Mizner said that he didn't write scenarios but that he telephoned them. Referring to a screen drama of which Mizner was the author, the opposing lawyer said, "Do you mean to say that you gave that to the motion-picture company by telephone?" "Yes," said Mizner, "and they paid me by telephone." Like most of the criminal charges against Mizner, the assault charge evaporated somewhere in the judicial processes.

While Mizner was devoting much of his leisure to the denunciation of suckers and chumps, his routine evening in Hollywood consisted of coming to the Brown Derby, of which he was part owner, with a thick roll of bills and giving them away a few at a time to professional moochers. By midnight he would be reduced to getting his paper from his newsboy on credit. He offered a feeble resistance to some of the demands on his purse. Once, when a borrower asked for fifty dollars, he said, "Here's twenty-five dollars. Let's both make twenty-five dollars." When a burglar came to him for a loan, he said, "Doesn't it get dark any more?"

For Mizner's protection, special glass was put into the front doors of the restaurant; a man inside could see out, but a man outside couldn't see in. With the help of this device, Mizner occasionally escaped. Once he jumped up at the sight of a small-loan nemesis and hurried to the washrooms. The knob of the washroom door was loose. It turned round and round in his hand and prevented his getaway. Mizner called to Robert Cobb, one of his Derby partners, "Hey, Bob! Take this knob and put it on the safe in your office. Jimmy Valentine couldn't crack it in three days."

Brusque and blasphemous in his own coterie, Mizner would put on an unctuous, ingratiating, Dale Carnegie manner at the approach of a stranger who appeared prosperous. His hope of finding new suckers to trim never deserted him. He would even stop eating a sizzling beefsteak in order to fawn upon a possible chump. In his later years he had almost entirely lost the sensation of taste; heat gave him an illusion of flavor, and his chief pleasure of the table was a blistering-hot sirloin. His regular crowd always preserved silence until he had consumed it. One night he was half through a hot steak when a well-groomed stranger appeared and offered to bet that Mizner couldn't remember him. Mizner sized up the stranger as a confidence man's dream. He forgot all about the steak and began to pour on the fraudulent camaraderie in his best how-to-win-friends manner. Didn't I meet you at Palm Beach? No. Monte Carlo? Wrong. Saratoga? Wrong again. Now I remember— Deauville? Still wrong. "Where was it?" Mizner finally demanded. "At the Hotel Ambassador last Wednesday," the man said. "Don't you remember? I showed you the samples of my new shirtings." Mizner picked up his steak knife, struggled to his feet, and chased the stranger into the night.

Most of Mizner's motion-picture work was done on the Warner Brothers lot. He was a writer who never wrote. His method of collaboration was unique. At the studio he slept most of the time in a huge red plush chair, which so closely resembled an archiepiscopal throne that he was called the Archbishop. When Mizner's literary partners needed some lines or ideas from him, they would shake him gently and start him talking. After half an hour or so they would order him back to sleep while they sat down at their typewriters and worked up his conversation into script form.

There were large gaps in Mizner's pose of being the hardest, coldest, and most callous man in the world. He used to visit narcotic hospitals to cheer up old pals. He had a real talent for comforting a friend in distress. One day he became greatly concerned over a change he saw in an old acquaintance, a screen writer who believed himself to be suffering from incipient insanity. The scenarist had just tried to introduce a man he had known for twenty-five years to another whom he had known for ten years. He had forgotten the names of both of them and was sure that his mind was cracking up. "I've known you for thirty years," said Mizner, "and that is the most hopeful sign I've seen in you. Now you're going to amount to something. Don't you know that when you forget your wife's name, your telephone number, and where you live, you're getting somewhere? Where would you be if you knew all the Vice-Presidents by their first names? You'd be getting thirty dollars a week!"

Mizner assumed that any friend of his would be in the wrong nine times out of ten. His advice to one of his young protégés was that if the man were ever in the right, he should waylay the other party in a crowded hotel lobby and carry on the discussion in ear-piercing screams.

In conversation Mizner did his best to suppress the instincts of humanity. His later comic style was largely ridicule of all sentiment and feeling. Although at times he could be soft in his behavior, he aimed at being as satanic as possible in speech. He and his brother Addison both maintained a pose of being completely divorced from human emotion. Anything shocking or saddening was made to order for their wit. Death was the finest of all comedy subjects, because it provided the largest amount of emotion to be deflated. When Wilson and Addison were living together in Palm Beach, Addison came in one day with the news that another brother, Lansing, a San Francisco lawyer, had been killed in an automobile accident. "Why didn't you tell me before I put on a red tie?" said Wilson.

A young woman with whom Wilson had quarreled threw herself from the eleventh floor of a Palm Beach hotel. The hotel clerk telephoned the news to Addison, who broke it to Wilson. Wilson picked up his hat and cane. "Where are you going?" asked Addison. "To Bradley's," said Wilson. "I'm going to lay a bet on No. 11. You can't tell me that isn't a hunch." This, to some of Wilson's admirers, was proof that his heart was broken.

He was working in Hollywood early in 1933 on a picture called "Merry Wives of Reno" when he received word that Addison was dying. He wired, "Stop dying. Am trying to write a comedy."

Singularly enough, the best-known and probably the greatest of Mizner's sayings is the only emotional line in his entire anthology, and it bears on the subject of death. In 1910, Mizner was the manager of Stanley Ketchel, the great middleweight who lasted twelve rounds with Jack Johnson. Ketchel was the embodiment of the fighting spirit. News was telephoned to Mizner that Ketchel had been shot and killed. "Tell 'em to start counting ten over him, and he'll get up," said Mizner.

Fatal illness was almost as happy a subject of merriment as death. One of Mizner's closest friends was Grant Clark, the songwriter. Like most other songwriters, Clark lived chiefly on advances from publishers. Shortly before his death he tottered up to Mizner's table in a restaurant. He wanted to borrow twenty dollars. "I'll tell you what I'll do," said Mizner. "I'll take you around to Campbell's and get an advance on you."

Mizner got all possible comedy value out of his own last illness. In March, 1933, in his fifty-seventh year, he had a heart attack at the Warner studio. When he recovered consciousness he was asked if he wanted a priest. "I want a priest, a rabbi, and a Protestant clergyman," he said. "I want to hedge my bets."

His heart attack, President Roosevelt's inauguration, the bank holiday, and a California earthquake came at almost the same time. Mizner criticized this piling up of climaxes. "Bad melodrama," he said.

Told that death was only a few hours away, Mizner rallied strength to send a postcard notifying a friend. "They're going to bury me at 9 A.M.," wrote Mizner. "Don't be a sucker and get up."

When they arranged a tent over him for the administration of oxygen, he said, "It looks like the main event."

Coming out of a coma shortly before his death, he waved a priest away disdainfully. "Why should I talk to you?" he said. "I've just been talking to your boss."

The priest gently reproached Mizner for levity at such a time. He told the sick man that his death might come at any moment. "What?" said Mizner. "No two weeks' notice?"

George S. Kaufman

George S. (for Simon or, according to the author, "for nothing") Kaufman has collaborated so spectacularly and with so many other dramatists that a published play bearing only his own name is one of the rarest of Kaufman items. His co-workers have been such diverse talents as Marc Connelly, Alexander Woollcott, Morrie Ryskind, Edna Ferber, and Moss Hart. "I have always been smart enough," said Kaufman, "to attach to myself the most promising lad that came along in the theater."

Born in Pittsburgh, Pennsylvania, in 1889, Kaufman found his way to the theater via the law, a clerkship in a county tax office, stenography, salesman for a ribbon company, daily contributor of trivia to newspapers, and the dramatic columns of The New York Times and Tribune. His first play, still unproduced, was written in his twenties; since then more than twenty successes have resulted from his shrewd sense of pace and extraordinary adaptability. Such a play as The Man Who Came to Dinner ("an unexpurgated biography of Alexander Woollcott") is continually being presented, and several others—notably the Pulitzer Prize-winning Of Thee I Sing—have been revived by Hollywood. It is true that the farce about life in the country, George Washington Slept Here, was dismissed as "George Kaufman slipped here," but, as Kaufman himself said, "One man's Mede is another man's Persian."

The playlet which follows has at least two distinctions: it represents Kaufman as a satirist—although, as a commercial man-of-the-theater he dislikes the appellation, saying that "satire is something that closes on a Saturday night"—and it presents him as a solo performer, unassisted by collaboration.

If Men Played Cards as Women Do

The scene is JOHN's *home—the living room. There are two doors, one leading to an outside hall, the other to the other rooms of the house. A card table has been set up in the middle of the room, with four chairs around it, and above it is another table on which are piled the necessary adjuncts for a poker game—a fancy cover for the table, cards, chips, a humidor. For the rest, you have only to imagine an average and good-looking room.*

As the curtain rises, JOHN *enters from another room, then turns and calls back through the open door, as though he had forgotten something.*

IMPERTINENCE FROM THE AUTHOR: *It is perhaps unnecessary to remark that the sketch derives its entire value from the fact that it is played in forthright and manly fashion. In other words, the actors must not imitate the voices of women.*

JOHN. And don't forget, I want things served very nicely. Use the best china and the filigree doilies. (*He starts to close the door—remembers another instruction.*) And at eleven o'clock just put the cigars and drinks right on the table and we'll stop playing. (*He closes the door and advances into the room. He looks the place over; rubs a suspecting finger along the table top in a quest for dust. He moves one chair a fraction of an inch and seems to think that that makes a difference in the appearance of the room. Then there comes a knock on the outer door.* JOHN *darts to the mirror and takes a quick look at himself; adjusts his tie.*) Come in! (BOB *enters.*) Hello, Bob!

BOB. Hello, John! I thought I'd run over early to see if I could help you with the lunch.

JOHN. Thanks—everything is ready. I baked a cake. Oh, say! That's a new hat, isn't it?

BOB. Why, no—don't you remember? It's the one I got at Knox's in the Spring. Then when they began wearing the bands higher, I said to myself, why should I buy a new hat when I can have a man in and get him to put on another band for me, just as easily as not? Do you like it?

JOHN. Very attractive. I wonder how it would look on me? (*Takes it; starts to try it on, then smooths his hair before he finally puts it on. He looks at himself in the mirror; turns.*) What do you think?

BOB. Lovely! Makes your face look thinner. (*Looks at the card table.*) Who's playing tonight?

349

JOHN. George and Marc.

BOB. Really? (*He takes his seat.*) Tell me—don't you think George is looking older these days? How are he and Ethel getting along? Any better?

JOHN. Not as good.

BOB. Funny what she saw in him. (*There is a knock on the door.*)

JOHN. Come in! (GEORGE *enters.*)

GEORGE. (*Greatly surprised, as though they were the last people he had expected to see*) Hello, boys!

JOHN. Hello, George! Well, well, well!

BOB. (*Rises*) Hello, George! Never saw you look so young!

GEORGE. (*In great excitement*) Say, I just met Ed Jennings down the street and what do you think? He says Jim Perkins told him that Will Harper's wife may leave him!

BOB. You don't say so! (*Sits again.*)

GEORGE. What do you think of that? (*His excitement dies a little; he looks around.*) The room looks lovely, John. You've changed things around, haven't you? Awfully nice. But if you don't mind just a little suggestion—I'm not sure that I like that table up there where you've got it. (*Another critical look.*) And if you had these chairs re-uphol-stered in blue——

JOHN. Well, what do you think of a plain chintz?

GEORGE. That would be nice. Oh, say! I've got a T.L. for you, Bob.

BOB. Oh, good! What is it?

GEORGE. Well, you owe me one first.

BOB. Oh, tell me mine! Don't be mean!

GEORGE. Well, all right. Frank Williams said you looked lovely in your dinner coat.

BOB. That *is* nice.

JOHN. How's the baby, George?

GEORGE. Awfully cranky lately. He's teething. I left him with the nurse tonight—first chance I've had to get out. (*Takes a seat at the table.*) Who else is coming?

JOHN. Just Marc.

GEORGE. (*With meaning*) Oh, is he? I want to speak to you boys about Marc. Don't you think he's been seeing a lot of that Fleming woman lately?

BOB. He certainly has. He was at the Biltmore, having tea with her yesterday—I know because a cousin of Tom Hennessey's saw him.

JOHN. Which cousin is that?

Bob. I don't know whether you know him—Ralph Wilson. He married that Akron girl—they have two children.

George. *You* remember—one of them is backward.

John. Oh, yes! I heard that. (*Another knock on the door.*) Come in! (Marc *enters.*)

Marc. Hello, everybody!

George, John *and* Bob. Hello, Marc!

Marc. I'm sorry to be the last, but we have a new maid, and you know what that means.

John. That's all right. Say, I like the cut of that vest, Marc. Look, boys! Don't you like that vest?

Marc. It is nice, isn't it?

George. Oh, lovely! Turn around and let's see the back. (George *and* John *both get up and examine his clothes, pull down his trousers, etc.*)

Marc. I had it made right in the house—I have a little tailor that comes in. Four dollars a day.

George. Excuse me—there's a little spot—— (*He moistens a finger and rubs* Marc's *lapel.*)

John. Well, shall we play a little poker?

Marc. (*Sitting*) Yes, sure. Oh, John, may I trouble you for a glass of water?

John. Why, of course, Marc. (George *and* Bob *sit again.*)

Marc. I'll get it myself if you'll tell me where——

John. Oh, no—that's all right. (*He goes out. A pause. The men look at each other, meaningly. Their heads come together.*)

Marc. John doesn't look well, does he?

Bob. No. Did you notice those lines? He can't hide them much longer.

Marc. He was very good-looking as a boy.

George. Isn't this room the most terrible thing you ever saw?

(Marc *goes to the table up stage; picks up a cigar and shows it to the others. They are scornful.*)

Marc. Huh! Ten cents. (*Pause.*) I really wanted to get that water myself. I'd like to see his kitchen. (John *re-enters with the water.*) Oh, thanks, John. (Marc *drinks.*)

John. Is it cold enough, Marc?

Marc. (*Indicating that it isn't*) Oh, yes. Of course, I generally put ice in, myself. (*Sits.*)

George. Say, we had the loveliest new dessert tonight!

BOB. Oh! What was it? It's awfully hard to find a new dessert.

MARC. (*With emphasis*) *Is* it?

GEORGE. Well, it was a sort of prune whip. You make it out of just nothing at all. And then, if company comes when you don't expect them——

BOB. I want the recipe.

MARC. How many eggs?

(JOHN *up at the rear table. Turns on this speech.*)

JOHN. Does it take much butter?

GEORGE. Oh, no—very little. I'll bring you the recipe Tuesday afternoon.

(MARC *feels a rough place on his chin. Rubs it, then takes a good-sized mirror out of his pocket and stands it on the table. Examines his chin. Then takes out a safety razor and starts to shave. After that he takes out two military brushes and combs his hair. The others pay no attention to this.* JOHN *is at the rear table, with his back to the audience;* BOB *is seated, fooling with the cards;* GEORGE *is seated, calmly smoking. After* MARC *has put everything away,* BOB *breaks the silence.*)

BOB. Are we ready?

JOHN. No! Wait just a minute. (*He brings down the fancy table cover, which he spreads on the table.*) There we are!

MARC. (*Feeling it*) That's nice, John. Where'd you get it?

JOHN. Why, I bought a yard of this plain sateen down at Macy's——

GEORGE. Really? How much was it?

JOHN. A dollar sixty-three. It was reduced. Then I had this edging in the house.

BOB. Awfully nice!

MARC. Oh, say! Walter Sharp just got back from Paris——

GEORGE. He did?

MARC. Yes. And *he* says they're wearing trousers longer over there.

GEORGE. Really? (*There is quite a fuss about it.*)

JOHN. (*Brings chips and takes his seat*) What'll we play for?

BOB. Oh, what's the difference? One cent limit?

GEORGE. Does it matter who deals? (*Takes the cards from* BOB.)

MARC. Say, did you hear about Eddie Parker?

JOHN. No.

MARC. Well, it seems he saw these advertisements about how to get thin, and he thought he'd try them. You know Eddie's taken on a lot of weight since his marriage.

GEORGE. Twenty pounds—absolutely.

MARC. Well, they sent him some powders and he began taking them, and what do you think?

GEORGE. Well? (MARC *whispers to him.*) You don't say so?

JOHN *and* BOB. (*Excited*) What was it? What was it? (GEORGE *whispers to* JOHN, *who whispers to* BOB. *Great excitement.*)

MARC. Who has the cards?

GEORGE. Here they are. (*Starts to deal—poker hands.*)

MARC. I don't want to play late. I've been shopping all day.

GEORGE. And I have an appointment at the barber's tomorrow. I'm going to try a new way of getting my hair cut. (*The deal is completed.*)

BOB. (*Picking up a few cards*) Which is higher—aces or kings?

GEORGE. Now, who bets first?

JOHN. Are these funny little things clubs?

MARC. What are the chips worth?

JOHN. Let's have them all worth the same thing.

BOB. A penny apiece. . . .

GEORGE. Say, Lord & Taylor are having a wonderful sale of night-gowns!

MARC. What do you pay your maid?

BOB. Sixty-five, but she isn't worth it. (*The three start talking at once about maids, and* JOHN *has a hard time being heard.*)

JOHN. (*Excited*) Boys! Boys! Listen to this! Boys!

ALL. Well?

JOHN. (*Excited*) I *knew* there was something I wanted to tell you!

ALL. (*They must not speak together*) What is it?

JOHN. Well, now in the first place you must promise not to breathe a word of it to anybody, because I got it in absolute confidence and I promised I wouldn't tell.

GEORGE. What is it?

MARC. Well?

BOB. Well?

JOHN. It's about Sid Heflin! Now, you won't tell anybody? At least, don't let on you got it from me!

ALL. No!

JOHN. Well, I'm told—and I got this pretty straight, mind you—I'm told that he's going to—ah——(*He puts the message across with his eyes.*)

MARC. I don't believe it!

BOB. What do you mean?

GEORGE. When?

JOHN. In April!

MARC. April! (*They count on their fingers, up to four.*)

GEORGE. What do you mean?

JOHN. Exactly! They were married late in January! (*They all throw down their hands and begin talking at once.*)

CURTAIN

Eric Knight

Eric Mobray Knight was born in Yorkshire in 1897. Two years later his father (a diamond merchant) died, and his mother, leaving her children with relatives in Yorkshire, went to St. Petersburg (now Leningrad) as governess for Princess Xenia's children. It was not until the boy was fifteen that he rejoined his mother, who had come to America. He had already earned his living in many ways: as worker in a steel mill, bobbin-boy in a cotton mill, extra hand in a saw mill, blower in a bottle glass factory. At sixteen he had the dialect scrubbed off his tongue and he became a copy boy on the Philadelphia Press. He began to educate himself in the arts. He attended the National Academy of Design in New York, enlisted in the first World War, returned to America and had to abandon his art career because he had become color-blind.

In his late thirties Knight turned to fiction, and was immediately successful as a short story writer and novelist. His range is indicated by the skylarking fantasy The Flying Yorkshireman, followed by the almost equally amusing Sam Small Flies Again, and the intensely dramatic This Above All, which made so exciting a film. Hollywood also benefited by his juvenile Lassie Come Home, one of the most appealing of dog stories.

In the second World War, Knight was a major in the United States Army. En route to North Africa, he was killed in a plane crash, January 15, 1943.

All Yankees Are Liars

You can always tell the Irish,
You can always tell the Dutch.
You can always tell a Yankee;
But you cannot tell him much.

Mr. Smith was pleased with The Spread Eagle. He was pleased with Polkingthorpe Brig. The village was off the beaten track—the truly rural sort of English village the American always wants to see.

The inn was low and rambling, with great sloping roofs. Over the door swung the sign—a darksome bird in a weather-beaten setting.

Everything justified his decision to take this bicycle trip up into the north—the mullioned windows, the roaring fire, the Yorkshire accents of the men who shuffled over the sanded stone floor of the low-ceilinged room as they played darts. Mr. Smith was almost beginning to understand what they were talking about. During his excellent high tea he had sorted out the four men playing darts. One was Saw Cooper, a farmer; a small old man was referred to as Sam; a young, bright-faced lad who played darts left-handed was Gollicker Pearson; and the fourth, a huge man, was just called Ian.

Mr. Smith watched them play, listening to the endless thwock of the darts in the cork board as he finished his meal. The barmaid, plump, corn-haired, came toward him, her apron rustling stiffly.

"Would there be owt else?"

"No. It was a very good meal." Mr. Smith smiled. He wanted to make the girl talk some more. "Er—what do they do for fun in this place of an evening?"

"Foon?" she repeated. "Well, they sit here—or o' Satday neights lots o'fowk goa ovver to Wuxley to t'pictures." She waited. "They gate Boock D'Arcy i' T' Singing Cowboy," she added suggestively.

Mr. Smith had already become acquainted with British cinemas in small towns. Also, he was a Southern Californian, and had that familiarity with movies that belongs to all Southern Californians. He had no inclination to go four miles to see a last year's Class B Western. "No. I think I'll have another ale and sit here," he said.

"If tha'll sit ovver by t' fire, Ah'll bring it to thee theer. Than Ah can clean oop here."

Mr. Smith sat on the bench by the generous fire and nursed his ale. The dart game came to an end with Saw Cooper losing and paying for the round. The men brought their mugs to the fire. Mr. Smith shifted politely. The men, in the presence of a stranger, grew quiet. Mr. Smith decided to put them at ease.

"Pretty chilly for an October evening, isn't it?"

The men considered the remark, as if looking at both sides of it. Finally Saw Cooper spoke.

"Aye," he said.

The others nodded. There was silence, and the five regarded the fire. Then, suddenly, young Gollicker smiled.

"Tha shouldn't heed t' cowd, being a Yankee," he said.

"Ah, but I'm not a Yankee," Mr. Smith said.

They stared at him in disbelief.

"Yankees," explained Mr. Smith, "come from New England."

They looked from Mr. Smith to one another. The big man named Ian took a deep breath.

"Yankees," he said, "come fro' t' United States."

"Well, yes. New England is a part of the United States," Mr. Smith said. "But it's thousands of miles away from where I live. In fact, believe it or not, I should think you're closer to the Yankees than I am. You see, the United States is a big country. In the part where the Yankees come from, it gets very cold in the winter. Where I am—in Southern California—it never snows. Why, I've never known it to snow there in all my life."

"No snow?" Gollicker breathed.

Mr. Smith smiled. For, after all, he was a Southern Californian—and they were discussing climate. "No snow," he said. "In wintertime we have a bit of a rainy season, but after February it clears, and then it doesn't even rain for nine months—not a drop."

"Noa rain for a nine month—noan at all?" Saw Cooper asked.

"Not a drop. Day after day, the sun comes out, clear skies, never a drop of rain for nine months. Never!"

"Whet do ye graw theer, lad?" Saw asked, slyly.

"Lots of things. Truck, vegetables, oranges—all kinds of things."

There was a silence again. Big Ian took a breath.

"Orinjis," he said, and then took another breath, "graw i' Spain."

He looked at Mr. Smith so emphatically that Mr. Smith nodded.

"Oh, yes," he said. "They grow in Spain, too, I understand."

"Orinjis," Ian repeated, "graw i' Spain."

That seemed to settle the question. They all looked in the fire in silence. Saw Cooper sniffed.

"Whet else graws theer?"

"Well, I have a ranch there; we grow alfalfa."

"Whet's that off to be?"

"Alfalfa? We use it for hay. It's a desert plant originally, but it thrives in California. We get eight cuttings a year."

"Eight cuttings o' hay a year?"

"Eight cuttings a year."

The little man, Sam, spoke for the first time: "Mister, if it doan't rain for a nine month, how can ye get eight cuttings o' hay a year?"

"Oh, that's easy," Mr. Smith said. "We irrigate the land." He went into a short but conclusive description of irrigating.

"Heh," Saw Cooper said. "Wheer's this heer water come from?"

"In the San Fernando Valley we buy it from the water company."

"Wheer do they get it?"

"From reservoirs."

"If it doan't rain, where's t' reservoys get t' watter?"

"Oh, we pipe it down from five hundred miles north. It rains a lot up there."

"And ye sprinkle t' farming land out o' t' watter tap. How mony acres hesta?"

"It isn't like sprinkling from the tap, of course. I used that to illustrate. The pipes are large—we have fourteen-inch valves on our pipes. We flood the land—cover it right over with water."

Saw looked in the fire. "Does corn graw theer?"

"Well, generally our land is too valuable to put into corn. But it will grow corn fourteen feet high."

They made noises in their throats and shifted their feet.

"Fohteen foot," Saw breathed. "Eigh, ba gum!"

"Mister," Sam said, "once Ah were oop to see t' Firth o' Forth brig. Ah suppose they hev bigger brigs i' Yankeeland?"

Mr. Smith should have touched on the new Oakland bridge, but then, he was a *Southern* Californian.

"We have bridges, but they're building tunnels under the rivers now."

"Whet for?"

"Well, there's so much motor traffic."

"How mony moatorcars goa through 'em?"

Mr. Smith lit his pipe happily. They seemed quite interested in America.

"I couldn't say. The way they turn 'em out. I should say there's hundreds of thousands."

"How fast do they turn 'em out?" Gollicker asked.

"I don't know. I know they roll out finished at the rate of one every couple of minutes."

"And they goa i' tunnels, not i' brigs?" Sam commented.

"Oh, we have some bridges."

"Big uns, Ah suppose."

"Well," Mr. Smith said modestly, thinking of the Pulaski Skyway coming into New York, "we have some that go right over entire towns. You're practically on one bridge for miles."

Saw Cooper spat in the fire. "How mony fowk is there in all America?"

Mr. Smith didn't know, but he felt expansive. And after all, there was South America too.

"A quarter of a billion, I should say," he hazarded.

"A quarter of a billion," they repeated. Then they stared at Mr. Smith, and he became aware of their disbelief.

"Wait a moment," he said. "I think a billion is different in America from here. It's a thousand million in America and a million million here, isn't it?"

"A billion," said Ian slowly, "is a billion."

The others nodded, and then Ian stood. The others rose too.

"Oh—er—wait a minute. Won't you all have a drink with me?" Mr. Smith invited.

"Us is off to play darts for a round—us four," Ian said, meaningly.

The other three laughed.

"Ah knew them theer brigs o' thine'd hev to be big," Saw Cooper said as a parting shot as he swung over the bench. "That's so's they'd be able to goa ovver wheat what graws fohteen foot high when ye sprinkle it fro' t' watter tap."

He grinned at the others in victory.

"I didn't say wheat; I said corn," Mr. Smith protested.

"Same thing," Saw snapped.

"It isn't. Wheat grows in an ear. Corn grows on a cob; it has broad long leaves."

"Heh! That's maize," Saw said.

Big Ian stepped between Saw Cooper and Mr. Smith.

"Now, lad," he said flatly, "tha said corn, and Ah heeard thee. Thee and thy orinjis, and farming out o' t' watter tap, and brigs ovver cities, and it nivver rains, and denying th' art a Yankee, and a billion is a billion and yet it ain't. Tha't tripped thysen oop a dozen times, it seems to me. Now, hesta owt to say?"

Mr. Smith looked at Big Ian, standing belligerently with legs widespread and his thumbs in the waistband of his corduroy trousers. He looked round and saw everyone in the inn waiting, silent.

Then a curious thing happened. In that minute the smell of soft-coal smoke and pig-twist tobacco and ale was gone, and instead Mr. Smith was smelling the mixed odor of sun-baked land and citrus blossom and jasmine and eucalyptus trees, just as you smell it in the cool darkness coming across the San Fernando Valley. And he was homesick. Suddenly it felt unreal that he should be so far from home, sitting in an English inn with these men about him. He looked up at the faces, forbidding in their expression of disapproval. And he began to laugh.

It was all so unreal that he laughed until he cried. Every time he looked up he saw the faces, now even more comical in their bewilderment than they had been in their disapproval. They stared at him, and then Big Ian began to laugh.

"Eigh, Ah'll be jiggered!" he roared. "Drat ma buttons if Ah won't!"

It was Mr. Smith's turn to be puzzled now.

Big Ian roared, and suddenly slapped Mr. Smith on the back so heartily that his chin flew up in the air and then banged back on his chest. The others looked on in amazement.

"Why, whet's oop, Ian?" Saw asked.

"Why, ye gowks!" Ian roared. "He's laughing at ye! He's been heving us on! Sitting theer for an hour, keeping his mug straight and telling us the tale! And us swallering it, thinking he was serious!"

"But," Mr. Smith said—"but you don't—"

"Nay, now no moar on it!" Ian roared. "Ye've codded us for fair, and done it champion! Lewk at owd Sam's face!"

The others regarded Ian and scratched their heads and grinned sheepishly, and finally looked at Mr. Smith in admiration.

"But—" Mr. Smith began again.

"Nay, now, ye copped us napping," Ian said, "and here's ma hand on it. Soa we'll hev noa moar—onless ye'd like to tell us whet Yankeeland's rightly like."

Mr. Smith drew a deep breath. "Well, what would you like to hear about?"

"About cowboys," young Gollicker breathed. "Werta ivver a cowboy?"

For a moment Mr. Smith stood on a brink, and then an imp pushed him over.

"Of course I've been a cowboy—naturally," Mr. Smith said. "What would you like to hear about it?"

"Wait a minute," Gollicker said. They all adjusted themselves on the bench. "Now," he went on, "tell us about a roundup—tha knaws, 'Ah'm heading for t' last roundup,' like Bing Crosby sings."

Mr. Smith held his mental breath and plunged.

"Ah," he said. "A roundup and the life of a cowboy. Up at the crack of dawn, mates, and down to the corral. There you rope your horse—"

"A mustang?" Gollicker asked.

"A mustang," Mr. Smith agreed.

"A wild one off'n the prairies, happen?"

"Indeed a wild one from off the prairies," Mr. Smith agreed. "I see you know America yourself."

Gollicker grinned modestly. "Doan't let me interrupt, measter," he apologized.

Mr. Smith drew another breath. He saw he was up against at least one expert, so he made it very good. He gave them, in more senses than one, a moving picture of the cowboy's life.

When he was done, Gollicker sighed and Big Ian nodded.

"Now," Sam said, "how about them buffalo?"

"Ah, the buffalo," Mr. Smith said. "The thundering herd! The bison! For a while there was danger or thought to be—that the herds were dying out. But now, I am glad to say—and no doubt you are just as glad to hear—the herds are increasing, and ere long, again the crack of a rifle will bring down a bull in full gallop."

"But how about them Indians?" Saw put in.

Mr. Smith considered the Indians at the station in Santa Fe. They didn't seem at all satisfactory. But he was inspired. He drew himself up.

"You will pardon me if I do not speak of that," he said. "We have not too much love for the paleface who stole our lands. I say 'we,' for my mother was Yellow Blanket, a princess of the Blackfoot tribe. Therefore, let us not speak of the white man and the red man."

He stared into the fire—majestically, he hoped.

"Now, see what tha's done?" Ian said to Saw. "Happen it'll learn thee to keep thy yapper shut once in a while. . . . Tha maun excuse him, measter. Tell us about gangsters instead. Didta ivver run into any gangsters?"

"Run into them? Why how could you help it?" Mr. Smith asked.

Swiftly and graphically he painted for them an America in which here was the town where the bullets of the gangs crackled day and night. Here was the last street, and on it the last house, and beyond that was the trackless prairie where the buffalo thundered, the cowboy rode and the Indian ever lurked.

As he finished, he looked up. Everyone in the inn was listening. At the bar, the maid leaned on her elbows, entranced.

"Ah, I talk too much," Mr. Smith said.

"Nay, goa on, lad," they said. "Goa on."

"Well, it's dry work. How about a drink?"

"Champion," said Saw.

"Owd on," Big Ian said. "Us'll play darts for a round."

"Now, Ian, if the lad wants to buy—"

"Ah said," Ian repeated, "us'll play darts—onybody that wishes to be in on t' round. And t' loser will pay."

Mr. Smith paid anyhow, for the dart game was trickier than he had thought, and they all seemed to be experts.

He was getting very much better when the barmaid called: "Time, gentlemen, please."

Mr. Smith was sorry. It had been a good evening. They all said good night cheerfully. Big Ian shook him by the hand.

"Well, soa long, lad. We had a champion time. But Ah just want to say, that didn't fool me when tha were kidding us at first. Tha sees, for one thing, us goas to t' pictures and so us knaws whet America's really like. And then Ah'd allus heeard tell that all Yankees were liars."

"Yes," Mr. Smith said, regarding his conscience, "I did tell some lies."

"Aye, but Ah suppose it's a way ye Yankees hev," Ian said. "But it's all right as long as tha told us t' trewth finally."

Arthur Kober

Arthur Kober has pursued a quietly mad career without losing his sanity. Born in 1900 in Brady, an Austro-Hungarian town which became part of Poland, Kober as a child was brought to America, where he grew up to be a bell-boy, stock-clerk, stenographer, press agent, columnist, Hollywood screen-writer, and, finally, an author in his own right, a recorder with a shrewd eye and an accurate but sympathetic ear. His comedy Having Wonderful Time is romantic, probing, and farcical—a combination which is equally true of Kober's New Yorker vignettes assembled in Thunder over the Bronx and My Dear Bella. Whether Kober portrays New York stenographers or Hollywood agents, his dislocations in language are as delicate as they are devastatingly funny.

Monroe Goes Back to the Indians

Bella Gross riffled the pages of the dictionary, paused at a leaf headed "dike," ran her finger down a column of words and, when she came to "dilatory," wrote "tardy and inactive" on a slip of paper. She thumbed the book again, hunted for "epistle," and snagged it after a little difficulty owing to her uncertainty over its spelling. She made the notation, "a formal letter."

Fortified by these two items, Bella was ready to plunge into the writing of the grave and important letter she had long planned. Whenever she engaged in such elaborate preliminaries—unearthing the coverless dictionary and bringing it into the dining room, placing pen, ink, and paper on the oilcloth table cover, using her "good" stationery, bought at a sale at Macy's—it was an indication that she was going to compose something of momentous importance.

And this letter to Monroe Rosenblatt, written in her mind time and time again, was of importance. Bella was finally going to do what she had so very often told her friends Jennie and Sarah she would do: "Give Monroe back to the Indians." It was one thing to make fine promises under a romantic summer moon at Kamp Kill Kare; it was another, she thought with burning indignation, to fulfill those pretty promises under the harsh and prosaic moon over the Bronx.

Bella reached for a sheet of her good stationery, so impressively monogrammed with the letter "G." No, she thought, no use wasting the paper. This letter needed careful construction. It would be better to make a rough draft first and then rewrite it. She disappeared into her bedroom for a moment and returned with several sheets of business stationery which she had filched from her office.

She dipped her pen in the ink, corrugated her forehead in deep reflection and then, under several printed lines which read "Solomon Silk Mills, Harry I. Solomon, Pres., Silks, Acetates—Plain and Novelty, 'A Satisfied Customer Is Our Best Recommendation,'" she wrote, "Dear Monroe."

She studied this a moment. "Dear Monroe." No, that sounded too warm, too inviting, too intimate. That was hardly her present attitude toward him. Dear Monroe, Indeed! She suddenly had it! All that was necessary was to add "Rosenblatt." That was it—formal, severe, cold, implacable. "I should have written"—she stopped to consult her notes, and then went on, slowly and painstakingly, employing an almost childish chirography—"this epistle before the present inst. but the reason"

364

—again there was a visual consultation with the notes—"I was so dilatory was because I wanted to carefully weigh what was on my chest. Now that I have weighed same I am going to get it off my chest irregardless of whom it affects even though it be—" There was only a moment's pause to consider grammar, and then she wrote, "I."

"First of all," she went on, "I don't want to throw up anything to your face but I feel this matter must be thrown up. Namely you might of forgotten about the fact that when I left 'Kamp Kill Kare' you declared yourself with all sorts of promises galore. I took you at your word in connection with the matter and gave up some 'contacts' which

to me I didn't want to give up, at the same time I thought inasmuch as you declared yourself the fair and square thing to do was not to go 'galvinating' around, not that I am the 'galvinating' type girl inasmuch as I wouldn't stoop to be that common. But still in all I wanted to be fair and square with you. In fact one 'contact' I had was very serious inasmuch as the certain party was 'matrimonyally-inclined' along the lines of marriage, only I thought he should have his two feet on the ground first because too many marriages end up on the rocks due to circumstances over which the girl in the matter has no controll. He's a professional person with a college degree."

Bella allowed her mind to dwell on Max Fine for a moment. Poor

Mac! A fine fellow—intelligent, well educated—a Certified Public Accountant. If only he had a substantial income. Well, what's done is done. It's silly to regret. Still in all, Mac's a fine boy, she thought, one whose friendship was certainly well worth keeping. Perhaps she ought to attend the regular meetings of the Excelsior Social Club. She had avoided these because of the embarrassment that would follow upon seeing and talking with Mac, the club's president. Oh, well. She sighed deeply, picked up the pen, and continued writing.

"For some time now we've been going out regularly with each other like clock-work. In fact, so regularly have we been going out with each other that one of my girl friend's (Jennie) remarked on same and said, 'We're beginning to look like two peas in a pot' and everybody was taking matters for granted. To be crudly blunt about the matter, I too thought that the issue was understood. I hope you won't think me 'mercinarilly-inclined' if I mention the fact that I didn't bring up the matter of a ring but the matter was brought up by you, yourself. Well all you did was to bring up the matter without bringing up the ring. We been seeing each other regularly like clock-work and not once did you lift a little finger to get same but all you did was to talk 'a poor mouth' about how business was bad and the responsibilities you got and gee whiz, people are not buying merchandise like they used to and this, that, and the other thing.

"In other words, Monroe, I suddenly came to the realization that I had no protection whatsoever in giving up my 'contacts' for what? So that you can keep me on tender hooks. So that you can come to my house for supper again and again, compliment my Mother on saying the food is very lucious, and then suddenly we wake up and find we got a boarder with us, only boarders at least pay the rent.

"Well I think that in view of this attitude on your part, in view of the fact that all the time you are saying that business conditions are bad so that we got to assume it don't warrant any serious step on your part, not even to the extent of a ring, in view of the fact that I am giving up chances which to me may prove valuable as I am not growing any younger each day and opportunities don't hang on trees, all a girl has to do is to go out and pick it off the tree just like it was an apple or some piece fruit, in view of all this, Monroe, suppose we better call it just 'quits.'

"Now please don't get the idea I am calling you 'A Cheap Skate' just because I haven't got a ring to show on my finger. I am not placing you in that catagory whatsoever inasmuch as you have on several occassions shown me a very good time. Still in all if you had merely said to me

'O. K. Billie. String along with me for another couple months till business conditions gets on its feet and then everything will be O. K.' I would of been only too pleased and happy to of strung along with you. But you didn't even have this common courtesy to the girl to who you apparently seemed so crazy about at camp last summer when you swore to me that this here was no typical summer romance you write down on ice it's quickly forgotten, but would culminate to a mutual union. Oh, no, not you! After all promises are cheap and cost nothing. What have you got to loose? Say, it's a wonder to me I'm opening my eyes now. God knows they were closed long enough before.

"So you see, Monroe, why it's better for me to get this matter off my chest once and for all rather than I should waste my time brooding about it because I just can't dismiss things with a snap of the fingers. Perhaps if I was the type girl who could dismiss things with a snap of the finger I would be better off today, believe me. So, Monroe, leave us call it 'quits' and just say it all comes under the heading of 'Experience.' I'm afraid that even if you should dig up a ring, and judgeing from the way your business is at the moment I can just imagine what type ring you would dig up, I'm afraid I'd still have to say 'I'm sorry, I'm not interested.' You had your chances and too bad, you didn't make the most of them. Better luck with some other girl next time. As for me, don't worry. I got along very nicely without you a long time before I met you, and I'll still get along without you inasmuch as I have some very worth-while 'contacts,' friends who don't talk a 'poor mouth' whenever they have to dig in their pockets, be it a ticket for a movie or just a chocolate ice-cream Sunday.

"This letter means 'finis' so please don't reply nor communicate with me via the phone or via the mails inasmuch as I will be out. I am not 'soreheaded' the least bit about the matter but I merely want to drop it once and for all.

"Assuring you of my sincerest feelings about the matter, and trusting that you meet a girl who appreciates you a little more than I do in view of the whole situation, I am—"

Bella wondered if "Very truly yours" wasn't just a bit formal and businesslike. But that was exactly what she wanted to be. She wrote, "Very truly yours, Bella Gross." There! Signing "Bella" instead of "Billie" would make him realize that their relationship was completely over.

She picked up the scribbled pages and read them carefully. Once or twice she stopped to make a correction and to consult the dictionary about spelling. When she had finished reading what she had written, she

added, "P. S. Please excuse the handwriting." She then reached for a
sheet of her good paper, inked her pen, glanced at the rough draft, and
started to write:

Dear Monroe Rosenblatt

Ring Lardner

He was christened Ringgold Wilmer Lardner, shortened the name to Ring W. Lardner, and then discarded the middle initial for fear that people might say it stood for Worm. Graduating from high school in his native Niles, he wanted to attend the University of Michigan to take "football and dentistry." Instead he enrolled at Armour Institute, Chicago, for the study of mechanical engineering; at the end of the first semester he "passed in rhetoric and out of Armour." A job as local freight agent (lost when a consignment of cream cheese was missing) was succeeded by a place on a newspaper where he was boy-of-all-work. A few years later Ring Lardner was a sports-writer whose style was both widely imitated and inimitable; at thirty his baseball stories created a new genre: stories that were broadly comic and unexpectedly caustic. His speech became a queer composite of American and English—a blend that has been referred to as "Ringlish."

At forty the humorist was supplanted by the satirist. The Lardner who lived to make people laugh became, according to William Bolitho, "the greatest and sincerest pessimist America has produced." After several years of illness, he died in 1933; he was forty-eight.

It will always be a question whether the "real" Lardner was the explorer of the American dialect, the sentimental reporter, the melancholy analyst, or the mad wag. Even his comprehensive collection Round Up omits the wild nonsense skits and the fantastically surrealist plays, such as "I Gaspiri," with its first act laid in "a public street in a bathroom."

alibi ike

His right name was Frank X. Farrell, and I guess the X stood for "Excuse me." Because he never pulled a play, good or bad, on or off the field, without apologizin' for it.

"Alibi Ike" was the name Carey wished on him the first day he reported down South. O' course we all cut out the "Alibi" part of it right away for the fear he would overhear it and bust somebody. But we called him "Ike" right to his face and the rest of it was understood by everybody on the club except Ike himself.

He ast me one time, he says:

"What do you all call me Ike for? I ain't no Yid."

"Carey give you the name," I says. "It's his nickname for everybody he takes a likin' to."

"He mustn't have only a few friends then," says Ike. "I never heard him say 'Ike' to nobody else."

But I was goin' to tell you about Carey namin' him. We'd been workin' out two weeks and the pitchers was showin' somethin' when this bird joined us. His first day out he stood up there so good and took such a reef at the old pill that he had everyone lookin'. Then him and Carey was together in left field, catchin' fungoes, and it was after we was through for the day that Carey told me about him.

"What do you think of Alibi Ike?" ast Carey.

"Who's that?" I says.

"This here Farrell in the outfield," says Carey.

"He looks like he could hit," I says.

"Yes," says Carey, "but he can't hit near as good as he can apologize."

Then Carey went on to tell me what Ike had been pullin' out there. He'd dropped the first fly ball that was hit to him and told Carey his glove wasn't broke in good yet, and Carey says the glove could easy of been Kid Gleason's gran'father. He made a whale of a catch out o' the next one and Carey says "Nice work!" or somethin' like that, but Ike says he could of caught the ball with his back turned only he slipped when he started after it and, besides that, the air currents fooled him.

"I thought you done well to get to the ball," says Carey.

"I ought to been settin' under it," says Ike.

"What did you hit last year?" Carey ast him.

"I had malaria most o' the season," says Ike. "I wound up with .356."

"Where would I have to go to get malaria?" says Carey, but Ike didn't wise up.

I and Carey and him set at the same table together for supper. It took him half an hour longer'n us to eat because he had to excuse himself every time he lifted his fork.

"Doctor told me I needed starch," he'd say, and then toss a shovelful o' potatoes into him. Or, "They ain't much meat on one o' these chops," he'd tell us, and grab another one. Or he'd say: "Nothin' like onions for a cold," and then he'd dip into the perfumery.

"Better try that apple sauce," says Carey. "It'll help your malaria."

"Whose malaria?" says Ike. He'd forgot already why he didn't only hit .356 last year.

I and Carey begin to lead him on.

"Whereabouts did you say your home was?" I ast him.

"I live with my folks," he says. "We live in Kansas City—not right down in the business part—outside a ways."

"How's that come?" says Carey. "I should think you'd get rooms in the post office."

But Ike was too busy curin' his cold to get that one.

"Are you married?" I ast him.

"No," he says. "I never run round much with girls, except to shows onct in a wile and parties and dances and roller skatin'."

"Never take 'em to the prize fights, eh?" says Carey.

"We don't have no real good bouts," says Ike. "Just bush stuff. And I never figured a boxin' match was a place for the ladies."

Well, after supper he pulled a cigar out and lit it. I was just goin' to ask him what he done it for, but he beat me to it.

"Kind o' rests a man to smoke after a good work-out," he says. "Kind o' settles a man's supper, too."

"Looks like a pretty good cigar," says Carey.

"Yes," says Ike. "A friend o' mine give it to me—a fella in Kansas City that runs a billiard room."

"Do you play billiards?" I ast him.

"I used to play a fair game," he says. "I'm all out o' practice now—can't hardly make a shot."

We coaxed him into a four-handed battle, him and Carey against Jack Mack and I. Say, he couldn't play billiards as good as Willie

Hoppe; not quite. But to hear him tell it, he didn't make a good shot all evenin'. I'd leave him an awful-lookin' layout and he'd gather 'em up in one try and then run a couple o' hundred, and between every carom he'd say he'd put too much stuff on the ball, or the English didn't take, or the table wasn't true, or his stick was crooked, or somethin'. And all the time he had the balls actin' like they was Dutch soldiers and him Kaiser William. We started out to play fifty points, but we had to make it a thousand so as I and Jack and Carey could try the table.

The four of us set round the lobby a wile after we was through playin', and when it got along toward bedtime Carey whispered to me and says:

"Ike'd like to go to bed, but he can't think up no excuse."

Carey hadn't hardly finished whisperin' when Ike got up and pulled it:

"Well, good night, boys," he says. "I ain't sleepy, but I got some gravel in my shoes and it's killin' my feet."

We knowed he hadn't never left the hotel since we'd came in from the grounds and changed our clo'es. So Carey says:

"I should think they'd take them gravel pits out o' the billiard room."

But Ike was already on his way to the elevator, limpin'.

"He's got the world beat," says Carey to Jack and I. "I've knew lots o' guys that had an alibi for every mistake they made; I've heard pitchers say that the ball slipped when somebody cracked one off'n 'em; I've heard infielders complain of a sore arm after heavin' one into the stand, and I've saw outfielders tooken sick with a dizzy spell when they've misjudged a fly ball. But this baby can't even go to bed without apologizin', and I bet he excuses himself to the razor when he gets ready to shave."

"And at that," says Jack, "he's goin' to make us a good man."

"Yes," says Carey, "unless rheumatism keeps his battin' average down to .400."

Well, sir, Ike kept whalin' away at the ball all through the trip till everybody knowed he'd won a job. Cap had him in there regular the last few exhibition games and told the newspaper boys a week before the season opened that he was goin' to start him in Kane's place.

"You're there, kid," says Carey to Ike, the night Cap made the 'nnouncement. "They ain't many boys that wins a big league berth their third year out."

"I'd of been up here a year ago," says Ike, "only I was bent over all season with lumbago."

It rained down in Cincinnati one day and somebody organized a little game o' cards. They was shy two men to make six and ast I and Carey to play.

"I'm with you if you get Ike and make it seven-handed," says Carey.

So they got a hold of Ike and we went up to Smitty's room.

"I pretty near forgot how many you deal," says Ike. "It's been a long wile since I played."

I and Carey give each other the wink, and sure enough, he was just as ig'orant about poker as billiards. About the second hand, the pot was opened two or three ahead of him, and they was three in when it come his turn. It cost a buck, and he throwed in two.

"It's raised, boys," somebody says.

"Gosh, that's right, I did raise it," says Ike.

"Take out a buck if you didn't mean to tilt her," says Carey.

"No," says Ike, "I'll leave it go."

Well, it was raised back at him and then he made another mistake and raised again. They was only three left in when the draw come. Smitty'd opened with a pair o' kings and he didn't help 'em. Ike stood pat. The guy that'd raised him back was flushin' and he didn't fill. So Smitty checked and Ike bet and didn't get no call. He tossed his hand away, but I grabbed it and give it a look. He had king, queen, jack and two tens. Alibi Ike he must have seen me peekin', for he leaned over and whispered to me.

"I overlooked my hand," he says. "I thought all the wile it was a straight."

"Yes," I says, "that's why you raised twice by mistake."

They was another pot that he come into with tens and fours. It was tilted a couple o' times and two o' the strong fellas drawed ahead of Ike. They each drawed one. So Ike throwed away his little pair and come out with four tens. And they was four treys against him. Carey'd look at Ike's discards and then he says:

"This lucky bum busted two pair."

"No, no, I didn't," says Ike.

"Yes, yes, you did," says Carey, and showed us the two fours.

"What do you know about that?" says Ike. "I'd of swore one was a five spot."

Well, we hadn't had no pay day yet, and after a wile everybody except Ike was goin' shy. I could see him gettin' restless and I was wonderin' how he'd make the get-away. He tried two or three times. "I got to buy some collars before supper," he says.

"No hurry," says Smitty. "The stores here keeps open all night in April."

After a minute he opened up again.

"My uncle out in Nebraska ain't expected to live," he says. "I ought to send a telegram."

"Would that save him?" says Carey.

"No, it sure wouldn't," says Ike, "but I ought to leave my old man know where I'm at."

"When did you hear about your uncle?" says Carey.

"Just this mornin'," says Ike.

"Who told you?" ast Carey.

"I got a wire from my old man," says Ike.

"Well," says Carey, "your old man knows you're still here yet this afternoon if you was here this mornin'. Trains leavin' Cincinnati in the middle o' the day don't carry no ball clubs."

"Yes," says Ike, "that's true. But he don't know where I'm goin' to be next week."

"Ain't he got no schedule?" ast Carey.

"I sent him one openin' day," says Ike, "but it takes mail a long time to get to Idaho."

"I thought your old man lived in Kansas City," says Carey.

"He does when he's home," says Ike.

"But now," says Carey, "I s'pose he's went to Idaho so as he can be near your sick uncle in Nebraska."

"He's visitin' my other uncle in Idaho."

"Then how does he keep posted about your sick uncle?" ast Carey.

"He don't," says Ike. "He don't even know my other uncle's sick. That's why I ought to wire and tell him."

"Good night!" says Carey.

"What town in Idaho is your old man at?" I says.

Ike thought it over.

"No town at all," he says. "But he's near a town."

"Near what town?" I says.

"Yuma," says Ike.

Well, by this time he'd lost two or three pots and he was desperate. We was playin' just as fast as we could, because we seen we couldn't hold him much longer. But he was tryin' so hard to frame an escape that he couldn't pay no attention to the cards, and it looked like we'd get his whole pile away from him if we could make him stick.

The telephone saved him. The minute it begun to ring, five of us jumped for it. But Ike was there first.

"Yes," he says, answerin' it. "This is him. I'll come right down."

And he slammed up the receiver and beat it out o' the door without even sayin' good-by.

"Smitty'd ought to locked the door," says Carey.

"What did he win?" ast Carey.

We figured it up—sixty-odd bucks.

"And the next time we ask him to play," says Carey, "his fingers will be so stiff he can't hold the cards."

Well, we set round a wile talkin' it over, and pretty soon the telephone rung again. Smitty answered it. It was a friend of his'n from Hamilton and he wanted to know why Smitty didn't hurry down. He was the one that had called before and Ike had told him he was Smitty.

"Ike'd ought to split with Smitty's friend," says Carey.

"No," I says, "he'll need all he won. It costs money to buy collars and to send telegrams from Cincinnati to your old man in Texas and keep him posted on the health o' your uncle in Cedar Rapids, D. C."

And you ought to heard him out there on that field! They wasn't a day when he didn't pull six or seven, and it didn't make no difference whether he was goin' good or bad. If he popped up in the pinch he should of made a base hit and the reason he didn't was so-and-so. And if he cracked one for three bases he ought to had a home run, only the ball wasn't lively, or the wind brought it back, or he tripped on a lump o' dirt, roundin' first base.

They was one afternoon in New York when he beat all records. Big Marquard was workin' against us and he was good.

In the first innin' Ike hit one clear over that right field stand, but it was a few feet foul. Then he got another foul and then the count come to two and two. Then Rube slipped one acrost on him and he was called out.

"What do you know about that!" he says afterward on the bench. "I lost count. I thought it was three and one, and I took a strike."

"You took a strike all right," says Carey. "Even the umps knowed it was a strike."

"Yes," says Ike, "but you can bet I wouldn't of took it if I'd knew it was the third one. The score board had it wrong."

"That score board ain't for you to look at," says Cap. "It's for you to hit that old pill against."

"Well," says Ike, "I could of hit that one over the score board if I'd knew it was the third."

"Was it a good ball?" I says.

"Well, no, it wasn't," says Ike. "It was inside."

"How far inside?" says Carey.

"Oh, two or three inches or half a foot," says Ike.

"I guess you wouldn't of threatened the score board with it then," says Cap.

"I'd of pulled it down the right foul line if I hadn't thought he'd call it a ball," says Ike.

Well, in New York's part o' the innin' Doyle cracked one and Ike run back a mile and a half and caught it with one hand. We was all sayin' what a whale of a play it was, but he had to apologize just the same as for gettin' struck out.

"That stand's so high," he says, "that a man don't never see a ball till it's right on top o' you."

"Didn't you see that one?" ast Cap.

"Not at first," says Ike; "not till it raised up above the roof o' the stand."

"Then why did you start back as soon as the ball was hit?" says Cap.

"I knowed by the sound that he'd got a good hold of it," says Ike.

"Yes," says Cap, "but how'd you know what direction to run in?"

"Doyle usually hits 'em that way, the way I run," says Ike.

"Why don't you play blindfolded?" says Carey.

"Might as well, with that big high stand to bother a man," says Ike. "If I could of saw the ball all the time I'd of got it in my hip pocket."

Along in the fifth we was one run to the bad and Ike got on with one out. On the first ball throwed to Smitty, Ike went down. The ball was outside and Meyers throwed Ike out by ten feet.

You could see Ike's lips movin' all the way to the bench and when he got there he had his piece learned.

"Why didn't he swing?" he says.

"Why didn't you wait for his sign?" says Cap.

"He give me his sign," says Ike.

"What is his sign with you?" says Cap.

"Pickin' up some dirt with his right hand," says Ike.

"Well, I didn't see him do it," Cap says.

"He done it all right," says Ike.

Well, Smitty went out and they wasn't no more argument till they come in for the next innin'. Then Cap opened it up.

"You fellas better get your signs straight," he says.

"Do you mean me?" says Smitty.

"Yes," Cap says. "What's your sign with Ike?"

"Slidin' my left hand up to the end o' the bat and back," says Smitty.

"Do you hear that, Ike?" ast Cap.

"What of it?" says Ike.

"You says his sign was pickin' up dirt and he says it's slidin' his hand. Which is right?"

"I'm right," says Smitty. "But if you're arguin' about him goin' last innin', I didn't give him no sign."

"You pulled your cap down with your right hand, didn't you?" ast Ike.

"Well, s'pose I did," says Smitty. "That don't mean nothin'. I never told you to take that for a sign, did I?"

"I thought maybe you meant to tell me and forgot," says Ike.

They couldn't none of us answer that and they wouldn't of been no more said if Ike had of shut up. But wile we was settin' there Carey got on with two out and stole second clean.

"There!" says Ike. "That's what I was tryin' to do and I'd of got away with it if Smitty'd swang and bothered the Indian."

"Oh!" says Smitty. "You was tryin' to steal then, was you? I thought you claimed I give you the hit and run."

"I didn't claim no such a thing," says Ike. "I thought maybe you might of gave me a sign, but I was goin' anyway because I thought I had a good start."

Cap prob'ly would of hit him with a bat, only just about that time Doyle booted one on Hayes and Carey come acrost with the run that tied.

Well, we go into the ninth finally, one and one, and Marquard walks McDonald with nobody out.

"Lay it down," says Cap to Ike.

And Ike goes up there with orders to bunt and cracks the first ball into that right-field stand! It was fair this time, and we're two ahead, but I didn't think about that at the time. I was too busy watchin' Cap's face. First he turned pale and then he got red as fire and then he got blue and purple, and finally he just laid back and busted out laughin'. So we wasn't afraid to laugh ourselfs when we seen him doin' it, and when Ike come in everybody on the bench was in hysterics.

But instead o' takin' advantage, Ike had to try and excuse himself. His play was to shut up and he didn't know how to make it.

"Well," he says, "if I hadn't hit quite so quick at that one I bet it'd of cleared the center-field fence."

Cap stopped laughin'.

"It'll cost you plain fifty," he says.

"What for?" says Ike.

"When I say 'bunt' I mean 'bunt,'" says Cap.

"You didn't say 'bunt,'" says Ike.

"I says 'Lay it down,'" says Cap. "If that don't mean 'bunt,' what does it mean?"

"'Lay it down' means 'bunt' all right," says Ike, "but I understood you to say 'Lay on it.'"

"All right," says Cap, "and the little misunderstandin' will cost you fifty."

Ike didn't say nothin' for a few minutes. Then he had another bright idear.

"I was just kiddin' about misunderstandin' you," he says. "I knowed you wanted me to bunt."

"Well, then, why didn't you bunt?" ast Cap.

"I was goin' to on the next ball," says Ike. "But I thought if I took

a good wallop I'd have 'em all fooled. So I walloped at the first one
to fool 'em, and I didn't have no intention o' hittin' it."

"You tried to miss it, did you?" says Cap.

"Yes," says Ike.

"How'd you happen to hit it?" ast Cap.

"Well," Ike says, "I was lookin' for him to throw me a fast one and
I was goin' to swing under it. But he come with a hook and I met it
right square where I was swingin' to go under the fast one."

"Great!" says Cap. "Boys," he says, "Ike's learned how to hit
Marquard's curve. Pretend a fast one's comin' and then try to miss it.
It's a good thing to know and Ike'd ought to be willin' to pay for the
lesson. So I'm goin' to make it a hundred instead o' fifty."

The game wound up 3 to 1. The fine didn't go, because Ike hit like a
wild man all through that trip and we made pretty near a clean-up.
The night we went to Philly I got him cornered in the car and I says
to him:

"Forget them alibis for a wile and tell me somethin'. What'd you do
that for, swing that time against Marquard when you was told to bunt?"

"I'll tell you," he says. "That ball he throwed me looked just like the
one I struck out on in the first innin' and I wanted to show Cap what
I could of done to that other one if I'd knew it was the third strike."

"But," I says, " the one you struck out on in the first innin' was a fast
ball."

"So was the one I cracked in the ninth," says Ike.

You've saw Cap's wife, o' course. Well, her sister's about twict as
good-lookin' as her, and that's goin' some.

Cap took his missus down to St. Louis the second trip and the other
one come down from St. Joe to visit her. Her name is Dolly, and some
doll is right.

Well, Cap was goin' to take the two sisters to a show and he wanted
a beau for Dolly. He left it to her and she picked Ike. He'd hit three
on the nose that afternoon—off'n Sallee, too.

They fell for each other that first evenin'. Cap told us how it come
off. She begin flatterin' Ike for the star game he'd played and o' course
he begin excusin' himself for not doin' better. So she thought he was
modest and it went strong with her. And she believed everything he said
and that made her solid with him—that and her make-up. They was
together every mornin' and evenin' for the five days we was there. In
the afternoons Ike played the grandest ball you ever see, hittin' and

runnin' the bases like a fool and catchin' everything that stayed in the park.

I told Cap, I says: "You'd ought to keep the doll with us and he'd make Cobb's figures look sick."

But Dolly had to go back to St. Joe and we come home for a long serious.

Well, for the next three weeks Ike had a letter to read every day and he'd set in the clubhouse readin' it till mornin' practice was half over. Cap didn't say nothin' to him, because he was goin' so good. But I and Carey wasted a lot of our time tryin' to get him to own up who the letters was from. Fine chanct!

"What are you readin'?" Carey'd say. "A bill?"

"No," Ike'd say, "not exactly a bill. It's a letter from a fella I used to go to school with."

"High school or college?" I'd ask him.

"College," he say.

"What college?" I'd say.

Then he'd stall a wile and then he'd say:

"I didn't go to the college myself, but my friend went there."

"How did it happen you didn't go?" Carey'd ask him.

"Well," he'd say, "they wasn't no colleges near where I lived."

"Didn't you live in Kansas City?" I'd say to him.

One time he'd say he did and another time he didn't. One time he says he lived in Michigan.

"Where at?" says Carey.

"Near Detroit," he says.

"Well," I says, "Detroit's near Ann Arbor and that's where they got the university."

"Yes," says Ike, "they got it there now, but they didn't have it there then."

"I come pretty near goin' to Syracuse," I says, "only they wasn't no railroads runnin' through there in them days."

"Where'd this friend o' yours go to college?" says Carey.

"I forget now," says Ike.

"Was it Carlisle?" ast Carey.

"No," says Ike, "his folks wasn't very well off."

"That's what barred me from Smith," I says.

"I was goin' to tackle Cornell's," says Carey, "but the doctor told me I'd have hay fever if I didn't stay up North."

"Your friend writes long letters," I says.

"Yes," says Ike; "he's tellin' me about a ball player."

"Where does he play?" ast Carey.

"Down in the Texas League—Fort Wayne," says Ike.

"It looks like a girl's writin'," Carey says.

"A girl wrote it," says Ike. "That's my friend's sister, writin' for him."

"Didn't they teach writin' at this here college where he went?" says Carey.

"Sure," Ike says, "they taught writin', but he got his hand cut off in a railroad wreck."

"How long ago?" I says.

"Right after he got out o' college," says Ike.

"Well," I says, "I should think he'd of learned to write with his left hand by this time."

"It's his left hand that was cut off," says Ike; "and he was left-handed."

"You get a letter every day," says Carey. "They're all the same writin'. Is he tellin' you about a different ball player every time he writes?"

"No," Ike says. "It's the same ball player. He just tells me what he does every day."

"From the size o' the letters, they don't play nothin' but double-headers down there," says Carey.

We figured that Ike spent most of his evenin's answerin' the letters from his "friend's sister," so we kept tryin' to date him up for shows and parties to see how he'd duck out of 'em. He was bugs over spaghetti, so we told him one day that they was goin' to be a big feed of it over to Joe's that night and he was invited.

"How long'll it last?" he says.

"Well," we says, "we're goin' right over there after the game and stay till they close up."

"I can't go," he says, "unless they leave me come home at eight bells."

"Nothin' doin'," says Carey. "Joe'd get sore."

"I can't go then," says Ike.

"Why not?" I ast him.

"Well," he says, "my landlady locks up the house at eight and I left my key home."

"You can come and stay with me," says Carey.

"No," he says, "I can't sleep in a strange bed."

"How do you get along when we're on the road?" says I.

"I don't never sleep the first night anywheres," he says. "After that I'm all right."

"You'll have time to chase home and get your key right after the game," I told him.

"The key ain't home," says Ike. "I lent it to one o' the other fellas and he's went out o' town and took it with him."

"Couldn't you borry another key off'n the landlady?" Carey ast him.

"No," he says, "that's the only one they is."

Well, the day before we started East again, Ike come into the club-house all smiles.

"Your birthday?" I ast him.

"No," he says.

"What do you feel so good about?" I says.

"Got a letter from my old man," he says. "My uncle's goin' to get well."

"Is that the one in Nebraska?" says I.

"Not right in Nebraska," says Ike. "Near there."

But afterwards we got the right dope from Cap. Dolly'd blew in from Missouri and was goin' to make the trip with her sister.

Well, I want to alibi Carey and I for what come off in Boston. If we'd of had any idear what we was doin', we'd never did it. They wasn't nobody outside o' maybe Ike and the dame that felt worse over it than I and Carey.

The first two days we didn't see nothin' of Ike and her except out to the park. The rest o' the time they was sight-seein' over to Cambridge and down to Revere and out to Brook-a-line and all the other places where the rubes go.

But when we come into the beanery after the third game Cap's wife called us over.

"If you want to see somethin' pretty," she says, "look at the third finger on Sis's left hand."

Well, o' course we knowed before we looked that it wasn't goin' to be no hangnail. Nobody was su'prised when Dolly blew into the dinin' room with it—a rock that Ike'd bought off'n Diamond Joe the first trip to New York. Only o' course it'd been set into a lady's-size ring instead o' the automobile tire he'd been wearin'.

Cap and his missus and Ike and Dolly ett supper together, only Ike didn't eat nothin', but just set there blushin' and spillin' things on the table-cloth. I heard him excusin' himself for not havin' no appetite. He says he couldn't never eat when he was clost to the ocean. He'd forgot about them sixty-five oysters he destroyed the first night o' the trip before.

He was goin' to take her to a show, so after supper he went upstairs to change his collar. She had to doll up, too, and o' course Ike was through long before her.

If you remember the hotel in Boston, they's a little parlor where the piano's at and then they's another little parlor openin' off o' that. Well, when Ike come down Smitty was playin' a few chords and I and Carey was harmonizin'. We seen Ike go up to the desk to leave his key and we called him in. He tried to duck away, but we wouldn't stand for it.

We ast him what he was all duded up for and he says he was goin' to the theayter.

"Goin' alone?" says Carey.

"No," he says, "a friend o' mine's goin' with me."

"What do you say if we go along?" says Carey.

"I ain't only got two tickets," he says.

"Well," says Carey, "we can go down there with you and buy our own seats; maybe we can all get together."

"No," says Ike. "They ain't no more seats. They're all sold out."

"We can buy some off'n the scalpers," says Carey.

"I wouldn't if I was you," says Ike. "They say the show's rotten."

"What are you goin' for, then?" I ast.

"I didn't hear about it bein' rotten till I got the tickets," he says.

"Well," I says, "if you don't want to go I'll buy the tickets from you."

"No," says Ike, "I wouldn't want to cheat you. I'm stung and I'll just have to stand for it."

"What are you goin' to do with the girl, leave her here at the hotel?" I says.

"What girl?" says Ike.

"The girl you ett supper with," I says.

"Oh," he says, "we just happened to go into the dinin' room together, that's all. Cap wanted I should set down with 'em."

"I noticed," says Carey, "that she happened to be wearin' that rock you bought off'n Diamond Joe."

"Yes," says Ike. "I lent it to her for a wile."

"Did you lend her the new ring that goes with it?" I says.

"She had that already," says Ike. "She lost the set out of it."

"I wouldn't trust no strange girl with a rock o' mine," says Carey.

"Oh, I guess she's all right," Ike says. "Besides, I was tired o' the stone. When a girl asks you for somethin', what are you goin' to do?"

He started out toward the desk, but we flagged him.

"Wait a minute!" Carey says. "I got a bet with Sam here, and it's up to you to settle it."

"Well," says Ike, "make it snappy. My friend'll be here any minute."

"I bet," says Carey, "that you and that girl was engaged to be married."

"Nothin' to it," says Ike.

"Now look here," says Carey, "this is goin' to cost me real money if I lose. Cut out the alibi stuff and give it to us straight. Cap's wife just as good as told us you was roped."

Ike blushed like a kid.

"Well, boys," he says, "I may as well own up. You win, Carey."

"Yatta boy!" says Carey. "Congratulations!"

"You got a swell girl, Ike," I says.

"She's a peach," says Smitty.

"Well, I guess she's O. K.," says Ike. "I don't know much about girls."

"Didn't you never run round with 'em?" I says.

"Oh, yes, plenty of 'em," says Ike. "But I never seen none I'd fall for."

"That is, till you seen this one," says Carey.

"Well," says Ike, "this one's O. K., but I wasn't thinkin' about gettin' married yet a wile."

"Who done the askin'—her?" says Carey.

"Oh, no," says Ike, "but sometimes a man don't know what he's gettin' into. Take a good-lookin' girl, and a man gen'ally almost always does about what she wants him to."

"They couldn't no girl lasso me unless I wanted to be lassoed," says Smitty.

"Oh, I don't know," says Ike. "When a fella gets to feelin' sorry for one of 'em it's all off."

Well, we left him go after shakin' hands all round. But he didn't take Dolly to no show that night. Some time wile we was talkin' she'd came into that other parlor and she'd stood there and heard us. I don't know how much she heard. But it was enough. Dolly and Cap's missus took the midnight train for New York. And from there Cap's wife sent her on her way back to Missouri.

She'd left the ring and a note for Ike with the clerk. But we didn't ask Ike if the note was from his friend in Fort Wayne, Texas.

When we'd came to Boston Ike was hittin' plain .397. When we got back home he'd fell off to pretty near nothin'. He hadn't drove one out o' the infield in any o' them other Eastern parks, and he didn't even give no excuse for it.

To show you how bad he was, he struck out three times in Brooklyn one day and never opened his trap when Cap ast him what was the matter. Before, if he'd whiffed oncet in a game he'd of wrote a book tellin' why.

Well, we dropped from first place to fifth in four weeks and we was still goin' down. I and Carey was about the only ones in the club that spoke to each other, and all as we did was remind ourself o' what a boner we'd pulled.

"It's goin' to beat us out o' the big money," says Carey.

"Yes," I says. "I don't want to knock my own ball club, but it looks like a one-man team, and when that one man's dauber's down we couldn't trim our whiskers."

"We ought to knew better," says Carey.

"Yes," I says, "but why should a man pull an alibi for bein' engaged to such a bearcat as she was?"

"He shouldn't," says Carey. "But I and you knowed he would or we'd never started talkin' to him about it. He wasn't no more ashamed o' the girl than I am of a regular base hit. But he just can't come clean on no subjec'."

Cap had the whole story, and I and Carey was as pop'lar with him as an umpire.

"What do you want me to do, Cap?" Carey'd say to him before goin' up to hit.

"Use your own judgment," Cap'd tell him. "We want to lose another game."

But finally, one night in Pittsburgh, Cap had a letter from his missus and he come to us with it.

"You fellas," he says, "is the ones that put us on the bum, and if you're sorry I think they's a chancet for you to make good. The old lady's out to St. Joe and she's been tryin' her hardest to fix things up. She's explained that Ike don't mean nothin' with his talk ; I've wrote and explained that to Dolly, too. But the old lady says that Dolly says that she can't believe it. But Dolly's still stuck on this baby, and she's pinin' away just the same as Ike. And the old lady says she thinks if you two fellas would write to the girl and explain how you was always kiddin' with Ike and leadin' him on, and how the ball club was all shot to pieces since Ike quit hittin', and how he acted like he was goin' to kill himself, and this and that, she'd fall for it and maybe soften down. Dolly, the old lady says, would believe you before she'd believe I and the old lady, because she thinks it's her we're sorry for, and not him."

Well, I and Carey was only too glad to try and see what we could do.

But it wasn't no snap. We wrote about eight letters before we got one that looked good. Then we give it to the stenographer and had it wrote out on a typewriter and both of us signed it.

It was Carey's idear that made the letter good. He stuck in somethin' about the world's serious money that our wives wasn't goin' to spend unless she took pity on a "boy who was so shy and modest that he was afraid to come right out and say that he had asked such a beautiful and handsome girl to become his bride."

That's prob'ly what got her, or maybe she couldn't of held out much longer anyway. It was four days after we sent the letter that Cap heard from his missus again. We was in Cincinnati.

"We've won," he says to us. "The old lady says that Dolly says she'll give him another chance. But the old lady says it won't do no good for Ike to write a letter. He'll have to go out there."

"Send him to-night," says Carey.

"I'll pay half his fare," I says.

"I'll pay the other half," says Carey.

"No," says Cap, "the club'll pay his expenses. I'll send him scoutin'."

"Are you goin' to send him to-night?"

"Sure," says Cap. "But I'm goin' to break the news to him right now. It's time we win a ball game."

So in the clubhouse, just before the game, Cap told him. And I certainly felt sorry for Rube Benton and Red Ames that afternoon! I and Carey was standin' in front o' the hotel that night when Ike come out with his suitcase.

"Sent home?" I says to him.

"No," he says, "I'm goin' scoutin'."

"Where to?" I says. "Fort Wayne?"

"No, not exactly," he says.

"Well," says Carey, "have a good time."

"I ain't lookin' for no good time," says Ike. "I says I was goin' scoutin'."

"Well, then," says Carey, "I hope you see somebody you like."

"And you better have a drink before you go," I says.

"Well," says Ike, "they claim it helps a cold."

Mr. and Mrs. Fix-It

They're certainly a live bunch in this town. We ain't only been here three days and had calls already from people representin' four different organizations—the Chamber of Commerce, Kiwanis, and I forget who else. They wanted to know if we was comfortable and did we like the town and is they anything they can do for us and what to be sure and see.

And they all asked how we happened to come here instead of goin' somewheres else. I guess they keep a record of everybody's reasons for comin' so as they can get a line on what features tourists is most attracted by. Then they play up them features in next year's booster advertisin'.

Well, I told them we was perfectly comfortable and we like the town fine and they's nothin' nobody can do for us right now and we'll be sure and see all the things we ought to see. But when they asked me how did we happen to come here, I said it was just a kind of a accident, because the real reason makes too long a story.

My wife has been kiddin' me about my friends ever since we was married. She says that judgin' by the ones I've introduced her to, they ain't nobody in the world got a rummier bunch of friends than me. I'll admit that the most of them ain't, well, what you might call hot; they're different somehow than when I first hung around with them. They seem to be lost without a brass rail to rest their dogs on. But of course they're old friends and I can't give 'em the air.

We have 'em to the house for dinner every little w'ile, they and their wives, and what my missus objects to is because they don't none of them play bridge or mah jong or do cross-word puzzles or sing or dance or even talk, but jest set there and wait for somebody to pour 'em a fresh drink.

As I say, my wife kids me about 'em and they ain't really nothin' I can offer in their defense. That don't mean, though, that the shoe is all on one foot. Because w'ile the majority of her friends may not be quite as dumb as mine, just the same they's a few she's picked out who I'd of had to be under the ether to allow anybody to introduce 'em to me in the first place.

Like the Crandalls, for instance. Mrs. Crandall come from my wife's home town and they didn't hardly know each other there, but they met again in a store in Chi and it went from bad to worse till finally Ada asked the dame and her husband to the house.

Well, the husband turns out to be the fella that win the war, w'ile it

387

seems that Mrs. Crandall was in Atlantic City once and some movin'
picture company was makin' a picture there and they took a scene of
what was supposed to be society people walkin' up and down the
Boardwalk and Mrs. Crandall was in the picture and people that seen it
when it come out, they all said that from the way she screened, why if
she wanted to go into the business, she could make Gloria Swanson look
like Mrs. Gump.

Now it ain't only took me a few words to tell you these things, but
when the Crandalls tells their story themselves, they don't hardly get
started by midnight and no chance of them goin' home till they're
through even when you drop 'em a hint that they're springin' it on you
for the hundred and twelfth time.

That's the Crandalls, and another of the wife's friends is the Thayers.
Thayer is what you might call a all-around handy man. He can mimic
pretty near all the birds and beasts and fishes, he can yodel, he can play
a ocarina, or he can recite Kipling or Robert H. Service, or he can do
card tricks, and strike a light without no matches, and tie all the
different knots.

And besides that, he can make a complete radio outfit and set it up,
and take pictures as good as the best professional photographers and a
whole lot better. He collects autographs. And he never had a sick day
in his life.

Mrs. Thayer gets a headache playin' bridge, so it's mah jong or rhum
when she's around. She used to be a teacher of elocution and she still
gives readin's if you coax her, or if you don't, and her hair is such a
awful nuisance that she would get it cut in a minute only all her friends
tells her it would be criminal to spoil that head of hair. And when she
talks to her husband, she always talks baby talk, maybe because somebody has told her that she'd be single if he wasn't childish.

And then Ada has got still another pal, a dame named Peggy Flood
who is hospital mad and ain't happy unless she is just goin' under the
knife or just been there. She's had everything removed that the doctors
knew the name of and now they're probin' her for new giblets.

Well, I wouldn't mind if they cut her up into alphabet soup if they'd
only do such a good job of it that they couldn't put her together again,
but she always comes through O. K. and she spends the intermissions at
our place, describin' what all they done or what they're plannin' to do
next.

But the cat's nightgown is Tom Stevens and his wife. There's the
team that wins the Olympics! And they're Ada's team, not mine.

Ada met Belle Stevens on the elevated. Ada was invited to a party out on the North Side and didn't know exactly where to get off and Mrs. Stevens seen her talkin' to the guard and horned in and asked her what was it she wanted to know and Ada told her, and Mrs. Stevens said she was goin' to get off the same station Ada wanted to get off, so they got off together.

Mrs. Stevens insisted on goin' right along to the address where Ada was goin' because she said Ada was bound to get lost if she wasn't familiar with the neighborhood.

Well, Ada thought it was mighty nice of her to do so much for a stranger. Mrs. Stevens said she was glad to because she didn't know what would of happened to her lots of times if strangers hadn't been nice and helped her out.

She asked Ada where she lived and Ada told her on the South Side and Mrs. Stevens said she was sure we'd like it better on the North Side if we'd leave her pick out a place for us, so Ada told her we had a year's lease that we had just signed and couldn't break it, so then Mrs. Stevens said her husband had studied law and he claimed they wasn't no lease that you couldn't break and some evening she would bring him out to call on us and he'd tell us how to break our lease.

Well, Ada had to say sure, come on out, though we was perfectly satisfied with our apartment and didn't no more want to break the lease than each other's jaw. Maybe not as much. Anyway, the very next night, they showed up, Belle and Tom, and when they'd gone, I give 'em the nickname—Mr. and Mrs. Fix-It.

After the introductions, Stevens made some remarks about what a cozy little place we had and then he asked if I would mind tellin' what rent we paid. So I told him a hundred and a quarter a month. So he said, of course, that was too much and no wonder we wanted to break the lease. Then I said we was satisfied and didn't want to break it and he said I must be kiddin' and if I would show him the lease he would see what loopholes they was in it.

Well, the lease was right there in a drawer in the table, but I told him it was in my safety deposit box at the bank. I ain't got no safety deposit box and no more use for one than Judge Landis has for the deef and dumb alphabet.

Stevens said the lease was probably just a regular lease and if it was, they wouldn't be no trouble gettin' out of it, and meanw'ile him and his wife would see if they couldn't find us a place in the same buildin' with them.

And he was pretty sure they could even if the owner had to give some other tenant the air, because he, the owner, would do anything in the world for Stevens.

So I said yes, but suppose we want to stay where we are. So he said I looked like a man with better judgment than that and if I would just leave everything to him he would fix it so's we could move within a month. I kind of laughed and thought that would be the end of it.

He wanted to see the whole apartment so I showed him around and when we come to the bathroom he noticed my safety razor on the shelf. He said, "So you use one of them things," and I said, "Yes," and he asked me how I liked it, and I said I liked it fine and he said that must be because I hadn't never used a regular razor.

He said a regular razor was the only thing to use if a man wanted to look good. So I asked him if he used a regular razor and he said he did, so I said, "Well, if you look good, I don't want to."

But that didn't stop him and he said if I would meet him downtown the next day he would take me to the place where he bought all his razors and help me pick some out for myself. I told him I was goin' to be tied up, so just to give me the name and address of the place and I would drop in there when I had time.

But, no, that wouldn't do; he'd have to go along with me and introduce me to the proprietor because the proprietor was a great pal of his and would do anything in the world for him, and if the proprietor vouched for the razors, I could be sure I was gettin' the best razors money could buy. I told him again that I was goin' to be tied up and I managed to get him on some other subject.

Meanw'ile, Mrs. Stevens wanted to know where Ada had bought the dress she was wearin' and how much had it cost and Ada told her and Mrs. Stevens said it was a crime. She would meet Ada downtown tomorrow morning and take her to the shop where she bought her clothes and help her choose some dresses that really was dresses.

So Ada told her she didn't have no money to spend on dresses right then, and besides, the shop Mrs. Stevens mentioned was too high priced. But it seems the dame that run the shop was just like a sister to Mrs. Stevens and give her and her friends a big reduction and not only that, but they wasn't no hurry about payin'.

Well, Ada thanked her just the same, but didn't need nothin' new just at present; maybe later on she would take advantage of Mrs. Stevens's kind offer. Yes, but right now they was some models in stock that would be just beautiful on Ada and they might be gone later on. They was nothin' for it but Ada had to make a date with her; she wasn't obliged to buy nothin', but it would be silly not to go and look at the stuff that was in the joint and get acquainted with the dame that run it.

Well, Ada kept the date and bought three dresses she didn't want and they's only one of them she's had the nerve to wear. They cost her a hundred dollars a smash and I'd hate to think what the price would of been if Mrs. Stevens and the owner of the shop wasn't so much like sisters.

I was sure I hadn't made no date with Stevens, but just the same he called me up the next night to ask why I hadn't met him. And a couple of days later I got three new razors in the mail along with a bill and a note from the store sayin' that these was three specially fine razors that had been picked out for me by Thomas J. Stevens.

I don't know yet why I paid for the razors and kept 'em. I ain't used 'em and never intended to. Though I've been tempted a few times to test their edge on Stevens's neck.

That same week, Mrs. Stevens called up and asked us to spend Sunday with them and when we got out there, the owner of the buildin' is there, too. And Stevens has told him that I was goin' to give up my apartment on the South Side and wanted him to show me what he had.

I thought this was a little too strong and I said Stevens must of misunderstood me, that I hadn't no fault to find with the place I was in and wasn't plannin' to move, not for a year anyway. You can bet this didn't make no hit with the guy, who was just there on Stevens's say-so that I was a prospective tenant.

Well, it was only about two months ago that this cute little couple come into our life, but I'll bet we seen 'em twenty times at least. They was always invitin' us to their place or invitin' themselves to our place and Ada is one of these here kind of people that just can't say no. Which may be why I and her is married.

Anyway, it begin to seem like us and the Stevenses was livin' together and all one family, with them at the head of it. I never in my life seen anybody as crazy to run other people's business. Honest to heavens, it's a wonder they let us brush our own teeth!

Ada made the remark one night that she wished the ski jumper who was doin' our cookin' would get married and quit so's she wouldn't have to can her. Mrs. Stevens was there and asked Ada if she should try and get her a new cook, but Ada says no, the poor gal might have trouble findin' another job and she felt sorry for her.

Just the same, the next afternoon a Jap come to the apartment and said he was ready to go to work and Mrs. Stevens had sent him. Ada had to tell him the place was already filled.

Another night, Ada complained that her feet was tired. Belle said her feet used to get tired, too, till a friend of hers recommended a chiropodist and she went to him and he done her so much good that she made a regular appointment with him for once every month and paid him a flat sum and no matter how much runnin' around she done, her dogs hadn't fretted her once since this corn-husker started tendin' to 'em.

She wanted to call up the guy at his home right then and there and make a date for Ada and the only way Ada could stop her was by promisin' to go and see him the next time her feet hurt. After that, whenever the two gals met, Belle's first question was "How is your feet?" and the answer was always "Fine, thanks."

Well, I'm quite a football fan and Ada likes to go, too, when it's a big game and lots of excitement. So we decided we'd see the Illinois-Chicago game and have a look at this "Red" Grange. I warned Ada to not say nothin' about it to Tom and Belle as I felt like we was entitled to a day off.

But it happened that they was goin' to be a game at Evanston that day and the Stevenses invited us to see that one with them. So we used the other game as a alibi. And when Tom asked me later on if I'd boughten my tickets yet, instead of sayin' yes, I told him the truth and said no.

So then he said:

"I'm glad you ain't, because I and Belle has made up our mind that the Chicago game is the one we ought to see. And we'll all go together. And don't you bother about tickets because I can get better ones than you can as Stagg and I is just like that."

So I left it to him to get the tickets and we might as well of set on the Adams Street bridge. I said to Stevens, I said:

"If these is the seats Mr. Stagg digs up for his old pals, I suppose he leads strangers twenty or thirty miles out in the country and blindfolds 'em and ties 'em to a tree."

Now of course it was the bunk about he and Stagg bein' so close. He may of been introduced to him once, but he ain't the kind of a guy that Stagg would go around holdin' hands with. Just the same, most of the people he bragged about knowin', why it turned out that he really did know 'em; yes, and stood ace high with 'em too.

Like, for instance, I got pinched for speedin' one night and they give me a ticket to show up in the Speeders' court and I told Stevens about it and he says, "Just forget it! I'll call up the judge and have it wiped off the book. He's a mighty good fella and a personal friend of mine."

Well, I didn't want to take no chances so I phoned Stevens the day before I was supposed to appear in court, and I asked him if he'd talked to the judge. He said he had and I asked him if he was sure. So he said, "If you don't believe me, call up the judge yourself." And he gave me the judge's number. Sure enough, Stevens had fixed it and when I thanked the judge for his trouble, he said it was a pleasure to do somethin' for a friend of Tom Stevens's.

Now, I know it's silly to not appreciate favors like that and not warm up to people that's always tryin' to help you along, but still a person don't relish bein' treated like they was half-witted and couldn't button their shirt alone. Tom and Belle meant all right, but I and Ada got kind of tired of havin' fault found with everything that belonged to us and everything we done or tried to do.

Besides our apartment bein' no good and our clothes terrible, we learned that my dentist didn't know a bridge from a mustache cup, and the cigarettes I smoked didn't have no taste to them, and the man that bobbed Ada's hair must of been mad at her, and neither of us would ever know what it was to live till we owned a wire-haired fox terrier.

And we found out that the liquor I'd been drinkin' and enjoyin' was a mixture of bath salts and assorted paints, and the car we'd paid seventeen hundred smackers for wasn't nowheres near as much of a car as one that Tom could of got for us for eight hundred on account of knowin' a brother-in-law of a fella that used to go to school with the president of the company's nephew, and that if Ada would take up aesthetic dancin' under a dame Belle knew about, why she'd never have no more trouble with her tonsils.

Nothin' we had or nothin' we talked about gettin' or doin' was worth a damn unless it was recommended or suggested by the Stevenses.

Well, I done a pretty good business this fall and I and Ada had always planned to spend a winter in the South, so one night we figured it out that this was the year we could spare the money and the time and if we didn't go this year we never would. So the next thing was where should we go, and we finally decided on Miami. And we said we wouldn't mention nothin' about it to Tom and Belle till the day we was goin'. We'd pretend we was doin' it out of a clear sky.

But a secret is just as safe with Ada as a police dog tethered with dental floss. It wasn't more than a day or two after we'd had our talk when Tom and Belle sprang the news that they was leavin' for California right after New Year's. And why didn't we go with them.

Well, I didn't say nothin' and Ada said it sounded grand, but it was impossible. Then Stevens said if it was a question of money, to not let that bother us as he would loan it to me and I could pay it back whenever I felt like it. That was more than Ada could stand, so she says we wasn't as poor as people seemed to think and the reason we couldn't go to California was because we was goin' to Miami.

This was such a surprise that it almost struck 'em dumb at first and all Tom could think of to say was that he'd been to Miami himself and it was too crowded and he'd lay off it if he was us. But the next time we seen 'em they had our trip all arranged.

First, Tom asked me what road we was goin' on and I told him the Big Four. So he asked if we had our reservations and I told him yes.

"Well," he said, "we'll get rid of 'em and I'll fix you up on the C. & E. I. The general passenger agent is a friend of mine and they ain't nothin' he won't do for my friends. He'll see that you're treated right and that you get there in good shape."

So I said:

"I don't want to put you to all that trouble, and besides I don't know nobody connected with the Big Four well enough for them to resent me travelin' on their lines, and as for gettin' there in good shape, even if I have a secret enemy or two on the Big Four, I don't believe they'd endanger the lives of the other passengers just to see that I didn't get there in good shape."

But Stevens insisted on takin' my tickets and sellin' 'em back to the Big Four and gettin' me fixed on the C. & E. I. The berths we'd had on the Big Four was Lower 9 and Lower 10. The berths Tom got us on the C. & E. I. was Lower 7 and Lower 8, which he said was better. I suppose he figured that the nearer you are to the middle of the car, the less chance there is of bein' woke up if your car gets in another train's way.

He wanted to know, too, if I'd made any reservations at a hotel. I showed him a wire I had from the Royal Palm in reply to a wire I'd sent 'em.

"Yes," he says, "but you don't want to stop at the Royal Palm. You wire and tell 'em to cancel that and I'll make arrangements for you at the Flamingo, over at the Beach. Charley Krom, the manager there, was born and raised in the same town I was. He'll take great care of you if he knows you're a friend of mine."

So I asked him if all the guests at the Flamingo was friends of his, and he said of course not; what did I mean?

"Well," I said, "I was just thinkin' that if they ain't, Mr. Krom probably makes life pretty miserable for 'em. What does he do, have the phone girl ring 'em up at all hours of the night, and hide their mail, and shut off their hot water, and put cracker crumbs in their beds?"

That didn't mean nothin' to Stevens and he went right ahead and switched me from one hotel to the other.

While Tom was reorganizin' my program and tellin' me what to eat in Florida, and what bait to use for barracuda and carp, and what time to go bathin' and which foot to stick in the water first, why Belle was makin' Ada return all the stuff she had boughten to wear down there and buy other stuff that Belle picked out for her at joints where Belle was so well known that they only soaked her twice as much as a stranger. She had Ada almost crazy, but I told her to never mind; in just a few more days we'd be where they couldn't get at us.

I suppose you're wonderin' why didn't we quarrel with 'em and break loose from 'em and tell 'em to leave us alone. You'd know why if you knew them. Nothin' we could do would convince 'em that we didn't want their advice and help. And nothin' we could say was a insult.

Well, the night before we was due to leave Chi, the phone rang and I answered it. It was Tom.

"I've got a surprise for you," he says. "I and Belle has give up the California idear. We're goin' to Miami instead, and on account of me knowin' the boys down at the C. & E. I., I've landed a drawin' room on the same train you're takin'. How is that for news?"

"Great!" I said, and I went back and broke it to Ada. For a minute I thought she was goin' to faint. And all night long she moaned and groaned and had hysterics.

So that's how we happened to come to Biloxi.

Cora, or Fun at a Spa

AN EXPRESSIONIST DRAMA OF LOVE AND DEATH AND SEX—IN THREE ACTS

CHARACTERS

(In the order in which I admire them)

A FRIEND OF THE PRESIDENT.
PLAGUE BENNETT, *an Embryo Steeplejack.*
ELSA, *their Ward.*
MANAGER OF THE PUMP ROOM.
A MAN WHO LOOKS A GOOD DEAL LIKE HEYWOOD BROUN.
MRS. TYLER.*
CORA.
POULTRY, GAME IN SEASON, ETC.

ACT I

A Pharmacy at a Spa. The Proprietor is at present out of the city and Mrs. Tyler is taking his place. She is a woman who seems to have been obliged to leave school while in the eighth grade. Plague Bennett enters. His mother named him Plague as tribute to her husband, who died of it. As Plague enters, Mrs. Tyler is seen replacing a small vial in a case behind the counter.

PLAGUE: Well, Mrs. T.

MRS. TYLER: "Mrs. T." indeed! I see you're still the same old Plague!

PLAGUE: What are you doing?

MRS. TYLER: What do I look like I was doing, spearing eels? I'm just putting this bottle of germs back in its place. The little fellows were trying to escape. They said they didn't like it here. I said, "Don't bacilli!"

(A Friend of the President enters)

PLAGUE: Hello, Doctor.

(He calls him Doctor)

FRIEND OF THE PRESIDENT: *(As if to himself)* That old devil sea!

PLAGUE: Well, Doctor, I'm going to Washington tomorrow.

(He repeatedly calls him Doctor)

---

* Mrs. Tyler appears only when one of the other characters is out of the city.

396

FRIEND OF THE PRESIDENT: What of it?

PLAGUE: Well, they tell me you and the President are pretty close.

FRIEND OF THE PRESIDENT: *He* is.

(END OF FIRST ACT)

ACT II

A poultry yard at a Spa. The chairs and tables are in disarray as if a blotter salesman had been making his rounds. The Manager of the Pump Room is out of the city and the poultry are being fed by Mrs. Tyler. A Dead Ringer for David Belasco enters, crosses stage.

MRS. TYLER: You old master you! (*Aside*) I can never tell whether he's in first speed or reverse.

(*Dead Ringer for David Belasco exits. Manager of the Pump Room returns to the city unexpectedly and Mrs. Tyler goes into pictures. Manager of the Pump Room stands in center stage as if he had been everywhere*)

MANAGER OF THE PUMP ROOM: (*Aside*) I wonder what is keeping Elsa. (*Looks right*) Ah! There she comes now, dancing as usual!

(*Elsa enters left, fooling him completely. She is not even dancing. She looks as if she had taken a bath*)

ELSA: Well——

MANAGER OF THE PUMP ROOM: (*Turns and sees her*) Elsa! I was just thinking about you. I was wondering what was keeping you.

ELSA: I presume you mean who.

(*The curtain is lowered and raised to see if it will work*)

MANAGER OF THE PUMP ROOM: What's the difference between that curtain and Ziegfeld?

ELSA: It works. And that reminds me that I just met a man who looks something like Heywood Broun. Here he comes now, dancing as usual.

(*A Man Who Looks a Good Deal Like Heywood Broun enters*)

MANAGER OF THE PUMP ROOM: (*Aside*) I'll say so!

MAN WHO LOOKS A GOOD DEAL LIKE HEYWOOD BROUN: What's that?

MANAGER OF THE PUMP ROOM: Why, this young lady was just saying she thought you looked something like Heywood Broun.

MAN WHO ETC.: (*Throwing confetti in all directions*) She's conservative.

(END OF SECOND ACT)

ACT III

A Mixed Grill at a Spa. Two Milch Cows sit at a table in one corner, playing draughts. In another corner is seated a gigantic zebu.

First Milch Cow: Don't you feel a draught?

Second Milch Cow: No. But we'd better be going. That gigantic zebu is trying to make us.

First Milch Cow: He thinks he is a cow catcher.

Second Milch Cow: (*As they rise*) They say there are still a great many buffaloes in Yellowstone Park.

First Milch Cow: So I herd.

(*The Milch Cows go out, followed at a distance by the zebu. Cora enters. She is dressed in the cat's pajamas. She looks as if she had once gone on an excursion to the Delaware Water Gap*)

Cora: (*Aside*) I wonder if it could be!

(*Plague Bennett and A Friend of the President enter in time to overhear her remark*)

Plague: (*To Friend of the President*) Go on without me, Doctor. (*He still calls him Doctor. Friend of the President exits and Plague turns to Cora*) You wonder if it could be who?

Cora: Why, I just met a man who looks a little like Heywood Broun. Here he comes now, dancing as usual.

(*A Man Who Looks a Good Deal Like Heywood Broun enters*)

Plague: (*Aside*) He does, at that!

Man Who Etc.: At what?

Plague: This little lady was just saying she thought you looked a little like Heywood Broun.

Man Who Etc.: A little! She's putting it mildly!

(*Finds he is out of confetti and exits. A poisoned rat dashes into the open air, seeking water*)

Plague: That rat acts like he was poisoned.

Cora: God! You ought to saw me last night!

(END OF THIRD ACT)

Clemo Uti—"The Water Lilies"

CHARACTERS

PADRE, *a Priest.*

SETHSO ⎫
GETHSO ⎬ *Both Twins.*

WAYSHATTEN, *a Shepherd's Boy.*

TWO CAPITALISTS.*

WAMA TAMMISCH, *her daughter.*

KLEMA, *a Janitor's third daughter.*

KEVELA, *their mother, afterwards their aunt.*

[TRANSLATOR'S NOTE: *This show was written as if people were there to see it.*]

ACT I

(*The Outskirts of a Parchesi Board. People are wondering what has become of the discs. They quit wondering and sit up and sing the following song.*)

CHORUS

> What has become of the discs?
> What has become of the discs?
> We took them at our own risks,
> But what has become of the discs?

(*Wama enters from an exclusive waffle parlor. She exits as if she had had waffles.*)

ACTS II and III

(*These two acts were thrown out because nothing seemed to happen.*)

ACT IV

(*A silo. Two rats have got in there by mistake. One of them seems diseased. The other looks at him. They go out. Both rats come in again and wait for a laugh. They don't get it, and go out. Wama enters from*

---

* NOTE: The two Capitalists don't appear in this show.

399

an off-stage barn. She is made up to represent the Homecoming of Casanova. She has a fainting spell. She goes out.)

KEVELA

Where was you born?

PADRE

In Adrian, Michigan.

KEVELA

Yes, but I thought I was confessing to you.
(The Padre goes out on an old-fashioned high-wheel bicycle. He acts as if he had never ridden many of them. He falls off and is brought back. He is in pretty bad shape.)

ACT V

(A Couple of Salesmen enter. They are trying to sell Portable Houses. The rest of the cast don't want Portable Houses.)

REST OF THE CAST

We don't want Portable Houses.
(The Salesmen become hysterical and walk off-stage left.)

KEVELA

What a man!

WAYSHATTEN (*the Shepherd's Boy*)

Why wasn't you out there this morning to help me look after my sheep?

CHORUS OF ASSISTANT SHEPHERDS

Why did you lay there asleep
When you should of looked after his sheep?
Why did you send telegrams
When you should of looked after his lambs?
Why did you sleep there, so old,
When you should of looked after his fold?

SETHSO

Who is our father?

GETHSO

What of it? We're twins, ain't we?

WAMA

Hush, clemo uti (*the Water Lilies*).

(*Two queels enter, overcome with water lilies. They both make fools of themselves. They don't seem to have any self-control. They quiver. They want to play the show over again, but it looks useless.*)

SHADES

I Gaspiri—"The Upholsterers"

A DRAMA IN THREE ACTS

Adapted from the Bukovinan of Casper Redmonda

CHARACTERS

IAN OBRI, *a Blotter Salesman.*
JOHAN WASPER, *his wife.*
GRETA, *their daughter.*
HERBERT SWOPE, *a nonentity.*
FFENA, *their daughter, later their wife.*
EGSO, *a Pencil Guster.*
TONO, *a Typical Wastebasket.*

ACT I

(*A public street in a bathroom. A man named Tupper has evidently just taken a bath. A man named Brindle is now taking a bath. A man*

named Newburn comes out of the faucet which has been left running. He exits through the exhaust. Two strangers to each other meet on the bath mat.)

FIRST STRANGER

Where was you born?

SECOND STRANGER

Out of wedlock.

FIRST STRANGER

That's a mighty pretty country around there.

SECOND STRANGER

Are you married?

FIRST STRANGER

I don't know. There's a woman living with me, but I can't place her.
(*Three outsiders named Klein go across the stage three times. They think they are in a public library. A woman's cough is heard off-stage left.*)

A New Character

Who is that cough?

Two Moors

That is my cousin. She died a little while ago in a haphazard way.

A Greek

And what a woman she was!
(*The curtain is lowered for seven days to denote the lapse of a week.*)

ACT III

(*The Lincoln Highway. Two bearded glue lifters are seated at one side of the road.*)

(Translator's Note: *The principal industry in Phlace is hoarding hay. Peasants sit alongside of a road on which hay wagons are likely to pass. When a hay wagon does pass, the hay hoarders leap from their points of vantage and help themselves to a wisp of hay. On an average a hay hoarder accumulates a ton of hay every four years. This is called Mah Jong.*)

First Glue Lifter

Well, my man, how goes it?

Second Glue Lifter

(*Sings "My Man," to show how it goes.*)
(*Eight realtors cross the stage in a friendly way. They are out of place.*)

Curtain

THOSE RADIO WITS

As if to prove Ring Lardner's burlesque of radio humor, Walter Winchell reports that a woebegone man was explaining his plight to the director of the Good Will hour.

"Mr. Anthony," he ended, "you see my position. My best friend ran away with my wife. They've been gone a month. And, Mr. Anthony, I miss him."

The program *Can You Top This* has specialized in stories of the incredible. One of the stories concerns a Vermont farmer who, plowing a field with his one mare, kept on calling, "Giddap, Babe. Giddap, Lady. Giddap, Sweetheart. Giddap, Queenie."

"But," said a passing stranger, "why has that mare got all those names?"

"Sh!" said the farmer. "Her name's Bess. But when I put blinders on her and yell those other names, she thinks she's got all those horses helping her."

"Abbott!" cried Costello, "Abbott! My feet are frozen and they're sticking out of the covers."

"You fool," answered Abbott, "why don't you pull them in?"

"Oh, no," said Costello, "I ain't putting those cold things in bed with me!"

Listeners on Kate Smith's hour listen to more than Kate Smith's soprano voice. They often hear quips as amusing as this one:

"Is he fickle? Why, he has gone around with more women than the revolving doors at Macy's!"

Or this one:

404

"That's the most terrible picture of me. It makes me look like a monkey!"

"You should have thought of that before you had it taken, dear."

Colonel Stoopnagle was complaining of his wife's extravagances. "She's always asking me for pin money," he concluded.

"Only pin money?" said his straight man. "Why don't you give it to her?"

"Because," said the Colonel, "the pin she wants has twelve diamonds in it."

This pun has been used over so many stations it is beginning to be a little shopworn, but it is still going the rounds:

Comedian: "Do you know who had the smallest radio and sending station ever made?"

His stooge, dutifully: "No. *Who* owned the smallest radio and sending station ever made?"

Comedian, triumphantly: "Paul Revere. He broadcast from one plug."

An experienced burglar wormed his way into the carefully guarded house. Without using his flashlight he felt along the wall, reached the knob, twisted it slowly, and waited to hear the tumblers click. What he heard was: ". . . and if you want to be loved, get rid of those dishpan hands. Here is a simple method: Rinse them three times a day in . . ."

Groucho Marx is as rapid with the comeback over the radio as he is on the stage and screen. His sense of timing is marvelous and is surpassed only by his sense of nonsense. Groucho Marx is the early worm that is always turning—and turning just in time to catch the bird. He has a way of entering a room with a blithe impertinence and leaving it with a light-hearted insult. "I've had a wonderful evening," he remarked to a Hollywood hostess. "But this wasn't it." Another hostess, unaware of Groucho's talent for deflation, exclaimed, "Oh, Mr. Marx, I just love nature!" "That's loyalty," said Groucho, "after what nature did to you." But perhaps his most devastating retort was to an officious celebrity chaser who approached Groucho at a party. "You remember me, of course, Mr. Marx. We met at the Redmans', remember?" "I never forget a face," replied Groucho. "But in your case I'll make an exception."

A good story is not only told to death, but is exhumed, revived and retold with countless variations. The following has been kicked around a lot by radio comedians:

Two Alabama boys met on the sidewalks of New York.

"What are you doing way up here in Yankee territory?" said the first.

"L-l-l-l-looking for a j-j-job," said the second.

"Any luck?"

"Had a c-c-c-c-conference this m-m-m-m-m-morning."

"What sort of work?"

"R-r-r-r-adio."

"Radio? In what capacity?"

"An-n-n-n-nouncer, of c-c-c-c-course."

"Announcer? Did you get the job?"

"W-w-w-w-what chance has a S-s-s-southerner!"

The mock feud between Jack Benny and Fred Allen had reached a new height—or a new low. In his broadcast Allen had made several disparaging remarks about his radio rival who, he claimed, was so stingy he wouldn't give a hoot.

"You wouldn't talk that way about me," retorted Benny, "if I had my gag writers here!"

Stephen Leacock

The most eminent Canadian humorist, Stephen Leacock (1869–1944) was born in Hampshire, England. His parents emigrated to Canada when he was a child; his father, by great diligence, was able to support a farm and, as a natural consequence, Leacock and his brothers became professors, businessmen, and engineers instead of farmers. At twenty-two he turned to teaching, "an experience which left me with a profound sympathy for those compelled to spend their lives in the most dreary, most thankless, and the worst-paid profession in the world." In 1908 he was head of the department of economics at McGill University in Canada, a position he held for twenty-eight years until his retirement.

The author of Elements of Political Science was always at variance with his alter ego, the creator of Literary Lapses. When the nonsense sketches were submitted to the publishers of Leacock's serious textbooks, they thought he had gone mad and rejected the manuscript, and Leacock had to print the pieces on his own account. Before his death he had published more than forty books with titles as grim as The Unsolved Riddle of Social Justice and as irresponsible as Moonbeams from the Larger Lunacy. "Personally," he once confessed, "I would rather have written Alice in Wonderland than the whole Encyclopaedia Britannica."

Gertrude the Governess: or, Simple Seventeen

Synopsis of Previous Chapters:
There are no Previous Chapters.

It was a wild and stormy night on the West Coast of Scotland. This, however, is immaterial to the present story, as the scene is not laid in the West of Scotland. For the matter of that the weather was just as bad on the East Coast of Ireland.

But the scene of this narrative is laid in the South of England and takes place in and around Knotacentinum Towers (pronounced as if written Nosham Taws), the seat of Lord Knotacent (pronounced as if written Nosh).

But it is not necessary to pronounce either of these names in reading them.

Nosham Taws was a typical English home. The main part of the house was an Elizabethan structure of warm red brick, while the elder portion, of which the Earl was inordinately proud, still showed the outlines of a Norman Keep, to which had been added a Lancastrian Jail and a Plantagenet Orphan Asylum. From the house in all directions stretched magnificent woodland and park with oaks and elms of immemorial antiquity, while nearer the house stood raspberry bushes and geranium plants which had been set out by the Crusaders.

About the grand old mansion the air was loud with the chirping of thrushes, the cawing of partridges and the clear sweet note of the rook, while deer, antelope and other quadrupeds strutted about the lawn so tame as to eat off the sun-dial. In fact, the place was a regular menagerie.

From the house downwards through the park stretched a beautiful broad avenue laid out by Henry VII.

Lord Nosh stood upon the hearthrug of the library. Trained diplomat and statesman as he was, his stern aristocratic face was upside down with fury.

"Boy," he said, "you shall marry this girl or I disinherit you. You are no son of mine."

Young Lord Ronald, erect before him, flung back a glance as defiant as his own.

"I defy you," he said. "Henceforth you are no father of mine. I will get another. I will marry none but a woman I can love. This girl that we have never seen—"

"Fool," said the Earl, "would you throw aside our estate and name of a thousand years? The girl, I am told, is beautiful; her aunt is willing; they are French; pah! they understand such things in France."

"But your reason—"

"I give no reason," said the Earl. "Listen, Ronald, I give one month. For that time you remain here. If at the end of it you refuse me, I cut you off with a shilling."

Lord Ronald said nothing; he flung himself from the room, flung himself upon his horse and rode madly off in all directions.

As the door of the library closed upon Ronald the Earl sank into a chair. His face changed. It was no longer that of the haughty nobleman, but of the hunted criminal. "He must marry the girl," he muttered. "Soon she will know all. Tutchemoff has escaped from Siberia. He knows and will tell. The whole of the mines pass to her, this property with it, and I—but enough." He rose, walked to the sideboard, drained a dipper full of gin and bitters, and became again a high-bred English gentleman.

It was at this moment that a high dogcart, driven by a groom in the livery of Earl Nosh, might have been seen entering the avenue of Nosham Taws. Beside him sat a young girl, scarce more than a child, in fact, not nearly so big as the groom.

The apple-pie hat which she wore, surmounted with black willow

plumes, concealed from view a face so face-like in its appearance as to be positively facial.

It was—need we say it—Gertrude the Governess, who was this day to enter upon her duties at Nosham Taws.

At the same time that the dogcart entered the avenue at one end there might have been seen riding down it from the other a tall young man, whose long, aristocratic face proclaimed his birth and who was mounted upon a horse with a face even longer than his own.

And who is this tall young man who draws nearer to Gertrude with every revolution of the horse? Ah, who, indeed? Ah, who, who? I wonder if any of my readers could guess that this was none other than Lord Ronald.

The two were destined to meet. Nearer and nearer they came. And then still nearer. Then for one brief moment they met. As they passed Gertrude raised her head and directed towards the young nobleman two eyes so eye-like in their expression as to be absolutely circular, while Lord Ronald directed towards the occupant of the dogcart a gaze so gazelike that nothing but a gazelle, or a gas-pipe, could have emulated its intensity.

Was this the dawn of love? Wait and see. Do not spoil the story.

Let us speak of Gertrude. Gertrude De Mongmorenci McFiggin had known neither father nor mother. They had both died years before she was born. Of her mother she knew nothing, save that she was French, was extremely beautiful, and that all her ancestors and even her business acquaintances had perished in the Revolution.

Yet Gertrude cherished the memory of her parents. On her breast the girl wore a locket in which was enshrined a miniature of her mother, while down her neck inside at the back hung a daguerreotype of her father. She carried a portrait of her grandmother up her sleeve and had pictures of her cousins tucked inside her boot, while beneath her—but enough, quite enough.

Of her father Gertrude knew even less. That he was a high-born English gentleman who had lived as a wanderer in many lands, this was all she knew. His only legacy to Gertrude had been a Russian grammar, a Roumanian phrase-book, a theodolite, and a work on mining engineering.

From her earliest infancy Gertrude had been brought up by her aunt. Her aunt had carefully instructed her in Christian principles. She had also taught her Mohammedanism to make sure.

When Gertrude was seventeen her aunt had died of hydrophobia.

The circumstances were mysterious. There had called upon her that day a strange bearded man in the costume of the Russians. After he had left, Gertrude had found her aunt in a syncope from which she passed into an apostrophe and never recovered.

To avoid scandal it was called hydrophobia. Gertrude was thus thrown upon the world. What to do? That was the problem that confronted her.

It was while musing one day upon her fate that Gertrude's eye was struck with an advertisement.

"Wanted a governess; must possess a knowledge of French, Italian, Russian, and Roumanian, Music, and Mining Engineering. Salary £1, 4 shillings and 4 pence halfpenny per annum. Apply between half-past eleven and twenty-five minutes to twelve at No. 41 A Decimal Six, Belgravia Terrace. The Countess of Nosh."

Gertrude was a girl of great natural quickness of apprehension, and she had not pondered over this announcement more than half an hour before she was struck with the extraordinary coincidence between the list of items desired and the things that she herself knew.

She duly presented herself at Belgravia Terrace before the Countess, who advanced to meet her with a charm which at once placed the girl at her ease.

"You are proficient in French?" she asked.

"*Oh, oui,*" said Gertrude modestly.

"And Italian?" continued the Countess.

"*Oh, si,*" said Gertrude.

"And German?" said the Countess in delight.

"*Ah, ja,*" said Gertrude.

"And Russian?"

"*Yaw.*"

"And Roumanian?"

"*Jep.*"

Amazed at the girl's extraordinary proficiency in modern languages, the Countess looked at her narrowly. Where had she seen those lineaments before? She passed her hand over her brow in thought, and spit upon the floor, but no, the face baffled her.

"Enough," she said. "I engage you on the spot; tomorrow you go down to Nosham Taws and begin teaching the children. I must add that in addition you will be expected to aid the Earl with his Russian Correspondence. He has large mining interests at Tschminsk."

Tschminsk! why did the simple word reverberate upon Gertrude's ears? Why? Because it was the name written in her father's hand on the title page of his book on mining. What mystery was here?

It was on the following day that Gertrude had driven up the avenue.

She descended from the dogcart, passed through a phalanx of liveried servants drawn up seven-deep, to each of whom she gave a sovereign as she passed and entered Nosham Taws.

"Welcome," said the Countess, as she aided Gertrude to carry her trunk upstairs.

The girl presently descended and was ushered into the library, where she was presented to the Earl. As soon as the Earl's eye fell upon the face of the new governess he started visibly. Where had he seen those lineaments? Where was it? At the races, or the theatre—on a bus—no. Some subtler thread of memory was stirring in his mind. He strode hastily to the sideboard, drained a dipper and a half of brandy, and became again the perfect English gentleman.

While Gertrude has gone to the nursery to make the acquaintance of the two tiny golden-haired children who are to be her charges, let us say something here of the Earl and his son.

Lord Nosh was the perfect type of the English nobleman and states-man. The years that he had spent in the diplomatic service at Constanti-nople, St. Petersburg, and Salt Lake City had given to him a peculiar finesse and noblesse, while his long residence at St. Helena, Pitcairn Island, and Hamilton, Ontario, had rendered him impervious to ex-ternal impressions. As deputy-paymaster of the militia of the county he had seen something of the sterner side of military life, while his hereditary office of Groom of the Sunday Breeches had brought him into direct contact with Royalty itself.

His passion for outdoor sports endeared him to his tenants. A keen sportsman, he excelled in fox-hunting, dog-hunting, pig-killing, bat-catching and the pastimes of his class.

In this latter respect Lord Ronald took after his father. From the start the lad had shown the greatest promise. At Eton he had made a splendid showing at battledore and shuttlecock, and at Cambridge had been first in his class at needlework. Already his name was whispered in connection with the All England ping-pong championship, a triumph which would undoubtedly carry with it a seat in Parliament.

Thus was Gertrude the Governess installed at Nosham Taws.

The days and the weeks sped past.

The simple charm of the beautiful orphan girl attracted all hearts. Her two little pupils became her slaves. "Me loves oo," the little Rasehellfrida would say, leaning her golden head in Gertrude's lap. Even the servants loved her. The head gardener would bring a bouquet of beautiful roses to her room before she was up, the second gardener a bunch of early cauliflowers, the third a spray of late asparagus, and even the tenth and eleventh a sprig of mangel-wurzel or an armful of hay. Her room was full of gardeners all the time, while at evening the aged butler, touched at the friendless girl's loneliness, would tap softly at her door to bring her a rye whisky and seltzer or a box of Pittsburg Stogies. Even the dumb creatures seemed to admire her in their own dumb way. The dumb rooks settled on her shoulder and every dumb dog around the place followed her.

And Ronald! ah, Ronald! Yes, indeed! They had met. They had spoken.

"What a dull morning," Gertrude had said. "*Quel triste matin! Was für ein allerverdamnter Tag!*"

"Beastly," Ronald had answered.

"Beastly!!" The word rang in Gertrude's ears all day.

After that they were constantly together. They played tennis and ping-pong in the day, and in the evening, in accordance with the stiff routine of the place, they sat down with the Earl and Countess to twenty-five-cent poker, and later still they sat together on the verandah and watched the moon sweeping in great circles around the horizon.

It was not long before Gertrude realised that Lord Ronald felt towards her a warmer feeling than that of mere ping-pong. At times in her presence he would fall, especially after dinner, into a fit of profound subtraction.

Once at night, when Gertrude withdrew to her chamber and before seeking her pillow, prepared to retire as a preliminary to disrobing—in other words, before going to bed, she flung wide the casement (opened the window) and perceived (saw) the face of Lord Ronald. He was sitting on a thorn bush beneath her, and his upturned face wore an expression of agonised pallor.

Meantime the days passed. Life at the Taws moved in the ordinary routine of a great English household. At 7 a gong sounded for rising, at 8 a horn blew for breakfast, at 8.30 a whistle sounded for prayers, at 1 a flag was run up at half-mast for lunch, at 4 a gun was fired for afternoon tea, at 9 a first bell sounded for dressing, at 9.15 a second bell for going on dressing, while at 9.30 a rocket was sent up to indicate that dinner was ready. At midnight dinner was over, and at 1 a.m. the tolling of a bell summoned the domestics to evening prayers.

Meanwhile the month allotted by the Earl to Lord Ronald was passing away. It was already July 15, then within a day or two it was July 17, and, almost immediately afterwards, July 18.

At times the Earl, in passing Ronald in the hall, would say sternly, "Remember, boy, your consent, or I disinherit you."

And what were the Earl's thoughts of Gertrude? Here was the one drop of bitterness in the girl's cup of happiness. For some reason that she could not divine the Earl showed signs of marked antipathy.

Once as she passed the door of the library he threw a bootjack at her. On another occasion at lunch alone with her he struck her savagely across the face with a sausage.

It was her duty to translate to the Earl his Russian correspondence. She sought in it in vain for the mystery. One day a Russian telegram was handed to the Earl. Gertrude translated it to him aloud.

"Tutchemoff went to the woman. She is dead."

On hearing this the Earl became livid with fury, in fact this was the day that he struck her with the sausage.

Then one day while the Earl was absent on a bat hunt, Gertrude, who was turning over his correspondence, with that sweet feminine instinct of interest that rose superior to ill-treatment, suddenly found the key to the mystery.

Lord Nosh was not the rightful owner of the Taws. His distant cousin of the older line, the true heir, had died in a Russian prison to which the machinations of the Earl, while Ambassador at Tschminsk, had consigned him. The daughter of this cousin was the true owner of Nosham Taws.

The family story, save only that the documents before her withheld the name of the rightful heir, lay bare to Gertrude's eye.

Strange is the heart of woman. Did Gertrude turn from the Earl with spurning? No. Her own sad fate had taught her sympathy.

Yet still the mystery remained! Why did the Earl start perceptibly each time that he looked into her face? Sometimes he started as much as four centimetres, so that one could distinctly see him do it. On such occasions he would hastily drain a dipper of rum and vichy water and become again the correct English gentleman.

The denouement came swiftly. Gertrude never forgot it.

It was the night of the great ball at Nosham Taws. The whole neighbourhood was invited. How Gertrude's heart had beat with anticipation, and with what trepidation she had overhauled her scant wardrobe in order to appear not unworthy in Lord Ronald's eyes. Her resources were poor indeed, yet the inborn genius for dress that she inherited from her French mother stood her in good stead. She twined a single rose in her hair and contrived herself a dress out of a few old newspapers and the inside of an umbrella that would have graced a court. Round her waist she bound a single braid of bag-string, while a piece of old lace that had been her mother's was suspended to her ear by a thread.

Gertrude was the cynosure of all eyes. Floating to the strains of the music she presented a picture of bright girlish innocence that no one could see undisenraptured.

The ball was at its height. It was away up!

Ronald stood with Gertrude in the shrubbery. They looked into one another's eyes.

"Gertrude," he said, "I love you."

Simple words, and yet they thrilled every fibre in the girl's costume.

"Ronald!" she said, and cast herself about his neck.

At this moment the Earl appeared standing beside them in the moonlight. His stern face was distorted with indignation.

"So!" he said, turning to Ronald, "it appears that you have chosen!"

"I have," said Ronald with hauteur.

"You prefer to marry this penniless girl rather than the heiress I have selected for you?"

Gertrude looked from father to son in amazement.

"Yes," said Ronald.

"Be it so," said the Earl, draining a dipper of gin which he carried, and resuming his calm. "Then I disinherit you. Leave this place, and never return to it."

"Come, Gertrude," said Ronald tenderly, "let us flee together."

Gertrude stood before them. The rose had fallen from her head. The lace had fallen from her ear and the bag-string had come undone from her waist. Her newspapers were crumpled beyond recognition. But dishevelled and illegible as she was, she was still mistress of herself.

"Never," she said firmly. "Ronald, you shall never make this sacrifice for me." Then to the Earl, in tones of ice, "There is a pride, sir, as great even as yours. The daughter of Metschnikoff McFiggin need crave a boon from no one."

With that she hauled from her bosom the daguerreotype of her father and pressed it to her lips.

The Earl started as if shot. "That name!" he cried, "that face! that photograph! stop!"

There! There is no need to finish; my readers have long since divined it. Gertrude was the heiress.

The lovers fell into one another's arms. The Earl's proud face relaxed. "God bless you," he said. The Countess and the guests came pouring out upon the lawn. The breaking day illuminated a scene of gay congratulations.

Gertrude and Ronald were wed. Their happiness was complete. Need we say more? Yes, only this. The Earl was killed in the hunting-field a few days later. The Countess was struck by lightning. The two children fell down a well. Thus the happiness of Gertrude and Ronald was complete.

My Financial Career

When I go into a bank, I get rattled. The clerks rattle me; the wickets rattle me; the sight of the money rattles me; everything rattles me.

The moment I cross the threshold of a bank and attempt to transact business there, I become an irresponsible idiot.

I knew this beforehand, but my salary had been raised to fifty dollars a month and I felt that the bank was the only place for it.

So I shambled in and looked timidly round at the clerks. I had an idea that a person about to open an account must needs consult the manager.

I went up to a wicket marked 'Accountant.' The accountant was a tall, cool devil. The very sight of him rattled me. My voice was sepulchral.

"Can I see the manager?" I said, and added solemnly, "alone." I don't know why I said "alone."

"Certainly," said the accountant, and fetched him.

The manager was a grave, calm man. I held my fifty-six dollars clutched in a crumpled ball in my pocket.

"Are you the manager?" I said. God knows I didn't doubt it.

"Yes," he said.

"Can I see you," I asked, "alone?" I didn't want to say "alone" again, but without it the thing seemed self-evident.

The manager looked at me in some alarm. He felt that I had an awful secret to reveal.

"Come in here," he said, and led the way to a private room. He turned the key in the lock.

"We are safe from interruption here," he said; "sit down."

We both sat down and looked at each other. I found no voice to speak.

"You are one of Pinkerton's men, I presume," he said.

He had gathered from my mysterious manner that I was a detective. I knew what he was thinking, and it made me worse.

"No, not from Pinkerton's," I said, seeming to imply that I came from a rival agency.

"To tell the truth," I went on, as if I had been prompted to lie about it, "I am not a detective at all. I have come to open an account. I intend to keep all my money in this bank."

The manager looked relieved, but still serious; he concluded now that I was a son of Baron Rothschild or a young Gould.

"A large account, I suppose," he said.

"Fairly large," I whispered. "I propose to deposit fifty-six dollars now and fifty dollars a month regularly."

The manager got up and opened the door. He called to the accountant.

"Mr. Montgomery," he said unkindly loud, "this gentleman is opening an account, he will deposit fifty-six dollars. Good morning."

I rose.

A big iron door stood open at the side of the room.

"Good morning," I said, and stepped into the safe.

"Come out," said the manager coldly, and showed me the other way.

I went up to the accountant's wicket and poked the ball of money at him with a quick convulsive movement as if I were doing a conjuring trick.

My face was ghastly pale.

"Here," I said, "deposit it." The tone of the words seemed to mean, "Let us do this painful thing while the fit is on us."

He took the money and gave it to another clerk.

He made me write the sum on a slip and sign my name in a book. I no longer knew what I was doing. The bank swam before my eyes.

"Is it deposited?" I asked in a hollow, vibrating voice.

"It is," said the accountant.

"Then I want to draw a check."

My idea was to draw out six dollars of it for present use. Someone gave me a check-book through a wicket and someone else began telling me how to write it out. The people in the bank had the impression that I was an invalid millionaire. I wrote something on the check and thrust it in at the clerk. He looked at it.

"What! are you drawing it all out again?" he asked in surprise. Then I realized that I had written fifty-six instead of six. I was too far gone to reason now. I had a feeling that it was impossible to explain the thing. All the clerks had stopped writing to look at me.

Reckless with misery, I made a plunge.

"Yes, the whole thing."

"You withdraw your money from the bank?"

"Every cent of it."

"Are you not going to deposit any more?" said the clerk, astonished.

"Never."

An idiot hope struck me that they might think something had insulted me while I was writing the check and that I had changed my mind. I made a wretched attempt to look like a man with a fearfully quick temper.

The clerk prepared to pay the money.

"How will you have it?" he said.

"What?"

"How will you have it?"

"Oh"—I caught his meaning and answered without even trying to think—"in fifties."

He gave me a fifty-dollar bill.

"And the six?" he asked dryly.

"In sixes," I said.

He gave it me and I rushed out.

As the big door swung behind me, I caught the echo of a roar of laughter that went up to the ceiling of the bank. Since then I bank no more. I keep my money in cash in my trousers pocket and my savings in silver dollars in a sock.

Edward Lear

Until he was in his mid-thirties Edward Lear (1812–1888) did everything he could to avoid being a humorist. He seriously devoted himself to natural history and art. He became a painter whose bird studies were favorably compared to Audubon's, a draftsman whose accuracy was such that experts could recognize the geology of a country from Lear's sketches. He was Queen Victoria's drawing master, and when he died he left innumerable canvases and water colors; one of his friends inherited some ten thousand designs. Lear also left an "incidental" collection of the most original nonsense ever imagined. His oils and pictorial notebooks are neglected, but "The Owl and the Pussy-Cat," "The Ahkond of Swat," and the whimsical limericks are firmly rooted in the world's affection. There is no limit to the enjoyment of Lear; ageless, he is eternal childhood's madcap laureate.

The Owl and the Pussy-Cat

The Owl and the Pussy-Cat went to sea
   In a beautiful pea-green boat:
They took some honey, and plenty of money
   Wrapped up in a five-pound note.
The Owl looked up to the stars above,
   And sang to a small guitar,
"Oh, lovely Pussy, oh, Pussy, my love,
   What a beautiful Pussy you are,
      You are,
      You are!
   What a beautiful Pussy you are!"

Pussy said to the Owl, "You elegant fowl,
   How charmingly sweet you sing!
Oh, let us be married; too long we have tarried:
   But what shall we do for a ring?"
They sailed away for a year and a day,
   To the land where the bong-tree grows;
And there in the wood a Piggy-wig stood,
   With a ring at the end of his nose,
      His nose,
      His nose,
   With a ring at the end of his nose.

"Dear Pig, are you willing to sell for one shilling
   Your ring?" Said the Piggy, "I will."
So they took it away and were married next day
   By the Turkey who lives on the hill.
They dined upon mince and slices of quince,
   Which they ate with a runcible spoon;
And hand in hand, on the edge of the sand,
   They danced by the light of the moon,
      The moon,
      The moon,
   They danced by the light of the moon.

The Ahkond of Swat

Who, or why, or which, or *what*
                    Is the Ahkond of Swat?
Is he tall or short, or dark or fair?
Does he sit on a stool or sofa or chair,
                    or Squat,
          The Ahkond of Swat?

Is he wise or foolish, young or old?
Does he drink his soup and his coffee cold
                    or Hot,
          The Ahkond of Swat?

Does he wear a turban, a fez, or a hat?
Does he sleep on a mattress, a bed or a mat,
                    or a Cot,
          The Ahkond of Swat?

Does he like to lie on his back in a boat
Like the lady who lived in that isle remote,
                    Shalott,
          The Ahkond of Swat?

Does he beat his wife with a gold-topped pipe,
When she lets the gooseberries grow too ripe,
                    or Rot,
          The Ahkond of Swat?

Does he like new cream, and hate mince-pies?
When he looks at the sun does he wink his eyes,
                    or Not,
          The Ahkond of Swat?

Someone, or nobody knows I wot
Who or which or why or what
                    Is the Ahkond of Swat?

Incidents in the Life of
My Uncle Arly

Oh! my aged Uncle Arly,
Sitting on a heap of barley
   Through the silent hours of night,
Close beside a leafy thicket;
On his nose there was a cricket,
In his hat a Railway Ticket,
   (But his shoes were far too tight).

Long ago, in youth, he squander'd
All his goods away, and wander'd
   To the Timskoop Hills afar.
There on golden sunsets glazing,
Every evening found him gazing,
Singing, "Orb! you're quite amazing!
   How I wonder what you are!"

Like the ancient Medes and Persians,
Always by his own exertions
   He subsisted on those hills;
Whiles, by teaching children spelling,
Or at times by merely yelling,
Or at intervals by selling
   "Propter's Nicodemus Pills."

Later, in his morning rambles,
He perceived the moving brambles
   Something square and white disclose:—
'Twas a First-class Railway Ticket;
But on stooping down to pick it
Off the ground, a pea-green cricket
   Settled on my uncle's nose.

Never, nevermore, oh! never
Did that cricket leave him ever,—
   Dawn or evening, day or night;
Clinging as a constant treasure,

Chirping with a cheerious measure,
Wholly to my uncle's pleasure,
  (Though his shoes were far too tight).

So for three and forty winters,
Till his shoes were worn to splinters,
  On he walked, till he was white,—
Sometimes silent, sometimes yelling;
Till he came to Borley-Melling,
Near his old ancestral dwelling,
  (But his shoes were far too tight).

On a little heap of barley
Died my aged Uncle Arly,
  And they buried him one night
Close beside the leafy thicket;
There, his hat and Railway Ticket;
There, his ever faithful cricket;
  (But his shoes were far too tight).

Lear's Limericks

There was an Old Man with a beard,
Who said, "It is just as I feared!
  Two Owls and a Hen,
  Four Larks and a Wren,
Have all built their nests in my beard."

There was a Young Person whose chin
Resembled the point of a pin;
  So she had it made sharp
  And purchased a harp,
And played several tunes with her chin.

There was an Old Man of Cape Horn,
Who wished he had never been born;
  So he sat on a chair
  Till he died of despair,
That dolorous Man of Cape Horn.

There was an Old Man who said, "Hush!
I perceive a young bird in this bush!"
  When they said, "Is it small?"
  He replied,"Not at all.
It is four times as big as the bush!"

There was an Old Man who supposed
That the street door was partially closed.
  But some very large rats
  Ate his coats and his hats
While that futile Old Gentleman dozed.

There was an Old Lady whose folly
Induced her to sit in a holly;
    Whereon, by a thorn
    Her dress being torn,
She quickly became melancholy.

There was an Old Man in a tree,
Who was horribly bored by a Bee.
    When they said, "Does it buzz?"
    He replied, "Yes, it does!
It's a regular brute of a Bee."

More Limericks

Scholars have had a hard time locating the author of the first limerick.
A few stubborn researchers have picked the Irish town of Limerick as
the place of origin, but the evidence is flimsy and founded on no ascer-
tainable fact. Edward Lear was the first to use the five-line form con-
sistently, but limericks existed long before Lear (see page 424) made
them popular. They also persisted long after Lear—some of the latest
and nimblest being by Morris Bishop on pages 58–60.

It is lamentable truth that the best limericks are the unprintable
ones. But everyone, seemingly, has tried his hand and cudgeled his
brain to produce new variations on these tricky rhymes without reason.
Six of the most famous printable limericks are (in the order printed)
by Robert Louis Stevenson, Cosmo Monkhouse, Rudyard Kipling,
Gelett Burgess, Carolyn Wells, and Dixon Merritt, once president of
the American Association of Humorists.

There was an old man of the Cape,
Who made himself garments of crêpe.
    When asked, "Do they tear?"
    He replied, "Here and there,
But they're perfectly splendid for shape."

There was a young lady of Niger,
Who smiled as she rode on a tiger.
   They returned from the ride
   With the lady inside,
And the smile on the face of the tiger.

There was a small boy in Quebec
Stood buried in snow to his neck.
   When asked, "Are you friz?"
   He said, "Yes, I is;
But we don't call this cold in Quebec!"

I'd rather have fingers than toes;
I'd rather have ears than a nose;
   And as for my hair,
   I'm glad it's all there.
I'll be awfully sad when it goes.

A tutor who tooted the flute
Tried to tutor two tooters to toot.
   Said the two to the tutor,
   "Is it harder to toot or
To tutor two tooters to toot?"

A rare old bird is the pelican;
His beak holds more than his belican.
   He can take in his beak
   Enough food for a week,
Though I'm darned if I see how the helican.

Carolyn Wells was a champion of the limerick whose point depended
upon absurdities of repetition, pronunciation or spelling. The first of
the following is hers; the others are worthy imitations.

There was a young fellow named Tait,
Who dined with his girl at 8 :08.
  But I'd hate to relate
  What that fellow named Tait
And his tête-à-tête ate at 8 :08.

A girl who weighs many an oz.,
Used language I will not pronoz.;
  Her brother one day
  Pulled her chair right away.
He wanted to see if she'd boz.

She frowned and called him Mr.
Because in sport he kr.
  And so in spite
  That very night
This Mr. kr. sr.

When you think of the hosts without No.
Who are slain by the deadly cuco.
  It's quite a mistake
  Of such food to partake;
It results in a permanent slo.

The bottle of perfume that Willie sent
Was highly displeasing to Millicent.
  Her thanks were so cold
  That they quarreled, I'm told,
Through that silly scent Willie sent Millicent.

Every reader has his own favorites, grotesque and giddy, delirious or indelicate, for public recital or private approval. Here are a mixed lot of
limericks, familiar as well as (the editor hopes) unfamiliar.

There once was a pious young priest
Who lived almost wholly on yeast;
  "For," said he, "it is plain
  We must all rise again.
And I want to get started at least."

The poor benighted Hindoo,
He does the best he kindo;
  He sticks to caste
  From first to last;
For pants he makes his skindo.

A diner while dining at Crewe
Found quite a large mouse in his stew.
  Said the waiter, "Don't shout
  And wave it about,
Or the rest will be wanting one, too."

There was a young man of Montrose,
Who had pockets in none of his clothes.
  When asked by his lass
  Where he carried his brass,
He said, "Darling, I pay through the nose."

There was a young lady of Twickenham,
Whose boots were too tight to walk quickenham.
  She bore them awhile,
  But at last, at a stile,
She pulled them both off and was sickenham.

There was an old man of Blackheath,
Who sat on his set of false teeth.
  Said he with a start,
  "O Lord, bless my heart!
I've bitten myself underneath!"

There once was an old man of Lyme.
Who married three wives at a time:
    When asked, "Why a third?"
    He replied, "One's absurd!
And bigamy, sir, is a crime."

There was an old man of Nantucket
Who kept all his cash in a bucket;
    But his daughter, named Nan,
    Ran away with a man—
And as for the bucket, Nantucket.

There was a young lady of Lynn,
    Who was so excessively thin,
    That when she assayed
    To drink lemonade
She slipped through the straw and fell in.

There was a young man from Ostend,
Who vowed he'd hold out to the end;
    But when half way over
    From Calais to Dover,
He did what he didn't intend.

There once was a maiden of Siam
Who said to her lover, young Kiam,
    "If you kiss me, of course,
    You will have to use force,
But God knows you are stronger than I am."

There was a young lady named Banker
Who slept while the ship lay at anchor.
    She woke in dismay
    When she heard the mate say,
"Now hoist up the topsheet and spanker."

A maiden at college, Miss Breeze,
Had B.A.'s and M.A.'s and Lit. D.'s.
　　Said her doctor, "It's plain
　　You'll collapse from the strain,
For you're killing yourself by degrees."

There was a young lady from Guam
Who observed, "The Pacific's so calm
　　That there can't be a shark.
　　I'll just swim for a lark."

Let us now sing the Twenty-third Psalm.

In conclusion, there is W. S. Gilbert's unrhymed burlesque of the limerick, a wholly Gilbertian conception.

There was an old man of St. Bees,
Who was stung in the arm by a wasp.
　　When asked, "Does it hurt?"
　　He replied, "No, it doesn't—
I'm so glad that it wasn't a hornet."

Newman Levy

Newman Levy, born in New York in 1888, contributed to F. P. A.'s column while in college, and won a watch for a collaboration in 1912. Nine years later he won another watch, this time unassisted. Plentifully supplied with watches, Levy discovered it was later than he thought; he also discovered that he could get paid for writing. From then on he pursued the double careers of attorney and versifier; he wrote with equal zest and distinction for The American Journal of Criminal Law and Criminology and for The Saturday Evening Post.

A quietly prolific author, Levy wrote many brilliant sketches for The Garrick Gaieties and other reviews, a surprisingly unsuccessful play with Edna Ferber entitled $1200 a Year, and Opera Guyed and Theater Guyed, two remarkably adroit volumes of light verse in which the madcap rhymes make their own reasons.

Rain

On the isle of Pago Pago, land of palm trees, rice and sago,
Where the Chinaman and Dago dwell with natives dusky hued,
Lived a dissolute and shady, bold adventuress named Sadie,
Sadie Thompson was the lady, and the life she lived was lewd.

She had practiced her profession in our insular possession,
Which, to make a frank confession, people call the Philippines.
There she'd made a tidy profit till the clergy, hearing of it,
Made her life as hot as Tophet, driving her to other scenes.

So this impudent virago hied herself to Pago Pago
Where the Chinaman and Dago to her cottage often came.
Trade was lucrative and merry, till one day the local ferry
Brought a noble missionary, Rev'rend Davidson by name.

Stern, austere and apostolic, life was no amusing frolic.
Braving fevers, cold and colic, he had come with prayers and hymns,
Most intolerant of wowsers, to those primitive carousers
Bearing chaste and moral trousers to encase their nether limbs.

In her quaint exotic bower, mid a never-ending shower,
Sadie Thompson, by the hour, entertained the local trade.
Every night brought more and more men, soldiers, natives, clerks and
   store-men,
Sailors, gallant man-of-war men, while her gay victrola played.

"Ha!" exclaimed the irate pastor, "straight you're headed for disaster
I'll convince you who's the master, shameless woman of the street!"
"Listen, Rev.," said Sadie tartly (pardon me for punning smartly),
"Though I get your meaning—partly—still, alas, a girl must eat."

"Girl," he cried in indignation, "choose at once between salvation
And immediate deportation from this charming tropic glade.
Like a devastating plague, O Scarlet Dame of Pago Pago
You're as welcome as lumbago, plying here your brazen trade."

Sadie said, "Though I'm no scoffer, that's a lousy choice you proffer,
Still I must accept your offer though my pride has been attacked.
432

Come on, Rev., and let us kill a flask or two of sa'sparilla
Here in my delightful villa while I watch you do your act."

Let us veil the tragic sequel, for a pious man but weak will
Find, alas, that he's unequal to a lady's potent charms.
So his long suppressed libido, sharp as steel of famed Toledo,
Spurning prayers and hymns and credo, found surcease in Sadie's arms.

There beside the waters tidal, urged by impulse suicidal
Lay, next day, the shattered idol, cleansed at last of sin and taint.
Here's the moral: Though a preacher fail to make a fallen creature
Pure and saintly as her teacher, she, perhaps, can make a saint.

The Belle of the Balkans

A BROADWAY OPERETTA

The scene: a public square in Ruritania,
Fair Ruritania, land of gay Romance,
Where the natives have a strange and curious mania
For gathering in public squares to dance.

Amid a scene of unrestricted gaiety,
They drink from cups of *papier-maché*.
The military mingle with the laity,
And sing an opening song that goes this way:

> *"Clink, clink, we merrily drink,*
> *Though the weather be sunny or rainier;*
> *Then we sing and we laugh as our vintage we quaff*
> *From the vines of our fair Ruritania."*

Among the local bourgeoisie and peasantry
There dwelt a maid who tended at the bar
Of all the girls, for beauty, charm and pleasantry,
Dolores was the loveliest by far.

She quite surpassed the other maidens vocally.
Her skill and grace at dancing took the prize;
But, strangely, it was not suspected locally
Dolores was their princess in disguise.

And now upon the scene in Ruritania
Arrives a gay adventurer named Cohn
A dashing lad from Scranton, Pennsylvania,
Who greets the maid in dulcet tenor tone:

> *"Dolores, my dearest, I love you,*
> *You are the ideal of my dreams.*
> *I never knew there was someone like you,*
> *You're fairer than princess or queen.*
> *Springtime you know, dear, is ring time,*

So let us get married in June.
Then we'll stroll down life's pathway together,
*   My darling,*
Beneath the Balkan moon."

And now, mid cheers the king appears,
A comic chap and rowdy,
A royal clown with tilted crown
Who greets the crowd with "Howdy!"

*   "Howdy, folks! I've got some jokes.*
*   What d'ye think of this?*
*   My Jester has written a brand new song*
*   Called 'Jester Little Kiss.'*
*   Come bring a drink for your noble kink.*
*   Don't think that I'm complaining,*
*   But it's strange that I am always dry,*
*   Although I'm always reigning.*

"I am searching with this large imposing retinue
For my daughter who is hiding here, I learn.
Which is nothing to the hiding, I am bettin' you
That she'll get from her old dad on her return.

"She is working in this picturesque locality
As a bar maid in a neighboring café,
An employment of debatable legality,
And unsuited to a princess, I must say.

"So my troops will search this section and vicinity—"
When, behold from out the crowd the maid appears
Quite disguised in simulated masculinity
In the costume of The Royal Grenadiers.

*   "With a rum tum tum of the fife and drum,*
*   While the banners gaily fly.*
*   For a soldier's life is a soldier's life,*
*   Which nobody can deny."*

There, beside her, stands the gallant Pennsylvanian,
As the natives gaily quench again their thirst,

Then they all join in an anthem Ruritanian
As the curtain quickly falls on Act the First.

Act Two. A scene of glittering aristocracy:
The Palace, filled with nobles gathered there,
Who remarkably resemble the democracy
Who were gathered in Act One about the square.

There they merrily imbibe the royal potables;
Mr. Cohn is seen commingling with the throng.
Then the king arrives and entertains the notables
With a tap dance and the chorus of a song.

> *"Dinah, no gal is finer,*
> *Say that you love me true,*
> *Boop-oopa-doop.*
> *Way down in Carolina, Dinah,*
> *We'll have a love nest*
> *Just built for two."*

Now once again the plot unreels,
(With time out for performing seals)
Upon the scene with royal mien
The princess enters stately.
She sings a song and does a dance,
While Cohn, amazed, looks on askance.
"Last week I saw her wearing pants,
This mystifies me greatly.
My dear," he cries with anguished moan,
"Oh say that you remember Cohn!
Can't you recall my face at all?
Please tell me that you know me!"
The princess says, "I quite regret
That you and I have never met."
And then they sing a love duet
Entitled "In Dahomey."

Now a telegram arrives in Ruritania
Which anounces that the gallant Mr. Cohn
Has been chosen Mayor of Scranton, Pennsylvania,
By the largest vote the city's ever known.

Then the king says, "Since, in your benighted domicile
That position corresponds to duke or earl,
If to love my child and cherish her you'll promise, I'll
Be proud to let you wed my charming girl."

Then the curtain falls upon an outburst lyrical,
As the critics rush to write their morning rave,
As they pen the words, "Delightfully satirical"
Mr. Gilbert does a handspring in his grave.

Howard Maier

Howard Maier, a born and bred New Yorker, has
been alternately—and often simultaneously—a
painter, an etcher, a gambler, a soldier in the U. S.
Army Air Forces, a member of the Office of War
Information, and an author. He wrote grimly for
The New Yorker, glibly for Colliers, patriotically
for Yank, and popularly for The Reader's Digest.
A novel, Undertow, managed to be both horrifying
and deeply moving. . . . In his idiom as a writer
for radio, Maier is both persuasive and inexplica-
ble. Summoned to explain himself, he submitted
the following improbable transcript of a day in
court.

The Editor Is Cross-Examined
by the Author

BAILIFF: Hear ye, hear ye . . . etc. . . .

CLERK: Do you solemnly swear . . . etc. . . .

MAIER: I do.

CLERK: Take the stand.

UNTERMEYER: (*Smugly . . . Leading witness*) Now, Mr. Maier, you say you were born in New York in 1905, and as a young boy, you always wanted to be a writer . . . yes?

MAIER: No . . . I always wanted to be—well, a policeman.

UNTERMEYER: A policeman? (*Decides to humor him*) Of course, of course, small boys want to be firemen, locomotive engineers . . . but why did you want to be a policeman?

MAIER: (*Weakly*) Well . . . I thought it would be sort of nice to be a policeman and be able to lock up my father and my mother, sisters and brothers, grandparents and aunts . . . you know, sort of lock them all up in jail.

UNTERMEYER: Yes, yes, of course . . . (*Little laugh for jury*) But of course that was only as a little boy?

MAIER: No.

UNTERMEYER: No what?

MAIER: Not only as a little boy . . . for a long, long while.

UNTERMEYER: We understand all that, Mr. Maier . . . but somewhere along the line you must have given up this idea?

MAIER: What idea?

UNTERMEYER: (*Impatiently*) This idea of becoming a policeman.

MAIER: Well, yes . . . I suppose you can put it that way if you want to.

UNTERMEYER: (*Triumphantly*) And you became a writer?

MAIER: Yes, I guess so . . . (*Then quickly*) . . . But I never gave up the other idea.

UNTERMEYER: What other idea?

MAIER: Of locking them up.

UNTERMEYER: (*Very impatiently*) But that was when you wanted to be a policeman . . . You just told us you became a writer.

MAIER: But I only became a writer so I could pretend I was a policeman. In that way, you see, I could lock up—

UNTERMEYER: (*Wearily*) I know, I know . . . You could lock up

439

your parents, your brothers, your sisters . . . your whole family, in fact.

MAIER: (*Excited*) That's it! But that's not the best . . . It's even better now.

UNTERMEYER: (*A bit dazed*) How better?

MAIER: Well, now that I'm a writer and therefore a policeman, I've built a big jail, the biggest jail in the whole world.

UNTERMEYER: Yes?

MAIER: And that's wonderful. You understand that, of course.

UNTERMEYER: Well—?

MAIER: (*Exultantly*) Because now—now I can lock up everybody!

UNTERMEYER: (*Quite dazed*) But—

MAIER: Yes, everybody—everybody in the whole world. (*Leans out of witness chair . . . and whispers dreamily*) I could even put you in my jail, Mr. Untermeyer. Yes, I can almost see you sitting there now, in a tiny cell . . . (*As if just remembering where he is . . . sits back and resumes normal tone*) But I beg your pardon—I will talk about myself. You were asking me about how I came to be a writer, I believe?

UNTERMEYER: (*Hurriedly*) No, no, it's quite all right, Mr. Maier . . . There are no further questions . . . You may step down.

What Price Heaven?

A PLAY FOR RADIO

MUSIC: *In . . . has a bubbling, gay quality . . . and blends into*:

SOUND: *Noise of homeward bound racetrack crowd . . . shouts of touts, sandwich vendors and newsboys.*

STATION MASTER: (*Calls*) Stand back from the edge of the platform! New York train'll be in any minute now.

1 MAN: Can't come too quick for me. Belmont Park! You can have it! I dropped a bundle—

2 MAN: Me, too.

DANNY: (*In quick*) Ahh, stop gripin', you guys. Whyn't you be like me? Happy, always smiling—

1 MAN: Happy. Smiling. Sure—when you beat four out of five races.

2 MAN: Lookit this mob. Everybody an' their sister. I'm sweatin'.

DANNY: Only the losers sweat.

1 MAN: Happy. Smiling—

DANNY: Okay, okay. Forget it. Only I gotta get a newspaper. Here, you guys, let me past. Now where's that kid? (*Up*) All right, people, let me through, huh? Comin' through. Sorry, comin' through.

CAST: *Ad lib adverse criticism as Danny pushes through toward newsboy's voice.*

1 MAN: (*Calls after him*) You'll never get through, Danny . . .

DANNY: Hey, kid! Let's have a paper . . .

1 VOICE: Watch out, you! Watch where you're goin'!

DANNY: I'm watchin' . . . *you* watch.

2 VOICE: Stop pushing!

WOMAN: Please . . . Please . . .

DANNY: (*Calls again*) Hey, kid . . .

WOMAN: Please! . . . (*In alarm*) . . . Oh . . . there! . . . now they've done it—pushed that poor boy off the platform . . . He's down on the tracks!

CAST: *Ad lib confusion at accident which mounts steadily behind:*

DANNY: Dummies! Knockin' the kid off . . . G'wan down and get him.

1 VOICE: Dummy yourself! Why don't *you* get him?

WOMAN: Oh, please . . . stop arguing! The boy's hurt his ankle.

SOUND: *Faint train whistle*

WOMAN: (*Up*) The train! The train's coming! . . . Please, please . . . somebody go down and get him!

DANNY: Okay, lady—keep your shirt on. I'll get him.

SOUND: *Danny jumps down*

DANNY: You all right, kid?

NEWSBOY: Yeah. Only my ankle—I can't stand . . .

SOUND: *Up steadily with approaching train*

DANNY: Just take it easy . . . don't try to move . . . Uncle Danny'll hoist you up on the platform . . . Ready? All set?

NEWSBOY: Ahuh.

DANNY: (*Grunts*) O-kay . . . up we go.

SOUND: *Train up very strong*

DANNY: There you are—safe and sound. (*Calls*) Hey—one of you mugs give me a lift.

1 VOICE: Hurry!

2 VOICE: Quick! Quick!

CAST: *Ad lib hysteria*

SOUND: *Overpowering train and brakes grinding right on mike*

WOMAN: *A high piercing scream that tops everything!*

MUSIC: *After long pause . . . a harp motif to establish heaven and under . . .*

ST. PETER: Good afternoon, Mr. McGuire.

DANNY: (*Casually*) How're yah? . . . Hey! What is this? This nightshirt stuff? Where's my pants?

ST. PETER: Your pants, Mr. McGuire?

DANNY: Yeah—my pants. I had four hundred bucks in my kick when I left the racetrack. Come on. Let's have my clothes.

ST. PETER: (*Sighing*) Oh my. So many people are like that when they first arrive. I wish the boss would get someone else for this job.

DANNY: Job?—what job?

ST. PETER: (*Ignoring him*) And anyway I'm more the executive type. Anyone can open and shut the gates of Heaven—

DANNY: Heaven?—what Heaven? . . . Ahhh, come off that stuff. Dish out my pants or I yell copper.

ST. PETER: Do you mind stepping over here a second, Mr. McGuire? That's it . . . just to the edge of this cloud. Now lean over—careful— there, that's it. Now—what do you see?

DANNY: Well, I'll be—it's Belmont Park! An' there's the railroad station. I was just on my way home—

ST. PETER: (*Patiently*) Do you see your pants, Mr. McGuire?

DANNY: (*As if to himself*) Lookit that crowd at the station . . . and there comes an ambulance down the road like a bat out of—

ST. PETER: (*Sighing*) Oh, yes—they always do send the wrong wagon . . . Mr. McGuire, do you see your pants?

DANNY: Hey! That's *me* down there on the tracks! An' here comes the docs with the stretcher. Hey—I must be sick.

ST. PETER: (*Gently*) Not sick, Mr. McGuire—

DANNY: No?

ST. PETER: No, Mr. McGuire—dead . . . But just for the record; so there can be no future complaints. (*Softly insistent*) *Your pants,* Mr. McGuire? Can you see them?

DANNY: Sure I see them—what would I be doin' layin' all over the railroad tracks without my pants? . . . Hey! What'd you say?

ST. PETER: (*Ignoring question*) Well, that's that—a fine thing if you'd run to the boss saying I had taken your trousers and stolen 400 something or other out of your—just what was that word again, Mr. McGuire?

DANNY: (*Absentmindedly*) Kick. . . . But you said something about somebody or other being dead?

ST. PETER: Not somebody or other—*You*, Mr. McGuire. You're dead.

DANNY: Me? I feel all right— Hey! Wait a minute! Then this must be—

ST. PETER: Heaven.

DANNY: An' you must be—

ST. PETER: St. Peter . . . (*Sighs*) . . . Oh what a life—the same questions year in and year out. It's a wonder I don't have a nervous breakdown . . . Oh well, here I go again. (*Formal speech*) Welcome to Heaven, Mr. McGuire. We are extremely happy to have you with us. May I have the honor of presenting you with your wings.

DANNY: (*Pause*) My wings? But—

ST. PETER: No—don't try to put them on. Just tuck them under your arm . . . That's it. It's a long time since anyone did any flying around here. The guests are all too bored. . . . Shall we go inside?

DANNY: Yeah. Sure . . . (*Start fading*) . . . Only I thought that when I died I'd go—

MUSIC: *Celestial theme up to bridge*

ST. PETER: (*Fades in*) Well, Mr. McGuire, what do you think of the place?

DANNY: (*Sarcastically*) Quite a layout. Must have been quite an architect to think of havin' the same clouds inside as outside . . . only more of them . . . (*Up sharp*) If you ask me—

ST. PETER: Shhhh—please, Mr. McGuire, please don't raise your voice. Not even in the slightest way. It's the first law of Heaven.

DANNY: Some law . . . why?

ST. PETER: Because any loud noise, or even a voice just a pitch above a conversational tone, disturbs the Gods.

DANNY: (*Whispers*) The Gods?

ST. PETER: That's right. They all live up there in that cloud.

DANNY: The bright green one, with all the flesh-colored ropes hanging down?

ST. PETER: That's the one. A little crowded perhaps—but then, if you must be a God, you should be prepared for a little discomfort.

DANNY: You talk like they were a football team . . . How many Gods you got, Pete?

ST. PETER: Pete? Pete? Why of course—Pete, a diminutive for Peter. You know—I like it. Pete. Sounds very friendly. You know, no one has ever called me that before, Mr. McGuire.

DANNY: Think nothing of it. And just call me Danny . . . Now— how about the low-down on all these Gods of yours?

ST. PETER: Well, Mr. Mc—I mean Danny—it's like this. Centuries ago, when Heaven was first conceived, there were not so many Gods. But people kept having them. The Chinese had one, and the Hindus another, and the Jews and the Christians and—oh, lots of others. And some people would pray to one, and some to another.

DANNY: So?

ST. PETER: So, we became sort of crowded up here and had to put them all together in one large cloud.

DANNY: Sort of Macy's basement stuff . . . But what're all those ropes that hang down?

ST. PETER: Ropes? What?— Oh those. They're not ropes, Danny. They're the ears of the Gods.

DANNY: The ears? Long and skinny like that?

ST. PETER: Why surely. You see, after years and years of listening to prayers they have become so attenuated that they almost reach to the earth.

DANNY: You don't tell me.

ST. PETER: I *am* telling you.

DANNY: So they pick up all the prayers, do they? Well, what do they do for the guys that set up the clamoring?

ST. PETER: Nothing.

DANNY: Nothing?

ST. PETER: Well—they listen.

DANNY: Come, come, Pete—no fibbing. I'm on the inside now.

ST. PETER: (*Heatedly*) Inside or outside—they *just* listen!

DANNY: Ah, ah, Pete—that's not what the rule book says.

ST. PETER: Rule book or *no* rule book—I said they do exactly *nothing!* . . . They're executives.

DANNY: Okay, okay, keep your shirt on, Pete . . .

SOUND: *Danny stumbles and falls heavily*

DANNY: (*Up loudly*) . . . Damn this nightshirt! How's a guy supposed to walk in one—

SOUND: *Whistle . . . from off-mike and approaching at terrific speed.*

ST. PETER: Shhhh, Danny, shhhh—

DANNY: (*Alarmed . . . as warning whistle approaches mike*) Hey! Watch it, Pete! Comin' straight at you—a little green cloud. Duck, Pete! Quick!

ST. PETER: Don't be alarmed, Danny. It'll stop. It's only our mail delivery. (*Warning speed sound stops abruptly*) See? Stopped right in front of my hand. (*Pause*) Oh, I knew it would happen. It's a letter concerning you, Danny. I'll read it to you . . . (*Reads*) To Saint Peter, Gatekeeper, First District, Second Assembly. Subject: One Daniel Phineas McGuire. (*Aside*) Ah, bureaucracy—I tell you, Danny, I'm fed up with it . . . (*Resumes reading*) Paragraph one: Under the civil penal code, section twelve, paragraph three—this warning is issued to one Daniel Phineas McGuire. If said guest once again breaks the law of Heaven by speaking in any but a normal tone—as put forth in section three, paragraph four—said guest will be subject to punishment. Punishment to be exile . . . And it's signed—Gods number one to two hundred inclusive.

DANNY: (*Whispers*) Exile? Where? How?

ST. PETER: Over there to your right. See that little black cloud like a puff-ball, with the long, spiral black chute going down and down?

DANNY: (*Still whispering*) I see it.

ST. PETER: Well, there are double doors on the top of it, with a sign which says—"To Hell! Beware the Doors!". . . So, you see, when you get a letter like—

DANNY: It's okay, Pete—you don't have to draw me no pictures—I get it.

ST. PETER: (*Dryly*) Most people do.

MUSIC: *Bridge*.

DANNY: (*Fades in*) Phew! What a joint this Heaven is. What's a guy to do with himself . . . (*Calls*) . . . Hey, Pete, what're you doin' with your head stuck through the gate? Lookin' for customers?

ST. PETER: Customers? Oh yes—you mean new arrivals.

DANNY: Yeah. Say—mind if I park the carcass and chew the fat a while? All right—don't say it—I'll translate . . . Do you mind if we have a little conversation?

ST. PETER: Why of course not, Danny. How did you like the gentlemen's club?

DANNY: A swell bunch of guys. So friendly. Each one a big shot. Each one a snob.

ST. PETER: Now, Danny . . . you must not mind the gentlemen too much. I admit they're a bit quiet.

DANNY: Quiet? Don't exaggerate, Pete. They don't even talk to each other. What do you do for excitement up here?

ST. PETER: Excitement?

DANNY: That's right. You know—horse races. The sport of kings and the racket of heels. Got any horses in Heaven?

ST. PETER: Horses?

DANNY: You know—things with four legs and a tail and a big long head?

ST. PETER: Oh, those. Sure. Plenty of them, over in Horse Heaven. All the most famous of all time.

DANNY: Must be good racing.

ST. PETER: Oh, but they never race. Wouldn't even think of it. That all goes on down there.

DANNY: (*Whispers*) In Hell?

ST. PETER: Ahuh. You see, long ago, Satan turned that Hell of his into one vast circuit of racetracks—newest gambling gadgets and what not. All the poor lost souls are encouraged to gamble.

DANNY: They are?

ST. PETER: Uhuh. Poor lost souls—they wager hours of frying and boiling against hours of *not* frying and boiling.

DANNY: Well, well, what'd you know. How do they do?

ST. PETER: Badly, very badly. I hear on the best authority that all of them spend most of their time in hot water.

DANNY: (*Thoughtfully*) It's a shame.

ST. PETER: What's a shame?

DANNY: That we got all the stake horses up here and the Devil's got all the racing down there.

ST. PETER: It is sort of peculiar, isn't it?

DANNY: Peculiar? . . . Look, Pete—how about me getting a gander at these famous nags of ours? . . . Can do?

ST. PETER: Now, Danny—I think you're going to be disappointed. . . . Oh, well, it does look as if you were the last guest of the day, so I guess no one can object if I leave a bit early. Come along; we'll fly over to Horse Heaven.

DANNY: Fly over?

ST. PETER: Of course. It's quite a ways, you know . . . Oh, I'm sorry; I've forgotten that you've never worn your wings . . . Put them on . . . No, no, not like that . . . stand still . . . now slip them over your shoulders and sort of wriggle back into the harness . . .

DANNY: (*Quite loud*) I'll be—

ST. PETER: Shhh! Remember! . . . Ah, that's better; that's it. Now just hook it together. That's right; now you've got it.

DANNY: Sort of like a bra.

ST. PETER: A what?

DANNY: A bra . . . like dames wear. You know—women.

ST. PETER: (*Interested*) They do? Would you mind explaining—

DANNY: (*Impatiently*) Not now, Pete, not now. One thing at a time. First horses . . . Now—how do you start this flying business?

ST. PETER: Just jump up a little. Like this. Then flap your wings.

SOUND: *Flap of heavy wings*

ST. PETER: (*Calls down*) Come on, Danny. It's quite simple . . .

SOUND: *Flap of Danny's wings*

ST. PETER: That's it; that's just fine. . . .

MUSIC: *Of celestial quality . . . fade in and keep in background and over it . . . sound of flapping wings close together.*

DANNY: (*Hums*) I got wings; you got wings; all God's chillun got wings—

ST. PETER: So you like flying, heh, Danny?

DANNY: Who wouldn't? It's like duck soup . . . Here! Watch this!

SOUND: *Rapid beat of wings simulating zoom of loop the loop*

DANNY: (*Calls excitedly*) How'm I doin', Pete?

ST. PETER: (*Alarmed*) Danny! Stop! If they ever see you—

SOUND: *Whistling warning sound approaching . . . stops dead on mike same as before*

ST. PETER: (*Tersely*) They have . . . Well, here we go again. Another directive . . . (*Reads*) Heaven ordinance number 32321352. I.E.: Stunt flying over the clouds of Heaven strictly forbidden and punishable by exile. . . . See, Danny, what I mean?

SOUND: *Long pause broken only by the regular flap of both pairs of wings.*

ST. PETER: Danny?

DANNY: Yeah?

ST. PETER: Danny—how does it—how does it feel to loop the loop?

DANNY: Well . . . Look—did you ever put up your last ten bucks, then take the dice and throw a natural?

ST. PETER: No.

DANNY: No? . . . Well then—did you ever have a blonde? You know, about five five, in your arms on the dance floor, say. An' the music playin' soft and low, and her lookin' up into your face outta baby-blue eyes?

ST. PETER: No.

DANNY: No? . . . Then I can't tell you how it feels to loop the loop.

ST. PETER: Oh.

DANNY: *(After pause)* Look, Pete, I was thinking—

ST. PETER: About what, Danny?

DANNY: About me—about me bein' in Heaven.

ST. PETER: What about it?

DANNY: Well, all those guys back in the Club, for instance. They're all big shots, famous guys—Aristotle, Lincoln, Wagner . . . But what I want to know is—is how does a mug like me rate Heaven?

ST. PETER: A mug, Danny?

DANNY: Okay then—a heel, a guy ain't never done nothin' all his life but hang around racetracks. How does he rate Heaven?

ST. PETER: Oh, that—you came in on our other quota.

DANNY: What other quota?

ST. PETER: The hero quota. I think it's number 6123. Something or other about meeting death at the instant of performing some heroic deed.

DANNY: What's all that got to do with me? I ain't no hero.

ST. PETER: Remember the little newsboy you saved from being crushed by the train . . . ?

DANNY: You mean that—well, I'll be—

ST. PETER: Here we are, Danny. Horse Heaven. Go ahead. Fly straight through that big orange cloud . . .

(Flap of wings and background music out)

DANNY: *(After pause)* Holy sufferin' catfish! Pete—do you see what I see? Horses, hundreds of 'em, all dressed up in *tuxedos!* In soup an' fish! High hats and all. Pete—get me out of here quick before I start seein' pink elephants.

St. Peter: Now take it gently, Danny. They're always like this.

Danny: Always? You mean horses sit around all dressed up like this, as if they was in the Stork Club, or somethin'? An' sippin' outta little demi-tassee cups. Don't tell me what they're drinkin' is . . . ?

St. Peter: Ambrosia—of course it is.

Danny: (*Groans*) I knew it; I knew it. Even the horses. It sure puts it on them; they all look pretty high to me.

St. Peter: High?

Danny: High in weight. Over 500 pounds overweight, everyone of 'em.

St. Peter: Yes, I guess they are pretty stout . . . Here, I'll introduce you. (*Up a little*) Mr. Eclipse; Mr. McGuire . . . (*Aside to Danny*) Careful, Danny—he's very English; quite standoff-ish.

Danny: How are you, Mr. Eclipse? Sure glad to meet you, after all these years of reading about you in the stud books.

Note: Throughout, horses speak in a high nasal twang, quite human, but with overtones of a horse's whinny.

Eclipse: (*Very bored*) How d'you do.

Danny: (*Enthusiastically*) Yes siree, from all I hear you were some punkins in your day. Never thought to meet you in the flesh.

Eclipse: How interesting.

Danny: (*Ire rising*) What is this, the brush-off—

St. Peter: (*In quick*) And, Danny, this is Mr. Star of India; Mr. India—Mr. McGuire. (*Aside to Danny*) He's Eclipse's right-hand horse. Careful what you say to him, to any of them for that matter—all very touchy, out of the top drawer, you know . . . (*Up a little*) And this is Mr. Salvator, Mr. Persimmon, Mr. Lexington and Mr. Broomstick, and—oh yes—Mr. Fair Play.

Danny: (*Again enthusiastic*) How'ya, Fair Play? My old man was nuts about your son—Man o' War . . . Thought he was the greatest horse to ever wear plates.

Fair Play: (*Haughtily*) We've had rumors. Probably a fair performer.

Danny: (*Angrily*) You weren't such a hot performer yourself!

St. Peter: (*In quick*) Careful, Danny!

Danny: (*Aside to Peter*) Look, I don't think I'm going to like this Horse Heaven of yours any better than I did your snob Gentlemen's Club—

St. Peter: (*Heartily*) Well, well, gentlemen—what about a race?

CAST: *Ad lib consternation . . . whispering . . . stamping of shod hooves.*

ECLIPSE: St. Peter—as our spokesman, I wish to say that we would no more consider racing before such common—

DANNY: (*Still angry*) Common is it? An' racing is it? Why you're all so fat you couldn't race your way out of a paper bag!

CAST: *Ad lib indignation.*

ST. PETER: Now Danny—

DANNY: All right, all right, I'll be good . . . I'm going for a walk. You want to try and convince them—you stay and convince them. Personally, I think you're wasting your breath on a bunch of snobs.

CAST: *Ad lib as if insulted and fade.*

DANNY: (*After long pause*) Well, well, well—as I live an' breathe—if it ain't my old friend, Larranaga, all dressed up in his soup and fish. You sure look right in the pink of condition, not like these other nags around here. How're'ya, Larranaga? How's tricks?

LARRANAGA: (*A sad woebegone horse, weighted with trouble*) Tricks are very bad, Mr. McGuire.

DANNY: (*Sympathetically*) Up here they're all bad . . . When did I see you last, boy?

LARRANAGA: I think at Hialeah Park—

DANNY: Oh, yeah—I remember now.

LARRANAGA: (*Sighs heavily*) Oh, I wish I had never come to Heaven. All the horses up here high-hat me so.

DANNY: I know just what you mean . . . Hey! Wait a minute. How come you rate Heaven? You were never nothin' more than a—

LARRANAGA: Go ahead and say it, Mr. McGuire. They all do. I was never anything more than a plater—a common, ordinary plater.

DANNY: There, there—at least you didn't run in the last race on the card. You were a high-class selling plater . . . But how come Heaven?

LARRANAGA: Do you recall my death at Hialeah Park, Mr. McGuire?

DANNY: Yeah—I guess so.

LARRANAGA: Well, all the sports writers had it incorrectly. I didn't step in a hole after the finish.

DANNY: No?

LARRANAGA: No. My leg was gone at least fifty feet from the finish, but I persevered and won the race. Remember? Right after crossing the line my leg gave way and I broke my neck. (*Sobs*) That made me a hero. So here I am. Worse luck. (*Continues to sob heartbrokenly*)

DANNY: Now take it easy, kid. Keep the old chin up out of the stiff shirt. And don't think I don't know how it is—because I do. (*Start fading*) Maybe I can sort of fix things. I got sort of an idea . . . you wait here . . .

St. Peter: (*Fading in*) Ah, there you are at last, Danny. Well, I have everything arranged. The gentlemen, here, have kindly consented to race.

Danny: Well, gentlemen, it'll be a pleasure to watch you perform. Oh, by the way—just bumped into an old friend of mine. Name of Larranaga. You gentlemen know him?

Cast: *Ad lib sniffs of scorn*

Danny: I can see that you do. I'd like to see him race.

St. Peter: Now, Danny, you're only complicating matters. Four of them are going to race—Diamond Jubilee and Persimmon and Broomstick and Lexington. Sort of an international affair.

Danny: (*Stubbornly*) I don't care; I want my friend Larranaga in it. Make it a five-horse go.

Eclipse: (*Haughtily*) That's impossible. Why this Larranaga, this bounder, is nothing but a plater.

Cast: *Ad libs approval*

Danny: (*Angry*) So what if he is? You're all so—

St. Peter: Gentlemen, gentlemen—we're wasting time. If Mr. McGuire wants his old friend Larranaga to race, then he races!

Cast: *Ad lib faint protest*

St. Peter: No, no, gentlemen, I will not listen. (*Authoritatively*) I have spoken! We will all meet in an hour at the edge of Heaven . . . (*Start fading*) The matter is settled. Good afternoon, gentlemen . . . Come, Danny . . .

Music: *Celestial theme in background as before.*

Sound: *Regular, rhythmical flap of wings as before.*

St. Peter: Happy, Danny?

Danny: (*In thought*) What? . . . Oh, sure, sure.

St. Peter: What's wrong, Danny? Aren't you interested in your race any more?

Danny: (*Heartily*) Sure, sure thing—it's going to be swell, and thanks. Come on, let's go look over the layout.

St. Peter: Layout?

Danny: The racetrack.

St. Peter: Racetrack?

Danny: (*Losing patience*) The place where the horses are going to run.

St. Peter: But—there is no such place in Heaven.

Danny: What? No racetrack? Well, we might just as well call off the whole shootin' match then. You just can't have horses—

ST. PETER: Now just a minute, Danny—not so fast. What does one of these racetracks of yours look like? I'll build you one.

DANNY: You'll what?

ST. PETER: I'll build one. You must have noticed the extreme pliability of our architecture up here. (*Soothingly*) Now just tell me what one of these things you want looks like and I have no doubt I can manage.

DANNY: (*Skeptically*) Oh you will, will you. . . . First off, you have to have a brown dirt track about a hundred an' fifty feet wide an' two miles around—

ST. PETER: This brown cloud do? See—I'll flatten it out like this and run it in a circle. (*Start fading*) Then I'll take this green cloud and . . .

MUSIC: *Background theme builds suddenly in volume and segues into "The Ride of the Valkyrie" furioso.*

DANNY: (*Calls excitedly over music*) Attaboy, Pete! It's a beaut! . . . Now another green cloud flat for the infield . . . an' one for the grandstand. . . .

MUSIC: *Swells to tremendous peak and crashes out.*

ST. PETER: (*After pause*) Well—will it do, Danny?

DANNY: It sure will. Stick a couple of mountains back of it and it'd look just like Santa Anita.

ST. PETER: (*Eagerly*) You want a few mountains?

DANNY: No, no. Thanks. Don't need 'em. They're just scenery for the suckers anyway. (*Pause*) Ah—here come the horses. Holy mackerel, Pete, don't tell me they're going to race in their tuxedos?

ST. PETER: Why of course. It's traditional here in Heaven . . . like our robes.

DANNY: (*Groans*) Everything's traditional . . . Say—will you look at those snob horses giving little Larranaga the high-hat!

ST. PETER: I can't see very well . . . I mean, not at a distance . . . It's all sort of blurred. I'm near-sighted, you know.

DANNY: (*Absentmindedly*) Too bad . . . oughta wear peepers.

ST. PETER: Peepers?

DANNY: Glasses . . . Never mind—I'll tell you what they're doing— all the horses are sitting around in a circle—all except poor Larranaga. He's out in the cold. They're not even talking to him. (*Up a little*) Come on, Pete, we'll give them their instructions. . . .

ST. PETER: (*Pause . . . fades in*) Good afternoon, gentlemen, good afternoon—nice of you to come.

CAST: *Horses sniff their disdain.*

St. Peter: Mr. McGuire, here, will take over . . .

Danny: All right now, you horses—pay attention. You—Larranaga, stop fidgetin'. Now listen—you all go down and wait at the bend. When I raise my hand like this, you start your post parade. Distance will be two miles. No jockeys. No weights. St. Peter will throw a little red cloud that breaks over your heads—that'll be the starting gun. Everybody understand? . . . Okay, get started then . . .

Sound: *Of hooves receding*

Danny: Get goin', Larranaga. What's the matter with you? You're as nervous as a witch.

Larranaga: (*Wails*) Oh, Mr. McGuire—

Danny: Don't "Oh, Mr. McGuire" me. Get out there and run. It's in the bag for you, chum. You're the only one of the lot anywhere near racing condition.

Larranaga: But I'm nervous.

Danny: Then stop being nervous.

Larranaga: I can't. Everything in Heaven makes me nervous.

Danny: Stop stamping an' twitchin' around, I say. You're sweating up your stiff shirt . . . Now do what I tell you—get out there and run, and no more nonsense. Remember, I'm betting on you to cop this heat.

Larranaga: Oh, Mr. McGuire, you shouldn't . . . (*Start fading . . . Sound of hooves*) . . . it only makes my nervousness worse . .

Danny: Okay, Pete, we're all set now, I guess. Where are the customers?

St. Peter: The customers?

Danny: Sure, customers. Fans. Can't run a horse race without people in the stands.

St. Peter: Oh yes—yes of course. Yes, yes—we must have customers . . . Just a second now . . . I think I can arrange it . . .

Music: *Muted bugle call "Assembly" up and under*

St. Peter: (*Proudly*) See—here come your customers, Danny.

Danny: (*Low whistle*) The Gentlemen's Club . . . They don't look none too happy about it though.

St. Peter: They're not. They hate being disturbed in the middle of the afternoon concert.

Danny: Well, okay, now we got customers we're ready to go. Where are the bookmakers?

St. Peter: Bookmakers?

Danny: Sure, bookmakers . . . pricemakers . . . layers . . . you know—the men who take the bets?

St. Peter: Oh yes—yes, of course. I'm sorry, Danny, but there is no such thing as a bookmaker in Heaven.

Danny: (*Bewildered*) No bookmakers?

St. Peter: I'm sorry, Danny, terribly sorry.

Danny: There, there, Pete—never you mind. Don't look so down in the mouth, it ain't your fault . . . (*Excited*) Tell you what—*I'll* be the bookmaker. How's that? All these gentlemen chumps can bet their money with me.

St. Peter: Money? Why, Danny, there's no money up here.

Danny: No money?

St. Peter: That's right—the gentlemen in the grandstand haven't a penny in their nightgowns.

Danny: Well then—all I can say is that this is gonna be a floperoo of a race . . . (*Disgustedly*) Let's call the whole thing off.

St. Peter: Just a minute, Danny—please, just a minute. Don't be so hasty. I think I can remedy the situation . . . Watch now . . .

Sound: *Quick flapping of wings in and out of mike as St. Peter circles audience*

Danny: (*After pause*) What'd you do now?

St. Peter: (*Winded*) I—I gave each gentleman ten gold pieces and told him to wager them with you . . . Look, here they come now.

Danny: (*In whisper to Peter*) Pete—you're a swell egg . . . (*Up a little*) All right, boys, don't crowd. And don't push. Stand in line. You'll all get down. Everybody gets a chance to place their dough on the gee-gee of his choice . . .

Cast: *Ad lib great betting ado*

Danny: (*Taking bets*) Eclipse?—Mr. Aristotle . . . he's a hundred to one. Broomstick?—Mr. Lincoln . . . fifty to one and your money back. What's that? No, you don't need a receipt . . . What's that, Mr. Wagner?—oh, Persimmon—he's ten to one . . .

Danny and cast: *Ad lib betting and gradually fade out*

Danny: (*Aside to Peter*) Phew!—that's the last of them. These gentlemen of yours, Pete, are certainly fast men with a dollar—especially when it's *your* dollar. . . . Okay, we're all set now. Send 'em to the post.

St. Peter: (*Pause . . . then*) I can't see a thing. They're so far away.

Danny: They're drawin' near the starting post. Gosh, that Larranaga's nervous—jumpin' and mincing around like a two-year-old. Hope he gets a hold of himself. Everything depends on him now.

St. Peter: Why?

DANNY: Why?—for the simple reason that those snob gentlemen of yours wouldn't wager on anything but the snob horses. So Larranaga's runnin' for the book. For us. You and me. If he wins, we win. If he loses—well, we're overboard and might as well climb the fence, see?

ST. PETER: No—not quite. Do you—

DANNY: Not now, Pete, not now . . . They're at the post. Throw 'em a cloud.

SOUND: *A soft continuous sputtering with a faint bang*

DANNY: They're off an' runnin'! Old fatty Diamond Jubilee broke on top. (*Groans*) That fool, that Larranaga—

ST. PETER: (*Excited*) What—what happened?

DANNY: (*Disgusted*) Larranaga—left flatfooted at the post.

ST. PETER: Is that bad?

DANNY: Bad? . . . Right now I'd sell the entire book for one Hong Kong dollar.

ST. PETER: (*Still excited*) Never mind that—where are *we?*

DANNY: We? Nowhere. At the post. Up front it's Diamond Jubilee a neck in front of Broomstick, who's two in front of Persimmon with Lexington lapped on—

ST. PETER: But where's Larranaga?

DANNY: Just leavin' the post, that's where he is.

ST. PETER: Can he make up the distance?

DANNY: Not even if he was to put on his wings. Looks like we're sunk, Pete . . . Here they come into the stretch!

SOUND: *Soft drum of hooves in distance*

CAST: *Ad lib whispering as they root for their horses*

DANNY: Broomstick's taken the lead; Diamond Jubilee's droppin' back, he's out of it; the others are comin' bunched. . . .

CAST: *Ad lib whispered consternation as drum of hooves stops suddenly*

DANNY: Well, I'll be—

ST. PETER: (*In quick*) Tell me! What happened?

DANNY: What happened? I never saw anything like it in my life! Why them four snob horses had the race between 'em—an' the second they hit the stretch they stopped runnin' and sat down and took them little demi-tassee cups of theirs out of a hunk of cloud and started drinking that ambrosia stuff. (*Groans*) Some race. Some horses. A regular little tea party right smack in the center of the stretch—

ST. PETER: Where's Larranaga?

DANNY: He's comin'—runnin' like the wind.

ST. PETER: Is he going to stop, too?

SOUND: *Faint hooves approaching mike*

DANNY: Yes, he's going to . . . *No!* . . . He's gone on past . . . he's tearin'—

ST. PETER: (*Very excited*) Quiet! Quiet! I can see him myself now . . . Oh, look at him run! (*Quite loud*) Come on, you beauty, run, run, run—

DANNY: (*In sharp*) Shhhh! Remember where you are.

SOUND: *Hooves up, on past mike and receding*

ST. PETER: Thank you, Danny . . . Oh, look at him come. Oh, you beauty! Look at him move! Isn't he beautiful, Danny? . . . And he's winning; he's winning.

DANNY: Well, that's that, I guess. As crazy a horse race as I ever heard of. But we got one consolation—we took the whole pot, Pete. We're the only winners.

SOUND: *Off mike flap of many wings receding in departure*

DANNY: Gee, I hate to see the boys go off like that; I've been a loser too many times myself not to know how it feels. Wait—I got an idea . . . (*Up a little*) Hey, just a second, Mr. Aristotle; you too, Mr. Beethoven. No hard feelings, I hope. Just the breaks of the game. Easy come, easy go, I always say. (*Brightly*) Hey—I got it! How about a little food? What say we put the feedbag on? Come on—I'm the winner —*I'll* buy dinner for the whole gang!

St. Peter: Forget it, Danny. No one up here eats food.

Danny: (*Slowly*) No food? No drinks? Then what good is all this dough I got loadin' down my nightshirt?

St. Peter: (*Sadly*) No good at all, Danny. We never use it up here. (*Hesitantly*) I—I just thought it would be a lot of fun for you—you wanted the race and everything so much. I'm—I'm sorry, Danny.

Danny: It's okay, Pete. Forget it. You did your best. Guess I'm just a fool up here . . . Oh, well, might as well dump these no-good gold pieces out then. There they go . . . (*Pause . . . and excitedly*) Holy mackerel! What a place! They don't even go with a bang—just drop down about ten feet and form a golden cloud . . . What is this? What kind of a place am I in? That's the last straw. I'm getting out of here, and right away. . . . So long, Pete, you've been swell . . .

Sound: *Flap of Danny's wings receding*

St. Peter: (*Calls*) Danny, Danny, where are you going?

Danny: (*From off mike*) Never mind where I'm going—I'm going, that's all, and as far as I can get . . . (*Fading*) . . . Take care of yourself, guy, you got what it takes . . . you're aces in my book, fella . . .

St. Peter: (*Calls*) Danny—wait!

Sound: *Flap of Peter's wings following*

St. Peter: Danny, wait . . . don't be rash . . .

Music: *Celestial theme as before played as chase music, sustain, then out*

Sound: *Flap of wings, first one stops, then after interval the other*

St. Peter: (*In fierce whisper*) Come down off of that cloud, Danny! Have you gone mad! No one has ever been up on that black cloud before. Danny—you so much as talk up there and it's all over. Come down instantly, do you hear, Danny? Come down this instant!

Danny: (*As if a distance above Peter's head*) Go away, Pete. Go'wan! I don't want you to get mixed up in this thing. I don't want you taking any raps for me.

St. Peter: Please, Danny—please think it over.

Danny: (*Firmly*) I have thought it over. I want to go to Hell; I'll go to Hell. You, you like this place, you stay here . . . Now go away, Pete, and let me alone.

St. Peter: Danny!

Danny: Go away!

ST. PETER: Danny! Stop! Oh my—

DANNY: *Starts singing in very loud off-key voice the opening of "Sweet Adeline"*

ST. PETER: (*Up and over*) That does it, sure. That's the end . . . Here, Danny, wait—

DANNY: (*Breaks off singing*) Go back down, Pete! Don't you come up here! You stay out of this—you're in the clear . . .

ST. PETER: (*Puffing as if climbing cloud*) Move over . . . Give me your hand . . . There now . . .

SOUND: *Of rusty iron doors opening slowly*

DANNY: The doors to Hell—they're opening! Get out of here, Pete!

ST. PETER: (*Calmly*) Let them open. Here—move over a bit and give a man with a voice a chance.

DANNY: (*Awestruck*) You wouldn't, would you, Pete?

ST. PETER: I certainly would. . . . Do you mind starting that tune of yours again?

DANNY AND ST. PETER: *Danny hesitantly starts song . . . After first line St. Peter's bass comes in good and strong . . . They achieve a sort of harmony*

SOUND: *Whistling warning from off mike swells until it tops duet*

MUSIC: *Curtain*

Don Marquis

Donald Robert Perry Marquis (1878–1937) had more friends and was compared to more famous figures than any other journalist of his day. Christopher Morley said that Marquis was "a careful blend of Falstaff and Napoleon III." Benjamin de Casseres likened him to "Shelley trying to lasso the Golden Calf." The incongruities were ingrained in Marquis' character. He was a schoolteacher, an actor, a reporter, a poet and playwright, always in revolt. His most ambitious work, The Dark Hours, a poetic drama of the Crucifixion, was a failure, whereas his lighthearted archy and mehitabel, a set of conversations between a cat and a cockroach, was joyfully hailed. Marquis tried to be casual about it, but he died a cynic. "It would be one on me if I should be remembered longest for creating a cockroach character," said Marquis. Time has proved the wry statement a truthful prediction.

FROM *"archy and mehitabel"*

i. the coming of archy

Dobbs Ferry possesses a rat which slips out of his lair at night and runs a typewriting machine in a garage. Unfortunately, he has always been interrupted by the watchman before he could produce a complete story.

It was at first thought that the power which made the typewriter run was a ghost, instead of a rat. It seems likely to us that it was both a ghost and a rat. Mme. Blavatsky's ego went into a white horse after she passed over, and someone's personality has undoubtedly gone into this rat. It is an era of belief in communications from the spirit land.

And since this matter had been reported in the public prints and seriously received we are no longer afraid of being ridiculed, and we do not mind making a statement of something that happened to our own typewriter only a couple of weeks ago.

We came into our room earlier than usual in the morning, and discovered a gigantic cockroach jumping about upon the keys.

He did not see us, and we watched him. He would climb painfully upon the framework of the machine and cast himself with all his force upon a key, head downward, and his weight and the impact of the blow were just sufficient to operate the machine, one slow letter after another. He could not work the capital letters, and he had a great deal of difficulty operating the mechanism that shifts the paper so that a fresh line may be started. We never saw a cockroach work so hard or perspire so freely in all our lives before. After about an hour of this frightfully difficult literary labor he fell to the floor exhausted, and we saw him creep feebly into a nest of the poems which are always there in profusion.

Congratulating ourself that we had left a sheet of paper in the machine the night before so that all this work had not been in vain, we made an examination, and this is what we found:

> expression is the need of my soul
> i was once a vers libre bard
> but i died and my soul went into the body of a cockroach
> it has given me a new outlook upon life
> i see things from the under side now
> thank you for the apple peelings in the wastepaper basket

but your paste is getting so stale i cant eat it
there is a cat here called mehitabel i wish you would have
removed she nearly ate me the other night why dont she
catch rats that is what she is supposed to be for
there is a rat here she should get without delay

most of these rats here are just rats
but this rat is like me he has a human soul in him
he used to be a poet himself
night after night i have written poetry for you
on your typewriter
and this big brute of a rat who used to be a poet
comes out of his hole when it is done
and reads it and sniffs at it
he is jealous of my poetry
he used to make fun of it when we were both human
he was a punk poet himself
and after he has read it he sneers
and then he eats it

i wish you would have mehitabel kill that rat
or get a cat that is onto her job

and i will write you a series of poems showing how things look
to a cockroach
that rats name is freddy
the next time freddy dies i hope he wont be a rat
but something smaller i hope i will be a rat
in the next transmigration and freddy a cockroach
i will teach him to sneer at my poetry then

dont you ever eat any sandwiches in your office
i havent had a crumb of bread for i don't know how long
or a piece of ham or anything but apple parings
and paste leave a piece of paper in your machine
every night you can call me archy

ii. mehitabel was once cleopatra

boss i am disappointed in
some of your readers they
are always asking how does
archy work the shift so as to get a
new line or how does archy do
this or do that they
are always interested in technical
details when the main question is
whether the stuff is
literature or not
i wish you would leave
that book of george moores on
the floor

mehitabel the cat and i want to
read it i have discovered that
mehitabel s soul formerly inhabited a
human also at least that
is what mehitabel is claiming these
days it may be she got jealous of
my prestige anyhow she and
i have been talking it over in a
friendly way who were you
mehitabel i asked her i was
cleopatra once she said well i said i

suppose you lived in a palace you bet
she said and what lovely fish dinners
we used to have and licked her chops

mehitabel would sell her soul for
a plate of fish any day i told her i thought
you were going to say you were
the favorite wife of the emperor
valerian he was some cat nip eh
mehitabel but she did not get me

                              archy

iii. the song of mehitabel

this is the song of mehitabel
of mehitabel the alley cat
as i wrote you before boss
mehitabel is a believer
in the pythagorean
theory of the transmigration
of the soul and she claims
that formerly her spirit
was incarnated in the body
of cleopatra
that was a long time ago
and one must not be
surprised if mehitabel
has forgotten some of her
more regal manners

i have had my ups and downs
but wotthehell wotthehell
yesterday sceptres and crowns
fried oysters and velvet gowns
and today i herd with bums
but wotthehell wotthehell
i wake the world from sleep
as i caper and sing and leap
when i sing my wild free tune
wotthehell wotthehell
under the blear eyed moon

i am pelted with cast off shoon
but wotthehell wotthehell

do you think that i would change
my present freedom to range
for a castle or moated grange
wotthehell wotthehell
cage me and i d go frantic
my life is so romantic
capricious and corybantic
and i m toujours gai toujours gai

i know that i am bound
for a journey down the sound
in the midst of a refuse mound
but wotthehell wotthehell
oh i should worry and fret
death and i will coquette
there s a dance in the old dame yet
toujours gai toujours gai

i once was an innocent kit
wotthehell wotthehell
with a ribbon my neck to fit
and bells tied onto it
o wotthehell wotthehell
but a maltese cat came by
with a come hither look in his eye
and a song that soared to the sky
and wotthehell wotthehell
and i followed adown the street
the pad of his rhythmical feet
o permit me again to repeat
wotthehell wotthehell

my youth i shall never forget
but there s nothing i really regret
wotthehell wotthehell
there s a dance in the old dame yet
toujours gai toujours gai

the things that i had not ought to
i do because i ve gotto
wotthehell wotthehell
and i end with my favorite motto
toujours gai toujours gai

boss sometimes i think
that our friend mehitabel
is a trifle too gay

David McCord

David (Thompson Watson) McCord has roamed
all over America since his birth in New York City
in 1897. His activities in the intervening years have
been multiple: associate editor of the Harvard
Alumni Bulletin and, subsequently, editor; music
and dramatic critic on the Boston Evening Transcript; literary agent for a particular publisher,
a second lieutenant, an excellent though little
known water-colorist, an essayist, and, first and
last, a poet.

McCord's serious poetry has been collected in
a volume entitled The Crows; but all his light
verse—for which he is not sufficiently famous—
has not yet been collected, although much of it
appears in Bay Window Ballads.

The Axolotl

"The axolotl
Looks a littl
like the ozelotl,
Itl

"Drink a greatl
more than whatl
Fill the fatl
Whiskey bottl.

"The food it eatsl
Be no morsl:
Only meatsl
Drive its dorsl.

"Such an awfl
Fish to kettl!"
"You said a mawfl,
Pop'epetl!"

Epitaph to a Waiter

By and by
God caught his eye.

History of Education

The decent docent doesn't doze:
He teaches standing on his toes.
His student dassn't doze—and does,
And that's what teaching is and was.

467

Of Time and the Reader

Reading all these long-gone-with-the-winded novels, some people are
    going gaga;
What this country needs is a good five-cent saga.

Ruth McKenney

Ruth McKenney was born in 1911 in the little Indiana town of Mishawaka, "*a town which took me nearly twenty years to learn how to spell. . . . I was graduated from high school in 1928 and I still have dismal memories of a class oration about taking the marines out of Nicaragua.*" While still in her teens, she became a printer, switched to newspaper reporting, and attended college. In between, she was "*an extremely bad waitress and an enormously unsuccessful book salesman.*"

In 1939, Ruth McKenney suddenly emerged from obscurity with My Sister Eileen, a gay autobiography and a lively picture of a period. It was equally successful as a book, a play, and a motion picture. Protesting that she was not a humorist, Miss McKenney has devoted herself to serious fiction—Industrial Valley was followed by Jake Home—but most readers still prefer her accounts of the amazing and slightly mad McKenneys.

The Sock Hunt

I suppose, what with the passing years and the girls he's met since, that young Mr. Randolph Churchill, the scion of the London Churchills, does not remember me. Still, looking back on it all, I should think he would. I certainly do. Precisely as I can never, for so long as I walk this earth, forget the time I fell down at my high-school senior prom, right smack in front of the orchestra with my best beau sprawled beside me, so can I never put aside the memory of young Mr. Churchill. My flesh still crawls. Not that Mr. Churchill is anything to make a girl's flesh crawl. Not at all. In a certain way, like the men in the breakfast-food ads, he is quite handsome.

Mr. Churchill and I met in a purely professional capacity. It was the late fall of 1930. He was touring America, speaking before literary clubs, Rotary Clubs, university clubs, and the like on a variety of light topics, including "Fate of an Empire" and "Why I Am a Conservative." He was then nineteen, and I was the daisy-eyed star reporter on the *Ohio State Lantern,* a newspaper published daily, except Saturday and Sunday, by the students of journalism at Ohio State University.

Young Mr. Churchill arrived in Columbus, Ohio, on the flood tide of a lot of awe-struck advance notices. He was to address a local men's dinner club which for pure hauteur would make the Union Club look sick any day. All the speeches before this tony outfit were dead secret; no reporters allowed. Furthermore, celebrities who appeared before these hallowed few were never interviewed by the Columbus press. The editors of the papers were all members of the club, and that was that.

Well, my mouth watered to interview Mr. Churchill. I had never seen a real Englishman in the flesh, for one thing. For another thing, my deadly rival on the *Lantern* staff, a chap of considerable energy and no ethics, had publicly stated that he considered the feat of obtaining an interview with Mr. Churchill too great even for his remarkable talents. After this, nothing could hold me. I marched forward with determination to my doom.

I arrived at the hotel lobby at 4:35 P.M. and briskly set about finding out Mr. Churchill's room number. Then, with success almost in the hollow of my hand, I collapsed on a lobby lounge with an attack of acute panic. This lasted until 5:22 P.M., when a man insulted me. At least he came directly over to my lounge and said, in a chummy tone, "Waiting for somebody?"

470

This drove me to Mr. Churchill. I fled from my insulter and arrived at the forbidding door of Mr. Churchill's hotel room, still unnerved. I knocked valiantly. I had mapped out my strategy well in advance. When Mr. Churchill asked, "Who's there?" I intended to reply, "Maid, with towels." Then, when he opened the door, I planned to stick my foot in the crack and ask him a lot of questions very fast. I think a scene such as this had been in a newspaper film about that time.

Anyway, Mr. Churchill ruined my pretty plans by replying, to the knock, "Come in." I hesitated, getting a burning sensation in my throat. I was nineteen and lived with my grandmother, who would have been absolutely horrified at the thought of any young woman traipsing into a man's hotel room alone.

"Come in!" roared Mr. Churchill from behind the door. He sounded rather angry. I kept telling myself that after I got out of school and got a real job on a newspaper, I would look back on this moment and laugh. As it turned out, however, in spite of a lot of jobs on newspapers, genuine daily ones, the mere thought of that frightful moment, with Mr. Churchill bellowing "Come in" on one side of the door and me trembling on the other, has never brought even the sickliest of smiles to my face. It still makes my hair prickle.

Finally I opened the door very timidly indeed, and beheld Mr. Churchill, surely the blondest young man in the world, seated at a desk, writing. He wore a smoking jacket over his dinner trousers, black vest, and starched shirt front. His bare feet were stuck in floppy leather slippers. Mr. Churchill looked so very public-school English he was faintly incredible. Maybe he's grown out of that now, but in 1930 he was certainly breath of Empire. You could—or at least I could—just see him wolfing down supper off in the tropics, dressed to the teeth in tails and white tie. Mr. Churchill's eyes were a china blue and his smoking jacket was the same, overlaid, however, with old rose and gold.

I stood by the door for several seconds while Mr. Churchill continued to scratch away at his desk. Now, a cynical old interviewer of ripened years, I fear that Mr. Churchill was attempting to impress me. But on that trying evening I felt that I had intruded on the literary labors of a young genius. Finally Mr. Churchill lifted his blue eyes to mine.

"Ah," he said, leaping gallantly to his feet, "a lady! I beg your pardon. Pray do forgive me."

My mouth sagged. Mr. Churchill drew up a chair beside his desk and, with a cozy gesture, beckoned me over. I went.

"Pray excuse me," said Mr. Churchill. "I must finish this wireless message." On his desk lay eleven or twelve Western Union blanks covered with writing.

"What?" I said. The reason I said this was that I could not understand very much of what he said. His accent, which I had so longed to hear, a real, bona-fide Oxford accent, was so broad that unfortunately he might as well have spoken French. I can get every other word a Frenchman says, too, which is fairly good, considering I studied French in the Ohio public schools for only eight years.

Young Mr. Churchill now turned to me and said in a fierce tone, "What would you say if you wanted to tell your manager you did not want ladies to give you flowers at lectures?" At least that is what I thought he said. It was so difficult for me to decipher Mr. Churchill's accent, and the question seemed so entirely improbable, that, after agonized reflection, I simply shook my head.

Mr. Churchill didn't note my silence. He apparently hit on just the right words, for he signed his name with a flourish I am sure no American operator ever spelled out, and turned briskly to me, saying, "Now, what may I do for you?"

I explained haltingly that I was a newspaper reporter. Mr. Churchill didn't ask, so I didn't find it necessary to tell him that the paper I was interviewing him for was only, alas, the university daily. I simply trotted out all my carefully prepared questions. I asked him about Ramsay MacDonald and Hoover and Briand and a few other such people. Mr. Churchill roundly denounced them all, for different reasons. MacDonald was too far left, and even Mr. Hoover was pretty much of a Socialist. I asked him about the future of English youth, and Mr. Churchill said that if only a few more young people of his class would awaken to their responsibility, the future of England was safe. I was slightly shaken at Mr. Churchill's firm Tory opinions. He seemed quite young to be so fierce.

However, I drew a breath and started off on the English public-school system. Just at this point Mr. Churchill created a diversion.

In an ordinary speaking voice, as distinguished from the voice in which he denounced Mr. Hoover or Mr. MacDonald, he said, "Would you care for a drink?"

This unnerved me again. I could explain the interview to Grandma and my conscience, but drinking with a total stranger in his hotel room certainly seemed excessive. In those days, most college students—at least at my school—still thought drinking, no matter where, was pretty darned daring. Mr. Churchill, however, had already unearthed from his suitcase a bottle of what he assured me was fine Scotch, straight from England.

I was no judge. Up to that very moment I had never tasted anything in alcoholic beverages except a variety of bootleg liquor called "New Straitsville corn," because it was distilled in some abandoned mines near New Straitsville, Ohio. New Straitsville corn burned your throat and made you sick. Also, it hurt so to choke down New Straitsville corn that you were acutely conscious of every drink. It was the suave, sneaking quality of Mr. Churchill's fine liquor which undid me. You hardly knew you were drinking it, until afterward.

Mr. Churchill and I soon forgot serious topics. I asked him whether he really enjoyed lecturing about "Fate of an Empire." He said he did not, and also that he hated America and couldn't wait to get home. After a while Mr. Churchill thought we ought to eat something.

"I say," he said, "how about a spot of food, what?" He really talked just like that.

"O.K.," I said. "Let me order, though. They can't understand you over the phone. You talk so funny."

Mr. Churchill glowered. He said I was the one who had a peculiar accent.

"You talk through your nose," he said, with truth, "and you pronounce all your 'r's. They aren't supposed to be pronounced."

"That's what you think," I said, feeling hilarious, "Old Mushmouth."

For some reason, Mr. Churchill thought that was very funny. " 'Mushmouth'!" he shouted joyously, amid peals of real upper-class English laughter, very high-pitched, like a whinny. " 'Mushmouth'! Deah me, I must remembaw that."

We ate lamb chops, a lot of them. "Tell them to send up a bally lot of them!" Mr. Churchill roared while I telephoned. "I want six lamb chops all for myself. After all, I must lecture on the 'Fate of an Empire.' "

While we were gnawing on lamb-chop bones we traded opinions on moving pictures. Mr. Churchill was a fan, and so was I. It turned out we both adored Vilma Banky. Suddenly Mr. Churchill said, "What about my lecture?"

"Well," I said, "what about it?"

"I won't do it," Mr. Churchill said. "Let the Empire go rot for to-night. Let's go to the cinema. You and I."

For a moment I was sorely tempted. Then I pictured the fearful scandal. The lecturer disappears. The town's leading citizens are left waiting. Among the leading citizens was the publisher of the Columbus *Dispatch*. I was the campus correspondent for the Columbus *Dispatch*, and I lived—in a very meagre way, to be sure, but still I lived—on the weekly wages the *Dispatch* paid me. In my fancy I saw the publisher of the *Dispatch* discovering that his most minor employee had practically kidnapped young Mr. Churchill.

"No," I said firmly. "You have to make that speech."

Mr. Churchill sighed. "Well, then," he said, "I have to put on my dinner jacket." He found that all right; also his white scarf and his black overcoat and his two patent-leather pumps. But alas, as the hour approached nine, he could find only one black sock. The club was to send a committee at nine, to escort Mr. Churchill to the lecture hall.

"What shall I do?" Mr. Churchill inquired frantically. "I can't lecture with only one sock." I rose from the dinner table, still gnawing a bone, and cast a quick look over the room.

"Be calm," I said. "They'll never notice."

"Oh, yes they will," Mr. Churchill said. "Besides, I won't go unless we find that sock. And I only have one black pair with me. The rest of them are in Pittsburgh."

"Wear another color," I said lightly. "What happened to the socks you had on this afternoon?"

"Tan socks," Mr. Churchill shouted, "with a dinner coat?"

I observed Mr. Churchill's frenzy with a motherly eye. "There, there," I said. "Relax. I'll find it."

Mr. Churchill sat down, putting a childish faith in me. I failed. I trotted around in circles, afraid to look in his luggage—for after all, that would hardly be proper—and unable to spot a stray black sock in the immediate surroundings.

Suddenly Mr. Churchill shouted, "I bet it's under the bed. I unpacked my things on the bed, and maybe it fell off on the floor." He threw himself down beside his bed and stuck his head under the springs.

"I can't see it," he said dismally, sounding muffled. "You have a look from the other side."

I obligingly sprawled out under the wall side of the bed, and peered around, coughing in the dust. At this moment precisely, there was a knock on the door.

"Come in!" bellowed Mr. Churchill, before he thought. I gave a faint scream, and too late Mr. Churchill considered the informality of his position. He tried to get up, too suddenly, and bumped his head severely on the bed slats. He relapsed, groaning, just as the committee of superleading citizens walked in.

Fortunately, I do not now remember the names of those three well-starched, beautifully tailored citizens who marched in on that sock-hunting expedition. It would be frightful to be haunted all my life by their names as well as their faces.

"Mr. Churchill?" said the first leading citizen, in a tone of pained surprise.

Young Mr. Churchill showed the heritage of generations of gentlemen. Still reclining on the floor, he turned his head, nodded an acknowledgment, and said in a loud, belligerent voice, "I'm looking for my lost black sock." The second leading citizen went directly to the bureau and picked up the lost black sock.

"Your sock, sir," he said. Mr. Churchill rose, bowed slightly, and said, "I thank you very much." Then he shouted to me, "Get up! We've found it."

I hesitated. I wanted to stay under that bed and just die there peacefully, without ever having to rise and face those three leading citizens. I did get up, though, feeling the way you do in dreams when you have no clothes on at a gala performance of "Aïda" in the Metropolitan. I suppose, from the expression on the faces of the three leading citizens, that they had not realized until the moment my face slowly emerged from behind the bed that there was a young lady in the room. Each leading citizen did a combination gasp and snort.

"She's coming to hear my lecture," Mr. Churchill announced as he put on his sock. The purple staining my cheeks now rose to my hairline.

"I couldn't," I said weakly. "I couldn't indeed. It's private. They don't allow women in."

"Nevertheless," said Mr. Churchill briskly, "I don't speak unless you come."

The three leading citizens looked so grim I thought I should really faint, although I never had in my whole life. Mr. Churchill and I and the committee now left the room and boarded the elevator. All the way down, Mr. Churchill maintained his position. I was to come or he wouldn't speak. The three leading citizens took turns saying, "But that is impossible, Mr. Churchill. The rules of the club do not permit ladies."

As we got off the elevator, one of the leading citizens, a tall, white-haired man with a large stomach, managed to fall in step with me while the two other leading citizens took Mr. Churchill by the arms.

"Now," said my sudden escort, "you go away fast, and stop bothering Mr. Churchill."

"Me?" I said in honest astonishment. "I never bothered him."

The leading citizen did not stop to argue. "Go away," he hissed, giving me a slight push into the lobby. I went. I was never so glad to leave any place in my life. I wrote my interview that night, and it was a big success. My rival, Ernest, was a picture of jealous confusion when he read it next day. But even the sweet rewards of college fame and my colleagues' envy did not erase the memory of that hideous moment when I was caught, red-handed, looking for Mr. Churchill's sock. It is comparatively easy to recover from honest sorrows, but I wake up in the dead of night at least twice a year and my heart fills with agony, remembering that unspeakable moment when, like a rising moon, my face slowly appeared from behind Mr. Churchill's bed, to confound the three leading citizens of Columbus, Ohio.

Life can hold no further terrors for me.

H. L. Mencken

No living writer has revealed himself more fully
and more frankly than Henry Louis Mencken,
born in Baltimore, Maryland, in 1880. All his
books are candid portrayals of a personality at once
sensitive and skeptical, rowdy and rebellious, full
of inextinguishable gusto. Happy Days and Newspaper Days are obviously autobiographical, but
even so impersonal a treatise as The American Language overflows with a spirit which is not only controversial but catalytic. A master of invective (see
Damn: A Book of Calumny and the various books
of Prejudices), Mencken is as much a pioneer as
a mischief-maker; a lifelong enemy of academicians
and demagogues, he has used his superb vocabulary to champion the unknown and the neglected.
The American literary scene is livelier for his de-
nunciations no less than for his enthusiasms.

Downfall of a Revolutionary

Of all the eminent characters who flourished in the West Baltimore of my infancy, the one most venerated by the boys of my generation was Hoggie Unglebower, an uncouth youth whose empire and influence, radiating out from an humble stable in the alley which ran behind our house in Hollins street, covered altogether an area of at least half a square mile. No storekeeper of that time and place was better known, whether for good or for evil, nor any cop, however heinous, nor any ma'am in the public school up Hollins street hill, nor bad nigger in Vincent alley, nor blind man in practice at Hollins market. Between the longitude of the market and the wilderness of Steuart's Hill, all through a chunk of territory four or five blocks thick, he was a hero to every boy above the age of seven.

The reader of today, soaked in the Freudian sewage for so many years, will assume at once, I suppose, that Hoggie must have been a Lothario, and his headquarters a seraglio. Nothing could have been further from the truth. He was actually almost a Trappist in his glandular life, and his hormones never gave him any visible trouble until much later on, as I shall show in due course. In the days of his greatest glory his view of all human females was predominantly disdainful, but it never led him to use them wickedly, or even impolitely. When a hired girl issued into the alley to flag a rag-and-bone man or hunt for a lost garbage box he would whistle at her satirically and shout "Ah, there!" but at the same time he always took off his hat. To women of greater age and station he was courteous to an extreme degree, and when he visited a neighboring dwelling with his terriers to purge it of rats he always wiped his feet at the back door, and never failed to address the lady of the house as Ma'am.

No, Hoggie was not carnal in the Catechism sense, and I incline to think that that was one of the reasons all the boys so greatly respected him. The male infantry of today, debauched by Progressive Education and the sex hygiene quackery, are said to be adepts at the arts of love before they are more than half house-broken, but that was certainly not true in my time. The boys of that Mousterian generation, until adolescence came down upon them, regarded girls with frank aversion, and had as little truck with them as with cats or cops. It is, of course, a fact that the probable delights of amour were occasionally discussed, but it was always vaguely and with a considerable uneasiness, for any move to put a concrete project into effect would have involved a close

478

approach to females, and that was never done if it could be helped. What made Hoggie a personage was nothing in that line; it was mainly, and perhaps even only, his successful and notorious resistance to the doctrine that cleanliness is next to godliness.

In his father's stable he led the life dreamed of as ideal by all normal boys, then, now, and forever. No one, it appeared, had any authority (at all events any authority that he recognized) to make him comb his hair, or brush his clothes, or shine his shoes, or wash behind the ears. He wallowed there day in and day out, including especially Sundays, in such slops as every normal boy longs to own, but is seldom permitted to have. Preferring the society of horses and dogs to that of men, he lived among them freely and unashamedly, sleeping with them, eating with them, and sharing his confidences with them. He got his hair cut when he damned well pleased, and it wasn't often. Hating neckties, he never wore them. When he thirsted, he drank from the end of the stable hose, and if anyone stopped to gape at him he squeezed the hose (which was old, soft and full of holes) and sent a fine stream into the gaper's eye.

In brief, a magnificent specimen of Natural Man, somehow surviving unscathed every corruption of an effete and pusillanimous civilization. He came of a bourgeois family and had been to school, but had fought off successfully every effort to denaturize him. His days were busy, and full of enterprises that, to us boys, were important, difficult and romantic. He was the architect, builder and navigator of the largest and fastest double-decker sleds known in West Baltimore, and probably the best repairer of boys' wagons ever seen in Christendom. He knew how to knock a barrel to pieces without splitting any of the staves, and how to put it together again. He could teach tricks to horses, and had so far mastered their vocabulary of whinnies and pawings that he carried on long conversations with them, often laughing at their pawky humor. He was a dog doctor of great gifts, and kept a large stock of medicines for his patients on a shelf in the stable. To cops, despite all their clubs, handcuffs and sidearms, he presented a calm and unflickering eye, and they had a high respect for him, for when he went to the aid of one who was overwhelmed by a passel of bad niggers, the bad niggers lost consciousness almost instantly, and awoke in the watch-house with huge bumps on their heads. Hoggie, disdaining firearms, did his fighting with clubs, and had an arsenal of them ready to hand—little ones for light jobs, and thick, warty shillalahs for really earnest work. When he came down upon a skull something gave way, and it was never Hoggie or his weapon.

He was the best dog-trainer for miles around, and could transfer even the sorriest mutt into a competent ratter. For this purpose he liked to have them young; indeed, he preferred to begin on them as soon as their eyes were open. At that age, of course, they were no match for actual rats, and even the more active sort of mice had the edge on them. To equalize the odds, Hoggie would catch infant rats in a trap, pull their teeth with a pair of pliers, and then throw them into a barrel with a couple of his pupils. As the latter gained in strength and technique, he would test them with rats of gradually larger growth, retaining at first one tooth each, and then two, and then four or five, and finally a whole set, upper and lower. Now and then a freshman was badly mauled in these exercises, but Hoggie did not despair, for he knew that any sort of educational process was bound to be painful, and he preferred the hard way for dogs as for men. His graduates were all recognized virtuosi. One day he let me go along as he took one to a hay-and-feed warehouse for a final examination. The candidate was only a spindly black-and-tan, but within three minutes by the watch he had unearthed, run down and killed a whole bucket of rats, some of them of the fearsome sewer variety, with fangs two inches long.

Hoggie admired dogs, and was admired by them in turn, though his medicating of them ran to heroic measures. His usual prescription for the common run of canine malaises was the better part of half a pound of Glauber's salts. The colored quacks who practised a Dahomeyan farriery in Reveille's livery stable down the street hesitated to give so large a dose to anything short of a cart horse, but Hoggie believed that it was foolish to temporize with disease, and proved it by curing most of his patients. He was also adept at surgery, and could point to at least a dozen dogs that he had treated successfully for broken bones. He sutured the lacerations that followed dog-fights with the thick, black thread used by shoemakers, and always waxed it carefully before setting to work. He was, I believe, the first canine dentist ever in practice in Baltimore; to this day, in fact, they are rare. He pulled the damaged teeth of his patients with the same pair of pliers that he employed to prepare rats for his academy, and sometimes he had to pull very hard. I heard him say once that most dogs, like most human beings, were born with too many teeth, and that getting rid of half a dozen or so toned up their systems and improved their dispositions.

No one that I ever heard of approached him in the delicate art of trimming puppies' tails. His technique was of the whirlwind variety: the tail was off before the puppy had a chance to be alarmed. In my earliest days he had a formidable rival in old Julius, an Aframerican with headquarters in Reveille's stable, but as the years passed he gobbled all of Julius's practice, and in the end his mastery was admitted by everyone. In that era the different breeds of dogs in vogue nearly all wore their tails clipped, so Hoggie was kept busy. I have seen him knock off six or eight of an afternoon, with the whole Hollins-street gang for a gallery. Our own dogs, from the early eighties onward to the middle nineties, all passed through his hands, and every one of them was friendly to him afterward, and wagged its stump whenever it encountered him. He also treated dogs when they took to nibbling grass in the yard or showed other signs of indisposition—always with that massive dose of Glauber's salts as a starter. He had plenty of other medicines, and used them freely on occasion, but he depended mainly on the Glauber's salts, just as Dr. Wiley, our family doctor, depended on castor oil.

Hoggie's incurable boyishness was shown by the fact that, for all his fondness for horses and dogs, he hated cats with a blind and implacable hatred, and spent a great deal of his time tracking them down and executing them. There was a time, indeed, when his chronic war upon them aroused some ill-will in the neighborhood—but not, of course, among the boys. What was done about it I forget, but for a while he locked himself in his stable, and refused to have any truck with human society. Even the cops were given to understand that their room was preferred to their company. But then a stray cat scratched a baby down the block, and under cover of the ensuing uproar Hoggie emerged from his solitude, and resumed his crusade. I well recall the day when, as a gesture of triumph, he threw eight dead cats into the alley in one lot, and got into a row with the street cleaner who had to haul them away.

The street cleaner, it appeared, held that a person engaged in such wholesale slaughters should dispose of his own dead, and not dump them on public officials. He cited the example of the hotels which carted off their own garbage, and that of the candy factory down the alley which kept a wagon to handle its own boiler ashes, but Hoggie refused to allow any weight to the argument. So far as he was concerned, he said, the cats could lie in the alley until the Judgment Day, along with the rats that he heaved out almost daily—the melancholy refuse of his college for puppies. The street cleaner muttered a while longer and threatened several times to submit the whole matter to Murphy the cop, but in the end he loaded the cats upon his cart, and during the weeks that followed he loaded many others. Until a fresh generation of kittens worked its way in from Hollins market, the Union Square neighborhood was almost as bare of *Felidae* as Greenland. A few, of course, survived in houses, but they were kept as closely penned as canary birds.

The boys of the Hollins-street gang believed, like well-educated American boys everywhere else, that cats had nine lives, but Hoggie dissented. He admitted freely that no cat within his experience ever had so little as one life, but he insisted that his researches indicated that five was the limit. Indeed, it was only battle-scarred old Toms who went even that far: the average free-lance cat, depleted by its wandering, precarious life, was disposed of finally after being killed three or four times. One day the alley metaphysician, Old Wesley, undertook to point out a possible statistical fallacy in this doctrine. What evidence was there, he demanded, that the Toms which Hoggie killed five times had not been killed four times before by other executioners, thus making up the classical nine? This argument, rather to the astonishment of his listening admirers, floored Hoggie completely. The louder he howled against it, the more he became confused and out of temper, and in the end he was reduced to the sorry expedient of denouncing Wesley as a sassy nigger, and threatening to set the medical students on him. His failure in the debate, and above all his resort to what amounted to forensic blackmail, lowered his stock with the boys of Hollins street, but not for long. In a little while he recovered face gloriously by staging, in the privacy of his stable, a dog-fight that went down into history as the most gory ever seen in West Baltimore.

Despite his unhappy encounter with Old Wesley, he was commonly on good terms with the colored people who lived in the alley, and exercised a general jurisdiction over them, milder and more understanding than that of the cops. They had a high respect for him, and went to him in their troubles, though in his practice as dog-doctor and cat-

DOWNFALL OF A REVOLUTIONARY

and-rat exterminator he was uncomfortably close to a medical student. He did not hold himself out as skilled at human medicine, but the bottles he kept for dosing dogs were at the disposal of any blackamoor who wanted to try them, and many professed to be benefited. In particular, the liniment he used on dogs run over by carts was said to be very efficacious against rheumatoid afflictions in *Anthropoidea*. Once he scared off all his Aframerican patients by stuffing a dead cat with oats, and using black shoe-buttons for its eyes. This gruesome object, while it remained on exhibition, kept all the colored people out of his stable, though we white boys thought it was very nobby. It didn't last long, for the huge, ferocious rats of Hollins market quickly heard of it, and one night they rushed the stable and devoured it, eyes and all. All that remained of it the next morning was a carriage-bolt that Hoggie had employed to counteract the flaccidity of the oats.

His downfall I can place with reasonable accuracy in the year 1890, when I was ten years old and he must have been about twenty-two or three. One afternoon in Summer, on my way to Reveille's livery stable to visit my father's horse, John, who was laid up with epizootic, I encountered Hoggie at the corner of Baltimore street in such vestments that I stopped dead in my tracks, and gaped at him as if he had been a cop in motley or a two-headed boy. He had on a brand-new suit of store clothes, golden brown in color, and wore a pair of the immense yellow shoes then in fashion—as wide, almost, as a street-car at the ball of the foot, but stretched out to a long point at the toe. On his head was a cart-wheel straw hat with a brim at least six inches deep, and a gorgeous red-and-white ribbon. His collar, which was of fresh celluloid, rose above a boiled shirt that gleamed like snow on the Alps, and around it he wore a bright green four-in-hand tie, with the ends tucked over to expose a stud that glittered like a diamond, but was no doubt something else. He was shaved so closely that his neck and chin were criss-crossed with red gashes, and the rest of his face was a brilliant vermilion. Finally, and most amazing of all, his hair—at least such of it as I could see below his hat—was cropped to its roots according to the best technique of Barber Lehnert. As I passed him, I caught a gust of Jockey Club scent, familiar to me as the special favorite of our current hired girl. I was so astonished that I passed him without greeting him, staring foolishly. He paid no attention to me, but stalked along painfully, like a man in a barrel. I spread the news over the neighborhood, and Hoggie's secret quickly leaked out.

He had succumbed at last, after all his years of outlawry, to one of the most conventional of human weaknesses: he had fallen in love. The ancient psychosis that had floored and made a mock of Marc Antony, Dante and Goethe—but *not* Shakespeare, Napoleon Bonaparte or George Washington—had now fetched him too. Some inconsiderable and probably pie-faced slip of a girl, name unknown, had collared him, tamed him, and made of him the dreadful popinjay that I had seen. The rest of the pathetic story follows classical lines, and is soon told. Hoggie disappeared from his stable, and was reported to be occupying a bedroom in the Unglebower family home, and actually eating at table. In a little while he vanished altogether, and reports came in that he was married to the lady, living in far Northwest Baltimore, and at work as a horse-car driver. That was the last I ever heard of him

Ogden Nash

Born in Rye, New York, August 19, 1902 (Frederic) Ogden Nash, like Caesar's Gaul, is divided into three parts. There is (1) the innovator, (2) the critic, and (3) the humorist. Sometimes Nash keeps these three selves fairly well separated; sometimes he lets them kick up their heels in hilarious unison. Readers were not slow to recognize that Nash had done something new and startling to light verse in America. They chuckled over his irregular lines, his words that nearly-but-do-not-quite match, words which never before had any relation with each other and which would never be on rhyming terms again. They were startled, when he disposed of such a subject as "The Baby" in two such nonchalant lines:

> A bit of talcum
> Is always walcum.

Readers had a good time deciphering Nash's reply to Dorothy Parker's "Men seldom make passes at girls who wear glasses." Nash wrote:

> A girl who is bespectacled,
> She may not get her necktacled;
> But safety pins and bassinets
> Await the girl who fassinets.

When Nash's lighter-than-air lyrics were first assembled it was inevitable that the book should be referred to as The Golden Trashery of Ogden Nashery, but it was soon evident that the slightly lunatic manner was purposely deceptive. Disguised as a clown, Nash was also a social critic, a subtle observer of the human heart, a surprising analyst of man's—and particularly woman's—foibles. He fashioned a kind of nonsense that made extremely good sense; his method of expression had just the right touch of madness, and his recklessness was never without reason.

485

To a Small Boy Standing on My Shoes While I Am Wearing Them

Let's straighten this out, my little man,
And reach an agreement if we can.
I entered your door as an honored guest.
My shoes are shined and my trousers are pressed,
And I won't stretch out and read you the funnies
And I won't pretend that we're Easter bunnies.
If you must get somebody down on the floor,
What in the hell are your parents for?
I do not like the things that you say
And I hate the games that you want to play.
No matter how frightfully hard you try,
We've little in common, you and I.
The interest I take in my neighbor's nursery
Would have to grow to be even cursory,
And I would that performing sons and nephews
Were carted away with the daily refuse,
And I hold that frolicsome daughters and nieces
Are ample excuse for breaking leases.
You may take a sock at your daddy's tummy
Or climb all over your doting mummy,
But keep your attentions to me in check
Or, sonny boy, I will wring your neck.
A happier man today I'd be
Had someone wrung it ahead of me.

The Evening Out

You have your hat and coat on and she says she will be right down,
And you hope so because it is getting late and you are dining on the other side of town,
And you are pretty sure she can't take long,

Because when you left her she already looked as neat and snappy as a
    Cole Porter song,
So you stand around thinking of various things and wondering why
    good rye costs more than Scotch.
And after a while you begin to look at your watch,
And so goes ten minutes, and then fifteen minutes, and then half an hour,
And you listen for the sound of water running because you suspect she
    may have gone back for a bath or a shower,
Or maybe she is taking a nap,
Or possibly getting up a subscription for the benefit of the children of
    the mouse that she said mean things about last night but she is now
    sorry got caught in a trap,
Or maybe she decided her hair was a mess and is now shampooing it,
But whatever she is up to, she is a long time doing it,
And finally she comes down and says she is sorry she couldn't find the
    right lipstick, that's why she was so slow,
And you look at her and she looks marvelous but not a bit more mar-
    velous than she did when you left her forty-five minutes ago,
And you tell her she looks ravishing and she says No, she is a sight,
And you reflect that you are now an hour late, but at any rate she is now
    groomed for the rest of the night,
So you get to your destination and there's the ladies dressing room and
    before you know it she's in it,
But she says she'll be back in a minute,
And so she is, but not to tarry,
No, only to ask you for her bag, which she has forgotten she had asked
    you to carry,
So you linger in the lobby
And wish you had a nice portable hobby,
And you try to pass the time seeing how much you can remember of
    the poetry you learned in school, both good verse and bad verse,
And eventually she re-appears just about as you have decided she was
    in the middle of *Anthony Adverse,*
And she doesn't apologize, but glances at you as if you were Bluebeard
    or Scrooge,
And says why didn't you tell her she had on too much rouge?
And you look to see what new tint she has acquired,
And she looks just the same as she did before she retired,
So you dine, and reach the theater in time for the third act, and then go
    somewhere to dance and sup,
And she says she looks like a scarecrow, she has to go straighten up,

OGDEN NASH

So then you don't see her for quite a long time,
But at last you see her for a moment when she comes out to ask if you
  will lend her a dime,
The moral of all which is that you will have just as much of her company and still save considerable on cover charges and beverages and
  grub
If instead of taking her out on the town, you settle her in a nice comfortable dressing room and then go off and spend the evening at
  the Club.

The Seven Spiritual Ages of
Mrs. Marmaduke Moore

Mrs. Marmaduke Moore, at the age of ten
(Her name was Jemima Jevons then),
Was the quaintest of little country maids.
Her pigtails slapped on her shoulderblades;
She fed the chickens, and told the truth
And could spit like a boy through a broken tooth.
She could climb a tree to the topmost perch,
And she used to pray in the Methodist church.

At the age of twenty her heart was pure,
And she caught the fancy of Mr. Moore.
He broke his troth (to a girl named Alice),
And carried her off to his city palace,
Where she soon forgot her childhood piety
And joined in the orgies of high society.
Her voice grew English, or, say, Australian,
And she studied to be an Episcopalian.

At thirty our lives are still before us,
But Mr. Moore had a friend in the chorus.
Connubial bliss was overthrown
And Mrs. Moore now slumbered alone.
Hers was a nature that craved affection;

She gave herself up to introspection;
Then, finding theosophy rather dry,
Found peace in the sweet Bahai and Bahai.

Forty! and still an abandoned wife.
She felt old urges stirring to life.
She dipped her locks in a bowl of henna
And booked a passage through to Vienna.
She paid a professor a huge emolument
To demonstrate what his ponderous volume meant.
Returning, she preached to the unemployed
The gospel according to St. Freud.

Fifty! she haunted museums and galleries,
And pleased young men by augmenting their salaries.
Oh, it shouldn't occur, but it does occur,
That poets are made by fools like her.
Her salon was full of frangipani,
Roumanian, Russian and Hindustani,
And she conquered par as well as bogey
By reading a book and going Yogi.

Sixty! and time was on her hands—
Maybe remorse and maybe glands.
She felt a need for a free confession
To publish each youthful indiscretion,
And before she was gathered to her mothers,
To compare her sinlets with those of others,
Mrs. Moore gave a joyous whoop,
And immersed herself in the Oxford group.

That is the story of Mrs. Moore,
As far as it goes. But of this I'm sure—
When seventy stares her in the face
She'll have found some other state of grace.
Mohammed may be her Lord and master,
Or Zeus, or Mithros or Zoroaster.
For when a lady is badly sexed
God knows what God is coming next.

The Common Cold

Go hang yourself, you old M.D.!
You shall no longer sneer at me.
Pick up your hat and stethoscope,
Go wash your mouth with laundry soap;
I contemplate a joy exquisite
In never paying you for your visit.
I did not call you to be told
My malady is a common cold.

By pounding brow and swollen lip;
By fever's hot and scaly grip;
By those two red redundant eyes
That weep like woeful April skies;
By racking snuffle, snort, and sniff;
By handkerchief after handkerchief;
This cold you wave away as naught
Is the damnedest cold man ever caught!

Give ear, you scientific fossil!
Here is the genuine Cold Colossal;
The Cold of which researchers dream,
The Perfect Cold, the Cold Supreme.
This honored system humbly holds
The Super-cold to end all colds;
The Cold Crusading for Democracy;
The Führer of the Streptococcracy.

Bacilli swarm within my portals
Such as were ne'er conceived by mortals,
But bred by scientists wise and hoary
In some Olympian laboratory;
Bacteria as large as mice,
With feet of fire and heads of ice
Who never interrupt for slumber
Their stamping elephantine rumba.

A common cold, gadzooks, forsooth!
Ah, yes. And Lincoln was jostled by Booth;

Don Juan was a budding gallant,
And Shakespeare's plays show signs of talent;
The Arctic winter is rather coolish,
And your diagnosis is fairly foolish.
Oh what a derision history holds
For the man who belittled the Cold of Colds!

Bill Nye

In common with Josh Billings and Artemus Ward, Edgar Wilson Nye (1850–1896) was a New England cracker-barrel philosopher. Born in Maine, his parents took him to northern Wisconsin when he was two years old. From Wisconsin Nye moved to Wyoming, where he founded the Laramie Boomerang, a paper which (according to literary historians) became a household word before Nye was thirty.

Nye's humor, like Billings' and Ward's, expresses the average man's reaction against intellectual pretentiousness. As opposed to synthetic culture, Nye offered bland exaggeration and straightfaced burlesque; for sophistication he proposed horse sense. Even his puns reflected the buffoon whose humor was homespun. Reviewing the performance of Peter Jackson, a Negro pugilist who made his theatrical debut in the role of Uncle Tom, Nye wrote: "Jackson was superb anatomically—but not Uncle-tomically."

Twombley's Tale

My name is Twombley, G. O. P. Twombley is my full name and I have had a checkered career. I thought it would be best to have my career checked right through, so I did so.

My home is in the Wasatch Mountains. Far up, where I can see the long, green, winding valley of the Jordan, like a glorious panorama below me, I dwell. I keep a large herd of Angora goats. That is my business. The Angora goat is a beautiful animal—in a picture. But out of a picture he has a style of perspiration that invites adverse criticism.

Still, it is an independent life, and one that has its advantages, too.

When I first came to Utah, I saw one day, in Salt Lake City, a young girl arrive. She was in the heyday of life, but she couldn't talk our language. Her face was oval; rather longer than it was wide, I noticed, and, though she was still young, there were traces of care and other foreign substances plainly written there.

She was an emigrant, about seventeen years of age, and, though she had been in Salt Lake City an hour and a half, she was still unmarried.

She was about the medium height, with blue eyes, that somehow, as you examined them carefully in the full, ruddy light of a glorious September afternoon, seemed to resemble each other. Both of them were that way.

I know not what gave me the courage, but I stepped to her side, and in a low voice told her of my love and asked her to be mine.

She looked askance at me. Nobody ever did that to me before and lived to tell the tale. But her sex made me overlook it. Had she been any other sex that I can think of, I would have resented it. But I would not strike a woman, especially when I had not been married to her and had no right to do so.

I turned on my heel and I went away. I most always turn on my heel when I go away. If I did not turn on my own heel when I went away, whose heel would a lonely man like me turn upon?

Years rolled by. I did nothing to prevent it. Still that face came to me in my lonely hut far up in the mountains. That look still rankled in my memory. Before that my memory had been all right. Nothing had ever rankled in it very much. Let the careless reader who never had his memory rankle in hot weather, pass this by. This story is not for him.

After our first conversation we did not meet again for three years, and then by the merest accident. I had been out for a whole afternoon, hunting an elderly goat that had grown childish and irresponsible. He had

wandered away, and for several days I had been unable to find him. So
I sought for him till darkness found me several miles from my cabin.
I realized at once that I must hurry back, or lose my way and spend the
night in the mountains. The darkness became more rapidly obvious.
My way became more and more uncertain.

Finally I fell down an old prospect shaft. I then resolved to remain
where I was until I could decide what was best to be done. If I had
known that the prospect shaft was there, I would have gone another
way. There was another way that I could have gone, but it did not occur
to me until too late.

I hated to spend the next few weeks in the shaft, for I had not locked
up my cabin when I left it, and I feared that someone might get in while
I was absent and play on the piano. I had also set a batch of bread and
two hens that morning, and all of these would be in sad knead of me
before I could get my business into such shape that I could return.

I could not tell accurately how long I had been in the shaft, for I had
no matches by which to see my watch. I also had no watch.

All at once, someone fell down the shaft. I knew that it was a woman,
because she did not swear when she landed at the bottom. Still, this
could be accounted for in another way. She was unconscious when I
picked her up.

I did not know what to do. I was perfectly beside myself, and so was
she. I had read in novels that when a woman became unconscious people
generally chafed her hands, but I did not know whether I ought to
chafe the hands of a person to whom I had never been introduced.

I could have administered alcoholic stimulants to her but I had
neglected to provide myself with them when I fell down the shaft. This
should be a warning to people who habitually go around the country
without alcoholic stimulants.

Finally she breathed a long sigh and murmured, "Where am I?" I
told her that I did not know, but wherever it might be, we were safe,
and that whatever she might say to me, I would promise her, should go
no farther.

Then there was a long pause.

To encourage further conversation I asked her if she did not think
we had been having a rather backward spring. She said we had, but she
prophesied a long, open fall.

Then there was another pause, after which I offered her a seat on an
old red empty powder can. Still, she seemed shy and reserved. I would
make a remark to which she would reply briefly, and then there would
be a pause of a little over an hour. Still it seemed longer.

Suddenly the idea of marriage presented itself to my mind. If we never got out of the shaft, of course an engagement need not be announced. No one had ever plighted his or her troth at the bottom of a prospect shaft before. It was certainly unique, to say the least. I suggested it to her.

She demurred to this on the ground that our acquaintance had been so brief, and that we had never been thrown together before. I told her that this would be no objection, and that my parents were so far away that I did not think they would make any trouble about it.

She said that she did not mind her parents so much as she did the violent temper of her husband.

I asked her if her husband had ever indulged in polygamy. She replied that he had, frequently. He had several previous wives. I convinced her that in the eyes of the law, and under the Edmunds bill, she was not bound to him. Still she feared the consequences of his wrath.

Then I suggested a desperate plan. We would elope!

I was now thirty-seven years old, and yet had never eloped. Neither had she. So, when the first streaks of rosy dawn crept across the soft, autumnal sky and touched the rich and royal coloring on the rugged sides of the grim old mountains, we got out of the shaft and eloped.

The Stars

There is much in the great field of astronomy that is discouraging to the savant who hasn't the time nor the means to rummage around through the heavens. At times I am almost hopeless, and feel like saying to the great yearnful, hungry world: "Grope on forever. Do not ask me for another scientific fact. Find it out yourself. Hunt up your own new-laid planets, and let me have a rest. Never ask me again to sit up all night and take care of a new-born world, while you lie in bed and reck not."

I get no salary for examining the trackless void night after night when I ought to be in bed. I sacrifice my health in order that the public may know at once of the presence of a red-hot comet, fresh from the factory. And yet, what thanks do I get?

Is it surprising that every little while I contemplate withdrawing from scientific research, to go and skin an eight-mule team down through the dim vista of relentless years?

Then, again, you take a certain style of star, which you learn from Professor Simon Newcomb is such a distance that it takes 50,000 years for its light to reach Boston. Now, we will suppose that after looking over the large stock of new and second-hand stars, and after examining the spring catalogue and price list, I decide that one of the smaller size will do me, and I buy it. How do I know that it was there when I bought it? Its cold and silent rays may have ceased 49,000 years before I was born and the intelligence to be still on the way. There is too much margin between sale and delivery. Every now and then another astronomer comes to me and says: "Professor, I have discovered another new star and intend to file it. Found it last night about a mile and a half south of the zenith, running loose. Haven't heard of anybody who has lost a star of the fifteenth magnitude, about thirteen hands high, with light mane and tail, have you?" Now, how do I know that he has discovered a brand new star? How can I discover whether he is or is not playing an old, threadbare star on me for a new one?

We are told that there has been no perceptible growth or decay in the star business since man began to roam around through space, in his mind, and make figures on the barn door with red chalk showing the celestial time table.

No serious accidents have occurred in the starry heavens since I began to observe and study their habits. Not a star has waxed, not a star has waned to my knowledge. Not a planet has season-cracked or shown any of the injurious effects of our rigorous climate. Not a star has ripened

prematurely or fallen off the trees. The varnish on the very oldest stars
I find on close and critical examination to be in splendid condition. They
will all no doubt wear as long as we need them, and wink on long after
we have ceased to wink back.

In 1866 there appeared suddenly in the northern crown a star of about
the third magnitude and worth at least $250. It was generally conceded
by astronomers that this was a brand new star that had never been used,
but upon consulting Argelander's star catalogue and price list it was
found that this was not a new star at all, but an old, faded star of the
ninth magnitude, with the front breadths turned wrong side out and
trimmed with moonlight along the seams. After a few days of phenome-
nal brightness, it gently ceased to draw a salary as a star of the third
magnitude, and walked home with an Uncle Tom's Cabin company.

It is such things as this that make the life of the astronomer one of
constant and discouraging toil. I have long contemplated, as I say, the
advisability of retiring from this field of science and allowing others to
light the northern lights, skim the milky way and do the other celestial
chores. I would do them myself cheerfully if my health would permit,
but for years I have realized, and so has my wife, that my duties as an
astronomer kept me up too much at night, and my wife is certainly right
about it when she says if I insist on scanning the heavens night after
night, coming home late with the cork out of my telescope and my eyes
red and swollen with these exhausting night vigils, I will be cut down
in my prime. So I am liable to abandon the great labor to which I had
intended to devote my life, my dazzling genius and my princely income.
I hope that other savants will spare me the pain of another refusal, for
my mind is fully made up that unless another skimmist is at once
secured, the milky way will henceforth remain unskum.

Dorothy Parker

Dorothy (Rothschild) Parker, born in 1893 in New Jersey, is not only the author of several books of prose and verse, but the accredited origin of a hundred real and apocryphal witticisms, wise-cracks, and epigrams. Several of these can be found in this volume, and most of them are more bitter than blithe. The humorist, Mrs. Parker insists, is not a funny fellow, but a desperately serious person— today more than ever. "The humorist has never been happy anyhow. Today he is whistling past worse graveyards to worse tunes." The sardonic character of her work is indicated by some of her titles: Enough Rope, Death and Taxes, Laments for the Living, Here Lies. Almost all her tart appraisals have been collected in The Portable Dorothy Parker.

You Were Perfectly Fine

The pale young man eased himself carefully into the low chair, and rolled his head to the side, so that the cool chintz comforted his cheek and temple.

"Oh, dear," he said. "Oh, dear, oh, dear, oh, dear. Oh."

The clear-eyed girl, sitting light and erect on the couch, smiled brightly at him.

"Not feeling so well today?" she said.

"Oh, I'm great," he said. "Corking, I am. Know what time I got up? Four o'clock this afternoon, sharp. I kept trying to make it, and every time I took my head off the pillow, it would roll under the bed. This isn't my head I've got on now. I think this is something that used to belong to Walt Whitman. Oh, dear, oh, dear, oh, dear."

"Do you think maybe a drink would make you feel better?" she said.

"The hair of the mastiff that bit me?" he said. "Oh, no, thank you. Please never speak of anything like that again. I'm through. I'm all, all through. Look at that hand; steady as a humming-bird. Tell me, was I very terrible last night?"

"Oh, goodness," she said, "everybody was feeling pretty high. You were all right."

"Yeah," he said. "I must have been dandy. Is everybody sore at me?"

"Good heavens, no," she said. "Everyone thought you were terribly funny. Of course, Jim Pierson was a little stuffy, there for a minute at dinner. But people sort of held him back in his chair, and got him calmed down. I don't think anybody at the other tables noticed it at all. Hardly anybody."

"He was going to sock me?" he said. "Oh, Lord. What did I do to him?"

"Why, you didn't do a thing," she said. "You were perfectly fine. But you know how silly Jim gets, when he thinks anybody is making too much fuss over Elinor."

"Was I making a pass at Elinor?" he said. "Did I do that?"

"Of course you didn't," she said. "You were only fooling, that's all. She thought you were awfully amusing. She was having a marvelous time. She only got a little tiny bit annoyed just once, when you poured the clam-juice down her back."

"My God," he said. "Clam-juice down that back. And every vertebra a little Cabot. Dear God. What'll I ever do?"

"Oh, she'll be all right," she said. "Just send her some flowers, or something. Don't worry about it. It isn't anything."

"No, I won't worry," he said. "I haven't got a care in the world. I'm sitting pretty. Oh, dear, oh, dear. Did I do any other fascinating tricks at dinner?"

"You were fine," she said. "Don't be so foolish about it. Everybody was crazy about you. The maître d'hôtel was a little worried because you wouldn't stop singing, but he really didn't mind. All he said was, he was afraid they'd close the place again, if there was so much noise. But he didn't care a bit, himself. I think he loved seeing you have such a good time. Oh, you were just singing away, there, for about an hour. It wasn't so terribly loud, at all.".

"So I sang," he said. "That must have been a treat. I sang."

"Don't you remember?" she said. "You just sang one song after another. Everybody in the place was listening. They loved it. Only you kept insisting that you wanted to sing some song about some kind of fusiliers or other, and everybody kept shushing you, and you'd keep trying to start it again. You were wonderful. We were all trying to make you stop singing for a minute, and eat something, but you wouldn't hear of it. My, you were funny."

"Didn't I eat any dinner?" he said.

"Oh, not a thing," she said. "Every time the waiter would offer you something, you'd give it right back to him, because you said that he was your long-lost brother, changed in the cradle by a gypsy band, and that anything you had was his. You had him simply roaring at you."

"I bet I did," he said. "I bet I was comical. Society's Pet, I must have been. And what happened then, after my overwhelming success with the waiter?"

"Why, nothing much," she said. "You took a sort of dislike to some old man with white hair, sitting across the room, because you didn't like his necktie and you wanted to tell him about it. But we got you out, before he got really mad."

"Oh, we got out," he said. "Did I walk?"

"Walk! Of course you did," she said. "You were absolutely all right. There was that nasty stretch of ice on the sidewalk, and you did sit down awfully hard, you poor dear. But good heavens, that might have happened to anybody."

"Oh, surely," he said. "Mrs. Hoover or anybody. So I fell down on the sidewalk. That would explain what's the matter with my— Yes. I see. And then what, if you don't mind?"

"Ah, now, Peter!" she said. "You can't sit there and say you don't remember what happened after that! I did think that maybe you were just a little tight at dinner—oh, you were perfectly all right, and all that, but I did know you were feeling pretty gay. But you were so serious from the time you fell down—I never knew you to be that way. Don't you know, how you told me I had never seen your real self before? Oh, Peter, I just couldn't bear it, if you didn't remember that lovely long ride we took together in the taxi! Please, you do remember that, don't you? I think it would simply kill me, if you didn't."

"Oh, yes," he said. "Riding in the taxi. Oh, yes, sure. Pretty long ride, hmm?"

"Round and round and round the park," she said. "Oh, and the trees were shining so in the moonlight. And you said you never knew before that you really had a soul."

"Yes," he said. "I said that. That was me."

"You said such lovely, lovely things," she said. "And I'd never known, all this time, how you had been feeling about me, and I'd never dared to let you see how I felt about you. And then last night—oh, Peter dear, I think that taxi ride was the most important thing that ever happened to us in our lives."

"Yes," he said. "I guess it must have been."

"And we're going to be so happy," she said. "Oh, I just want to tell everybody! But I don't know—I think maybe it would be sweeter to keep it all to ourselves."

"I think it would be," he said.

"Isn't it lovely?" she said.

"Yes," he said. "Great."

"Lovely!" she said.

"Look here," he said, "do you mind if I have a drink? I mean, just medicinally, you know. I'm off the stuff for life, so help me. But I think I feel a collapse coming on."

"Oh, I think it would do you good," she said. "You poor boy, it's a shame you feel so awful. I'll go make you a highball."

"Honestly," he said, "I don't see how you could ever want to speak to me again, after I made such a fool of myself, last night. I think I'd better go join a monastery in Thibet."

"You crazy idiot!" she said. "As if I could ever let you go away now! Stop talking like that. You were perfectly fine."

She jumped up from the couch, kissed him quickly on the forehead, and ran out of the room.

The pale young man looked after her and shook his head long and slowly, then dropped it in his damp and trembling hands.

"Oh, dear," he said. "Oh, dear, oh, dear, oh, dear."

Little Words

When you are strayed, there is nor bloom nor leaf
    Nor singing sea at night, nor silver birds.
And I may only stare, and shape my grief
    In little words.

I cannot conjure loveliness, to drown
    The bitter woe that racks my chords apart.
The staggering pen that sets my sorrow down
    Feeds at my heart.

There is no mercy in the shifting year;
    No beauty wraps me tenderly about.
I turn to little words—so you, my dear,
    Can spell them out.

S. J. Perelman

A quiet, bespectacled graduate of Brown University, S. (for Sidney) J. (for Joseph) Perelman has driven writing to the verge of irresponsibility and clear across the borders of insanity. "In the dementia praecox field," said Robert Benchley, "he is in a class by himself." Actually Perelman is a master of dead-pan parody. He fashions a prose that, seemingly capricious, is coldly critical; his surrealism is not merely a set of free associations, but a series of satires on high pressure salesmanship, publishers' blurbs, and lush advertising copy. His volumes reveal a genius for garbled non sequiturs: Dawn Ginsbergh's Revenge; Parlor, Bedlam and Bath; Strictly from Hunger; Look Who's Talking; Crazy Like a Fox.

Perelman's is a strange kind of humor. It is the humor of applying logic to the illogical, the intellectual knockabout humor of the mad Marx Brothers and the carefully lunatic manner of Dali. Perelman collects clichés only to detonate them with vicious delight.

Reticent about his personal life—he was born in 1904 in New York—Perelman originally wrote (presumably with a straight face) the following "autobiographical note" for that strictly factual periodical Time, and reprinted it on the jacket of his volume appropriately entitled The Dream Department.

Perelman the Man

A TIMEPORTRAIT

Button-cute, rapier-keen, wafer-thin, and pauper-poor is S. J. Perelman, whose tall, stooping figure is better known to the twilit half-world of five continents than to Publishers' Row. That he possesses the power to become invisible to finance companies; that his laboratory is tooled up to manufacture Frankenstein-type monsters on an incredible scale; and that he owns one of the rare mouths in which butter has never melted are legends treasured by every schoolboy.

Perelman's life reads like a picaresque novel. It began on a bleak shelf of rock in mid-Atlantic near Tristan da Cunha. Transplanted to Rhode Island by a passing Portuguese, he became a man of proverbial strength around the Providence wharves; he could drive a spike through an oak plank with his fist. As there was constant need for this type of skilled labor, he soon acquired enough tuition to enter Brown University. He is chiefly remembered there for translating the epigrams of Martial into colloquial Amharic and designing Brooks Bros.' present trademark, a sheep suspended in a diaper.

Perelman, like many another fledgling writer, headed posthaste for Montparnasse. A redoubtable tosspot and coxcomb, he was celebrated throughout the Quarter for drinking Modigliani under the table; his fondness for this potent Italian *apéritif* still remains unabated. In 1925, disguised as Ashton-Wolfe of the Sûreté, he took to frequenting the *milieu,* the sinister district centering about the rue de Lappe. As "Papa" Thernardier, he organized the gang that stole a towel from the Hotel Claridge and defaced the blotters at the American Express Co. A *démarche* from the Quai d'Orsay shortly forced him to flee Paris.

When, in 1928, the meteoric career of Joe Strong, the Boy Plunger, ended abruptly with the latter's disappearance from Wall Street, few knew that Perelman had ended another chapter. In bloody Cicero, Illinois, swart Sicilian mobsters fingered their roscoes uneasily, dismayed at lightning forays by a new rival. In a scant eight months, no shell of needled beer touched lip in Chicago County without previous tribute to "Nails" Perelman. Implacable, deadly as a puff adder, the hand that triggered a steely automatic could caress a first Folio with equal relish. Able to snatch in fifteen minutes the rest most men required a night for, Perelman spent the balance dictating novels (*Jo Bracegirdle's Ordeal,*

504

The Splendid Sinners), essays (*Winnowings, The Anatomy of Gluttony, Turns with a Stomach*), plays (*Are You There, Wimperis?, Musclebound, Philippa Steps Out*), and scenarios (*She Married Her Double, He Married Himself*).

Retired today to peaceful Erwinna, Pa., Perelman raises turkeys which he occasionally displays on Broadway, stirs little from his alembics and retorts. Those who know hint that the light burning late in his laboratory may result in a breathtaking electric bill. Queried, he shrugs with the fatalism of your true Oriental. *"Mektoub,"* he observes curtly, "It is written."

Nothing But the Tooth

I am thirty-eight years old, have curly brown hair and blue eyes, own a uke and a yellow roadster, and am considered a snappy dresser in my crowd. But the thing I want most in the world for my birthday is a free subscription to *Oral Hygiene,* published by Merwin B. Massol, 1005 Liberty Avenue, Pittsburgh, Pa. In the event you have been repairing your own teeth, *Oral Hygiene* is a respectable smooth-finish technical magazine circulated to your dentist with the compliments of his local supply company. Through its pages runs a recital of the most horrendous and fantastic deviations from the dental norm. It is a confessional in which dentists take down their back hair and stammer out the secrets of their craft. But every time I plunge into its crackling pages at my dentist's, just as I get interested in the story of the Man with the Alveolar Dentures or Thirty Reasons Why People Stay Away from Dentists, the nurse comes out slightly flushed and smoothing her hair to tell me that the doctor is ready. Last Thursday, for example, I was head over heels in the question-and-answer department of *Oral Hygiene.* A frankly puzzled extractionist, who tried to cloak his agitation under the initials "J. S. G.," had put his plight squarely up to the editor: "I have a patient, a woman of 20, who has a full complement of teeth. All of her restorations are gold foils or inlays. She constantly grinds her teeth at night. How can I aid her to stop grinding them? Would it do any good to give her a vellum rubber bite?" But before I could learn whether it was a bite or just a gentle hug the editor recommended, out popped Miss Inchbald with lipstick on her nose, giggling, "The Doctor is free now."

"Free" indeed—"running amok" would be a better way to put it.

I had always thought of dentists as of the phlegmatic type—square-jawed sadists in white aprons who found release in trying out new kinds of burs on my shaky little incisors. One look at *Oral Hygiene* fixed that. Of all the inhibited, timorous, uncertain fumble-bunnies who creep the earth, Mr. Average Dentist is the worst. A filing clerk is a veritable sabre-toothed tiger by comparison. Faced with a decision, your dentist's bones turn to water and he becomes all hands and feet. He muddles through his ordinary routine with a certain amount of bravado, plugging a molar here with chewing gum, sinking a shaft in a sound tooth there. In his spare time he putters around his laboratory making tiny cement cup-cakes, substituting amber electric bulbs for ordinary bulbs in his waiting-room to depress patients, and jotting down nasty little innuendoes about people's gums in his notebook. But let an honest-to-goodness sufferer stagger in with his face out of drawing, and Mr. Average Dentist's nerves go to hell. He runs sobbing to the "Ask *Oral Hygiene*" department and buries his head in the lap of V. C. Smedley, its director. I dip in for a typical sample:

Question—A patient of mine, a girl, 18, returned from school recently with a weird story of lightning having struck an upper right cuspid tooth and checked the enamel on the labial surface nearly two-thirds of the way from the incisal edge toward the neck. The patient was lying on a bed looking out an open window during an electric storm, and this one flash put out the lights of the house, and at the same time, the patient felt a burning sensation (like a burning wire) along the cuspid tooth. She immediately put her tongue on the tooth which felt rough, but as the lights were out she could not see it so she went to bed. (A taste as from a burnt match accompanied the shock.)

Next morning she found the labial of the tooth black. Some of the color came off on her finger. By continually brushing all day with the aid of peroxide, salt, soda and vinegar she removed the remainder of the black, after which the tooth was a yellow shade and there was some roughness on the labial surface.

Could the lightning have caused this and do you recommend smoothing the surface with discs?—R.D.L., D.D.S., Oregon.

Well, Doctor, let us take your story step by step. Miss Muffet told you the sensation was like a burning wire, and she tasted something like a burnt match. Did you think, by any chance, of looking into her mouth for either wire or matches? Did you even think of looking into her mouth? I see no mention of the fact in your letter. You state that she walked in and told you the story, that's all. Of course it never occurred to you that she had brought along her mouth for a reason. Then you say, "she removed the remainder of the black after which the tooth was a yellow shade." Would it be asking too much of you to make up your mind? Was it a tooth or a yellow shade? You're quite sure it wasn't a Venetian blind? Or a gaily striped awning? Do you ever take a drink in the daytime, Doctor?

Frankly, men, I have no patience with such idiotic professional behavior. An eighteen-year-old girl walks into a dentist's office exhibiting obvious symptoms of religious hysteria (stigmata, etc.). She babbles vaguely of thunderstorms and is patently a confirmed drunkard. The dentist goes to pieces, forgets to look in her mouth, and scurries off to *Oral Hygiene* asking for permission to smooth her surface with discs. It's mercy he doesn't take matters into his own hands and try to plough every fourth tooth under. This is the kind of man to whom we intrust our daughters' dentures.

There is practically no problem so simple that it cannot confuse a dentist. For instance, thumb-sucking. "Could you suggest a method to correct thumb and index finger sucking by an infant of one year?" flutters a Minnesota orthodontist, awkwardly digging his toe into the hot sand. Dr. Smedley, whose patience rivals Job's, has an answer for everything: "Enclose the hand by tying shut the end of the sleeve of a sleeping garment, or fasten a section of a pasteboard mailing tube to the sleeping garment in such a position as to prevent the bending of the elbow sufficiently to carry the thumb or index finger to the mouth." Now truly, Dr. Smedley, isn't that going all the way around Robin Hood's barn? Nailing the baby's hand to the high-chair is much more cozy, or, if no nail is available, a smart blow with the hammer on Baby's fingers will slow him down. My grandfather, who was rather active in the nineties (between Columbus and Amsterdam Avenues—they finally got him for breaking and entering), always used an effective method to break children of this habit. He used to tie a Mills grenade to the baby's thumb with cobbler's waxed thread, and when the little spanker pulled out the detonating pin with his teeth, Grandpa would stuff his fingers into his ears and run like the wind. Ironically enough, the people with whom Grandpa now boards have the same trouble keeping him from biting his thumbs, but overcome it by making him wear a loose jacket with very long sleeves, which they tie to the bars.

I have always been the mildest of men, but you remember the old saying "Beware the fury of a patient man." (I remember it very well and put my finger on it instantly, page 269 of Bartlett's book of quotations.) For years I have let dentists ride rough-shod over my teeth; I have been sawed, hacked, chopped, whittled, bewitched, bewildered, tattooed, and signed on again; but this is cuspid's last stand. They'll never get *me* into that chair again. I'll dispose of my teeth as I see fit, and after they're gone, I'll get along. I started off living on gruel, and, by God, I can always go back to it again.

Hold That Christmas Tiger!

Some few years ago there was translated to the screen as a vessel for the talents of Warner Baxter a play called "I Loved You Wednesday." The result was an amiable little film which undoubtedly recovered its investment, earned a snug profit, and in the normal course of things was retired to be cut into mandolin picks. What makes it still verdant in the memory of connoisseurs, however, is a patch of dialogue that came about the end of the first reel. Mr. Baxter, in beautifully tailored breeches and cordovans, had been established as a construction engineer on a vast, unidentified power project, barking crisp commands at giant cranes and chivying steam shovels. The scene then dissolved to his home, and as the work-worn engineer entered, his wife looked up eagerly from her sewing. "What's new, dear?" she inquired. "Well, darling," replied Baxter, inhaling deeply and brushing clouds of alkali from his shoulders, "I just finished Boulder Dam." "Oh, *Jim!*" murmured his wife adoringly.

It may be presumptuous of me to compare myself in any sense with Mr. Baxter (I am twenty pounds lighter, not quite as photogenic, and infinitely less solvent), but if sheer doggedness and fighting heart mean anything, the undertaking I have just completed may yet outclass his. At ten o'clock this morning, fortified with a bottle of benzedrine and a stoup of black coffee, I kissed my newsdealer good-bye and set out to read through the Christmas-party suggestions in *Mademoiselle*, *Vogue*, and *House & Garden*. "It's madness, Derek!" implored the handful of friends who had come down to see me off. "Think it over, old man! You'll never get through!" I smiled grimly, set my jaw as well as a serious case of malocclusion would allow, and plunged into the perfume advertising. Hours later, gray with fatigue and my eyes those of a man who had looked on things better left veiled from mortal gaze, I stumbled out of the back cover of *House & Garden* and fell forward into the waiting arms of my friends.

Perhaps the most soaring imagination displayed in any of the three magazines is that of a Mr. Lester Gaba, whom *Mademoiselle* called in to advise its readers regarding their Christmas décor. It is Mr. Gaba's thesis that, given a little energy and a few everyday materials, Christmas need never be stodgy. His first target is the tree itself. "Dip tips of twisted cotton strips into India ink and trim your tree entirely with 'ermine tails,' " he orders. "Pin a fresh mauve orchid to the treetop." Arresting as the effect might be, the actual execution seems a bit less simple. "Well, what do we do next?" I can hear a Mr. Kapustin asking his wife as he finishes tacking up the last holly wreath. Mrs. Kapustin peers uncertainly at her copy of *Mademoiselle*. " 'Tip dips of twisted crotton sips—' " she begins. "No, wait a minute. 'Sip dips of cristed totton tips—' " Obviously, such an enterprise can only end in disaster. Either Mr. Kapustin, who is extremely short-tempered, snatches the magazine from his wife, provoking a free-for-all, or the dawn discloses two pallid householders on the verge of a breakdown, mumbling, "Dip, dip, dip."

Next turning his attention to the lighting, Mr. Gaba says, "Go medieval: get Gothic-lantern effects by shielding ceiling bulbs with pierced, rectangular tin food-graters." It might be well to temper your enthusiasm for this novel hint with a pinch of caution, unless you want a dusky handmaiden mounted on a chair right in the middle of your party, grating carrots over the shoulders of your guests and murmuring bitterly to herself in Gullah. In the event you do, the best plan would be to sprinkle artificial snow around her feet and drape her with silver festoons and candy canes. It is certainly just as feasible as another of Mr. Gaba's suggestions: "Tie blown-up, red penny balloons to your outdoor Christmas trees. The kids in the block will pop them quick like a flash—but who cares?" Who indeed but an old Scrooge? I, for one, can think of no more diverting pastime than beating off stinging pellets from a bean-blower while setting 'em up in the next alley for a little marksman. The same promise of high adventure pervades still another of Mr. Gaba's proposals: "Decorate your mantel with a begged, borrowed, or stolen French horn filled cornucopia-style with holly and mistletoe." No French-horn player around Carnegie Hall will refuse to turn over his instrument to you once the purpose is explained to him. Should he prove reluctant, simply read him Mr. Gaba's article, and if that fails to stun him, sap him just below the left ear with a blackjack. Anybody so deficient in Christmas spirit, and above all a French-horn player, is hardly worth your sympathy.

Conscious of its august tradition, *Vogue* naturally scorns any such pinchpenny devices as the foregoing. Its article on the subject permits the reader to flatten his nose against the windows of several great houses and watch their occupants celebrate. Mrs. Frederick Frelinghuysen, for instance, occasionally "masques all the curtains in great lengths of red mosquito netting," a mystifying rite, since there are surely no red mosquitoes in Mrs. Frelinghuysen's well-ordered home. (Who the devil Mrs. Frelinghuysen is I have no idea, but it is a cinch from the context that she has a well-ordered home.) Another family brews up an appalling mixture of port, brandy, Burgundy, almonds and raisins, called *glögg*, and then, I presume, proceeds to get quietly glöggy. A deeply religious bachelor, whose name is unfortunately not given, "once set his Christmas table with all sorts of mechanical toys. As the guests entered the dining room, the wound-up dolls, acrobats, animals, merry-go-rounds began performing their mechanical tricks." The effect on the guests, already reeling with *glögg*, must have been a curious one. Somehow, I have the feeling that everybody started turning handsprings, tearing down the smilax, and beating the tar out of the host—a thing he richly deserved.

No such chronicle, of course, would be complete without mention of Hollywood's method of observing the holiday. Mrs. Richard Barthelmess, I discovered, "often trims her trees with Cellophane tassels or opalescent glass bubbles," so refreshing after the opalescent iron bubbles one encounters everywhere. The Charles Boyers "cajole little pickaninnies to sing the Christmas carols." As one who in eight years has yet to see a pickaninny, big or little, within the confines of Beverly Hills, I can only conclude that the Boyers must range all the way to Georgia and Mississippi for their tiny songsters. Mr. Boyer is a very persuasive article, but that threatens to stand as an all-time high in cajolery.

It was left to that ordinarily staid journal of gracious living, *House & Garden*, however, to emerge with the one truly brilliant inspiration of the season—an upside-down evergreen tree swung from the ceiling. To any human flies within the sound of my voice, here is an open invitation: Drop around at my flat whenever you like on Christmas Eve with your suction shoes and have a cup of *glögg* on our ceiling. The Kapustins will be there and so will Mr. Gaba, if he isn't tied up (figuratively speaking, of course). You'll know me right away because my eyes will be so radiant; and, besides, I'll have a fresh mauve orchid in my hair—to say nothing of *Mademoiselle, Vogue,* and *House & Garden.*

The Lunatic Fringe

As early as Shakespeare's time, and probably long before, people laughed at simpletons. The zany is still one of our most popular clowns. Perhaps it is because we all have a touch of madness that we can smile at the absurdities of the village idiot. Perhaps it flatters our sense of superiority to chuckle at the remarks of fools.

Lately there has been a flood of stories about morons, a mildly patronizing term for those who are halfway between low grade intellects and high class idiots, the unfortunates who win our sympathy even while they rouse our derision. Here are a few choice specimens.

Two patients of the asylum were looking over the wall, watching the gardener.

"What's he doing?" said the first.

"Putting fertilizer on the strawberries," said the second.

"Fertilizer on the strawberries!" exclaimed the first. "We put sugar and cream on ours—and they call *us* crazy!"

"Young man," said the professor to the student who kept on interrupting, "are you trying to instruct this class?"

"Certainly not, sir," said the student.

"Well, then, don't talk like an idiot."

Two men just released from the lunatic asylum meet on the street.

"Bet you," says the first, "you can't guess what I've got in my hand."

"A battleship?" asks the second.

The first looks in his closed hand a moment, and then says "No."

"An automobile?" hazards the second.

Another cautious look, and "No," says the first. "Try once more."

"A horse!" shouts the second.

"Darn it," says the first. "But what color?"

"Green," says the second.

"Ah," says the first, "you peeked!"

One moron was painting the ceiling as the other entered the room.

"Got a good grip on your brush?" asked the newcomer.

"Sure," said the painter.

"Well, hold tight to it. I'm taking away the ladder."

"I can do anything in the world, for I am the master of space and time," said the first lunatic. "Nothing is impossible for me."

"There's one thing you can't do," said the second. "When I throw a beam of light from my flashlight I'll bet you can't walk up on it."

"Do you think I'm an idiot?" said the first. "When I'm half way up you'll turn off the light."

"Is this number 1—1—1—1?" asked the voice over the telephone.

"No," replied the moron. "This is eleven-eleven."

"Sorry to have bothered you," said the voice.

"No bother," said the moron. "I was getting up anyway to answer the phone."

Once more the telephone rang. "What is it?" asked the moron.

"It's a Long Distance from New York," replied the operator.

"I know it is," said the moron, and went back to bed.

An eccentric millionaire decided to build a log-house entirely of knot-holes. He was explaining it to his even more eccentric companion. "See?" said the first. "These are all knot-holes."

"Perhaps," said the second. "But they look like holes to me."

Two morons had remarkable good luck on a fishing expedition. Toward the end of the day one of them said, "This is a good spot. I wish we had some way of finding it tomorrow."

"Why don't you put a mark on the boat?" said the other.

"That sounds reasonable," said the first. "But how do you know that we'll get the same boat?"

The fighting between the Germans and the Russians had come to an end in the middle of a field belonging to a stupid Russian peasant. Both sides determined to give him a choice of nationality.

"If he has any sense," said the Nazi general, "he'll become a German."

"Nonsense," retorted the Soviet leader. "Naturally, he'll remain Russian."

When the peasant decided that he and his field should be part of the German Reich the Russian general was astounded. "But why?" he asked.

"Well, you see," replied the peasant, "the winters in Soviet Russia are so cold."

The fashionable psychiatrist finished his notes and turned to the lady in front of him. "I'll be perfectly frank," he said. "I find nothing the matter—nothing abnormal—and I shall so inform your relatives."

"Thank you, doctor, I was sure you'd say that," she replied. "I only came here to please my family. After all, there's nothing very strange about a fondness for pancakes, is there?"

"Pancakes?" repeated the psychiatrist. "Certainly not. I'm fond of them myself."

"Are you?" she queried brightly. "Then you must come over to my house. I have trunks full of them!"

Leonard Q. Ross

Leo Calvin Rosten was born in Poland in 1908. Educated in Chicago, he studied to be a lawyer, became an economist, and wrote such sharp analyses as The Washington Correspondents and Hollywood: The Movie Colony. A job teaching English to adult foreigners in a night school led to the creation of Rosten's alter ego, Leonard Q. Ross, and the inimitable The Education of H*y*m*a*n K*a*p*l*a*n.

The humorist (Ross) and the economist (Rosten) are not as far apart as the record indicates. The sketches originally published in The New Yorker are the result of a sensitive eye and a delicately recording ear; the blushing Miss Mitnick, the plodding Mr. Bloom, and the irrepressible Hyman Kaplan are all the more comic for being entirely convincing.

The Education of
H·Y·M·A·N K·A·P·L·A·N

In the third week of the new term, Mr. Parkhill was forced to the conclusion that Mr. Kaplan's case was rather difficult. Mr. Kaplan first came to his special attention, out of the thirty-odd adults in the beginners' grade of the American Night Preparatory School for Adults ("English—Americanization—Civics—Preparation for Naturalization"), through an exercise the class had submitted. The exercise was entitled "Fifteen Common Nouns and Their Plural Forms." Mr. Parkhill came to one paper which included the following:

house	makes	houses
dog	"	dogies
library	"	Public library
cat	"	Katz

Mr. Parkhill read this over several times, very thoughtfully. He decided that here was a student who might, unchecked, develop into a "problem case." It was clearly a case that called for special attention. He turned the page over and read the name. It was printed in large, firm letters with red crayon. Each letter was outlined in blue. Between every two letters was a star, carefully drawn, in green. The multi-colored whole spelled, unmistakably, H*Y*M*A*N K*A*P*L*A*N.

This Mr. Kaplan was in his forties, a plump, red-faced gentleman, with wavy blond hair, *two* fountain pens in his outer pocket, and a perpetual smile. It was a strange smile, Mr. Parkhill remarked: vague, bland, and consistent in its monotony. The thing that emphasized it for Mr. Parkhill was that it never seemed to leave the face of Mr. Kaplan, even during Recitation and Speech period. This disturbed Mr. Parkhill considerably, because Mr. Kaplan was particularly bad in Recitation and Speech.

Mr. Parkhill decided he had not applied himself as conscientiously as he might to Mr. Kaplan's case. That very night he called on Mr. Kaplan first.

"Won't *you* take advantage of Recitation and Speech practice, Mr. Kaplan?" he asked, with an encouraging smile.

Mr. Kaplan smiled back and answered promptly, "Vell, I'll tell abot Prazidents United States. Fife Prazidents United States is Abram Lin-
516

cohen, he vas freeink de neegers; Hodding, Coolitch, Judge Vashington, an' Banjamin Frenklin."

Further encouragement revealed that in Mr. Kaplan's literary Valhalla the "most famous tree American wriders" were Jeck Laundon, Valt Viterman, and the author of "Hawk L. Barry-Feen," one Mocktvain. Mr. Kaplan took pains to point out that he did not mention Relfvaldo Amerson because "He is a poyet, an' I'm talkink abot wriders."

Mr. Parkhill diagnosed the case as one of "inability to distinguish between 'a' and 'e.' " He concluded that Mr. Kaplan *would* need special attention. He was, frankly, a little disturbed.

Mr. Kaplan's English showed no improvement during the next hard weeks. The originality of his spelling and pronunciation, however, flourished—like a sturdy flower in the good, rich earth. A man to whom "Katz" is the plural of "cat" soon soars into higher and more ambitious endeavor. As a one-paragraph "Exercise in Composition," Mr. Kaplan submitted:

When people is meating on the boulvard, on going away one is saying, "I am glad I mat you," and the other is giving answer, "Mutual."

Mr. Parkhill felt that perhaps Mr. Kaplan had overreached himself, and should be confined to the simpler exercises.

Mr. Kaplan was an earnest student. He worked hard, knit his brows regularly (albeit with that smile), did all his homework, and never missed a class. Only once did Mr. Parkhill feel that Mr. Kaplan might, perhaps, be a little more *serious* about his work. That was when he asked Mr. Kaplan to "give a noun."

"Door," said Mr. Kaplan, smiling.

It seemed to Mr. Parkhill that "door" had been given only a moment earlier, by Miss Mitnick.

"Y-es," said Mr. Parkhill. "Er—and another noun?"

"Another door," Mr. Kaplan replied promptly.

Mr. Parkhill put him down as a doubtful "C." Everything pointed to the fact that Mr. Kaplan might have to be kept on an extra three months before he was ready for promotion to Composition, Grammar, and Civics, with Miss Higby.

One night Mrs. Moskowitz read a sentence, from "English for Beginners," in which "the vast deserts of America" were referred to. Mr. Parkhill soon discovered that poor Mrs. Moskowitz did not know the meaning of "vast." "Who can tell us the meaning of 'vast'?" asked Mr. Parkhill lightly.

Mr. Kaplan's hand shot up, volunteering wisdom. He was all proud grins. Mr. Parkhill, in the rashness of the moment, nodded to him.

Mr. Kaplan rose, radiant with joy. "'Vast!' It's commink fromm *diraction*. Ve have four diractions: de naut, de sot, de heast, and de vast."

Mr. Parkhill shook his head. "Er—that is 'west,' Mr. Kaplan." He wrote "VAST" and "WEST" on the blackboard. To the class he added, tolerantly, that Mr. Kaplan was apparently thinking of "west," whereas it was "vast" which was under discussion.

This seemed to bring a great light into Mr. Kaplan's inner world. "So is 'vast' vat you eskink?"

Mr. Parkhill admitted that it was "vast" for which he was asking.

"Aha!" cried Mr. Kaplan. "You minn *'vast,'* not"—with scorn— "'vast.'"

"Yes," said Mr. Parkhill, faintly.

"Hau Kay!" said Mr. Kaplan, essaying the vernacular. "Ven I'm buyink a suit clothes, I'm gattink de cawt, de pents, an' de vast!"

Stunned, Mr. Parkhill shook his head, very sadly. "I'm afraid that you've used still another word, Mr. Kaplan."

Oddly enough, this seemed to give Mr. Kaplan great pleasure.

Several nights later Mr. Kaplan took advantage of Open Questions period. This ten-minute period was Mr. Parkhill's special innovation in the American Night Preparatory School for Adults. It was devoted to answering any questions which the students might care to raise about any difficulties which they might have encountered during the course of their adventures with the language. Mr. Parkhill enjoyed Open Questions. He liked to clear up *practical* problems. He felt he was being ever so much more constructive that way. Miss Higby had once told him that he was a born Open Questions teacher.

"Plizz, Mr. Pockheel," asked Mr. Kaplan as soon as the period opened. "Vat's de minnink fromm—" It sounded, in Mr. Kaplan's rendition, like "a big department."

" 'A big department,' Mr. Kaplan?" asked Mr. Parkhill, to make sure.

"Yassir!" Mr. Kaplan's smile was beauteous to behold. "In de stritt, ven I'm valkink, I'm hearink like 'I big de pottment.' "

It was definitely a pedagogical opportunity.

"Well, class," Mr. Parkhill began. "I'm sure that you have all——"

He told them that they had all probably done some shopping in the large downtown stores. (Mr. Kaplan nodded.) In these large stores, he said, if they wanted to buy a pair of shoes, for example, they went to a special *part* of the store, where only shoes were sold—a *shoe* department. (Mr. Kaplan nodded.) If they wanted a table, they went to a different *part* of the store, where *tables* were sold. (Mr. Kaplan nodded.) If they wanted to buy, say, a goldfish, they went to still another part of the store, where goldfish . . . (Mr. Kaplan frowned; it was clear that Mr. Kaplan had never bought a goldfish.)

"Well, then," Mr. Parkhill summed up hastily, "each article is sold in a different *place*. These different and special places are called *departments*." He printed "D-E-P-A-R-T-M-E-N-T" on the board in large, clear capitals. "And a *big* department, Mr. Kaplan, is merely such a department which is large—*big*!"

He put the chalk down and wiped his fingers.

"Is that clear now, class?" he asked, with a little smile. (It was rather an ingenious explanation, he thought; it might be worth repeating to Miss Higby during the recess.)

It *was* clear. There were thirty nods of approval. But Mr. Kaplan looked uncertain. It was obvious that Mr. Kaplan, a man who would not compromise with truth, did *not* find it clear.

"Isn't that clear *now*, Mr. Kaplan?" asked Mr. Parkhill anxiously.

Mr. Kaplan pursed his lips in thought. "It's a *fine* haxplination, Titcher," he said generously, "but I don' unnistand vy I'm hearink de voids de vay I do. Simms to me it's used in annodder minnink."

"There's really only one meaning for 'a big department.' " Mr. Parkhill was definitely worried by this time. "*If* that's the phrase you mean."

Mr. Kaplan nodded gravely. "Oh, dat's de phrase—ufcawss! It sonds like dat—or maybe a lettle more like '*I* big de pottment.' "

Mr. Parkhill took up the chalk. ("*I* big department" was obviously a case of Mr. Kaplan's own curious audition.) He repeated the explanation carefully, this time embellishing the illustrations with a shirt department, a victrola section, and "a separate part of the store where, for example, you buy canaries, or other birds."

Mr. Kaplan sat entranced. He followed it all politely, even the part about "canaries, or other birds." He smiled throughout with consummate reassurance.

Mr. Parkhill was relieved, assuming, in his folly, that Mr. Kaplan's smiles were a testimony to his exposition. But when he had finished, Mr. Kaplan shook his head once more, this time with a new and superior firmness.

"Is the explanation *still* not clear?" Mr. Parkhill was genuinely concerned by this time.

"Is de haxplination clear!" cried Mr. Kaplan with enthusiasm. "Ha! I should live so! Soitinly! Clear like *gold!* So clear! An' netcheral too! But Mr. Pockheel——"

"Go on, Mr. Kaplan," said Mr. Parkhill, studying the white dust on his fingers. There was, after all, nothing more to be done.

"Vell! I think it's more like '*I* big de pottment.' "

"Go on, Mr. Kaplan, go on." (*Domine, dirige nos.*)

Mr. Kaplan rose. His smile was broad, luminous, transcendent; his manner was regal.

"I'm hearink it in de stritt. Somtimes I'm stendink in de stritt, talkink to a frand, or mine vife, mine brodder—or maybe only stendink. An' somvun is pessink arond me. An' by hexident he's givink me a bump, you know, a *poosh!* Vell, he says, 'Axcuse me!' no? But somtimes, an' *dis* is vat I minn, he's sayink '*I big de pottment!*' "

Mr. Parkhill studied the picture of "Abram Lincohen" on the back wall, as if reluctant to face reality. He wondered whether he could reconcile it with his conscience if he were to promote Mr. Kaplan to Composition, Grammar, and Civics—at once. Another three months of Recitation and Speech might, after all, be nothing but a waste of Mr. Kaplan's valuable time.

JEWISH LOGIC

Jewish humor is essentially logical. It is often so *painstakingly* logical that it reduces reason to absurdity. Argument becomes an art that is both hair-splitting and side-splitting.

There are, for example, countless variations on the theme of the two business rivals who are always outwitting each other. But the classic version concerns two pedlars who meet early one morning in the railway station.

Says the first, "Where are you going today?"

The second hesitates a moment and then replies, "I'm going to Minsk."

"Shame upon you!" says the first. "When you say you're going to Minsk you want me to believe you're going to Lemberg. Now I happen to know that you *are* going to Minsk. What are you lying for!"

"The house may seem a little shabby, but the people are well off," said the marriage-broker to his prospective but hesitant client. "Observe the expensive furnishings. Examine those delicate china dishes. Look at this elegant silver service. Feel these fine linens—"

"But," interrupted the suspicious young bridegroom-to-be, "to make a good impression they may have borrowed those things."

"Borrowed!" snorted the marriage-broker. "Borrowed! Who'd lend anything to such paupers!"

"Don't worry about her family," said the marriage-broker to the reluctant young man. "Her family is one of the best. Besides, you'll never have to support any member of it; the girl is an orphan."

A few days after the engagement was announced the young man assaulted the marriage-broker.

"You fraud!" he shouted. "An orphan indeed! I've found out that the girl's father is not only living, but is in prison!"

"Ah," groaned the marriage-broker, "you can't call that 'living'!"

521

Law has its own brand of logic. It follows an intricate rabbinical form of reasoning.

Mandelstam was brought into court for having damaged a precious jar borrowed from Ginsberg. But Mandelstam's lawyer was equal to the emergency.

"We have three lines of defense, your Honor," began the attorney. "In the first place we will prove that Mandelstam never borrowed the jar from Ginsberg. In the second place we will prove that when Mandelstam borrowed the jar, it was already damaged beyond repair. And in the third place, we will prove that when Mandelstam returned it, it was in absolutely perfect condition."

The Schnorrer is, to put it meagerly, a beggar. But he is a beggar plus tradition, a beggar with a combination of dignity and effrontery, a beggar with joy in his calling and pride in his craft. He accepts gratuities not as a dole, but as his right.

One of the stories which illustrates the Schnorrer's pride is at least a hundred years old and concerns an encounter with Baron Rothschild.

"Look," said the great philanthropist, "you know you will receive your weekly gift, so it's not necessary to whine so much about your condition. A little less cringing, a little less sniveling would be better not only for your patrons but for you."

"Baron Rothschild," said the Schnorrer stiffly, "I don't teach you how to be a millionaire. Please don't teach me how to schnorr!"

Most of the Schnorrer stories revolve about the fabulously wealthy Baron Rothschild. One in particular is a perfect example of logic and effrontery.

A Schnorrer had coughed so alarmingly and told so pitiful a story that Baron Rothschild had sent him to his physician, adding that he would pay the bill.

"Well," said the Schnorrer a few days later, "the doctor says I must go to the seashore for two weeks. So I've chosen Ostend."

"But," exclaimed Rothschild, "why Ostend, the gayest of watering places, and the most expensive?"

"Baron Rothschild," replied the Schnorrer in a tone of reproof, "for my health nothing is too expensive!"

Lachs, or smoked salmon, is considered a great Jewish delicacy, particularly by those who cannot afford it.

"My wife is dangerously ill, my son is in debt, my daughter's clothes are in rags, and I owe three months' rent. I simply must have twenty gold marks," pleaded the Schnorrer.

"All right," said Baron Rothschild, "I'll give them to you." Then, turning to his major-domo, the philanthropist whispered, "I don't quite trust that fellow. Follow him and see what becomes of the money."

When the Schnorrer came for next week's contribution, Baron Rothschild was in a rage. "You scoundrel!" he cried. "You wheedling rogue! As soon as you left my house you went to a delicatessen and spent the entire twenty gold marks on *lachs*."

"It's true," said the Schnorrer sadly. "But put yourself in my position. When I've got no money I can't buy *lachs*. When I *have* money I can't buy *lachs*. Tell me, Baron Rothschild, when *can* I buy *lachs*!"

"Pay attention to this problem, Ikey," said the teacher. "If you had ten pennies and lost three, how many would you have left?"

"But, teacher," said little Ikey, "why should I lose three pennies?"

In the middle of the night Isaac Levy was wakened by a phone call. The voice at the other end inquired, "Is this the residence of Mr. Frederick Jay Van Norden?"

"Oy!" laughed Levy. "Have *you* got a wrong number!"

Two good friends, Father Kelly and Rabbi Levi, sat opposite each other at a banquet where roast ham was served. After Father Kelly had helped himself liberally, he turned to his friend and said:

"Rabbi Levi, when are you going to become liberal enough to eat ham?"

"At your wedding, Father Kelly," retorted the rabbi.

"One of my ancestors," the Virginian boasted, "signed the Declaration of Independence."

"Indeed," replied the Jew. "One of mine signed the Ten Commandments."

The old shopkeeper was dying; his whole family was gathered about him. Just before he lost consciousness, he asked: "Is momma here?"

"Yes, poppa," answered his wife.

"Is Jakey here?"

"Yes, poppa."

"Is Rifke here?"

"Yes, poppa—right here."

"Is my nephew Milton here?"

"Yes, uncle—we're all here."

"All of you!" cried the dying man. "Then who's minding the store!"

George Jessel swears that he was on his way to the theater when a stranger gave him a terrific thump on the back and cried, "Hello, Finkelstein."

"I'm not Finkelstein," protested Jessel.

"You're not Finkelstein?" said the stranger.

"I certainly am not," said Jessel indignantly. "And even if I were, is that a way to greet a friend by punching him hard in the back?"

"Say," replied the walloper, "who are you to tell me how to treat Finkelstein?"

The synagogue was crowded during the high Holy Days and the pews were reserved for ticket-holders. Lapidis tried to get past the usher. "It's my brother—I've got to see him—it's very important."

"Have you got a ticket?" asked the usher.

"No," said Lapidis. "But I just *got* to see my brother—it's a matter of life or death."

"All right," said the usher. "Go inside and talk to your brother. But don't let me catch you praying!"

"The food at 'Paradise Manor' was awful," complained Mrs. Feitel-baum. "Every mouthful was poison, positive poison. And, to make it worse, the portions were so small!"

After T. Whitney Nadelson had entered the upper income tax brackets, Mrs. Nadelson entertained heavily. Her proudest moment came when she gave an afternoon tea for the literary lion of the day. "Do have another of those delicious little cakes," she urged.

"Thank you," said the lion. "But I've already had two."

"You've had five," Mrs. Nadelson corrected him. "But *who's counting?*"

Perhaps the most logical of Jewish jokes is the one about Otto H. Kahn, the eminent banker. Driving through New York's East Side, he saw a huge sign over a small clothing store. The sign read:

Abram Cahn
Cousin of Otto H. Kahn

Indignantly the financier called his attorney and the latter threatened suit. The East Side merchant promised to take down the sign. A week later the banker drove past to see whether the offending sign had been removed. It had. There was a new sign, and it read:

Abram Cahn
Formerly cousin of
OTTO H. KAHN

Count Esterhazy was organizing an expedition to the Near East and beyond. He had engaged most of the helpers, but he needed a general factotum for the long journey. Knowing the position was hard to fill, he advertised for a seasoned traveler who spoke the languages of the Near East, a fearless swordsman, an intrepid rider, etcetera. The advertisement was worded to attract only the right man—and there were no applicants. After a week, the butler announced that a small and shabby looking fellow had come in response to the ad.

"He doesn't sound very promising," said Count Esterhazy, "but show him up."

The man proved to be even less prepossessing than the butler's description. But clothes do not always make the man, and the Count began by asking, "You like to travel?"

"Me?" said the little man. "I hate traveling. Boats make me seasick. And trains are worse."

"But you are a linguist," continued the Count. "I presume you speak Arabian, Persian, Turkish, Hindustani—"

"Who? Me?" gasped the candidate. "I talk nothing but Yiddish."

"Your swordsmanship?" inquired the Count.

"What do you mean, swordsmanship? What should I do with a sword?"

"And as a horseman?"

"I hate horses. I wouldn't go near one."

"But," said the Count, "what did you come here for?"

"I saw your ad," said the man, "and I just came to tell you that on me you shouldn't depend."

After the usual haggling, the coachman agreed to drive the Rabbi to Minsk. "But I warn you," said the driver, "it's a hard road and I can't hurry my horse. Rifke—that's my horse—has been with me so long she's like one of the family."

They had proceeded only a few miles when the driver stopped. "See that hill?" he said to the Rabbi. "Rifke could never make it with both of us. You'll have to get out and walk while I guide her."

It was a long hill and the Rabbi was barely seated when the driver stopped again. "There's another bad hill ahead," he said. "But this time to spare Rifke I'll get out and walk."

After a short interval, the driver said, "I told you it was a hard road, and the hill we're coming to is the worst of the lot. This time both of us will have to walk. Rifke is getting tired out."

Finally they reached Minsk, having walked at least three quarters of the distance. Ruefully the Rabbi paid the amount agreed upon. And then he said, "I had to come to Minsk for the sake of my congregation. You had to come to Minsk for the sake of money. But, for God's sake, why did we bring Rifke?"

Damon Runyon

By a pretty trick of geography Damon Runyon
was born in one Manhattan and became the inexhaustible voice of another. From Manhattan,
Kansas, where he was born in 1880, Runyon
roamed the country as itinerant reporter until he
became the laureate of the semi-literate, hard-
boiled (but always sentimental) sports, kidnappers,
beer barons, safe-blowers, gangsters and slangsters
of Manhattan-on-the-Subway. Runyon, said Walter Winchell, "is the most exciting and spell-bind-
ing of historians, whether his assignment is the
Kentucky Derby or the current murder mystery."
His success in America was followed by a vogue in
England, even though all of his books had to be
supplied with glossaries so that English readers
could follow Runyon's rapid-fire Broadwayese.

Runyon died at the age of 62 on December 10,
1946.

Butch Minds the Baby

One evening along about seven o'clock I am sitting in Mindy's restaurant putting on the gefillte fish, which is a dish I am very fond of, when in comes three parties from Brooklyn wearing caps as follows: Harry the Horse, Little Isadore and Spanish John.

Now these parties are not such parties as I will care to have much truck with, because I often hear rumors about them that are very discreditable, even if the rumors are not true. In fact, I hear that many citizens of Brooklyn will be very glad indeed to see Harry the Horse, Little Isadore and Spanish John move away from there, as they are always doing something that is considered a knock to the community, such as robbing people, or maybe shooting or stabbing them, and throwing pineapples, and carrying on generally.

I am really much surprised to see these parties on Broadway, as it is well known that the Broadway coppers just naturally love to shove such parties around, but here they are in Mindy's, and there I am, so of course I give them a very large hello, as I never wish to seem inhospitable, even to Brooklyn parties. Right away they come over to my table and sit down, and Little Isadore reaches out and spears himself a big hunk of my gefillte fish with his fingers, but I overlook this, as I am using the only knife on the table.

Then they all sit there looking at me without saying anything, and the way they look at me makes me very nervous indeed. Finally I figure that maybe they are a little embarrassed being in a high-class spot such as Mindy's, with legitimate people around and about, so I say to them, very polite:

"It is a nice night."

"What is nice about it?" asks Harry the Horse, who is a thin man with a sharp face and sharp eyes.

Well, now that it is put up to me in this way, I can see there is nothing so nice about the night, at that, so I try to think of something else jolly to say, while Little Isadore keeps spearing at my gefillte fish with his fingers, and Spanish John nabs one of my potatoes.

"Where does Big Butch live?" Harry the Horse asks.

"Big Butch?" I say, as if I never hear the name before in my life, because in this man's town it is never a good idea to answer any question without thinking it over, as some time you may give the right answer to the wrong guy, or the wrong answer to the right guy. "Where does Big Butch live?" I ask them again.

"Yes, where does he live?" Harry the Horse says, very impatient. "We wish you to take us to him."

"Now wait a minute, Harry," I say, and I am now more nervous than somewhat. "I am not sure I remember the exact house Big Butch lives in, and furthermore I am not sure Big Butch will care to have me bringing people to see him, especially three at a time, and especially from Brooklyn. You know Big Butch has a very bad disposition, and there is no telling what he may say to me if he does not like the idea of me taking you to him."

"Everything is very kosher," Harry the Horse says. "You need not be afraid of anything whatever. We have a business proposition for Big Butch. It means a nice score for him, so you take us to him at once, or the chances are I will have to put the arm on somebody around here."

Well, as the only one around there for him to put the arm on at this time seems to be me, I can see where it will be good policy for me to take these parties to Big Butch, especially as the last of my gefillte fish is just going down Little Isadore's gullet, and Spanish John is finishing up my potatoes, and is dunking a piece of rye bread in my coffee, so there is nothing more for me to eat.

So I lead them over into West Forty-ninth Street, near Tenth Avenue, where Big Butch lives on the ground floor of an old brownstone-front house, and who is sitting out on the stoop but Big Butch himself. In fact, everybody in the neighborhood is sitting out on the front stoops over there, including women and children, because sitting out on the front stoops is quite a custom in this section.

Big Butch is peeled down to his undershirt and pants, and he has no shoes on his feet, as Big Butch is a guy who likes his comfort. Furthermore, he is smoking a cigar, and laid out on the stoop beside him on a blanket is a little baby with not much clothes on. This baby seems to be asleep, and every now and then Big Butch fans it with a folded newspaper to shoo away the mosquitoes that wish to nibble on the baby. These mosquitoes come across the river from the Jersey side on hot nights and they seem to be very fond of babies.

"Hello, Butch," I say, as we stop in front of the stoop.

"Sh-h-h-h!" Butch says, pointing at the baby, and making more noise with his shush than an engine blowing off steam. Then he gets up and tiptoes down to the sidewalk where we are standing, and I am hoping that Butch feels all right, because when Butch does not feel so good he is apt to be very short with one and all. He is a guy of maybe six foot two and a couple of feet wide, and he has big hairy hands and a mean look.

In fact, Big Butch is known all over this man's town as a guy you must not monkey with in any respect, so it takes plenty of weight off of me when I see that he seems to know the parties from Brooklyn, and nods at them very friendly, especially at Harry the Horse. And right away Harry states a most surprising proposition to Big Butch.

It seems that there is a big coal company which has an office in an old building down in West Eighteenth Street, and in this office is a safe, and in this safe is the company pay roll of twenty thousand dollars cash money. Harry the Horse knows the money is there because a personal friend of his who is the paymaster for the company puts it there late this very afternoon.

It seems that the paymaster enters into a dicker with Harry the Horse and Little Isadore and Spanish John for them to slug him while he is carrying the pay roll from the bank to the office in the afternoon, but something happens that they miss connections on the exact spot, so the paymaster has to carry the sugar on to the office without being slugged, and there it is now in two fat bundles.

Personally it seems to me as I listen to Harry's story that the paymaster must be a very dishonest character to be making deals to hold still while he is being slugged and the company's sugar taken away from him, but of course it is none of my business, so I take no part in the conversation.

Well, it seems that Harry the Horse and Little Isadore and Spanish John wish to get the money out of the safe, but none of them knows anything about opening safes, and while they are standing around over in Brooklyn talking over what is to be done in this emergency Harry suddenly remembers that Big Butch is once in the business of opening safes for a living.

In fact, I hear afterwards that Big Butch is considered the best safe opener east of the Mississippi River in his day, but the law finally takes to sending him to Sing Sing for opening these safes, and after he is in and out of Sing Sing three different times for opening safes Butch gets sick and tired of the place, especially as they pass what is called the Baumes Law in New York, which is a law that says if a guy is sent to Sing Sing four times hand running, he must stay there the rest of his life, without any argument about it.

So Big Butch gives up opening safes for a living, and goes into business in a small way, such as running beer, and handling a little Scotch now and then, and becomes an honest citizen. Furthermore, he marries one of the neighbor's children over on the West Side by the name of Mary Murphy, and I judge the baby on this stoop comes of this mar-

riage between Big Butch and Mary because I can see that it is a very
homely baby, indeed. Still, I never see many babies that I consider rose
geraniums for looks, anyway.

Well, it finally comes out that the idea of Harry the Horse and Little
Isadore and Spanish John is to get Big Butch to open the coal company's safe and take the pay-roll money out, and they are willing to
give him fifty per cent of the money for his bother, taking fifty per
cent for themselves for finding the plant, and paying all the overhead,
such as the paymaster, out of their bit, which strikes me as a pretty
fair sort of deal for Big Butch. But Butch only shakes his head.

"It is old-fashioned stuff," Butch says. "Nobody opens pete boxes for
a living any more. They make the boxes too good, and they are all
wired up with alarms and are a lot of trouble generally. I am in a legitimate business now and going along. You boys know I cannot stand
another fall, what with being away three times already, and in addition
to this I must mind the baby. My old lady goes to Mrs. Clancy's wake
tonight up in the Bronx, and the chances are she will be there all night,
as she is very fond of wakes, so I must mind little John Ignatius
Junior."

"Listen, Butch," Harry the Horse says, "this is a very soft pete. It is
old-fashioned, and you can open it with a toothpick. There are no wires
on it, because they never put more than a dime in it before in years.
It just happens they have to put the twenty G's in it tonight because
my pal the paymaster makes it a point not to get back from the jug
with the scratch in time to pay off today, especially after he sees we
miss out on him. It is the softest touch you will ever know, and where
can a guy pick up ten G's like this?"

I can see that Big Butch is thinking the ten G's over very seriously,
at that, because in these times nobody can afford to pass up ten G's,
especially a guy in the beer business, which is very, very tough just
now. But finally he shakes his head again and says like this:

"No," he says, "I must let it go, because I must mind the baby. My
old lady is very, very particular about this, and I dast not leave little
John Ignatius Junior for a minute. If Mary comes home and finds I
am not minding the baby she will put the blast on me plenty. I like to
turn a few honest bobs now and then as well as anybody, but," Butch
says, "John Ignatius Junior comes first with me."

Then he turns away and goes back to the stoop as much as to say he
is through arguing, and sits down beside John Ignatius Junior again
just in time to keep a mosquito from carrying off one of John's legs.
Anybody can see that Big Butch is very fond of this baby, though

personally I will not give you a dime a dozen for babies, male and female.

Well, Harry the Horse and Little Isadore and Spanish John are very much disappointed, and stand around talking among themselves, and paying no attention to me, when all of a sudden Spanish John, who never has much to say up to this time, seems to have a bright idea. He talks to Harry and Isadore, and they get all pleasured up over what he has to say and finally Harry goes to Big Butch.

"Sh-h-h-h!" Big Butch says, pointing to the baby as Harry opens his mouth.

"Listen, Butch," Harry says in a whisper, "we can take the baby with us, and you can mind it and work, too."

"Why," Big Butch whispers back, "this is quite an idea indeed. Let us go into the house and talk things over."

So he picks up the baby and leads us into his joint, and gets out some pretty fair beer, though it is needled a little, at that, and we sit around the kitchen chewing the fat in whispers. There is a crib in the kitchen, and Butch puts the baby in this crib, and it keeps on snoozing away first rate while we are talking. In fact, it is sleeping so sound that I am commencing to figure that Butch must give it some of the needled beer he is feeding us, because I am feeling a little dopey myself.

Finally Butch says that as long as he can take John Ignatius Junior with him he sees no reason why he shall not go and open the safe for them, only he says he must have five per cent more to put in the baby's bank when he gets back, so as to round himself up with his ever-loving wife in case of a beef from her over keeping the baby out in the night air. Harry the Horse says he considers this extra five per cent a little strong, but Spanish John, who seems to be a very square guy, says that after all it is only fair to cut the baby in if it is to be with them when they are making the score, and Little Isadore seems to think this is all right, too. So Harry the Horse gives in, and says five per cent it is.

Well, as they do not wish to start out until after midnight, and as there is plenty of time, Big Butch gets out some more needled beer, and then he goes looking for the tools with which he opens safes, and which he says he does not see since the day John Ignatius Junior is born and he gets them out to build the crib.

Now this is a good time for me to bid one and all farewell, and what keeps me there is something I cannot tell you to this day, because personally I never before have any idea of taking part in a safe opening, especially with a baby, as I consider such actions very dishonorable. When I come to think things over afterwards, the only thing I can figure is the needled beer, but I wish to say I am really very much surprised at myself when I find myself in a taxicab along about one o'clock in the morning with these Brooklyn parties and Big Butch and the baby.

Butch has John Ignatius Junior rolled up in a blanket, and John is still pounding his ear. Butch has a satchel of tools, and what looks to me like a big flat book, and just before we leave the house Butch hands me a package and tells me to be very careful with it. He gives Little Isadore a smaller package, which Isadore shoves into his pistol pocket, and when Isadore sits down in the taxi something goes wa-wa, like a sheep, and Big Butch becomes very indignant because it seems Isadore is sitting on John Ignatius Junior's doll, which says "Mamma" when you squeeze it.

It seems Big Butch figures that John Ignatius Junior may wish something to play with in case he wakes up, and it is a good thing for Little Isadore that the mamma doll is not squashed so it cannot say "Mamma" any more, or the chances are Little Isadore will get a good bust in the snoot.

We let the taxicab go a block away from the spot we are headed for in West Eighteenth Street, between Seventh and Eighth Avenues, and walk the rest of the way two by two. I walk with Big Butch, carrying my package, and Butch is lugging the baby and his satchel and the flat thing that looks like a book. It is so quiet down in West Eighteenth Street at such an hour that you can hear yourself think, and in fact I hear myself thinking very plain that I am a big sap to be on a job like this, especially with a baby, but I keep going just the same, which shows you what a very big sap I am, indeed.

There are very few people in West Eighteenth Street when we get there, and one of them is a fat guy who is leaning against a building almost in the center of the block, and who takes a walk for himself as soon as he sees us. It seems that this fat guy is the watchman at the coal company's office and is also a personal friend of Harry the Horse, which is why he takes the walk when he sees us coming.

It is agreed before we leave Big Butch's house that Harry the Horse and Spanish John are to stay outside the place as lookouts, while Big Butch is inside opening the safe, and that Little Isadore is to go with Butch. Nothing whatever is said by anybody about where I am to be at any time, and I can see that, no matter where I am, I will still be an outsider, but, as Butch gives me the package to carry, I figure he wishes me to remain with him.

It is no bother at all getting into the office of the coal company, which is on the ground floor, because it seems the watchman leaves the front door open, this watchman being a most obliging guy, indeed. In fact he is so obliging that by and by he comes back and lets Harry the Horse and Spanish John tie him up good and tight, and stick a handkerchief in his mouth and chuck him in an areaway next to the office, so nobody will think he has anything to do with opening the safe in case anybody comes around asking.

The office looks out on the street, and the safe that Harry the Horse and Little Isadore and Spanish John wish Big Butch to open is standing up against the rear wall of the office facing the street windows. There is one little electric light burning very dim over the safe so that when anybody walks past the place outside, such as a watchman, they can look in through the window and see the safe at all times, unless they are blind. It is not a tall safe, and it is not a big safe, and I can see Big Butch grin when he sees it, so I figure this safe is not much of a safe, just as Harry the Horse claims.

Well, as soon as Big Butch and the baby and Little Isadore and me get into the office, Big Butch steps over to the safe and unfolds what I think is the big flat book, and what is it but a sort of screen painted on one side to look exactly like the front of a safe. Big Butch stands this screen up on the floor in front of the real safe, leaving plenty of space in between, the idea being that the screen will keep anyone passing in the street outside from seeing Butch while he is opening the safe, because when a man is opening a safe he needs all the privacy he can get.

Big Butch lays John Ignatius Junior down on the floor on the blanket behind the phony safe front and takes his tools out of the satchel and starts to work opening the safe, while Little Isadore and me get back in a corner where it is dark, because there is not room for all of us back of the screen. However, we can see what Big Butch is doing, and I wish to say while I never before see a professional safe opener at work, and never wish to see another, this Butch handles himself like a real artist.

He starts drilling into the safe around the combination lock, working very fast and very quiet, when all of a sudden what happens but John Ignatius Junior sits up on the blanket and lets out a squall. Naturally this is most disquieting to me, and personally I am in favor of beaning John Ignatius Junior with something to make him keep still, because I am nervous enough as it is. But the squalling does not seem to bother Big Butch. He lays down his tools and picks up John Ignatius Junior and starts whispering, "There, there, there, my itty oddleums. Da-dad is here."

Well, this sounds very nonsensical to me in such a situation, and it makes no impression whatever on John Ignatius Junior. He keeps on squalling, and I judge he is squalling pretty loud because I see Harry the Horse and Spanish John both walk past the window and look in very anxious. Big Butch jiggles John Ignatius Junior up and down and keeps whispering baby talk to him, which sounds very undignified coming from a high-class safe opener, and finally Butch whispers to me to hand him the package I am carrying.

He opens the package, and what is in it but a baby's nursing bottle full of milk. Moreover, there is a little tin stew pan, and Butch hands the pan to me and whispers to me to find a water tap somewhere in the joint and fill the pan with water. So I go stumbling around in the dark in a room behind the office and bark my shins several times before I find a tap and fill the pan. I take it back to Big Butch, and he squats there with the baby on one arm, and gets a tin of what is called canned heat out of the package, and lights this canned heat with his cigar lighter, and starts heating the pan of water with the nursing bottle in it.

Big Butch keeps sticking his finger in the pan of water while it is heating, and by and by he puts the rubber nipple of the nursing bottle in his mouth and takes a pull at it to see if the milk is warm enough, just like I see dolls who have babies do. Apparently the milk is okay, as Butch hands the bottle to John Ignatius Junior, who grabs hold of it with both hands and starts sucking on the business end. Naturally he has to stop squalling, and Big Butch goes to work on the safe again, with John Ignatius Junior sitting on the blanket, pulling on the bottle and looking wiser than a treeful of owls.

It seems the safe is either a tougher job than anybody figures, or Big Butch's tools are not so good, what with being old and rusty and used for building baby cribs, because he breaks a couple of drills and works himself up into quite a sweat without getting anywhere. Butch afterwards explains to me that he is one of the first guys in this country to open safes without explosives, but he says to do this work properly you have to know the safes so as to drill to the tumblers of the lock just right, and it seems that this particular safe is a new type to him, even if it is old, and he is out of practice.

Well, in the meantime John Ignatius Junior finishes his bottle and starts mumbling again, and Big Butch gives him a tool to play with, and finally Butch needs this tool and tries to take it away from John Ignatius Junior, and the baby lets out such a squawk that Butch has to let him keep it until he can sneak it away from him, and this causes more delay.

Finally Big Butch gives up trying to drill the safe open, and he whispers to us that he will have to put a little shot in it to loosen up the lock, which is all right with us, because we are getting tired of hanging around and listening to John Ignatius Junior's glug-glugging. As far as I am personally concerned, I am wishing I am home in bed.

Well, Butch starts pawing through his satchel looking for something and it seems that what he is looking for is a little bottle of some kind of explosive with which to shake the lock on the safe up some, and at first he cannot find this bottle, but finally he discovers that John Ignatius Junior has it and is gnawing at the cork, and Butch has quite a battle making John Ignatius Junior give it up.

Anyway, he fixes the explosive in one of the holes he drills near the combination lock on the safe, and then he puts in a fuse, and just before he touches off the fuse Butch picks up John Ignatius Junior and hands him to Little Isadore, and tells us to go into the room behind the office. John Ignatius Junior does not seem to care for Little Isadore, and I do not blame him, at that, because he starts to squirm around quite some in Isadore's arms and lets out a squall, but all of a sudden he becomes very quiet indeed, and, while I am not able to prove it, something tells me that Little Isadore has his hand over John Ignatius Junior's mouth.

Well, Big Butch joins us right away in the back room, and sound comes out of John Ignatius Junior again as Butch takes him from Little Isadore, and I am thinking that it is a good thing for Isadore that the baby cannot tell Big Butch what Isadore does to him.

"I put in just a little bit of a shot," Big Butch says, "and it will not make any more noise than snapping your fingers."

But a second later there is a big whoom from the office, and the whole joint shakes, and John Ignatius Junior laughs right out loud. The chances are he thinks it is the Fourth of July.

"I guess maybe I put in too big a charge," Big Butch says, and then he rushes into the office with Little Isadore and me after him, and John Ignatius Junior still laughing very heartily for a small baby. The door of the safe is swinging loose, and the whole joint looks somewhat wrecked, but Big Butch loses no time in getting his dukes into the safe and grabbing out two big bundles of cash money, which he sticks inside his shirt.

As we go into the street Harry the Horse and Spanish John come running up much excited, and Harry says to Big Butch like this:

"What are you trying to do," he says, "wake up the whole town?"

"Well," Butch says, "I guess maybe the charge is too strong, at that, but nobody seems to be coming, so you and Spanish John walk over to Eighth Avenue, and the rest of us will walk to Seventh, and if you go along quiet, like people minding their own business, it will be all right."

But I judge Little Isadore is tired of John Ignatius Junior's company by this time, because he says he will go with Harry the Horse and Spanish John, and this leaves Big Butch and John Ignatius Junior and me to go the other way. So we start moving, and all of a sudden two cops come tearing around the corner toward which Harry and Isadore and Spanish John are going. The chances are the cops hear the earthquake Big Butch lets off and are coming to investigate.

But the chances are, too, that if Harry the Horse and the other two keep on walking along very quietly like Butch tells them to, the coppers will pass them up entirely, because it is not likely that coppers will figure anybody to be opening safes with explosives in this neighborhood. But the minute Harry the Horse sees the coppers he loses his nut, and he outs with the old equalizer and starts blasting away, and what does Spanish John do but get his out, too, and open up.

The next thing anybody knows, the two coppers are down on the ground with slugs in them, but other coppers are coming from every which direction, blowing whistles and doing a little blasting themselves, and there is plenty of excitement, especially when the coppers who are not chasing Harry the Horse and Little Isadore and Spanish John start poking around the neighborhood and find Harry's pal, the watchman, all tied up nice and tight where Harry leaves him, and the watchman explains that some scoundrels blow open the safe he is watching.

All this time Big Butch and me are walking in the other direction toward Seventh Avenue, and Big Butch has John Ignatius in his arms, and John Ignatius is now squalling very loud, indeed. The chances are he is still thinking of the big whoom back there which tickles him so and is wishing to hear some more whooms. Anyway, he is beating his own best record for squalling, and as we go walking along Big Butch says to me like this:

"I dast not run," he says, "because if any coppers see me running they will start popping at me and maybe hit John Ignatius Junior, and besides running will joggle the milk up in him and make him sick. My old lady always warns me never to joggle John Ignatius Junior when he is full of milk."

"Well, Butch," I say, "there is no milk in me, and I do not care if I am joggled up, so if you do not mind, I will start doing a piece of running at the next corner."

But just then around the corner of Seventh Avenue toward which we are headed comes two or three coppers with a big fat sergeant with them, and one of the coppers, who is half out of breath as if he has been doing plenty of sprinting, is explaining to the sergeant that somebody blows a safe down the street and shoots a couple of coppers in the getaway.

And there is Big Butch, with John Ignatius Junior in his arms and twenty G's in his shirt front and a tough record behind him, walking right up to them.

I am feeling very sorry, indeed, for Big Butch, and very sorry for myself, too, and I am saying to myself that if I get out of this I will never associate with anyone but ministers of the gospel as long as I live. I can remember thinking that I am getting a better break than Butch, at that, because I will not have to go to Sing Sing for the rest of my life, like him, and I also remember wondering what they will give John Ignatius Junior, who is still tearing off these squalls, with Big Butch saying, "There, there, there, Daddy's itty woogleums." Then I hear one of the coppers say to the fat sergeant :

"We better nail these guys. They may be in on this."

Well, I can see it is good-by to Butch and John Ignatius Junior and me, as the fat sergeant steps up to Big Butch, but instead of putting the arm on Butch, the fat sergeant only points at John Ignatius Junior and asks very sympathetic:

"Teeth?"

"No," Big Butch says. "Not teeth. Colic. I just get the doctor here out of bed to do something for him, and we are going to a drug store to get some medicine."

Well, naturally I am very much surprised at this statement, because of course I am not a doctor, and if John Ignatius Junior has colic it serves him right, but I am only hoping they do not ask for my degree, when the fat sergeant says:

"Too bad. I know what it is. I got three of them at home. But," he says, "it acts more like it is teeth than colic."

Then as Big Butch and John Ignatius Junior and me go on about our business I hear the fat sergeant say to the copper, very sarcastic:

"Yea, of course a guy is out blowing safes with a baby in his arms! You will make a great detective, you will!"

I do not see Big Butch for several days after I learn that Harry the Horse and Little Isadore and Spanish John get back to Brooklyn all right, except they are a little nicked up here and there from the slugs the coppers toss at them, while the coppers they clip are not damaged so very much. Furthermore, the chances are I will not see Big Butch for several years, if it is left to me, but he comes looking for me one night, and he seems to be all pleasured up about something.

"Say," Big Butch says to me, "you know I never give a copper credit for knowing any too much about anything, but I wish to say that this fat sergeant we run into the other night is a very, very smart duck. He is right about it being teeth that is ailing John Ignatius Junior, for what happens yesterday but John cuts in his first tooth."

Carl Sandburg

Carl Sandburg's poetry, composed of "limber, lasting, fierce words," is matched by the vigor of his humor. Born in Galesburg, Illinois, in 1878, Sandburg explored the folkways of his country while earning a living as delivery boy, porter in a barbershop, dishwasher, truck-handler, scene-shifter, and harvest hand. His love of the native spirit found expression in such indigenous volumes as Good Morning, America; The People, Yes; The American Songbag; and the panoramic six-volume biography of Abraham Lincoln, a monument of industry and understanding.

Lincoln, the Laughing President

Respectable friends, who cared about reputations as gentlemen and scholars, took it as a little queer, a little like "a country Jake," beneath dignity, that Lincoln should carry with him the book "Joe Miller's Jests," generally called Joe Miller's joke book.[1] English puns, Irish bulls, Greek repartee, folk tales of Jews and Egyptians, brisk anecdotes, filled the book—more than a thousand, each with a serial number. No. 997 told of "the celebrated organist Abbe Vogler, once imitating a thunderstorm so well that for miles round all the milk turned sour." The Irishman was told of, who had been living in Scotland and was asked how he liked the country, replying, "I was sick all the time I was there, and if I had lived there till this time, I'd been dead a year ago." Lord Russell on the scaffold ready to have his head cut off, handed his watch to a bishop, with the remark, "Take this—it shows time; I am going into eternity and no longer need it." Another lord, owing many debts, was asked how he could sleep at night, and answered: "I sleep very well, but I wonder how my creditors can." A wounded officer on a bloody battlefield was howling with pain when another wounded officer near by called to him: "What do you make such a noise for? Do you think nobody is killed but yourself?"

Such was some of the foolery in the book that Lincoln occasionally took out of his carpetbag and read aloud to other lawyers. Some had the pith and poignancy of the grave-digger in the play of Hamlet, one joke reading: "An Irishman going to be hanged, begged that the rope might be tied under his arms instead of round his neck; for, said Pat, I am so remarkably ticklish in the throat, that if tied there, I will certainly kill myself with laughing." Or again Joke No. 506, reading: "Lieutenant Connolly, an Irishman in the service of the United States, during the American war, chanced to take three Hessian prisoners himself, without any assistance; being asked by the commander-in-chief how he had taken them—'I surrounded them,' was the answer."

There were tales of the people. A traveler in Egypt said to a worker on the land: "I suppose you are quite happy now; the country looks like a garden and every village has its minaret." "God is great," replied the worker. "Our master gives with one hand and takes with two." Another traveler, reporting that he and his servant had made fifty wild Arabs run, said there was nothing surprising about it. "We ran and they

---

[1] See "Who Was Joe Miller?" on page 246.

ran after us." And again and again little tales of the people, the people. Into the street before Dean Swift's deanery came "a great rabble," waiting "to see the eclipse." And Dean Swift had the big bell rung, and a crier bawling: "O Yes, O Yes, all manner of persons here concerned take notice the eclipse be put off till to-morrow this time! So God save the King and his Reverence the dean." And the rabble went away, all but one Irishman who said he would stay because "the dean might change his mind and have the eclipse that day after all."

Thus Joe Miller's jests. They were a nourishing company to Lincoln. Once in a while he told a story that seemed to have been made over from Joe Miller and placed in Indiana. In his lighter moods his humors matched with the Rabelais definition, "a certain jollity of mind, pickled in the scorn of fortune."

He told of the long-legged boy "spark-ing" a farmer's daughter when the hostile farmer came in with a shotgun; the boy jumped through a window, and running across the cabbage patch scared up a rab-bit; in about two leaps the boy caught up with the rabbit, kicked it high in the air, and grunted, "Git out of the road and let somebody run that knows how." He told of a Kentucky horse sale where a small boy was riding a fine horse to show off points, when a man whispered to the boy, "Look here, boy, hain't that horse got the splints?" and the boy answered: "Mister, I don't know what the splints is, but if it's good for him, he has got it; if it ain't good for him, he ain't got it."

Riding to Lewiston an old acquaint-ance, a weather-beaten farmer, spoke of going to law with his next neighbor. "Been a neighbor of yours for long?" "Nigh onto fifteen year." "Part of the time you get along all right, don't you?" "I reckon we do." "Well, see this horse of mine? I sometimes get out of patience with him. But I know his faults; he does fairly well as horses go; it might take me a long time to get used to some other horse's faults: for all horses have faults."

The instant dignity became bogus his eye caught it. He enjoyed such anecdotes as the one of a Brown County, Indiana, man who killed a neighbor's dog, and the proof of guilt was clear. The defendant's attorney cleared his throat and began a speech, "May it please the court, we are proud to live in a land where justice is administered to the king on the throne and the beggar on his dunghill." The squire then interrupted, "You may go ahead with your speech, but the case *are* decided."

Little folk tales and snatches of odd wisdom known to common people of the ancient kingdoms of the Persians and the Arabians, came to be known among the common people of the farming districts in Illinois, hitched up somehow to Abe Lincoln. When a story or saying had a certain color or smack, it would often be tagged as coming from Lincoln. He had said to a book agent, "For those who like that kind of a book, that's the kind of a book they'll like." He was the man walking along a dusty road when a stranger, driving a buggy came along. And he asked the stranger, "Will you be so good as to take my overcoat to town for me?" And the man in the buggy said he would. "But how will you get your overcoat back again?" "Oh, that's easy! I'm going to stay right inside of it." And of course, said some jokers, it was Abe Lincoln who first told a hotel waiter, "Say, if this is coffee, then please bring me some tea, but if this is tea, please bring me some coffee." And on Abe Lincoln was laid the remark, after tasting ice cream, "Say, waiter, I don't want to slander this hotel, but this here pudding's froze."

He had come out of a slushy snow into a courtroom to try a case and sat down to dry his feet at the stove. The words of the lawyer arguing against him came to his ears. All of a sudden he was out in the middle of the courtroom, one shoe off, calling: "Now, judge, that isn't fair. I'm not going to have this jury all fuddled up."

Did he not say when he met a man somewhat matching his own height, "Well, you're up some"—had they not seen how the clay of the earth clung to him? Before posing for a photographer, he stepped into a barber shop, saying, "I better get my hair slicked up." Then, sitting before the camera, he ran his fingers through his hair, caught himself, and said, "Guess I've made a bird's nest of it again." It was he who agreed to make a horse trade, sight unseen, with a judge. First came the judge the next morning with a broken-down bone-rack of a horse; then came Lincoln carrying a wooden sawhorse on his shoulders, saying, "Well, judge, this is the first time I ever got the worst of it in a horse trade."

A walking, stalking library of stories he was. Some of them could have had musical accompaniments from barn-dance fiddles. The prize story tellers of one neighborhood and another had met him and they had competed. "That reminds me." "That's like the feller down at Goose Holler." And occasionally was one with a shine of many cross-lights in it. Lincoln told of a balloonist going up in New Orleans, sailing for hours, and dropping his parachute over a cotton field. The gang of Negroes picking cotton saw a man coming down from the sky in blue silk, in silver spangles, wearing golden slippers. They ran—all but one old timer who had the rheumatism and couldn't get away. He waited till the balloonist hit the ground and walked toward him. Then he mumbled: "Howdy, Massa Jesus. How's yo' Pa?"

Lincoln had stood with two umbrellas at an imaginary rat hole, impersonating Sam'l, the Quaker boy whose father wanted to stop the boy's using swear words. The two umbrellas were blacksmith tongs. Sam'l's father had said, "Now, Sam'l, thee will sit here until thee has a rat. If I hear thee swear, thee will sit here till thee has another." And Sam'l had sat there for hours, snipping the tongs a few times, but no rat caught. At last one came out from the rat hole, the whiskers peeping up, then the black nose, and the eyes blinking. And the two umbrella tongs snapped together in a flash. And Sam'l yelled, "By God, I have thee at last!" And Lincoln with a shaking, swaying frame let out a squeal and stood holding an imaginary wriggling rat between the two umbrellas. He had told this in Illinois towns during the debates with Douglas. And Robert R. Hitt, the phonographic reporter, said he forgot himself and politics and business and nearly believed there was a live squeaking rat caught between the two umbrellas. For a roomful of men in a hotel, Lincoln would perform this drama of Sam'l, Sam'l's father, and the rat, acting subtly the rôles of the earnest father, the obstreperous boy, and the furtive rat.

He picked up comedy, as he met it, and passed it on to others. In Cumberland County, one Dr. Hamburgher, a Democrat, forced his way to the front to reply to Lincoln's speech. As Hamburgher worked into a frothy and threatening speech, a little man with a limp came over to Lincoln and said: "Don't mind *him*. I know *him*; I live here! I'll take care of *him*. Watch me." And he took the platform, and replying brought from Hamburgher the cry, "That's a lie." To which the little man with the limp called out with high defiance, "Never mind, I'll take that from *you*—yes, I'll take anything from you, except your pills." At the mention of pills, the doctor snorted, "You scoundrel, you know I've quit practicing medicine." And the little man dropped down on the knee of his best leg, raised his hands toward the sky in thankfulness, and shouted, "Then, thank God! The country is safe."

Plato, the Kane County lawyer, had told him a story about a man who had beaten a dog to death and was in such a rage that he would go out of the house and again beat the dog to death. When Plato came one day to Lincoln's office in Springfield, Lincoln's greeting was, "Well, Plato, have you got that dog killed yet?"

A family in Indiana, according to Lincoln, picked dandelion tops or other leaves and boiled "greens" for dinner in the spring and early summer. Once after a mess of greens the whole family went out of commission. After that when they had greens a big helping would first be forked out for Zerah, a half-wit boy, as the family said: "Try it on Zerah. If he stands it, it won't hurt the rest of us." And a man had a horse that would balk and settle down on all four legs like a bird dog. He traded off the horse as good for hunting birds. As the horse crossed a creek he settled down in the middle of it like a bird dog and the man who had owned him called to the new rider: "Ride him! Ride him! He's as good for fish as he is for birds."

People looked at Lincoln, searching his face, thinking about his words and ways, ready to believe he was a Great Man. Then he would spill over with a joke or tell of some new horse-play of wit or humor in the next county. The barriers tumbled. He was again a strange friend, a neighbor, a friendly stranger, no far-off Great Man at all. "His face," Moncure D. Conway noted, "had a battered and bronzed look, without being hard." He fitted the measurements, "three parts sublime to one grotesque."

A crowd was bubbling with mirth in an Ohio town as a short friend stood alongside Lincoln to introduce him. Lincoln, pointing at himself, said, "This is the long of it," and putting an arm on the friend's shoulder, "and this is the short of it."

Joe Fifer, an eighteen-year-old corn husker, heard Lincoln at Bloomington after Swett made the opening address. "When Lincoln was starting to speak," Fifer noticed, "some men near me said Lincoln was no great shakes as a public speaker and Swett would make a better showing against Douglas. But when Lincoln got to going they listened; they stood still without moving out of their foot tracks. Lincoln looked out on a wall of faces still as if they had been made of stone."

The Springfield doctor, William Jayne, trying to fathom why Lincoln had carried the crowds with him usually in debating with Douglas, said: "Everybody thinks he is honest and believes what he says. If he was really a great man, or if people regarded him as a great man, he could not do half so much."

He was the man who had started a little circle of people to giggling one morning in Judge Davis's courtroom, and the judge sputtered out: "I am not going to stand this any longer, Mr. Lincoln. You're always disturbing this court with your tomfoolery." The fine was $5.00, for disorderly conduct. Lincoln sat with his hand over his mouth trying to keep his face straight. Later the judge called Lawrence Weldon to him and Weldon whispered into his ear what it was that Lincoln had told. Then the judge giggled. Getting his face straight, he announced, "The clerk may remit Mr. Lincoln's fine." The joke had to do with "taking up a subscription to buy Jim Wheeler a new pair of pants."

He could speak of So-and-So as "a quiet, orderly, faithful man." And he could hand a bottle to a baldheaded man he wished to get rid of, with the remarks: "Try this stuff for your hair. Keep it up. They say it will grow hair on a pumpkin. Come back in ten months and tell me how it works." When it was intimated to him that he was consulting too much with Judge Davis, he told of a New Hampshire judge who said: "The only time the chief judge ever consulted was at the close of a long day's session, when he turned and whispered, 'Don't your back ache?'" He liked to tell of the strict judge of whom it was said: "He would hang a man for blowing his nose in the street, but he would quash the indictment if it failed to specify which hand he blew it with."

When he presented Coles County relatives with a sad-faced photograph of himself, he said, "This is not a very good-looking picture, but it's the best that could be produced from the poor subject."

"Saki"

Son of an inspector-general of Irish descent, Hector Hugh Munro was born in Akyab, Burma, in 1870. Following his father's profession, he received an appointment with the Burma police but poor health made him abandon it. At twenty-five he began writing political satires, adopting the pseudonym "Saki," the cupbearer in The Rubáiyát of Omar Khayyám. Although he was forty-five at the beginning of the first World War, he immediately enlisted. A year later he was killed in action.

A deft fashioner of polished tea-table trivialities, "Saki" is both suave and startling; he could, as Christopher Morley wrote, "purge the decorous amenities of an English week-end party with blasts of cyclonic force." Like John Collier (see page 140), "Saki" found nothing incongruous in the combination of humor and horror.

A master of surprise, "Saki" is captivating when he is dealing with the macabre, and most urbane when he is most absurd.

The Mouse

Theodoric Voler had been brought up, from infancy to the confines of middle age, by a fond mother whose chief solicitude had been to keep him screened from what she called the coarser realities of life. When she died she left Theodoric alone in a world that was as real as ever, and a good deal coarser than he considered it had any need to be. To a man of his temperament and upbringing even a simple railway journey was crammed with petty annoyances and minor discords, and as he settled himself down in a second-class compartment one September morning he was conscious of ruffled feelings and general mental discomposure. He had been staying at a country vicarage, the inmates of which had been certainly neither brutal nor bacchanalian, but their supervision of the domestic establishment had been of that lax order which invites disaster. The pony carriage that was to take him to the station had never been properly ordered, and when the moment for his departure drew near the handyman who should have produced the required article was nowhere to be found. In this emergency Theodoric, to his mute but very intense disgust, found himself obliged to collaborate with the vicar's daughter in the task of harnessing the pony, which necessitated groping about in an ill-lighted outhouse called a stable, and smelling very like one—except in patches where it smelt of mice. Without being actually afraid of mice, Theodoric classed them among the coarser incidents of life, and considered that Providence, with a little exercise of moral courage, might long ago have recognized that they were not indispensable, and have withdrawn them from circulation. As the train glided out of the station Theodoric's nervous imagination accused himself of exhaling a weak odour of stable-yard, and possibly of displaying a mouldy straw or two on his usually well-brushed garments. Fortunately the only other occupant of the compartment, a lady of about the same age as himself, seemed inclined for slumber rather than scrutiny; the train was not due to stop till the terminus was reached, in about an hour's time, and the carriage was of the old-fashioned sort, that held no communication with a corridor, therefore no further travelling companions were likely to intrude on Theodoric's semi-privacy. And yet the train had scarcely attained its normal speed before he became reluctantly but vividly aware that he was not alone with the slumbering lady; he was not even alone in his own clothes. A warm, creeping movement over his flesh betrayed the unwelcome and highly resented presence, unseen but poignant, of a strayed mouse, that had evidently

548

dashed into its present retreat during the episode of the pony harnessing. Furtive stamps and shakes and wildly directed pinches failed to dislodge the intruder, whose motto, indeed, seemed to be Excelsior; and the lawful occupant of the clothes lay back against the cushions and endeavoured rapidly to evolve some means for putting an end to the dual ownership. It was unthinkable that he should continue for the space of a whole hour in the horrible position of a Rowton House for vagrant mice (already his imagination had at least doubled the numbers of the alien invasion). On the other hand, nothing less drastic than partial disrobing would ease him of his tormentor, and to undress in the presence of a lady, even for so laudable a purpose, was an idea that made his ear-tips tingle in a blush of abject shame. He had never been able to bring himself even to the mild exposure of open-work socks in the presence of the fair sex. And yet—the lady in this case was to all appearances soundly and securely asleep; the mouse, on the other hand, seemed to be trying to crowd a Wanderjahr into a few strenuous minutes. If there is any truth in the theory of transmigration, this particular mouse must certainly have been in a former state a member of the Alpine Club. Sometimes in its eagerness it lost its footing and slipped for half an inch or so; and then, in fright, or more probably temper, it bit. Theodoric was goaded into the most audacious undertaking of his life. Crimsoning to the hue of a beetroot and keeping an agonized watch on his slumbering fellow-traveller, he swiftly and noiselessly secured the ends of his railway-rug to the racks on either side of the carriage, so that a substantial curtain hung athwart the compartment. In the narrow dressing-room that he had thus improvised he proceeded with violent haste to extricate himself partially and the mouse entirely from the surrounding casings of tweed and half-wool. As the unravelled mouse gave a wild leap to the floor, the rug, slipping its fastening at either end, also came down with a heart-curdling flop, and almost simultaneously the awakened sleeper opened her eyes. With a movement almost quicker than the mouse's, Theodoric pounced on the rug, and hauled its ample folds chin-high over his dismantled person as he collapsed into the further corner of the carriage. The blood raced and beat in the veins of his neck and forehead, while he waited dumbly for the communication-cord to be pulled. The lady, however, contented herself with a silent stare at her strangely muffled companion. How much had she seen, Theodoric queried to himself, and in any case what on earth must she think of his present posture?

"I think I have caught a chill," he ventured desperately.

"Really, I'm sorry," she replied. "I was just going to ask you if you would open this window."

"I fancy it's malaria," he added, his teeth chattering slightly, as much from fright as from a desire to support his theory.

"I've got some brandy in my hold-all, if you'll kindly reach it down for me," said his companion.

"Not for worlds—I mean, I never take anything for it," he assured her earnestly.

"I suppose you caught it in the Tropics?"

Theodoric, whose acquaintance with the Tropics was limited to an annual present of a chest of tea from an uncle in Ceylon, felt that even the malaria was slipping from him. Would it be possible, he wondered, to disclose the real state of affairs to her in small instalments?

"Are you afraid of mice?" he ventured, growing, if possible, more scarlet in the face.

"Not unless they came in quantities, like those that ate up Bishop Hatto. Why do you ask?"

"I had one crawling inside my clothes just now," said Theodoric in a voice that hardly seemed his own. "It was a most awkward situation."

"It must have been, if you wear your clothes at all tight," she observed; "but mice have strange ideas of comfort."

"I had to get rid of it while you were asleep," he continued; then, with a gulp, he added, "it was getting rid of it that brought me to—to this."

"Surely leaving off one small mouse wouldn't bring on a chill," she exclaimed, with a levity that Theodoric accounted abominable.

Evidently she had detected something of his predicament, and was enjoying his confusion. All the blood in his body seemed to have mobilized in one concentrated blush, and an agony of abasement, worse than a myriad mice, crept up and down over his soul. And then, as reflection began to assert itself, sheer terror took the place of humiliation. With every minute that passed the train was rushing nearer to the crowded and bustling terminus where dozens of prying eyes would be exchanged for the one paralyzing pair that watched him from the further corner of the carriage. There was one slender despairing chance, which the next few minutes must decide. His fellow-traveller might relapse into a blessed slumber. But as the minutes throbbed by that chance ebbed away. The furtive glance which Theodoric stole at her from time to time disclosed only an unwinking wakefulness.

"I think we must be getting near now," she presently observed.

Theodoric had already noted with growing terror the recurring stacks of small, ugly dwellings that heralded the journey's end. The words acted as a signal. Like a hunted beast breaking cover and dashing madly towards some other haven of momentary safety he threw aside his rug, and struggled frantically into his dishevelled garments. He was conscious of dull suburban stations racing past the window, of a choking, hammering sensation in his throat and heart, and of an icy silence in that corner towards which he dared not look. Then as he sank back in his seat, clothed and almost delirious, the train slowed down to a final crawl, and the woman spoke.

"Would you be so kind," she asked, "as to get me a porter to put me into a cab? It's a shame to trouble you when you're feeling unwell, but being blind makes one so helpless at a railway station."

The Story-Teller

It was a hot afternoon, and the railway carriage was correspondingly sultry, and the next stop was at Templecombe, nearly an hour ahead. The occupants of the carriage were a small girl, and a smaller girl, and a small boy. An aunt belonging to the children occupied one corner seat, and the further corner seat on the opposite side was occupied by a bachelor who was a stranger to their party, but the small girls and the small boy emphatically occupied the compartment. Both the aunt and the children were conversational in a limited, persistent way, reminding one of the attentions of a housefly that refused to be discouraged. Most of the aunt's remarks seemed to begin with "Don't," and nearly all of the children's remarks began with "Why?" The bachelor said nothing out loud.

"Don't, Cyril, don't," exclaimed the aunt, as the small boy began smacking the cushions of the seat, producing a cloud of dust at each blow.

"Come and look out of the window," she added.

The child moved reluctantly to the window. "Why are those sheep being driven out of that field?" he asked.

"I expect they are being driven to another field where there is more grass," said the aunt weakly.

"But there is lots of grass in that field," protested the boy; "there's nothing else but grass there. Aunt, there's lots of grass in that field."

"Perhaps the grass in the other field is better," suggested the aunt fatuously.

"Why is it better?" came the swift, inevitable question.

"Oh, look at those cows!" exclaimed the aunt. Nearly every field along the line had contained cows or bullocks, but she spoke as though she were drawing attention to a rarity.

"Why is the grass in the other field better?" persisted Cyril.

The frown on the bachelor's face was deepening to a scowl. He was a hard, unsympathetic man, the aunt decided in her mind. She was utterly unable to come to any satisfactory decision about the grass in the other field.

The smaller girl created a diversion by beginning to recite "On the Road to Mandalay." She only knew the first line, but she put her limited knowledge to the fullest possible use. She repeated the line over and over again in a dreamy but resolute and very audible voice; it seemed to the bachelor as though some one had had a bet with her that she could not repeat the line aloud two thousand times without stopping. Whoever it was who had made the wager was likely to lose his bet.

"Come over here and listen to a story," said the aunt, when the bachelor had looked twice at her and once at the communication cord.

The children moved listlessly towards the aunt's end of the carriage. Evidently her reputation as a story-teller did not rank high in their estimation.

In a low, confidential voice, interrupted at frequent intervals by loud, petulant questions from her listeners, she began an unenterprising and deplorably uninteresting story about a little girl who was good, and made friends with every one on account of her goodness, and was finally saved from a mad bull by a number of rescuers who admired her moral character.

"Wouldn't they have saved her if she hadn't been good?" demanded the bigger of the small girls. It was exactly the question that the bachelor had wanted to ask.

"Well, yes," admitted the aunt lamely, "but I don't think they would have run quite so fast to her help if they had not liked her so much."

"It's the stupidest story I've ever heard," said the bigger of the small girls, with immense conviction.

"I didn't listen after the first bit, it was so stupid," said Cyril.

The smaller girl made no actual comment on the story, but she had long ago recommenced a murmured repetition of her favourite line.

"You don't seem to be a success as a story-teller," said the bachelor suddenly from his corner.

The aunt bristled in instant defence at this unexpected attack.

"It's a very difficult thing to tell stories that children can both understand and appreciate," she said stiffly.

"I don't agree with you," said the bachelor.

"Perhaps *you* would like to tell them a story," was the aunt's retort.

"Tell us a story," demanded the bigger of the small girls.

"Once upon a time," began the bachelor, "there was a little girl called Bertha, who was extraordinarily good."

The children's momentarily-aroused interest began at once to flicker; all stories seemed dreadfully alike, no matter who told them.

"She did all that she was told, she was always truthful, she kept her clothes clean, ate milk puddings as though they were jam tarts, learned her lessons perfectly, and was polite in her manners."

"Was she pretty?" asked the bigger of the small girls.

"Not as pretty as any of you," said the bachelor, "but she was horribly good."

There was a wave of reaction in favour of the story; the word horrible in connection with goodness was a novelty that commended itself. It seemed to introduce a ring of truth that was absent from the aunt's tales of infant life.

"She was so good," continued the bachelor, "that she won several medals for goodness, which she always wore, pinned on to her dress. There was a medal for obedience, another medal for punctuality, and a third for good behaviour. They were large metal medals and they clicked against one another as she walked. No other child in the town where she lived had as many as three medals, so everybody knew that she must be an extra good child."

"Horribly good," quoted Cyril.

"Everybody talked about her goodness, and the Prince of the country got to hear about it, and he said that as she was so very good she might be allowed once a week to walk in his park, which was just outside the town. It was a beautiful park, and no children were ever allowed in it, so it was a great honour for Bertha to be allowed to go there."

"Were there any sheep in the park?" demanded Cyril.

"No," said the bachelor, "there were no sheep."

"Why weren't there any sheep?" came the inevitable question arising out of that answer.

The aunt permitted herself a smile, which might almost have been described as a grin.

"There were no sheep in the park," said the bachelor, "because the Prince's mother had once had a dream that her son would either be killed by a sheep or else by a clock falling on him. For that reason the Prince never kept a sheep in his park or a clock in his palace."

The aunt suppressed a gasp of admiration.

"Was the Prince killed by a sheep or by a clock?" asked Cyril.

"He is still alive, so we can't tell whether the dream will come true," said the bachelor unconcernedly; "anyway, there were no sheep in the park, but there were lots of little pigs running all over the place."

"What colour were they?"

"Black with white faces, white with black spots, black all over, grey with white patches, and some were white all over."

The story-teller paused to let a full idea of the park's treasures sink into the children's imaginations; then he resumed:

"Bertha was rather sorry to find that there were no flowers in the park. She had promised her aunts, with tears in her eyes, that she would not pick any of the kind Prince's flowers, and she had meant to keep her promise, so of course it made her feel silly to find that there were no flowers to pick."

"Why weren't there any flowers?"

"Because the pigs had eaten them all," said the bachelor promptly. "The gardeners had told the Prince that you couldn't have pigs and flowers, so he decided to have pigs and no flowers."

There was a murmur of approval at the excellence of the Prince's decision; so many people would have decided the other way.

"There were lots of other delightful things in the park. There were ponds with gold and blue and green fish in them, and trees with beautiful parrots that said clever things at a moment's notice, and humming-birds that hummed all the popular tunes of the day. Bertha walked up and down and enjoyed herself immensely, and thought to herself: 'If I were not so extraordinarily good I should not have been allowed to come into this beautiful park and enjoy all that there is to be seen in it,' and her three medals clinked against one another as she walked and helped to remind her how very good she really was. Just then an enormous wolf came prowling into the park to see if it could catch a fat little pig for its supper."

"What colour was it?" asked the children, amid an immediate quickening of interest.

"Mud-colour all over, with a black tongue and pale grey eyes that gleamed with unspeakable ferocity. The first thing that it saw in the park was Bertha; her pinafore was so spotlessly white and clean that it could be seen from a great distance. Bertha saw the wolf and saw that it was stealing towards her, and she began to wish that she had never been allowed to come into the park. She ran as hard as she could, and the wolf came after her with huge leaps and bounds. She managed to reach a shrubbery of myrtle bushes and she hid herself in one of the thickest of the bushes. The wolf came sniffing among the branches, its black tongue lolling out of its mouth and its pale grey eyes glaring with rage. Bertha was terribly frightened, and thought to herself: 'If I had not been so extraordinarily good I should have been safe in the town at this moment.' However, the scent of the myrtle was so strong that the wolf could not sniff out where Bertha was hiding, and the bushes were so thick that he might have hunted about in them for a long time without catching sight of her, so he thought he might as well go off and catch a little pig instead. Bertha was trembling very much at having the wolf prowling and sniffing so near her, and as she trembled the medal for obedience clinked against the medals for good conduct and punctuality. The wolf was just moving away when he heard the sound of the medals clinking and stopped to listen; they clinked again in a bush quite near him. He dashed into the bush, his pale grey eyes gleaming with ferocity and triumph, and dragged Bertha out and devoured her to the last morsel. All that was left of her were her shoes, bits of clothing and the three medals for goodness."

"Were any of the little pigs killed?"

"No, they all escaped."

"The story began badly," said the smaller of the small girls, "but it had a beautiful ending."

"It is the most beautiful story that I ever heard," said the bigger of the small girls, with immense decision.

"It is the *only* beautiful story I have ever heard," said Cyril.

A dissentient opinion came from the aunt.

"A most improper story to tell to young children! You have undermined the effect of years of careful teaching."

"At any rate," said the bachelor, collecting his belongings preparatory to leaving the carriage, "I kept them quiet for ten minutes, which was more than you were able to do."

"Unhappy woman!" he observed to himself as he walked down the platform of Templecombe station; "for the next six months or so those children will assail her in public with demands for an improper story!"

William Saroyan

He was a legend in the literary world before he was twenty-six. Born in 1908 in Fresno, California, the son of Armenian immigrants, William Saroyan turned handsprings almost as soon as he could walk. He has been turning them ever since. No writer of his day has had more verve—or, according to his detractors, nerve—and none has shown more originality in blending the naïve and the noble, the ridiculous and the profound, the spontaneously simple and the elaborately sentimental. Saroyan's indiscriminate love of everything led one critic to dub him "the St. Francis of Fresno"; another critic, commenting on his weakness for thinned-out platitudes, said that Saroyan suffered from "pernicious Armenia."

Meanwhile, Saroyan went blithely on his career "to write the best stories ever written" and "to change the world." "I don't want to brag," he said, "but I would like to know why it snowed the year I began to write, when never before in the history of San Joaquin Valley since 1856, had it snowed." A superb attention-getter, he stops the reader short with titles like The Daring Young Man on the Flying Trapeze; Love, Here Is My Hat; Ever Fall in Love With a Midget?; Comedy Is Where You Die and They Don't Bury You Because You Can Still Walk—stories that seem fabulously improvised rather than thought out and written down. The formula is his own. As the author himself has written in an introduction to one of his own books: "The Saroyan story is simultaneously American and international. It sings mainly, and for the most part it sings the song of people and the way they live, or would like to live, or dream, or kill time, or wait, or hurry." Or something.

Ever Fall in Love with a Midget?

I don't suppose you ever fell in love with a midget weighing thirty-nine pounds, did you?

No, I said, but have another beer.

Down in Gallup, he said, twenty years ago. Fellow by the name of Rufus Jenkins came to town with six white horses and two black ones. Said he wanted a man to break the horses for him because his left leg was wood and he couldn't do it. Had a meeting at Parker's Mercantile Store and finally came to blows, me and Henry Walpal. Bashed his head with a brass cuspidor and ran away to Mexico, but he didn't die.

Couldn't speak a word. Took up with a cattle-breeder named Diego, educated in California. Spoke the language better than you and me. Said, Your job, Murph, is to feed them prize bulls. I said, Fine; what'll I feed them? He said, Hay, lettuce, salt, and beer. I said, Fine; they're your bulls.

Came to blows two days later over an accordion he claimed I stole. I borrowed it and during the fight busted it over his head; ruined one of the finest accordions I ever saw. Grabbed a horse and rode back across the border. Texas. Got to talking with a fellow who looked honest. Turned out to be a Ranger who was looking for me.

Yeah, I said. You were saying, a thirty-nine pound midget.

Will I ever forget that lady? he said. Will I ever get over that amazon of small proportions?

Will you? I said.

If I live to be sixty, he said.

Sixty? I said. You look more than sixty now.

That's trouble showing in my face. Trouble and complications. I was fifty-six three months ago.

Oh.

Told the Texas Ranger my name was Rothstein, mining engineer from Pennsylvania, looking for something worth while. Mentioned two places in Houston. Nearly lost an eye early one morning, going down the stairs. Ran into a six-footer with an iron-claw where his right hand was supposed to be. Said, You broke up my home. Told him I was a stranger in Houston. The girls gathered at the top of the stairs to see a fight. Seven of them. Six feet and an iron claw. That's bad on the nerves. Kicked him in the mouth when he swung for my head with the claw. Would have lost an eye except for quick thinking. Rolled into the gutter and pulled a gun. Fired seven times, but I was back upstairs.

558

Left the place an hour later, dressed in silk and feathers, with a hat swung around over my face. Saw him standing on the corner, waiting. Said, Care for a wiggle? Said he didn't. Went on down the street, left town.

I don't suppose you ever had to put on a dress to save your skin, did you?

No, I said, and I never fell in love with a midget weighing thirty-nine pounds. Have another beer.

Thanks. Ever try to herd cattle on a bicycle?

No, I said.

Left Houston with sixty cents in my pocket, gift of a girl named Lucinda. Walked fourteen miles in fourteen hours. Big house with barbwire all around, and big dogs. One thing I never could get around. Walked past the gate, anyway, from hunger and thirst. Dogs jumped up and came for me. Walked right into them, growing older every second. Went up to the door and knocked. Big negress opened the door, closed it quick. Said, On your way, white trash.

Knocked again. Said, On your way. Again, On your way. Again. This time the old man himself opened the door, ninety if he was a day. Sawed-off shotgun too.

Said, I ain't looking for trouble, Father. I'm hungry and thirsty, name's Cavanaugh.

Took me in and made mint juleps for the two of us.

Said, Living here alone, Father?

Said, Drink and ask no questions; maybe I am and maybe I ain't. You saw the negress. Draw your own conclusions.

I'd heard of that, but didn't wink out of tact.

Called out, Elvira, bring this gentleman sandwiches.

Young enough for a man of seventy, probably no more than forty, and big.

Said, Any good at cards? Said, No.

Said, Fine, Cavanaugh, take a hand of poker.

Played all night.

If I told you that old Southern gentleman was my grandfather, you wouldn't believe me, would you?

No.

Well, it so happens he wasn't, although it would have been remarkable if he had been.

Where did you herd cattle on a bicycle?

Toledo, Ohio, 1918.

Toledo, Ohio? I said. They don't herd cattle up there.

They don't any more. They did in 1918. One fellow did, leastways. Bookkeeper named Sam Gold. Only Jewish cowboy I ever saw. Straight from the Eastside New York. Sombrero, lariats, Bull Durham, two head of cattle, and two bicycles. Called his place Gold Bar Ranch, two acres, just outside the city limits.

That was the year of the War, you'll remember.

Yeah, I said.

Remember a picture called *Shoulder Arms?*

Sure. Saw it five times.

Remember when Charlie Chaplin thought he was washing *his* foot, and the foot turned out to be another man's?

Sure.

You may not believe me, but I was the man whose foot was washed by Chaplin in that picture.

It's possible, I said, but how about herding them two cows on a bicycle? How'd you do it?

Easiest thing in the world. Rode no hands. Had to, otherwise couldn't lasso the cows. Worked for Sam Gold till the cows ran away. Bicycles scared them. They went into Toledo and we never saw hide or hair of them again. Advertised in every paper, but never got them back. Broke his heart. Sold both bikes and returned to New York.

Took four aces from a deck of red cards and walked to town. Poker. Fellow in the game named Chuck Collins, liked to gamble. Told him with a smile I didn't suppose he'd care to bet a hundred dollars I wouldn't hold four aces the next hand. Called it. My cards were red on the blank side. The other cards were blue. Plumb forgot all about it. Showed him four aces. Ace of spades, ace of clubs, ace of diamonds, ace of hearts. I'll remember them four cards if I live to be sixty. Would have been killed on the spot except for the hurricane that year.

Hurricane?

You haven't forgotten the Toledo hurricane of 1918, have you?

No, I said. There was no hurricane in Toledo, in 1918, or any other year.

For the love of God, then, what do you suppose that commotion was? And how come I came to in Chicago? Dream-walking down State Street?

I guess they scared you.

No, that wasn't it. You go back to the papers of November, 1918, and I think you'll find there was a hurricane in Toledo. I remember sitting on the roof of a two-story house, floating northwest.

Northwest?

Sure.

Okay, have another beer.

Thaaaaanks. Thanks, he said.

I don't suppose *you* ever fell in love with a midget weighing thirty-nine pounds, did you? I said.

Who? he said.

You. I said.

No, he said, can't say I have.

Well, I said, let *me* tell *you* about it.

The Fifty-Yard Dash

After a certain letter came to me from New York the year I was twelve, I made up my mind to become the most powerful man in my neighborhood. The letter was from my friend Lionel Strongfort. I had clipped a coupon from *Argosy All-Story Magazine*, signed it, placed it in an envelope, and mailed it to him. He had written back promptly, with an enthusiasm bordering on pure delight, saying I was undoubtedly a man of uncommon intelligence, potentially a giant, and—unlike the average run-of-the-mill people of the world who were, in a manner of speaking, dreamwalkers and daydreamers—a person who would some day be somebody.

His opinion of me was very much like my own. It was pleasant, however, to have the opinion so emphatically corroborated, particularly by a man in New York—and a man with the greatest chest expansion in the world. With the letter came several photographic reproductions of Mr. Strongfort wearing nothing but a little bit of leopard skin. He was a tremendous man and claimed that at one time he had been puny. He was loaded all over with muscle and appeared to be somebody who could lift a 1920 Ford roadster and tip it over.

It was an honor to have him for a friend.

The only trouble was—I didn't have the money. I forget how much the exact figure was at the beginning of our acquaintanceship, but I haven't forgotten that it was an amount completely out of the question. While I was eager to be grateful to Mr. Strongfort for his enthusiasm, I didn't seem to be able to find words with which to explain about not having the money, without immediately appearing to be a dream-walker and a daydreamer myself. So, while waiting from one day to another, looking everywhere for words that would not blight our friendship and degrade me to commonness, I talked the matter over with my uncle Gyko, who was studying Oriental philosophy at the time. He was amazed at my curious ambition, but quite pleased. He said the secret of greatness, according to Yoga, was the releasing within one's self of those mysterious vital forces which are in all men.

These strength, he said in English which he liked to affect when speaking to me, ease from God. I tell you, Aram, eat ease wonderful.

I told him I couldn't begin to become the powerful man I had decided to become until I sent Mr. Strongfort some money.

Mohney! my uncle said with contempt. I tell you, Aram, mohney is nawthing. You cannot bribe God.

Although my uncle Gyko wasn't exactly a puny man, he was certainly not the man Lionel Strongfort was. In a wrestling match I felt certain Mr. Strongfort would get a headlock or a half-nelson or a toe hold on my uncle and either make him give up or squeeze him to death. And then again, on the other hand, I wondered. My uncle was nowhere near as big as Mr. Strongfort, but neither was Mr. Strongfort as dynamically furious as my uncle. It seemed to me that, at best, Mr. Strongfort, in a match with my uncle, would have a great deal of unfamiliar trouble—I mean with the mysterious vital forces that were always getting released in my uncle, so that very often a swift glance from him would make a big man quail and turn away, or, if he had been speaking, stop quickly.

Long before I had discovered words with which to explain to Mr. Strongfort about the money, another letter came from him. It was as cordial as the first, and as a matter of fact, if anything, a little more cordial. I was delighted and ran about, releasing mysterious vital forces, turning handsprings, scrambling up trees, turning somersaults, trying to tip over 1920 Ford roadsters, challenging all comers to wrestle, and in many other ways alarming my relatives and irritating the neighbors.

Not only was Mr. Strongfort not sore at me, he had reduced the cost of the course. Even so, the money necessary was still more than I could get hold of. I was selling papers every day, but *that* money was for bread and stuff like that. For a while I got up very early every morning and went around town looking for a small satchel full of money. During six days of this adventuring I found a nickel and two pennies. I found also a woman's purse containing several foul-smelling cosmetic items, no money, and a slip of paper on which was written in an ignorant hand: Steve Hertwig, 3764 Ventura Avenue.

Three days after the arrival of Mr. Strongfort's second letter, his third letter came. From this time on our correspondence became one-sided. In fact, I didn't write at all. Mr. Strongfort's communications were overpowering and not at all easy to answer, without money. There was, in fact, almost nothing to say.

It was wintertime when the first letter came, and it was then that I made up my mind to become the most powerful man in my neighborhood and ultimately, for all I knew, one of the most powerful men in the world. I had ideas of my own as to how to go about getting that way, but I had also the warm friendship and high regard of Mr. Strongfort in New York, and the mystical and furious guardianship of my uncle Gyko, at home.

The letters from Mr. Strongfort continued to arrive every two or three days all winter and on into springtime. I remember, the day apricots were ripe enough to steal, the arrival of a most charming letter from my friend in New York. It was a hymn to newness on earth, the arrival of springtime, the time of youth in the heart, of renewal, fresh strength, fresh determination, and many other things. It was truly a beautiful epistle, probably as fine as any to the Romans or anybody else. It was full of the legend-quality, the world-feeling, and the dignity-of-strength-feeling so characteristic of Biblical days. The last paragraph of the lovely hymn brought up, apologetically, the coarse theme of money. The sum was six or seven times as little as it had been originally, and a new element had come into Mr. Strongfort's program of changing me over from a nobody to a giant of tremendous strength, and extreme attractiveness to women. Mr. Strongfort had decided, he said, to teach me everything in one fell swoop, or one sweep fall, or something of that sort. At any rate, for three dollars, he said, he would send me all his precious secrets in one envelope and the rest would be up to me, and history.

I took the matter up with my uncle Gyko, who by this time had reached the stage of fasting, meditating, walking for hours, and vibrating. We had had discussions two or three times a week all winter and he had told me in his own unique broken-English way all the secrets *he* had been learning from Yoga.

I tell you, Aram, he said, I can do *anything*. Eat ease wonderful.

I believed him, too, even though he had lost a lot of weight, couldn't sleep, and had a strange dynamic blaze in his eyes. He was very scornful of the world that year and was full of pity for the dumb beautiful animals that man was mistreating, killing, eating, domesticating, and teaching to do tricks.

I tell you, Aram, he said, eat ease creaminal to make the horses work. To keal the cows. To teach the dogs to jump, and the monkeys to smoke pipes.

I told him about the letter from Mr. Strongfort.

Mohney! he said. Always he wants mohney. I do not like heem.

My uncle was getting all his dope free from the theosophy-philosophy-astrology-and-miscellaneous shelf at the Public Library. He believed, however, that he was getting it straight from God. Before he took up Yoga he had been one of the boys around town and a good drinker of *rakhi,* but after the light began to come to him he gave up drinking. He said he was drinking liquor finer than *rakhi* or anything else.

What's that? I asked him.

Aram, he said, eat ease weasdom.

Anyhow, he had little use for Mr. Strongfort and regarded the man as a charlatan.

He's all right, I told my uncle.

But my uncle became furious, releasing mysterious vital forces, and said, I wheel break hease head, fooling all you leatle keads.

He ain't fooling, I said. He says he'll give me all his secrets for three dollars.

I tell you, Aram, my uncle Gyko said, he does not know any seacrets. He ease a liar.

I don't know, I said. I'd like to try that stuff out.

Eat ease creaminal, my uncle Gyko said, but I wheel geave you tree dollar.

My uncle Gyko gave me the necessary three dollars and I sent them along to Mr. Strongfort. The envelope came from New York, full of Mr. Strongfort's secrets. They were strangely simple. It was all stuff I had known anyhow but had been lazy to pay any attention to. The idea was to get up early in the morning and for an hour or so to do various kinds of acrobatic exercises, which were illustrated. Also to drink plenty of water, get plenty of fresh air, eat good wholesome food, and keep it up until you were a giant.

I felt a little let down and sent Mr. Strongfort a short polite note saying so. He ignored the note and I never heard from him again. In the meantime, I had been following the rules and growing more powerful every day. When I say *in the meantime,* I mean for four days I followed the rules. On the fifth day I decided to sleep instead of getting up and filling the house with noise and getting my grandmother sore. She used to wake up in the darkness of early morning and shout that I was an impractical fool and would never be rich. She would go back to

sleep for five minutes, wake up, and then shout that I would never buy and sell for a profit. She would sleep a little more, waken, and shout that there were once three sons of a king; one was wise like his father; the other was crazy about girls; and the third had less brains than a bird. Then she would get out of bed, and, shouting steadily, tell me the whole story while I did my exercises.

The story would usually warn me to be sensible and not go around waking her up before daybreak all the time. That would always be the moral, more or less, although the story itself would be about three sons of some king, or three brothers, each of them very wealthy and usually very greedy, or three daughters, or three proverbs, or three roads, or something else like that.

She was wasting her breath, though, because I wasn't enjoying the early-morning acrobatics any more than she was. In fact, I was beginning to feel that it was a lot of nonsense, and that my uncle Gyko had been right about Mr. Strongfort in the first place.

So I gave up Mr. Strongfort's program and returned to my own, which was more or less as follows: to take it easy and grow to be the most powerful man in the neighborhood without any trouble or exercise. Which is what I did.

That spring Longfellow School announced that a track meet was to be held, one school to compete against another; *everybody* to participate.

Here, I believed, was my chance. In my opinion I would be first in every event.

Somehow or other, however, continuous meditation on the theme of athletics had the effect of growing into a fury of anticipation that continued all day and all night, so that before the day of the track meet I had run the fifty-yard dash any number of hundreds of times, had jumped the running broad jump, the standing broad jump, and the high jump, and in each event had made my competitors look like weaklings.

This tremendous inner activity, which was strictly Yoga, changed on the day of the track meet into fever.

The time came at last for me and three other athletes, one of them a Greek, to go to our marks, get set, and go; and I did, in a blind rush of speed which I knew had never before occurred in the history of athletics.

It seemed to me that never before had any living man moved so swiftly. Within myself I ran the fifty yards fifty times before I so much as opened my eyes to find out how far back I had left the other runners. I was very much amazed at what I saw.

Three boys were four yards ahead of me and going away.

It was incredible. It was unbelievable, but it was obviously the truth. There ought to be some mistake, but there wasn't. There they were, ahead of me, going away.

Well, it simply meant that I would have to overtake them, with my eyes open, and win the race. This I proceeded to do. They continued, incredibly, however, to go away, in spite of my intention. I became irritated and decided to put them in their places for the impertinence, and began releasing all the mysterious vital forces within myself that I had. Somehow or other, however, not even this seemed to bring me any closer to them and I felt that in some strange way I was being betrayed. If so, I decided, I would shame my betrayer by winning the race in spite of the betrayal, and once again I threw fresh life and energy into my running. There wasn't a great distance still to go, but I knew I would be able to do it.

Then I knew I wouldn't.

The race was over.

I was last, by ten yards.

Without the slightest hesitation I protested and challenged the runners to another race, same distance, back. They refused to consider the proposal, which proved, I knew, that they were afraid to race me. I told them they knew very well I could beat them.

It was very much the same in all the other events.

When I got home I was in high fever and very angry. I was delirious all night and sick three days. My grandmother took very good care of me and probably was responsible for my not dying. When my uncle Gyko came to visit me he was no longer hollow-cheeked. It seems he had finished his fast, which had been a long one—forty days or so; and nights, too, I believe. He had stopped meditating, too, because he had practically exhausted the subject. He was again one of the boys around town, drinking, staying up all hours, and following the women.

I tell you, Aram, he said, we are a great family. We can do *anything*.

THE · CIRCUS

Any time a circus used to come to town, that was
all me and my old pal Joey Renna needed to make us
run hog-wild, as the saying is. All we needed to do was see
the signs on the fences and in the empty store windows to start
going to the dogs and neglecting our educations. All we needed to know
was that a circus was on its way to town for me and Joey to start wanting to know what good a little education ever did anybody anyway.

After the circus *reached* town we were just no good at all. We spent
all our time down at the trains, watching them unload the animals, walking out Ventura Avenue with the wagons with lions and tigers in them
and hanging around the grounds, trying to win the favor of the animal
men, the workers, the acrobats, and the clowns.

The circus was everything everything else we knew wasn't. It was
adventure, travel, danger, skill, grace, romance, comedy, peanuts, pop-
corn, chewing-gum and soda-water. We used to carry water to the elephants and stand around afterwards and try to seem associated with the
whole magnificent affair, the putting up of the big tent, the getting
everything in order, and the worldly-wise waiting for the people to come
and spend their money.

One day Joey came tearing into the classroom of the fifth grade at
Emerson School ten minutes late, and without so much as removing his
hat or trying to explain his being late, shouted, Hey, Aram, what the
hell are you doing here? The circus is in town.

And sure enough I'd forgotten. I jumped up and ran out of the room
with poor old Miss Flibety screaming after me, Aram Garoghlanian,
you stay in this room. Do you hear me, Aram Garoghlanian?

I heard her all right and I knew what my not staying would mean. It
would mean another powerful strapping from old man Dawson. But I
568

couldn't help it. I was just crazy about a circus.

I been looking all over for you, Joey said in the street. What happened?

I forgot, I said. I knew it was coming all right, but I forgot it was today. How far along are they?

I was at the trains at five, Joey said. I been out at the grounds since seven. I had breakfast at the circus table. Boy, it was good.

Honest, Joey? I said. How were they?

They're all swell, Joey said. Couple more years, they told me, and I'll be ready to go away with them.

As what? I said. Lion-tamer, or something like that?

I guess maybe not as a lion-tamer, Joey said. I figure more like a workman till I learn about being a clown or something, I guess. I don't figure I could work with lions right away.

We were out on Ventura Avenue, headed for the circus grounds, out near the County Fairgrounds, just north of the County Hospital.

Boy, what a breakfast, Joey said. Hot-cakes, ham and eggs, sausages, coffee. Boy.

Why didn't you tell me? I said.

I thought you knew, Joey said. I thought you'd be down at the trains same as last year. I would have told you if I knew you'd forgotten. What made you forget?

I don't know, I said. Nothing, I guess.

I was wrong there, but I didn't know it at the time. I hadn't really forgotten. What I'd done was *remembered*. I'd gone to work and remembered the strapping Dawson gave me last year for staying out of school the day the circus was in town. That was the thing that had kind of kept me sleeping after four-thirty in the morning when by rights I should have been up and dressing and on my way to the trains. It was the memory of that strapping old man Dawson had given me, but I didn't know it at the time. We used to take them strappings kind of for granted, me and Joey, on account of we wanted to be fair and square with the Board of Education and if it was against the rules to stay out of school when you weren't sick, and if you were supposed to get strapped for doing it, well, there we were, we'd done it, so let the Board of Education balance things the best way they knew how. They did that with a strapping. They used to threaten to send me and Joey to Reform School but they never did it.

Circus? old man Dawson used to say. I see. *Circus*. Well, bend down, boy.

So, first Joey, then me, would bend down and old man Dawson would get some powerful shoulder exercise while we tried not to howl. We wouldn't howl for five or six licks, but after that we'd howl like Indians coming. They used to be able to hear us all over the school and old man Dawson, after our visits got to be kind of regular, urged us politely to try to make a little less noise, inasmuch as it was a school and people were trying to study.

It ain't fair to the others, old man Dawson said. They're trying to learn something for themselves.

We can't help it, Joey said. It hurts.

That I know, old man Dawson said, but it seems to me there's such a thing as modulation. I believe a lad can overdo his howling if he ain't thoughtful of others. Just try to modulate that awful howl a little. I think you can do it.

Then he gave Joey a strapping of twenty and Joey tried his best not to howl so loud. After the strapping his face was very red and old man Dawson was very tired.

How was that? Joey said.

That was better, old man Dawson said. By far the most courteous you've managed yet.

I did my best, Joey said.

I'm grateful to you, old man Dawson said.

He was tired and out of breath. I moved up to the chair in front of him that he furnished during these matters to help us suffer the stinging pain. I got in the right position and he said, Wait a minute, Aram. Give a man a chance to get his breath. I'm not twenty-three years old. I'm *sixty*-three. Let me rest a minute.

All right, I said, but I sure would like to get this over with.

Don't howl too loud, he said. Folks passing by in the street are liable to think this is a veritable chamber of tortures. Does it really hurt that much?

You can ask Joey, I said.

How about it, Joey? old man Dawson said. Aren't you lads exaggerating just a little? Perhaps to impress someone in your room? Some girl, perhaps?

We don't howl to impress anybody, Mr. Dawson, Joey said. We wouldn't howl if we could help it. Howling makes us feel ashamed, doesn't it, Aram?

It's awfully embarrassing to go back to our seats in our room after howling that way, I said. We'd rather not howl if we could help it.

Well, old man Dawson said, I'll not be unreasonable. I'll only ask you to try to modulate it a little.

I'll do my best, Mr. Dawson, I said. Got your breath back?

Give me just a moment longer, Aram, Mr. Dawson said.

When he got his breath back he gave me my twenty and I howled a little louder than Joey and then we went back to class. It was awfully embarrassing. Everybody was looking at us.

Well, Joey said, what did you expect? The rest of you would fall down and die if you got twenty. You wouldn't *howl a little*, you'd die.

That'll be enough out of you, Miss Flibety said.

Well, it's true, Joey said. They're all scared. A circus comes to town and what do they do? They come to school. They don't go out to the circus.

That'll be enough, Miss Flibety said.

Who do they think they are, giving us dirty looks? Joey said.

Miss Flibety lifted her hand, hushing Joey.

Now the circus was back in town, another year had gone by, it was April again, and we were on our way out to the grounds. Only this time it was worse than ever because they'd seen us at school and knew we were going out to the circus.

Do you think they'll send Stafford after us? I said.

Stafford was truant officer.

We can always run, Joey said. If he comes, I'll go one way, you go another. He can't chase *both* of us. At least one of us will get away.

All right, I said. Suppose one of us gets caught?

Well, let's see, Joey said. Should the one who isn't caught give himself up or should he wreck Stafford's Ford?

I vote for wreck, I said.

So do I, Joey said, so wreck it is.

When we got out to the grounds a couple of the little tents were up, and the big one was going up. We stood around and watched. It was great the way they did it. Just a handful of guys who looked like tramps doing work you'd think no less than a hundred men could do. Doing it with style, too.

All of a sudden a man everybody called Red hollered at me and Joey.

Here, you Arabs, he said, give us a hand.

Me and Joey ran over to him.

Yes, sir, I said.

He was a small man with very broad shoulders and very big hands. You didn't feel that he was small, because he seemed so powerful and because he had so much thick red hair on his head. You thought he was practically a giant.

He handed me and Joey a rope. The rope was attached to some canvas that was lying on the ground.

This is going to be easy, Red said. As the boys lift the pole and get it in place you keep pulling the rope, so the canvas will go up with the pole.

Yes, sir, Joey said.

Everybody was busy when we saw Stafford.

We can't run now, I said.

Let him come, Joey said. We told Red we'd give him a hand and we're going to do it.

I'll tell you what, I said. We'll tell him we'll go with him after we get the canvas up; then we'll run.

All right, Joey said.

Stafford was a big fellow in a business suit who had a beef-red face and looked as if he ought to be a lawyer or something. He came over and said, All right, you hooligans, come along with me.

We promised to give Red a hand, Joey said. We'll come just as soon as we get this canvas up.

We were pulling for all we were worth, slipping and falling. The men were all working hard. Red was hollering orders, and then the whole thing was over and we had done our part.

We didn't even get a chance to find out what Red was going to say to us, or if he was going to invite us to sit at the table for lunch, or what.

Joey busted loose and ran one way and I ran the other and Stafford came after *me*. I heard the circus men laughing and Red hollering, Run, boy, run. He can't catch *you*. He's soft. Give him a good run. He needs the exercise.

I could hear Stafford, too. He was very sore and he was cussing.

I got away, though, and stayed low until I saw him drive off in his Ford. Then I went back to the big tent and found Joey.

We'll get it this time, Joey said.

I guess it'll be Reform School this time, I said.

No, Joey said. I guess it'll be thirty. We're going to do some awful howling if it is. Thirty's a lot of whacks even if he *is* sixty-three years old. He ain't exactly a weakling.

Thirty? I said. Ouch. That's liable to make me cry.

Maybe, Joey said. Me too, maybe. Seems like ten can make you cry, then you hold off till it's eleven, then twelve, and you think you'll start crying on the next one, but you don't. We haven't so far, anyway. Maybe we will when it's thirty.

Oh, well, I said, that's tomorrow.

Red gave us some more work to do around the grounds and let us sit next to him at lunch. It was swell. We talked to some acrobats who were Spanish, and to a family of Italians who worked with horses. We saw both shows, the afternoon one and the evening one, and then we helped with the work, taking the circus to pieces again; then we went down to the trains, and then home. I got home real late. In the morning I was sleepy when I had to get up for school.

They were waiting for us. Miss Flibety didn't even let us sit down for the roll call. She just told us to go to the office. Old man Dawson was waiting for us, too. Stafford was there, too, and very sore.

I figured, Well, here's where we go to Reform School.

Here they are, Mr. Dawson said to Stafford. Take them away, if you like.

It was easy to tell they'd been talking for some time and hadn't been getting along any too well. Old man Dawson seemed irritated and Stafford seemed sore at him.

In *this* school, old man Dawson said, I do any punishing that's got to be done. Nobody else. I can't stop you from taking them to Reform School, though.

Stafford didn't say anything. He just left the office.

Well, lads, old man Dawson said. How was it?

We had lunch with them, Joey said.

Let's see now, old man Dawson said. What offense is this, the sixteenth or the seventeenth?

It ain't that many, Joey said. Must be eleven or twelve.

Well, old man Dawson said, I'm sure of one thing. This is the time I'm supposed to make it thirty.

I think the next one is the one you're supposed to make thirty, Joey said.

No, Mr. Dawson said, we've lost track somewhere, but I'm sure this is the time it goes up to thirty. Who's going to be first?

Me, I said.

All right, Aram, Mr. Dawson said. Take a good hold on the chair, brace yourself, and try to modulate your howl.

Yes, sir, I said. I'll do my best, but thirty's an awful lot.

Well, a funny thing happened. He gave me thirty all right and I howled all right, but it *was* a modulated howl. It was the most modulated howl I ever howled; because it was the *easiest* strapping I ever got. I counted them and there were thirty all right, but they didn't hurt, so I didn't cry, as I was afraid I might.

It was the same with Joey. We stood together waiting to be dismissed.

I'm awfully grateful to you boys, old man Dawson said, for modulating your howls so nicely this time. I don't want people to think I'm killing you.

We wanted to thank him for giving us such easy strappings, but we couldn't say it. I think he knew the way we felt, though, because he smiled in a way that gave us an idea he knew.

Then we went back to class.

It was swell because we knew everything would be all right till the County Fair opened in September.

Donald Ogden Stewart

The biography of Donald Ogden Stewart in Twentieth Century Authors concludes with this accurate but unfeeling sentence: "He is tall, bald, and very near-sighted." In compensation for that disposal, the same volume quotes pieces of Stewart's own autobiography. We learn, for example, that Stewart, born in 1894, in Columbus, Ohio, "in his early years gave manifold evidences of his gift for humor, and many of his bright remarks are still related by his proud mother upon the slightest provocation or, in fact, upon no provocation at all. There were others, however, who did not think this child prodigy was so funny. Mr. Stewart still bears a long red scar on his forehead as mute evidence of one little red-headed girl's particular lack of appreciation of his early efforts. At fourteen he was sent to Phillips Exeter because it was a good preparatory school for Harvard. At eighteen he entered Yale."

Groomed, but not too well-groomed, for a business career, he worked in states as far apart as Alabama and Minnesota, and thereupon decided that he wanted to go in for literature. It was as a parodist that Stewart made his literary debut, with A Parody Outline of History, Aunt Polly's Story of Mankind, and Mr. and Mrs. Haddock Abroad, burlesques that were light-hearted but not too light-minded. The satirical implications suggested the next step, the turn from the humorist to the outspoken liberal. Writing scenarios in Hollywood and plays in New York he managed, somehow, to preserve, edit, and utter fighting as well as fooling words.

FROM *"The Crazy Fool"*

The twelve-forty-five left at twelve-forty-five. "We're off!" cried Charlie, with all the eager, excited assurance of eternal Youth in the face of the Great Adventure. The old gentleman only smiled—the wise smile of Age —Age mellowed and saddened by Experience.

Five minutes later, Charlie again looked out of the window.

"If I'm not too inquisitive," he said, "may I ask a question?"

"My name is King," said the old gentleman, "Horace King. You may ask me anything."

"Well, in the first place," said Charlie, "isn't that the same man out there we saw back at the station?"

Mr. King looked out.

"Yes," he said, "I believe it is."

Charlie took out an envelope and did some figuring on the back.

"Well, then," he said, at last, "either he is moving—or we're not."

"I'll ask him," said the old gentleman affably, and he tried to raise the window.

"Here, I'll help you," said Charlie, and together they succeeded in getting their hands very dirty.

"It won't raise," said Charlie.

"Ah, my boy," said the old man patiently, "maybe it's *us* who won't *lower*. Did you ever stop to think of that?"

"No," replied Charlie, so he and the old man lowered.

"Maybe if I had a diamond," said Mr. King, "I could cut a hole in the glass and get out."

Just then an employee in overalls walked through the car, carrying a pail and a mop.

"I beg your pardon," said Mr. King, "but have you a diamond?"

The man stared dumbly.

"*Pardonnez-moi,*" said Charlie quickly, "*mais est-ce que vous avez une diamant . . .*"

"It's masculine, I think," said Mr. King.

"Isn't he, though!" said Charlie. "And what a mustache!"

"I meant the word," explained Mr. King; "*diamant*—it's '*un diamant*,' if I'm not too mistaken."

"*Un diamant,*" repeated Charlie to the man, but with no better result.

"*Bitte,*" began Mr. King. "*Haben Sie vielleicht . . .*"

The man turned and left the car.

"In my time," said Mr. King, "employees were taught courtesy."

"And French and dancing," said Charlie. "And ladies were ladies and did the gavotte," and he pretended to execute a few quaint steps in the aisle. "Will you join me?"

"Ah, me," sighed Mr. King. "The good old days."

"Maybe," said Charlie, "if we don't let the window know we are trying to open it, we can catch it unawares."

"All right," said Mr. King, and they sat down and pretended to go to sleep. Suddenly Charlie leaped up and grabbed the window and after a tremendous struggle forced it open.

"See!" he said triumphantly, "I told you."

Mr. King, however, still had his eyes closed and did not answer.

"That's a wonderful piece of acting," said Charlie, and he held a mirror in front of Mr. King's mouth to see if by any chance he were dead.

Mr. King soon opened his eyes and looked out the window.

"That's the same man," he said, somewhat petulantly. "I wish he would go away"—and he called to the man.

"I beg your pardon," he said, "but can you tell me what station this is?"

"New York," replied the man.

"New York," repeated Mr. King, with a puzzled look. "I see. Thank you."

He turned to Charlie. "We left New York at twelve-forty-five," he said.

"I know it," said Charlie. "I was there," and he turned to the man. "We left New York at twelve-forty-five," he said.

"Did you?" replied the man.

"Yes, we 'did you,'" said Charlie, somewhat irritated.

"Careful," said Mr. King. "Let me talk to him. Are you sure," he said presently, "that this is New York? Are you acquainted here?"

The man put his fingers to his mouth and whistled shrilly. "Hey, Bill!" he called.

Bill came, wiping his hands on a piece of waste.

"Here's a couple of guys," said the man, "want to know if this is New York."

Bill looked at Charlie and Mr. King, then tossed the waste onto the next track.

"Come on, Eddie," he said. "We've got to finish that truck on thirteen."

Bill and Eddie left to finish the truck on thirteen. Charlie looked at Mr. King. Then they picked up their baggage and walked out of the car by the front end.

"I guess they didn't take this car," said Charlie, somewhat crest-fallen.

"You'll learn, my boy," said Mr. King wisely, "not to count on any-thing."

Charlie was looking through a time-table.

"That's not the right railroad," said Mr. King.

"I know it," said Charlie, "but it's the only time-table I've ever had. We were Southerners," he added, "and proud."

"Time-tables are like women," said Mr. King. "The more you some-thing or other them, the more they—I forget the exact words."

"How's the tune go?" asked Charlie. "Maybe I can help you out."

"There used to be a two-thirteen," said Mr. King, "but I can't remem-ber where it was a two-thirteen from. My memory is getting worse every day."

"New York?" suggested Charles. "Chicago?"

"Maybe," replied Mr. King. "Anyway, we can ask. It never does any harm to ask, my boy."

So they picked up their bags and walked back through the gate to the Information Bureau.

"Is there a two-thirteen?" asked Mr. King politely, but the informa-tion man was talking on the telephone and did not answer.

"It's your turn to ask a question now," said Mr. King to Charlie when the man had finished. So Charlie asked a question.

The man reached under the counter, handed Charlie a purple time-table and answered a call on another telephone.

"Now I'll ask one," said Mr. King, so the next time the man seemed to be free, Mr. King asked one.

"What great English statesman," he began, "is sometimes referred to as——"

Mr. King was handed a time-table—a red-and-black one.

"Dear, dear," he said. "We don't seem to be getting anywhere. And it gets dark early around here, too."

"It's the fault of our colleges," said Charlie. "College graduates don't know anything."

"When I was at college," said Mr. King, "a young man had to work," and he glared at the smooth-faced youngster behind the counter.

"I tell you what," suggested Charlie. "Let's get all the time-tables and go over in a corner and look for a two-thirteen—and the first one who finds it can sit next the window all the way."

So, with a little patience, they collected a large assortment of time-

tables and retired to a cold marble bench on which Mr. King spread
out a newspaper before he sat down.

"You'll understand," he explained to Charlie, "when you're older."

"Oh, go on, tell me now," said Charlie, but Mr. King wisely refused.

"Here's a two-thirteen!" he cried. "I get the seat."

"Let's see," said Charlie. "The only trouble is," he said, "that that
train goes to St. Louis."

"I've been to St. Louis," said Mr. King. "I was there in '84—no, '85—
I can remember just as well. We got there about two in the afternoon—
phew, wasn't it hot—and I kept saying——"

"Here's a train," interrupted Charlie, "which might do."

"You mustn't hesitate to interrupt me," said Mr. King, "any time. I'm
old and I get to talking and I know it doesn't interest anyone, so don't
you hesitate to cut right in. So that afternoon in St. Louis, I kept saying,
'My, but I wish it would rain,' and the man I was with, John Bradshaw——"

"Do you think this is our train?" asked Charlie, holding up the time-
table.

"That's right—you just interrupt whenever you want," said Mr.
King. "Well, John Bradshaw—he was from Cleveland, then, although
he came originally from Albany and I had known him for several years
—oh, ever since he and I were youngsters——"

"All I want to know is," asked Charlie, "if you think this is our train," and he pointed to a column on the forty-second page.

"That's what I like to see," said Mr. King, taking out his spectacles, "a young man who isn't afraid to ask questions. So John Bradshaw said, 'I bet it doesn't rain before night,' and I said, 'I bet it does'—and along about five-thirty, it began to look as if it might rain and, sure enough, just about six o'clock, it began to rain and it rained all night. Now, isn't that about as dull a story as you ever heard?"

"It's pretty dull," said Charlie. "And yet it's probably true."

"Well, as a matter of fact," said Mr. King, "it isn't true. I never knew any John Bradshaw."

"Do you mean to say," asked Charlie, "that you made that all up out of your own head?"

Mr. King smiled. "Most of it," he said. "The part about the rain I got from watching rain."

"With an imagination like that," said Charlie, "you ought to write books."

"I wrote a book," said Mr. King.

"I bet you did," said Charlie, "and I bet I've read it a hundred times without knowing it."

"The book's not so bad," said Mr. King. "It's got more of a plot."

"More of a plot than *what?*" asked Charlie.

"Than the story that I just told," replied Mr. King.

"About John Bradshaw?" asked Charlie.

"Yes," replied the old man, "I told that story more or less just for the dialogue—and the character study."

"The dialogue was a knockout," said Charlie, "and that reminds me— I'm going over and find out the truth about our train."

"The truth never hurt anyone," said Mr. King.

"Now you sit right here," said Charlie, "and be quiet, and Charlie will be back as quick as you can say Jack Robinson."

"Jack Robinson," said Mr. King.

"You've got to shut your eyes," said Charlie, "and count up to a hundred."

"But when I shut my eyes," protested Mr. King, "I go to sleep."

"Not if you drink coffee," said Charlie. "I'll bring you some."

"And a cheese sandwich," added the old man, but Charlie had gone. So Mr. King shut his eyes and when Charlie came back, he was asleep.

"This is very discouraging," said Charlie. "I'll never make good and marry Judith if this nice old gentleman is going to go to sleep all the time," and he woke Mr. King up by laying him flat on the bench, loosening his collar and working his arms up and down and backward and forward until artificial respiration began.

"Where am I?" asked Mr. King, opening his eyes.

"In St. Louis," replied Charlie, "and it is just beginning to rain and we'll have to hurry if we want to catch the two-thirteen. My name's Bradshaw."

"Where's my cheese sandwich?" asked Mr. King.

"We haven't time," replied Charlie.

"Time and tide——" began Mr. King, but Charlie picked up the bags and started for the gate.

"You promised me a cheese sandwich," said Mr. King reproachfully, as he hurried along beside the young man.

"Later," said Charlie.

"But I want it *now*," said Mr. King.

"Later—Charlie said '*later*.'"

"But——"

"Do you want Charlie to give you a good sock in the eye?"

Mr. King was silent, and they reached the gates.

"Have you got the tickets?" asked Charlie.

Mr. King began fumbling through his pockets.

"Maybe you swallowed them," suggested the gate-keeper, sarcastically.

Mr. King stopped and considered.

"No," he said at last, "I don't think I did. That was a hat-check I swallowed."

"He puts everything in his mouth," explained Charlie.

"I was only kidding," said the gateman. "Hurry up."

"Maybe they dropped down inside your trousers," said Charlie. "You might take them off and look."

"You can't do that here," warned the gate-keeper, instantly.

"Why not?" asked Charlie, looking around for a "No-Taking-Off-of-Trousers" sign.

"Say, are you two trying to kid me?" asked the gateman.

"Dear me, no," exclaimed Charlie. "Not *you*."

"Here they are," said Mr. King. "They were on my forehead all the time." And after the tickets had been indignantly punched, they passed through the gates and onto the train.

"Are you sure this train stops at our station?" asked Charlie nervously, after the bags had been swung up into the rack. "I can't afford to make any mistakes at the start."

"There's only one way to be sure," replied Mr. King, "and that's the right way," and so together they walked through the coach, out onto the platform, and up to where the engine was standing.

"That's quite an engine you've got there," remarked Mr. King, looking up pleasantly at the engineer and resting one hand on the cab.

"Mustn't touch!" cautioned Charlie.

The engineer regarded Mr. King in silence.

"Yes, sir," went on the old gentleman, "that's certainly quite an engine."

"Yeh?" said the engineer.

"Tell me," said Mr. King—"and I don't want to seem inquisitive—but are you connected with this road?"

"I'm the engineer," replied the other.

"Ah," said Mr. King. "I thought so. The engineer—well, well," and he turned to Charlie with a smile. "He says he's the engineer."

Charlie raised his hat, deferentially.

"And this is certainly quite an engine," went on Mr. King. "Yes, sir—quite an engine. I suppose these engines go in and out of the station pretty regularly?"

There was no answer.

"I should imagine they did," said Mr. King. "Yes, sir—pretty regularly. On schedules, probably—or am I presuming too much?"

"They have regular schedules, if that's what you mean," said the engineer.

"Well, now, that's very interesting," said Mr. King, and he turned once more to Charlie. "They have regular schedules, he says."

"And I suppose," went on Mr. King, "that you have a perfectly definite list of places where you are expected to stop—of course, I'm not a railroad man in any sense of the word—but that is what I would suppose."

There was no response from the cab.

"They tell me," continued Mr. King, "that one of these trains used to stop at a place called Lodge Junction—I think that was the name———"

"This train stops at Lodge Junction, if that's what you want to know," said the engineer.

"Thank you," said Mr. King. "That's just what I wanted to know. Come, Charles," and they walked triumphantly back to their seats.

"Yes, sir," explained Mr. King. "You can get anything you wish if you only go about it in the right way."

"Well, I wish this train would start," said Charlie, looking at his watch.

"It will," said Mr. King, "with time and patience," and at that, the train gave a couple of tugs and started.

"See?" said Mr. King, smiling wisely at the impatient youth. "When you're as old as I am——" But just then the train stopped suddenly with a jerk and Charlie's golf bag crashed down from the rack onto Mr. King's straw hat.

"I didn't need to have brought my extra putter," said Charlie apologetically.

"That's perfectly all right," said Mr. King, rubbing his head. "That's what I get for being selfish. I should have given *you* that seat."

For the first hour or so, Charlie and Mr. King gazed out of the window, more or less in silence.

"It's sort of an unusual place you're going to," said Mr. King at last. "The people may strike you as a little—well, different—but I think you'll learn to enjoy them."

"If they're at all like you," replied Charlie, "I will."

"Well, they're like me," said Mr. King, pleased, "and they're not— that's quite a paradox, isn't it?" he said. "I'll have to remember that."

Charlie leaned back in his seat and began to think about Judith.

"It must be great to be married," he murmured, but Mr. King did not answer, so Charlie turned to the lady sitting alone across the aisle.

"It must be great to be married," he said.

She was reading, but looked up with a smile. There was something unusual about her, too—and something quite interesting. Beautiful, well-dressed, veiled, and with a curious birdlike voice.

"It's terrible to be married," she said, with a faint shrug of one small shoulder.

"Why, you're crazy," replied Charlie. "And, besides, you don't know Judith."

"There are lots of people I don't know," she said. "I don't know you, for example."

· "I'm just old Charlie Hatch," he explained. "I was born in a log cabin and then I became a surveyor, and many stories are told about my honesty and my marksmanship, until one day I came across a copy of Shakespeare in the pocket of an old Indian chief and that made me want to go to college. So I walked twenty-one miles to the little old schoolhouse, but it wasn't there, and just then a kind old gentleman, driving by in his automobile, saw me splitting rails in my coonskin cap and asked me if this was the road to New York and I said, 'No.' 'A bright lad,' he said, turning to his wife, who was driving. 'How would you like to go to college?' 'Fine,' I replied, so they laughed and drove on, and sometimes, as I sit around the fire with my wife and kiddies I think I am the happier, don't you?"

"I think you are very nice," said the lady. "And now I will tell you who I am. I was a poor little girl born in a tenement and my mother and father used to be drunk all the time and beat me so I grew up to be sweet and pure and beautiful and one day when the Prince of Wales knocked a polo ball into our alley he saw me and fell in love with me and married me and we lived happily ever after and now I think I shall return to my book," and with another intriguing smile, she began to read and Charlie noticed that it was a French book written in French.

Suddenly, as though a thought had just come to her, she wrote something on a piece of paper, got up and walked past Charlie to the front of the car and out, and when Charlie looked down he saw that the slip of paper was in his lap.

"There is a man in the third seat back of you," he read, "who has been annoying me. If he follows me out of the car, and you are an American gentleman, you will take care of him for me."

"Say, listen——" said Charlie, but she had disappeared, so he slowly and cautiously turned around to look.

The gentleman in the third seat back of him was one of the largest men Charlie had ever seen. And as he looked, the fellow slowly got up out of his seat and started forward.

When he was opposite Charlie, Charlie stood up.

"Take that, you cad," he said, and he aimed a blow at the man's jaw, but missed.

"Down where ah come from," said Charlie, "they string 'em up for less than that," and he swung, and missed again.

"Say, listen," said Charlie. "How can I knock you down if you don't hold still?"

"All right," said the man, and he stood still and Charlie knocked him down.

"Now *you* hold still," said the stranger, getting up, "and I'll knock *you* down."

"What for?" asked Charlie.

"I don't know," said the man. "I've never been down South," and with that he knocked Charlie down.

"Now what do we do?" he asked, picking Charlie up.

"I don't know," confessed Charlie. "How do you feel?"

"My jaw hurts a little," said the man.

"So does mine," said Charlie. "I tell you what—if you apologize to the lady, my honor will be satisfied."

"All right," said the man. "I'm sort of shy with ladies, though. Who is she?"

"Why, don't you know?" and Charlie looked at the big man angrily.

"No. I was just going up to get a drink of water," explained the man.

"Well," said Charlie, "you want to be careful about that in the future."

"Yes, sir," said the man.

Charlie relented, held out his hand, and smiled. "No hard feelings, stranger," he said, and the two men shook hands.

"Now can I get my drink of water?" asked the man.

"You sure can," said Charlie heartily, and so the stranger passed forward out of his life and so, apparently, had the interesting lady.

After the second hour, the train seemed to become considerable of a local—at least, it made a great many unnecessary stops for such a nice train, and Charlie impatiently woke Mr. King up and suggested that they go forward again and ask the engineer if there was anything they could do about it.

"He's probably just lonely," said Charlie, as the train once more came to a halt. "Or maybe it's his wind. Too many cigarettes are very harmful in excess."

"Perhaps he ate something which didn't agree with him," said Mr. King. "I wonder what it could have been?"

"Eggplant," suggested Charlie. "That doesn't go with some things at all."

"I've got some bicarbonate of soda in my bag," said Mr. King, and Charlie took down the suitcase and opened it.

"The only drawback," said Charlie, "is that it might offend him to have us comparative strangers climb up into his cab with some bicarbonate, especially if he is just renting the cab for the afternoon."

"Not if you do it in the right way," said Mr. King. "Leave it to me."

So Mr. King dug around in his bag until he found some notepaper and then he sat down and began to write.

"Would you say, 'Dear Engineer,'" he asked, "or, 'Dear Mr. Engineer'?"

"'Dear Mr. Engineer,'" replied Charlie, "unless it is a relative, or a very dear friend."

"I don't think he's a relative," said Mr. King, "most of our family were professional men," so he wrote, "Dear Mr. Engineer," and stopped.

"Unless," he added thoughtfully, "it is Cousin Lemuel. Cousin Lemuel was sort of a black sheep of the family—he eloped with an actress his sophomore year at Columbia. It might just possibly be Cousin Lemuel and he was always very sensitive," so he crossed out the "Mr." and wrote "Dear Engineer," and then added, apologetically, "(If I may call you so)."

"There," he said, and waited for an inspiration.

" 'In reply to yours of even date,' " suggested Charlie.

Mr. King shook his head.

"Too formal," he said, "and, besides, there wasn't any 'yours of even date.' "

"It's just a business form," said Charlie. "I learned it in the bank."

The two men were silent in the face of what seemed an insurmountable difficulty. Charlie at last took out a pencil and wrote something on the back of an envelope. "Here," and he read: " 'I suppose you are bothered with letters like this all the time, but I have always been a great admirer of your work and I just couldn't refrain from writing to tell you how much I enjoy the way you handle that engine and if you ever need any bicarbonate of soda, I hope you will let me be the first to know about it.' "

Mr. King shook his head.

"You forgot to ask him for a photograph," he said, "and, besides, those letters are always answered by the engineer's mother or his secretary."

Charlie chewed the pencil disconsolately.

"No," said Mr. King, "I think it would probably be better to start with something a little less stereotyped—a little more personal," and after a long interval, he began to write.

" 'It is very pleasant here now,' " he read, as he went along, " 'with just the right amount of tang in the air, and I often think of you up there in that hot cab and wish you were here.' "

The train came to a stop.

" 'Although quite warm at noon,' " continued Mr. King, " 'the nights are always cool and Thursday we actually slept between blankets. Think of that!' "

"Now for the body of the letter," said Mr. King.

" 'As I sit at my window and look out, I see——' " The train started and Mr. King looked out.

"Oh, good Heavens!" he cried. "This is our station!" and he slammed the bag shut and jumped up. Charlie grabbed everything in sight and they fled down the aisle and off the moving train.

Frank Sullivan

Francis John Sullivan is another example of America's favorite success story, the local boy who makes good—at practically everything. Born in 1892, in Saratoga Springs, a graduate of the Saratoga High School, Sullivan got his degree at Cornell and a second lieutenancy in the First World War. A journalist since youth, he perfected a kind of commentary which was a little like a brief informal essay and a lot like a brisk extravaganza.

A calculating humorist, Sullivan remains incalculable. He loves children and animals and sometimes understands them; he loathes clichés and has become America's outstanding collector of trite phrases. His curiously assorted passions and exasperations are candidly exposed in The Adventures of an Oaf, Innocent Bystanding, Broccoli and Old Lace, and the explicit Sullivan at Bay.

A Trip to Hollywood

'Hollywood! All out!''

The voice of the conductor rang through the crack flier which had borne us westward.

Was it possible that I was really in Hollywood, the Citadel of Glamour? I pinched myself. It was.

A young woman stood beside me in the aisle. Probably one of that army that descends upon the film capital each year seeking the bubble reputation even in the camera's eye.

"You have, perhaps, come to Hollywood to break into the movies?" I ventured to ask her.

She looked at me dreamily.

"I have come to Hollywood to see Clark Gable," she said in a reverent voice. "I stuck up a filling station in Tonawanda to get the money. I had to do it. I was desperate."

"I know, and understand," I told her gently.

The young lady said her name was Twistle—Miss Millicent Twistle.

"You may call me Milly, if you like, or Twiss," she said. "Have you come all the way to Hollywood to see Clark too?"

"I wouldn't mind seeing him, of course," I said, "only I must confess I want to see more of Hollywood than him."

The Gable-maddened maiden looked at me with an expression of contempt not unmixed with disdain, as if to say, what more could anyone wish to see than Clark Gable.

"Don't misunderstand me," I said. "I yield to no one in my admiration for Mr. Gable, but, after all, he is only one phase of this magic place. I want to see all the phases. I want to see Malibu Beach. I want to see a yes man in action, and I would like to crash one of those famous Hollywood parties where they play practical jokes and push you into the swimming pool. I also want to see the Brown Derby and Joan Crawford."

"Do you?" came a silvery voice behind us.

I turned, and there stood absolutely the most ravishingly beautiful woman I had ever in all my born days beheld. She smiled. Our eyes met. Somehow we both—knew. I clasped her in my arms.

"I have always known that someday I would—find you," I said brokenly.

"I knew that someday you would—come," she said simply.

"No, no, no, no, no," came an irritated, weary voice. I looked behind

us and saw a portly gentleman seated in a chair labeled "Director." H
seemed to be supervising the operations of several cameras which wer
trained on my radiant vis-à-vis and myself.

"You said that as though you were asking her to pass the catsup," h
rebuked. "Man alive, put some fire into it! You love her. You're crazy
for her. Come on now, once again. Ready! Set! Camera! Go!"

Came the strains of a violin playing Love's Old Sweet Song. Tear:
come to my eyes. Something in me snapped. Clasping the young lady t
me again, I said chokingly, "Oh, my loved one, I always knew that some
day I would—find you."

"I knew that someday you would—come," she said simply.

"That's more like it," applauded the director. "That was titanic. You
were only colossal before. . . . Come on, boys."

They took their cameras and marched away.

"Your face is familiar," I said to my loved one. "Haven't we me
before?"

"I am Joan Crawford," said the vision simply.

Ten minutes in Hollywood and Joan Crawford already clasped in my
arms!

"Could this happen any place else?" I asked Twiss, over Joan':
shoulder.

"It certainly beats the Dutch," Twiss admitted.

"Who is that you're talking to back there?" demanded Joan.

"It's a little girl who thumbed her way three thousand miles to feas:
her eyes on Clark Gable. Miss Crawford, do you suppose you can fix i
so she can see Mr. Gable?"

"I certainly can," said Miss Crawford. "She's just in time. Clark i
granting audience at three this afternoon to all the girls who hav
traveled from afar for that purpose."

"Where?" cried Twiss frantically.

"In the Hollywood Bowl," said Miss Crawford, "but you better star
right now or you may not get a seat."

Miss Twistle was off like the Burlington Zephyr.

"Have you lunched?" said Miss Crawford.

I hadn't.

"Then let's go to the Brown Derby," she suggested.

"Oh, the Brown Derby. Good."

Happy in our new-found love, we went to the Brown Derby. Four o
five thousand movie stars were having lunch, or crackers and milk, a
the famous restaurant, and there was a busy hum of conversation fron
which one's ear could occasionally pick such Hollywood colloquialism:

as "Terrific," "Montage," "Dub in," "Not the type," "Yes, Mr. Warner," and "So they jumped her salary from $75 a week to $3500."

Miss Crawford took me to a table where sat twelve young women,
each one of them absolutely the most ravishingly beautiful vision I had
ever seen.

"These are the Misses Loy, Davies, Young, Lombard, Shearer, West,
Del Rio, Sullavan, Francis, Hopkins, Temple and Hepburn," said Miss
Crawford.

"How do you do, Miss Loy, Miss Davies, Miss——" I began.

"Oh, call us Myrna, Marion, Loretta, Carole, Norma, Mae, Dolores,
Margaret, Kay, Miriam, Shirley and Katharine," said Myrna, Marion,
Loretta, Carole, and so on.

Our eyes met—a total of twenty-six eyes—and somehow, by that ineffable magic that Cupid weaves, we—knew. It was love at first, second,
third, fourth, fifth, sixth, seventh, eighth, ninth, tenth, eleventh and
twelfth sights, not necessarily in the order named.

"I always knew that somehow, someday, I would—find you," I said
brokenly.

"We always knew that you would—come," they said simply.

"Speech!" cried Miss West. The others took up the cry. I rose, took a sip of water and cleared my throat:

"Madame Chairman, Ladies: I am no speechmaker, as you know. What few words I have to say to you here today will not take long. If you want flowery speeches and sweet nothings, I am afraid you will have to go to one more versed in that sort of thing than I am. All I can say is that I love you with a love that is as eternal as the snows on yonder alp, and that life without you would be unthinkable, unendurable. All that I am and have, I offer you. Will you cast your lot with mine? Will you walk with me down life's pathway, hand in hand, secure in the knowledge that our love is all that matters? In other words, will you be mine? All in favor say 'aye.' All opposed, 'nay.' The ayes have it. Is there any unfinished business? Any committee reports?"

There were none.

We fourteen, including Miss Crawford, were very happy in our new-found love. They promised to do all in their power to help me see the Hollywood of my dreams.

"You look hungry," said Miss Loy hospitably. "Have something to eat. Here's the waitress."

I looked up, and there stood absolutely the most ravishingly glamorous creature I had ever seen in my life.

"Waitress?" I gasped, in a kind of daze from the impact of her loveliness on my already beauty-befuddled senses. "You a waitress?"

"Yes," said the waitress simply, smiling down at me with great sad brown eyes.

I rose and clasped her in my arms.

"I always knew that someday, and so on," I said.

"I knew that someday, and so on," she said brokenly. "Be careful of my tray."

"Tray. Tray. What care we twain for trays? Let the world and its trays go by. Our love is all that matters."

"I have always dreamed that someday, somehow, a golden knight would come riding through clouds of sapphire, coral and ebony," said the beautiful slavey.

"Oh, my darling," I said. "Why do you tremble? What kind of pie have you got?"

"Huckleberry, raspberry, lemon meringue, custard——"

"Ah, I don't want pie," I said fiercely. "I don't need pie. With you at my side, I no longer fear destiny. But why aren't you in the movies?"

"I'm too beautiful," she said sadly. "The law of diminishing returns got me. I'm so beautiful I don't photograph well. Mr. Goldwyn, Mr. Van Dyke, Mr. Lubitsch, Mr. Mayer, Mr. Milestone, Mr. Selznick and Mr. Capra tried to figure every possible way to lop off enough looks to put me over, but no use. I remained a raving, tearing beauty."

"You poor kid!"

"Oh, Hollywood's full of us," she sighed. "Butterflies broken on the wheel of fortune. Unsuccessful eyefuls doomed to a life of waiting."

"You said you wanted to see a picture being made," one of the girls said to me. "They're shooting a love scene with Diane d'Amour on the Metro-Paramount-Warner lot across the street this afternoon. Why don't you run over?"

Diane d'Amour! The great French actress. Most colossal Hollywood sensation since Garbo's debut. Would I like to see her playing a love scene? I grabbed at the chance. Over at the M-P-W lot, I found Miss d'Amour sitting on the set, surrounded by klieg lights, supervisors, yes men, yes maids, four screen lovers—one limbering up and three in reserve—and an anxious-looking director.

"I can't tell you how grateful I am for this opportunity of seeing Miss d'Amour in action," I told the director. "Look at her. What marvelous restraint!"

"That's not restraint," said the director. "She isn't acting."

"Not acting? The great d'Amour not acting? I thought she was always acting. What's the trouble?"

"I don't know," said he gloomily. "She just don't seem to come to a boil today."

"Maybe the part isn't worthy of her genius," I suggested indignantly.

"Same part she's always had. She's the wickedest woman in Paris and has had a quarrel with her lover. She's supposed to be pleading with him; she's supposed to say, 'Jacques, won't you please try to—understand?' No use. We've shot her a hundred times and she still says it as if Jacques were a wooden Indian."

"Have you tried music?" I asked, recalling from my own recent experience how music can inspire one to heights of dramatic power one has hitherto considered one's self incapable of reaching. "The violin, for instance?"

"I've tried violins," said the director, "and I've tried lutes. I've tried rebecs, harps, lyres, zithers, banjos and the dulcimer."

"Have you tried the viola da gamba," I asked, "or the xanorphica?"

"Yes, and the double bassoon and the contrafagotto, not to speak of the pitch pipe, the ophicleide, the oboe and the doodlesack. Yesterday I hired the entire Los Angeles Symphony Orchestra to come out here and play, and they couldn't budge her. I'm beginning to doubt if Stokowski, leading the massed Boston, Philadelphia and New York symphonies, together with the Chicago Fire Department band, could start her to acting. She says she don't feel it—here."

He indicated a point just below the left lapel of his coat.

Miss d'Amour heard all this, glanced haughtily yet beseechingly at the director. Even in adversity she was lovely. She had that Gallic chic which is the mark of your true Parisienne.

"Have you tried the comb?" I asked, as an idea struck me.

"The comb?"

"The old-fashioned comb with tissue paper over it. Probably I'm a fool rushing in, but I don't think I've lost my old skill at getting a tune out of a comb. Care to have me try it on her?"

"No," said the director. Then he thumped a table.

"By George, why not?" he said desperately. "What harm can it do?"

"None that time cannot heal," I assured him.

The director seemed to be infused with new hope suddenly.

"All right," he megaphoned. "Who's the lover on duty? Watson? . . . All right, Watson; get in there and fight now. Give Miss d'Amour all you got. . . . Miss d'Amour, we're going to try it once again, with a new kind of music. Please give Mr. Watson all you got. All set?"

I adjusted the comb and slid a lip up and down it a few times to get the feel of it. Then I winked a signal to the director.

"One, two, three! Camera!" he shouted, and I started playing Love's Old Sweet Song.

Miss d'Amour looked startled for a few seconds, and then an amazing thing happened. Something seemed to come over her. She began to give. The comb had broken the log jam! Softly, pleadingly, she said, "Jacques, won't you please try to—onderstand?"

Never in the history of the movies had the classic line been rendered with such consummate artistry.

"Diane, that was terrific," the director enthused.

Miss d'Amour hurried over, rubbing off her make-up excitedly.

"Who was that playing on the comb?" she demanded.

I acknowledged the soft impeachment. She clasped me in her arms.

"I never had anything get me so," she said. "When I was a kid back in Attleboro, I used to go on straw rides with a boy I was terribly stuck on, and he used to play that tune on the comb as we glided through the golden October evenings. I haven't heard it played for ages, especially on the comb. It took me right back. You're a dear. How about dinner with me tonight, just for two?"

Dinner with the great d'Amour, toast of half Paris!

"Oh, Miss d'Amour, that sounds marvelous," I said.

"It will be," she assured me cordially.

"I can't thank you enough, old man, for helping us out of that dilemma," said the director. He scribbled something on a piece of paper and handed it to me. "Just present this at this cashier's office as you go out, and they will give you $3500 and a percentage of the gross."

I had heard of the fabulous Hollywood salaries, but this was the first time I had actually received one.

Well, the rest of the afternoon was a rapid succession of parties at the palatial bungalows of one or another glamorous movie star. Social life in Hollywood is bizarre. Guests have a habit of moving on from one party to another, sometimes taking the entire party with them. One star may be giving a party and may suddenly get the idea of taking all fifty of her guests to another star's party. That party may go on to another party in toto like a snowball going downhill. So that what starts as a friendly call on, let us say, Joan Crawford by two or three pals in search of a dish of tea and a crumpet, may eventually turn into a costume ball for twelve hundred at the Countess di Frasso's. In fact, usually does. The custom makes Hollywood social life unpredictable, but adds zest to it.

I couldn't for the life of me remember a tenth of the glamorous people I met that afternoon. The time passed so quickly that, before I realized it, it was five minutes to nine. Fortunately, anticipating some such emergency, I had put on my evening clothes and white tie underneath my mufti that morning, so I knew it would be the work of a second to moult the outer suit and present myself at Miss d'Amour's suitably clad.

"I've got to run," I apologized to my hostess of the moment. "I'm due at Diane d'Amour's for dinner at nine o'clock."

"A splendid idea!" exclaimed a star who was loitering near the caviar bin. "We'll all go to d'Amour's for dinner."

This was rather embarrassing.

"I'm terribly sorry, but I—uh—I believe Miss d'Amour said it was to be a dinner for—uh—two."

"Oh, that's all right. We don't stand on formality in Hollywood. There's always room for a hundred more," said another star, bristling with ermine.

But there happened to be about two hundred more. Well, it wasn't my funeral, so I made no further comment. Away we went, two hundred strong, to Diane d'Amour's palatial Beverly Hills estate, a château imported stone by stone from Normandy, Devonshire and Spain.

Miss d'Amour herself met us at the third gatekeeper's lodge. She was simply yet richly costumed in a cloth-of-gold dress with several ropes of perfectly matched pearls draped about that classic ivory column called her neck.

"So sorry to be late, Miss d'Amour," I apologized.

"Why, you're not late, you're early," she soothed. "I was just going in to dress. I've been puttering in the garden."

"In your Sunday clothes!"

"Sunday clothes? These old rags my Sunday clothes?"

She gave a light laugh, and one thought of larks singing at sunrise in a French garden.

"Why, these are my gardening clothes," she explained. "I love to putter in the garden. I've been spading truffles. Nothing rests me so much after a hard day's work at the studio as a putter with a truffle in the garden."

"But those magnificent pearls," I could not help saying.

"These old pearls magnificent!" Again she laughed, and it was like silver chimes caressed by a Provençal zephyr. "These are just my puttering pearls. I picked 'em up from a Gaekwar in India. They get in the way sometimes, but they keep me warm. The garden is rather drafty and I am subject to colds."

"Miss d'Amour, I'm terribly sorry to have brought along so many extra guests. It really wasn't my idea."

"How many are there?" she asked, surveying the line of expensive limousines still filing into the grounds.

"About two hundred, I'm afraid."

"Two hundred. Pooh! What's two hundred extra guests for dinner at Well Kum Inn? Don't you think that's a cute name for my shack here?"

"If you must slander such a magnificent château, imported stone by stone from Tuscany, Sussex and Wales, by calling it a shack," I said, with a bow. "But I thought you said dinner for two."

"Sure I did. For two hundred. You know the old saying: Two hundred's company, three hundred's a crowd."

She seized a gold megaphone and addressed the throng:

"Make yourself at home, folks. There'll be a tun of sherry right out, so you can wet your whistles. Excuse me now while I dress."

She explained later that she used the gold megaphone ordinarily for summoning her maids when they were at the other end of her boudoir, which is seven hundred and fifty feet long.

D'Amour reappeared shortly, this time a vision in cloth of platinum, with ropes of diamonds.

"I'm going to give you a treat," she said, tapping me with her fan. "I hear you want to see a Hollywood swimming party."

She reached an elegantly shod foot for a button which lay concealed in the grass, and pressed it five times. Five butlers responded. "We shall swim this evening, Meadows," she said.

"Very good, madame. Which swimming pool does madame wish filled?" said the dignified old fellow who seemed to be the head Meadows.

"All four of them, of course," said Miss d'Amour, with an imperious wave of the hand.

Four swimming pools! I'm in Hollywood, all right, I thought.

"Very good, madame. Does madame wish the pools to be filled with the usual——"

"With the usual champagne, of course. You know very well I do."

Swimming pools filled with champagne! Whew, I thought, for I am an accomplished whew-thinker.

"Diane, dear——"

That voice! I recognized it instantly. It had come to me from the silver screen so often. It was Carmencita Passion, the glamorous film star, of course.

"Diane, dear, I'd love to take a dip, but my doctor says I absolutely must not swim in champagne. Could you——"

"Oh, Carmencita, dear, I forgot," said Miss d'Amour. . . . "Meadows, Miss Passion is on the wagon. Fill her up a pool of iced tea. . . . With lemon, dear?"

"Yes, darling."

"How many lumps of sugar?"

"No sugar, thank you."

"Perhaps it's just as well, dear," said Miss d'Amour sweetly, "although, you know, they tell me plump women are coming back in style."

"How nice for you, dear," said Miss Passion, also sweetly.

After dinner, which was a simple meal of *pâté de foie gras*, since most of the folks in the picture business must watch their calories carefully, we adjourned to the swimming pools for our dip.

I was walking with Morrison Turnsour, the director.

"Imagine having four swimming pools to your name," I said admiringly.

"Confidentially," he said, "I believe d'Amour would gladly exchange all four of them for the one La Passion has."

"You mean?" I said simply.

"Passion and d'Amour are great rivals," he explained. "When

d'Amour got her fourth pool, Passion knew she must top d'Amour in order to save face. Saving face is very important here. Passion determined to have something different, a pool that would be like no other pool in Hollywood. For a while she was stumped, because there is every known kind of swimming pool in Hollywood, including one lined with fur. Then La Passion got a brilliant idea. All the swimming pools are on land, she figured. So she decided to build one in the ocean. She bought a twenty-acre tract of water forty-five miles offshore in the Pacific, and built herself a cork pool out there. Said she wanted to have some place where she could get away from It All. D'Amour was fit to be tied. Passion's one simple little cork pool out there in the briny deep made her four onyx pools look ostentatious. Yet I understand it costs Passion seven dollars a quart to have fresh water hauled out to her pool, as against the four and half dollars d'Amour pays for her champagne, wholesale."

"Did Passion save her face?" I asked.

"Yes, but d'Amour said it was only for a rainy day."

With that someone tripped me and pushed me into the pool, fully clad. I found out later it was Vince Barnett who pushed me. Vince Barnett is the chief ribber, or perpetrator of practical jokes, in Hollywood. I considered it quite an honor to have been pushed in by the chief ribber.

Everyone who was anyone in Hollywood was in the pools. Some wore bathing suits and some had been pushed in, fully dressed, as a joke. It was a beautiful sight. Handsome men and glamorous women, ornaments of the silver screen, swimming about, laughing and joking and spouting iridescent jets of sparkling Burgundy into the air. The magnates were there too—the producers and bankers and big shots of the financial end of the industry. You could tell the magnates because they floated. The champagne bubbled and effervesced and broke into millions of tiny jewels as the colored lights played upon them. Although I had never been in the Orient, I knew instinctively, by some age-old racial stirring, that this was none other than a scene of Oriental splendor.

I began to have a pleasant sense of well-being, and in a burst of enthusiasm, struck out for the middle of the pool, but collided with a young fellow before I had gone a yard. He was a magnificent figure of a lad, with long hair, white tie and bathing trunks.

"Excuse me, friend, but aren't you Johnny Weissmuller?" I asked.

He said he was.

"Your face is familiar too," he added.

"I know it," I apologized. "Maybe you will think it fresh of me, Mr.

Weissmuller, but I have never been in Hollywood before. I am here to see the sights, and I have read so much in the papers about the famous arguments that you and Mrs. Weissmuller have, that I was hoping to see one before I left."

"I'll see if I can fix it," Mr. Weissmuller said pleasantly. . . . "Lupe! Lupe!"

Absolutely the most ravishingly beautiful girl I had ever seen in my life swam up.

"What you want now, John-ee?" she exploded. "Always you call, 'Lupe, Lupe, Lupe.' Why do you not leave me alone?"

"This gentleman wanted to see you and me have a little spat."

"I am beezy sweeming," stormed Miss Velez. "I have no time to spat wiz you."

"I was only trying to be agreeable and do this gentleman a fa——"

"Always I must have ze spat wiz you," cried Lupe. "I am tired of having ze spat. I will not have ze spat."

"This man is a stranger in Hollywood and he wanted to see——"

"I do not care. I weel not spat. You hear, John-ee?"

"I guess you'll spat if I want you to," said Mr. W., his dander aroused.

Lupe said she wouldn't. He said she would. She said she wouldn't, and the fight was on. She swam away, and Johnny chased her.

"Thank you very much, Mr. Weissmuller," I called after him.

By this time I was getting a little tired treading champagne, so I struck out for the edge of the pool and pulled myself up. There, standing on the edge of the pool, stood absolutely the most ravishingly beautiful girl I had ever seen in my life, and I was just about to push her in, fully clad, as a joke, when I saw, to my astonishment, that she was my old friend of the morning, Milly Twistle.

"Twiss!"

"You?"

"How did you get here? Did you see Clark Gable?"

"No," said Milly bitterly.

"What happened?"

"The gatekeepers wouldn't let me in the bowl."

"Why not?"

"He was seeing only the girls whose names began with U, today. It seems there is such a mob he has to see 'em one letter a day. Wouldn't it be my luck that he would see my letter the day before I get here? Now, I either wait twenty-five days until he gets around to T again, or I go home. I tried to pull a fast one on the gatekeeper. I told him my name was Unglefinger, but he just laughed, and said, 'Where's your birth certificate?' I'm so mad I could cry. I'd o' had to walk back from the Bowl, too, if I hadn't o' got a lift from this gentleman here."

She pointed to a handsome chap in evening clothes.

It was Clark Gable.

I introduced her to him, then pushed them both into the pool, fully clad, as a joke.

I got home, dog tired but lark happy, at four in the morning. I figured I had seen about as much of Hollywood as anyone could see in one day. And it had all been just as exciting and glamorous as I had hoped, if not more so.

Around noontime Claudette Colbert, Ann Sheridan, Jeanette MacDonald, Minnie Mouse, Vivian Leigh, Merle Oberon and Ginger Rogers telephoned and asked me to stay over for a few more days, but I said no.

"It's been swell here and you've all been perfectly dandy to me," I said, "but I guess I'm about ready to make tracks for back home. I like to visit Hollywood," I said, "but I wouldn't live here if you gave me the place."

Howlers from the Press

We are always amused at blunders—someone else's blunders. There is something comforting to all of us when somebody else commits a *faux pas*, when he not only opens his mouth and puts his foot in it—but swallows the foot. We laugh with a certain condescension at a schoolboy's boners, such as those on pages 654–657, but we are not so quick to appreciate our own slips of the tongue. The Reverend Spooner did not find it amusing when, instead of speaking of his "half-formed wish" he heard himself say, "I have been nursing a half-warmed fish." Berating his congregation for its small attendance, he intended to emphasize the "weary benches"; instead he shouted, "I am tired of addressing these beery wenches." It is said that the Reverend Spooner went on to speak of someone "occupewing his pie" and said he had just ridden from town on "a well-boiled icicle."

There will always be something incalculably comic in the surprise of a word misplaced or the twist caused by an omitted letter. Jack Goodman and Albert Rice call it "the law of the bungle" in their *I Wish I'd Said That!* As an example of humor in typographical errors they quote a New Zealand paper which stated that a Mr. X was a "defective in the police force." When the error was pointed out, the paper ran a retraction: "We regret the typographical mistake which made us refer to Mr. X as a 'defective in the police force.' Obviously the sentence should have read: 'Mr. X is a detective in the police farce.'"

Closely allied to this blunder is the obituary of a war casualty which paid a tribute to the "bottle-scarred" veteran. When friends of the deceased wrote outraged letters of protest, the paper corrected itself: "Last week we spoke of a certain veteran as 'bottle-scarred.' We are deeply mortified, and we apologize. We meant to say 'battle-scared.'"

The misplaced word is responsible for some amazing results. The reader knows what the advertiser meant, but he is nevertheless startled to read: "Wanted—a folding table by a woman with detachable legs." The same is true of the advertisement which read: "Wanted—a boy to take care of horses who can speak German." And this one: "Sale—25 Men's Wool Suits: $15.00—They Won't Last an Hour."

Observe what the omission of the letter "k" did to this advertisement: "Experienced but young Swiss girl able to do fancy cooing." And see what the addition of another letter made of this insect ad: "One bottle —Get Rid of Aunts." A slight fault in phrasing was responsible for this howler from an Ohio newspaper: "Easter Matinée for the Kiddies.

Every child laying an egg in the doorman's hand will be admitted free."

The absence of the letter "g" caused havoc in several headlines. One of them read: "Keeseville bride can bear 50 tons"; another read: "The new bride is twenty feet wide from buttress to buttress." A slip of the typographical machine changed Smetana's "The Bartered Bride" to "The Battered Bride." And another verbal lapse made a handsome wedding unite the couple in "holy deadlock."

Freud insists that our subconscious self prompts us to commit errors which reveal our hidden desires. This certainly seems true of the writer who inserted the word "not" in the following brief newspaper item: "Rudy Vallee, the well-known crooner and radio singer was shaken up and bruised when his car left the highway and turned over. It is feared that his vocal cords were not injured."

The substitution of an "l" for a "d" turned a dull statement into a startling truth: "Mrs. Robbins, President of the Woman's Club, announces that on Wednesday, June 15th, the final meeting will be hell." The substitution of an "a" for an "o" caused something even more dramatic. "Gypsy Rose Lee," so ran the announcement, "the well-known strip-tease artist and author has turned playwright; she is having her navel dramatized."

Here are a few other instances in which a misplaced letter or an inverted clause created some choice journalistic headlines:

ROBBERS EAT THEN HOLD UP
RESTAURANT PROPRIETOR

CRIMINAL JURY DISMISSED:
HAMM FAILS TO IDENTIFY YEGGS

MADDENED STEER INJURES FARMER WITH AX

FORT WORTH RANCHER HAS LONGEST
HORNS IN TEXAS

PAMPERED DOG IN BED, ASKS DIVORCE

Twisted words, faulty punctuation, and mixed metaphors have occasioned howlers that are not easily forgotten. The following are among the most persistent:

"It is only a snake in the grass who will attempt to knife a man in the back with so evil-smelling a report."

"Most people know the position assumed by the present recumbent. But where will he stand when he takes his seat?"

"It is with real regret that we learn of Mr. Wayne's recovery from an automobile accident."

"At the Ladies' Aid Society Meeting many interesting articles were raffled off. Every member had brought something they no longer needed. Many members brought their husbands."

"Frank Cape is at the Massachusetts General Hospital. He is suffering from head injuries and shock caused by coming into contact with a live wife."

An advertisement in a Pennsylvania paper attracted a great deal of notice, especially as it was headed "Mother's Day Special." It read: "Don't Kill Your Wife. Let Our Washing Machine Do the Dirty Work."

"Having broken both ankles in a collision, Mrs. McKnight is recovering under the car of her physician."

A fish story from the *Northwest Organizer* ended with this startling statement: "That's a lot of fish in any language—thirty-nine pounds—and all in one piece. Still, as Fred Simmons says, 'For sheer tricks, fight and stamina, give me a small-mouthed lass at sundown, any time.'"

The prize for moral standards must be awarded to that combination of primness and fashion, *Godey's Lady's Book*. A household authority about the middle of the nineteenth century, the journal even told its readers how to arrange their bookshelves properly. "The perfect hostess," wrote the editor, "will see to it that the works of male and female authors are strictly separated. Their proximity on the shelves—unless they happen to be married—should not be tolerated."

"James Harper had his finger badly chewed by his dog last week. Thinking that the animal was poisoned, Harper administered to him, but the dog did not respond to the anecdote."

"Fifty guests assembled at the Domestic Forum, and thirty have been married to the same man for more than twenty years."

"The fatal accident occurred at the corner of Broadway and Fourth Street just as the dead man attempted to cross."

"After ten years of marriage, two happy parents, Mr. and Mrs. Jay V. Door, announce the birth of their first child, a son."
Remember, Champlain County Want Ads Bring Results.

"The Sunday School picnic held at Ocean Grove last Sunday was a hug success."

Finally, there is this slightly misworded ad, which has been reprinted in many different forms: "Why go elsewhere to be cheated? You can trust us to do the job!"

Booth Tarkington

In more than half a hundred works Booth Tarkington raced back and forth between sheer escapism and frank realism, between characters as spuriously romantic as Monsieur Beaucaire and as painstakingly honest as Alice Adams, between books as comically juvenile as Penrod and Sam and as bitterly mature as The Magnificent Ambersons.

Born in 1869, in Indianapolis, Indiana, he paid a tribute to his native state by calling his first book The Gentleman from Indiana, and the best of Tarkington's subsequent work is stubbornly Hoosier in spirit. Although he lived extensively on the Atlantic seacoast and in Europe, and although the Indianapolis in which he was born "exists no more than Carthage existed after the Romans had driven ploughs over the ground where it had stood," Tarkington remained a Middle Westerner, alternately sentimental and cynical, accurate, forthright, and conservatively idealistic. He died May 19, 1946.

The Quiet Afternoon

Perhaps middle-aged people might discern Nature's real intentions in the matter of pain if they would examine a boy's punishments and sorrows, for he prolongs neither beyond their actual duration. With a boy, trouble must be of Homeric dimensions to last overnight. To him, every next day is really a new day. Thus, Penrod woke, next morning, with neither the unspared rod, nor Mr. Kinosling in his mind. Tar, itself, so far as his consideration of it went, might have been an undiscovered substance. His mood was cheerful and mercantile; some process having worked mysteriously within him, during the night, to the result that his first waking thought was of profits connected with the sale of old iron—or perhaps a ragman had passed the house, just before he woke.

By ten o'clock he had formed a partnership with the indeed amiable Sam, and the firm of Schofield and Williams plunged headlong into commerce. Heavy dealings in rags, paper, old iron and lead gave the firm a balance of twenty-two cents on the evening of the third day; but a venture in glassware, following, proved disappointing on account of the scepticism of all the druggists in that part of town, even after seven laborious hours had been spent in cleansing a wheelbarrow-load of old medicine bottles with hydrant water and ashes. Likewise, the partners were disheartened by their failure to dispose of a crop of "greens," although they had uprooted specimens of that decorative and unappreciated flower, the dandelion, with such persistence and energy that the Schofields' and Williams' lawns looked curiously haggard for the rest of that summer.

The fit passed: business languished; became extinct. The dog-days had set in.

One August afternoon was so hot that even boys sought indoor shade. In the dimness of the vacant carriage-house of the stable, lounged Masters Penrod Schofield, Samuel Williams, Maurice Levy, Georgie Bassett, and Herman. They sat still and talked. It is a hot day, in rare truth, when boys devote themselves principally to conversation, and this day was that hot.

Their elders should beware such days. Peril hovers near when the fierceness of weather forces inaction and boys in groups are quiet. The more closely volcanoes, Western rivers, nitroglycerin, and boys are pent, the deadlier is their action at the point of outbreak. Thus, parents and guardians should look for outrages of the most singular violence and of the most peculiar nature during the confining weather of February and August.

The thing which befell upon this broiling afternoon began to brew and stew peacefully enough. All was innocence and languor; no one could have foretold the eruption.

They were upon their great theme: "When I get to be a man!" Being human, though boys, they considered their present estate too commonplace to be dwelt upon. So, when the old men gather, they say: "When I was a boy!" It really is the land of nowadays that we never discover.

"When I'm a man," said Sam Williams, "I'm goin' to hire me a couple of coloured waiters to swing me in a hammock and keep pourin' ice-water on me all day out o' those waterin'-cans they sprinkle flowers from. I'll hire you for one of 'em, Herman."

"No; you ain' goin' to," said Herman promptly. "You ain' no flowuh. But nev' min' nat, anyway. Ain' nobody goin' hiah me whens I'm a man. Goin' be my own boss. I'm go' be a rai'road man!"

"You mean like a superintendent, or sumpthing like that, and sell tickets?" asked Penrod.

"Sup'in—nev' min' nat! Sell ticket? No suh! Go' be a po'tuh! My uncle a po'tuh right now. Solid gole buttons—oh, oh!"

"Generals get a lot more buttons than porters," said Penrod. "Generals——"

"Po'tuhs make the bes' livin'," Herman interrupted. "My uncle spen' mo' money 'n any white man n'is town."

"Well, I rather be a general," said Penrod, "or a senator, or sumpthing like that."

"Senators live in Warshington," Maurice Levy contributed the information. "I been there. Washington ain't so much; Niag'ra Falls is a hundred times as good as Warshington. So's 'Tlantic City, I was there, too. I been everywhere there is. I——"

"Well, anyway," said Sam Williams, raising his voice in order to obtain the floor, "anyway, I'm goin' to lay in a hammock all day, and have ice-water sprinkled on top o' me, and I'm goin' to lay there all night, too, and the next day. I'm goin' to lay there a couple o' years, maybe."

"I bet you don't!" exclaimed Maurice. "What'd you do in winter?"

"What?"

"What you goin' to do when it's winter, out in a hammock with water sprinkled on top o' you all day? I bet you——"

"I'd stay right there," Sam declared, with strong conviction, blinking as he looked out through the open doors at the dazzling lawn and trees, trembling in the heat. "They couldn't sprinkle too much for me!"

"It'd make icicles all over you, and——"

"I wish it would," said Sam. "I'd eat 'em up."

"And it'd snow on you——"

"Yay! I'd swaller it as fast as it'd come down. I wish I had a *barrel* o' snow right now. I wish this whole barn was full of it. I wish they wasn't anything in the whole world except just good ole snow."

Penrod and Herman rose and went out to the hydrant, where they drank long and ardently. Sam was still talking about snow when they returned.

"No, I wouldn't just roll in it. I'd stick it all round inside my clo'es, and fill my hat. No, I'd freeze a big pile of it all hard, and I'd roll her out flat and then I'd carry her down to some ole tailor's and have him make me a *suit* out of her, and——"

"Can't you keep still about your ole snow?" demanded Penrod petulantly. "Makes me so thirsty I can't keep still, and I've drunk so much now I bet I bust. That ole hydrant water's mighty near hot anyway."

"I'm goin' to have a big store, when I grow up," volunteered Maurice.

"Candy store?" asked Penrod.

"*No*, sir! I'll have candy in it, but not to eat, so much. It's goin' to be a deportment store: ladies' clothes, gentlemen's clothes, neckties, china goods, leather goods, nice lines in woollings and lace goods——"

"Yay! I wouldn't give a five-for-a-cent marble for your whole store," said Sam. "Would you, Penrod?"

"Not for ten of 'em; not for a million of 'em! *I'm* goin' to have——"

"Wait!" clamoured Maurice. "You'd be foolish, because they'd be a toy deportment in my store where they'd be a hundred marbles! So, how much would you think your five-for-a-cent marble counts for? And when I'm keepin' my store I'm goin' to get married."

"Yay!" shrieked Sam derisively. "*Married!* Listen!" Penrod and Herman joined in the howl of contempt.

"Certumly I'll get married," asserted Maurice stoutly. "I'll get married to Marjorie Jones. She likes me awful good, and I'm her beau."

"What makes you think so?" inquired Penrod in a cryptic voice.

"Because she's my beau, too," came the prompt answer. "I'm her beau because she's my beau; I guess that's plenty reason! I'll get married to her as soon as I get my store running nice."

Penrod looked upon him darkly, but, for the moment, held his peace.

"Married!" jeered Sam Williams. "Married to Marjorie Jones! You're the only boy I ever heard say he was going to get married. I wouldn't get married for—why, I wouldn't for—for——" Unable to think of any inducement the mere mention of which would not be ridiculously incommensurate, he proceeded: "I wouldn't do it! What you want to get married for? What do married people do, except just come home tired, and worry around and kind of scold? You better not do it, M'rice; you'll be mighty sorry."

"Everybody gets married," stated Maurice, holding his ground. "They gotta."

"I'll bet *I* don't!" Sam returned hotly. "They better catch me before they tell *me* I have to. Anyway, I bet nobody has to get married unless they want to."

"They do, too," insisted Maurice. "They *gotta!*"

"Who told you?"

"Look at what my own papa told me!" cried Maurice, heated with argument. "Didn't he tell me your papa had to marry your mamma, or else he never'd got to handle a cent of her money? Certumly, people gotta marry. Everybody. You don't know anybody over twenty years old that isn't married—except maybe teachers."

"Look at policemen!" shouted Sam triumphantly. "You don't s'pose anybody can make policemen get married, I reckon, do you?"

"Well, policemen, maybe," Maurice was forced to admit. "Policemen and teachers don't, but everybody else gotta."

"Well, I'll be a policeman," said Sam. "*Then* I guess they won't come around tellin' me I have to get married. What you goin' to be, Penrod?"

"Chief police," said the laconic Penrod.

"What you?" Sam inquired of quiet Georgie Bassett.

"I am going to be," said Georgie, consciously, "a minister."

This announcement created a sensation so profound that it was followed by silence. Herman was the first to speak.

"You mean preachuh?" he asked incredulously. "You goin' *preach?*"

"Yes," answered Georgie, looking like Saint Cecilia at the organ.

Herman was impressed. "You know all 'at preachuh talk?"

"I'm going to learn it," said Georgie simply.

"How loud kin you holler?" asked Herman doubtfully.

"He can't holler at all," Penrod interposed with scorn. "He hollers like a girl. He's the poorest hollerer in town!"

Herman shook his head. Evidently he thought Georgie's chance of being ordained very slender. Nevertheless, a final question put to the candidate by the coloured expert seemed to admit one ray of hope.

"How good kin you clim a pole?"

"He can't climb one at all," Penrod answered for Georgie. "Over at Sam's turning-pole you ought to see him try to——"

"Preachers don't have to climb poles," Georgie said with dignity.

"*Good* ones do," declared Herman. "Bes' one ev' *I* hear, he clim up an' down same as a circus man. One n'em big 'vivals outen whens we livin' on a fahm, preachuh clim big pole right in a middle o' the church, what was to hol' roof up. He clim way high up, an' holler: "Goin' to heavum, goin' to heavum, goin' to heavum *now*. Hallelujah, praise my Lawd!' An' he slide down little, an' holler: 'Devil's got a hol' o' my coat-tails; devil tryin' to drag me down! Sinnuhs, take wawnun! Devil got a hol' o' my coat-tails; I'm a-goin' to hell, oh Lawd!' Nex', he clim up little mo', an' yell an' holler: 'Done shuck ole devil loose; goin' straight to heavum again! Goin' to heavum, goin' to heavum, my Lawd!' Nex', he slide down some mo' an' holler, 'Leggo my coat-tails, ole devil! Goin' to hell agin, sinnuhs! Goin' straight to hell, my Lawd!' An' he clim an' he slide, an' he slide, an' he clim, an' all time holler: 'Now 'm a-goin' to heavum; now 'm a-goin' to hell! Goin' to heavum, heavum, heavum, my Lawd!' Las' he slide all a-way down, jes' a-squallin' an' a-kickin' an' a-rarin' up an' squealin', 'Goin' to hell. Goin' to hell! Ole Satum got my soul! Goin' to hell! Goin' to hell! Goin' to hell, hell, hell!'"

Herman possessed that extraordinary facility for vivid acting which is the great native gift of his race, and he enchained his listeners. They sat fascinated and spellbound.

"Herman, tell that again!" said Penrod, breathlessly.

Herman, nothing loath, accepted the encore and repeated the Miltonic episode, expanding it somewhat, and dwelling with a fine art upon those portions of the narrative which he perceived to be most exciting to his audience. Plainly, they thrilled less to Paradise gained than to its losing, and the dreadful climax of the descent into the Pit was the greatest treat of all.

The effect was immense and instant. Penrod sprang to his feet.

"Georgie Bassett couldn't do that to save his life," he declared. "*I'm* goin' to be a preacher! *I'd* be all right for one, wouldn't I, Herman?"

"So am I!" Sam Williams echoed loudly. "I guess I can do it if *you* can. I'd be better'n Penrod, wouldn't I, Herman?"

"I am, too!" Maurice shouted. "I got a stronger voice than anybody here, and I'd like to know what——"

The three clamoured together indistinguishably, each asserting his qualifications for the ministry according to Herman's theory, which had been accepted by these sudden converts without question.

"Listen to *me!*" Maurice bellowed, proving his claim to at least the voice by drowning the others. "Maybe I can't climb a pole so good, but who can holler louder'n this? Listen to *me-e-e!*"

"Shut up!" cried Penrod, irritated. "Go to heaven; go to hell!"

"Oo-o-oh!" exclaimed Georgie Bassett, profoundly shocked.

Sam and Maurice, awed by Penrod's daring, ceased from turmoil, staring wide-eyed.

"You cursed and swore!" said Georgie.

"I did not!" cried Penrod, hotly. "That isn't swearing."

"You said, 'Go to a big H'!" said Georgie.

"I did not! I said, 'Go to heaven,' before I said a big H. That isn't swearing, is it, Herman? It's almost what the preacher said, ain't it, Herman? It ain't swearing now, any more—not if you put 'go to heaven' with it, is it, Herman? You can say it all you want to, long as you say 'go to heaven' first, *can't* you, Herman? Anybody can say it if the preacher says it, can't they, Herman? I guess I know when I ain't swearing, don't I, Herman?"

Judge Herman ruled for the defendant, and Penrod was considered to have carried his point. With fine consistency, the conclave established that it was proper for the general public to "say it," provided "go to heaven" should in all cases precede it. This prefix was pronounced a perfect disinfectant, removing all odour of impiety or insult; and, with the exception of Georgie Bassett (who maintained that the minister's words were "going" and "gone," not "go"), all the boys proceeded to exercise their new privilege so lavishly that they tired of it.

But there was no diminution of evangelical ardour; again were heard the clamours of dispute as to which was the best qualified for the ministry, each of the claimants appealing passionately to Herman, who, pleased but confused, appeared to be incapable of arriving at a decision.

During a pause, Georgie Bassett asserted his prior rights. "Who said it first, I'd like to know?" he demanded. "I was going to be a minister from long back of to-day, I guess. And I guess I said I was going to be a minister right to-day before any of you said anything at all. *Didn't* I, Herman? *You* heard me, didn't you, Herman? That's the very thing started you talking about it, wasn't it, Herman?"

"You' right," said Herman. "You the firs' one to say it."

Penrod, Sam, and Maurice immediately lost faith in Herman. They turned from him and fell hotly upon Georgie.

"What if you did say it first?" Penrod shouted. "You couldn't *be* a minister if you were a hundred years old!"

"I bet his mother wouldn't let him be one," said Sam. "She never lets him do anything."

"She would, too," retorted Georgie. "Ever since I was little, she——"

"He's too sissy to be a preacher!" cried Maurice. "Listen at his squeaky voice!"

"I'm going to be a better minister," shouted Georgie, "than all three of you put together. I could do it with my left hand!"

The three laughed bitingly in chorus. They jeered, derided, scoffed, and raised an uproar which would have had its effect upon much stronger nerves than Georgie's. For a time he contained his rising choler and chanted monotonously, over and over: *"I could! I could, too! I could! I could, too!"* But their tumult wore upon him, and he decided to avail himself of the recent decision whereby a big H was rendered innocuous and unprofane. Having used the expression once, he found it comforting, and substituted it for: "I could! I could, too!"

But it relieved him only temporarily. His tormentors were unaffected by it and increased their howlings, until at last Georgie lost his head altogether. Badgered beyond bearing, his eyes shining with a wild light, he broke through the besieging trio, hurling little Maurice from his path with a frantic hand.

"I'll show you!" he cried, in this sudden frenzy. "You give me a chance, and I'll prove it right *now!*"

"That's talkin' business!" shouted Penrod. "Everybody keep still a minute. Everybody!"

He took command of the situation at once, displaying a fine capacity for organization and system. It needed only a few minutes to set order in the place of confusion and to determine, with the full concurrence of all parties, the conditions under which Georgie Bassett was to defend his claim by undergoing what may be perhaps intelligibly defined as the Herman test. Georgie declared he could do it easily. He was in a state of great excitement and in no condition to think calmly or, probably, he would not have made the attempt at all. Certainly he was overconfident.

It was during the discussion of the details of this enterprise that Georgie's mother, a short distance down the street, received a few female callers, who came by appointment to drink a glass of iced tea with her, and to meet the Rev. Mr. Kinosling. Mr. Kinosling was proving almost formidably interesting to the women and girls of his own and other flocks. What favour of his fellow clergymen a slight precociousness of manner and pronunciation cost him was more than balanced by the visible ecstasies of ladies. They blossomed at his touch.

He had just entered Mrs. Bassett's front door, when the son of the house, followed by an intent and earnest company of four, opened the alley gate and came into the yard. The unconscious Mrs. Bassett was about to have her first experience of a fatal coincidence. It was her first, because she was the mother of a boy so well behaved that he had become a proverb of transcendency. Fatal coincidences were plentiful in the Schofield and Williams families, and would have been familiar to Mrs. Bassett had Georgie been permitted greater intimacy with Penrod and Sam.

Mr. Kinosling sipped his iced tea and looked about him approvingly. Seven ladies leaned forward, for it was to be seen that he meant to speak.

"This cool room is a relief," he said, waving a graceful hand in a neatly limited gesture, which everybody's eyes followed, his own included. "It is a relief and a retreat. The windows open, the blinds closed—that is as it should be. It is a retreat, a fastness, a bastion against the heat's assault. For me, a quiet room—a quiet room and a book, a volume in the hand, held lightly between the fingers. A volume of poems, lines metrical and cadenced; something by a sound Victorian. We have no later poets."

"Swinburne?" suggested Miss Beam, an eager spinster. "Swinburne, Mr. Kinosling? Ah, *Swinburne!*"

"Not Swinburne," said Mr. Kinosling chastely. "No."

That concluded all the remarks about Swinburne.

Miss Beam retired in confusion behind another lady; and somehow there became diffused an impression that Miss Beam was erotic.

"I do not observe your manly little son," Mr. Kinosling addressed his hostess.

"He's out playing in the yard," Mrs. Bassett returned. "I heard his voice just now, I think."

"Everywhere I hear wonderful report of him," said Mr. Kinosling. "I may say that I understand boys, and I feel that he is a rare, a fine, a pure, a lofty spirit. I say spirit, for spirit is the word I hear spoken of him."

A chorus of enthusiastic approbation affirmed the accuracy of this proclamation, and Mrs. Bassett flushed with pleasure. Georgie's spiritual perfection was demonstrated by instances of it, related by the visitors; his piety was cited, and wonderful things he had said were quoted.

"Not all boys are pure, of fine spirit, of high mind," said Mr. Kinosling, and continued with true feeling: "You have a neighbour, dear Mrs. Bassett, whose household I indeed really feel it quite impossible to visit until such time when better, firmer, stronger handed, more determined discipline shall prevail. I find Mr. and Mrs. Schofield and their daughter charming——"

Three or four ladies said "Oh!" and spoke a name simultaneously. It was as if they had said, "Oh, the bubonic plague!"

"Oh! Penrod Schofield!"

"Georgie does not play with him," said Mrs. Bassett quickly—"that is, he avoids him as much as he can without hurting Penrod's feelings. Georgie is very sensitive to giving pain. I suppose a mother should not tell these things, and I know people who talk about their own children are dreadful bores, but it was only last Thursday night that Georgie looked up in my face so sweetly, after he had said his prayers and his little cheeks flushed, as he said: "Mamma, I think it would be right for me to go more with Penrod. I think it would make him a better boy.""

A sibilance went about the room. "Sweet! How sweet! The sweet little soul! Ah, *sweet!*"

"And that very afternoon," continued Mrs. Bassett, "he had come home in a dreadful state. Penrod had thrown tar all over him."

"Your son has a forgiving spirit!" said Mr. Kinosling with vehemence. "A too forgiving spirit, perhaps." He set down his glass. "No more, I thank you. No more cake, I thank you. Was it not Cardinal Newman who said——"

He was interrupted by the sounds of an altercation just outside the closed blinds of the window nearest him.

"Let him pick his tree!" It was the voice of Samuel Williams. "Didn't we come over here to give him one of his own trees? Give him a fair show, can't you?"

"The little lads!" Mr. Kinosling smiled. "They have their games, their outdoor sports, their pastimes. The young muscles are toughening. The sun will not harm them. They grow; they expand; they learn. They learn fair play, honour, courtesy, from one another, as pebbles grow round in the brook. They learn more from themselves than from us. They take shape, form, outline. Let them."

"Mr. Kinosling!" Another spinster—undeterred by what had happened to Miss Beam—leaned far forward, her face shining and ardent. "Mr. Kinosling, there's a question I *do* wish to ask you."

"My dear Miss Cosslit," Mr. Kinosling responded, again waving his hand and watching it, "I am entirely at your disposal."

"*Was* Joan of Arc," she asked fervently, "inspired by spirits?"

He smiled indulgently. "Yes—and no," he said. "One must give both answers. One must give the answer, yes; one must give the answer, no."

"Oh, *thank* you!" said Miss Cosslit, blushing. "She's one of my great enthusiasms, you know."

"And I have a question, too," urged Mrs. Lora Rewbush, after a moment's hasty concentration. "I've never been able to settle it for myself, but *now*——"

"Yes?" said Mr. Kinosling encouragingly.

"Is—ah—is—oh, yes: Is Sanskrit a more difficult language than Spanish, Mr. Kinosling?"

"It depends upon the student," replied the oracle, smiling. "One must not look for linguists everywhere. In my own especial case—if one may cite one's self as an example—I found no great, no insurmountable difficulty in mastering, in conquering either."

"And may *I* ask one?" ventured Mrs. Bassett. "Do you think it is right to wear egrets?"

"There are marks of quality, of caste, of social distinction," Mr. Kinosling began, "which must be permitted, allowed, though perhaps regulated. Social distinction, one observes, almost invariably implies spiritual distinction as well. Distinction of circumstances is accompanied by mental distinction. Distinction is hereditary; it descends from father to son, and if there is one thing more true than 'Like father, like son,' it

is—" he bowed gallantly to Mrs. Bassett—"it is, 'Like mother, like son.'
What these good ladies have said this afternoon of *your*——"

This was the fatal instant. There smote upon all ears the voice of
Georgie, painfully shrill and penetrating—fraught with protest and
protracted strain. His plain words consisted of the newly sanctioned
and disinfected curse with a big H.

With an ejaculation of horror, Mrs. Bassett sprang to the window and
threw open the blinds.

Georgie's back was disclosed to the view of the tea-party. He was en-
deavouring to ascend a maple tree about twelve feet from the window.
Embracing the trunk with arms and legs, he had managed to squirm to
a point above the heads of Penrod and Herman, who stood close by,
watching him earnestly—Penrod being obviously in charge of the performance. Across the yard were Sam Williams and Maurice Levy,
acting as a jury on the question of voice-power, and it was to a complaint of theirs that Georgie had just replied.

"That's right, Georgie," said Penrod encouragingly. "They can, too,
hear you. Let her go!"

"Going to heaven!" shrieked Georgie, squirming up another inch.
"Going to heaven, heaven, heaven!"

His mother's frenzied attempts to attract his attention failed utterly.
Georgie was using the full power of his lungs, deafening his own ears
to all other sounds. Mrs. Bassett called in vain; while the tea-party
stood petrified in a cluster about the window.

"Going to heaven!" Georgie bellowed. "Going to heaven! Going to
heaven, my Lord! Going to heaven, heaven, heaven!"

He tried to climb higher, but began to slip downward, his exertions
causing damage to his apparel. A button flew into the air, and his
knickerbockers and his waistband severed relations.

"Devil's got my coat-tails, sinners! Old devil's got my coat-tails!" he
announced appropriately. Then he began to slide. He relaxed his clasp
of the tree and slid to the ground.

"Going to hell!" shrieked Georgie, reaching a high pitch of enthusiasm in this great climax. "Going to hell! Going to hell! I'm gone to
hell, hell, hell!"

With a loud scream, Mrs. Bassett threw herself out of the window,
alighting by some miracle upon her feet with ankles unsprained.

Mr. Kinosling, feeling that his presence as spiritual adviser was demanded in the yard, followed with greater dignity through the front
door. At the corner of the house a small departing figure collided with

him violently. It was Penrod, tactfully withdrawing from what promised to be a family scene of unusual painfulness.

Mr. Kinosling seized him by the shoulders and, giving way to emotion, shook him viciously.

"You horrible boy!" exclaimed Mr. Kinosling. "You ruffianly creature! Do you know what's going to happen to you when you grow up?
Do you realize what you're going to *be!*"

With flashing eyes, the indignant boy made known his unshaken purpose. He shouted the reply:

"A minister!"

William Makepeace Thackeray

Born in India, educated in England, William
Makepeace Thackeray (1811–1863) tried a little of
everything before he settled down to be a serious
novelist. He prepared himself for the law, which
he soon abandoned, studied art in Paris, published
caricatures of ballet dancers, dabbled in rhyme,
and wrote satirical pieces under such pseudonyms
as "Théophile Wagstaff," "Michael Angelo Tit-
marsh," "George Savage Fitzboodle." A lecture
trip in America resulted in The Virginians, a sequel to Henry Esmond.

It is too bad that this book cannot include some
of Thackeray's characteristic attacks on social pretentiousness. But his prose passages are inseparable
from their context, and Thackeray's wit is most
condensed in his verse and his conversation. When
Thackeray attempted to become a politician, his
opponent for a seat in the House of Commons was
Edward Cardwell. During the campaign the two
men met; Cardwell hoped it would be a sporting
fight and concluded with the trite remark, "May
the best man win." "Oh, I hope not," said Thackeray. "But perhaps I am being too modest."

Sorrows of Werther

Werther had a love for Charlotte
  Such as words could never utter;
Would you know how first he met her?
  She was cutting bread and butter.

Charlotte was a married lady,
  And a moral man was Werther,
And, for all the wealth of Indies,
  Would do nothing for to hurt her.

So he sighed and pined and ogled,
  And his passion boiled and bubbled,
Till he blew his silly brains out,
  And no more was by it troubled.

Charlotte, having seen his body
  Borne before her on a shutter,
Like a well-conducted person,
  Went on cutting bread and butter.

A Credo

I

For the sole edification
Of this decent congregation,
Goodly people, by your grant
I will sing a holy chant—
  I will sing a holy chant.
If the ditty sound but oddly,
'Twas a father, wise and godly,
  Sang it so long ago—
Then sing as Martin Luther sang,
As Doctor Martin Luther sang:

"Who loves not wine, woman and song,
He is a fool his whole life long!"

II

He, by custom patriarchal,
Loved to see the beaker sparkle;
And he thought the wine improved,
Tasted by the lips he loved—
    By the kindly lips he loved.
Friends, I wish this custom pious
Duly were obsérved by us,
    To combine love, song, wine,
And sing as Martin Luther sang,
As Doctor Martin Luther sang:
"Who loves not wine, woman, and song,
He is a fool his whole life long!"

Ernest Lawrence Thayer

"Casey at the Bat" is the acknowledged classic of baseball, its anthem and its theme song. Yet, when it was first printed under a pseudonym in 1888, in the San Francisco Examiner, it was received without enthusiasm and even without comment. It was not until De Wolf Hopper made it the feature of his repertoire that the verses entered the national consciousness. They were recited up and down the country; they were dramatically declaimed from the stages of countless theaters and raucously echoed from every bar-room. They were attributed to several vociferous claimants, one of whom tried to collect illegal royalties from Hopper for making the poem famous.

In Famous Single Poems Burton Egbert Stevenson gives sufficient evidence to prove that the poem was the work of Ernest Lawrence Thayer, who had been an editor and president of the Harvard Lampoon and who had been coaxed to California by William Randolph Hearst to contribute light verse and casual editorials to the San Francisco Examiner. "Casey at the Bat" was one of the many occasional pieces written by Thayer over the signature "Phin." Thayer thought it neither better nor worse than his usual output; he considered its vogue "simply unaccountable" and the controversy incredible. Resigning from the newspaper, he went back East, became a successful manufacturer of woolens, and was glad to be forgotten as a humorist. But no one who has ever yelled at an umpire or jumped to his feet at the crack of a bat can ever forget the mighty Casey and the Mudville nine.

Casey at the Bat

It looked extremely rocky for the Mudville nine that day;
The score stood two to four, with but one inning left to play.
So, when Cooney died at second, and Burrows did the same,
A pallor wreathed the features of the patrons of the game.

A straggling few got up to go, leaving there the rest,
With that hope which springs eternal within the human breast.
For they thought: "If only Casey could get a whack at that,"
They'd put even money now, with Casey at the bat.

But Flynn preceded Casey, and likewise so did Blake,
And the former was a pudd'n, and the latter was a fake.
So on that stricken multitude a deathlike silence sat;
For there seemed but little chance of Casey's getting to the bat.

But Flynn let drive a single, to the wonderment of all.
And the much-despisèd Blakey "tore the cover off the ball."
And when the dust had lifted, and they saw what had occurred,
There was Blakey safe at second, and Flynn a-huggin' third.

Then from the gladdened multitude went up a joyous yell—
It rumbled in the mountaintops, it rattled in the dell;
It struck upon the hillside and rebounded on the flat;
For Casey, mighty Casey, was advancing to the bat.

There was ease in Casey's manner as he stepped into his place,
There was pride in Casey's bearing and a smile on Casey's face;
And when responding to the cheers he lightly doffed his hat,
No stranger in the crowd could doubt 'twas Casey at the bat.

Ten thousand eyes were on him as he rubbed his hands with dirt,
Five thousand tongues applauded when he wiped them on his shirt;
Then when the writhing pitcher ground the ball into his hip,
Defiance glanced in Casey's eye, a sneer curled Casey's lip.

And now the leather-covered sphere came hurtling through the air,
And Casey stood a-watching it in haughty grandeur there.
Close by the sturdy batsman the ball unheeded sped;
"That ain't my style," said Casey. "Strike one," the umpire said.

From the benches, black with people, there went up a muffled roar,
Like the beating of the storm waves on the stern and distant shore.
"Kill him! kill the umpire!" shouted someone on the stand;
And it's likely they'd have killed him had not Casey raised his hand.

With a smile of Christian charity great Casey's visage shone;
He stilled the rising tumult, he made the game go on;
He signaled to the pitcher, and once more the spheroid flew;
But Casey still ignored it, and the umpire said, "Strike two."

"Fraud!" cried the maddened thousands, and the echo answered
    "Fraud!"
But one scornful look from Casey and the audience was awed;
They saw his face grow stern and cold, they saw his muscles strain,
And they knew that Casey wouldn't let the ball go by again.

The sneer is gone from Casey's lips, his teeth are clenched in hate,
He pounds with cruel vengeance his bat upon the plate;
And now the pitcher holds the ball, and now he lets it go,
And now the air is shattered by the force of Casey's blow.

Oh, somewhere in this favored land the sun is shining bright,
The band is playing somewhere, and somewhere hearts are light;
And somewhere men are laughing, and somewhere children shout,
But there is no joy in Mudville—mighty Casey has struck out.

James Thurber

The mind of James Thurber (born in Columbus, Ohio, in 1894) is as restless as it is irresistible. It deals with everything, seemingly at the same time. My World—and Welcome to It (his tenth, and in many ways his best, book) ranges all the way from speculations on Life and Letters to an account of colored maids out of Lewis Carroll; a startling analysis of Macbeth as a detective story; an interview with a lemming; the tale of a man of our time who, in a dream, is shot to death by Aaron Burr; a triple murder caused by a whippoorwill. A few years after it was published, one of his stories became a much-quoted classic; "The Secret Life of Walter Mitty," which first appeared in The New Yorker, reached millions in The Reader's Digest version, was published in two of Thurber's own volumes, was dramatized for radio, and finally turned into a Hollywood super-fable.

Thurber is at his best when he is nocturnal or grim or slightly mad, or all three simultaneously— a fact borne out by some of his other books: My Life and Hard Times, The Seal in the Bedroom, The Middle-Aged Man on the Flying Trapeze, and Men, Women and Dogs, which is a book of indescribable drawings of "hugely resigned dogs, determined and sometimes frightening women, and globular men who try so hard to think so unsuccessfully."

Thurber's work has always provoked wonder, and his comprehensive collection, The Thurber Carnival, is something of a landmark. Whether he is tracing a nightmare battle between the sexes or toying with a delicate whimsy about a polar bear, Thurber is one of the wisest commentators and one of the funniest recorders of his day—or, one is tempted to add, of any other day.

The Secret Life of Walter Mitty

"We're going through!" The Commander's voice was like thin ice breaking. He wore his full-dress uniform, with the heavily braided white cap pulled down rakishly over one cold gray eye. "We can't make it, sir. It's spoiling for a hurricane, if you ask me." "I'm not asking you, Lieutenant Berg," said the Commander. "Throw on the power lights! Rev her up to 8,500! We're going through!" The pounding of the cylinders increased: ta-pocketa-pocketa-pocketa-*pocketa-pocketa.* The Commander stared at the ice forming on the pilot window. He walked over and twisted a row of complicated dials. "Switch on No. 8 auxiliary!" he shouted. "Switch on No. 8 auxiliary!" repeated Lieutenant Berg. "Full strength in No. 3 turret!" shouted the Commander. "Full strength in No. 3 turret!" The crew, bending to their various tasks in the huge, hurtling eight-engined Navy hydroplane, looked at each other and grinned. "The Old Man'll get us through," they said to one another. "The Old Man ain't afraid of Hell!". . .

"Not so fast! You're driving too fast!" said Mrs. Mitty. "What are you driving so fast for?"

"Hmm?" said Walter Mitty. He looked at his wife, in the seat beside him, with shocked astonishment. She seemed grossly unfamiliar, like a strange woman who had yelled at him in a crowd. "You were up to fifty-five," she said. "You know I don't like to go more than forty.

You were up to fifty-five." Walter Mitty drove on toward Waterbury in silence, the roaring of the SN202 through the worst storm in twenty years of Navy flying fading in the remote, intimate airways of his mind. "You're tensed up again," said Mrs. Mitty. "It's one of your days. I wish you'd let Dr. Renshaw look you over."

Walter Mitty stopped the car in front of the building where his wife went to have her hair done. "Remember to get those overshoes while I'm having my hair done," she said. "I don't need overshoes," said Mitty. She put her mirror back into her bag. "We've been all through that," she said, getting out of the car. "You're not a young man any longer." He raced the engine a little. "Why don't you wear your gloves? Have you lost your gloves?" Walter Mitty reached in a pocket and brought out the gloves. He put them on, but after she had turned and gone into the building and he had driven on to a red light, he took them off again. "Pick it up, brother!" snapped a cop as the light changed, and Mitty hastily pulled on his gloves and lurched ahead. He drove around the streets aimlessly for a time, and then he drove past the hospital on his way to the parking lot.

. . . "It's the millionaire banker, Wellington McMillan," said the pretty nurse. "Yes?" said Walter Mitty, removing his gloves slowly. "Who has the case?" "Dr. Renshaw and Dr. Benbow, but there are two specialists here, Dr. Remington from New York and Mr. Pritchard-Mitford from London. He flew over." A door opened down a long, cool corridor and Dr. Renshaw came out. He looked distraught and haggard. "Hello, Mitty," he said. "We're having the devil's own time with Mc-Millan, the millionaire banker and close personal friend of Roosevelt. Obstreosis of the ductal tract. Tertiary. Wish you'd take a look at him." "Glad to," said Mitty.

In the operating room there were whispered introductions: "Dr. Remington, Dr. Mitty. Mr. Pritchard-Mitford, Dr. Mitty." "I've read your book on streptothricosis," said Pritchard-Mitford, shaking hands. "A brilliant performance, sir." "Thank you," said Walter Mitty. "Didn't know you were in the States, Mitty," grumbled Remington. "Coals to Newcastle, bringing Mitford and me up here for a tertiary." "You are very kind," said Mitty. A huge, complicated machine, connected to the operating table, with many tubes and wires, began at this moment to go pocketa-pocketa-pocketa. "The new anesthetizer is giving way!" shouted an interne. "There is no one in the East who knows how to fix it!" "Quiet, man!" said Mitty, in a low, cool voice. He sprang to the machine, which was now going pocketa-pocketa-queep-pocketa-queep. He began fingering delicately a row of glistening dials.

"Give me a fountain pen!" he snapped. Someone handed him a fountain pen. He pulled a faulty piston out of the machine and inserted the pen in its place. "That will hold for ten minutes," he said. "Get on with the operation." A nurse hurried over and whispered to Renshaw, and Mitty saw the man turn pale. "Coreopsis has set in," said Renshaw nervously. "If you would take over, Mitty?" Mitty looked at him and at the craven figure of Benbow, who drank, and at the grave, uncertain faces of the two great specialists. "If you wish," he said. They slipped a white gown on him; he adjusted a mask and drew on thin gloves; nurses handed him shining . . .

"Back it up, Mac! Look out for that Buick!" Walter Mitty jammed on the brakes. "Wrong lane, Mac," said the parking-lot attendant, looking at Mitty closely. "Gee. Yeh," muttered Mitty. He began cautiously to back out of the lane marked "Exit Only." "Leave her sit there," said the attendant. "I'll put her away." Mitty got out of the car. "Hey, better leave the key." "Oh," said Mitty, handing the man the ignition key. The attendant vaulted into the car, backed it up with insolent skill, and put it where it belonged.

They're so damn cocky, thought Walter Mitty, walking along Main Street; they think they know everything. Once he had tried to take his chains off, outside New Milford, and he had got them wound around the axles. A man had had to come out in a wrecking car and unwind them, a young, grinning garageman. Since then Mrs. Mitty always made him drive to a garage to have the chains taken off. The next time, he thought, I'll wear my right arm in a sling; they won't grin at me then. I'll have my right arm in a sling and they'll see I couldn't possibly take the chains off myself. He kicked at the slush on the sidewalk. "Overshoes," he said to himself, and he began looking for a shoe store.

When he came out into the street again, with the overshoes in a box under his arm, Walter Mitty began to wonder what the other thing was his wife had told him to get. She had told him, twice, before they set out from their house for Waterbury. In a way he hated these weekly trips to town—he was always getting something wrong. Kleenex, he thought, Squibb's, razor blades? No. Toothpaste, toothbrush, bicarbonate, carborundum, initiative and referendum? He gave it up. But she would remember it. "Where's the what's-its-name?" she would ask. "Don't tell me you forgot the what's-its-name." A newsboy went by shouting something about the Waterbury trial.

. . . "Perhaps this will refresh your memory." The District Attorney suddenly thrust a heavy automatic at the quiet figure on the witness stand. "Have you ever seen this before?" Walter Mitty took the gun and examined it expertly. "This is my Webley-Vickers 50.80," he said calmly. An excited buzz ran around the courtroom. The Judge rapped for order. "You are a crack shot with any sort of firearms, I believe?" said the District Attorney, insinuatingly. "Objection!" shouted Mitty's attorney. "We have shown that the defendant could not have fired the shot. We have shown that he wore his right arm in a sling on the night of the fourteenth of July." Walter Mitty raised his hand briefly and the bickering attorneys were stilled. "With any known make of gun," he said evenly, "I could have killed Gregory Fitzhurst at three hundred feet *with my left hand*." Pandemonium broke loose in the courtroom. A woman's scream rose above the bedlam and suddenly a lovely, dark-haired girl was in Walter Mitty's arms. The District Attorney struck at her savagely. Without rising from his chair, Mitty let the man have it on the point of the chin. "You miserable cur!" . . .

"Puppy biscuit," said Walter Mitty. He stopped walking and the buildings of Waterbury rose up out of the misty courtroom and surrounded him again. A woman who was passing laughed. "He said 'Puppy biscuit,'" she said to her companion. "That man said 'Puppy biscuit' to himself." Walter Mitty hurried on. He went into an A. & P., not the first one he came to but a smaller one farther up the street. "I want some biscuit for small, young dogs," he said to the clerk. "Any special brand, sir?" The greatest pistol shot in the world thought a moment. "It says 'Puppies Bark for It' on the box," said Walter Mitty.

His wife would be through at the hairdresser's in fifteen minutes, Mitty saw in looking at his watch, unless they had trouble drying it; sometimes they had trouble drying it. She didn't like to get to the hotel first; she would want him to be there waiting for her as usual. He found a big leather chair in the lobby, facing a window, and he put the overshoes and the puppy biscuit on the floor beside it. He picked up an old copy of *Liberty* and sank down into the chair. "Can Germany Conquer the World Through the Air?" Walter Mitty looked at the pictures of bombing planes and of ruined streets.

. . . "The cannonading has got the wind up in young Raleigh, sir," said the sergeant. Captain Mitty looked up at him through touseled hair. "Get him to bed," he said wearily. "With the others. I'll fly alone." "But you can't, sir," said the sergeant anxiously. "It takes two men to handle that bomber and the Archies are pounding hell out of the air. Von Richtman's circus is between here and Saulier." "Somebody's got to get that ammunition dump," said Mitty. "I'm going over. Spot of brandy?" He poured a drink for the sergeant and one for himself. War thundered and whined around the dugout and battered at the door. There was a rending of wood and splinters flew through the room. "A bit of a near thing," said Captain Mitty carelessly. "The box barrage is closing in," said the sergeant. "We only live once, Sergeant," said Mitty, with his faint, fleeting smile. "Or do we?" He poured another brandy and tossed it off. "I never see a man could hold his brandy like you, sir," said the sergeant. "Begging your pardon, sir." Captain Mitty stood up and strapped on his huge Webley-Vickers automatic. "It's forty kilometers through hell, sir," said the sergeant. Mitty finished one last brandy. "After all," he said softly, "what isn't?" The pounding of the cannon increased; there was the rat-tat-tatting of machine guns, and from somewhere came the menacing pocketa-pocketa-pocketa of the new flame-throwers. Walter Mitty walked to the door of the dugout humming "Auprès de Ma Blonde." He turned and waved to the sergeant. "Cheerio!" he said. . . .

Something struck his shoulder. "I've been looking all over this hotel for you," said Mrs. Mitty. "Why do you have to hide in this old chair? How did you expect me to find you?" "Things close in," said Walter Mitty vaguely. "What?" Mrs. Mitty said. "Did you get the what's-its-

name? The puppy biscuit? What's in that box?" "Overshoes," said Mitty. "Couldn't you have put them on in the store?" "I was thinking," said Walter Mitty. "Does it ever occur to you that I am sometimes thinking?" She looked at him. "I'm going to take your temperature when I get you home," she said.

They went out through the revolving doors that made a faintly derisive whistling sound when you pushed them. It was two blocks to the parking lot. At the drugstore on the corner she said, "Wait here for me. I forgot something. I won't be a minute." She was more than a minute. Walter Mitty lighted a cigarette. It began to rain, rain with sleet in it. He stood up against the wall of the drugstore, smoking. . . . He put his shoulders back and his heels together. "To hell with the handkerchief," said Walter Mitty scornfully. He took one last drag on his cigarette and snapped it away. Then, with that faint, fleeting smile playing about his lips, he faced the firing squad; erect and motionless, proud and disdainful, Walter Mitty the Undefeated, inscrutable to the last.

What Do You Mean It Was Brillig?

I was sitting at my typewriter one afternoon several weeks ago, staring at a piece of blank white paper, when Della walked in. "They are here with the reeves," she said. It did not surprise me that they were. With a colored woman like Della in the house it would not surprise me if they showed up with the toves. In Della's afternoon it is always brillig; she could outgrabe a mome rath on any wabe in the world. Only Lewis Carroll would have understood Della completely. I try hard enough. "Let them wait a minute," I said. I got out the big Century Dictionary and put it on my lap and looked up "reeve." It is an interesting word, like all of Della's words; I found out that there are four kinds of reeves. "Are they here with strings of onions?" I asked. Della said they were not. "Are they here with enclosures or pens for cattle, poultry, or pigs; sheepfolds?" Della said no sir. "Are they here with administrative officers?" From a little nearer the door Della said no again. "Then they've got to be here," I said, "with some females of the common European sandpiper." These scenes of ours take as much out of Della as they do out of me, but she is not a woman to be put down by a crazy man with a dictionary. "They are here with the reeves for the windas," said Della with brave stubbornness. Then, of course, I understood what they were there with: they were there with the Christmas wreaths for the windows. "Oh, *those* reeves!" I said. We were both greatly relieved; we both laughed. Della and I never quite reach the breaking point; we just come close to it.

Della is a New England colored woman with nothing of the South in her accent; she doesn't say "d" for "th" and she pronounces her "r's." Hearing her talk in the next room, you might not know at first that she was colored. You might not know till she said some such thing as "Do you want cretonnes in the soup tonight?" (She makes wonderful cretonnes for the soup.) I have not found out much about Della's words, but I have learned a great deal about her background. She told me one day that she has three brothers and that one of them works into a garage and another works into an incinerator where they burn the refuge. The one that works into the incinerator has been working into it since the Armitage. That's what Della does to you; she gives you incinerator perfectly and then she comes out with the Armitage. I spent most of an hour one afternoon trying to figure out what was wrong with the Armitage; I thought of Armistead and armature and Armentières, and when I finally hit on Armistice it sounded crazy. It still does. Della's third and youngest brother is my favorite; I think he'll be yours, too, and everybody else's. His name is Arthur and it seems that he has just passed with commendably high grades, his silver-service eliminations. Della is delighted about that, but she is not half so delighted about it as I am.

Della came to our house in Connecticut some months ago, trailing her glory of cloudiness. I can place the date for you approximately: it was while there were still a great many fletchers about. "The lawn is full of fletchers," Della told me one morning, shortly after she arrived, when she brought up my orange juice. "You mean neighbors?" I said. "This early?" By the way she laughed I knew that fletchers weren't people; at least not people of flesh and blood. I got dressed and went downstairs and looked up the word in the indispensable Century. A fletcher, I found, is a man who makes arrows. I decided, but without a great deal of conviction, that there couldn't be any arrow-makers on my lawn at that hour in the morning and at this particular period in history. I walked cautiously out the back door and around to the front of the house—and there they were. I don't know many birds but I do know flickers. A flicker is a bird which, if it were really named fletcher, would be called flicker by all the colored cooks in the United States. Out of a mild curiosity I looked up "flicker" in the dictionary and I discovered that he is a bird of several aliases. When Della brought my toast and coffee into the dining room I told her about this. "Fletchers," I said, "are also golden-winged woodpeckers, yellowhammers, and high-holders." For the first time Della gave me the look that I was to recognize later, during the scene about the reeves. I have become very familiar with that look and I believe I know the thoughts that lie behind it. Della was puzzled at first because I work at home instead of in an office, but I think she has it figured out now. This man, she thinks, used to work into an office like anybody else, but he had to be sent to an institution; he got well enough to come home from the institution, but he is still not well enough to go back to the office. I could have avoided all these suspicions, of course, if I had simply come out in the beginning and corrected Della when she got words wrong. Coming at her obliquely with a dictionary only enriches the confusion; but I wouldn't have it any other way. I share with Della a form of escapism that is the most mystic and satisfying flight from actuality I have ever known. It may not always comfort me, but it never ceases to beguile me.

Every Thursday when I drive Della to Waterbury in the car for her day off, I explore the dark depths and the strange recesses of her nomenclature. I found out that she had been married for ten years but was now divorced; that is, her husband went away one day and never came back. When I asked her what he did for a living, she said he worked into a dove-wedding. "Into a what?" I asked. "Into a dove-wedding," said Della. It is one of the words I haven't figured out yet, but I am still working on it. "Where are you from, Mr. Thurl?" she asked me one day. I told her Ohio, and she said, "Ooooh, to be sure!" as if I had given her a clue to my crazy definitions, my insensitivity to the ordinary household nouns, and my ignorance of the commoner migratory birds. "Semantics, Ohio," I said. "Why, there's one of them in Massachusetts, too," said Della. "The one I mean," I told her, "is bigger and more confusing." "I'll bet it is," said Della.

Della told me the other day that she had had only one sister, a beautiful girl who died when she was twenty-one. "That's too bad," I said. "What was the matter?" Della had what was the matter at her tongue's tip. "She got tuberculosis from her teeth," she said, "and it went all through her symptom." I didn't know what to say to that except that my teeth were all right but that my symptom could probably be easily gone all through. "You work too much with your brain," said Della. I knew she was trying to draw me out about my brain and what had happened to it so that I could no longer work into an office, but I changed the subject. There is no doubt that Della is considerably worried about my mental condition. One morning when I didn't get up till noon because I had been writing letters until three o'clock, Della told my wife at breakfast what was the matter with me. "His mind works so fast his body can't keep up with it," she said. This diagnosis has shaken me not a little. I have decided to sleep longer and work less. I know exactly what will happen to me if my mind gets so far ahead of my body that my body can't catch up with it. They will come with a reeve and this time it won't be a red-and-green one for the window, it will be a black one for the door.

The Greatest Man in the World

Looking back on it now, from the vantage point of 1940, one can only marvel that it hadn't happened long before it did. The United States of America had been, ever since Kitty Hawk, blindly constructing the elaborate petard by which, sooner or later, it must be hoist. It was inevitable that some day there would come roaring out of the skies a national hero of insufficient intelligence, background, and character successfully to endure the mounting orgies of glory prepared for aviators who stayed up a long time or flew a great distance. Both Lindbergh and Byrd, fortunately for national decorum and international amity, had been gentlemen; so had our other famous aviators. They wore their laurels gracefully, withstood the awful weather of publicity, married excellent women, usually of fine family, and quietly retired to private life and the enjoyment of their varying fortunes. No untoward incidents, on a worldwide scale, marred the perfection of their conduct on the perilous heights of fame. The exception to the rule was, however, bound to occur and it did, in July, 1935, when Jack ("Pal") Smurch, erstwhile mechanic's helper in a small garage in Westfield, Iowa, flew a second-hand, single-motored Bresthaven Dragon-Fly III monoplane all the way around the world, without stopping.

Never before in the history of aviation had such a flight as Smurch's ever been dreamed of. No one had ever taken seriously the weird floating auxiliary gas tanks, invention of the mad New Hampshire professor of astronomy, Dr. Charles Lewis Gresham, upon which Smurch placed full reliance. When the garage worker, a slightly built, surly, unprepossessing young man of twenty-two, appeared at Roosevelt Field early in July, 1935, slowly chewing a great quid of scrap tobacco, and announced "Nobody ain't seen no flyin' yet," the newspapers touched briefly and satirically upon his projected twenty-five-thousand-mile flight. Aëronautical and automotive experts dismissed the idea curtly, implying that it was a hoax, a publicity stunt. The rusty, battered, second-hand plane wouldn't go. The Gresham auxiliary tanks wouldn't work. It was simply a cheap joke.

Smurch, however, after calling on a girl in Brooklyn who worked in the flap-folding department of a large paper-box factory, a girl whom he later described as his "sweet patootie," climbed nonchalantly into his ridiculous plane at dawn of the memorable seventh of July, 1935, spit a curve of tobacco juice into the still air, and took off, carrying with him only a gallon of bootleg gin and six pounds of salami.

When the garage boy thundered out over the ocean the papers were forced to record, in all seriousness, that a mad, unknown young man—his name was variously misspelled—had actually set out upon a preposterous attempt to span the world in a rickety, one-engined contraption, trusting to the long-distance refuelling device of a crazy schoolmaster. When, nine days later, without having stopped once, the tiny plane appeared above San Francisco Bay, headed for New York, spluttering and choking, to be sure, but still magnificently and miraculously aloft, the headlines, which long since had crowded everything else off the front page—even the shooting of the Governor of Illinois by the Capone gang —swelled to unprecedented size, and the news stories began to run to twenty-five and thirty columns. It was noticeable, however, that the accounts of the epoch-making flight touched rather lightly upon the aviator himself. This was not because facts about the hero as a man were too meager, but because they were too complete.

Reporters, who had been rushed out to Iowa when Smurch's plane was first sighted over the little French coast town of Serly-le-Mer, to dig up the story of the great man's life, had promptly discovered that the story of his life could not be printed. His mother, a sullen short-order cook in a shack restaurant on the edge of a tourists' camping ground near Westfield, met all inquiries as to her son with an angry "Ah, the hell with him; I hope he drowns." His father appeared to be in jail somewhere for stealing spotlights and laprobes from tourists' automobiles; his young brother, a weakminded lad, had but recently escaped from the Preston, Iowa, Reformatory and was already wanted in several

Western towns for the theft of money-order blanks from post offices. These alarming discoveries were still piling up at the very time that Pal Smurch, the greatest hero of the twentieth century, blear-eyed, dead for sleep, half-starved, was piloting his crazy junkheap high above the region in which the lamentable story of his private life was being unearthed, headed for New York and a greater glory than any man of his time had ever known.

The necessity for printing some account in the papers of the young man's career and personality had led to a remarkable predicament. It was of course impossible to reveal the facts, for a tremendous popular feeling in favor of the young hero had sprung up, like a grass fire, when he was halfway across Europe on his flight around the globe. He was, therefore, described as a modest chap, taciturn, blond, popular with his friends, popular with girls. The only available snapshot of Smurch, taken at the wheel of a phony automobile in a cheap photo studio at an amusement park, was touched up so that the little vulgarian looked quite handsome. His twisted leer was smoothed into a pleasant smile. The truth was, in this way, kept from the youth's ecstatic compatriots; they did not dream that the Smurch family was despised and feared by its neighbors in the obscure Iowa town, nor that the hero himself, because of numerous unsavory exploits, had come to be regarded in Westfield as a nuisance and a menace. He had, the reporters discovered, once knifed the principal of his high school—not mortally, to be sure, but he had knifed him; and on another occasion, surprised in the act of stealing an altarcloth from a church, he had bashed the sacristan over the head with a pot of Easter lilies; for each of these offenses he had served a sentence in the reformatory.

Inwardly, the authorities, both in New York and in Washington, prayed that an understanding Providence might, however awful such a thing seemed, bring disaster to the rusty, battered plane and its illustrious pilot, whose unheard-of-flight had aroused the civilized world to hosannas of hysterical praise. The authorities were convinced that the character of the renowned aviator was such that the limelight of adulation was bound to reveal him, to all the world, as a congenital hooligan mentally and morally unequipped to cope with his own prodigious fame. "I trust," said the Secretary of State, at one of many secret Cabinet meetings called to consider the national dilemma, "I trust that his mother's prayer will be answered," by which he referred to Mrs. Emma Smurch's wish that her son might be drowned. It was, however, too late for that—Smurch had leaped the Atlantic and then the Pacific as if they were millponds. At three minutes after two o'clock on the

afternoon of July 17, 1935, the garage boy brought his idiotic plane into
Roosevelt Field for a perfect three-point landing.

It had, of course, been out of the question to arrange a modest little
reception for the greatest flier in the history of the world. He was received at Roosevelt Field with such elaborate and pretentious ceremonies as rocked the world. Fortunately, however, the worn and spent
hero promptly swooned, had to be removed bodily from his plane, and
was spirited from the field without having opened his mouth once. Thus
he did not jeopardize the dignity of this first reception, a reception
illumined by the presence of the Secretaries of War and the Navy,
Mayor Michael J. Moriarity of New York, the Premier of Canada, Governors Fanniman, Groves, McFeely, and Critchfield, and a brilliant ar-
ray of European diplomats. Smurch did not, in fact, come to in time to
take part in the gigantic hullabaloo arranged at City Hall for the next
day. He was rushed to a secluded nursing home and confined in bed. It
was nine days before he was able to get up, or to be more exact, before he
was permitted to get up. Meanwhile the greatest minds in the country,
in solemn assembly, had arranged a secret conference of city, state, and
government officials, which Smurch was to attend for the purpose of
being instructed in the ethics and behavior of heroism.

On the day that the little mechanic was finally allowed to get up and
dress and, for the first time in two weeks, took a great chew of tobacco,
he was permitted to receive the newspapermen—this by way of testing
him out. Smurch did not wait for questions. "Youse guys," he said—and
the *Times* man winced—"youse guys can tell the cockeyed world dat I
put it over on Lindbergh, see? Yeh—an' made an ass o' them two frogs."
The "two frogs" was a reference to a pair of gallant French fliers who,
in attempting a flight only halfway round the world, had, two weeks
before, unhappily been lost at sea. The *Times* man was bold enough, at
this point, to sketch out for Smurch the accepted formula for interviews
in cases of this kind; he explained that there should be no arrogant
statements belittling the achievements of other heroes, particularly
heroes of foreign nations. "Ah, the hell with that," said Smurch. "I did it,
see? I did it, an' I'm talkin' about it." And he did talk about it.

None of this extraordinary interview was, of course, printed. On the
contrary, the newspapers, already under the disciplined direction of a
secret directorate created for the occasion and composed of statesmen
and editors, gave out to a panting and restless world that "Jacky," as he
had been arbitrarily nicknamed, would consent to say only that he was
very happy and that anyone could have done what he did. "My achieve-

ment has been, I fear, slightly exaggerated," the *Times* man's article had him protest, with a modest smile. These newspaper stories were kept from the hero, a restriction which did not serve to abate the rising malevolence of his temper. The situation was, indeed, extremely grave, for Pal Smurch was, as he kept insisting, "rarin' to go." He could not much longer be kept from a nation clamorous to lionize him. It was the most desperate crisis the United States of America had faced since the sinking of the Lusitania.

On the afternoon of the twenty-seventh of July, Smurch was spirited away to a conference-room in which were gathered mayors, governors, government officials, behaviorist psychologists, and editors. He gave them each a limp, moist paw and a brief unlovely grin. "Hah ya?" he said. When Smurch was seated, the Mayor of New York arose and, with obvious pessimism, attempted to explain what he must say and how he must act when presented to the world, ending his talk with a high tribute to the hero's courage and integrity. The Mayor was followed by Governor Fanniman of New York, who, after a touching declaration of faith, introduced Cameron Spottiswood, Second Secretary of the American Embassy in Paris, the gentleman selected to coach Smurch in the amenities of public ceremonies. Sitting in a chair, with a soiled yellow tie in his hand and his shirt open at the throat, unshaved, smoking a rolled cigarette, Jack Smurch listened with a leer on his lips. "I get ya, I get ya," he cut in, nastily. "Ya want me to ack like a softy, huh? Ya want me to ack like that— —— baby-faced Lindbergh, huh? Well, nuts to that, see?" Everyone took in his breath sharply; it was a sigh and a hiss. "Mr. Lindbergh," began a United States Senator, purple with rage, "and Mr. Byrd—" Smurch, who was paring his nails with a jackknife, cut in again. "Byrd!" he exclaimed. "Aw, fa God's sake, *dat* big—" Somebody shut off his blasphemies with a sharp word. A newcomer had entered the room. Everyone stood up, except Smurch, who, still busy with his nails, did not even glance up. "Mr. Smurch," said someone, sternly, "the President of the United States!" It had been thought that the presence of the Chief Executive might have a chastening effect upon the young hero, and the former had been, thanks to the remarkable coöperation of the press, secretly brought to the obscure conference-room.

A great, painful silence fell. Smurch looked up, waved a hand at the President. "How ya comin'?" he asked, and began rolling a fresh cigarette. The silence deepened. Someone coughed in a strained way. "Geez, it's hot, ain't it?" said Smurch. He loosened two more shirt buttons, revealing a hairy chest and the tattooed word "Sadie" enclosed in a stenciled heart. The great and important men in the room, faced by the most serious crisis in recent American history, exchanged worried frowns. Nobody seemed to know how to proceed. "Come awn, come awn," said Smurch. "Let's get the hell out of here! When do I start cuttin' in on de parties, huh? And what's they goin' to be *in* it?" He rubbed a thumb and forefinger together meaningly. "Money!" exclaimed a state senator, shocked, pale. "Yeh, money," said Pal, flipping his cigarette out of a window. "An' big money." He began rolling a fresh cigarette. "Big money," he repeated, frowning over the rice paper. He tilted back in his chair, and leered at each gentleman, separately, the leer of an animal that knows its power, the leer of a leopard loose in a bird-and-dog shop. "Aw fa God's sake, let's get some place where it's cooler," he said. "I been cooped up plenty for three weeks!"

Smurch stood up and walked over to an open window, where he stood staring down into the street, nine floors below. The faint shouting of newsboys floated up to him. He made out his name. "Hot dog!" he cried, grinning, ecstatic. He leaned out over the sill. "You tell 'em, babies!" he shouted down. "Hot diggity dog!" In the tense little knot of men standing behind him, a quick, mad impulse flared up. An unspoken word of appeal, of command, seemed to ring through the room. Yet it was deadly silent. Charles K. L. Brand, secretary to the Mayor of New York City, happened to be standing nearest Smurch; he looked in-

quiringly at the President of the United States. The President, pale, grim, nodded shortly. Brand, a tall, powerfully built man, once a tackle at Rutgers, stepped forward, seized the greatest man in the world by his left shoulder and the seat of his pants, and pushed him out the window.

"My God, he's fallen out the window!" cried a quick-witted editor.

"Get me out of here!" cried the President. Several men sprang to his side and he was hurriedly escorted out of a door toward a side-entrance of the building. The editor of the Associated Press took charge, being used to such things. Crisply he ordered certain men to leave, others to stay; quickly he outlined a story which all the papers were to agree on, sent two men to the street to handle that end of the tragedy, commanded a Senator to sob and two Congressmen to go to pieces nervously. In a word, he skillfully set the stage for the gigantic task that was to follow, the task of breaking to a grief-stricken world the sad story of the untimely, accidental death of its most illustrious and spectacular figure.

The funeral was, as you know, the most elaborate, the finest, the solemnest, and the saddest ever held in the United States of America. The monument in Arlington Cemetery, with its clean white shaft of marble and the simple device of a tiny plane carved on its base, is a place for pilgrims, in deep reverence, to visit. The nations of the world paid lofty tributes to little Jacky Smurch, America's greatest hero. At a given hour there were two minutes of silence throughout the nation. Even the inhabitants of the small, bewildered town of Westfield, Iowa, observed this touching ceremony; agents of the Department of Justice saw to that. One of them was especially assigned to stand grimly in the doorway of a little shack restaurant on the edge of the tourists' camping ground just outside the town. There, under his stern scrutiny, Mrs. Emma Smurch bowed her head above two hamburger steaks sizzling on her grill—bowed her head and turned away, so that the Secret Service man could not see the twisted, strangely familiar, leer on her lips.

Mark Twain

Nearing thirty, unsure of himself and his world, Samuel L. Clemens took the river pilot's call, "Mark Twain," for his pseudonym. Before he died, at the age of seventy-five, the pseudonym had become not only a trade-mark but a hall-mark of a new kind of American writing. Born in 1835 in one small Missouri town (Florida) and raised in another (Hannibal), a Mississippi pilot at twenty-one, a Nevada journalist at twenty-seven, Twain became known as a frontier humorist with the publication of The Celebrated Jumping Frog. Twelve years later he extended the frontier with Tom Sawyer; seven years after that he enlarged it with Huckleberry Finn—the only sequel in literature which is greater than the original from which it stemmed. These two masterpieces are an eternal nostalgia for boyhood. They reach further than their backgrounds—together with Twain's other irreverences and easy exaggerations, they are not only pieces of his autobiography, but part of the biography of America.

Although Twain's purpose was anything but academic, there is (as he wrote in the preface to Roughing It) a good deal of information in his work. "I regret this very much but really it could not be helped: information appears to stew out of me naturally, like the precious ottar of roses out of the otter. Sometimes it has seemed to me that I would give worlds if I could retain my facts; but it cannot be. The more I calk up the sources, and the tighter I get, the more I leak wisdom. Therefore, I can only claim indulgence at the hands of the reader, not justification."

The Celebrated Jumping Frog of Calaveras County

In compliance with the request of a friend of mine, who wrote me from the East, I called on good-natured, garrulous old Simon Wheeler, and inquired after my friend's friend, Leonidas W. Smiley, as requested to do, and I hereunto append the result. I have a lurking suspicion that *Leonidas W.* Smiley is a myth; and that my friend never knew such a personage; and that he only conjectured that if I asked old Wheeler about him, it would remind him of his infamous *Jim Smiley*, and he would go to work and bore me to death with some exasperating reminiscence of him as long and as tedious as it should be useless to me. If that was the design, it succeeded.

I found Simon Wheeler dozing comfortably by the bar-room stove of the dilapidated tavern in the decayed mining camp of Angel's, and I noticed that he was fat and bald-headed, and had an expression of winning gentleness and simplicity upon his tranquil countenance. He roused up, and gave me good-day. I told him a friend had commissioned me to make some inquiries about a cherished companion of his boyhood named *Leonidas W.* Smiley—*Rev. Leonidas W.* Smiley, a young minister of the Gospel, who he had heard was at one time a resident of Angel's Camp. I added that if Mr. Wheeler could tell me anything about this Rev. Leonidas W. Smiley, I would feel under many obligations to him.

Simon Wheeler backed me into a corner and blockaded me there with his chair, and then sat down and reeled off the monotonous narrative which follows this paragraph. He never smiled, he never frowned, he never changed his voice from the gentle-flowing key to which he tuned his initial sentence, he never betrayed the slightest suspicion of enthusiasm; but all through the interminable narrative there ran a vein of impressive earnestness and sincerity, which showed me plainly that, so far from his imagining that there was anything ridiculous or funny about his story, he regarded it as a really important matter, and admired its two heroes as men of transcendent genius in *finesse*. I let him go on in his own way, and never interrupted him once.

"Rev. Leonidas W. H'm, Reverend Le—well, there was a feller here once by the name of *Jim* Smiley, in the winter of '49—or maybe it was the spring of '50—I don't recollect exactly, somehow, though what makes me think it was one or the other is because I remember the big flume warn't finished when he first came to the camp; but any way, he was the curiousest man about always betting on anything that turned up you ever see, if he could get anybody to bet on the other side; and if he couldn't he'd change sides. Any way that suited the other man would suit *him*—any way just so's he got a bet, *he* was satisfied. But still he was lucky, uncommon lucky; he most always come out winner. He was always ready and laying for a chance; there couldn't be no solit'ry thing mentioned but that feller'd offer to bet on it, and take ary side you please, as I was just telling you. If there was a horse-race, you'd find him flush or you'd find him busted at the end of it; if there was a dog-fight, he'd bet on it; if there was a cat-fight, he'd bet on it; if there was a chicken-fight, he'd bet on it; why, if there was two birds setting on a fence, he would bet you which one would fly first; or if there was a camp-meeting, he would be there reg'lar to bet on Parson Walker, which he judged to be the best exhorter about here, and he was, too, and a good man. If he even see a straddle-bug start to go anywheres, he would bet you how long it would take him to get to— to wherever he was going to, and if you took him up, he would foller that straddle-bug to Mexico but what he would find out where he was bound for and how long he was on the road. Lots of the boys here has seen that Smiley and can tell you about him. Why, it never made no difference to *him*—he'd bet on *any* thing—the dangest feller. Parson Walker's wife laid very sick once, for a good while, and it seemed as if they warn't going to save her; but one morning he come in, and Smiley up and asked him how she was, and he said she was considerable better —thank the Lord for his inf'nit' mercy—and coming on so smart that with the blessing of Prov'dence she'd get well yet; and Smiley, before he thought, says, "Well, I'll risk two-and-a-half she don't anyway."

Thish-yer Smiley had a mare—the boys called her the fifteen-minute nag, but that was only in fun, you know, because, of course, she was faster than that—and he used to win money on that horse, for all she was so slow and always had the asthma, or the distemper, or the consumption, or something of that kind. They used to give her two or three hundred yards start, and then pass her under way; but always at the fag-end of the race she'd get excited and desperate-like, and come cavorting and straddling up, and scattering her legs around limber, sometimes in the air, and sometimes out to one side amongst the fences, and kicking up m-o-r-e dust and raising m-o-r-e racket with her coughing and sneezing and blowing her nose—and *always* fetch up at the stand just about a neck ahead, as near as you could cipher it down.

And he had a little small bull-pup, that to look at him you'd think he warn't worth a cent but to set around and look ornery and lay for a chance to steal something. But as soon as money was up on him he was a different dog; his under-jaw'd begin to stick out like the fo'-castle of a steamboat, and his teeth would uncover and shine like the furnaces. And a dog might tackle him and bully-rag him, and bite him, and throw him over his shoulder two or three times, and Andrew Jackson—which was the name of the pup—Andrew Jackson would never let on but what *he* was satisfied, and hadn't expected nothing else—and the bets being doubled and doubled on the other side all the time, till the money was all up; and then all of a sudden he would grab that other dog jest by the j'int of his hind leg and freeze to it—not chaw, you understand, but only just grip and hang on till they throwed up the sponge, if it was a year. Smiley always come out winner on that pup, till he harnessed a dog once that didn't have no hind legs, because they'd been sawed off in a circular saw, and when the thing had gone along far enough, and the money was all up, and he come to make a snatch for his pet holt, he see in a minute how he'd been imposed on, and how the other dog had him in the door, so to speak, and he 'peared surprised, and then he looked sorter discouraged-like, and didn't try no more to win the fight, and so he got shucked out bad. He gave Smiley a look, as much as to say his heart was broke, and it was *his* fault, for putting up a dog that hadn't no hind legs for him to take holt of, which was his main dependence in a fight, and then he limped off a piece and laid down and died. It was a good pup, was that Andrew Jackson, and would have made a name for hisself if he'd lived, for the stuff was in him and he had genius—I know it, because he hadn't no opportunities to speak of, and it don't stand to reason that a dog could make such a fight as he could under them circumstances if he hadn't no talent. It always makes me feel sorry when I think of that last fight of his'n, and the way it turned out.

Well, thish-yer Smiley had rat-tarriers, and chicken cocks, and tom-cats and all of them kind of things, till you couldn't rest, and you couldn't fetch nothing for him to bet on but he'd match you. He ketched a frog one day, and took him home, and said he cal'lated to educate him; and so he never done nothing for three months but set in his back yard and learn that frog to jump. And you bet you he *did* learn him, too. He'd give him a little punch behind, and the next minute you'd see that frog whirling in the air like a doughnut—see him turn one summerset, or maybe a couple, if he got a good start, and come down flat-footed and all right, like a cat. He got him up so in the matter of ketching flies, and kep' him in practice so constant, that he'd nail a fly every time as fur as he could see him. Smiley said all a frog wanted was education, and he could do 'most anything—and I believe him. Why, I've seen him set Dan'l Webster down here on this floor— Dan'l Webster was the name of the frog—and sing out, "Flies, Dan'l, flies!" and quicker'n you could wink he'd spring straight up and snake a fly off'n the counter there, and flop down on the floor ag'in as solid as a gob of mud, and fall to scratching the side of his head with his hind foot as indifferent as if he hadn't no idea he'd been doin' any more'n any frog might do. You never see a frog so modest and straightfor'ard as he was, for all he was so gifted. And when it come to fair and square jumping on a dead level, he could get over more ground at one straddle than any animal of his breed you ever see. Jumping on a dead level was his strong suit, you understand; and when it come to that, Smiley would ante up money on him as long as he had a red. Smiley was monstrous proud of his frog, and well he might be, for fellers that had traveled and been everywheres, all said he laid over any frog that ever *they* see.

Well, Smiley kep' the beast in a little lattice box, and he used to fetch him downtown sometimes and lay for a bet. One day a feller—a stranger in the camp, he was—come acrost him with his box, and says:

"What might be that you've got in the box?"

And Smiley says, sorter indifferent-like, "It might be a parrot, or it might be a canary, maybe, but it ain't—it's only just a frog."

And the feller took it, and looked at it careful, and turned it round this way and that, and says, "H'm—so 'tis. Well, what's *he* good for?"

"Well," Smiley says, easy and careless, "he's good enough for *one* thing, I should judge—he can outjump any frog in Calaveras County."

The feller took the box again, and took another long, particular look, and give it back to Smiley, and says, very deliberate, "Well," he says, "I don't see no p'ints about that frog that's any better'n any other frog."

"Maybe you don't," Smiley says. "Maybe you understand frogs and maybe you don't understand 'em; maybe you've had experience, and maybe you ain't only a amature, as it were. Anyways, I've got *my* opinion and I'll risk forty dollars that he can outjump any frog in Calaveras County."

And the feller studied a minute, and then says, kinder sad like, "Well, I'm only a stranger here, and I ain't got no frog; but if I had a frog, I'd bet you."

And then Smiley says, "That's all right—that's all right—if you'll hold my box a minute, I'll go and get you a frog." And so the feller took the box, and put up his forty dollars along with Smiley's, and set down to wait.

So he set there a good while thinking and thinking to hisself, and then he got the frog out and prized his mouth open and took a teaspoon and filled him full of quail shot—filled him pretty near up to his chin—and set him on the floor. Smiley he went to the swamp and slopped around in the mud for a long time, and finally he ketched a frog, and fetched him in, and give him to this feller, and says:

"Now, if you're ready, set him alongside of Dan'l, with his forepaws just even with Dan'l's, and I'll give the word." Then he says, "One—two—three—*git!*" and him and the feller touched up the frogs from behind, and the new frog hopped off lively, but Dan'l give a heave, and hysted up his shoulders—so—like a Frenchman, but it warn't no use—he couldn't budge; he was planted as solid as a church, and he couldn't no more stir than if he was anchored out. Smiley was a good deal surprised, and he was disgusted too, but he didn't have no idea what the matter was, of course.

The feller took the money and started away; and when he was going out at the door, he sorter jerked his thumb over his shoulder—so—at Dan'l, and says again, very deliberate, "Well," he says, "*I* don't see no p'ints about that frog that's any better'n any other frog."

Smiley he stood scratching his head and looking down at Dan'l a long time, and at last says, "I do wonder what in the nation that frog throwed off for—I wonder if there ain't something the matter with him

—he 'pears to look mighty baggy, somehow." And he ketched Dan'l up by the nap of the neck, and hefted him, and says, "Why blame my cats if he don't weigh five pounds!" and turned him upside down and he belched out a double handful of shot. And then he see how it was, and he was the maddest man—he set the frog down and took out after that feller, but he never ketched him. And——"

(Here Simon Wheeler heard his name called from the front yard, and got up to see what was wanted.) And turning to me as he moved away, he said: "Jest set where you are, stranger, and rest easy—I ain't going to be gone a second."

But, by your leave, I did not think that a continuation of the history of the enterprising vagabond *Jim* Smiley would be likely to afford me much information concerning the Rev. *Leonidas W.* Smiley, and so I started away.

At the door I met the sociable Wheeler returning, and he buttonholed me and recommenced:

"Well, thish-yer Smiley had a yaller, one-eyed cow that didn't have no tail, only jest a short stump like a bannanner, and——"

However, lacking both time and inclination, I did not wait to hear about the afflicted cow, but took my leave.

Tom Whitewashes the Fence

(FROM "THE ADVENTURES OF TOM SAWYER")

Saturday morning was come, and all the summer world was bright and fresh, and brimming with life. There was a song in every heart; and if the heart was young the music issued at the lips. There was cheer in every face and a spring in every step. The locust trees were in bloom and the fragrance of the blossoms filled the air. Cardiff Hill, beyond the village and above it, was green with vegetation, and it lay just far enough away to seem a Delectable Land, dreamy, reposeful, and inviting.

Tom appeared on the sidewalk with a bucket of whitewash and a long-handled brush. He surveyed the fence, and all gladness left him and a deep melancholy settled down upon his spirit. Thirty yards of board fence nine feet high. Life to him seemed hollow, and existence but a burden. Sighing he dipped his brush and passed it along the topmost plank; repeated the operation; did it again; compared the insignificant whitewashed streak with the far-reaching continent of unwhitewashed fence, and sat down on a tree-box discouraged. Jim came skipping out at the gate with a tin pail, and singing "Buffalo Gals." Bringing water from the town pump had always been hateful work in Tom's eyes, before, but now it did not strike him so. He remembered that there was company at the pump. White, mulatto, and Negro boys and girls were always there waiting their turns, resting, trading playthings, quarreling, fighting, skylarking. And he remembered that although the pump was only a hundred and fifty yards off, Jim never got back with a bucket of water under an hour—and even then somebody generally had to go after him. Tom said:

"Say, Jim, I'll fetch the water if you'll whitewash some."

Jim shook his head and said:

"Can't, Mars Tom. Ole missis, she tole me I got to go an' git dis water an' not stop foolin' roun' wid anybody. She says she spec' Mars Tom gwine to ax me to whitewash, an' so she tole me go 'long an' 'tend to my own business—she 'lowed *she'd* 'tend to de whitewashin'."

"O, never you mind what she said, Jim. That's the way she always talks. Gimme the bucket—I won't be gone only a minute. *She* won't ever know."

"Oh, I dasn't, Mars Tom. Ole missis she'd take an' tar de head off'n me. Deed she would."

"*She!* She never licks anybody—whacks 'em over the head with her thimble—and who cares for that, I'd like to know. She talks awful, but talk don't hurt—anyways it don't if she don't cry. Jim, I'll give you a marvel. I'll give you a white alley!"

Jim began to waver.

"White alley, Jim! And it's a bully taw."

"My! Dat's a mighty gay marvel, I tell you! But Mars Tom I's powerful 'fraid ole missis—"

"And, besides, if you will I'll show you my sore toe."

Jim was only human—this attraction was too much for him. He put down the pail, took the white alley, and bent over the toe with absorbing interest while the bandage was being unwound. In another moment he was flying down the street with his pail and a tingling rear, Tom was whitewashing with vigor, and Aunt Polly was retiring from the field with a slipper in her hand and triumph in her eye.

But Tom's energy did not last. He began to think of the fun he had planned for this day, and his sorrows multiplied. Soon the free boys would come tripping along on all sorts of delicious expeditions, and they would make a world of fun of him for having to work—the very thought of it burnt him like fire. He got out his worldly wealth and examined it—bits of toys, marbles, and trash; enough to buy an exchange of *work*, maybe, but not half enough to buy so much as half an hour of pure freedom. So he returned his straitened means to his pocket, and gave up the idea of trying to buy the boys. At this dark and hopeless moment an inspiration burst upon him! Nothing less than a great, magnificent inspiration.

He took up his brush and went tranquilly to work. Ben Rogers hove in sight presently—the very boy, of all boys, whose ridicule he had been dreading. Ben's gait was the hop-skip-and-jump—proof enough that his heart was light and his anticipations high. He was eating an apple, and giving a long, melodious whoop, at intervals, followed by a deep-toned ding-dong-dong, for he was personating a steamboat. As he drew near, he slackened speed, took the middle of the street, leaned far over to starboard and rounded to ponderously and with laborious pomp and circumstance—for he was personating the *Big Missouri,* and considered himself to be drawing nine feet of water. He was boat and captain and engine-bells combined, so he had to imagine himself standing on his own hurricane-deck giving the orders and executing them:

"Stop her, sir! Ting-a-ling-ling!" The headway ran almost out and he drew up slowly toward the sidewalk.

"Ship up to back! Ting-a-ling-ling!" His arms straightened and stiffened down his sides.

"Set her back on the starboard! Ting-a-ling-ling! Chow! ch-chow-wow! Chow!" His right hand, meantime, describing stately circles—for it was representing a forty-foot wheel.

"Let her go back on the labboard! Ting-a-ling-ling! Chow-ch-chow-chow!" The left hand began to describe circles.

"Stop the stabboard! Ting-a-ling-ling! Stop the labboard! Come ahead on the stabboard! Stop her! Let your outside turn over slow! Ting-a-ling-ling! Chow-ow-ow! Get out that head-line! *Lively* now! Come—out with your spring-line—what're you about there! Take a turn round that stump with the bight of it! Stand by that stage, now—let her go! Done with the engines, sir! Ting-a-ling-ling! Sh't! Sh't!" (trying the gauge-cocks.)

Tom went on whitewashing—paid no attention to the steamboat. Ben stared a moment and then said:

"Hi-*yi! You're* up a stump, ain't you!"

No answer. Tom surveyed his last touch with the eye of an artist, then he gave his brush another gentle sweep and surveyed the result, as before. Ben ranged up alongside of him. Tom's mouth watered for the apple, but he stuck to his work. Ben said:

"Hello, old chap, you got to work, hey?"

Tom wheeled suddenly and said:

"Why, it's you, Ben! I warn't noticing."

"Say—I'm going in a-swimming, I am. Don't you wish you could? But of course you'd druther *work*—wouldn't you? Course you would!"

Tom contemplated the boy a bit, and said:

"What do you call work?"

"Why, ain't *that* work?"

Tom resumed his whitewashing and answered carelessly:

"Well, maybe it is, and maybe it ain't. All I know is, it suits Tom Sawyer."

"Oh come, now, you don't mean to let on that you *like* it?"

The brush continued to move.

"Like it? Well, I don't see why I oughtn't to like it. Does a boy get a chance to whitewash a fence every day?"

That put the thing in a new light. Ben stopped nibbling his apple. Tom swept his brush daintily back and forth—stepped back to note the effect—added a touch here and there—criticized the effect again—Ben watching every move and getting more and more interested, more and more absorbed. Presently he said:

"Say, Tom, let *me* whitewash a little."

Tom considered, was about to consent; but he altered his mind:

"No—no—I reckon it wouldn't hardly do, Ben. You see, Aunt Polly's awful particular about this fence—right here on the street, you know—but if it was the back fence I wouldn't mind and *she* wouldn't. Yes, she's awful particular about this fence; it's got to be done very careful; I reckon there ain't one boy in a thousand, maybe two thousand, that can do it the way it's got to be done."

"No—is that so? Oh, come, now—lemme just try. Only just a little— I'd let *you,* if you was me, Tom."

"Ben, I'd like to, honest injun; but Aunt Polly—well, Jim wanted to do it, but she wouldn't let him; Sid wanted to do it, and she wouldn't let Sid. Now don't you see how I'm fixed? If you was to tackle this fence and anything was to happen to it—"

"Oh, shucks, I'll be just as careful. Now lemme try. Say—I'll give you the core of my apple."

"Well, here— No, Ben, now don't. I'm afeard—"

"I'll give you *all* of it!"

Tom gave up the brush with reluctance in his face, but alacrity in his heart. And while the late steamer *Big Missouri* worked and sweated in the sun, the retired artist sat on a barrel in the shade close by, dangled his legs, munched his apple, and planned the slaughter of more innocents. There was no lack of material; boys happened along every little while; they came to jeer, but remained to whitewash. By the time Ben

was fagged out, Tom had traded the next chance to Billy Fisher for a kite, in good repair; and when *he* played out, Johnny Miller bought in for a dead rat and a string to swing it with—and so on, and so on, hour after hour. And when the middle of the afternoon came, from being a poor poverty-stricken boy in the morning, Tom was literally rolling in wealth. He had, beside the things before mentioned, twelve marbles, part of a jew's-harp, a piece of blue bottle-glass to look through, a spool cannon, a key that wouldn't unlock anything, a fragment of chalk, a glass stopper of a decanter, a tin soldier, a couple of tadpoles, six firecrackers, a kitten with only one eye, a brass door-knob, a dog-collar —but no dog—the handle of a knife, four pieces of orange-peel, and a dilapidated old window-sash.

He had had a nice, good, idle time all the while—plenty of company
—and the fence had three coats of whitewash on it! If he hadn't run
out of whitewash, he would have bankrupted every boy in the village.

Tom said to himself that it was not such a hollow world, after all.
He had discovered a great law of human action, without knowing it—
namely, that in order to make a man or boy covet a thing, it is only
necessary to make the thing difficult to attain. If he had been a great
and wise philosopher, like the writer of this book, he would now have
comprehended that Work consists of whatever a body is *obliged* to do,
and that Play consists of whatever a body is not obliged to do. And
this would help him to understand why constructing artificial flowers
or performing on a treadmill is work, while rolling tenpins or climbing
Mont Blanc is only amusement. There are wealthy gentlemen in England who drive four-horse passenger-coaches twenty or thirty miles
on a daily line, in the summer, because the privilege costs them considerable money; but if they are offered wages for the service, that
would turn it into work and then they would resign.

The boy mused awhile over the substantial change which had taken
place in his worldly circumstances, and then wended toward headquarters to report.

The Camel's Appetite

FROM "ROUGHING IT"

Mules and donkeys and camels have appetites that anything will relieve
temporarily, but nothing satisfy. In Syria, once, at the headwaters of
the Jordan, a camel took charge of my overcoat while the tents were
being pitched, and examined it with a critical eye, all over, with as
much interest as if he had the idea of getting one made like it. Then,
after he was done figuring on it as an article of apparel, he began to
contemplate it as an article of diet. He put his foot on it, and lifted one
of the sleeves out with his teeth, and chewed and chewed at it, gradually
taking it in, and all the while opening and closing his eyes in a kind of
religious ecstasy, as if he had never tasted anything as good as an overcoat before in his life. Then he smacked his lips once or twice, and
reached after the other sleeve. Next he tried the velvet collar, and

smiled a smile of such contentment that it was plain to see that he regarded that as the daintiest thing about an overcoat. The tails went next, along with some percussion-caps and cough-candy, and some fig-paste from Constantinople. And then my newspaper correspondence dropped out, and he took a chance on that—manuscript letters written for the home papers. But he was treading on dangerous ground now. He began to come across solid wisdom in those documents that was rather weighty on his stomach; and occasionally he would take a joke that would shake him up till it loosened his teeth; it was getting to be perilous times with him, but he held his grip with good courage and hopefully, till at last he began to stumble on statements that not even a camel could swallow with impunity. He began to gag and gasp, and his eyes to stand out, and his forelegs to spread, and in about a quarter of a minute he fell over as stiff as a carpenter's work-bench, and died a death of indescribable agony.

I went and pulled the manuscript out of his mouth, and found that the sensitive creature had choked to death on one of the mildest and gentlest statements of fact that I ever laid before a trusting public.

Fifty Boners

A boner is a howler, a misprint, a right word in the wrong place (or vice versa), a slight error in association that turns a simple fact into a side-splitting absurdity.

But definitions are unsatisfactory; an example is more illuminating. The class is studying Greek mythology and is devoting some attention to the heroes. Billy, his mind as much on batting averages as on Bulfinch, hears something about the hero Achilles being dipped in the river Styx to make him invulnerable. But on the examination paper, it comes out this way: "Achilles was the boy whose mother held him under the River Stinx until he was intolerable."

That's how boners are made.

Mark Twain was so impressed with the astounding errors made by the public-school pupils of his day that he published an article entitled "English as She Is Taught." The following fifty boners illustrate what has been happening to education since 1887, when Twain wrote his piece.

HISTORY

Abraham Lincoln wrote the Gettysburg Address while traveling from Washington to Gettysburg on the back of an envelope.

Nero was a cruel tyrant who would torture his poor subjects by playing the fiddle to them.

The government of England is a limited mockery.

Columbus was a great navigator who cursed about the Atlantic.

Many of the Indian heroes were killed, which proved very fatal to them.

What part did the U. S. Navy play in the war?
It played the Star Spangled Banner.

Martin Luther died a horrible death. He was excommunicated by a bull.

Watchword of the French Revolution: Liberty, Equality and Maternity.

Queen Elizabeth rode through Coventry with nothing on, and Raleigh offered her his cloak.

Magna Charta said that the King was not to order taxis without the consent of Parliament.

They gave William IV a lovely funeral. It took six men to carry the beer.

The chief executive of Massachusetts is the electric chair.

The English planted colonels when they came to America, some of which grew rapidly.

Henry VIII had an abbess on his knee, which made walking difficult.

What did Paul Revere say at the end of his famous ride? "Whoa."

LANGUAGE AND THE ARTS

Since pro means the opposite of con, can you give me an illustration? Progress and Congress

The Scarlet Letter griped me intensely.

Shakespeare wrote tragedies, comedies and errors.

Donatello's interest in the female nude made him the father of the Renaissance.

Milton wrote "Paradise Lost"; then his wife died and he wrote "Paradise Regained."

The dome of St. Paul's is supported by eight peers, all of which are unfortunately cracked.

A metaphor is a thing you shout through.

DEFINITIONS

A bamboo is an Italian baby.

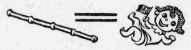

Staying married to one woman is known as monotony.

Trigonometry is when a lady marries three men at the same time.

Gorilla warfare means when the sides get up to monkey tricks.

An octopus is a person who hopes for the best.

The Kodak is the Bible of the Mohammedans.

Ibid was a famous Latin poet.

The letters M.D. signify "mentally deficient."

The Papal Bull was really a cow that was kept at the Vatican to supply milk for the Pope's children.

A polygon is a man who has many wives.

A Senator is half horse and half man.

A millennium is something like a centennial, only it has more legs.

Acrimony is what a man gives his divorced wife.

An illiterate child is one whose parents are not married.

A yokel is the way people talk to each other in the Alps.

ODD FACTS

In the middle of the nineteenth century, all the morons moved to Utah.

As she is going to be married next month, she is very busy getting her torso ready.

Capital punishment should not be used too frequently in schools.

The witness was warned not to purge himself.

Socrates died from an overdose of wedlock.

There are only two crimes visited with capital punishment, murder and suicide.

A horse divided against itself cannot stand.

Three shots rang out. Two of the servants fell dead, the other went through his hat.

Herrings go about the sea in shawls.

Our forefathers are not living as long as they did.

Mushrooms always grow in damp places and so they always look like umbrellas.

Most of the houses in France are made of Plaster of Paris.

During the Napoleonic Wars crowned heads were trembling in their shoes.

Louis Untermeyer

Because he failed three times in geometry and was unable to graduate from high school, Louis Untermeyer (born in 1885 in New York City) considers himself the least educated author in America. In youth he wrote poems and parodies; in middle age he edited them.

A Bachelor Keeps House

A year ago had anyone accused me of having lived a sheltered life, I would have been outraged. "Sheltered!" I would have snorted. "My youth was spent in the hurlyburly of New York, where I was ruggedly miseducated. For twenty years I commuted to a jewelry factory which I, somehow, managed in the wilds of Newark, New Jersey. I gave myself a tough two-year sabbatical in pre-Hitler Vienna, and I returned to America to rough it on an Adirondack farm. Sheltered indeed!"

Yet, for all my changes in jobs and geography, it is true that I have been sheltered. Someone has always taken care of my larger needs and, what is more important, my smaller whims. Some domestic ministering angel, some motherly soul, has usually kept my house in order; some inexhaustible hired man has seen to it that my larder is stocked; some impersonal deity has created maids who kept me lavishly supplied with free soap and fragrant towels, changed the sheets, cleaned the tub, and made my occasional hotel room "a home away from home."

Suddenly something went out of this world. In fact several things went out—all of them simultaneously: hired men, maids, ministering angels. They found employment elsewhere. The ministering angels spread their wings and ascended into a well-rationed heaven; the maids reaped a richer reward in overtime munitions factories; the inexhaustible hired men discovered that farm work was too exhausting and built bombers. I was faced with the prospect of not merely getting my own meat but shooting, skinning, cutting, curing and cooking it. It was then that I decided to be independent of men—and especially of women. I determined to prove to myself, and as much of the world as might be interested, that Emerson's philosophy of self-reliance was as good today as ever, and now was the time to rediscover the virtues of the simple life. In short I decided to do my own housekeeping.

Living a sheltered pre-war life, I had not heard of the housing shortage. I heard of it now—heard of it until my days stretched into a nightmare of endless streets all placarded "No rooms." Finally, thanks to a good friend and a thumping bribe, I secured one floor of a metropolitan house. It was situated on what, in a burst of poetic exaggeration, was named Brooklyn Heights. There was, obviously, a tree growing in the back yard—hereinafter referred to as "the garden"—there was (and still is) a magnificent view of the harbor with the point of Manhattan plowing into the water like the prow of a great stone ship. But there was no furniture. The bedroom was innocent of beds; no single pot or pan disfigured the newly installed kitchen.

The living room, I concluded, could wait until I could fix upon a design for living in it. The kitchen, too, could remain barren of cooking utensils while I explored the neighborhood restaurants. But I refused to sleep in a bedroom without a bed.

At this crisis my friend's wife came to my aid. "You'll need more than a bed, of course," she said. "There'll be a dresser or a bureau or a chest of drawers—or do you prefer a commode?"

"A bureau, by all means," I said, not knowing the difference, but feeling that it sounded more masculine. "But let's concentrate on the bed."

"Well," she went on, "you must know about linens and things. Sheets, for example; at least six."

"Six!" I exclaimed. "I'm not running a hotel! I've never slept in a bed with more than two sheets—one above and one below."

"At least six," she insisted. "Two on the bed, two in the laundry, two on the shelf. And be sure to get a good mattress; and, if you'll take my advice, one with covered springs. And covers for them."

This, I felt, was going too far. "Isn't that overdoing it?" I asked. "Does even a covered box-spring have to have a cover—and," I added sarcastically, "undoubtedly a cover charge?"

"Undoubtedly," she said. "And blankets and a bed-pad and a bright satin comforter—"

"Of course," I interrupted. "As if I didn't know!"

"And a bed-spread," she continued.

"But a bed-spread will hide the comforter. Why this passion for concealment?" I objected. "Why another cover to go on top of all the other covers?"

"So you can take it off," she said with firm feminine logic. "And now about your cleaning materials—perhaps I'd better give you a list."

"Don't bother," I said. "I know."

An hour later I clattered up the stairs, carrying the major part of a looted hardware store. "It's all here," I gasped, "the whole outfit. A pail, a dustpan, a broom, steel wool, furniture polish, chamois, cheesecloth, a mop—"

"A dry mop?" she asked.

"Naturally," I replied. "What other kind would anyone get?"

"Well, many housewives buy a wet mop, too."

"Just like them," I retorted. "No man would think of parading through the streets dragging a dripping mop."

"You don't buy it wet," she explained sweetly. "The two mops serve different purposes. There are, you will discover, various ways of keeping a house clean. You see—"

I saw. I got the second mop. Not to be outdone by any woman, I also purchased a complete collection of brushes—brushes with short handles and with long handles, brushes with soft cotton-like ends and with thick hard bristles, wooden brushes, plastic brushes, and brushes that were triumphs of a bizarre imagination. I arranged everything carefully in front of the kitchen closet, left a note for the girl who was to give the place a "general going over," and went to the office.

When I returned everything was in its place—untouched. I called up my friend's wife, with proper indignation. "You can't trust anyone nowadays," I complained bitterly. "The place is no cleaner than when I left it."

"You wouldn't let me give you a list," she said with maddening reasonableness. "Perhaps you forgot something. Perhaps there's a note around somewhere."

"There's an impertinent phrase scribbled on a piece of paper," I said angrily. "If it's a note, it's a decidedly jarring one."

"What does it say?" she asked, trying not to seem amused.

" 'No soap!' " I growled.

"You must have seen soap somewhere," she went on in exasperating detail. "It's usually rectangular and comes in cakes. It also comes in flakes, in boxes and wrappers, in—"

"Don't be so smart," I interrupted. "A man can't think of everything!"

It was then I became involved in chemistry. I discovered there were separate chemicals to wash windows and brighten dishes, highly specialized powders and solutions, half a hundred cleansers, spot-removers, leather-preservers, smoke-destroyers, dog-discouragers, moth-repellants, air-fresheners. I bought them all. They overflowed out of the kitchen, past the pantry, into the living room; I moved books into a borrowed attic to make room for them.

And the gadgets! I couldn't resist the magic labor-saving devices that always demanded more work: the elaborate can-openers which only a skilled burglar could operate, the bean-shellers which spilled the beans and kept the pods, the mechanical grapefruit seed-remover and scalloper which left the grapefruit intact but which seemed designed to make mincemeat of masculine fingers. One gadget called for another; there was no way of stopping. My once spare rooms bristled with shining and mysterious metal—a cross between an arsenal and torture-chamber. "Ah," I said, paraphrasing the proverb:

"Woman works till set of sun,
But man's work is never done."

I was being possessed by my own possessions, a slave to things. Suddenly a mood of revolt swept over me. The only bondage I desired was vagabondage. I cried out with Richard Hovey, that wanderlusty poet:

"I said in my heart, 'I am sick of four walls and a ceiling.
I have need of the sky.
I have business with the grass.
I will up and get me away where the hawk is wheeling,
Lone and high,
And the slow clouds go by. . . .'"

It was only a mood. I did not depart with the irresponsible sky-soaring, free-wheeling hawk. I clung to earth; I was grateful for four

walls and a ceiling. But every once in a while I dream of keeping house in a cave—none of your streamlined caves either, but a simple pre-historic cave where the only gadgets are a couple of flints and a primi-tive knife of stone, where the cleansing chemicals are free air and lavish water, and the warm and ever-restful bed is a bed of earth. That, I sometimes say to myself, is the way a bachelor should keep house.

Meanwhile I am installing a weird and wonderful self-operating, self-chopping, and self-dissolving garbage disposal system in my place on Brooklyn Heights.

MOTHER GOOSE UP TO DATE

WALTER DE LA MARE tells the Listener about "Jack and Jill"

Up to the top of the haunted turf
   They climbed on the moonlit hill;
Not a leaf rustled in the underbrush,
   The listening air was still.

And only the noise of the water pail
   As it struck on a jutting stone,
Clattered and jarred against the silence
   As the two trod on alone.

Up to the moonlit peak they went;
   And, though not a word would they say,
Their thoughts outnumbered a poet's love-songs
   In the first green weeks of May.

The stealthy shadows crept closer;
    They clutched at the hem of Jill's gown;
And there at the very top she stumbled,
    And Jack came shuddering down.

Their cries rang out against the stillness,
    Pitiful and high and thin.
And the echoes edged back still further
    As the silence gathered them in.

EDGAR A. GUEST glorifies

THE OLD WOMAN WHO LIVED IN A SHOE

It takes a heap o' children to make a home that's true,
And home can be a palace grand, or just a plain, old shoe;
But if it has a mother dear, and a good old dad or two,
Why, that's the sort of good old home for good old me and you.

Of all the institutions this side the Vale o' Rest
Howe'er it be, it seems to me a good old mother's best;
And fathers are a blessing, too, they give the place a tone;
In fact each child should try and have some parents of its own.

The food can be quite simple; just a sop of milk and bread
Are plenty when the kiddies know it's time to go to bed.
And every little sleepy-head will dream about the day
When he can go to work because a Man's Work is his Play.

And, oh, how sweet his life will seem, with nought to make him cross;
And he will never watch the clock and always mind the boss.
And when he thinks (as may occur), this thought will please him best:
That ninety million think the same—including   *Eddie Guest.*

Artemus Ward

"I am no politician, and my other habits are good," wrote Artemus Ward, the rural philosopher whom Abraham Lincoln often quoted to his startled Cabinet. Born in 1834 in Maine, Charles Farrar Browne became a roving reporter and printer. In his twenties he contributed a series of seemingly illiterate letters to the Cleveland Plain Dealer and signed them "A. Ward, Showman." Readers were fascinated by his "Grate Moral Show"; the public demanded him in person, and the author turned lecturer. His reputation took him abroad; he was as popular in England as in America; he was hailed as our first national humorist. Few people knew he was suffering from tuberculosis; he was not quite thirty-three when he died.

Ward excelled in shrewd colloquialisms. His humor, as Walter Blair has pointed out, is characteristically local, compounded of mother wit and gumption, of horse sense and the horse laugh. Even his unpublished anecdotes were pointed with robustiousness. Ward liked to tell of a Southern major who reproached a railroad conductor for the way the train was crawling along, puffing and stopping every few minutes.

"But what can I do?" asked the conductor.

"Do?" stormed the major. "Why don't you take the cow-catcher from the front of the engine and hitch it to the rear of the train! We'll never catch up with a cow. But what's to prevent a cow from strolling into the car and biting a passenger for getting in his way!"

Among the Spirits

My naburs is mourn harf crazy on the new fangled idear about Sperrets. Sperretooul Sircles is held nitely & 4 or 5 long hared fellers has settled here and gone into the sperret biznis excloosively. A atemt was made to git Mrs. A. Ward to embark into the Sperret biznis but the atemt faled. 1 of the long hared fellers told her she was a ethereal creeter & wood make a sweet mejium, whareupon she attact him with a mop handle & drove him out of the house. I will hear obsarve that Mrs. Ward is a invalerble womun—the partner of my goys & the shairer of my sorrers. In my absunse she watchis my interests & things with a Eagle Eye & when I return she welcums me in afectionate stile. Trooly it is with us as it was with Mr. & Mrs. Ingomer in the Play, to whit—

> 2 soles with but a single thawt
> 2 harts which beet as 1.

My naburs injooced me to atend a Sperretooul Sircle at Squire Smith's. When I arrove I found the east room chock full includin all the old maids in the village & the long hared fellers a4sed. When I went in I was saluted with "hear cums the benited man"—"hear cums the horyheded unbeleever"—"hear cums the skoffer at trooth," etsettery, etsettery.

Sez I, "my frens, it's troo I'm hear, & now bring on your Sperrets."

1 of the long hared fellers riz up and sed he would state a few remarks. He sed man was a critter of intelleck & was movin on to a Gole. Sum men had bigger intellecks than other men had and thay wood git to the Gole the soonerest. Sum men was beests & wood never git into the Gole at all. He sed the Erth was materiel but man was immateriel, and hens man was different from the Erth. The Erth, continnered the speakers, resolves round on its own axeltree onct in 24 hours, but as man haint gut no axeltree he can't resolve. He sed the ethereal essunce of the koordinate branchis of superhuman natur becum mettymorfussed as man progrest in harmonial coexistunce & eventooally anty humanized theirselves & turned into reglar sperretuellers. [This was versifferusly applauded by the cumpany, and as I make it a pint to get along as pleasant as possible, I sung out "bully for you, old boy."]

The cumpany then drew round the table and the Sircle kommenst to go it. They axed me if thare was anbody in the Sperrit land which I wood like to convarse with. I sed if Bill Tompkins, who was onct my partner in the show biznis, was sober, I should like to convarse with him a few periods.

"Is the Sperret of William Tompkins present?" sed 1 of the long hared chaps, and there was three knox on the table.

Sez I, "William, how goze it, Old Sweetness?"

"Pretty ruff, old hoss," he replide.

That was a pleasant way we had of addressin each other when he was in the flesh.

"Air you in the show biznis, William?" sed I.

He sed he was. He sed he & John Bunyan was travelin with a side show in connection with Shakspere, Jonson & Co.'s Circus. He sed Old Bun (meaning Mr. Bunyan), stired up the animils & ground the organ while he tended door. Occasshunally Mr. Bunyan sung a comic song. The Circus was doin middlin well. Bill Shakspere had made a grate hit with old Bob Ridley, and Ben Jonson was delitin the peple with his trooly grate ax of hossmanship without saddul or bridal. Thay was rehersin Dixey's Land & expected it would knock the peple.

Sez I, "William, my luvly frend, can you pay me that 13 dollars you owe me?" He sed no with one of the most tremenjis knox I ever experiunsed.

The Sircle sed he had gone. "Air you gone, William?" I axed.

"Rayther," he replide, and I know it was no use to pursoo the subject furder.

I then called fur my farther.

"How's things, daddy?"

"Middlin, my son, middlin."

"Ain't you proud of your orfurn boy?"

"Scacely."

"Why not, my parient?"

"Becawz you hav gone to writin for the noospapers, my son. Bimeby you'll lose all your character for trooth and verrasserty. When I helpt you into the show biznis I told you to dignerfy that there profeshun. Litteratoor is low."

He also statid that he was doin middlin well in the peanut biznis & liked it putty well, tho' the climit was rather warm.

When the Sircle stopt they axed me what I thawt of it.

Sez I, "my frends I've been into the show biznis now goin on 23 years. Theres a artikil in the Constitooshun of the United States which sez in effeck that everybody may think just as he darn pleazes, & them is my sentiments to a hare. You dowtlis beleeve this Sperret doctrin while I think it is a little mixt. Just so soon as a man becums a reglar out & out

Sperret rapper he leeves orf workin, lets his hare grow all over his face & commensis spungin his livin out of other peple. He eats all the dickshunaries he can find & goze round chock full of big words, scarein the wimmin folks & little children & destroyin the piece of mind of evry famerlee he enters. He don't do nobody no good & is a cuss to society & a pirit on honest peple's corn beef barrils. Admittin all you say abowt the doctrin to be troo, I must say the reglar professional Sperret rappers —them as makes a biznis on it—air abowt the most ornery set of cusses I ever enkountered in my life."

So sayin I put on my surtoot and went home.

Edward Noyes Westcott

Until he was fifty Edward Noyes Westcott never intended to be anything but a banker who, except for business letters, avoided writing. Son of a dentist, born in Syracuse, New York, in 1846, he had followed a humdrum and moderately rewarding career as clerk in an insurance company, bankteller, and broker. Suddenly, in his fiftieth year he was afflicted with tuberculosis and was forced to retire to the Adirondack Mountains. There, having nothing else to do, he began to write about an old codger, a shrewd rapscallion who mixed country banking with horse-trading. Weaving the episodes into a kind of novel, David Harum, Westcott sent off the manuscript. It was returned by publisher after publisher; one of them voiced the general objection that the book was "vulgar and smelled of the stables." Finally the firm of D. Appleton thought it had possibilities and so informed Westcott. But the sick man did not live to see his work in print. Three months after receiving the publisher's letter of acceptance, he succumbed to his disease.

Westcott's single volume was the runaway best seller of his day. Half a million copies were sold in two years; it was successful as a play and as a motion picture; it still persists (in name only) as a radio serial. The old horse-trader, with the proverbial tongue of vinegar and heart of gold, refuses to die.

David Harum's Horse Trade

Mrs. Bixbee, known to most of those who enjoyed the privilege of her acquaintance as "Aunt Polly," though nieces and nephews of her blood there were none in Homeville, Freeland County, looked curiously at her brother, as, in fact, she had done at intervals as he read. Twice or thrice she opened her lips as if to address him, but apparently some restraining thought interposed. Finally, the impulse to utter her mind culminated. "Dave," she said, "d' you know what Deakin Perkins is sayin' about ye?"

David opened his paper so as to hide his face, and the corners of his mouth twitched as he asked in return, "Wa'al, what's the deakin sayin' now?"

"He's sayin'," she replied, in a voice mixed of indignation and apprehension, "thet you sold him a balky horse, an' he's goin' to hev the law on ye." David's shoulders shook behind the sheltering page, and his mouth expanded in a grin.

"Wa'al," he replied after a moment, lowering the paper and looking gravely at his companion over his glasses, "next to the deakin's religious experience, them of lawin' an' horse-tradin' air his strongest p'ints, an' he works the hull on 'em to once sometimes."

The evasiveness of this generality was not lost on Mrs. Bixbee, and she pressed the point with, "Did ye? an' will he?"

"Yes, an' no, an' mebbe, an' mebbe not," was the categorical reply.

"Wa'al," she answered with a snap, "mebbe you call that an answer. I s'pose if you don't want to let on you won't, but I do believe you've ben playin' some trick on the deakin, an' won't own up. I do wish," she added, "that if you hed to get rid of a balky horse onto somebody you'd hev picked out somebody else."

"When you got a balker to dispose of," said David gravely, "you can't alwus pick an' choose. Fust come, fust served." Then he went on more seriously: "Now I'll tell ye. Quite a while ago—in fact, not long after I come to enjoy the priv'lidge of the deakin's acquaintance—we hed a deal. I wasn't jest on my guard, knowin' him to be a deakin an' all that, an' he lied to me so splendid that I was took in, clean over my head. He done me so brown I was burnt in places, an' you c'd smell smoke 'round me for some time."

"Was it a horse?" asked Mrs. Bixbee gratuitously.

"Wa'al," David replied, "mebbe it *had* ben some time, but at that partic'lar time the only thing to determine that fact was that it wa'n't nothin' else.''

"Wa'al, I declare!" exclaimed Mrs. Bixbee, wondering not more at the deacon's turpitude than at the lapse in David's acuteness, of which she had an immense opinion, but commenting only on the former. "I'm 'mazed at the deakin.''

"Yes'm," said David with a grin, "I'm quite a liar myself when it comes right down to the hoss bus'nis, but the deakin c'n give me both bowers ev'ry hand. He done it so slick that I had to laugh when I come to think it over—an' I had witnesses to the hull confab, too, that he didn't know of, an' I c'd 've showed him up in great shape if I'd had a mind to.''

"Why didn't ye?" said Aunt Polly, whose feelings about the deacon were undergoing a revulsion.

"Wa'al, to tell ye the truth, I was so completely skunked that I hadn't a word to say. I got rid o' the thing fer what it was wuth fer hide an' taller, an' stid of squealin' 'round the way you say he's doin', like a stuck pig, I kep' my tongue between my teeth an' laid to git even some time.''

"You ort to 've hed the law on him," declared Mrs. Bixbee, now fully converted. "The old scamp!"

"Wa'al," was the reply, "I gen'ally prefer to settle out of court, an' in this partic'lar case, while I might 'a' been willin' t' admit that I hed ben did up, I didn't feel much like swearin' to it. I reckoned the time 'd come when mebbe I'd git the laugh on the deakin, an' it did, an' we're putty well settled now in full.''

"You mean this last pufformance?" asked Mrs. Bixbee. "I wish you'd quit beatin' about the bush, an' tell me the hull story.''

"Wa'al, it's like this, then, if you *will* hev it. I was over to Whiteboro a while ago on a little matter of worldly bus'nis an' I seen a couple of fellers halter-exercisin' a hoss in the tavern yard. I stood 'round a spell watchin' 'em, an' when he come to a standstill I went an' looked him over, an' I liked his looks fust rate.

" 'Fer sale?' I says.

" 'Wa'al,' says the chap that was leadin' him, 'I never see the hoss that wa'n't if the price was right.'

" 'Your'n?' I says.

" 'Mine an' his'n,' he says, noddin' his head at the other feller.

" 'What ye askin' fer him?' I says.

" 'One-fifty,' he says.

"I looked him all over agin putty careful, an' once or twice I kind o' shook my head's if I didn't quite like what I seen, an' when I got through I sort o' half turned away without sayin' anythin', 's if I'd seen enough.

" 'The' ain't a scratch ner a pimple on him,' says the feller, kind o' resentin' my looks. 'He's sound an' kind, an' 'll stand without hitchin', an' a lady c'n drive him's well's a man.'

" 'I ain't got anythin' agin him,' I says, 'an' prob'ly that's all true, ev'ry word on't; but one-fifty's a consid'able price fer a hoss these days. I hain't no pressin' use fer another hoss, an', in fact,' I says, 'I've got one or two fer sale myself.'

" 'He's wuth two hundred jest as he stands,' the feller says. 'He hain't had no trainin', an' he c'n draw two men in a road-wagin bet-ter'n fifty.'

"Wa'al, the more I looked at him the better I liked him, but I only says, 'Jes' so, jes' so, he may be wuth the money, but jest as I'm fixed now he ain't wuth it to me, an' I hain't got that much money with me if he was,' I says. The other feller hadn't said nothin' up to that time, an' he broke in now. 'I s'pose you'd take him fer a gift, wouldn't ye?' he says, kind o' sneerin'.

" 'Wa'al, yes,' I says, 'I dunno but I would if you'd throw in a pound of tea an' a halter.'

"He kind o' laughed an' says, 'Wa'al, this ain't no gift enterprise, an' I guess we ain't goin' to trade, but I'd like to know,' he says, 'jest as a matter of curios'ty, what you'd say he *was* wuth to ye?'

" 'Wa'al,' I says, 'I come over this mornin' to see a feller that owed me a trifle o' money. Exceptin' of some loose change, what he paid me 's all I got with me,' I says, takin' out my wallet. 'That wad's got a hundred an' twenty-five into it, an' if you'd sooner have your hoss an' halter than the wad,' I says, 'why, I'll bid ye good-day.'

" 'You're offerin' one-twenty-five fer the hoss an' halter?' he says.

" 'That's what I'm doin',' I says.

" 'You've made a trade,' he says, puttin' out his hand fer the money an' handin' the halter over to me."

"An' didn't ye suspicion nuthin' when he took ye up like that?" asked Mrs. Bixbee.

"I did smell woolen some," said David, "but I had the *hoss* an' they had the *money*, an', as fur's I c'd see, the critter was all right. How-somever, I says to 'em: 'This here's all right, fur's it's gone, but you've talked putty strong 'bout this hoss. I don't know who you fellers be, but I c'n find out,' I says. Then the fust feller that done the talkin' 'bout the hoss put in an' says, 'The' hain't ben one word said to you about this hoss that wa'n't gospel truth, not one word.' An' when I come to think on't afterward," said David with a half laugh, "it mebbe wa'n't *gospel* truth, but it was good enough *jury* truth. I guess this ain't over 'n' above interestin' to ye, is it?" he asked after a pause, looking doubt-fully at his sister.

"Yes, 'tis," she asserted. "I'm lookin' forrered to where the deakin comes in, but you jest tell it your own way."

"I'll git there all in good time," said David, "but some of the point of the story'll be lost if I don't tell ye what come fust."

"I allow to stan' it's long's you can," she said encouragingly, "seein' what work I had gettin' ye started. Did ye find out anythin' 'bout them fellers?"

"I ast the barn man if he knowed who they was, an' he said he never seen 'em till the yestiddy before, an' didn't know 'em f'm Adam. They come along with a couple of hosses, one drivin' an' t'other leadin'—the one I bought. I ast him if they knowed who I was, an' he said one on 'em ast him, an' he told him. The feller said to him, seein' me drive up: 'That's a putty likely-lookin' hoss. Who's drivin' him?' An' he says to the feller: 'That's Dave Harum, f'm over to Homeville. He's a great feller fer hosses,' he says."

"Dave," said Mrs. Bixbee, "them chaps jest laid fer ye, didn't they?"

"I reckon they did," he admitted; "an' they was as slick a pair as was ever drawed to," which expression was lost upon his sister. David rubbed the fringe of yellowish-gray hair which encircled his bald pate for a moment.

"Wa'al," he resumed, "after the talk with the barn man, I smelt woolen stronger'n ever, but I didn't say nothin', an' had the mare hitched an' started back. Old Jinny drives with one hand, an' I c'd watch the new one all right, an' as we come along I begun to think I wa'n't stuck after all. I never see a hoss travel evener an' nicer, an' when we come to a good level place I sent the old mare along the best she knew, an' the new one never broke his gait, an' kep' right up 'ithout 'par'ntly half tryin'; an' Jinny don't take most folks' dust neither. I swan! 'fore I got home I reckoned I'd jest as good as made seventy-five anyway."

"Then the' wa'n't nothin' the matter with him, after all," commented Mrs. Bixbee in rather a disappointed tone.

"The meanest thing top of the earth was the matter with him," de-clared David, "but I didn't find it out till the next afternoon, an' then I found it out good. I hitched him to the open buggy an' went 'round by the East Road, 'cause that ain't so much travelled. He went along all right till we got a mile or so out of the village, an' then I slowed him down to a walk. Wa'al, sir, scat my—! He hadn't walked more'n a rod 'fore he come to a dead stan'still. I clucked an' gitapp'd, an' finely took the gad to him a little; but he only jest kind o' humped up a little, an' stood like he'd took root."

"Wa'al, now!" exclaimed Mrs. Bixbee.

"Yes'm," said David; "I was stuck in ev'ry sense of the word."

"What d'ye do?"

"Wa'al, I tried all the tricks I knowed—an' I could lead him—but when I was in the buggy he wouldn't stir till he got good an' ready; 'n' then he'd start of his own accord an' go on a spell, an'—"

"Did he keep it up?" Mrs. Bixbee interrupted.

"Wa'al, I s'd say he did. I finely got home with the critter, but I thought one time I'd either hev to lead him or spend the night on the East Road. He balked five sep'rate times, varyin' in length, an' it was dark when we struck the barn."

"I should hev thought you'd a wanted to kill him," said Mrs. Bixbee; "an' the fellers that sold him to ye, too."

"The' *was* times," David replied, with a nod of his head, "when if he'd a fell down dead I wouldn't hev figgered on puttin' a band on my hat, but it don't never pay to git mad with a hoss; an' as fur's the feller I bought him of, when I remembered how he told me he'd stand without hitchin', I swan! I had to laugh. I did, fer a fact. 'Stand without hitchin'!' He, he, he!"

"I guess you wouldn't think it was so awful funny if you hadn't gone an' stuck that horse onto Deakin Perkins—an' I don't see how you done it."

"Mebbe that *is* part of the joke," David allowed, "an' I'll tell ye th' rest on't. Th' next day I hitched the new one to th' dem'crat wagin an' put in a lot of straps an' rope, an' started off fer the East Road agin. He went fust rate till we come to about the place where we had the fust trouble, an', sure enough, he balked agin. I leaned over an' hit him a smart cut on the off shoulder, but he only humped a little, an' never lifted a foot. I give him another lick, with the self-same result. Then I got down an' I strapped that animal so't he couldn't move nothin' but his head an' tail, an' got back into the buggy. Wa'al, bimby, it may 'a' ben ten minutes, or it may 'a' ben more or less—it's slow work settin' still behind a balkin' hoss—he was ready to go on his own account, but he couldn't budge. He kind o' looked around, much as to say, 'What on earth's the matter?' an' then he tried another move, an' then another, but no go. Then I got down an' took the hopples off an' then climbed back into the buggy, an' says 'Cluck' to him, an' off he stepped as chipper as could be, an' we went joggin' along all right mebbe two mile, an' when I slowed up, up he come agin. I gin him another clip in the same place on the shoulder, an' I got down an' tied him up agin, an' the same thing happened as before, on'y it didn't take him quite so long to make up his mind about startin', an' we went some further without a hitch. But I had to go through the puformance the third time before he got it into his head that if he didn't go when *I* wanted he couldn't go when *he* wanted, an' that didn't suit him; an' when he felt the whip on his shoulder it meant bus'nis."

"Was that the end o' his balkin'?" asked Mrs. Bixbee.

"I had to give him one more go-round," said David, "an' after that I didn't have no more trouble with him. He showed symptoms at times, but a touch of the whip on the shoulder alwus fetched him. I alwus carried them straps, though, till the last two or three times."

"Wa'al, what's the deakin kickin' about, then?" asked Aunt Polly. "You're jest sayin' you broke him of balkin'."

"Wa'al," said David slowly, "some hosses will balk with some folks an' not with others. You can't most alwus gen'ally tell."

"Didn't the deakin have a chance to try him?"

"He had all the chance he ast fer," replied David. "Fact is, he done most of the sellin', as well's the buyin', himself."

"How's that?"

"Wa'al," said David, "it come about like this: After I'd got the hoss where I c'd handle him I begun to think I'd had some int'restin' an' valu'ble experience, an' it wa'n't scurcely fair to keep it all to myself. I didn't want no patent on't, an' I was willin' to let some other feller git a piece. So one mornin', a week before last—let's see, week ago Tuesday it was, an' a mighty nice mornin' it was, too—one o' them days that kind o' lib'ral up your mind—I allowed to hitch an' drive up past the deakin's an' back, an' mebbe git somethin' to strengthen my faith, et cetery, in case I run acrost him. Wa'al, 's I come along I seen the deakin putterin' 'round, an' I waved my hand to him an' went by a-kitin'. I went up the road a ways an' killed a little time, an' when I come back there was the deakin, as I expected. He was leanin' over the fence, an' as I jogged up he hailed me, an' I pulled up.

" 'Mornin', Mr. Harum,' he says.

" 'Mornin', deakin,' I says. 'How are ye? an' how's Mis' Perkins these days?'

" 'I'm fair,' he says; 'fair to middlin', but Mis' Perkins is ailin' some —*as usyul*,' he says."

"They do say," put in Mrs. Bixbee, "thet Mis' Perkins don't hev much of a time herself."

"Guess she hez all the time the' is," answered David. "Wa'al," he went on, "we passed the time o' day, an' talked a spell about the weather an' all that, an' finely I straightened up the lines as if I was goin' on, an' then I says: 'Oh, by the way,' I says, 'I jest thought on't. I heard Dominie White was lookin' fer a hoss that'd suit him.' 'I hain't heard,' he says; but I see in a minute he had—an' it really was a fact —an' I says: 'I've got a roan colt risin' five, that I took on a debt a spell ago, that I'll sell reasonable, that's as likely an' nice ev'ry way a young hoss as ever I owned. I don't need him,' I says, 'an' didn't want to take him, but it was that or nothin' at the time an' glad to git it, an' I'll sell him a barg'in. Now what I want to say to you, deakin, is this: That hoss'd suit the dominie to a tee in my opinion, but the dominie won't come to me. Now if *you* was to say to him—bein' in his church an' all that,' I says, 'that you c'd get him the right kind of a hoss, he'd believe you, an' you an' me'd be doin' a little stroke of bus'nis, an' a favor to the dominie into the bargain. The dominie's well off,' I says, 'an' c'n afford to drive a good hoss.'"

"What did the deakin say?" asked Aunt Polly as David stopped for breath.

"I didn't expect him to jump down my throat," he answered; "but I seen him prick up his ears, an' all the time I was talkin' I noticed him lookin' my hoss over, head an' foot. 'Now I 'member,' he says, 'hearin' sunthin' 'bout Mr. White's lookin' fer a hoss, though when you fust spoke on't it had slipped my mind. Of course,' he says, 'the' ain't any real reason why Mr. White shouldn't deal with you direct, an' yit mebbe I *could* do more with him 'n you could. But,' he says, 'I wa'n't cal'latin' to go t' the village this mornin', an' I sent my hired man off with my drivin' hoss. Mebbe I'll drop 'round in a day or two,' he says, 'an' look at the roan.'

"'You mightn't ketch me,' I says, 'an' I want to show him myself; an' more'n that,' I says, 'Dug Robinson's after the dominie. I'll tell ye,' I says, 'you jest git in 'ith me an' go down an' look at him, an' I'll send ye back or drive ye back, an' if you've got anythin' special on hand you needn't be gone three quarters of an hour,' I says."

"He come, did he?" inquired Mrs. Bixbee.

"He done *so*," said David sententiously. "Jest as I knowed he would, after he'd hem'd an' haw'd about so much, an' he rode a mile an' a half livelier 'n he done in a good while, I reckon. He had to pull that old broadbrim of his'n down to his ears, an' don't you fergit it. He, he, he, he! The road was jest *full* o' hosses. Wa'al, we drove into the yard, an' I told the hired man to unhitch the bay hoss an' fetch out the roan, an' while he was bein' unhitched the deakin stood 'round an' never took his eyes off'n him, an' I knowed I wouldn't sell the deakin no roan hoss *that* day, even if I wanted to. But when he come out I begun to crack him up, an' I talked hoss fer all I was wuth. The deakin looked him over in a don't-care kind of a way, an' didn't 'parently give much heed to what I was sayin'. Finely I says, 'Wa'al, what do you think of him?' 'Wa'al,' he says, 'he seems to be a likely enough critter, but I don't believe he'd suit Mr. White—'fraid not,' he says. 'What you askin' fer him?' he says. 'One-fifty,' I says, 'an' he's a cheap hoss at the money'; but," added the speaker with a laugh, "I knowed I might's well of said a thousan'. The deakin wa'n't buyin' no roan colts that mornin'."

"What did he say?" asked Mrs. Bixbee.

" 'Wa'al,' he says, 'wa'al, I guess you ought to git that much fer him, but I'm 'fraid he ain't what Mr. White wants.' An' then, 'That's quite a hoss we come down with,' he says. 'Had him long?' 'Jest long 'nough to git 'quainted with him,' I says. 'Don't you want the roan fer your own use?' I says. 'Mebbe we c'd shade the price a little.' 'No,' he says. 'I guess not. I don't need another hoss jest now.' An' then, after a minute he says: 'Say, mebbe the bay hoss we drove'd come nearer the mark fer White, if he's all right. Jest as soon I'd look at him?' he says. 'Wa'al, I hain't no objections, but I guess he's more of a hoss than the dominie'd care for, but I'll go an' fetch him out,' I says. So I brought him out, an' the deakin looked him all over. I see it was a case of love at fust sight, as the storybooks says. 'Looks all right,' he says. 'I'll tell ye,' I says, 'what the feller I bought him off told me.' 'What's that?' says the deakin. 'He said to me,' I says, ' "that hoss ain't got a scratch ner a pimple on him. He's sound an' kind, an' 'll stand without hitchin', an' a lady c'd drive him as well's a man."

" 'That's what he said to me,' I says, 'an' it's every word on't true. You've seen whether or not he c'n travel,' I says, 'an', so fur's I've seen, he ain't 'fraid of nothin'.' 'D'ye want to sell him?' the deakin says. 'Wa'al, I says, 'I ain't offerin' him fer sale. You'll go a good ways,' I says, ' 'fore you'll strike such another; but, of course, he ain't the only hoss in the world, an' I never had anythin' in the hoss line I wouldn't sell at *some* price.' 'Wa'al,' he says, 'what d'ye ask fer him?' 'Wa'al,' I says, 'if my own brother was to ask me that question I'd say to him two hundred dollars, cash down, an' I wouldn't hold the offer open an hour,' I says."

"My!" ejaculated Aunt Polly. "Did he take you up?"

" 'That's more'n I give fer a hoss 'n a good while,' he says, shakin' his head, 'an' more'n I c'n afford, I'm 'fraid.' 'All right,' I says; 'I c'n afford to keep him'; but I knew I had the deakin same as the wood-chuck had Skip. 'Hitch up the roan,' I says to Mike; 'the deakin wants to be took up to his house.' 'Is that your last word?' he says. 'That's what it is,' I says. 'Two hundred, cash down.' "

"Didn't ye dast to trust the deakin?" asked Mrs. Bixbee.

"Polly," said David, "the's a number of holes in a ten-foot ladder." Mrs. Bixbee seemed to understand this rather ambiguous rejoinder.

"He must 'a' squirmed some," she remarked. David laughed.

"The deakin ain't much used to payin' the other feller's price," he said, "an' it was like pullin' teeth; but he wanted that hoss more'n a cow wants a calf, an' after a little more squimmidgin' he hauled out his wallet an' forked over. Mike come out with the roan, an' off the deakin went, leadin' the bay hoss."

"I don't see," said Mrs. Bixbee, looking up at her brother, "thet after all the' was anythin' you said to the deakin thet he could ketch holt on."

"The' wa'n't nothin'," he replied. "The only thing he c'n complain about's what I *didn't* say to him."

"Hain't he said anythin' to ye?" Mrs. Bixbee inquired.

"He, he, he, he! He hain't but once, an' the' wa'n't but little of it then."

"How?"

"Wa'al, the day but one after the deakin sold himself Mr. Stickin'-Plaster I had an arrant three, four mile or so up past his place, an' when I was comin' back, along 'bout four or half past, it come on to rain like all possessed. I had my old umbrel'—though it didn't hender me f'm gettin' more or less wet—an' I sent the old mare along fer all she knew. As I come along to within a mile f'm the deakin's house I sen somebody in the road, an' when I come up closter I see it was the deakin himself, in trouble, an' I kind o' slowed up to see what was goin' on. There he was, settin' all humped up with his ole broad-brim hat slopin' down his back, a-sheddin' water like a roof. Then I seen him lean over an' larrup the hoss with the end of the lines fer all he was wuth. It appeared he hadn't no whip, an' it wouldn't done him no good if he'd had. Wa'al, sir, rain or no rain, I jest pulled up to watch him. He'd larrup a spell, an' then he'd set back; an' then he'd lean over an' try it agin, harder'n ever. Scat my—! I thought I'd die a-laughin'. I couldn't hardly cluck to the mare when I got ready to move on. I drove alongside an' pulled up. 'Hullo, deakin,' I says, 'what's the matter?' He looked up at me, an' I won't say he was the maddest man I ever see, but he was long ways the maddest-*lookin'* man, an' he shook his fist at me jest like one o' the unregen'rit. 'Consarn ye, Dave Harum!' he says, 'I'll hev the law on ye fer this.' 'What fer?' I says. 'I don't make it come on to rain, did I?' I says. 'You know mighty well what fer,' he says. 'You sold me this *damned beast,'* he says, 'an' he's balked with me *nine* times this afternoon, an' I'll fix ye for 't,' he says. 'Wa'al, deakin,' I says, 'I'm 'fraid the squire's office 'll be shut up 'fore you *git* there, but I'll take any word you'd like to send. You know I told ye,' I says, 'that he'd stand 'ithout hitchin'.' An' at that he only jest kind o' choked an' sputtered. He was so mad he couldn't say nothin', an' on I drove, an' when I got about forty rod or so I looked back, an' there was the deakin a-comin' along the road with as much of his shoulders as he could git under his hat an' *leadin'* his new hoss. He, he, he, he! Oh, my stars an' garters! Say, Polly, it paid me fer bein' born into this vale o' tears. It did, I declare for't!" Aunt Polly wiped her eyes on her apron.

"But, Dave," she said, "did the deakin really say—*that word?*"

"Wa'al," he replied, "if 'twa'n't that it was the puttiest imitation on't that ever I heard."

"David," she continued, "don't you think it putty mean to badger the deakin so't he swore, an' then laugh 'bout it? An' I s'pose you've told the story all over."

"Mis' Bixbee," said David emphatically, "if I'd paid good money to see a funny show I'd be a blamed fool if I didn't laugh, wouldn't I? That specticle of the deakin cost me consid'able, but it was more'n wuth it. But," he added, "I guess, the way the thing stands now, I ain't so much out on the hull."

Mrs. Bixbee looked at him inquiringly.

"Of course, you know Dick Larrabee?" he asked.

She nodded.

"Wa'al, three four days after the shower, an' the story'd got aroun' some—as *you* say, the deakin *is* consid'able of a talker—I got holt of Dick—I've done him some favors an' he natur'ly expects more—an' I says to him: 'Dick,' I says, 'I hear 't Deakin Perkins has got a hoss that don't jest suit him—hain't got knee-action enough at times,' I says, 'an' mebbe he'll sell him reasonable.' 'I've heard somethin' about it,' says Dick, laughin'. 'One of them kind o' hosses 't you don't like to git ketched out in the rain with,' he says. 'Jes' so,' I says. 'Now,' I says, 'I've got a notion 't I'd like to own that hoss at a price, an' that mebbe *I* c'd git him home even if it did rain. Here's a hundred an' ten,' I says, 'an' I want you to see how fur it'll go to buyin' him. If you git me the hoss you needn't bring none on't back. Want to try?' I says. 'All right,' he says, an' took the money. 'But,' he says, 'won't the deakin suspicion that it comes from you?' 'Wa'al,' I says, 'my portrit ain't on none o' the bills, an' I reckon *you* won't tell him so, out an' out,' an' off he went. Yistidy he come in, an' I says, 'Wa'al, done anythin'?' 'The hoss is in your barn,' he says. 'Good fer you!' I says. 'Did you make anythin'?' 'I'm satisfied,' he says. 'I made a ten-dollar note.' An' that's the net results on't," concluded David, "that I've got the hoss, an' he's cost me jest thirty-five dollars."

P. G. Wodehouse

Born in 1881 at Guilford, England, educated at Dulwich College, P. G. Wodehouse—or, to give him his full name, Pelham Grenville Wodehouse —seems like one of his own incredible characters: the Honorable Bertie Wooster, Frederick Altamount Cornwallis Twistleton, fifth earl of Ickenham, Mr. Mulliner, Ukridge, Psmith, and the incomparable Jeeves. Wodehouse's first book was published before he was twenty-one; since 1908 he has written an average of more than a book a year. Cast in the form of novels and short stories, his work is the exploitation of oddities; Wodehouse's gallery of eccentrics is crowded with young nincompoops, formidable aunts, uncles who are imbeciles, and valets who should have been statesmen. It has been said that Wodehouse has more gusto than invention, that he is indefatigable rather than versatile, and that his people are not characters but caricatures. But the high spirits compensate for depth, and the wild or inane figures turn their world into ultimate and irresistible farce.

Uncle Fred Flits By

In order that they might enjoy their after-luncheon coffee in peace, the Crumpet had taken the guest whom he was entertaining at the Drones Club to the smaller and less frequented of the two smoking-rooms. In the other, he explained, though the conversation always touched an exceptionally high level of brilliance, there was apt to be a good deal of sugar thrown about.

The guest said he understood.

"Young blood, eh?"

"That's right. Young blood."

"And animal spirits."

"And animal, as you say, spirits," agreed the Crumpet. "We get a fairish amount of those here."

"The complaint, however, is not, I observe, universal."

"Eh?"

The other drew his host's attention to the doorway, where a young man in form-fitting tweeds had just appeared. The aspect of this young man was haggard. His eyes glared wildly and he sucked at an empty cigarette-holder. If he had a mind, there was something on it. When the Crumpet called to him to come and join the party, he merely shook his head in a distraught sort of way and disappeared, looking like a character out of a Greek tragedy pursued by the Fates.

The Crumpet sighed.

"Poor old Pongo!"

"Pongo?"

"That was Pongo Twistleton. He's all broken up about his Uncle Fred."

"Dead?"

"No such luck. Coming up to London again tomorrow. Pongo had a wire this morning."

"And that upsets him?"

"Naturally. After what happened last time."

"What was that?"

"Ah!" said the Crumpet.

"What happened last time?"

"You may well ask."

"I do ask."

"Ah!" said the Crumpet.

684 P. G. WODEHOUSE

Poor old Pongo (said the Crumpet) has often discussed his Uncle Fred with me, and if there weren't tears in his eyes when he did so, I don't know a tear in the eye when I see one. In round numbers the Earl of Ickenham, of Ickenham Hall, Ickenham, Hants, he lives in the country most of the year, but from time to time has a nasty way of slipping his collar and getting loose and descending upon Pongo at his flat in the Albany. And every time he does so, the unhappy young blighter is subjected to some soul-testing experience. Because the trouble with this uncle is that, though sixty if a day, he becomes on arriving in the metropolis as young as he feels—which is, apparently, a youngish twenty-two. I don't know if you happen to know what the word "excesses" means, but those are what Pongo's Uncle Fred from the country, when in London, invariably commits.

It wouldn't so much matter, mind you, if he would confine his activities to the club premises. We're pretty broad-minded here, and if you stop short of smashing the piano, there isn't much that you can do at the Drones that will cause the raised eyebrow and the sharp intake of breath. The snag is that he will insist on lugging Pongo out in the open and there, right in the public eye, proceeding to step high, wide and plentiful.

So when, on the occasion to which I allude, he stood pink and genial on Pongo's hearth-rug, bulging with Pongo's lunch and wreathed in the smoke of one of Pongo's cigars, and said: "And now, my boy, for a pleasant and instructive afternoon," you will readily understand why the unfortunate young clam gazed at him as he would have gazed at two-penn'orth of dynamite, had he discovered it lighting up in his presence.

"A what?" he said, giving at the knees and paling beneath the tan a bit.

"A pleasant and instructive afternoon," repeated Lord Ickenham, rolling the words round his tongue. "I propose that you place yourself in my hands and leave the program entirely to me."

Now, owing to Pongo's circumstances being such as to necessitate his getting into the aged relative's ribs at intervals and shaking him down for an occasional much-needed tenner or what not, he isn't in a position to use the iron hand with the old buster. But at these words he displayed a manly firmness.

"You aren't going to get me to the dog races again."

"No, no."

"You remember what happened last June?"

"Quite," said Lord Ickenham, "quite. Though I still think that a wiser magistrate would have been content with a mere reprimand."

"And I won't—"

"Certainly not. Nothing of that kind at all. What I propose to do this afternoon is to take you to visit the home of your ancestors."

Pongo did not get this.

"I thought Ickenham was the home of my ancestors."

"It is one of the homes of your ancestors. They also resided rather nearer the heart of things, at a place called Mitching Hill."

"Down in the suburbs, do you mean?"

"The neighbourhood is now suburban, true. It is many years since the meadows where I sported as a child were sold and cut up into building lots. But when I was a boy Mitching Hill was open country. It was a vast, rolling estate belonging to your great-uncle, Marmaduke, a man with whiskers of a nature which you with your pure mind would scarcely credit, and I have long felt a sentimental urge to see what the hell the old place looks like now. Perfectly foul, I expect. Still, I think we should make the pious pilgrimage."

Pongo absolutely-ed heartily. He was all for the scheme. A great weight seemed to have rolled off his mind. The way he looked at it was that even an uncle within a short jump of the loony bin couldn't very well get into much trouble in a suburb. I mean, you know what suburbs are. They don't, as it were, offer the scope. One follows his reasoning, of course.

"Fine!" he said. "Splendid! Topping!"

"Then put on your hat and rompers, my boy," said Lord Ickenham, "and let us be off. I fancy one gets there by omnibuses and things."

Well, Pongo hadn't expected much in the way of mental uplift from the sight of Mitching Hill, and he didn't get it. Alighting from the bus, he tells me, you found yourself in the middle of rows and rows of semi-detached villas, all looking exactly alike, and you went on and you came to more semi-detached villas, and those all looked exactly alike, too. Nevertheless, he did not repine. It was one of those early spring days which suddenly change to mid-winter and he had come out without his overcoat, and it looked like rain and he hadn't an umbrella, but despite this his mood was one of sober ecstasy. The hours were passing and his uncle had not yet made a goat of himself. At the Dog Races the other had been in the hands of the constabulary in the first ten minutes.

It began to seem to Pongo that with any luck he might be able to keep the old blister pottering harmlessly about here till nightfall, when he could shoot a bit of dinner into him and put him to bed. And as Lord Ickenham had specifically stated that his wife, Pongo's Aunt Jane, had expressed her intention of scalping him with a blunt knife if he wasn't back at the Hall by lunch time on the morrow, it really looked as if he might get through this visit without perpetrating a single major outrage on the public weal. It is rather interesting to note that as he thought this Pongo smiled, because it was the last time he smiled that day.

All this while, I should mention, Lord Ickenham had been stopping at intervals like a pointing dog and saying that it must have been just about here that he plugged the gardener in the trousers seat with his bow and arrow and that over there he had been sick after his first cigar, and he now paused in front of a villa which for some unknown reason called itself The Cedars. His face was tender and wistful.

"On this very spot, if I am not mistaken," he said, heaving a bit of a sigh, "on this very spot, fifty years ago come Lammas Eve, I . . . Oh, blast it!"

The concluding remark had been caused by the fact that the rain, which had held off until now, suddenly began to buzz down like a shower-bath. With no further words, they leaped into the porch of the villa and there took shelter, exchanging glances with a gray parrot which hung in a cage in the window.

Not that you could really call it shelter. They were protected from above all right, but the moisture was now falling with a sort of swivel action, whipping in through the sides of the porch and tickling them up properly. And it was just after Pongo had turned up his collar and was huddling against the door that the door gave way. From the fact that a female of general-servant aspect was standing there he gathered that his uncle must have rung the bell.

This female wore a long mackintosh, and Lord Ickenham beamed upon her with a fairish spot of suavity.

"Good afternoon," he said.

The female said good afternoon.

"The Cedars?"

The female said yes, it was The Cedars.

"Are the old folks at home?"

The female said there was nobody at home.

"Ah? Well, never mind. I have come," said Lord Ickenham, edging in, "to clip the parrot's claws. My assistant, Mr. Walkinshaw, who applies the anaesthetic," he added, indicating Pongo with a gesture.

"Are you from the bird shop?"

"A very happy guess."

"Nobody told me you were coming."

"They keep things from you, do they?" said Lord Ickenham, sympathetically. "Too bad."

Continuing to edge, he had got into the parlor by now, Pongo following in a sort of dream and the female following Pongo.

"Well, I suppose it's all right," she said. "I was just going out. It's my afternoon."

"Go out," said Lord Ickenham cordially. "By all means go out. We will leave everything in order."

And presently the female, though still a bit on the dubious side, pushed off, and Lord Ickenham lit the gas-fire and drew a chair up.

"So here we are, my boy," he said. "A little tact, a little address, and here we are, snug and cozy and not catching our deaths of cold. You'll never go far wrong if you leave things to me."

"But, dash it, we can't stop here," said Pongo.

Lord Ickenham raised his eyebrows.

"Not stop here? Are you suggesting that we go out into that rain? My dear lad, you are not aware of the grave issues involved. This morning, as I was leaving home, I had a rather painful disagreement with your aunt. She said the weather was treacherous and wished me to take my woolly muffler. I replied that the weather was not treacherous and that I would be dashed if I took my woolly muffler. Eventually, by the exercise of an iron will, I had my way, and I ask you, my dear boy, to envisage what will happen if I return with a cold in the head. I shall sink to the level of a fifth-class power. Next time I came to London, it would be with a liver pad and a respirator. No! I shall remain here, toasting my toes at this really excellent fire. I had no idea that a gas-fire radiated such warmth. I feel all in a glow."

So did Pongo. His brow was wet with honest sweat. He is reading for the Bar, and while he would be the first to admit that he hasn't yet got a complete toe-hold on the Law of Great Britain he had a sort of notion that oiling into a perfect stranger's semi-detached villa on the pretext of pruning the parrot was a tort or misdemeanor, if not actually barratry or soccage in fief or something like that. And apart from the legal aspect of the matter there was the embarrassment of the thing. Nobody is more of a whale on correctness and not doing what's not done than Pongo, and the situation in which he now found himself caused him to chew the lower lip and, as I say, perspire a goodish deal.

"But suppose the blighter who owns this ghastly house comes back?"

he asked. "Talking of envisaging things, try that one over on your pianola."

And, sure enough, as he spoke, the front doorbell rang.

"There!" said Pongo.

"Don't say 'There!' my boy," said Lord Ickenham reprovingly. "It's the sort of thing your aunt says. I see no reason for alarm. Obviously this is some casual caller. A ratepayer would have used his latchkey. Glance cautiously out of the window and see if you can see anybody."

"It's a pink chap," said Pongo, having done so.

"How pink?"

"Pretty pink."

"Well, there you are, then. I told you so. It can't be the big chief. The sort of fellows who own houses like this are pale and sallow, owing to working in offices all day. Go and see what he wants."

"You go and see what he wants."

"You go and see what he wants."

"We'll both go and see what he wants," said Lord Ickenham.

So they went and opened the front door, and there, as Pongo had said, was a pink chap. A small young pink chap, a bit moist about the shoulder-blades.

"Pardon me," said this pink chap, "is Mr. Roddis in?"

"No," said Pongo.

"Yes," said Lord Ickenham. "Don't be silly, Douglas—of course I'm in. I am Mr. Roddis," he said to the pink chap. "This, such as he is, is my son Douglas. And you?"

"Name of Robinson."

"What about it?"

"My name's Robinson."

"Oh, *your* name's Robinson? Now we've got it straight. Delighted to see you, Mr. Robinson. Come right in and take your boots off."

They all trickled back to the parlour, Lord Ickenham pointing out objects of interest by the wayside to the chap, Pongo gulping for air a bit and trying to get himself abreast of this new twist in the scenario. His heart was becoming more and more bowed down with weight of woe. He hadn't liked being Mr. Walkinshaw, the anaesthetist, and he didn't like it any better being Roddis Junior. In brief, he feared the worst. It was only too plain to him by now that his uncle had got it thoroughly up his nose and had settled down to one of his big afternoons, and he was asking himself, as he had so often asked himself before, what would the harvest be?

Arrived in the parlor, the pink chap proceeded to stand on one leg and look coy.

"Is Julia here?" he asked, simpering a bit, Pongo says.

"Is she?" said Lord Ickenham to Pongo.

"No," said Pongo.

"No," said Lord Ickenham.

"She wired me she was coming here today."

"Ah, then we shall have a bridge four."

The pink chap stood on the other leg.

"I don't suppose you've ever met Julia. Bit of trouble in the family, she gave me to understand."

"It is often the way."

"The Julia I mean is your niece Julia Parker. Or, rather, your wife's niece Julia Parker."

"Any niece of my wife's is a niece of mine," said Lord Ickenham heartily. "We share and share alike."

"Julia and I want to get married."

"Well, go ahead."

"But they won't let us."

"Who won't?"

"Her mother and father. And Uncle Charlie Parker and Uncle Henry Parker and the rest of them. They don't think I'm good enough."

"The morality of the modern young man is notoriously lax."

"Class enough, I mean. They're a haughty lot."

"What makes them haughty? Are they earls?"

"No, they aren't earls."

"Then why the devil," said Lord Ickenham warmly, "are they haughty? Only earls have a right to be haughty. Earls are hot stuff. When you get an earl, you've got something."

"Besides, we've had words. Me and her father. One thing led to another, and in the end I called him a perishing old—— Coo!" said the pink chap, breaking off suddenly.

He had been standing by the window, and he now leaped lissomely into the middle of the room, causing Pongo, whose nervous system was by this time definitely down among the wines and spirits and who hadn't been expecting this *adagio* stuff, to bite his tongue with some severity.

"They're on the doorstep! Julia and her mother and father. I didn't know they were all coming."

"You do not wish to meet them?"

"No, I don't!"

"Then duck behind the settee, Mr. Robinson," said Lord Ickenham, and the pink chap, weighing the advice and finding it good, did so. And as he disappeared the doorbell rang.

Once more, Lord Ickenham led Pongo out into the hall.

"I say!" said Pongo, and a close observer might have noted that he was quivering like an aspen.

"Say on, my dear boy."

"I mean to say, what?"

"What?"

"You aren't going to let these bounders in, are you?"

"Certainly," said Lord Ickenham. "We Roddises keep open house. And as they are presumably aware that Mr. Roddis has no son, I think we had better return to the old layout. You are the local vet, my boy, come to minister to my parrot. When I return, I should like to find you by the cage, staring at the bird in a scientific manner. Tap your teeth from time to time with a pencil and try to smell of iodoform. It will help to add conviction."

So Pongo shifted back to the parrot's cage and stared so earnestly that it was only when a voice said "Well!" that he became aware that there was anybody in the room. Turning, he perceived that Hampshire's leading curse had come back, bringing the gang.

It consisted of a stern, thin, middle-aged woman, a middle-aged man and a girl.

You can generally accept Pongo's estimate of girls, and when he says that this one was a pippin one knows that he uses the term in its most exact sense. She was about nineteen, he thinks, and she wore a black béret, a dark-green leather coat, a shortish tweed skirt, silk stockings and high-heeled shoes. Her eyes were large and lustrous and her face like a dewy rosebud at daybreak on a June morning. So Pongo tells me. Not that I suppose he has ever seen a rosebud at daybreak on a June morning, because it's generally as much as you can do to lug him out of bed in time for nine-thirty breakfast. Still, one gets the idea.

"Well," said the woman, "you don't know who I am, I'll be bound. I'm Laura's sister Connie. This is Claude, my husband. And this is my daughter Julia. Is Laura in?"

"I regret to say, no," said Lord Ickenham.

The woman was looking at him as if he didn't come up to her specifications.

"I thought you were younger," she said.

"Younger than what?" said Lord Ickenham.

"Younger than you are."

"You can't be younger than you are, worse luck," said Lord Ickenham. "Still, one does one's best, and I am bound to say that of recent years I have made a pretty good go of it."

The woman caught sight of Pongo, and he didn't seem to please her, either.

"Who's that?"

"The local vet, clustering round my parrot."

"I can't talk in front of him."

"It is quite all right," Lord Ickenham assured her. "The poor fellow is stone deaf."

And with an imperious gesture at Pongo, as much as to bid him stare less at girls and more at parrots, he got the company seated.

"Now, then," he said.

There was silence for a moment, then a sort of muffled sob, which Pongo thinks proceeded from the girl. He couldn't see, of course, because his back was turned and he was looking at the parrot, which looked back at him—most offensively, he says, as parrots will, using one eye only for the purpose. It also asked him to have a nut.

The woman came into action again.

"Although," she said, "Laura never did me the honour to invite me to her wedding, for which reason I have not communicated with her for five years, necessity compels me to cross her threshold today. There comes a time when differences must be forgotten and relatives must stand shoulder to shoulder."

"I see what you mean," said Lord Ickenham. "Like the boys of the old brigade."

"What I say is, let bygones be begones. I would not have intruded on you, but needs must. I disregard the past and appeal to your sense of pity."

The thing began to look to Pongo like a touch, and he is convinced that the parrot thought so, too, for it winked and cleared its throat. But they were both wrong. The woman went on.

"I want you and Laura to take Julia into your home for a week or so, until I can make other arrangements for her. Julia is studying the piano, and she sits for her examination in two week's time, so until then she must remain in London. The trouble is, she has fallen in love. Or thinks she has."

"I know I have," said Julia.

Her voice was so attractive that Pongo was compelled to slew round and take another look at her. Her eyes, he says, were shining like twin stars and there was a sort of Soul's Awakening expression on her face, and what the dickens there was in a pink chap like the pink chap, who even as pink chaps go wasn't much of a pink chap, to make her look like ·that, was frankly, Pongo says, more than he could understand. The thing baffled him. He sought in vain for a solution.

"Yesterday, Claude and I arrived in London from our Bexhill home to give Julia a pleasant surprise. We stayed, naturally, in the boarding-house where she has been living for the past six weeks. And what do you think we discovered?"

"Insects."

"Not insects. A letter. From a young man. I found to my horror that a young man of whom I knew nothing was arranging to marry my daughter. I sent for him immediately, and found him to be quite impossible. He jellies eels!"

"Does what?"

"He is an assistant at a jellied eel shop."

"But surely," said Lord Ickenham, "that speaks well for him. The capacity to jelly an eel seems to me to argue intelligence of a high order. It isn't everybody who can do it, by any means. I know if some one came to me and said, 'Jelly this eel!' I should be nonplussed. And so, or I am very much mistaken, would Ramsay MacDonald and Winston Churchill."

The woman did not seem to see eye to eye.

"Tchah!" she said. "What do you suppose my husband's brother Charlie Parker would say if I allowed his niece to marry a man who jellies eels?"

"Ah!" said Claude, who, before we go any further, was a tall, droop-ing bird with a red soup-strainer mustache.

"Or my husband's brother, Henry Parker."

"Ah!" said Claude. "Or Cousin Alf Robbins, for that matter."

"Exactly. Cousin Alfred would die of shame."

The girl Julia hiccoughed passionately, so much so that Pongo says it was all he could do to stop himself nipping across and taking her hand in his and patting it.

"I've told you a hundred times, mother, that Wilberforce is only jellying eels till he finds something better."

"What is better than an eel?" asked Lord Ickenham, who had been following this discussion with the close attention it deserved. "For jellying purposes, I mean."

"He is ambitious. It won't be long," said the girl, "before Wilberforce suddenly rises in the world."

She never spoke a truer word. At this very moment, up he came from behind the settee like a leaping salmon.

"Julia!" he cried.

"Wilby!" yipped the girl.

And Pongo says he never saw anything more sickening in his life than the way she flung herself into the blighter's arms and clung there like the ivy on the old garden wall. It wasn't that he had anything specific against the pink chap, but this girl had made a deep impression on him and he resented her glueing herself to another in this manner.

Julia's mother, after just that brief moment which a woman needs in which to recover from her natural surprise at seeing eel-jelliers pop up from behind sofas, got moving and plucked her away like a referee breaking a couple of welter-weights.

"Julia Parker," she said, "I'm ashamed of you!"

"So am I," said Claude.

"I blush for you."

"Me, too," said Claude. "Hugging and kissing a man who called your father a perishing old bottle-nosed Gawd-help-us."

"I think," said Lord Ickenham, shoving his oar in, "that before proceeding any further we ought to go into that point. If he called you a perishing old bottle-nosed Gawd-help-us, it seems to me that the first thing to do is to decide whether he was right, and frankly, in my opinion . . ."

"Wilberforce will apologize."

"Certainly I'll apologize. It isn't fair to hold a remark passed in the heat of the moment against a chap . . ."

"Mr. Robinson," said the woman, "you know perfectly well that whatever remarks you may have seen fit to pass don't matter one way or the other. If you were listening to what I was saying you will understand . . ."

"Oh, I know, I know. Uncle Charlie Parker and Uncle Henry Parker and Cousin Alf Robbins and all that. Pack of snobs!"

"What!"

"Haughty, stuck-up snobs. Them and their class distinctions. Think themselves everybody just because they've got money. I'd like to know how they got it."

"What do you mean by that?"

"Never mind what I mean."

"If you are insinuating—"

"Well, of course, you know, Connie," said Lord Ickenham mildly, "he's quite right. You can't get away from that."

I don't know if you have ever seen a bull-terrier embarking on a scrap with an Airedale and just as it was getting down nicely to its work suddenly having an unexpected Kerry Blue sneak up behind it and bite it in the rear quarters. When this happens, it lets go of the Airedale and swivels round and fixes the butting-in animal with a pretty nasty eye. It was exactly the same with the woman Connie when Lord Ickenham spoke these words.

"What!"

"I was only wondering if you had forgotten how Charlie Parker made his pile."

"What are you talking about?"

"I know it is painful," said Lord Ickenham, "and one doesn't mention it as a rule, but, as we are on the subject, you must admit that lending money at two hundred and fifty per cent interest is not done in the best circles. The judge, if you remember, said so at the trial."

"I never knew that!" cried the girl Julia.

"Ah," said Lord Ickenham. "You kept it from the child? Quite right, quite right."

"It's a lie!"

"And when Henry Parker had all that fuss with the bank it was touch and go they didn't send him to prison. Between ourselves, Connie, has a bank official, even a brother of your husband, any right to sneak fifty pounds from the till in order to put it on a hundred to one shot for the Grand National? Not quite playing the game, Connie. Not the straight bat. Henry, I grant you, won five thousand of the best and never looked back afterwards, but, though we applaud his judgment of form, we must surely look askance at his financial methods. As for Cousin Alf Robbins . . ."

The woman was making rummy stuttering sounds. Pongo tells me he once had a Pommery Seven which used to express itself in much the same way if you tried to get it to take a hill on high. A sort of mixture of gurgles and explosions.

"There is not a word of truth in this," she gasped at length, having managed to get the vocal cords disentangled. "Not a single word. I think you must have gone mad."

Lord Ickenham shrugged his shoulders.

"Have it your own way, Connie. I was only going to say that, while the jury were probably compelled on the evidence submitted to them to give Cousin Alf Robbins the benefit of the doubt when charged with smuggling dope, everybody knew that he had been doing it for years. I am not blaming him, mind you. If a man can smuggle cocaine and get away with it, good luck to him, say I. The only point I am trying to make is that we are hardly a family that can afford to put on dog and sneer at honest suitors for our daughters' hands. Speaking for myself, I consider that we are very lucky to have the chance of marrying even into eel-jellying circles."

"So do I," said Julia firmly.

"You don't believe what this man is saying?"

"I believe every word."

"So do I," said the pink chap.

The woman snorted. She seemed overwrought.

"Well," she said, "goodness knows I have never liked Laura, but I would never have wished her a husband like you!"

"Husband?" said Lord Ickenham, puzzled. "What gives you the impression that Laura and I are married?"

There was a weighty silence, during which the parrot threw out a general invitation to the company to join it in a nut. Then the girl, Julia spoke.

"You'll have to let me marry Wilberforce now," she said. "He knows too much about us."

"I was rather thinking that myself," said Lord Ickenham. "Seal his lips, I say."

"You wouldn't mind marrying into a low family, would you, darling?" asked the girl, with a touch of anxiety.

"No family could be too low for me, dearest, if it was yours," said the pink chap.

"After all, we needn't see them."

"That's right."

"It isn't one's relations that matter: it's oneselves."

"That's right, too."

"Wilby!"

"Julia!"

They repeated the old ivy on the garden wall act. Pongo says he didn't like it any better than the first time, but his distaste wasn't in it with the woman Connie's.

"And what, may I ask," she said, "do you propose to marry on?"

This seemed to cast a damper. They came apart. They looked at each other. The girl looked at the pink chap, and the pink chap looked at the girl. You could see that a jarring note had been struck.

"Wilberforce is going to be a very rich man some day."

"Some day!"

"If I had a hundred pounds," said the pink chap, "I could buy a half-share in one of the best milk walks in South London tomorrow."

"If!" said the woman.

"Ah!" said Claude.

"Where are you going to get it?"

"Ah!" said Claude.

"Where," repeated the woman, plainly pleased with the snappy crack and loath to let it ride without an encore, "are you going to get it?"

"That," said Claude, "is the point. Where are you going to get a hundred pounds?"

"Why, bless my soul," said Lord Ickenham jovially, "from me, of course. Where else?"

And before Pongo's bulging eyes he fished out from the recesses of his costume a crackling bundle of notes and handed it over. And the agony of realizing that the old bounder had had all that stuff on him all this time and that he hadn't touched him for so much as a tithe of it was so keen, Pongo says, that before he knew what he was doing he had let out a sharp, whinnying cry which rang through the room like the yowl of a stepped-on puppy.

"Ah," said Lord Ickenham. "The vet wishes to speak to me. Yes, vet?"

This seemed to puzzle the cerise bloke a bit.

"I thought you said this chap was your son."

"If I had a son," said Lord Ickenham, a little hurt, "he would be a good deal better-looking than that. No, this is the local veterinary surgeon. I may have said I *looked* on him as a son. Perhaps that was what confused you."

He shifted across to Pongo and twiddled his hands enquiringly. Pongo gaped at him, and it was not until one of the hands caught him smartly in the lower ribs that he remembered he was deaf and started to twiddle back. Considering that he wasn't supposed to be dumb, I can't see why he should have twiddled, but no doubt there are moments when twiddling is about all a fellow feels himself equal to. For what seemed to him at least ten hours Pongo had been undergoing great mental stress, and one can't blame him for not being chatty. Anyway, be that as it may, he twiddled.

"I cannot quite understand what he says," announced Lord Ickenham at length, "because he sprained a finger this morning and that makes him stammer. But I gather that he wishes to have a word with me in private. Possibly my parrot has got something the matter with it which he is reluctant to mention even in sign language in front of a young unmarried girl. You know what parrots are. We will step outside."

"*We* will step outside," said Wilberforce.

"Yes," said the girl Julia. "I feel like a walk."

"And you?" said Lord Ickenham to the woman Connie, who was looking like a female Napoleon at Moscow. "Do you join the hikers?"

"I shall remain and make myself a cup of tea. You will not grudge us a cup of tea, I hope?"

"Far from it," said Lord Ickenham cordially. "This is Liberty Hall. Stick around and mop it up till your eyes bubble."

Outside, the girl, looking more like a dewy-rosebud than ever, fawned on the old buster pretty considerably.

"I don't know how to thank you!" she said. And the pink chap said he didn't, either.

"Not at all, my dear, not at all," said Lord Ickenham.

"I think you're simply wonderful."

"No, no."

"You are. Perfectly marvellous."

"Tut, tut," said Lord Ickenham. "Don't give the matter another thought."

He kissed her on both cheeks, the chin, the forehead, the right eyebrow, and the tip of the nose, Pongo looking on the while in a baffled and discontented manner. Everybody seemed to be kissing this girl except him.

Eventually the degrading spectacle ceased and the girl and the pink chap shoved off, and Pongo was enabled to take up the matter of that hundred quid.

"Where," he asked, "did you get all that money?"

"Now, where did I?" mused Lord Ickenham. "I know your aunt gave it to me for some purpose. But what? To pay some bill or other, I rather fancy."

This cheered Pongo up slightly.

"She'll give you the devil when you get back," he said, with not a little relish. "I wouldn't be in your shoes for something. When you tell Aunt Jane," he said, with confidence, for he knew his Aunt Jane's emotional nature, "that you slipped her entire roll to a girl, and explain, as you will have to explain, that she was an extraordinarily pretty girl—a girl, in fine, who looked like something out of a beauty chorus of the better sort, I should think she would pluck down one of the ancestral battle-axes from the wall and jolly well strike you on the mazzard."

"Have no anxiety, my dear boy," said Lord Ickenham. "It is like your kind heart to be so concerned, but have no anxiety. I shall tell her that I was compelled to give the money to you to enable you to buy back some compromising letters from a Spanish *demimondaine*. She will scarcely be able to blame me for rescuing a fondly-loved nephew from the clutches of an adventuress. It may be that she will feel a little vexed with you for a while, and that you may have to allow a certain time to elapse before you visit Ickenham again, but then I shan't be wanting you at Ickenham till the ratting season starts, so all is well."

At this moment, there came toddling up to the gate of The Cedars a large red-faced man. He was just going in when Lord Ickenham hailed him.

"Mr. Roddis?"

"Hey?"

"Am I addressing Mr. Roddis?"

"That's me."

"I am Mr. J. G. Bulstrode from down the road," said Lord Ickenham. "This is my sister's husband's brother, Percy Frensham, in the lard and imported-butter business."

The red-faced bird said he was pleased to meet them. He asked Pongo if things were brisk in the lard and imported-butter business, and Pongo said they were all right, and the red-faced bird said he was glad to hear it.

"We have never met, Mr. Roddis," said Lord Ickenham, "but I think it would be only neighbourly to inform you that a short while ago I observed two suspicious-looking persons in your house."

"In my house? How on earth did they get there?"

"No doubt through a window at the back. They looked to me like cat burglars. If you creep up, you may be able to see them."

The red-faced bird crept, and came back not exactly foaming at the mouth but with the air of a man who for two pins would so foam.

"You're perfectly right. They're sitting in my parlor as cool as dammit, swigging my tea and buttered toast."

"I thought as much."

"And they've opened a pot of my raspberry jam."

"Ah, then you will be able to catch them red-handed. I should fetch a policeman."

"I will. Thank you, Mr. Bulstrode."

"Only too glad to have been able to render you this little service, Mr. Roddis," said Lord Ickenham. "Well, I must be moving along. I have an appointment. Pleasant after the rain, is it not? Come, Percy."

He lugged Pongo off.

"So that," he said, with satisfaction, "is that. On these visits of mine to the metropolis, my boy, I always make it my aim, if possible, to spread sweetness and light. I look about me, even in a foul hole like Mitching Hill, and I ask myself—How can I leave this foul hole a better and happier foul hole than I found it? And if I see a chance, I grab it. Here is our omnibus. Spring aboard, my boy, and on our way home we will be sketching out rough plans for the evening. If the old Leicester Grill is still in existence, we might look in there. It must be fully thirty-five years since I was last thrown out of the Leicester Grill. I wonder who is the bouncer there now."

Such (concluded the Crumpet) is Pongo Twistleton's Uncle Fred from the country, and you will have gathered by now a rough notion of why it is that when a telegram comes announcing his impending arrival in the great city Pongo blenches to the core and calls for a couple of quick ones.

The whole situation, Pongo says, is very complex. Looking at it from one angle, it is fine that the man lives in the country most of the year. If he didn't, he would have him in his midst all the time. On the other hand, by living in the country he generates, as it were, a store of loopiness which expends itself with frightful violence on his rare visits to the center of things.

What it boils down to is this—Is it better to have a loopy uncle whose loopiness is perpetually on tap but spread out thin, so to speak, or one who lies low in distant Hants for three hundred and sixty days in the year and does himself proud in London for the other five? Dashed moot, of course, and Pongo has never been able to make up his mind on the point.

Naturally, the ideal thing would be if some one would chain the old hound up permanently and keep him from Jan. one to Dec. thirty-one where he wouldn't do any harm—viz. among the spuds and tenantry. But this, Pongo admits, is a Utopian dream. Nobody could work harder to that end than his Aunt Jane, and she has never been able to manage it.

Alexander Woollcott

Fat, owlish, insolent—his favorite way of addressing his "eight hundred intimate friends" was "Hello, repulsive!"—exhibitionistic, but always an original, he was called "all Woollcott and a yard wide." Born in Phalanx, New Jersey, in 1887, fatally stricken by a heart attack while appearing on a broadcast in 1943, Alexander Woollcott became a legend for his oddity even before he was graduated from Hamilton College. As a reporter he was, according to Wolcott Gibbs, "not exactly hostile to facts, but apathetic about them.' As a dramatic critic he was explosive in furious praise and prejudice; George Jean Nathan dubbed him "the Seidlitz Powder of Times Square." Edna Ferber spoke of him as "a New Jersey Nero who mistook his pinafore for a toga," and Howard Dietz ridiculed his combination of malice and mawkishness by calling him "Louisa M. Woollcott." His appetite was large and eccentric; his taste was wayward; he idolized Dickens, Mrs. Fiske, and the very best second-rate literature.

A malicious wit, a bad actor, a good friend, and a sentimental story-teller, Woollcott made much of worn anecdotes. He collected them with profitable pleasure. While Rome Burns is, for the most part, trivial in subject matter and precious in tone; yet the combination of enthusiasm and mockery, of rudeness and mincing urbanity, was relished by half a million readers. Woollcott played himself in life as he did upon the stage: an improbable character unaccountably in love with his own portly shadow.

Entrance Fee

This, then, is the story of Cosette and the Saint-Cyrien, much as they tell it (and these many years have been telling it) in the smoky *popotes* of the French army.

In the nineties, when one heard less ugly babel of alien tongues in the sidewalk cafés, the talk at the *apéritif* hour was sure to turn sooner or later on Cosette—Mlle. Cosette of the *Variétés*, who was regarded by common consent as the most desirable woman in France. She was no hedged-in royal courtesan, as her possessive fellow-citizens would point out with satisfaction, but a distributed du Barry, the *chère amie* of a republic.

Her origins were misty. Some said she had been born of fisher folk at Ploubazlanec on the Brittany coast. Others preferred the tale that she was the love-child of a famous actress by a very well-known king. In any case, she was now a national legend, and in her preeminence the still-bruised French people found in some curious way a balm for their wounded self-esteem. Her photographs, which usually showed her sitting piquantly on a café table, were cut from *L'Illustration* and pinned up in every barracks. Every French lad dreamed of her, and every right-minded French girl quite understood that her sweetheart was saying in effect, "Since I cannot hope to have Cosette, will you come to the river's edge at sundown?" Quite understood, and did not blame him.

Everyone had seen the pictures of Cosette's tiny, vine-hung villa at Saint-Cloud, with its high garden wall and its twittering aviary. And even those for whom that wall was hopelessly high took morbid pride in a persistent detail of the legend which said that no man was ever a guest there for the night who could not bring five thousand francs with him. This was in the nineties, mind you, when francs were francs, and men—by a coincidence then more dependable—were men.

The peasant blend of charm and thrift in Cosette filled the cadets at Saint-Cyr with a gentle melancholy. In their twilight hours of relaxation they talked it over, and all thought it a sorrowful thing that, so wretched is the soldier's pittance, not one of those who must some day direct the great *Revanche* would ever carry into battle a memory of the fairest woman in France. For what cadet could hope to raise five thousand francs? It was very sad. But, cried one of their number, his voice shaking, his eyes alight, there were a thousand students at Saint-Cyr, and not one among them so lacking in resource that he could not, if given time, manage to raise at least five francs.

That was how the Cosette Sweepstakes were started. There followed then all the anxious distraction of ways and means, with such Spartan exploits in self-denial, such Damon-and-Pythias borrowings, such flagrant letters of perjured appeal to unsuspecting aunts and godmothers, as Saint-Cyr had never known. But by the appointed time the last man had his, or somebody's, five francs.

The drawing of numbers was well under way when a perplexed instructor stumbled on the proceedings and reported his discovery to the Commandant. When the old General heard the story he was so profoundly moved that it was some time before he spoke.

"The lad who wins the lottery," he said at last, "will be the envy of his generation. But the lad who conceived the idea—ah, he, my friend, will some day be a Marshal of France!"

Then he fell to laughing at the thought of the starry-eyed youngster arriving at the stage door of the *Variétés* with nothing but his youth and his entrance fee. The innocent budget had made no provision for the trip to Paris, none for a carriage, a bouquet, perhaps a supper party. The Commandant said that he would wish to meet this margin of contingency from his own fatherly pocket.

"There will be extras," he said. "Let the young rascal who wins be sent to me before he leaves for Paris."

It was a cadet from the Vendée who reported to the Commandant next afternoon—very trim in his red breeches and blue tunic, his white gloves spotless, his white cockade jaunty, his heart in his mouth. The Commandant said no word to him, but put a little purse of gold *louis* in his hand, kissed him on both cheeks in benediction, and stood at his window, moist-eyed and chuckling, to watch until the white cockade disappeared down the avenue of trees.

The sunlight, latticed by the *jalousies,* was making a gay pattern on Cosette's carpet the next morning when she sat up and meditated on the day which stretched ahead of her. Her little cadet was cradled in a sweet, dreamless sleep, and it touched her rather to see how preposterously young he was. Indeed, it quite set her thinking of her early days, and how she had come up in the world. Then she began speculating on *his* early days, realized with a pang that he was still in the midst of them, and suddenly grew puzzled. Being a woman of action, she prodded him.

"Listen, my old one," she said, "how did a cadet at Saint-Cyr ever get hold of five thousand francs?"

Thus abruptly questioned, he lost his head and blurted out the tale of the sweepstakes. Perhaps he felt it could do no harm now, and anyway she listened so avidly, with such flattering little gasps of surprise and such sunny ripples of laughter, that he quite warmed to his story. When he came to the part about the Commandant, she rose and strode up and down, the lace of her peignoir fluttering behind her, tears in her violet eyes.

"Saint-Cyr has paid me the prettiest compliment I have ever known," she said, "and I am the proudest woman in France this day. But surely I must do my part. You shall go back and tell them all that Cosette is a woman of sentiment. When you are an old, old man in the Vendée you shall tell your grandchildren that once in your youth you knew the dearest favors in France, and they cost you not a sou. Not a sou."

At that she hauled open the little drawer where he had seen her lock up the lottery receipts the night before.

"Here," she said, with a lovely gesture. "I give you back your money." And she handed him his five francs.

The Art of Insult
OR, THE DEVASTATING CRUSHER

The art of insult is one of the oldest forms of repartee. Perhaps the finest of all examples of the retort discourteous is the one uttered by the philosopher Diogenes to Alexander the Great. Seeing the impoverished philosopher with no more possessions than a large tub, the world-conquering Alexander inquired, "Is there something I can do for you?" "Yes," replied Diogenes, "stand out of my sun."

About two thousand years later the art of insult had reached a devastating and almost fatal viciousness. The antagonism between William Pitt, first Earl of Chatham, and Robert Walpole, Earl of Orford, led to some of the most severe diatribes ever recorded. The climax was reached when, after a particularly heated speech, Walpole met Pitt outside of Parliament. The older man furiously taunted the younger. "Sir," said Walpole, "you will either die on the gallows or of some unspeakable disease!"

"That, my Lord," replied Pitt, "depends upon whether I embrace your policies or your mistress."

The genial Irvin Cobb was not above an occasional malicious thrust. He was working for Charles E. Chapin, the famous city editor of *The New York World*, a man who later killed his own wife and died in prison, but who was even then building up a reputation as the severest editor who ever scowled at a cub reporter. One day young Cobb, asking where his employer was, learned that Chapin was at home ill.

"I trust," said Cobb, "that it is nothing trivial."

When ladies engage in thrust and counter-thrust, the pointed barb may be more delicate, but it is no less deadly.

Most of her adversaries have learned that it is dangerous to challenge Dorothy Parker, but there were many foolhardy antagonists. On one occasion Miss Parker and Clare Boothe Luce met in front of a revolving door. The poetic Miss Parker, who was both in a daze and in a hurry, entered first. "After you, my dear," purred Mrs. Luce. "Age before beauty, you know."

"Yes," replied Miss Parker. "And pearls before swine."

Although Dorothy Parker's most celebrated ripostes were directed against women, she did not spare the opposite sex. Once, after a dinner party, Miss Parker was laughing at the antics of a wit who was something of a clown. But her partner, an overeducated young snob, was disdainful. "I'm afraid I can't join in the merriment," he said. "I can't bear fools."

"That's queer," said Miss Parker. "Your mother could."

She was a famous motion-picture star, but she did not impress Broadway. "What was the matter?" a mutual friend asked Dorothy Parker. "Didn't she run the whole gamut of emotions?"

"Well," said Miss Parker, "she ran the gamut of emotions from A to B."

Voltaire and Heine sharpened their wit with the keenest irony. A trouble-maker once said to the great Frenchman, "It is strange that you speak so well of Monsieur X when he always speaks so badly about you."

"Really?" said Voltaire. "Perhaps we are both wrong."

Heine's thrusts were as penetrating as they were surprising. He spared neither friends nor foes. Of a fellow-poet he said, "All women love him—all except the Muses." Of a woman who, no longer young, still prided herself on her figure, Heine wrote, "She is truly like the Venus de Milo. She is unbelievably old; she has no teeth; and her body is covered with yellow spots."

Unsparing in his attacks on the aristocracy, Heine recalled the Napoleonic days when "coffee was made out of acorns, and princes out of nothing at all." Dying of his long illness, he commented, "My constitution grows worse—worse even than the Constitution of Prussia."

But Heine's chief crushers were directed against the puritans and pedagogs. His tribute to the pedantic Professor Saalfeld is immortal: "Curious how Napoleon's greatest detractors have all come to horrible ends. Castlereagh cut his throat. Louis the Eighteenth rotted to death on his throne. And Professor Saalfeld still teaches at Göttingen."

A. E. Housman, Latin scholar and author of *A Shropshire Lad*, had something of Heine's epigrammatic sarcasm, a killing form of criticism. He deflated Swinburne's windy rhetoric by saying, "Swinburne has now said not only all he has to say about everything, but all he has to say about nothing." One of his pedagogic victims drew this verdict: "Nature, not content with denying to Mr. Y the faculty of thinking, has endowed him with the faculty of writing."

The antagonism between Gladstone and Disraeli (see page 86) and Pitt and Walpole was matched by the violent quarrels between John Randolph and Henry Clay. Once, after they had not spoken to each other for a long while, they met in a narrow street. It was plain that one would have to step aside to let the other pass.

Randolph held his ground. "I never give way to scoundrels," said he.

Clay stepped into the muddy gutter. "I *always* do," he said.

Sydney Smith was made a canon of St. Paul's in 1831. But that did not prevent him from continuing to be one of the keenest wits of his day. His conversation was not only droll but delightfully malicious. His phrasing and his timing were equally perfect. He called Macaulay "a book in breeches," a man who laid society waste "with his waterspouts of talk."

Speaking of the excessive heat of an English summer, Smith said, "Heat! It was so dreadful that I found there was nothing for me to do but take off my flesh and sit in my bones." Asked to give a name to a lady's dog, Smith said it should be called "Spot," preferably with the rest of the Shakespearean quotation: "Out, damned Spot!" Describing the sloth, Smith said that this lazy animal "moves suspended, rests suspended, sleeps suspended, and passes his life in suspense—like a young clergyman distantly related to a bishop."

Alexander Woollcott (see page 700) was renowned for his backhanded compliments. Some victim had attacked Oscar Levant for his habit of interrupting serious conversation with ill-timed flippancies. Woollcott defended him by saying, "There's nothing wrong with Oscar —nothing that a miracle couldn't cure." It was Woollcott also who was reputed to have defended Michael Arlen by saying, "Arlen, for all his reputation, is not a bounder. He is every other inch a gentleman."

Noel Coward, the versatile English actor, playwright, composer, author and scenarist, can slay an opponent before he knows he has even been assailed. Lady Diana Manners once tried to put Coward in his place. "I saw you in your play *The Vortex*," said the titled lady who was also on the stage, "and I didn't think you were very funny."

"My dear Lady Manners," replied Coward, "I saw you as the madonna in *The Miracle* and I thought you were a scream!"

No list of insults can be compiled without Mark Twain's reply to Paul Bourget. Bourget had been baiting his visitor about America's lack of traditions. "When an American has nothing else to do he can always spend some time trying to trace his ancestry back to his grandfather," said Bourget.

"Yes," said Twain, "and when a Frenchman has nothing better to do, he can always try to find out who his father was."

G. B. Shaw and G. K. Chesterton were great friends and greater opposites. Shaw was quietly sardonic, heretical, a lean vegetarian; Chesterton was loudly affirmative, orthodox, and a heartily obese meat-eater. Once, at a public dinner, Chesterton stared pointedly at Shaw's thin figure and remarked, "Looking at you, Shaw, people would think there was a famine in England."

Turning to his rotund companion, Shaw observed, "And looking at you, Chesterton, people would think you were the cause of it."

It takes a wit to catch a wit. Perhaps the most devastating thing ever said about Shaw was uttered by his fellow-playwright and critic, Oscar Wilde. Shortly after Shaw appeared in print with a weekly London column, Wilde commented, "As yet Shaw isn't prominent enough to have any enemies. But none of his friends like him."

The puzzle of relations is an endless theme for stories. One of the most recent concerns a socially prominent woman who, while traveling, was greeted by another woman whose face was familiar but, somehow, could not be placed. "How wonderful," said the stranger, "to see you here. It's been too long since we visited."

Terribly embarrassed because of this evidence of intimacy, the first woman tried to recall some connection which would reveal who her companion was. Nothing was forthcoming until the unknown said, "And only yesterday my brother was saying—"

This seemed a promising clue, and the woman interrupted, "Your brother—of course—I couldn't forget your brother. Tell me, what is he doing now?"

"My brother," said the unknown coolly, "is still President of the United States."

Index of Authors and Titles